*View*points 12

Authors

Robert Dawe

Margaret Iveson

Sharon Jeroski

Christel Kleitsch

Wendy Mathieu

Robin Pearson

Dirk Verhulst

Series Consultants

John Borovilos

Robert Dawe

Margaret Iveson

Wendy Mathieu

Dirk Verhulst

Publishing Consultant

Anthony Luengo

Assessment Consultant

Sharon Jeroski

Prentice
Hall

Toronto

National Library of Canada Cataloguing in Publication Data

Main entry under title:
    Viewpoints 12

ISBN 0-13-092462-8 (bound)   ISBN 0-13-092450-4 (pbk.)

    1. Readers (Secondary). I. Dawe, Robert T. (Robert Thomas), 1948– II. Mathieu,
Wendy Lee, 1959–

PE1121.V55 2002   428.6   C2001-903519-5

ISBN 0-13-092462-8 (hardcover)   ISBN 0-13-092450-4 (paperback)

Publisher: Mark Cobham
Product Manager: Anita Borovilos
Managing Editor: Elynor Kagan
Project Manager: Anthony Luengo
Anthologist and Developmental Editor: Irene Cox
Production Editor: Angelie Kim
Text Researchers: Angelie Kim, Stephen Sanborn, Rebecca Vogan
Visuals Researchers: Krista Alexander, Angelie Kim
Contributing Writer: Laura Edlund
Copy Editor: Sarah Swartz
Proofreaders: Gail Copeland, Milena Mazzolin, Geri Savitz-Fine, Rebecca Vogan
Production Coordinator: Zane Kaneps
Art Direction: Zena Denchik
Cover Design: Jennifer Federico
Cover Image: Freeman Patterson/Masterfile
Interior Design: Zena Denchik
Page Layout: David Cheung Design Inc.
Permissions: Karen Hunter, Elizabeth Kelly, Michaele Sinko

1 2 3 4 5 TCP 06 05 04 03 02

Printed and bound in Canada

The publisher has taken every care to meet or exceed industry specifications for the
manufacturing of textbooks. The cover of this sewn book is a premium, polymer-reinforced
material designed to provide long life and withstand rugged use. Mylar gloss lamination has
been applied for further durability.

Contents by Genre and Form

Preface. xviii

Acknowledgements xix

Invitation to Literature   2

The Word   *poem*
Pablo Neruda 4

Reading on "the Rez"   *memoir*
Tomson Highway 6

For the Love of Books   *memoir*
Rita Dove 7

Not a Boyhood Passion   *memoir*
Mordecai Richler 10

How Reading Changed My Life   *memoir*
Anna Quindlen 12

The Secret   *poem*
Denise Levertov 14

Invitation to Literature: Activities 15

Unit 1   Short Fiction   16

The Rocking-Horse Winner   *short story*
D.H. Lawrence 18

Write Me Sometime   *short story*
Taien Ng-Chan 36

Calgary from Sunnyside   *woodblock print*
Margaret Shelton 46

Outside Edges   *short story*
Ivan Dorin 48

Twisted Roots   *photograph*
Lyle McIntyre 60

The Shining Houses   *short story*
Alice Munro 62

A Devoted Son   *short story*
Anita Desai 74

Magpies   *short story*
Thomas King 87

The Winner   *short story*
Barbara Kimenye 96

Windows   *short story*
Bernice Morgan 109

Easter at My Aunt's   *lithograph*
Christopher Pratt 118

War   *short story*
Timothy Findley 120

Peace and War   *short story*
Moacyr Scliar 138

The Spirit of Haida Gwaii   *sculpture*
Bill Reid 142

Mazes   *speculative fiction*
Ursula K. Le Guin 144

Was It a Dream?   *ghost story*
Guy de Maupassant 150

From **No Great Mischief**   *novel excerpt*
Alistair MacLeod 155

Unit Wrap-Up Activities 163

In-Depth: Universal Themes and Patterns   **164**

From The Archetypes of Literature   *literary criticism*
Northrop Frye 166

The Hero's Adventure   *interview*
Joseph Campbell with Bill Moyers 171

Ode to the West Wind   *poem*
Percy Bysshe Shelley 177

Araby *from* Dubliners   *short story*
James Joyce 181

Utopian Dreams   *book review*
Val Ross 188

Universal Themes and Patterns: Activities 193

Unit 2 Essays, Articles, and Media 194

Essays

Portrait of the Essay as a Warm Body   *expository essay*
Cynthia Ozick 196

Personal and Reflective Essays

Ka-Ching!   *personal essay*
Margaret Atwood 205

Afternoon of an American Boy   *personal essay*
E.B. White. 209

A Place to Stand On   *reflective essay*
Margaret Laurence 216

Chameleons and Codas   *personal essay*
Patricia Conrad 224

Elegy in Stone   *reflective essay*
Steven Heighton 229

The Death of the Moth   *reflective essay*
Virginia Woolf. 236

Biographical Essays

Guy Lafleur   *biographical essay*
Ken Dryden 242

My Mother's Blue Bowl   *biographical essay*
Alice Walker 251

Migrant Mother   *photograph*
Dorothea Lange 256

Expository and Analytical Essays

Of Youth and Age   *analytical essay*
Francis Bacon 258

Why I Write   *analytical essay*
George Orwell 263

The Not-So-Deadly Sin   *expository essay*
Barbara Kingsolver 272

Call of the Weird   *expository essay*
Drew Hayden Taylor 279

Argumentative and Persuasive Essays

A Modest Proposal   *persuasive essay*
Jonathan Swift 283

Get Beyond Babel   *argumentative essay*
Ken Wiwa 294

The Death of History Is Bunk   *persuasive essay*
Patrick Watson 300

Wanderers by Choice   *argumentative essay*
Eva Hoffman 306

Peace, Technology, and the Role of Ordinary People
speech
Ursula Franklin 313

Articles

Slide to Entropy   *newspaper column*
Kathleen Winter 323

Paradise, a Poet, and Promised Land   *magazine article*
George Elliott Clarke 327

Hockey Night in Port Hawkesbury   *magazine article*
Lynn Coady 331

The Sixth Flight   *magazine article*
Chantal Tranchemontagne 336

Buying Your Next Synthesizer   *tech-advice column*
Amin Bhatia 345

A Chat with Al Purdy   *interview*
Kate Climenhage 349

Ours by Design   *magazine feature article*
Alison Blackduck 354

Media

Look What I Found   *cartoon*
Marian Henley 364

Landscape with the Fall of Icarus   *painting*
Pieter Brueghel 366

Shower at Ohashi Bridge   *print*
Hiroshige Utagawa 368

The Poetry of Earth and Sky   *photo essay*
Courtney Milne with Ormond and Barbara Mitchell . . 370

Canada: A Virtual History *newspaper feature article*
Ray Conlogue 380

Unzipped *annotated graphic*
Anna Husarska. 389

The Humpback of Notre Dame *print advertisement*
Government of Newfoundland and Labrador 392

Morty Mania *trade magazine article*
Judy Waytiuk 394

The Monkey's Paw *magazine feature article*
Daniel Wood. 403

Restoring Life on the Edge *newspaper article*
Chris Rose 421

Unit Wrap-Up Activities. 429

In-Depth: Media on Media   **430**

Aphorisms *aphorisms*
Marshall McLuhan 431

The News *analytical essay*
Neil Postman 434

Learning Without Lectures *newspaper article*
Ann Rees 443

King Zog's Birthday *radio script*
Bob Elliott and Ray Goulding 446

almost visible *poem*
Kenneth J. Harvey 449

Media on Media: Activities 451

In-Depth: Argument and Persuasion   **452**

Effective Persuasion *from* **Rhetoric** *argument*
Aristotle. 454

Giant Database Is Ripe for Abuse *newspaper editorial*
Edmonton Journal 456

**Let's Stop Being Hysterical, Shall We, and Start Selling
Water to Those Who Need It** *opinion piece*
Lee Morrison 459

Our Water Sovereignty Is at Risk *opinion piece*
Eric Reguly 463

From **Water**   *non-fiction book excerpt*
Marq de Villiers 466

Poetry   *poem*
Marianne Moore 473

Argument and Persuasion: Activities 475

Unit 3   P o e t r y   4 7 6

T h e   T w e n t i e t h   C e n t u r y   a n d
B e y o n d

Engineers' Corner   *light verse*
Wendy Cope 478

Is the Pathetic Fallacy True?   *lyric*
Elizabeth Brewster 481

Evening   *etching*
Mary Cassatt 484

Birch Bark   *lyric*
Michael Ondaatje 486

vancouver–courtenay–calgary   *free verse*
George Bowering 489

Prairie Flight   *free verse*
Dorothy Livesay 492

Fern Hill   *lyric*
Dylan Thomas 494

Amiri Baraka   *photograph*
C. Daniel Dawson 498

The Committee to Upgrade Celestial Signs   *shape poem*
Kurt Brown 500

The Heroes You Had as a Girl   *free verse*
Bronwen Wallace 503

foremother   *narrative*
Lillian Bouzane 507

To You Who Would Wage War Against Me   *dramatic
monologue*
Kateri Akiwenzie Damm 511

I, Icarus   *free verse*
Alden Nowlan 515

Musée des Beaux Arts *reflective verse*
W.H. Auden 518

People on the Bridge *reflective verse*
Wislawa Szymborska 521

Progress *free verse*
Emma LaRocque 524

Summer Night *lyric*
Langston Hughes 527

The Love Song of J. Alfred Prufrock *dramatic monologue*
T.S. Eliot 530

Afternoons & Coffeespoons *song lyrics*
Brad Roberts of The Crash Test Dummies 539

The River *lyric*
Derek Walcott 542

grammar poem *shape poem*
Rita Wong 545

Traditions

Mu-lan *ballad*
Anonymous 548

From **Beowulf** *epic*
Anonymous, Translated by Seamus Heaney 553

From **The Canterbury Tales: General Prologue** *narrative*
Geoffrey Chaucer 560

Sonnet 116 *sonnet*
William Shakespeare 570

A Poison Tree *engraving*
William Blake 572

The Rime of the Ancient Mariner *narrative*
Samuel Taylor Coleridge 574

O Can You Leave Your Native Land? *quatrain*
Susanna Moodie 601

Dover Beach *dramatic monologue*
Matthew Arnold 604

Because I Could Not Stop for Death— *allegorical verse*
Emily Dickinson 608

Unit Wrap-Up Activities 611

Unit 4 **D r a m a**   612

A Marriage Proposal   *stage play*
Anton Chekhov 614

***Set Design for* The Foreigner**   *set design*
Karen Schulz Gropman 634

***From* Acoose: Man Standing Above Ground**   *monologue*
Janice Acoose and Brenda Zeman 636

***Film Location for* Random Passage**   *film location*
CBC Television 640

Stop!   *stage play*
Donna Lewis. 642

Dead Parrot   *television script*
Monty Python 650

Unit Wrap-Up Activities. 655

In-Depth: Shakespeare   656

Invisible Genius: The Quiet Talent of Tanya Moiseiwitsch
magazine article
Therese Greenwood 658

From Hamlet   *film script*
William Shakespeare and Kenneth Branagh 666

Shakespeare in the Cinema: A Film Directors' Symposium
symposium 677

The Shakespearean Tragic Hero   *literary criticism*
A.C. Bradley. 687

From Strong Women Prevail in Shakespeare's Comedies
literary criticism
Angela Pitt 692

Saloonio   *short story*
Stephen Leacock 696

Shakespeare: Activities 700

Glossary 701

Another Viewpoint Index 714

Author Index 715

Credits. 716

Contents by Theme

Sense of Self

The Rocking-Horse Winner *18* ■ Outside Edges *48* ■ A Devoted Son *74* ■ War *120* ■ No Great Mischief *155* ■ The Hero's Adventure *171* ■ Araby *181* ■ Ka-Ching! *205* ■ Afternoon of an American Boy *209* ■ A Place to Stand On *216* ■ Chameleons and Codas *224* ■ My Mother's Blue Bowl *251* ■ Of Youth and Age *258* ■ Why I Write *263* ■ The Not-So-Deadly Sin *272* ■ Wanderers by Choice *306* ■ Paradise, a Poet, and Promised Land *327* ■ Hockey Night in Port Hawkesbury *331* ■ Is the Pathetic Fallacy True? *481* ■ Fern Hill *494* ■ The Heroes You Had as a Girl *503* ■ I, Icarus *515* ■ Summer Night *527* ■ The Love Song of J. Alfred Prufrock *530* ■ Afternoons & Coffeespoons *539* ■ grammar poem *545* ■ Stop! *642*

Personal Challenges

The Rocking-Horse Winner *18* ■ Outside Edges *48* ■ The Hero's Adventure *171* ■ Chameleons and Codas *224* ■ Wanderers by Choice *306* ■ The Sixth Flight *336* ■ Landscape with the Fall of Icarus *366* ■ Restoring Life on the Edge *421* ■ foremother *507* ■ I, Icarus *515* ■ The Canterbury Tales *560* ■ Acoose *636* ■ Hamlet *666*

Creating and Breaking Stereotypes

The Shining Houses *62* ■ Chameleons and Codas *224* ■ Elegy in Stone *229* ■ Call of the Weird *279* ■ Mu-lan *548*

Close Connections

The Rocking-Horse Winner *18* ■ Write Me Sometime *36* ■ Outside Edges *48* ■ A Devoted Son *74* ■ Magpies *87* ■ The Winner *96* ■ Windows *109* ■ Easter at My Aunt's *118* ■ War *120* ■ Was It a Dream? *150* ■ No Great Mischief *155* ■ Araby *181* ■ Afternoon of an American Boy *209* ■ A Place to Stand On *216* ■ Chameleons and Codas *224* ■ My Mother's Blue Bowl *251* ■ Look What I Found *364* ■ The Monkey's Paw *403* ■ Evening *484* ■ Birch Bark *486* ■ The Heroes You Had as a Girl *503* ■ foremother *507* ■ To You Who Would Wage War Against Me *511*

■ The Love Song of J. Alfred Prufrock *530* ■ Sonnet 116 *570* ■ Dover Beach *604* ■ A Poison Tree *572* ■ A Marriage Proposal *614* ■ Hamlet *666*

Heroes and Rebels

The Archetypes of Literature *166* ■ The Hero's Adventure *171* ■ Elegy in Stone *229* ■ Guy Lafleur *242* ■ Amiri Baraka *498* ■ The Heroes You Had as a Girl *503* ■ foremother *507* ■ I, Icarus *515* ■ Mu-lan *548* ■ Beowulf *553* ■ The Canterbury Tales *560* ■ Acoose *636* ■ The Shakespearean Tragic Hero *687* ■ Strong Women Prevail *692*

Loss

A Devoted Son *74* ■ Magpies *87* ■ Was It a Dream? *150* ■ No Great Mischief *155* ■ The Archetypes of Literature *166* ■ The Death of the Moth *236* ■ Migrant Mother *256* ■ The Rime of the Ancient Mariner *574* ■ Because I Could Not Stop for Death— *608* ■ Hamlet *666*

Creativity

Calgary from Sunnyside *46* ■ Twisted Roots *60* ■ Easter at My Aunt's *118* ■ The Spirit of Haida Gwaii *142* ■ Portrait of the Essay *196* ■ A Place to Stand On *216* ■ Guy Lafleur *242* ■ Why I Write *263* ■ The Not-So-Deadly Sin *272* ■ Ours by Design *354* ■ Shower at Ohashi Bridge *368* ■ The Poetry of Earth and Sky *370* ■ Morty Mania *394* ■ Aphorisms *431* ■ Engineers' Corner *478* ■ Is the Pathetic Fallacy True? *481* ■ Evening *484* ■ Amiri Baraka *498* ■ People on the Bridge *521* ■ Progress *524* ■ Set Design for The Foreigner *634* ■ Invisible Genius *658* ■ Shakespeare in the Cinema *677*

Learning

A Devoted Son *74* ■ The Death of History Is Bunk *300* ■ Learning Without Lectures *443* ■ grammar poem *545* ■ Saloonio *696*

Work and Careers

Write Me Sometime *36* ■ Ka-Ching! *205* ■ Guy Lafleur *242* ■ Unzipped *389* ■ Morty Mania *394* ■ Engineers' Corner *478* ■ Prairie Flight *492* ■ Amiri Baraka *498* ■ Set Design for The Foreigner *634* ■ Invisible Genius *658*

Recreation

The Winner *96* ■ Guy Lafleur *242* ■ Hockey Night in Port Hawkesbury *331* ■ The Sixth Flight *336* ■ Buying Your Next Synthesizer *345*

Rights and Responsibilities

The Shining Houses *62* ■ Utopian Dreams *188* ■ Chameleons and Codas *224* ■ Why I Write *263* ■ A Modest Proposal *283* ■ The Death of History Is Bunk *300* ■ Peace, Technology *313* ■ Ours by Design *354* ■ Look What I Found *364* ■ Restoring Life on the Edge *421* ■ Giant Database Is Ripe for Abuse *456*

Nature and the Environment

Outside Edges *48* ■ Twisted Roots *60* ■ The Shining Houses *62* ■ Windows *109* ■ No Great Mischief *155* ■ The Archetypes of Literature *166* ■ Ode to the West Wind *177* ■ The Death of the Moth *236* ■ Peace, Technology *313* ■ Paradise, a Poet, and Promised Land *327* ■ Look What I Found *364* ■ The Poetry of Earth and Sky *370* ■ The Humpback of Notre Dame *392* ■ Restoring Life on the Edge *421* ■ Let's Stop Being Hysterical *459* ■ Our Water Sovereignty Is at Risk *463* ■ Water *466* ■ Is the Pathetic Fallacy True? *481* ■ Birch Bark *486* ■ vancouver–courtenay –calgary *489* ■ Prairie Flight *492* ■ Fern Hill *494* ■ Progress *524* ■ The River *542* ■ The Rime of the Ancient Mariner *574* ■ Dover Beach *604* ■ *Film Location for* Random Passage *640*

Science and Technology

Peace, Technology *313* ■ Buying Your Next Synthesizer *345* ■ Canada: A Virtual History *380* ■ The Monkey's Paw *403* ■ Aphorisms *431* ■ Learning Without Lectures *443* ■ Engineers' Corner *478*

Media

The Winner *96* ■ Canada: A Virtual History *380* ■ The Humpback of Notre Dame *392* ■ Morty Mania *394* ■ Aphorisms *431* ■ The News *434* ■ Learning Without Lectures *443* ■ King Zog's Birthday *446* ■ almost visible *449* ■ The Committee to Upgrade Celestial Signs *500* ■ Shakespeare in the Cinema *677*

Home and Exile

How Reading Changed My Life *12* ▪ Calgary from Sunnyside *46* ▪ Outside Edges *48* ▪ Twisted Roots *60* ▪ The Shining Houses *62* ▪ Windows *109* ▪ Easter at My Aunt's *118* ▪ Peace and War *138* ▪ Utopian Dreams *188* ▪ A Place to Stand On *216* ▪ Elegy in Stone *229* ▪ Migrant Mother *256* ▪ Wanderers by Choice *306* ▪ Paradise, a Poet, and Promised Land *327* ▪ The Poetry of Earth and Sky *370* ▪ vancouver–courtenay–calgary *489* ▪ Prairie Flight *492* ▪ Fern Hill *494* ▪ Summer Night *527* ▪ The Love Song of J. Alfred Prufrock *530* ▪ The River *542* ▪ O Can You Leave Your Native Land? *601*

Aboriginal Cultures

Reading on "the Rez" *6* ▪ Magpies *87* ▪ The Spirit of Haida Gwaii *142* ▪ Call of the Weird *279* ▪ Ours by Design *354* ▪ To You Who Would Wage War Against Me *511* ▪ Progress *524* ▪ Acoose *636*

Canada

Reading on "the Rez" *6* ▪ Not a Boyhood Passion *10* ▪ Write Me Sometime *36* ▪ Calgary from Sunnyside *46* ▪ Outside Edges *48* ▪ Twisted Roots *60* ▪ The Shining Houses *62* ▪ Magpies *87* ▪ Windows *109* ▪ Easter at My Aunt's *118* ▪ War *120* ▪ The Spirit of Haida Gwaii *142* ▪ No Great Mischief *155* ▪ The Archetypes of Literature *166* ▪ Utopian Dreams *188* ▪ Ka-Ching! *205* ▪ A Place to Stand On *216* ▪ Chameleons and Codas *224* ▪ Elegy in Stone *229* ▪ Guy Lafleur *242* ▪ Call of the Weird *279* ▪ Get Beyond Babel *294* ▪ The Death of History Is Bunk *300* ▪ Peace, Technology *313* ▪ Slide to Entropy *323* ▪ Paradise, a Poet, and Promised Land *327* ▪ Hockey Night in Port Hawkesbury *331* ▪ The Sixth Flight *336* ▪ Buying Your Next Synthesizer *345* ▪ A Chat with Al Purdy *349* ▪ Ours by Design *354* ▪ The Poetry of Earth and Sky *370* ▪ Canada: A Virtual History *380* ▪ The Humpback of Notre Dame *392* ▪ Morty Mania *394* ▪ The Monkey's Paw *403* ▪ Restoring Life on the Edge *421* ▪ Aphorisms *431* ▪ Learning Without Lectures *443* ▪ almost visible *449* ▪ Giant Database Is Ripe for Abuse *456* ▪ Let's Stop Being Hysterical *459* ▪ Our Water Sovereignty Is at Risk *463* ▪ Water *466* ▪ Is the Pathetic Fallacy True? *481* ▪ Birch Bark *486* ▪ vancouver–courtenay–calgary *489* ▪ Prairie Flight *492* ▪ The Heroes You Had as a Girl *503* ▪ foremother *507* ▪ To You Who Would Wage War Against Me *511* ▪

I, Icarus *515* ▪ Progress *524* ▪ Afternoons & Coffeespoons *539* ▪
grammar poem *545* ▪ O Can You Leave Your Native Land? *601* ▪ Acoose
636 ▪ *Film Location for* Random Passage *640* ▪ Stop! *642* ▪ Invisible
Genius *658* ▪ Saloonio *696*

Caribbean

The River *542*

South America

The Word *4* ▪ Peace and War *138*

Africa

The Winner *96* ▪ Get Beyond Babel *294* ▪ Water *466*

Europe

The Rocking-Horse Winner *18* ▪ Was It a Dream? *150* ▪ Ode to the West
Wind *177* ▪ Araby *181* ▪ The Death of the Moth *236* ▪ Of Youth and
Age *258* ▪ Why I Write *263* ▪ A Modest Proposal *283* ▪ Wanderers by
Choice *306* ▪ Landscape with the Fall of Icarus *366* ▪ Effective Persuasion
454 ▪ Engineers' Corner *478* ▪ Fern Hill *494* ▪ Musée des Beaux Arts
518 ▪ People on the Bridge *521* ▪ The Love Song of J. Alfred Prufrock
530 ▪ Beowulf *553* ▪ The Canterbury Tales *560* ▪ Sonnet 116 *570* ▪
A Poison Tree *572* ▪ The Rime of the Ancient Mariner *574* ▪ Dover
Beach *604* ▪ A Marriage Proposal *614* ▪ Dead Parrot *650* ▪ Hamlet *666*
▪ Shakespeare in the Cinema *677* ▪ The Shakespearean Tragic Hero *687* ▪
Strong Women Prevail *692*

Asia

A Devoted Son *74* ▪ Shower at Ohashi Bridge *368* ▪ Birch Bark *486* ▪
grammar poem *545* ▪ Mu-lan *548*

Myth and Archetypes

The Rocking-Horse Winner *18* ▪ Outside Edges *48* ▪ The Spirit of Haida
Gwaii *142* ▪ The Archetypes of Literature *166* ▪ The Hero's Adventure
171 ▪ Araby *181* ▪ Utopian Dreams *188* ▪ Elegy in Stone *229* ▪
Landscape with the Fall of Icarus *366* ▪ The Committee to Upgrade

Celestial Signs *500* ▪ I, Icarus *515* ▪ Musée des Beaux Arts *518* ▪ Mu-lan *548* ▪ Because I Could Not Stop for Death— *608*

Oral Traditions and Language

The Word *4* ▪ Reading on "the Rez" *6* ▪ Magpies *87* ▪ The Spirit of Haida Gwaii *142* ▪ Chameleons and Codas *224* ▪ Get Beyond Babel *294* ▪ Effective Persuasion *454* ▪ Birch Bark *486* ▪ grammar poem *545* ▪ Mu-lan *548* ▪ Beowulf *553* ▪ Shakespeare in the Cinema *677*

Reading and Writing

The Word *4* ▪ Reading on "the Rez" *6* ▪ For the Love of Books *7* ▪ Not a Boyhood Passion *10* ▪ How Reading Changed My Life *12* ▪ The Secret *14* ▪ Write Me Sometime *36* ▪ Portrait of the Essay *196* ▪ A Place to Stand On *216* ▪ Why I Write *263* ▪ The Not-So-Deadly Sin *272* ▪ Paradise, a Poet, and Promised Land *327* ▪ A Chat with Al Purdy *349* ▪ The Poetry of Earth and Sky *370* ▪ Poetry *473* ▪ Engineers' Corner *478* ▪ Evening *484* ▪ Amiri Baraka *498*

Humour

Not a Boyhood Passion *10* ▪ Magpies *87* ▪ The Winner *96* ▪ Was It a Dream? *150* ▪ Ka-Ching! *205* ▪ Afternoon of an American Boy *209* ▪ The Not-So-Deadly Sin *272* ▪ Call of the Weird *279* ▪ Slide to Entropy *323* ▪ Hockey Night in Port Hawkesbury *331* ▪ Look What I Found *364* ▪ King Zog's Birthday *446* ▪ Engineers' Corner *478* ▪ The Committee to Upgrade Celestial Signs *500* ▪ A Marriage Proposal *614* ▪ Stop! *642* ▪ Dead Parrot *650* ▪ Saloonio *696*

Parody and Satire

A Modest Proposal *283* ▪ Poetry *473* ▪ The Love Song of J. Alfred Prufrock *530* ▪ Afternoons & Coffeespoons *539*

Mystery and Intrigue

The Secret *14* ▪ Peace and War *138* ▪ Mazes *144* ▪ Was It a Dream? *150* ▪ almost visible *449* ▪ People on the Bridge *521* ▪ The Rime of the Ancient Mariner *574* ▪ Because I Could Not Stop for Death— *608*

Conflict and War

War *120* ■ Peace and War *138* ■ Elegy in Stone *229* ■ Peace, Technology *313* ■ Unzipped *389* ■ The News *434* ■ King Zog's Birthday *446* ■ To You Who Would Wage War Against Me *511* ■ Musée des Beaux Arts *518* ■ Mu-lan *548* ■ Beowulf *553* ■ The Canterbury Tales *560* ■ A Poison Tree *572* ■ The Rime of the Ancient Mariner *574* ■ Dover Beach *604* ■ A Marriage Proposal *614* ■ Hamlet *666*

Ethical and Moral Questions

The Rocking-Horse Winner *18* ■ The Shining Houses *62* ■ A Devoted Son *74* ■ Peace and War *138* ■ Mazes *144* ■ The Archetypes of Literature *166* ■ The Hero's Adventure *171* ■ Araby *181* ■ Utopian Dreams *188* ■ Chameleons and Codas *224* ■ Elegy in Stone *229* ■ The Death of the Moth *236* ■ Why I Write *263* ■ A Modest Proposal *283* ■ Peace, Technology *313* ■ Ours by Design *354* ■ Look What I Found *364* ■ Landscape with the Fall of Icarus *366* ■ The Monkey's Paw *403* ■ Effective Persuasion *454* ■ Giant Database Is Ripe for Abuse *456* ■ To You Who Would Wage War Against Me *511* ■ Musée des Beaux Arts *518* ■ People on the Bridge *521* ■ The Love Song of J. Alfred Prufrock *530* ■ A Poison Tree *572* ■ The Rime of the Ancient Mariner *574* ■ Dover Beach *604* ■ Hamlet *666* ■ The Shakespearean Tragic Hero *687*

Preface

The thinkers and dreamers gathered in this anthology—writers of fiction, essayists, poets, dramatists, literary critics, journalists, artists, photographers—all have one thing in common. They invite you to experience the world from their perspective. Their goal is to present their ideas to their audience in exciting, appealing, and thought-provoking ways. This is what the painter Edgar Degas meant when he said: "Art is not what you see but what you make others see." These outstanding works of literature and art will help you to see the world through the eyes of their creators, challenge you with their vision and insights, and stimulate you to formulate your own viewpoints.

Viewpoints 12 features a collection of compelling texts ranging from the traditional to the contemporary. The four main units are organized by genre—short fiction; essays, articles, and media; poetry; and drama. Interspersed among them are multi-genre "In-Depth" sections that explore Universal Themes and Patterns, Media on Media, Argument and Persuasion, and Shakespeare. Many styles and modes of writing are represented and numerous media texts are recreated in their original formats. The five essay sections provide a rich range of argument and reflection.

Each selection begins with an introduction that provides relevant background about the life and times of its creator, and ends with notes that offer information to enhance your understanding of the work. The activities at the end of each "In-Depth" section encourage your personal response to the text and challenge you to react critically as well as creatively through words and images. Many selections are followed by "Another Viewpoint," which broadens your perspective by examining the selection through a critical lens that might be historical, archetypal, or sociological. The wrap-up activities at the end of each unit make connections among the selections.

Without you, the reader, the words and images on these pages would have no purpose. By engaging with them, you bring the ideas they contain to life. Their example and inspiration will help you to understand and interpret the world around you as you consolidate the skills you have been building throughout your high-school years. This book will be a doorway to appreciating and enjoying literature in your post-secondary education and beyond.

Acknowledgements

The editors and publisher would like to thank all the reviewers of Prentice Hall Senior English.

Philip Allingham
Susan Balfe
Alice Barlow-Kedves
Jamie Bell
John Borovilos
Connie Bray
Danielle Brown
Mike Budd
Jane Burningham-Ernst
Terri Carleton
Scott Carter
Jackie Chambers
Annette Chiu
Carrie Collins
Mary Conway
Owen Davis
Dan DiGravio
Sandy Dobec
Janis Fertuck
Linda Ferworn
Barbara Fullerton
Ross Garnett
Margie Gartland
Gail Grant
Bryan Harrigan
Amanda Joseph
Myra Junyk
Gabriel Kampf
Michelle Kennedy
Diana Knight
Marty Kofsky
Lorne Kulak
Patricia Lachance

Gerd Laudenbach
Kathryn Lemmon
Elaine Leslie
Noël Lim
Cheryl Manny
Janie McTavish
Ian Mills
Yula Nouragas
Victoria Nutting
Adam Oberfrank
Keith Pearce
Larry Peters
Frank Petruzella
Louise Pivato
Sheila Powell
Peter Purcell
Judith Robinson
Tom Sbrocchi
Richard Schultz
Lawrence Smith
Sally Spofforth
Jim Stewart
Brian Switzer
Jean Szeles
Cornelia Wagner
Judy Wedeles
Darlene White
Stephen Willcock

Ian Esquivel, Media Consultant
Linda Laliberté, Equity and
    Aboriginal Consultant
Hari Lalla, Equity Consultant

The Library, 1960, Jacob Lawrence

What comes to mind when we talk about a *text*? Why does this concept matter? Every one of us is surrounded daily by books, magazines, television, CDs, DVDs, e-mail, the Internet, cell phone screens, billboards, virtual reality arcades—all of them texts. How do we sift through these texts and make sense of them? How do we sort out which ones are important to us? Texts contain words, images, sounds, textures, or a combination of all four. They may embody information that we need. Many texts hold a story or a narrative. These texts form *literature*, a body of work that communicates meaningful information and insights into ideas, culture, and history.

Literature is more than simply information; it is information with lasting significance, created because someone has a story to tell. As Ezra Pound said, "Literature is news that stays news." Literature is unique because it allows direct access into the mind of the person who created it. When you become engaged with a piece of literature, what began as a *writer* addressing a *reader* becomes a two-way conversation. As you react to the text with your own experiences, thoughts, and emotions, it becomes an invigorating exchange that engages your intellect and your imagination as you form your own meaning from the text in front of you. Literature is about ideas, but it is also about people. It broadens your understanding of human nature by giving you the opportunity to view life through the eyes of someone in a different time or place, or someone of a different gender, ethnicity, or age.

This anthology contains selections of many kinds. Some of the selections will entertain you. Some will challenge you, making you reconsider things you already know something about. This book contains texts that open up new worlds, introducing you to cultures that are new to you, as well as to people—real and imagined—who are leading remarkable lives. There are texts that will take you to places you've never been and ones that will transport you to distant times. There, long ago, you will recognize some things that are different, and much that is the same, about human beings and how they think, feel, and behave.

In this introductory section, you will experience poetry by the Chilean poet Pablo Neruda, who speaks of "the word" as something "in the blood," elemental, oral, and existing before words were ever written down. Tomson Highway, Rita Dove, Mordecai Richler, Anna Quindlen, and Denise Levertov will share their experiences with literature and articulate its power. As you read through this section, think of how works of literature, and texts in general, are part of your life. They were there when you were first read to and they will continue to exist for you in meaningful ways in your future.

The Word

Pablo Neruda

Translated by Alastair Reid

The word
was born in the blood,
grew in the dark body, beating,
and flew through the lips and the mouth.

Farther away and nearer
still, still it came
from dead fathers and from wandering races,
from lands that had returned to stone
weary of their poor tribes,
because when pain took to the roads   10
the settlements set out and arrived
and new lands and water reunited
to sow their word anew.

And so, this is the inheritance—
this is the wavelength which connects us
with the dead man and the dawn
of new beings not yet come to light.

Still the atmosphere quivers
with the initial word
dressed up   20
in terror and sighing.
It emerged
from the darkness
and until now there is no thunder
that rumbles yet with all the iron
of that word,

the first
word uttered—
perhaps it was only a ripple, a drop,
and yet its great cataract falls and falls.   30

Later on, the word fills with meaning.
It remained gravid and it filled up with lives.
Everything had to do with births and sounds—
affirmation, clarity, strength,
negation, destruction, death—
the verb took over all the power
and blended existence with essence
in the electricity of its beauty.

Human word, syllable, combination
of spread light and the fine art of the silversmith,   40
hereditary goblet which gathers
the communications of the blood—
here is where silence was gathered up
in the completeness of the human word
and, for human beings, not to speak is to die—
language extends even to the hair,
the mouth speaks without the lips moving—
all of a sudden the eyes are words.

I take the word and go over it
as though it were nothing more than a human shape,   50
its arrangements awe me and I find my way
through each variation in the spoken word—
I utter and I am and without speaking I approach
the limit of words and the silence.

I drink to the word, raising
a word or a shining cup,
in it I drink
the pure wine of language
or inexhaustible water,
maternal source of words,   60
and cup and water and wine
give rise to my song
because the verb is the source
and vivid life—it is blood,
blood which expresses its substance
and so implies its own unwinding—
words give glass-quality to glass, blood to blood,
and life to life itself.

*Born in 1904 in Chile, **Pablo Neruda** is generally considered to be one of the greatest poets who wrote in Spanish in the twentieth century. An avowed Marxist, he was very politically active and served his country as a professional diplomat in a number of countries. His work has been widely translated and was awarded the Nobel Prize in Literature in 1971. He died in 1973.*

Reading on "the Rez"

Tomson Highway

Well, you see, up where I was born and grew up—the wilds of northern Manitoba and the Territories, everybody born in tents, dogsleds, caribou herds, etc., Cree country to the hilt—there weren't any books. So I never grew up with those little kiddie books that all other kids did. Plus, English wasn't our language. Our version of books was "oral" storytelling sessions with elders, in the Cree language, fabulous, mystical, hilarious tales about the Trickster, mostly, and about other mythological beasts, creatures, and heroes. That was our world of magic.

By the time I got comfortably conversant with the English language, I was about fifteen years old. I just could never learn the damn thing before then.

So I remember reading the summer I was fifteen, late into at least three nights, back on "the Rez," a ratty old copy of Victor Hugo's *The Hunchback of Notre-Dame*. Really the first novel I ever read. And I couldn't stop. I remember that, back in those days, there was no electricity on the Rez so I read by the light of one candle until five in the morning, as I say, three nights in a row. I started wearing glasses the next year—and have ever since. So that's one way that book changed my life. Darn!

But I couldn't stop, because I was so enthralled by the tale. Just a plain, rollicking good yarn. I was amazed, more than anything else, at the skill, the magic, the spell that a really good storyteller wields. Ever since then, I've always wanted to be like Esmeralda when I grow up. Just kidding…

Tomson Highway was born in northwestern Manitoba in 1951 and spoke only Cree until he was six years old. He received degrees in English and music from the University of Western Ontario. An Aboriginal activist and writer, he is best known as a playwright. He has won several Dora Mavor Moore Awards for plays including The Rez Sisters *and* Dry Lips Oughta Move to Kapuskasing.

For the Love of Books

Rita Dove

When I am asked: "What made you want to be a writer?" my answer has always been: "Books." First and foremost, now, then, and always, I have been passionate about books. From the time I began to read, as a child, I loved to feel their heft in my hand and the warm spot caused by their intimate weight in my lap: I lived the crisp whisper of a page turning, the musky odour of old paper and the sharp inky whiff of new pages. Leather bindings sent me into ecstasy. I even loved to gaze at a closed book and daydream about the possibilities inside—it was like contemplating a genie's lamp. Of course, my favourite fairy tale was *A Thousand and One Nights*—imagine buying your life with stories!—and my favourite cartoons were those where animated characters popped out of books and partied while the unsuspecting humans slept. In books, I could travel anywhere, be anybody, understand worlds long past and imaginary colonies in the future. My idea of a bargain was to go to the public library, wander along the bookshelves, and emerge with a chin-high stack of books that were mine, all mine, for two weeks—free of charge!

What I remember most about long summer days is browsing the bookshelves in our solarium to see if there were any new additions. I grew up with those rows of books; I knew where each one was shelved and immediately spotted newcomers. And after months had gone by and there'd be no new books, I would think: Okay, I guess I'll try this one—and then discover that the very book I had been avoiding because of a drab cover or small print was actually a wonderful read. Louis Untermeyer's *Treasury of Best Loved Poems* had a sickeningly sweet lilac and gold cover and was forbiddingly thick, but I finally pulled it off the shelf and discovered a cornucopia of emotional and linguistic delights, from "The Ballad of Barbara Fritchie," which I adored for its sheer length and rather numbing rhymes, to Langston Hughes' dazzlingly syncopated "Dream Boogie." Then there was Shakespeare—daunting for many years because it was his entire oeuvre, in matching wine-red volumes that were so thick they looked more like oversized bouillon cubes than books, and yet it was that ponderous title—*The Complete Works of William Shakespeare*—that enticed me, because here was a lifetime's work—a lifetime!—in two compact, dense packages. I began with the long poem "The Rape of Lucrece"...I sampled a few sonnets, which I found beautiful but rather adult; and finally wandered into the plays—first *Romeo and Juliet*, then *Macbeth, Julius Caesar, A Midsummer Night's Dream, Twelfth Night*—enthralled by the language, by the fact that poetry was spinning the story. Of course I did not understand every single word, but I was too young to know that this was supposed to be difficult; besides, no one was waiting to test me on anything, so, free from pressure, I dove in.

Although I loved books, for a long time I had no aspirations to be a writer. The possibility was beyond my imagination. I liked to write, however—and on long summer days when I ran out of reading material or my legs had fallen asleep because I had been curled up on the couch for hours on end, I made up my own stories. Most were abandoned midway. Those that I did bring to a conclusion I neither showed to others nor considered saving.

My first piece of writing I thought enough of to keep was a novel called *Chaos*, which was about robots taking over the earth. I had just entered third or fourth grade; the novel had forty-three chapters, and each chapter was twenty lines or less because I used each week's spelling list as the basis for each chapter, and there were twenty words per list. In the course of the year I wrote one installment per week, and I never knew what was going to happen next—the words led me, not the other way around.

At that time I didn't think of writing as an activity people admitted doing. I had no living role models—a "real" writer was a long-dead white male, usually with a white beard to match. Much later, when I was in eleventh grade, my English teacher, Miss Oechsner, took me to a book-signing in a downtown hotel. She didn't ask me if I'd like to go— she asked my parents instead, signed me and a classmate (who is now a professor of literature) out of school one day, and took us to meet a writer. The writer was John Ciardi, a poet who also had translated Dante's *Divine Comedy*, which I had heard of, vaguely. At that moment I realized that writers were real people and how it was possible to write down a poem or story in the intimate sphere of one's own room and then share it with the world.

Born in Akron, Ohio, in 1952, the African American writer **Rita Dove** *is a renowned poet, novelist, short story writer, and educator. Among her many achievements, she was the poet laureate of the United States in 1993 and was awarded the Pulitzer Prize for Poetry in 1987.*

Not a Boyhood Passion

Mordecai Richler

Reading was not one of my boyhood passions. Girls, or rather the absence of girls, drove me to it. When I was thirteen years old, short for my age, more than somewhat pimply, I was terrified of girls. As far as I could make out, they were only attracted to boys who were tall or played for the school basketball team or at least shaved. Unable to qualify on all three counts, I resorted to subterfuge. I set out to call attention to myself by becoming a character. I acquired a pipe, which I chewed on ostentatiously, and made it my business to be seen everywhere, even at school basketball games, pretending to be absorbed by books of daunting significance: say, H.G. Wells' *The Outline of History,* or Paul de Kruif's *Microbe Hunters,* or John Gunther inside one continent or another. I rented these thought-provoking books for three cents a day from a neighbourhood lending library that was across the street from a bowling alley where I used to spot pins four nights a week.

O my God, I would not be thirteen again for anything. The sweetly scented girls of my dreams, wearing lipstick and tight sweaters and nylon stockings, would sail into the bowling alley holding hands with the boys from the basketball team. "Hi," they would call out, giggly, nudging each other, even as I bent over the pins: "How goes the reading?"

The two ladies who ran the lending library, possibly amused by my pretensions, tried to interest me in fiction.

"I want fact. I can't be bothered with *stories,*" I protested, waving my pipe at them, affronted.

I knew what novels were, of course. I had read *Scaramouche,* by Rafael Sabatini, at school, as well as *Treasure Island* and some Ellery Queen and a couple of thumpers by G.A. Henty. Before that there had been *Action Comics, Captain Marvel, Batman,* and—for educational reasons—either *Bible Comics* or *Classic Comics.*

Novels, I knew, were mere romantic make-believe, not as bad as poetry, to be fair, but bad enough. Our high-school class master, a dedicated Scot, was foolish enough to try to interest us in poetry. A veteran of World War I, he told us that during the nightly bombardments on the Somme he had fixed a candle to his steel helmet so that he could read poetry in the trenches. A scruffy lot, we were not moved. Instead, we exchanged knowing winks behind that admirable man's back. Small wonder, we agreed, that he drove an ancient Austin and had ended up no better than a high-school teacher.

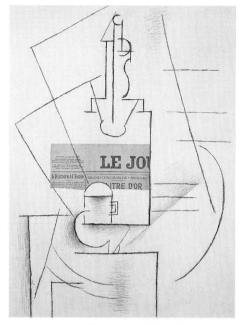

Bottle, Cup and Newspaper, 1912–13, Pablo Picasso

My aunts consumed historical novels like pastries. My father read *Black Mask* and *True Detective.* My mother would read anything on a Jewish subject, preferably by I.J. Singer or Sholem Asch, though she would never forgive Asch for having written *The Nazarene,* never mind *Mary and the Apostle.* My older brother kept a novel, *Topper Takes a Trip,* secure under his mattress in the bedroom we shared, assuring me that it was placed at just such an angle on the springs that if it were moved so much as a millimetre in his absence he would know and bloody well make me pay for it.

I fell ill with a childhood disease, I no longer remember which, but one obviously meant as a rebuke for those girls in tight sweaters who continued to ignore me. Never mind, they would mourn at my funeral, burying me with my pipe. Too late they would say, "Boy, was he ever an intellectual!"

*Novelist, journalist, scriptwriter, and essayist, **Mordecai Richler** was born in Montreal in 1931, where he died in 2001. He first achieved* *international recognition with his 1959 novel* The Apprenticeship of Duddy Kravitz, *which was made into a film. Among his many awards are the Order of Canada, the Governor General's Award (twice), and the Giller Prize.*

How Reading Changed My Life

Anna Quindlen

My home was in that pleasant place outside Philadelphia, but I really lived somewhere else. I lived within the covers of books and those books were more real to me than any other thing in my life. One poem committed to memory in grade school survives in my mind. It is by Emily Dickinson: "There is no Frigate like a Book / To take us Lands away / Nor any coursers like a Page / Of prancing Poetry."

Perhaps only a truly discontented child can become as seduced by books as I was. Perhaps restlessness is a necessary corollary of devoted literacy. There was a club chair in our house, a big one, with curled arms and a square ottoman; it sat in one corner of the living room, catty-corner to the fireplace, with a barrel table next to it. In my mind I am always sprawled in it, reading with my skinny, scabby legs slung over one of its arms. "It's a beautiful day," my mother is saying; she said that always, often, autumn, spring, even when there was a fresh snowfall. "All your friends are outside." It was true; they always were. Sometimes I went out with them, coaxed into the street, out into the fields, down by the creek, by the lure of what I knew intuitively was normal childhood, by the promise of being what I knew instinctively was a normal child, one who lived, raucous, in the world.

I have clear memories of that sort of life, of lifting the rocks in the creek that trickled through Naylor's Run to search for crayfish, of laying pennies on the tracks of the trolley and running to fetch them, flattened, when the trolley had passed. But at base it was never any good. The best part of me was always at home, within some book that had been laid flat on the table to mark my place, its imaginary people waiting for me to return and bring them to life. That was where the real people were, the trees that moved in the wind, the still, dark waters. I won a bookmark in a spelling bee during that time with these words of Montaigne upon it in gold: "When I am reading a book, whether wise or silly, it seems to me to be alive and talking to me." I found that bookmark not long ago, at the bottom of a box, when my father was moving.

Years later I would come to discover, as Robinson Crusoe did when he found Man Friday, that I was not alone in that world or on that island. I would discover (through reading, naturally) that while I was sprawled, legs akimbo, in that chair with a book, Jamaica Kincaid was sitting in the glare of the Caribbean sun in Antigua reading in that same way that I did, as though she was starving and the book was bread. When she was grown-up, writing books herself, winning awards for her work, she talked in one of her memoirs of ignoring her little brother when she was supposed to be looking after him: "I liked reading a book much more than I liked looking after him."

While I was in that club chair with a book, Hazel Rochman and her husband were in South Africa, burying an old tin trunk heavy with hardcovers in the backyard, because the police might raid their house and search it for banned books. Rochman, who left Johannesburg for Chicago and became an editor for the American Library Association's *Booklist,* summed up the lessons learned from that night, about the power of reading, in a way I would have recognized even as a girl. "Reading makes immigrants of us all," she wrote years later. "It takes us away from home, but, most important, it finds homes for us everywhere."

Born in Philadelphia in 1953, **Anna Quindlen** *was a journalist with the* Washington Post *and the* New York Times *before becoming a full-time novelist. She won the Pulitzer Prize in 1992 for her journalism.*

The Secret

Denise Levertov

Two girls discover
the secret of life
in a sudden line of
poetry.

I who don't know the
secret wrote
the line. They
told me

(through a third person)
they had found it   10
but not what it was
not even

what line it was. No doubt
by now, more than a week
later, they have forgotten
the secret,

the line, the name of
the poem. I love them
for finding what
I can't find,   20

and for loving me
for the line I wrote,
and for forgetting it
so that

a thousand times, till death
finds them, they may
discover it again, in other
lines

in other
happenings. And for   30
wanting to know it,
for

assuming there is
such a secret, yes,
for that
most of all.

*Poet and essayist **Denise Levertov** was born in Ilford, England, in 1923. She worked as a nurse during World War II and moved to the United States in 1948 with her American husband. She published her first collection of poetry in 1946. Most of her writing from the late 1960s and 1970s focuses on political and social issues such as the Vietnam War and racial unrest in American cities. She died in 1997.*

Invitation to Literature: Activities

1. In a small group or as a class, discuss the ways in which literature affected the lives of the writers in this section. How do your own earlier and later experiences with literature compare with those described here?

2. Identify a world—fictional or factual—that one or more texts opened up for you. Describe the way in which this text or texts led you into this new world.

3. Think of an image combined with words that you are familiar with, such as an advertisement. To what extent does the image alone have an impact on you? To what extent do the words affect you? How do the image and words work together to convey a message?

1

short fiction

"The act of writing is
the creation of some-
thing in the world that
hasn't existed before in
just this form, and
while I'm engaged in it
I am at a very high level
of concentration,
absorption, and joy."

— *Alice Walker*

"I find the world around
me much more inter-
esting than what I can
come up with inside
my own head. If you
write just what you
have experienced,
you've only got about a
book and a half in you."

— *Michael Ondaatje*

The Rocking-Horse Winner

D.H. Lawrence

David Herbert Lawrence was born into poverty in Nottinghamshire, England, in 1885. He attended university, where he began publishing poems and briefly worked as a teacher. Lawrence wrote novels, poetry, plays, travel books, and essays; he was also a painter. His work often featured themes of freedom, redemption, and tormented family relationships. When talking about writers, he said: "His art, if it be art, will tell you the truth of his day. And that is all that matters. Away with eternal truth." A controversial writer, he experienced the banning of several of his books. He died in France in 1930. "The Rocking-Horse Winner" explores class issues and the notion of luck. What does it mean to be a lucky person? To what extent do you think luck and success are the same?

There was a woman who was beautiful, who started with all the advantages, yet she had no luck. She married for love, and the love turned to dust. She had bonny children, yet she felt they had been thrust upon her, and she could not love them. They looked at her coldly, as if they were finding fault with her. And hurriedly she felt she must cover up some fault in herself. Yet what it was that she must cover up she never knew. Nevertheless, when her children were present, she always felt the centre of her heart go hard. This troubled her, and in her manner she was all the more gentle and anxious for her children, as if she loved them very much. Only she herself knew that at the centre of her heart was a hard little place that could not feel love, no, not for anybody. Everybody else said of her: "She is such a good mother. She adores her children." Only she herself, and her children themselves, knew it was not so. They read it in each other's eyes.

There were a boy and two little girls. They lived in a pleasant house, with a garden, and they had discreet servants, and felt themselves superior to anyone in the neighbourhood.

Although they lived in style, they felt always an anxiety in the house. There was never enough money. The mother had a small income, and the father had a small income, but not nearly enough for the social position which they had to keep up. The father went in to town to some office. But though he had good prospects, these prospects never materialized. There was always the grinding sense of the shortage of money, though the style was always kept up.

At last the mother said, "I will see if I can't make something." But she did not know where to begin. She racked her brains, and tried this thing and the other, but could not find anything successful. The failure made deep lines come into her face. Her children were growing up, they would have to go to school. There must be more money, there must be more money. The father, who was always very handsome and expensive in his tastes, seemed as if he never would be able to do anything worth doing. And the mother, who had a great belief in herself, did not succeed any better, and her tastes were just as expensive.

And so the house came to be haunted by the unspoken phrase: There must be more money! There must be more money! The children could hear it all the time, though nobody said it aloud. They heard it at Christmas, when the expensive and splendid toys filled the nursery. Behind the shining modern rocking horse, behind the smart doll's house, a voice would start whispering: "There must be more money! There must be more money!" And the children would stop playing, to listen for a moment. They would look into each other's eyes, to see if they had all heard. And each one saw in the eyes of the other two that they too had heard. "There must be more money! There must be more money!"

It came whispering from the springs of the still-swaying rocking horse, and even the horse, bending his wooden, champion head, heard it. The big doll, sitting so pink and smirking in her new pram, could hear it quite plainly, and seemed to be smirking all the more self-consciously because of it. The foolish puppy, too, that took the place of the Teddy bear, he was looking so extraordinarily foolish for no other reason but that he heard the secret whisper all over the house: "There must be more money!"

Yet nobody ever said it aloud. The whisper was everywhere, and therefore no one spoke it. Just as no one ever says: "We are breathing!" in spite of the fact that breath is coming and going all the time.

"Mother," said the boy Paul one day, "why don't we keep a car of our own? Why do we always use Uncle's, or else a taxi?"

"Because we're the poor members of the family," said the mother.

"But why are we, Mother?"

"Well—I suppose," she said slowly and bitterly, "it's because your father has no luck."

The boy was silent for some time.

"Is luck money, Mother?" he asked, rather timidly.

"No, Paul. Not quite. It's what causes you to have money."

"Oh!" said Paul vaguely. "I thought when Uncle Oscar said filthy lucker, it meant money."

"Filthy lucre does mean money," said the mother. "But it's lucre, not luck."

"Oh!" said the boy. "Then what is luck, Mother?"

"It's what causes you to have money. If you're lucky you have money. That's why it's better to be born lucky than rich. If you're rich, you may lose your money. But if you're lucky, you will always get more money."

"Oh! Will you? And is Father not lucky?"

"Very unlucky, I should say," she said bitterly.

The boy watched her with unsure eyes.

"Why?" he asked.

"I don't know. Nobody ever knows why one person is lucky and another unlucky."

"Don't they? Nobody at all? Does nobody know?"

"Perhaps God. But He never tells."

"He ought to, then. And aren't you lucky either, Mother?"

"I can't be, if I married an unlucky husband."

"But by yourself, aren't you?"

"I used to think I was, before I married. Now I think I am very unlucky indeed."

"Why?"

"Well—never mind! Perhaps I'm not really," she said.

The child looked at her, to see if she meant it. But he saw, by the lines of her mouth, that she was only trying to hide something from him.

"Well, anyhow," he said stoutly, "I'm a lucky person."

"Why?" said his mother, with a sudden laugh.

He stared at her. He didn't even know why he had said it.

"God told me," he asserted, brazening it out.

"I hope He did, dear!" she said, again with a laugh, but rather bitter.

"He did, Mother!"

"Excellent!" said the mother, using one of her husband's exclamations.

The boy saw she did not believe him; or rather, that she paid no attention to his assertions. This angered him somewhere, and made him want to compel her attention.

He went off by himself, vaguely, in a childish way, seeking for the clue to "luck." Absorbed, taking no heed of other people, he went about with a sort of stealth, seeking inwardly for luck. He wanted luck, he wanted it, he wanted it. When the two girls were playing dolls in the nursery, he would sit on his big rocking horse, charging madly into space, with a frenzy that made the little girls peer at him uneasily. Wildly the horse careered, the waving dark hair of the boy tossed, his eyes had a strange glare in them. The little girls dared not speak to him.

When he had ridden to the end of his mad little journey, he climbed down and stood in front of his rocking horse, staring fixedly into its lowered face. Its red mouth was slightly open, its big eye was wide and glassy-bright.

"Now!" he would silently command the snorting steed. "Now, take me to where there is luck! Now take me!"

And he would slash the horse on the neck with the little whip he had asked Uncle Oscar for. He knew the horse could take him to where there was luck, if only he forced it. So he would mount again, and start on his furious ride, hoping at last to get there. He knew he could get there.

"You'll break your horse, Paul!" said the nurse.

"He's always riding like that! I wish he'd leave off!" said his sister Joan.

But he only glared down on them in silence. Nurse gave him up. She could make nothing of him. Anyhow, he was growing beyond her.

One day his mother and his Uncle Oscar came in when he was on one of his furious rides. He did not speak to them.

"Hallo, you young jockey! Riding a winner?" said his uncle.

"Aren't you growing too big for a rocking horse? You're not a very little boy any longer, you know," said his mother.

But Paul only gave a blue glare from his big, rather close-set eyes. He would speak to nobody when he was in full tilt. His mother watched him with an anxious expression on her face.

At last he suddenly stopped forcing his horse into the mechanical gallop, and slid down.

"Well, I got there," he announced fiercely, his blue eyes still flaring, and his sturdy long legs straddling apart.

"Where did you get to?" asked his mother.

"Where I wanted to go," he flared back at her.

"That's right, son!" said Uncle Oscar. "Don't you stop till you get there. What's the horse's name?"

"He doesn't have a name," said the boy.

"Gets on without all right?" asked the uncle.

"Well, he has different names. He was called Sansovino last week."

"Sansovino, eh? Won the Ascot. How did you know his name?"

"He always talks about horse races with Bassett," said Joan.

The uncle was delighted to find that his small nephew was posted with all the racing news. Bassett, the young gardener, who had been wounded in the left foot in the war and had got his present job through Oscar Cresswell, whose batman he had been, was a perfect blade of the "turf." He lived in the racing events, and the small boy lived with him.

Oscar Cresswell got it all from Bassett.

"Master Paul comes and asks me, so I can't do more than tell him, sir," said Bassett, his face terribly serious, as if he were speaking of religious matters.

"And does he ever put anything on a horse he fancies?"

"Well—I don't want to give him away—he's a young sport, a fine sport, sir. Would you mind asking him himself? He sort of takes a pleasure in it, and perhaps he'd feel I was giving him away, sir, if you don't mind."

Bassett was serious as a church.

The uncle went back to his nephew, and took him off for a ride in the car.

"Say, Paul, old man, do you ever put anything on a horse?" the uncle asked.

The boy watched the handsome man closely.

"Why, do you think I oughtn't to?" he parried.

"Not a bit of it! I thought perhaps you might give me a tip for the Lincoln."

The car sped on into the country, going down to Uncle Oscar's place in Hampshire.

"Honour bright?" said the nephew.

"Honour bright, son!" said the uncle.

"Well, then, Daffodil."

"Daffodil! I doubt it, sonny. What about Mirza?"

"I only know the winner," said the boy. "That's Daffodil."

"Daffodil, eh?"

There was a pause. Daffodil was an obscure horse comparatively.

"Uncle!"

"Yes, son?"

"You won't let it go any further, will you? I promised Bassett."

"Bassett be damned, old man! What's he got to do with it?"

"We're partners. We've been partners from the first. Uncle, he lent me my first five shillings, which I lost. I promised him, honour bright, it was only between me and him; only you gave me that ten-shilling note I started winning with, so I thought you were lucky. You won't let it go any further, will you?"

The boy gazed at his uncle from those big, hot, blue eyes, set rather close together. The uncle stirred and laughed uneasily.

"Right you are, son! I'll keep your tip private. Daffodil, eh? How much are you putting on him?"

"All except twenty pounds," said the boy. "I keep that in reserve."

The uncle thought it a good joke.

"You keep twenty pounds in reserve, do you, you young romancer? What are you betting, then?"

"I'm betting three hundred," said the boy gravely. "But it's between you and me, Uncle Oscar! Honour bright?"

The uncle burst into a roar of laughter.

"It's between you and me all right, you young Nat Gould," he said, laughing. "But where's your three hundred?"

"Bassett keeps it for me. We're partners."

"You are, are you! And what is Bassett putting on Daffodil?"

"He won't go quite as high as I do, I expect. Perhaps he'll go a hundred and fifty."

"What, pennies?" laughed the uncle.

"Pounds," said the child, with a surprised look at his uncle. "Bassett keeps a bigger reserve than I do."

Between wonder and amusement Uncle Oscar was silent. He pursued the matter no further, but he determined to take his nephew with him to the Lincoln races.

"Now, son," he said, "I'm putting twenty on Mirza, and I'll put five for you on any horse you fancy. What's your pick?"

"Daffodil, Uncle."

"No, not the fiver on Daffodil!"

"I should if it was my own fiver," said the child.

"Good! Good! Right you are! A fiver for me and a fiver for you on Daffodil."

The child had never been to a race meeting before, and his eyes were blue fire. He pursed his mouth tight, and watched. A Frenchman just in front had put his money on Lancelot. Wild with excitement, he flayed his arms up and down, yelling "Lancelot! Lancelot!" in his French accent.

Daffodil came in first, Lancelot second, Mirza third. The child, flushed with eyes blazing, was curiously serene. His uncle brought him four five-pound notes, four to one.

"What am I to do with these?" he cried, waving them before the boy's eyes.

"I suppose we'll talk to Bassett," said the boy. "I expect I have fifteen hundred now; and twenty in reserve; and this twenty."

His uncle studied him for some moments.

"Look here, son!" he said. "You're not serious about Bassett and that fifteen hundred, are you?"

"Yes, I am. But it's between you and me, Uncle. Honour bright!"

"Honour bright all right, son! But I must talk to Bassett."

"If you'd like to be a partner, Uncle, with Bassett and me, we could all be partners. Only, you'd have to promise, honour bright, Uncle, not to let it go beyond us three. Bassett and I are lucky, and you must be lucky, because it was your ten shillings I started winning with…."

Uncle Oscar took both Bassett and Paul into Richmond Park for an afternoon, and there they talked.

"It's like this, you see, sir," Bassett said. "Master Paul would get me talking about racing events, spinning yarns, you know, sir. And he was always keen on knowing if I'd made or if I'd lost. It's about a year since, now, that I put five shillings on Blush of Dawn for him: and we lost. Then the luck turned, with that ten shillings he had from you: that we put on Singhalese. And since that time, it's been pretty steady, all things considering. What do you say, Master Paul?"

"We're all right when we're sure," said Paul. "It's when we're not quite sure that we go down."

"Oh, but we're careful then," said Bassett.

"But when are you sure?" smiled Uncle Oscar.

"It's Master Paul, sir," said Bassett, in a secret, religious voice. "It's as if he had it from heaven. Like Daffodil, now, for the Lincoln. That was as sure as eggs."

"Did you put anything on Daffodil?" asked Oscar Cresswell.

"Yes, sir. I made my bit."

"And my nephew?"

Bassett was obstinately silent, looking at Paul.

"I made twelve hundred, didn't I, Bassett? I told Uncle I was putting three hundred on Daffodil."

"That's right," said Bassett, nodding.

"But where's the money?" asked the uncle.

"I keep it safe locked up, sir. Master Paul he can have it any minute he likes to ask for it."

"What, fifteen hundred pounds?"

"And twenty! And forty, that is, with the twenty he made on the course."

"It's amazing!" said the uncle.

"If Master Paul offers you to be partners, sir, I would, if I were you: if you'll excuse me," said Bassett.

Oscar Cresswell thought about it.

"I'll see the money," he said.

They drove home again, and, sure enough, Bassett came round to the gardenhouse with fifteen hundred pounds in notes. The twenty pounds' reserve was left with Joe Glee, in the Turf Commission deposit.

"You see, it's all right, Uncle, when I'm sure! Then we go strong, for all we're worth. Don't we, Bassett?"

"We do that, Master Paul."

"And when are you sure?" said the uncle, laughing.

"Oh, well, sometimes I'm absolutely sure, like about Daffodil," said the boy; "and sometimes I have an idea; and sometimes I haven't even an idea, have I, Bassett? Then we're careful, because we mostly go down."

"You do, do you! And when you're sure, like about Daffodil, what makes you sure, sonny?"

"Oh, well, I don't know," said the boy uneasily. "I'm sure, you know, Uncle, that's all."

"It's as if he had it from heaven, sir," Bassett reiterated.

"I should say so!" said the uncle.

But he became a partner. And when the Leger was coming on, Paul was "sure" about Lively Spark, which was a quite inconsiderable horse. The boy insisted on putting a thousand on the horse, Bassett went for five hundred, and Oscar Cresswell two hundred. Lively Spark came in first, and the betting had been ten to one against him. Paul had made ten thousand.

"You see," he said, "I was absolutely sure of him."

Even Oscar Cresswell had cleared two thousand.

"Look here, son," he said, "this sort of thing makes me nervous."

"It needn't, Uncle! Perhaps I shan't be sure again for a long time."

"But what are you going to do with your money?" asked the uncle.

"Of course," said the boy, "I started it for Mother. She said she had no luck, because Father is unlucky, so I thought if I was lucky, it might stop whispering."

"What might stop whispering?"

"Our house. I hate our house for whispering."

"What does it whisper?"

"Why—why"—the boy fidgeted—"why, I don't know, But it's always short of money, you know, Uncle."

"I know it, son, I know it."

"You know people send Mother writs, don't you, Uncle?"

"I'm afraid I do," said the uncle.

"And then the house whispers, like people laughing at you behind your back. It's awful, that is! I thought if I was lucky—"

"You might stop it," added the uncle.

The boy watched him with big blue eyes, that had an uncanny cold fire in them, and he said never a word.

"Well, then!" said the uncle. "What are we doing?"

"I shouldn't like Mother to know I was lucky," said the boy.

"Why not, son?"

"She'd stop me."

"I don't think she would."

"Oh!"—and the boy writhed in an odd way—"I don't want her to know, Uncle."

"All right, son! We'll manage it without her knowing."

They managed it very easily. Paul, at the other's suggestion, handed over five thousand pounds to his uncle, who deposited it with the family lawyer, who was then to inform Paul's mother that a relative had put five thousand pounds into his hands, which sum was to be paid out a thousand pounds at a time, on the mother's birthday, for the next five years.

"So she'll have a birthday present of a thousand pounds for five successive years," said Uncle Oscar. "I hope it won't make it all the harder for her later."

Paul's mother had her birthday in November. The house had been "whispering" worse than ever lately, and, even in spite of his luck, Paul could not bear up against it. He was very anxious to see the effect of the birthday letter, telling his mother about the thousand pounds.

When there were no visitors, Paul now took his meals with his parents, as he was beyond the nursery control. His mother went into town nearly every day. She had discovered that she had an odd knack of sketching furs and dress materials, so she worked secretly in the studio of a friend who was the chief "artist" for the leading drapers. She drew the figures of ladies in furs and ladies in silk and sequins for the newspaper advertisements. This young woman artist earned several thousand pounds a year, but Paul's mother only made several hundreds, and she was again dissatisfied. She so wanted to be first in something, and she did not succeed, even in making sketches for drapery advertisements.

She was down to breakfast on the morning of her birthday. Paul watched her face as she read her letters. He knew the lawyer's letter. As his mother read it, her face hardened and became more expressionless. Then a cold, determined look came on her mouth. She hid the letter under the pile of others, and said not a word about it.

"Didn't you have anything nice in the post for your birthday, Mother?" asked Paul.

"Quite moderately nice," she said, her voice cold and absent.

She went away to town without saying more.

But in the afternoon Uncle Oscar appeared. He said Paul's mother

had had a long interview with the lawyer, asking if the whole five thousand could not be advanced at once, as she was in debt.

"What do you think, Uncle?" said the boy.

"I leave it to you, son."

"Oh, let her have it, then! We can get some more with the other," said the boy.

"A bird in the hand is worth two in the bush, laddie!" said Uncle Oscar.

"But I'm sure to know for the Grand National; or the Lincolnshire; or else the Derby. I'm sure to know for one of them," said Paul.

So Uncle Oscar signed the agreement, and Paul's mother touched the whole five thousand. Then something very curious happened. The voices in the house suddenly went mad, like a chorus of frogs on a spring evening. There were certain new furnishings, and Paul had a tutor. He was really going to Eton, his father's school, in the following autumn. There were flowers in the winter, and blossoming of the luxury Paul's mother had been used to. And yet the voices in the house, behind the sprays of mimosa and almond blossom, and from under the piles of iridescent cushions, simply trilled and screamed in a sort of ecstasy: "There must be more money; Oh-h-h; there must be more money. Oh, now, now-w! Now-w-w—there must be more money!—more than ever! More than ever!"

It frightened Paul terribly. He studied away at his Latin and Greek with his tutor, but his intense hours were spent with Bassett. The Grand National had gone by: he had not "known," and had lost a hundred pounds. Summer was at hand. He was in agony for the Lincoln. But even for the Lincoln he didn't "know," and he lost fifty pounds. He became wild-eyed and strange, as if something were going to explode in him.

"Let it alone, son! Don't you bother about it!" urged Uncle Oscar. But it was as if the boy couldn't really hear what his uncle was saying.

"I've got to know for the Derby! I've got to know for the Derby," the child reiterated, his big blue eyes blazing with a sort of madness.

His mother noticed how overwrought he was.

"You'd better go to the seaside. Wouldn't you like to go now to the seaside, instead of waiting? I think you'd better," she said, looking down at him anxiously, her heart curiously heavy because of him.

But the child lifted his uncanny blue eyes.

"I couldn't possibly go before the Derby, Mother!" he said. "I couldn't possibly!"

"Why not?" she said, her voice becoming heavy when she was opposed. "Why not? You can still go from the seaside to see the Derby with your Uncle Oscar, if that's what you wish. No need for you to wait here. Besides, I think you care too much about these races. It's a bad sign. My family has been a gambling family, and you won't know till you grow up how much damage it has done. But it has done damage. I shall have to send Bassett away, and ask Uncle Oscar not to talk racing to you, unless you promise to be reasonable about it: go away to the seaside and forget it. You're all nerves!"

"I'll do what you like, Mother, so long as you don't send me away till after the Derby," the boy said.

"Send you away from where? Just from this house?"

"Yes," he said, gazing at her.

"Why, you curious child, what makes you care about this house so much, suddenly? I never knew you loved it."

He gazed at her without speaking. He had a secret within a secret, something he had not divulged, even to Bassett or to his Uncle Oscar.

But his mother, after standing undecided and a little bit sullen for some moments, said:

"Very well, then! Don't go to the seaside till after the Derby, if you don't wish it. But promise me you won't let your nerves go to pieces. Promise you won't think so much about horse racing and events, as you call them!"

"Oh, no," said the boy casually. "I won't think much about them, Mother. You needn't worry. I wouldn't worry, Mother, if I were you."

"If you were me and I were you," said his mother, "I wonder what we should do!"

"But you know you needn't worry, Mother, don't you?" the boy repeated.

"I should be awfully glad to know it," she said wearily.

"Oh, well, you can, you know. I mean, you ought to know you needn't worry," he insisted.

"Ought I? Then I'll see about it," she said.

Paul's secret of secrets was his wooden horse, that which had no name. Since he was emancipated from a nurse and a nursery governess, he had had his rocking horse removed to his own bedroom at the top of the house.

"Surely, you're too big for a rocking horse!" his mother had remonstrated.

"Well, you see, Mother, till I can have a real horse, I like to have some sort of animal about," had been his quaint answer.

"Do you feel he keeps you company?" she laughed.

"Oh, yes! He's very good, he always keeps me company, when I'm there," said Paul.

So the horse, rather shabby, stood in an arrested prance in the boy's bedroom.

The Derby was drawing near, and the boy grew more and more tense. He hardly heard what was spoken to him, he was very frail, and his eyes were really uncanny. His mother had sudden strange seizures of uneasiness about him. Sometimes, for half-an-hour, she would feel a sudden anxiety about him that was almost anguish. She wanted to rush to him at once, and know he was safe.

Two nights before the Derby, she was at a big party in town, when one of her rushes of anxiety about her boy, her firstborn, gripped her heart till she could hardly speak. She fought with the feeling, might and main, for she believed in common sense. But it was too strong. She had to leave the dance and go downstairs to telephone to the country. The children's nursery governess was terribly surprised and startled at being rung up in the night.

"Are the children all right, Miss Wilmot?"

"Oh, yes, they are quite all right."

"Master Paul? Is he all right?"

"He went to bed as right as a trivet. Shall I run up and look at him?"

"No," said Paul's mother reluctantly. "No! Don't trouble. It's all right. Don't sit up. We shall be home fairly soon." She did not want her son's privacy intruded upon.

"Very good," said the governess.

It was about one o'clock when Paul's mother and father drove up to their house. All was still. Paul's mother went to her room and slipped off her white fur cloak. She had told her maid not to wait up for her. She heard her husband downstairs, mixing a whisky and soda.

And then, because of the strange anxiety at her heart, she stole upstairs to her son's room. Noiselessly she went along the upper corridor. Was there a faint noise? What was it?

She stood, with arrested muscles, outside his door, listening. There was a strange, heavy, and yet not loud noise. Her heart stood still. It was a soundless noise, yet rushing and powerful. Something huge, in violent, hushed motion. What was it? What in God's name was it? She ought to know. She felt that she knew the noise. She knew what it was.

Yet she could not place it. She couldn't say what it was. And on and on it went, like a madness.

Softly, frozen with anxiety and fear, she turned the door handle.

The room was dark. Yet in the space near the window, she heard and saw something plunging to and fro. She gazed in fear and amazement.

Then suddenly she switched on the light, and saw her son, in his green pyjamas, madly surging on the rocking horse. The blaze of light suddenly lit him up, as he urged the wooden horse, and lit her up, as she stood, blonde, in her dress of pale green and crystal, in the doorway.

"Paul!" she cried. "Whatever are you doing?"

"It's Malabar!" he screamed, in a powerful, strange voice. "It's Malabar!"

His eyes blazed at her for one strange and senseless second, as he ceased urging his wooden horse. Then he fell with a crash to the ground, and she, all her tormented motherhood flooding upon her, rushed to gather him up.

But he was unconscious, and unconscious he remained, with some brain fever. He talked and tossed, and his mother sat stonily by his side.

"Malabar! It's Malabar! Bassett, Bassett, I know! It's Malabar!"

So the child cried, trying to get up and urge the rocking horse that gave him his inspiration.

"What does he mean by Malabar?" asked the heart-frozen mother.

"I don't know," said the father stonily.

"What does he mean by Malabar?" she asked her brother Oscar.

"It's one of the horses running for the Derby," was the answer.

And, in spite of himself, Oscar Cresswell spoke to Bassett, and himself put a thousand on Malabar; at fourteen to one.

The third day of the illness was critical; they were waiting for a change. The boy, with his rather long, curly hair, was tossing ceaselessly on the pillow. He neither slept nor regained consciousness, and his eyes were like blue stones. His mother sat, feeling her heart had gone, turned actually into a stone.

In the evening, Oscar Cresswell did not come, but Bassett sent a message saying could he come up for one moment, just one moment? Paul's mother was very angry at the intrusion, but on second thoughts she agreed. The boy was the same. Perhaps Bassett might bring him to consciousness.

The gardener, a shortish fellow with a little brown moustache, and sharp little brown eyes, tiptoed into the room, touched his imaginary cap to Paul's mother, and stole to the bedside, staring with glittering, smallish eyes at the tossing, dying child.

"Master Paul!" he whispered. "Master Paul! Malabar came in first all right, a clean win. I did as you told me. You've made over seventy thousand pounds, you have; you've got over eighty thousand. Malabar came in all right, Master Paul."

"Malabar! Malabar! Did I say Malabar, Mother? Did I say Malabar? Do you think I'm lucky, Mother? I knew Malabar, didn't I? Over eighty thousand pounds! I call that lucky, don't you, Mother? Over eighty thousand pounds! I knew, didn't I know I knew? Malabar came in all right. If I ride my horse till I'm sure, then I tell you, Bassett, you can go as high as you like. Did you go for all you were worth, Bassett?"

"I went a thousand on it, Master Paul."

"I never told you, Mother, that if I can ride my horse, and get there, then I'm absolutely sure—oh, absolutely! Mother, did I ever tell you? I am lucky!"

"No, you never did," said the mother.

But the boy died in the night.

And even as he lay dead, his mother heard her brother's voice saying to her: "My God, Hester, you're eighty-odd thousand to the good, and a poor devil of a son to the bad. But, poor devil, poor devil, he's best gone out of a life where he rides his rocking horse to find a winner."

Notes

Ascot a race course in Ascot, England, founded by Queen Anne in 1711. The first four-day annual Royal Meeting horse race took place there in 1768 and continues to this day. From this race course came the use of the word *ascot,* meaning a broad-necked scarf knotted so that one end lies flat against the other. This apparel was customarily worn by the upper-class spectators at Ascot.

batman an attendant who serves a military officer

blade of the "turf" a gambler on horse races

writs a written order issued by a court, stating that the addressee must legally either engage in or stop engaging in a specified act

Activities

1. Write a journal entry in which you first summarize the story. Next describe your responses to the characters and events at various points. Then develop two open-ended questions you are interested in discussing. Work with others in the class to develop a structured discussion around the group's questions. Afterward add one or two paragraphs to your journal entry, incorporating new insights or interpretations from your discussion.

2. Create a visual representation, such as a collage, collection of objects, or a sketch, that conveys the overall mood and theme of this story without including any of the characters. Reread the story closely, noting descriptions of objects and the physical setting. Then consider the mood, or *emotional setting*, of the story. Identify which objects, if any, might play a symbolic role in "The Rocking-Horse Winner" and include those in your visual. Display your work and invite others to comment on your interpretation.

3. "The Rocking-Horse Winner" is set in an upper middle-class home in England, early in the twentieth century. Choose a passage of dialogue that reflects this context, both in the language and speech patterns of the characters and in the values and beliefs that underlie their words. Then create a new version of the passage by rewriting the dialogue to reflect a contemporary context of your choice. Which elements of the story are specific to the context in which it was written? Which elements are universal?

Another Viewpoint: Archetypal Patterns

In literary traditions from various cultures, the horse has functioned as an omen of death and symbolized the transport of the soul. How might Paul's rides be interpreted as a journey of the soul to the "other world"? What does he gain from these journeys? Do research to learn more about symbolism connected both with the horse and with visits to another world beyond life. Then present an argument for or against this interpretation of "The Rocking-Horse Winner."

Storefronts, Jose Luis Ortiz

Write Me Sometime

Taien Ng-Chan

Taien Ng-Chan is a playwright, poet, editor, producer, and photographer, as well as a writer of fiction. Born in Vancouver in 1970, she is currently based in Montreal. Ng-Chan was a winner of the CBC New Voices Radio Drama Competition in 2000. She has also served as a contributing editor and Web site designer at *Matrix* magazine, as well as editor and producer of *Speakeasy*, a webzine. Ng-Chan has said, "I often find it painful to read my older writings, but there are certain pieces that work for me every time I read them, and that's when I think I've been successful." When have you considered your writing successful? What are some of the qualities of a piece of writing that make it a success?

Whenever I think of my father, I think of food. I think of the years we spent eating at McDonald's and the Old Spaghetti Factory and pizza parlours galore. From as far back as I can remember, I saw my dad only once a week, when he picked me up every Saturday afternoon to go out for lunch. I'd get to choose which restaurant we'd go to, and then he'd ask me about school, my mother and assorted things that I can't remember now. I was probably too busy eating. My mother did come along with us at first, mainly to keep an eye on me, but she eventually stopped because she didn't want to deal with my father. I don't blame her.

When I turned ten, my six-year-old half sister started joining our Saturday excursions. Suddenly, I had a weekend sibling, which was strange because I had always thought I was an only child. The three of us would argue about where to go for lunch, but as my sister liked the same things I did, it wouldn't take too long for us to decide. Every now and then we'd let Dad choose, but we knew he'd just want to go for dim sum, which we thought was boring.

I used to look forward to these Saturdays because I could eat anything I wanted. As I got older, we started going out for steak and seafood, but for the longest time, I just wanted pizza. My mother never made pizza, or even spaghetti. Sometimes she made pork chops or shepherd's pie or soya sauce chicken and rice, which I liked well enough. But I loved my pizza. Thin crust with extra sauce, sometimes ham and pineapple, sometimes all dressed but no olives. My dad and I were harsh pizza critics: the sauce had to be spicy, and the vegetables cut and arranged just right. An abundance of pineapple was a must, and the cheese had to pull away into long, thin strands between the slices. One particular restaurant failed abysmally to meet our standards and was forever dubbed "The Yucky House of Pizza," which we'd shout every time we drove past it.

After lunch, we'd go bowling, or to the dinosaur park at the zoo, or paddle boating at Prince's Island in the summer, or skating and tobogganing in the winter. Sometimes, Dad would take us to IKEA and spend an hour pretending to look at furniture while we jumped around in the room full of blue and red plastic balls. Other times, we'd go to the bakery at the mall and each pick out two slices of cake, plus a couple for my mom. Chocolate cheesecake, fruit tarts, danishes. We'd make a pot of tea and pretend to have a party. Then, just before dinnertime, my dad and my sister would go home.

The images I have in my head of these Saturdays are blurry, happy pictures that go with my dad's stories like illustrations. There was the time he ate two slices of a pizza and I ate the rest. I must have been only six or seven at the time, and I see myself sitting small in the corner of a restaurant booth with dark brown vinyl seats, a huge pizza in front of me. "The whole pizza!" my dad exclaims every time he brings up that story.

Or the time we went for spaghetti, and the top fell off the container as I was shaking out some parmesan over the spicy meat sauce, spilling a ton of cheese like a snowfall over the entire plate. That's the picture I have, me with the container still in my hand, the lid in the spaghetti. From then on, we made a great ritual of checking the lids every time.

If I could look just at these pictures, I'd think that my childhood was made up of fifty-two happy lunches a year. But somewhere along the way, I stopped looking forward to Saturdays. I'd listen to my sister talk about playing basketball with Dad after supper, or the way they both called grilled cheese sandwiches "grouchy" sandwiches. Or notice how my sister knew all the songs on the tape of Chinese opera that my dad liked to play in the car. It left me with the taste of something sharp and grey under my tongue, like a tiny piece of rock had slipped into my food. If I wasn't careful, I'd break my teeth on it. Once I told him not to bother coming any more, that I had lots of friends and needed more time to play with them. But I felt sad about it afterwards, remembering how his face had changed. After that, I seemed to go into automatic cheer whenever I saw him. Our Saturday lunch rituals continued right up until the time I moved out to go to university.

We live in different cities now, and I only see my father once or twice a year, when I come home to Calgary for Christmas or if he happens to come by Vancouver on business. I see my half sister even less, and I'm still apt to think of myself as an only child. I think she feels the same way, because we've never tried to stay in touch.

I don't know why I feel the need to keep in touch with my father, when he wasn't much more in my life than lunch once a week. But somehow I think that the lines have to be kept open. My mom thinks so too, oddly enough.

"Have you heard from your dad lately?" she says every time she phones. "What did he say? You should write him."

And I do write him. I write him longer letters than I write my friends. I write him about what I've been doing, how my classes are going, what projects I've been working on. I sent him the entire movie script that I had gotten funding to write, and the last essay I researched about the effects of Darwinism on Victorian literature. I tell him about newspaper articles I've been reading on the controversy over the age of the universe, and what I've been thinking about our last conversation on artificial intelligence.

My father, you see, is a scientist. More precisely, a geophysicist. When I was younger, he used to tell me he sat at a desk and drank lots of coffee for a living. When I found out that he flew all over the world to look at rocks and stuff, I wanted to be a scientist too. Or an artist. "A scientist or an artist, I haven't made up my mind yet," I used to tell people who asked what I wanted to be when I grew up. In my letters to my dad, I guess I try to be both.

He hardly ever writes back to me, but every so often he calls. Every time we talk, we say that we should write more often, get to know each other better. And then I won't hear from him for another year. I feel as if I'm trying to communicate with outer-space life-forms, my satellite dish sending out signals just in case.

The last time I saw my father was about a year ago, when he was in Vancouver for a business meeting. He called me just before noon and wanted to take me out for lunch. I had already eaten an avocado and tomato sandwich.

"That's okay," Dad said. "You can eat more!"

"Well, maybe we can go for a walk instead," I suggested. "We could go to Stanley Park."

"I can't do too much walking," he said. "I've been having a little trouble with my feet lately. Your dad's getting old, you know…"

"Oh, Dad, you're not getting old," I said, as cheerfully as I could. "We can do something else. Maybe we can go to the art gallery. Or what else do you want to see?"

"I don't have too much time," he said. "Why don't we go have lunch anyway? We can go a little later if you like."

So I gave up and let him take me out for lunch. We ended up at a trendy restaurant on Robson Street, since it was close by, and Dad tried to order me everything on the menu.

"How about an appetizer?" he said, poking his finger at the description of the liver pâté. "This sounds good. Or how about a salad? That's good for you. How are you eating these days? You should have some soup, too."

"I'm really not that hungry," I said. "I can't eat like I used to. What about you? What are you going to have?"

"I'm not too hungry either. I'll just have a beer," he said. I'd never seen him have a drink before. "Maybe we should've gone to the pub," I said jokingly.

The waiter came over and waited.

"I guess I'll have the spinach salad," I said, handing him my menu. "And a glass of white wine, please."

"I'll have a beer," Dad said. "Any kind."

The waiter nodded and smiled and went away. Dad looked at me funny for a second, probably because he'd never seen me drink before, either.

"Is that all you're having?" he said. "You should have an entrée. The veal looked very good."

"Veal…," I said, screwing up my nose. "Dad, I'm a vegetarian."

"Oh. That's right." He scratched his head.

I could see him wanting to debate the issue, just as he had when I first explained to him why I was a vegetarian. I was back in Calgary for Christmas. I hadn't seen my dad or my sister in quite a while, and we were about to go out for lunch when I told them the big news.

"So," he had said, "that means you don't eat meat any more." My sister looked at me as if I was crazy.

"What about chicken?" Dad asked. "Do you eat chicken? Seafood?"

"No, Dad, chickens aren't vegetables. Fish aren't vegetables either."

"What's your reason for not eating meat? It's not just because you have to kill animals, is it? After all, death is a part of life."

"I know. If you went out and killed your own animal and ate it, that'd be fine with me."

I had launched into the whole thing about battery cages and steroids and how you could feed the world with the grain that goes to feeding cows and how the rainforests of Brazil were being destroyed for hamburgers. Dad countered each point. We ended up discussing the impact individuals could make, and why Buddhists didn't eat meat. My sister just looked on.

Finally, Dad asked us what we wanted for lunch. My sister suggested pizza.

"Uh," I said, "actually, I don't eat pizza much any more. I try to stay away from dairy products. Hard to digest."

But there weren't too many places to go to in Calgary, so I compromised. "Wow," my sister said after lunch. "I never had a pizza without meat before."

When the waiter came back with our drinks and my spinach salad, there were bacon bits that I had to pick out. My dad watched me for a while and fiddled with his beer glass. Then he started what had become our usual routine.

"So," he began, "what do you think of what's been happening in the news lately?"

We had an ongoing discussion about politics and the economy and the state of the world—it gave us something to talk about. These talks always started and ended the same way. He would ask me what I thought about recent events, and then we would talk about the future, the need to adapt to change, the impact of technology. Dad always got very animated when talking about technology. I would bring up the need for human responsibility in science, and he would agree with me wholeheartedly. They were good conversations.

My father likes to debate things, to argue for the sake of argument. My mother said he had wanted to be a philosopher when he was young and idealistic. A lot like you, she said. That was when she first met him. That was before he decided there was no living to be made in philosophy and went into the oil industry.

"Arts," he said to me once, "are for the weekends." I told him then that I wanted to be a writer. "Journalism?" he said.

"No, writing," I said. "Stories and plays and stuff."

"Write for the newspapers," he said. "That's what you should do if you like writing."

I told him I would think about it.

But he never did ask me what I wrote about. And I never asked what he thought of the things I sent him, either. Except once, about the Darwin essay.

"Interesting," he said. "Very interesting. Why don't you write a book about the relationship between science and the arts?"

I said I might do that. And we haven't mentioned it since.

By the time I had finished my salad, Dad had convinced me to have dessert. I mulled over the menu, torn between the chocolate hazelnut torte and the blueberry apple flan.

"Aren't you going to have any?" I asked, hoping we could swap bites. Dad shook his head.

"Why don't you get both anyway?" he said. "After all, how often do you get to have lunch with your dad?"

I settled for the flan.

The rest of the lunch was spent in polite enquiry. We had run out of politics and technology, so I asked him how his work was, and how my sister was. He asked me how my work was, and how my mother was. She's fine, we both said. Things are going fine.

After I had finished eating, we walked up Robson Street. We passed chocolate shops and pizza joints, and every time I looked in the window of a store, Dad would ask me if I wanted anything. When we passed a frozen yogurt shop he wanted to buy a tub of frozen yogurt for me.

"Yogurt's very healthy," he said. "I want you to eat right."

"But I just ate."

"You can eat it later," he said. "You're a growing girl!"

"Not any more," I said. "I haven't grown an inch in years."

"Remember that time you ate a whole pizza?"

"I was seven years old, Dad."

"A whole pizza! How about getting some pizza now? You can bring it home for dinner."

"That's okay."

"You don't eat much any more. Are you getting enough protein? You have to be careful, being vegetarian."

I nodded and smiled. "Yes, Dad."

We went on like this all the way up the street, with Dad ducking into a store every now and then despite my protests. By the time we reached my apartment, my arms were laden with bags of food. I invited him in, but he said he had had only a couple of hours to spare.

"Write me sometime," he said. "Let me know if there's anything you need."

I closed the door behind him, my insides feeling forlorn and empty. I went into the kitchen to put the pizza in the fridge, the frozen yogurt in the freezer, the chocolate in the cupboard. But I didn't feel like eating again for days.

When I told my mother about Dad's visit, she wanted to know all the details. Where we ate, what we talked about, what he had bought me.

"Did he give you any spending money?" she said. "Well, he should have. He's your father. And he can afford it."

"I don't want him to," I said.

I could hear her clucking her tongue over the phone. "You're his *daughter*," she said. "You shouldn't even have to *ask*."

I haven't seen my father since that lunch, although he did call me a couple of weeks ago. I was out at the time. When I came home, I found my father's voice on my answering machine, sounding almost querulous. He said that he'd call back some other time. I called him a few days later. The phone rang twice before he picked it up.

"Hi, Dad," I said, only to be greeted enthusiastically with my sister's name. "Uh, no," I said. I felt almost apologetic. "It's your other daughter."

"Oh," Dad said. There was a moment's silence, then he cleared his throat. "You sound very much alike."

"Well," I said, as cheerfully as I could. "We are sisters, after all." The conversation went downhill from there.

"Are you in town?" my father asked.

"No, I just called to say hi. And to return your call."

"Ah," he said.

I asked him how his work was, and how my sister was; he asked me how my work was, and how my mother was. She's fine, we both said. Things are going fine.

Notes

dim sum traditional Chinese breakfast dish of steamed dumplings and pastry, filled with meat and vegetables

IKEA a Scandinavian furniture warehouse store, featuring "assemble-it-yourself" furniture displayed in room-like settings

Darwinism the theory of evolution first put forward by Charles Darwin in his book *On the Origin of Species* (1859); subsequently used as the basis for theories about social evolution in the Victorian era (1832–1901)

geophysicist a scientist who studies the physics of the earth

Activities

1. The story begins with the narrator's observation that "whenever I think of my father, I think of food." Explain how the changes in the relationship between the girl and her father are reflected in the changes in what, when, where, and under what circumstances they meet and eat.

2. The story concludes with these lines: "She's fine, we both said. Things are going fine." Find another point in the story where these lines are used. How does their repetition add to the pathos of the story? Explain the irony in these words.

3. The narrator is a creative writer and her father is a geophysicist. With a partner, locate a creative writer and scientist in your community. Interview each, specifically asking them in what ways their professions are similar to and different from other professions. In a short essay, use specific examples from the story to assess the extent to which you think the conflict between the girl and her father is the result of the differing perspectives of a writer and a scientist.

Calgary from Sunnyside

Margaret Shelton

About the Visual   Margaret Shelton was born in Bruce, Alberta, in 1915 and has spent most of her life in Calgary. As a young woman, she studied at Calgary's Provincial Institute of Technology and Art (now The Alberta College of Art and Design). Shelton has produced a large body of work that includes watercolours, prints, and drawings. *Calgary from Sunnyside* is a woodblock print, made by cutting a design in a block of wood and using ink to transfer the image to paper. In an artwork representing a familiar place, do you prefer the work to feature recognizable landmarks and reflect your mental images or would you rather have it offer a unique perspective? Why?

Activities

1. Record your first impression of *Calgary from Sunnyside* by jotting down the initial words that come to mind. Use your notes to write a dialogue journal entry to exchange with a partner. Read and respond to each other's writing. What factors in your own experiences and preferences affected your reactions?

2. In preparation for a class discussion, analyze some of the key visual elements and principles of design that Shelton has used in this print. How has she used contrast to emphasize parts of the picture? What texture and shapes has she used? What observation or "truth" about an urban landscape does the print convey?

woodblock print, 12 cm x 24.4 cm

Outside Edges

Ivan Dorin

Ivan Dorin lives in Calgary, Alberta. He is an earth scientist who has worked at the Royal Tyrrell Museum of Palaeontology in Drumheller, Alberta. He writes in his spare time and his stories have appeared in literary journals, including *Alberta Rebound* and *Vox*. "Outside Edges" explores a young man's goals and his relationship with his father. Think about a personal goal you had when you were young. Did you share your goal with anyone and, if so, what was that person's reaction? How did the goal change as you got older? What are some of the benefits of setting goals? Are there any drawbacks?

I always wanted my feelings for David to be understated, a tastefully drawn picture in a smooth-edged rectangular frame. I didn't want something too big for me to express. I didn't want to gush; to take endless rolls of baby pictures or display my kid's sports trophies for everyone to see. I was surprised at how difficult it was. I restrained myself constantly. I didn't just believe that my kid was special; that he could do anything he set his mind to. I *knew* it, and that made it even harder for me to find the right words. Once when he was seven, I was boring everyone at the supper table by talking about my latest real estate deal, so I asked David what he had learned in school that day. He said the teacher talked about Christopher Columbus and his four ships. I chewed over the names for a minute: Nina, Pinta, Santa Maria; Nina, Pinta, Santa Maria. Finally I swallowed.

"Are you sure about that? I thought Columbus had three ships."

"Well," he said expressionlessly, pausing to wash down his broccoli, "he started out with four, but one went off the edge."

He didn't crack a smile all through dinner. I started to think the world *was* flat before Columbus. My favourite line came when he was eight years old, on the way home from school.

"Daddy?"

"Uh huh?"

"When I grow up, I'm gonna skate across the country."

I started to smile, but that little face looked so determined. (If anyone could do it, you could.) "It's a big country."

"But people have run across it, haven't they? And skating's easier than running, once you get good. I'm sure I could skate faster than that Terry Fox guy. He had to run, and he had only one leg."

"He ran along the highway though. How would you skate on the highway?"

"I could have a Zamboni drive along in front of me."

No, I thought, the ice wouldn't be thick enough. Then I got this image of a convoy of Zambonis steaming down the Trans-Canada, past a signpost saying "Wawa 46," past some disconsolate hitchhikers ("Wawa's the armpit of Canada," I remember them saying. "If you get left there, you can be stranded for days") framed against the snow-covered pines. Then came David in his hockey gear, just far enough behind for the water to freeze in front of him, pausing from his shuffle to scoop a puck out of the ditch, deking out an invisible defender, and getting a breakaway on the Pacific.

I really shouldn't have laughed.

"Well, I could, couldn't I?"

(You bet. Will you let me drive the Zamboni?)

"I don't think the government would let you flood the highway. It wouldn't be safe."

"But I wouldn't need much. Just the part on the side."

"Not all the highways in this country are as good as ours, son. Some shoulders are just dirt and gravel. Others aren't even there at all."

"Oh."

"You just worry about skating across the rink for now, okay?"

"Yeah."

It was a long drive home. He hardly moved except when we crossed the Bow River, and he craned his neck for a better view. I wanted to rewind and start the conversation over somehow, but all I could think of was how simple it would be to have a son who just wanted to be a fireman. We didn't talk again until after supper.

"Where does the Bow River come from, Dad?"

"Somewhere in Banff, I guess."

"But where does it really start?"

I had to admit I didn't know. I found a road map, and we traced the thin blue line to Bow Lake, but he wasn't satisfied.

"Well, this is a road map of Alberta," I explained. "They can't show every little creek."

"Are there ones where they do have all the creeks on?"

"The University library has some, I think. I'm going there tomorrow, if you'd like to look at some."

"Really? Could I? Mum, guess what! Dad's taking me to the library tomorrow."

I expected him to forget about it overnight, but he didn't. I told him that I had my own work to do and he would have to be by himself part of the time, but he didn't mind. I think I helped him with the map index, so that he could find out which maps he wanted to look at. In hopes that his interest might lead him into real estate someday, I showed him how the township and range system worked. It was the last thing I ever told him about maps.

When I got home from work the next day, he was poring over a pair of brand new topographic maps. He had obtained the address of the government map office from the librarian at the University, dumped out his piggy bank and begged Marie to drive him there at lunchtime. "Look, Dad! We live at 51 degrees 2 minutes north, 114 degrees 5 minutes west. And here's where the Elbow River meets the Bow." He wasn't satisfied for long. For one thing, Calgary falls on a four-corner junction in the topographic system, and even at a scale of 1 to 250,000 or four miles to the inch, it takes four maps to show the whole city. He liked the 1 to 50,000 (1.24 inches to the mile) Calgary map best, but its edges frustrated him. There were always so many more hills and valleys and creeks just beyond the edge of the map. His allowance couldn't come in fast enough. His favourite map had a little tic-tac-toe style grid in the bottom right-hand corner, labelled "Index to adjoining sheets of National Topographic System," with Calgary in the middle. As his eye spiralled outward from our house, he wanted more and more to have those eight adjoining sheets. We didn't have a maid then; Marie paid him for doing chores around the house, and she said she'd never had it so good. One by one the maps came in: Dalroy, Dalemead, Priddis, Bragg Creek, Jumpingpound Creek, Wildcat Hills, Crossfield, Irricana.

His ninth birthday presented us with a dilemma. We weren't strapped for money, even then; there just weren't that many things he wanted. We'd bought him things like a bicycle and a baseball glove and a new hockey stick, and he hadn't touched some of his toys. As a last resort I asked him, rather sheepishly, if he'd like me to go to the map office with him and pick up a couple of maps for his birthday.

The map office had a large index map on one wall, dividing Canada into more than a hundred blocks arranged in north-south columns, with numbers increasing from east to west. The women at the desk greeted him by name, and asked all sorts of questions about him while he flipped through the sample maps of block 82.

"I don't really know what got him started," I told them. "He wanted to know about the Bow River first, and it just mushroomed from there." He closed the cover of block 82, and wandered from one sample pile to another, northward through Alberta, 83, 84, 85.

"How many maps per block?" I asked, eyeing the map on the wall.

"Sixteen, at 1:250,000 scale, A through P. Some blocks are mostly ocean. The 1:250,000 series covers the whole country with 917 sheets. Each of those is subdivided into sixteen 1:50,000 scale maps."

"My God. I'll be ruined."

We watched him move north through Saskatchewan. 72, 73, 74.

"Well, we have some extra maps. Sometimes we order too many, or they go out of print. Maybe he might be interested in those."

We expected a couple of rolls of maps sitting on a desk somewhere. He was intrigued at the prospect of getting some maps for free, of course, but wasn't prepared to be led around the counter and find rolls stacked three feet high. It was like seeing Anthony Henday climb one of thousands of ordinary prairie hills, reach the top with his eyes to the ground, and look up to see for the first time the blue and white wall of the Rockies spread before him.

Mackenzie Delta. "Ooh, look at all the *lakes*!" Spence Bay. "Look at how high the raised beaches are, Dad! That's where the ocean used to be. The ice is gone so the land is bouncing back now. See? It came up 400 feet here." Tammarvi River. "Why do the lakes and rivers all run the same way, Dad? And they're so straight." Tanquary Fiord. "This part goes all the way across the map. I bet the whole thing would run from here to Lethbridge." Azure River. "The glacier goes all the way down to 5,200 feet. They must get tons of snow there." We must have been there for a couple of hours at least, rolling and unrolling the maps. It astounded him that such treasures could remain unclaimed. We had time to examine only a few maps closely; we had all we could carry by the time we were finished. Then he turned to the clerk and asked, as if opening his last Christmas present, "Is that all?"

"We order maps all the time," she smiled. "If you check back in a couple of months, we'll probably have some more."

He was content to leave then. We were partway out the door when I stopped.

"What is it, Dad?"

"Well, uh, haven't we forgotten something?"

"What?"

"Your birthday present."

"Oh."

"We don't have to, now I mean—"

"No, that's okay, Dad." He put on his best smile for me. "I know some I really want." He turned back to the index map on the wall. "This one," he said, pointing just west of Lake Superior. Then he took a step west. "And this one," just west of Calgary. 52B, Quetico, and 82N, Golden. There was no hesitation; no implication that he was just being kind. But after that, it seemed that he was happiest with his maps for company, and there was nothing more I could give him.

Sometimes I thought about that day in the car, and would imagine us on skating expeditions. Once I saw some figure skaters drawing circles on the ice with scribes, telescoping metal rods with screws at both ends and foldout handles. As I watched, I began to see myself and David at the bottom of a frozen waterfall. I stood on the bank with a duffel bag, awaiting his instructions like a surgical caddy as he scanned what I thought would be a portage.

"Hmmn," he said, frowning in concentration, "I'll need the figure skates for this one." I passed the skates to him efficiently. He changed out of his hockey skates without taking his eyes off the curtain of ice, stood up and held out his right hand, palm upward.

"Scribe," he said solemnly.

"Scribe," I answered, passing it to him.

"Other scribe."

"Other scribe."

He skated to the bottom of the waterfall, rechecked his route, and then drove one skate, toe pick first, into the vertical ice face. Then he extended the scribes to full length, stuck them into the ice above, and shortened them as he climbed. At first, he looked as if he were being pulled upward by two thin metal caterpillars, but as he climbed higher, he used them less and less. His toes turned outward too; with each step, he put more weight on the blades. Then his skates began to slide upward a little more with each step, and as he approached the top, I realized that he wasn't climbing anymore. And I wanted to tell him, hold on, I'll just run up and throw down a rope for you.

Sipanok Channel, Oskikebuk Lake, Ne-Parle-Pas Rapids, Potter Landing. He kept the index maps beside his bed and coloured them in, one square at a time, as his pile of maps grew thicker and thicker. He never folded them, and rolled them up only for transport. When the older kids were still at home, we went on Sunday drives to Moraine Lake (the one on the back of the $20 bill), and he studied the route in keen anticipation. But when we reached the turnoff just below Lake Louise, he always wanted me to avoid the familiar left-hand route. "Can't we go toward Field this time, Dad? Just a few miles?" Sure, I told him. Today Field, tomorrow Japan. (If I went everywhere I wanted to go with you, we'd never get home.) Eventually, he stopped mentioning that stretch of road directly. He talked intermittently about the sights to be seen just across the border in Yoho: Takakkaw Falls, Emerald Lake, Lake O'Hara, the Natural Bridge. We never had quite enough time. I had to draw the line somewhere.

Nova Zembia Island, Sabine Peninsula, Coral Harbour, Laredo Sound. As a teenager, David didn't put up posters of rock singers or women in wet T-shirts. When he found enough adjoining maps, he wallpapered the ceiling and walls of his room with them. He cut away the white borders and fitted the edges together, so that his room became a chunk of northwestern Ontario. I always closed his door when we had company. It wasn't the maps themselves that bothered me, but the way I was forced to look at them. I felt distanced and suffocated at the same time, as if part of the globe had been turned inside out.

Pointe Louis XIV, Cape Krusenstern, Queen Maud Gulf, Sault Ste. Marie. His supply network extended across the country: friends and relatives, retiring geologists, oil companies, librarians, someone who knew someone in the Ottawa map office. The maps filled his room, overflowed into the basement and attic, formed isolated blocks, lines and checkerboard patterns that grew and filled and reached toward each other across the vast jigsaw puzzle. By the time he graduated from high school, the gaps on the 1:250,000 index map had become lonely outposts in an expanse of pencil crayon, but he was more interested in completing his 1:50,000 collection. I tried to get him to tell me why, but he only said, "I'd map the country at one to one if I could."

He left home to go to university, got a student loan and a place just big enough for him and his maps. He worked in the map office during the summer. I felt more at ease after he moved out; the further apart we were, the more I enjoyed the reunions.

Smoky Falls, Grinnell Glacier, Tute Inlet, Swift Current, Lac Mesgouez, Washahigan Lake. The summers flew by; he graduated and got a job at the main map office in Ottawa. He came home for Christmas, without a wife or girlfriend, and always made one visit to the map office. He told me about how more of the Arctic was being mapped at 1:50,000, and that the whole country would probably be covered soon. I told him about my plans to make West Edmonton Mall look like the corner grocery store. I wanted to build sort of a Disneyland North and call it Western Canada Mall. Each year Marie, the other "kids" and I had a few more plans drawn up. By the time David was 32, we had the land and were ready to break ground. We were still unsatisfied about the skating facilities, though. We wanted them bigger and better than those at West Edmonton Mall, and indoors, but that was all we could agree on. David listened to us argue over turkey. After dinner, he brought me a piece of paper with an irregular triangle shape drawn on it in pencil.

"It should be about 350 feet across, this way. The other directions would be a little less. It would probably be the biggest indoor ice surface in the world. What do you think? Could you do it?"

"Well, sure we could do it. That's about the right size. But why the shape?"

"Well, it's Canada, of course. One unit of ice for every 50,000 of Canada."

I said it would be too expensive to hire people to cut and assemble all those maps, and we wouldn't be able to get the right plastic to cover them, and even with uncoloured ice, we'd have to keep replacing it to keep it transparent, and maybe the maps should be displayed some other way. "No!" he said. "This isn't just the biggest map in the world, of the most glaciated country in the world, with the largest area of fresh water in the world, and most of the largest lakes. It's fur and fish and floating logs and Toller Cranston and Gaetan Boucher and Gordie Howe and voyageurs and cold and people who are supposed to know how to make love in a canoe! If you can't skate on it, it's not Canadian."

The rest of the family eventually convinced me. I guess I really wanted to be convinced. But I held out until David had gone back to Ottawa.

Port aux Basques, Kananaskis Lakes, Seymour Arm, Pipmuacan Reservoir, Snowbird Lake, Lac la Ronge, Trois Rivières, Kiyiu Lake, Carcajou Canyon. When he came home the next Christmas, he looked like he hadn't slept in days. He didn't say hi or anything, just walked straight across the carpet and handed me the index map, worn and starting to curl up at the corners. I saw nothing but coloured pencil.

"That's great," I said. "Amazing. Should I arrange for a truck to have them moved?"

He looked at me as if I had slapped him. Then he turned and walked back out the door.

I went and sat in his old room. Somehow, I'd never arranged to have the maps taken down. I looked at that tangle of lakes, rivers and muskeg for I don't know how long, squinting, running my fingers along the lines. I even got a stepladder to get a closer look at the ones on the ceiling. Then I saw a faint pencil line. It followed the Nipigon River upstream from Lake Superior to Lake Nipigon, then went up the Little Jackfish River past the Summit Control Dam to the Ogoki Reservoir, west and south up the Ogoki River, Allan Water, Brightsand River and Wowing River to Wowing Lake, along a tiny creek into McCausland Lake, down the McCausland River and then down the English River. The line crossed two drainage divides without ever leaving the water.

I looked at the coloured index map again. My eyes followed the English and Winnipeg rivers to Lake Winnipeg, then followed the Saskatchewan, South Saskatchewan and Bow rivers. Just west of Lake Louise, there was a tiny blank rectangle.

I went to the map office and tried to buy him a copy, but the clerk wouldn't accept money. "I'll take care of it," she said. "I'd be honoured. Just tell him who it's from." I thanked her, and then drove west. Below Lake Louise, near the map's eastern edge. I turned right and took the old highway toward Field. I stopped at the Continental Divide, where the map showed a creek on the Alberta side, gradually flowing closer to the border, and ending in an arrow. I puffed uphill through the snow and found the creek, or creeks. The main stream divided; half flowed to Hudson Bay, and half to the Pacific. And I saw him eight years old again, in his hockey jersey, with one skate on each frozen branch. See, Dad? I told you I could do it.

When I got back, he was waiting for me. "I talked to Francine at the map office," I said, passing him the map. "She wants you to have this." He didn't say anything. I coughed and continued. "Funny thing about maps. The more you look at them, the less you need them." I paused again. "I often thought about you skating across the country, but each time, it seemed to get easier for you. I guess I figured that all you really had to do was put on your skates." (I'm sorry.) "I'm sorry I didn't tell you before."

It wasn't an instant reconciliation. We did make one trip to the Divide, though. We also spent a lot of hours at the construction site, quietly watching the edges of the maps merge and spread in a great carpet from east to west.

David would have made a great real estate developer. We filled Hudson Bay in with blue paper, but our tenants had other ideas. Everybody from furriers to fast food chains wanted to locate there. One guy wanted to rename his franchise Hudson Bay Hot Dogs and had already drawn up an advertising campaign, with Sir John Franklin's last expedition abandoning their ships in open water and trekking across the frozen tundra to sample his wares. Finally I got tired of refusing offers and had a 30-foot tall NOT FOR SALE sign erected in the middle of the Bay. David just beamed when he saw it. When the offers finally stopped, we decided to leave it there.

On opening day, the ice cover was still being completed. The Mayor and Miss Calgary and thousands of people waited outside with the ribbon and scissors as the workmen finished. Then they cleared the place, and David and I sat down on a bench just east of St. John's to put on our skates. He had chosen speed skates for the occasion, and he was finished lacing them before I was done with my hockey skates. He stood at the last edge, much as one climber might pause to allow the other to reach the summit with him.

"No, that's okay," I said, "you go ahead. I'll catch up."

He smiled then, and skated smoothly over the forests and hills of Newfoundland, leaning over and swinging one arm. I watched his strides grow longer as he sailed over Québec, and then finished tying my skates. When I looked up again, he was gone. I followed the offset herringbone pattern of his traces over James Bay and Lake Winnipeg, across the prairies and the mountains, to a final thin line. There was no wobble or curve to that trace, no second trace beside it, no telltale line of snow. He hadn't slowed down or even broken stride as he glided over South Moresby Island and off the edge of the Pacific. But it was only by knowing exactly where to look, getting down on my hands and knees, and placing my head sideways on the ice, that I could trace the faint lines across the concrete and out the door.

Notes

Terry Fox a young runner, recovering from the loss of his leg due to cancer, who decided to run across Canada to raise money for cancer research. At the age of 21, he began his "Marathon of Hope" at St. John's, Newfoundland, on April 12, 1980, but was forced to abandon his run on September 1 in Thunder Bay, Ontario, when cancer had spread to his lungs. He died in 1981. Thousands of people continue to participate in an annual fundraising run held in his memory.

Zamboni a machine used by a driver to prepare and clean the ice surface in a skating arena

National Topographic System an agency developed by the Canadian federal government in the 1920s to provide detailed maps of Canada for military, geological, and aeronautical uses, among others. Full map coverage of Canada was not completed until the 1990s.

West Edmonton Mall the world's largest shopping mall, located in the suburbs of Edmonton. It contains over 800 stores, including eleven major department stores, seven amusement parks, twenty-five salt water aquariums, nineteen movie theatres, and an NHL-sized rink.

Sir John Franklin an arctic explorer who charted much of Canada's arctic seaboard. He died tragically in 1847 when his ships, the Erebus and the Terror, became locked in the frozen ice. The surviving crew members tried to trek southward, but all perished.

Activities

1. This is a story about hopes, dreams, and the determination to make them come true. What is David's goal? Why is it important to him? What obstacles must he overcome to reach his goal? In what ways do people help him along the way? How does his personal goal eventually become a vision shared with others?

2. In writing this story, Dorin has made frequent use of proper nouns. In a language handbook, look up the differences between the following kinds of nouns: proper and common, specific and general, concrete and abstract. Have a class discussion about ways in which language is more vivid and descriptive when a writer uses proper, specific, and concrete nouns instead of nouns that are common, general, and abstract. Find examples from the story that demonstrate this.

3. Find a detailed map of Canada and make a copy of it. On your copy, locate as many of the places mentioned in the story as possible. Connect them with a pencil, trying to follow the route David used to "skate" across Canada. Imagine that David kept a diary as he crossed the country. Write an entry for a journal that he might have written while skating through *your* part of the country. Include in your description the places and people that he might have encountered along the way.

Another Viewpoint: Archetypal Patterns

Locate a reference book on mythology, such as *The Hero with a Thousand Faces* by Joseph Campbell, and do research on myths that depict the quests of heroes or heroines. What patterns emerge that are characteristic of each of these quests? What do these myths reveal to us about patterns of personal growth and development? In what ways does "Outside Edges" follow the archetypal pattern of quest myths?

Twisted Roots

Lyle McIntyre

About the Visual Lyle McIntyre was born in Huntsville, Ontario, in 1937. McIntyre began his photographic career in 1971. His work has been published in international photographic magazines and he has won numerous awards, including the Canadian Professional Photographer of the Year Award in 1986. McIntyre describes his love of photography this way: "Photography allows me to see and feel without being disturbed, to drink in nature, and to escape the everyday." What locations have inspired you to take landscape photographs? How would you describe your results? What are the challenges of capturing natural beauty through landscape photography?

Activities

1. Photographer Bill Brandt wrote: "We look at a thing and think we have seen it and yet what we see is only what our prejudices tell us should be seen, or what our desires want to see. Very rarely are we able to free our minds of thought and emotions and just see for the simple pleasure of seeing, and so long as we fail to do this, so long will the essence of things be hidden from us." Discuss the meaning of Brandt's words and then consider your response to *Twisted Roots* in terms of *thought*, *emotions*, and *essence*.

2. Lyle McIntyre has said that he works in black and white because he feels it can "communicate texture, mood, and depth to a greater degree." Write a paragraph in which you analyze which of these three elements contributes most to the impact of *Twisted Roots*. In your writing, consider the photographer's purpose in creating this image.

1992, black-and-white print

The Shining Houses

Alice Munro

Alice Munro, one of Canada's most distinguished writers, was born in Huron County, Ontario, in 1931. Her stories frequently appear in prestigious international publications such as *The New Yorker, The Atlantic Monthly,* and *The Paris Review* and have been translated into many languages. Munro has won many prizes, including three Governor General's Awards and the Giller Prize. Praised for being able to "create an entire life in a page," she has a keen eye for domestic detail and has said, "I know I get excited by ordinary things." To what extent are people's homes an extension of themselves? What dangers are there in stereotyping people by the appearance or location of their homes?

Mary sat on the back steps of Mrs. Fullerton's house, talking—or really listening—to Mrs. Fullerton, who sold her eggs. She had come in to pay the egg money, on her way to Edith's Debbie's birthday party. Mrs. Fullerton did not pay calls herself and she did not invite them, but, once a business pretext was established, she liked to talk. And Mary found herself exploring her neighbour's life as she had once explored the lives of grandmothers and aunts—by pretending to know less than she did, asking for some story she had heard before; this way, remembered episodes emerged each time with slight differences of content, meaning, colour, yet with a pure reality that usually attaches to things which are at least part legend. She had almost forgotten that there are people whose lives can be seen like this. She did not talk to many old people any more. Most of the people she knew had lives like her own, in which things were not sorted out yet, and it is not certain if this thing, or that, should be taken seriously. Mrs. Fullerton had no doubts or questions of this kind. How was it possible, for instance, not to take seriously the broad blithe back of Mr. Fullerton, disappearing down the road on a summer day, not to return?

"I didn't know that," said Mary. "I always thought Mr. Fullerton was dead."

"He's no more dead than I am," said Mrs. Fullerton, sitting up straight. A bold Plymouth Rock walked across the bottom step and Mary's little boy, Danny, got up to give rather cautious chase. "He's just gone off on his travels, that's what he is. May of gone up north, may of gone to the States, I don't know. But he's not dead. I would of felt it. He's not old neither, you know, not old like I am. He was my second husband, he was younger. I never made any secret of it. I had this place and raised my children and buried my first husband, before ever Mr. Fullerton came upon the scene. Why, one time down in the post office we was standing together by the wicket and I went over to put a letter in the box and left my bag behind me, and Mr. Fullerton turns to go after me and the girl calls to him, she says, here, your mother's left her purse!"

Mary smiled, answering Mrs. Fullerton's high-pitched and not trustful laughter. Mrs. Fullerton was old, as she had said—older than you might think, seeing her hair still fuzzy and black, her clothes slatternly-gay, dime-store brooches pinned to her ravelling sweater. Her eyes showed it, black as plums, with a soft inanimate sheen; things sank into them and they never changed. The life in her face was all in the nose and mouth, which were always twitching, fluttering, drawing tight grimace-lines down her cheeks. When she came around every Friday on her egg deliveries her hair was curled, her blouse held together by a bunch of cotton flowers, her mouth painted, a spidery and ferocious line of red; she would not show herself to her new neighbours in any sad old-womanish disarray.

"Thought I was his mother," she said. "I didn't care. I had a good laugh. But what I was telling you," she said, "a day in summer, he was off work. He had the ladder up and he was picking me the cherries off of my black-cherry tree. I came out to hang my clothes and there was this man I never seen before in my life, taking the pail of cherries my husband hands down to him. Helping himself, too, not backward, he sat down and ate cherries out of my pail. Who's that, I said to my husband, and he says, just a fellow passing. If he's a friend of yours, I said, he's welcome to stay for supper. What are you talking about, he says, I never seen him before. So I never said another thing. Mr. Fullerton went and talked to him, eating my cherries I intended for a pie, but that man would talk to anybody, tramp, Jehovah's Witness, anybody—that didn't need to mean anything.

"And half an hour after that fellow went off," she said, "Mr. Fullerton comes out in his brown jacket and his hat on. I have to meet a man downtown. How long will you be, I said. Oh, not long. So off he goes down the road, down to where the old tram went—we was all in the bush then—and something made me look after him. He must be hot in that coat, I said. And that's when I knew he wasn't coming back. Yet I couldn't've expected it, he liked it here. He was talking about putting chinchillas in the back yard. What's in a man's mind even when you're living with him you will never know."

"Was it long ago?" said Mary.

"Twelve years. My boys wanted me to sell then and go and live in rooms. But I said no. I had my hens and a nanny goat too at that time. More or less a pet. I had a pet coon too for a while, used to feed him chewing gum. Well, I said, husbands maybe come and go, but a place you've lived fifty years is something else. Making a joke of it with my family. Besides, I thought, if Mr. Fullerton was to come back, he'd come back here, not knowing where else to go. Of course he'd hardly know where to find me, the way it's changed now. But I always had the idea he might of suffered a loss of memory and it might come back. That has happened.

"I'm not complaining. Sometimes it seems to me about as reasonable a man should go as stay. I don't mind changes, either, that helps out my egg business. But this baby-sitting. All the time one or the other is asking me about baby-sitting. I tell them I got my own house to sit in and I raised my share of children."

Mary, remembering the birthday party, got up and called to her little boy. "I thought I might offer my black cherries for sale next summer," Mrs. Fullerton said. "Come and pick your own and they're fifty cents a box. I can't risk my old bones up a ladder no more."

"That's too much," Mary said, smiling. "They're cheaper than that at the supermarket." Mrs. Fullerton already hated the supermarket for lowering the price of eggs. Mary shook out her last cigarette and left it with her, saying she had another package in her purse. Mrs. Fullerton was fond of a cigarette but would not accept one unless you took her by surprise. Baby-sitting would pay for them, Mary thought. At the same time she was rather pleased with Mrs. Fullerton for being so unaccommodating. When Mary came out of this place, she always felt as if she were passing through barricades. The house and its surroundings were so self-sufficient, with their complicated and seemingly unalterable layout of vegetables and flower beds, apple and cherry trees, wired chicken-run, berry patch and wooden walks, woodpile, a great many roughly built dark little sheds, for hens or rabbits or a goat. Here was no open or straightforward plan, no order that an outsider could understand; yet what was haphazard time had made final. The place had become fixed, impregnable, all its accumulations necessary, until it seemed that even the washtubs, mops, couch springs and stacks of old police magazines on the back porch were there to stay.

Mary and Danny walked down the road that had been called, in Mrs. Fullerton's time, Wicks Road, but was now marked on the maps of the subdivision as Heather Drive. The name of the subdivision was Garden Place, and its streets were named for flowers. On either side of the road the earth was raw; the ditches were running full. Planks were laid across the open ditches, planks approached the doors of the newest houses. The new, white and shining houses, set side by side in long rows in the wound of the earth. She always thought of them as white houses, though of course they were not entirely white. They were stucco and siding, and only the stucco was white; the siding was painted in shades of blue, pink, green and yellow, all fresh and vivid colours. Last year, just at this time, in March, the bulldozers had come in to clear away the brush and second-growth and great trees of the mountain forest; in a little while the houses were going up among the boulders, the huge torn stumps, the unimaginable upheavals of that earth. The houses were frail at first, skeletons of new wood standing up in the dusk of the cold spring days. But the roofs went on, black and green, blue and red, and the stucco, the siding; the windows were put in, and plastered with signs that said, Murry's Glass, French's Hardwood Floors; it could be seen that the houses were real. People who would live in them came out and tramped around in the mud on Sundays. They were for people like Mary and her husband and their child, with not much money but expectations of more; Garden Place was already put down, in the minds of people who understood addresses, as less luxurious than Pine Hills but more desirable than Wellington Park. The bathrooms were beautiful, with three-part mirrors, ceramic tile, and coloured plumbing. The cupboards in the kitchen were light birch or mahogany, and there were copper lighting fixtures there and in the dining ells. Brick planters, matching the fireplaces, separated the living rooms and halls. The rooms were all large and light and the basements dry, and all this soundness and excellence seemed to be clearly, proudly indicated on the face of each house—those ingenuously similar houses that looked calmly out at each other, all the way down the street.

Today, since it was Saturday, all the men were out working around their houses. They were digging drainage ditches and making rockeries and clearing off and burning torn branches and brush. They worked with competitive violence and energy, all this being new to them; they were not men who made their livings by physical work. All day Saturday and Sunday they worked like this, so that in a year or two there should be green terraces, rock walls, shapely flower beds and ornamental shrubs. The earth must be heavy to dig now; it had been raining last night and this morning. But the day was brightening; the clouds had broken, revealing a long thin triangle of sky, its blue still cold and delicate, a winter colour. Behind the houses on one side of the road were pine trees, their ponderous symmetry not much stirred by any wind. These were to be cut down any day now, to make room for a shopping centre, which had been promised when the houses were sold.

And under the structure of this new subdivision, there was still something else to be seen; that was the old city, the old wilderness city that had lain on the side of the mountain. It had to be called a city because there were tramlines running into the woods, the houses had numbers and there were all the public buildings of a city, down by the water. But houses like Mrs. Fullerton's had been separated from each other by uncut forest and a jungle of wild blackberry and salmonberry bushes; these surviving houses, with thick smoke coming out of their chimneys, walls unpainted and patched and showing different degrees of age and darkening, rough sheds and stacked wood and compost heaps and grey board fences around them—these appeared every so often among the large new houses of Mimosa and Marigold and Heather Drive—dark, enclosed, expressing something like savagery in their disorder and the steep, unmatched angles of roofs and lean-tos; not possible on these streets, but there.

*   *   *

"What are they saying," said Edith, putting on more coffee. She was surrounded in her kitchen by the ruins of the birthday party—cake and moulded jellies and cookies with animal faces. A balloon rolled underfoot. The children had been fed, had posed for flash cameras and endured the birthday games; now they were playing in the back bedrooms and the basement, while their parents had coffee. "What are they saying in there?" said Edith.

"I wasn't listening," Mary said, holding the empty cream pitcher in her hand. She went to the sink window. The rent in the clouds had been torn wide open and the sun was shining. The house seemed too hot.

"Mrs. Fullerton's house," said Edith, hurrying back to the living-room. Mary knew what they were talking about. Her neighbours' conversation, otherwise not troubling, might at any moment snag itself on this subject and eddy menacingly in familiar circles of complaint, causing her to look despairingly out of windows, or down into her lap, trying to find some wonderful explanatory word to bring it to a stop; she did not succeed. She had to go back; they were waiting for cream.

A dozen neighbourhood women sat around the living room, absently holding the balloons they had been given by their children. Because the children on the street were so young, and also because any gathering-together of the people who lived there was considered a healthy thing in itself, most birthday parties were attended by mothers as well as children. Women who saw each other every day met now in earrings, nylons and skirts, with their hair fixed and faces applied. Some of the men were there too—Steve, who was Edith's husband, and others he had invited in for beer; they were all in their work clothes. The subject just introduced was one of the few on which male and female interest came together.

"I tell you what I'd do if I was next door to it," Steve said, beaming good-naturedly in expectation of laughter. "I'd send my kids over there to play with matches."

"Oh, funny," Edith said. "It's past joking. You joke, I try to do something. I even phoned the Municipal Hall."

"What did they say?" said Mary Lou Ross.

"Well I said couldn't they get her to paint it, at least, or pull down some of the shacks, and they said no they couldn't. I said I thought there must be some kind of ordinance applied to people like that and they said they knew how I *felt* and they were very *sorry*—"

"But no?"

"But no."

"But what about the chickens, I thought—"

"Oh, they wouldn't let you or me keep chickens, but she has some special dispensation about that too, I forgot how it goes."

"I'm going to stop buying them," Janie Inger said. "The supermarket's cheaper and who cares that much about fresh? And my God, the smell. I said to Carl I knew we were coming to the sticks but I somehow didn't picture us next door to a barnyard."

"Across the street is worse than next door. It makes me wonder why we ever bothered with a picture window, whenever anybody comes to see us I want to draw the drapes so they won't see what's across from us."

"Okay, okay," Steve said, cutting heavily through these female voices. "What Carl and I started out to tell you was that, if we can work this lane deal, she has got to go. It's simple and it's legal. That's the beauty of it."

"What lane deal?"

"We are getting to that. Carl and I been cooking this for a couple of weeks, but we didn't like to say anything in case it didn't work out. Take it, Carl."

"Well she's on the lane allowance, that's all," Carl said. He was a real estate salesman, stocky, earnest, successful. "I had an idea it might be that way, so I went down to the Municipal Hall and looked it up."

"What does that mean, dear?" said Janie, casual, wifely.

"This is it," Carl said. "There's an allowance for a lane, there always has been, the idea being if the area ever got built up they would put a lane through. But they never thought that would happen, people just built where they liked. She's got part of her house and half a dozen shacks sitting right where the lane has to go through. So what we do now, we get the municipality to put through a lane. We need a lane anyway. Then she has to get out. It's the law."

"It's the law," said Steve, radiating admiration. "What a smart boy. These real estate operators are smart boys."

"Does she get anything?" said Mary Lou. "I'm sick of looking at it and all but I don't want to see anybody in the poorhouse."

"Oh, she'll get paid. More than it's worth. Look, it's to her advantage. She'll get paid for it, and she couldn't sell it, she couldn't give it away."

Mary set her coffee cup down before she spoke and hoped her voice would sound all right, not emotional or scared. "But remember she's been here a long time," she said. "She was here before most of us were born." She was trying desperately to think of other words, words more sound and reasonable than these; she could not expose to this positive tide any notion that they might think flimsy and romantic, or she would destroy her argument. But she had no argument. She could try all night and never find any words to stand up to their words, which came at her now invincibly from all sides: *shack, eyesore, filth, property, value.*

"Do you honestly think that people who let their property get so rundown have that much claim to our consideration?" Janie said, feeling her husband's plan was being attacked.

"She's been here forty years, now we're here," Carl said. "So it goes. And whether you realize it or not, just standing there that house is bringing down the resale value of every house on this street. I'm in the business, I know."

And these were joined by other voices; it did not matter much what they said as long as they were full of self-assertion and anger. That was their strength, proof of their adulthood, of themselves and their seriousness. The spirit of anger rose among them, bearing up their young voices, sweeping them together as on a flood of intoxication, and they admired each other in this new behaviour as property-owners as people admire each other for being drunk.

*   *   *

"We might as well get everybody now," Steve said. "Save going around to so many places."

It was supper time, getting dark out. Everybody was preparing to go home, mothers buttoning their children's coats, children clutching, without much delight, their balloons and whistles and paper baskets full of jelly beans. They had stopped fighting, almost stopped noticing each other; the party had disintegrated. The adults too had grown calmer and felt tired.

"Edith! Edith, have you got a pen?"

Edith brought a pen and they spread the petition for the lane, which Carl had drawn up, on the dining-room table, clearing away the paper plates with smears of dried ice cream. People began to sign mechanically as they said goodbye. Steve was still scowling slightly; Carl stood with one hand on the paper, businesslike, but proud. Mary knelt on the floor and struggled with Danny's zipper. She got up and put on her own coat, smoothed her hair, put on her gloves and took them off again. When she could not think of anything else to do she walked past the dining-room table on her way to the door. Carl held out the pen.

"I can't sign that," she said. Her face flushed up, at once, her voice was trembling. Steve touched her shoulder.

"What's the matter, honey?"

"I don't think we have the right. We haven't the right."

"Mary, don't you care how things look? You live here too."

"No, I—I don't care." Oh, wasn't it strange, how in your

imagination, when you stood up for something, your voice rang, people started, abashed; but in real life they all smiled in rather a special way and you saw that what you had really done was serve yourself up as a conversational delight for the next coffee party.

"Don't worry, Mary, she's got money in the bank," Janie said. "She must have. I asked her to baby-sit for me once and she practically spit in my face. She isn't exactly a charming old lady, you know."

"I know she isn't a charming old lady," Mary said.

Steve's hand still rested on her shoulder. "Hey what do you think we are, a bunch of ogres?"

"Nobody wants to turn her out just for the fun of it," Carl said. "It's unfortunate. We all know that. But we have to think of the community."

"Yes," said Mary. But she put her hands in the pockets of her coat and turned to say thank you to Edith, thank you for the birthday party. It occurred to her that they were right, for themselves, for whatever it was they had to be. And Mrs. Fullerton was old, she had dead eyes, nothing could touch her. Mary went out and walked with Danny up the street. She saw the curtains being drawn across living-room windows; cascades of flowers, of leaves, of geometrical designs, shut off these rooms from the night. Outside it was quite dark, the white houses were growing dim, the clouds breaking and breaking, and smoke blowing from Mrs. Fullerton's chimney. The pattern of Garden Place, so assertive in the daytime, seemed to shrink at night into the raw black mountainside.

· · ·

The voices in the living room have blown away, Mary thought. If they would blow away and their plans be forgotten, if one thing could be left alone. But these are people who win, and they are good people; they want homes for their children, they help each other when there is trouble, they plan a community—saying that word as if they found a modern and well-proportioned magic in it, and no possibility anywhere of a mistake.

There is nothing you can do at present but put your hands in your pockets and keep a disaffected heart.

Notes

Plymouth Rock in this instance, refers to a breed of hen; named after the place in Massachusetts where the Pilgrims from England are said to have first set foot on North American soil after disembarking from *The Mayflower* ship

Jehovah's Witness a member of a religious Christian sect. Members of this sect canvass door-to-door as witnesses for their faith.

Activities

1. Create a two-column chart. In the first column, record three quotations that you believe are central to the story. In the second column, explain the context and significance of each. With a group, compare and discuss your choices.

2. In a group, consider characterization by discussing the motivation of the "people who win" in this story: Why is Mrs. Fullerton's house so important to them? What underlying beliefs and values are revealed in their words and behaviour? Do you agree with Mary that "they are good people"? To what extent does Alice Munro offer a fair and balanced portrait of these characters?

3. Work with a group to create a script for a dramatization of a scene that might result from the conflicts in "The Shining Houses." Before presenting, prepare an audience-response form to collect feedback about your production. Afterward, have your group evaluate both your collaborative skills and the quality of your presentation.

Another Viewpoint: Culture

Consider the following statement: "The main character in 'The Shining Houses' is a quintessential Canadian character—she would not exist in any other culture." To what extent do you agree with this statement? Make a "top ten" list of Canadian characters in fiction—characters who represent something essential about Canada and who would not be "at home" in any other context. Be prepared to defend your choices.

A Devoted Son

Anita Desai

Anita Desai was born in India, in 1937, to a German mother and a Bengali father. She attended Delhi University, where she studied English literature. Although her family spoke German at home and Hindi to their friends, she has always written in English. Desai published her first story in a children's magazine at the age of nine. She published her first book in 1963. A recent novel, *Fasting, Feasting*, was published in 2000. Desai has received a number of international awards and has been short-listed for the prestigious Booker Prize three times. What are some frequent causes of tensions within families? Do these causes change at different stages of life? As parents age, to what extent do power and control shift from parents to their children?

When the results appeared in the morning papers, Rakesh scanned them, barefoot and in his pyjamas, at the garden gate, then went up the steps to the veranda where his father sat sipping his morning tea and bowed down to touch his feet.

"A first division, son?" his father asked, beaming, reaching for the papers.

"At the top of the list, Papa," Rakesh murmured, as if awed. "First in the country."

Bedlam broke loose then. The family whooped and danced. The whole day long visitors streamed into the small yellow house at the end of the road, to congratulate the parents of this *Wunderkind*, to slap Rakesh on the back and fill the house and garden with the sounds and colours of a festival. There were garlands and *halwa*, party clothes and gifts (enough fountain pens to last years, even a watch or two), nerves and temper and joy, all in a multicoloured whirl of pride and great shining vistas newly opened: Rakesh was the first son in the family to receive an education, so much had been sacrificed in order to send him to school and then medical college, and at last the fruits of their sacrifice had arrived, golden and glorious.

To everyone who came to say, "*Mubarak, Varma-ji*, your son has brought you glory," the father said, "Yes, and do you know what is the first thing he did when he saw the results this morning? He came and touched my feet. He bowed down and touched my feet." This moved many of the women in the crowd so much that they were seen to raise the ends of their saris and dab at their tears while the men reached out for the betel leaves and sweetmeats that were offered around on trays and shook their heads in wonder and approval of such exemplary filial behaviour. "One does not often see such behaviour in sons any more," they all agreed, a little enviously perhaps. Leaving the house, some of the women said, sniffing, "At least on such an occasion they might have served pure *ghee* sweets," and some of the men said, "Don't you think old Varma was giving himself airs? He needn't think we don't remember that he comes from the vegetable market himself, his father used to sell vegetables, and he has never seen the inside of a school." But there was more envy than rancour in their voices and it was, of course, inevitable— not every son in that shabby little colony at the edge of the city was destined to shine as Rakesh shone, and who knew that better than the parents themselves?

And that was only the beginning, the first step in a great, sweeping ascent to the radiant heights of fame and fortune. The thesis he wrote for his M.D. brought Rakesh still greater glory, if only in select medical circles. He won a scholarship. He went to the U.S.A. (that was what his father learnt to call it and taught the whole family to say—not America, which was what the ignorant neighbours called it, but, with a grand familiarity, "the U.S.A.") where he pursued his career in the most prestigious of all hospitals and won encomiums from his American colleagues which were relayed to his admiring and glowing family. What was more, he came *back*, he actually returned to that small yellow house in the once-new but increasingly shabby colony, right at the end of the road where the rubbish vans tipped out their stinking contents for pigs to nose in and rag-pickers to build their shacks on, all steaming and smoking just outside the neat wire fences and well-tended gardens. To this Rakesh returned and the first thing he did on entering the house was to slip out of the embraces of his sisters and brothers and bow down and touch his father's feet.

As for his mother, she gloated chiefly over the strange fact that he had not married in America, had not brought home a foreign wife as all her neighbours had warned her he would, for wasn't that what all Indian boys went abroad for? Instead, he agreed, almost without argument, to marry a girl she had picked out for him in her own village, the daughter of a childhood friend, a plump and uneducated girl, it was true, but so old-fashioned, so placid, so complaisant that she slipped into the household and settled in like a charm, seemingly too lazy and too good-natured to even try and make Rakesh leave home and set up independently, as any other girl might have done. What was more, she was pretty—really pretty, in a plump, pudding way that only gave way to fat—soft, spreading fat, like warm wax—after the birth of their first baby, a son, and then what did it matter?

For some years Rakesh worked in the city hospital, quickly rising to the top of the administrative organization, and was made a director before he left to set up his own clinic. He took his parents in his car—a new, sky-blue Ambassador with a rear window full of stickers and charms revolving on strings—to see the clinic when it was built, and the large sign-board over the door on which his name was printed in letters of red, with a row of degrees and qualifications to follow it like so many little black slaves of the regent. Thereafter his fame seemed to grow just a little dimmer—or maybe it was only that everyone in town had grown accustomed to it at last—but it was also the beginning of his fortune for he now became known not only as the best but also the richest doctor in town.

However, all this was not accomplished in the wink of an eye. Naturally not. It was the achievement of a lifetime and it took up Rakesh's whole life. At the time he set up his clinic his father had grown into an old man and retired from his post at the kerosene dealer's depot at which he had worked for forty years, and his mother died soon after, giving up the ghost with a sigh that sounded positively happy, for it was her own son who ministered to her in her last illness and who sat pressing her feet at the last moment—such a son as few women had borne.

For it had to be admitted—and the most unsuccessful and most rancorous of neighbours eventually did so—that Rakesh was not only a devoted son and a miraculously good-natured man who contrived somehow to obey his parents and humour his wife and show concern equally for his children and his patients, but there was actually a brain inside this beautifully polished and formed body of good manners and kind nature and, in between ministering to his family and playing host to many friends and coaxing them all into feeling happy and grateful and content, he had actually trained his hands as well and emerged an excellent doctor, a really fine surgeon. How one man—and a man born to illiterate parents, his father having worked for a kerosene dealer and his mother having spent her life in a kitchen—had achieved, combined and conducted such a medley of virtues, no one could fathom, but all acknowledged his talent and skill.

It was a strange fact, however, that talent and skill, if displayed for too long, cease to dazzle. It came to pass that the most admiring of all eyes eventually faded and no longer blinked at his glory. Having retired from work and having lost his wife, the old father very quickly went to pieces, as they say. He developed so many complaints and fell ill so frequently and with such mysterious diseases that even his son could no longer make out when it was something of significance and when it was merely a peevish whim. He sat huddled on his string bed most of the day and developed an exasperating habit of stretching out suddenly and lying absolutely still, allowing the whole family to fly around him in a flap, wailing and weeping, and then suddenly sitting up, stiff and gaunt, and spitting out a big gob of betel juice as if to mock their behaviour.

He did this once too often: there had been a big party in the house, a birthday party for the youngest son, and the celebrations had to be suddenly hushed, covered up and hustled out of the way when the daughter-in-law discovered, or thought she discovered, that the old man stretched out from end to end of his string bed had lost his pulse; the party broke up, dissolved, even turned into a band of mourners, when the old man sat up and the distraught daughter-in-law received a gob of red spittle right on the hem of her new organza sari. After that no one much cared if he sat up cross-legged on his bed, hawking and spitting, or lay down flat and turned grey as a corpse. Except, of course, for that pearl amongst pearls, his son Rakesh.

It was Rakesh who brought him his morning tea, not in one of the china cups from which the rest of the family drank, but in the old man's favourite brass tumbler, and sat at the edge of his bed, comfortable and relaxed with the string of his pyjamas dangling out from under his fine lawn night-shirt, and discussed or, rather, read out the morning news to his father. It made no difference to him that his father made no response apart from spitting. It was Rakesh, too, who on returning from the clinic in the evening, persuaded the old man to come out of his room, as bare and desolate as a cell, and take the evening air out in the garden, beautifully arranging the pillows and bolsters on the divan in the corner of the open veranda. On summer nights he saw to it that the servants carried the old man's bed onto the lawn and himself helped his father down the steps and onto the bed, soothing him and settling him down for a night under the stars.

All this was very gratifying for the old man. What was not so gratifying was that he even undertook to supervise his father's diet. One day when the father was really sick, having ordered his daughter-in-law to make him a dish of *soojie halwa* and eaten it with a saucerful of cream, Rakesh marched into the room, not with his usual respectful step but with the confident and rather contemptuous stride of the famous doctor, and declared, "No more *halwa* for you, Papa. We must be sensible, at your age. If you must have something sweet, Veena will cook you a little *kheer*, that's light, just a little rice and milk. But nothing fried, nothing rich. We can't have this happening again."

The old man who had been lying stretched out on his bed, weak and feeble after a day's illness, gave a start at the very sound, the tone of these words. He opened his eyes—rather, they fell open with shock—and he stared at his son with disbelief that darkened quickly to reproach. A son who actually refused his father the food he craved? No, it was unheard of, it was incredible. But Rakesh had turned his back to him and was cleaning up the litter of bottles and packets on the medicine shelf and did not notice while Veena slipped silently out of the room with a little smirk that only the old man saw, and hated.

Halwa was only the first item to be crossed off the old man's diet. One delicacy after the other went—everything fried to begin with, then everything sweet, and eventually everything, everything the old man enjoyed. The meals that arrived for him on the shining stainless steel tray twice a day were frugal to say the least—dry bread, boiled lentils, boiled vegetables and, if there were a bit of chicken or fish, that was boiled too. If he called for another helping—in a cracked voice that quavered the- atrically—Rakesh himself would come to the door, gaze at him sadly and shake his head, saying, "Now, Papa, we must be careful, we can't risk another illness, you know," and although the daughter-in-law kept tact- fully out of the way, the old man could just see her smirk sliding merrily through the air. He tried to bribe his grandchildren into buying him sweets (and how he missed his wife now, that generous, indulgent and illit- erate cook), whispering, "Here's fifty *paise*" as he stuffed the coins into a tight, hot fist. "Run down to the shop at the crossroads and buy me thirty *paise* worth of *jalebis*, and you can spend the remaining twenty *paise* on yourself. Eh? Understand? Will you do that?" He got away with it once or twice but then was found out, the conspirator was scolded by his father and smacked by his mother and Rakesh came storming into the room, almost tearing his hair as he shouted through compressed lips, "Now, Papa, are you trying to turn my little son into a liar? Quite apart from spoil- ing your own stomach, you are spoiling him as well—you are encourag- ing him to lie to his own parents. You should have heard the lies he told his mother when she saw him bringing back those *jalebis* wrapped up in filthy newspaper. I don't allow anyone in my house to buy sweets in the bazaar, Papa, surely you know that. There's cholera in the city, typhoid, gastro-enteritis—I see these cases daily in the hospital, how can I allow my own family to run such risks?" The old man sighed and lay down in the corpse position. But that worried no one any longer.

There was only one pleasure left the old man now (his son's early morning visits and readings from the newspaper could no longer be called that) and those were visits from elderly neighbours. These were not frequent as his contemporaries were mostly as decrepit and helpless as he and few could walk the length of the road to visit him any more. Old Bhatia, next door, however, who was still spry enough to refuse, adamantly, to bathe in the tiled bathroom indoors and to insist on carrying out his brass mug and towel, in all seasons and usually at impossible hours, into the yard and bathe noisily under the garden tap, would look over the hedge to see if Varma were out on his veranda and would call to him and talk while he wrapped his *dhoti* about him and dried the sparse hair on his head, shivering with enjoyable exaggeration. Of course these conversations, bawled across the hedge by two rather deaf old men conscious of having their entire households overhearing them, were not very satisfactory but Bhatia occasionally came out of his yard, walked down the bit of road and came in at Varma's gate to collapse onto the stone plinth built under the temple tree. If Rakesh were at home he would help his father down the steps into the garden and arrange him on his night bed under the tree and leave the two old men to chew betel leaves and discuss the ills of their individual bodies with combined passion.

"At least you have a doctor in the house to look after you," sighed Bhatia, having vividly described his martyrdom to piles.

"Look after me?" cried Varma, his voice cracking like an ancient clay jar. "He—he does not even give me enough to eat."

"What?" said Bhatia, the white hairs in his ears twitching. "Doesn't give you enough to eat? Your own son?"

"My own son. If I ask him for one more piece of bread, he says no, Papa, I weighed out the *ata* myself and I can't allow you to have more than two hundred grammes of cereal a day. He *weighs* the food he gives me, Bhatia—he has scales to weigh it on. That is what it has come to."

"Never," murmured Bhatia in disbelief. "Is it possible, even in this evil age, for a son to refuse his father food?"

"Let me tell you," Varma whispered eagerly. "Today the family was having fried fish—I could smell it. I called to my daughter-in-law to bring me a piece. She came to the door and said No…"

"Said No?" It was Bhatia's voice that cracked. A *drongo* shot out of the tree and sped away. "*No?*"

"No, she said no, Rakesh has ordered her to give me nothing fried. No butter, he says, no oil—"

"No butter? No oil? How does he expect his father to *live*?"

Old Varma nodded with melancholy triumph. "That is how he treats me—after I have brought him up, given him an education, made him a great doctor. Great doctor! This is the way great doctors treat their fathers, Bhatia," for the son's sterling personality and character now underwent a curious sea change. Outwardly all might be the same but the interpretation had altered: his masterly efficiency was nothing but cold heartlessness, his authority was only tyranny in disguise.

There was cold comfort in complaining to neighbours and, on such a miserable diet, Varma found himself slipping, weakening and soon becoming a genuinely sick man. Powders and pills and mixtures were not only brought in when dealing with a crisis like an upset stomach but became a regular part of his diet—became his diet, complained Varma, supplanting the natural foods he craved. There were pills to regulate his bowel movements, pills to bring down his blood pressure, pills to deal with his arthritis and, eventually, pills to keep his heart beating. In between there were panicky rushes to the hospital, some humiliating experiences with the stomach pump and enema, which left him frightened and helpless. He cried easily, shrivelling up on his bed, but if he complained of a pain or even a vague, grey fear in the night, Rakesh would simply open another bottle of pills and force him to take one. "I have my duty to you, Papa," he said when his father begged to be let off.

"Let me be," Varma begged, turning his face away from the pills on the outstretched hand. "Let me die. It would be better. I do not want to live only to eat your medicines."

"Papa, be reasonable."

"I leave that to you," the father cried with sudden spirit. "Let me alone, let me die now, I cannot live like this."

"Lying all day on his pillows, fed every few hours by his daughter-in-law's own hands, visited by every member of his family daily—and then he says he does not want to live 'like this,'" Rakesh was heard to say, laughing, to someone outside the door.

"Deprived of food," screamed the old man on the bed, "his wishes ignored, taunted by his daughter-in-law, laughed at by his grandchildren—*that* is how I live." But he was very old and weak and all anyone heard was an incoherent croak, some expressive grunts and cries of genuine pain. Only once, when old Bhatia had come to see him and they sat together under the temple tree, they heard him cry, "God is calling me—and they won't let me go."

The quantities of vitamins and tonics he was made to take were not altogether useless. They kept him alive and even gave him a kind of strength that made him hang on long after he ceased to wish to hang on. It was as though he were straining at a rope, trying to break it, and it would not break, it was still strong. He only hurt himself, trying.

In the evening, that summer, the servants would come into his cell, grip his bed, one at each end, and carry it out to the veranda, there setting it down with a thump that jarred every tooth in his head. In answer to his agonized complaints they said the Doctor Sahib had told them he must take the evening air and the evening air they would make him take—thump. Then Veena, that smiling, hypocritical pudding in a rustling sari, would appear and pile up the pillows under his head till he was propped up stiffly into a sitting position that made his head swim and his back ache. "Let me lie down," he begged. "I can't sit up any more."

"Try, Papa, Rakesh said you can if you try," she said, and drifted away to the other end of the veranda where her transistor radio vibrated to the lovesick tunes from the cinema that she listened to all day.

So there he sat, like some stiff corpse, terrified, gazing out on the lawn where his grandsons played cricket, in danger of getting one of their hard-spun balls in his eye, and at the gate that opened onto the dusty and rubbish-heaped lane but still bore, proudly, a newly touched-up signboard that bore his son's name and qualifications, his own name having vanished from the gate long ago.

At last the sky-blue Ambassador arrived, the cricket game broke up in haste, the car drove in smartly and the doctor, the great doctor, all in white, stepped out. Someone ran up to take his bag from him, others to escort him up the steps. "Will you have tea?" his wife called, turning down the transistor set, "or a Coca Cola? Shall I fry you some *samosas*?" But he did not reply or even glance in her direction. Ever a devoted son, he went first to the corner where his father sat gazing, stricken, at some undefined spot in the dusty yellow air that swam before him. He did not turn his head to look at his son. But he stopped gobbling air with his uncontrolled lips and set his jaw as hard as a sick and very old man could set it.

"Papa," his son said, tenderly, sitting down on the edge of the bed and reaching out to press his feet.

Old Varma tucked his feet under him, out of the way, and continued to gaze stubbornly into the yellow air of the summer evening.

"Papa, I'm home."

Varma's hand jerked suddenly, in a sharp, derisive movement, but he did not speak.

"How are you feeling, Papa?"

Then Varma turned and looked at his son. His face was so out of control, and all in pieces, that the multitude of expressions that crossed it could not make up a whole and convey to the famous man exactly what his father thought of him, his skill, his art.

"I'm dying," he croaked. "Let me die, I tell you."

"Papa, you're joking," his son smiled at him, lovingly. "I've brought you a new tonic to make you feel better. You must take it, it will make you feel stronger again. Here it is. Promise me you will take it regularly, Papa."

Varma's mouth worked as hard as though he still had a gob of betel in it (his supply of betel had been cut off years ago). Then he spat out some words, as sharp and bitter as poison, into his son's face. "Keep your tonic—I want none—I want none—I won't take any more of—of your medicines. None. Never," and he swept the bottle out of his son's hand with a wave of his own, suddenly grand, suddenly effective.

His son jumped, for the bottle was smashed and thick brown syrup had splashed up, staining his white trousers. His wife let out a cry and came running. All around the old man was hubbub once again, noise, attention.

He gave one push to the pillows at his back and dislodged them so he could sink down on his back, quite flat again. He closed his eyes and pointed his chin at the ceiling, like some dire prophet, groaning, "God is calling me—now let me go."

Notes

first division the highest level of achievement in a high school based on the British academic model

Wunderkind a person who achieves great success while very young; from the Old High German *wuntar*, meaning "wonder," and from the German *kind*, meaning "child"

halwa a popular Indian dessert

ghee clarified butter, a common ingredient in Indian cooking

little black slaves of the regent a reference to enslaved servants of the regent or viceroy, the representative of the British crown. Viceroys ruled India from the seventeenth century until the country's independence in 1947. The slave trade, mainly of African peoples, was abolished in the British Empire in 1807.

betel juice juice of a leaf that is chewed with parings of the areca nut

lawn linen or cotton fabric; from the Middle English word *laun*, which is probably a reference to Laon, a city in northern France

soojie halwa a dessert made with semolina

kheer a rice pudding

paise a coin equal to one-hundredth of a rupee, the main monetary unit in South Asian countries such as India, Pakistan, and Sri Lanka; a Hindi word, originally from the Sanskrit word *rūpya*, meaning "wrought silver"

jalebis pretzel-shaped sweets that are fried to a golden crisp and soaked in saffron syrup

dhoti a loincloth worn as ceremonial dress by male Hindus

ata corn flour

drongo a type of blackbird

samosas triangular fried pastries with meat or vegetable filling; a word in
the Persian and Urdu languages

Activities

1. Write a journal response in which you describe your feelings toward
Rakesh and his father as the story progressed. Did your feelings remain
consistent or did they change? Which character did you most identify with at
the beginning, middle, and end of the story? How might your own experiences have shaped your reactions to these characters?

2. Discuss the title of the story. Do you think that Desai intends it to be interpreted literally or ironically? How does the title contribute to the meaning and
the theme? With whom—the "devoted son" or the father—do the author's
sympathies seem to lie?

3. Desai has commented that she is more influenced by poets than by fiction writers: "Poets use language in a way I would like to emulate. I would
like to achieve that gravity, compression, the intensity of their language."
Find a passage in "A Devoted Son" where Desai's language reflects the
intensity and imagery of poetry. Write a short analysis of the style in the
passage you have selected. What do you notice about the diction, sentence
structure, and use of literary devices? Next, use Desai's passage as a model
for a short piece of descriptive writing in which you try to achieve the same
precision and intensity of language.

Another Viewpoint: Culture

In a recent interview, Anita Desai commented that "Indians manage to slip
back and forth between the modern world and ancient world, the Indian
world and the Western world, with a great ease, without feeling any strain."
If possible, find several people of South Asian descent in your community and
interview them about whether Desai's statement is true for them. Then
consider how the dualities represented in her quotation are reflected in "A
Devoted Son."

Magpies

Thomas King

Thomas King is an award-winning novelist, short story writer, children's writer, scriptwriter, and photographer. Born in California, in 1943, of Greek and Cherokee descent, he has spent much of his adult life in Canada, first teaching at the University of Lethbridge for ten years, and more recently at the University of Guelph. His first novel, *Medicine River*, was published in 1990 and became a television movie. King has twice been nominated for the Governor General's Award, was runner-up for the 1991 Commonwealth Writer's Prize, and won the Canadian Authors Association Award for Fiction. Central to "Magpies" is the act of making a promise. When you make a promise, how far will you go to keep it? How do you feel and behave when you have difficulty keeping your word?

This one is about Granny. Reserve story. Everyone knows this story. Wilma knows it. Ambrose knows it. My friend, Napioa. Lionel James. Billy Frank knows it, too. Billy Frank hears this story in Calgary. He hears it three times. Maybe six. Boy, he tells me, here comes that story again.

Sometimes this story is about Wilma. Some people tell it so Ambrose is all over the place. The way I tell it is this way and I tell it this way all the time.

Sometimes I tell you about those Magpies first. With those noses. Good noses, those ones. Magpies talk all the time, you know. Good gossips, those. Hahahahaha. Good jokes, too. Sometimes I start that way.

Okay. Here comes that story again.

Granny falls and hurts her leg. So, that leg is pink. Then it looks blue. Another time it is black. Yellow for a long time. That leg. Granny's leg.

Granny looks at that leg and thinks about dying. So she talks about falling over dead. When that Granny starts talking about being dead, Wilma says no, no, no. That is just a bruise. Yellow bruise. Those ones are okay.

Granny talks to everyone she see about dying. I'm going to die, she says to me and I say yes, that's right. Old people know these things. It happens. Maybe that blood thing. Maybe cigarettes. Maybe a truck. Maybe that bottle. Granny likes to talk of dying. I'm going to be dead real soon, she says. Going to rot and nobody comes by but those birds tell all those stories and laugh.

Watch those Magpies, that old woman tells Ambrose. You see them?

Sure, says Ambrose.

They smell death, she says. Isn't that right?

Yes, I says, that's true.

Those ones take the eyes first, she says, soft parts. Nice round parts they like first. Ripe. That's why you got to wrap them tight.

That's right, I says.

You listening, Ambrose? That old Granny shake Ambrose so he is awake. They smell death, those birds, like you smell chokecherries on the boil. When I die, they'll come to me like that.

You can count on me, says Ambrose.

I'm going to die, then, Granny tells me, and I says okay.

Wilma takes that old woman to the hospital to see two, maybe five white doctors. They took at the leg. They look at that leg again. They do it some more times, too. Ummmm, ummmm, ummmm. That way. In the mouth. They don't dance. They don't sing. They think they talking to Granny. Ummmm, ummmm, ummmm.

Granny says to me there are good places to die. River is a good one. Coulees is okay, too. Maybe a mountain. Bad places, too, she says. Grocery store. Shopping mall. Movie show. Hospital.

That hospital is one bad place to die. See-po-aah-loo. See-po-aah-loo is like a hole. In the ground. See-po-aah-loo is one old word. Where you put stew bones. Where you put old things that are broke. Where you put old things that smell bad. Where you put beer cans. Coffee grounds. Fish guts. Milk cartons. Newspapers. Tractor oil. That black dog Walter Turnbull hit with his truck. Everything you don't want people to see. You put them there. See-po-aah-loo.

Then you cover it up. Go someplace else.

Hospital.

Those doctors tell Granny, ummmm, ummmm, ummmm. Maybe you better stay here. One day. Four days. Maybe we see something. Ummmm, ummmm, ummmm. Ambrose says Whites go to that hospital to get a new nose. Get good breasts. Fix up that old butt. Haul out things you don't need no more. Ambrose tells me that. Fix you up. Like a car. Run better. Ummmm, ummmm, ummmm.

Those ones don't fool Granny. I can tell you that.

That Granny nod her head. Look at that floor. Look at that door. Shuffle her feet. Like a Round dance. Ho-ho-ho-ho, that one dances out of See-po-aah-loo. Don't want to be in no hole, she says.

God loves you, Granny, Wilma says. Good woman, that Wilma. Loves Granny. Fixes her food. Washes her clothes. Wilma is mostly Catholic in the middle. Knows about dying. Reads those papers you get from church. In that wood pocket. Near that water.

When God takes you, Momma, you'll be real happy. This is how Wilma talks. Dead is okay, Wilma says. That God fellow just waiting for you. Good to see you. Howdy-do.

Don't put me in that grave, See-po-aah-loo, Granny tell Wilma.

Garbage hole.

Hospital.

One word. You see?

Yes, says Wilma, that's the modern way. You need a priest. He can make it clean.

Holes are cold, Granny says.

God will keep you warm, Wilma says.

So, Granny finds Ambrose.

Ambrose is a big man. Big chest. Big legs. Big head. Friendly man that Ambrose. Have a joke. Have a story. Always thinking about things to do. Going to fix this thing. Going to fix that thing. Granny finds Ambrose. You fix this thing for me, she says. Yes, that one says, I will do it. You can count on me.

Granny brings that boy to my house. Ho, I says, you got your big boy with you. Yes, she says, we come to see you, talk with you. Sit down, I says. Coffee is here. Tea, too. Sit down and eat some food.

You must talk to my big boy, Granny says. Tell him the way. Show him how to do this thing. You listen to this old one, Granny says. You can count on me, Ambrose says.

Granny squeeze her eyes. You be here when I die. You tell Wilma how to do this thing. You look out for me, take care of me, my big boy.

You can count on me.

I'm counting on you, says Granny. In that cottonwood at Heavyshield's cabin. Aoo-lee-sth. That's the one. Other ways that hole will get me and I'll come back.

You can count on me.

That leg get better. Granny's leg. But Granny dies anyway. Later. Not right now. Two, maybe four years. Maybe more. She falls over dead then. Like that. It is finished.

Ambrose is not there when Granny dies. Someone says he is in Edmonton at those meetings. Someone says, no, he is in Toronto. Someone says he is across the line. Wilma sniff her nose this way and that one sniff her nose that way. We can't wait for that Ambrose maybe come along. We going to do this thing right, Wilma says. We going to do this thing now.

So they get a priest.

So they put Granny in a box.

So they stick Granny in the church.

So they throw her in a hole.

Just like that. Pretty quick. They put her in that hole before Ambrose comes home. Everyone stands there. Ho ho ho ho. All of them feel bad, Granny in that hole. Wilma cries, too. Smack her hands and says, that's okay now. Everything is done now. It is finished.

Aoh-quwee.

That's the end of the story.

No, I was just fooling.

There's more.

Stick around.

Okay. Ambrose comes home. Everyone figures out this part, Ambrose comes home. No smile. No happy joke. Momma is with God, Wilma says. She's happy. Nothing for you to do.

I gave her this promise, Ambrose says, and I says, yes, that's right.

Keep your promise in your pocket, Wilma says. Momma don't need that promise. Everything is pretty good. God's got her.

God don't live in a hole, says Ambrose.

God is everywhere, says Wilma.

Those two talk like that. One day, maybe two, three weeks. Talk about God. Talk about that promise. You make lots of promises, Wilma says. Those things are easy for you to make. They fall out of your mouth like spit. Everybody got three or four of them.

That part is true. I can tell you that. Ambrose is generous with those things. Those promises. I help you chop wood for winter, Ambrose tells my friend Napioa. Fix that truck for you, he says to Billy Frank. Going to dig that ditch tomorrow, he tells his uncle.

You can count on me.

Keep that promise in your pocket, Wilma tells that one.

Ambrose comes to my house. Ho, he says, we got to fix that window. Yes, I says, it is broke alright. Maybe I'll bring some tools out next week, he says. Yes, I says, that would be good.

That Ambrose sits down and starts to cry. Hoo hoo hoo hoo. Like that. That big boy cries like that. Sit down, I says. Have some tea.

You got to help me, he says. Sure, I says. I can do that.

Granny's in that hole, he says. She's going to come back. You got to help me do this thing. We got to get her out and do it right. Put her in that tree. Heavyshield's tree. In the mountains. Like she said.

Boy, I says, lots of work that. They put her in pretty deep. Way down there. With that God fellow.

I can dig her up, Ambrose says. You don't have to do anything. I'll dig her up and get you and you can tell me how to do this thing. Got to keep that promise.

Okay, I says.

So.

That Ambrose gets everything we need. Wilma watches him and sniffs with her nose. Tonight I'm going to do it, Ambrose says. But he doesn't. Flat tire, he says.

Tonight I'm going to do it, that one tells me. But he doesn't. No moon.

Tonight I'm going to do it. That big boy has one good memory. But he doesn't do it then, either. Got the flu.

Ambrose gets a skin and he keeps that skin in the back of his truck. Green. Getting to smell, I think. Maybe not. Those Magpies hang around that truck. What you got in that truck, Wilma says. Nothing, says Ambrose. Just some stuff.

But you know, he does it. That big boy comes to my house early in the morning. With his truck. With that skin. With Granny sewed up in that skin. Just like I said. Ho, I says, you got that Granny. Yes, says Ambrose, I dig her up last night. Now we can do it right.

So we do. Ambrose drives that truck with Granny sewed up in the skin to Heavyshield's cabin and that good boy climbs that tree and that one drags Granny up that tree with a rope. High. On those skinny branches. Near the sun. He puts that old woman. Then he climbs down. There, he says, and smacks his hands together. That does it.

I make some tea. Ambrose sits on the ground, watches Granny in the tree. Pretty soon he is asleep.

Let's see what happens.

Well, pretty quick those Magpies come along and look in that tree. And they fly in that tree. And they sit in that tree. Talking. They sit on that hide has Granny hid inside and talk to her. Hello. Nice day.

Then that sun comes down. Into the tree. With those birds. With Granny. Ho, that sun says, what we got here? Granny and a bunch of Magpies. That's right, I says.

Then that big dust ball comes along, right up to the house. Heavyshield's place. Rolls into the yard.

Then Wilma gets out.

Then the RCMP gets out.

Then Benny Goodrunner, tribal policeman, gets out.

Out of that dust ball.

Boy, those birds are some fast talkers.

Where's Granny, Wilma says. Where's Ambrose? She says that, too. Where's Ambrose Standing Bull, RCMP says. Benny don't say nothing. He just stand there. Look embarrassed.

Ambrose wakes up. Wilma sees him wake up. There he is, she says. There is that criminal. There is that thief. Then she uses words I don't understand.

Ambrose stands right up. I'm just doing what Granny asked. Nothing wrong with that.

That RCMP got his bright uniform on. Body-stealing is against the law, he says.

This is reserve land, Ambrose says.

Benny's going to arrest you, Ambrose, says Wilma. Going to put you in jail for digging up Granny.

Lots of Magpies in the tree now. They just listening. All ears.

Wilma looks in that tree. She sees those birds. She sees that sun. She sees that hide. He's already stuck her in that tree. We got to bring her down.

RCMP man looks at Wilma and looks at Benny. Wilma looks at Benny. Ambrose looks at Benny. Maybe you boys want some tea, I says. Nice evening. Maybe you want to sit and have some tea.

No time for tea, old one, Wilma says in our language. My mother's in that tree. We got to get her down.

So. Benny is the one. Have to climb that tree. All the way. So, he starts up. Those birds stop walking on Granny and watch Benny. Ambrose watches Benny. Wilma watches Benny. RCMP man watches Benny. That Benny is a rodeo man, rides those bulls. Strong legs, that one. He climbs all the way to Granny. Then he sits down. On a limb. Like those birds. Hey, he says, I can see the river. Real good view.

Look for Granny, says that Wilma.

Leave her alone, says Ambrose.

Boy, those Magpies are jumping around in that tree. Dancing. Choosing sides. Singing songs. Telling jokes.

Milk carton comes out of that tree.

Peach can comes out of that tree.

Bottle of Wesson cooking oil comes down. Empty.

Carburetor.

Magazine.

Hey, says Benny. Granny's not here. She's not in this skin. She's gone. Nothing here but garbage. Benny comes down that tree.

Everybody looks at Ambrose.

Must be magic, says Ambrose and he walks into that cabin and closes the door.

Wilma stands up straight and she looks at that RCMP man. Benny has his clothes all dirty. That RCMP is mostly clean. Nothing but garbage in that tree, Benny says. Alright, says Wilma. She gets back in the truck, that one. Benny gets in that truck. RCMP gets in that truck.

Boy, pretty exciting.

That sun gets down behind the mountain. Ambrose comes out of that house, says, everybody gone? Yes, I says. Good trick, that one, he says. Yes, I says, that one had me fooled. My shovel broke, says Ambrose. I'm going to get her tonight. Nobody will see me this time. I would have got her that other time but my shovel broke. You got a shovel I can borrow? Sure, I say, you can use my good shovel.

You watch, says Ambrose. This is my plan. Benny saw that bag of garbage. So now I get Granny and put her up there. Take that garbage down and put Granny in that tree like I promise. No one will look there again. That's my plan.

That's a good plan, I says. That should fool them. Good thing you got some of that garbage out of the ground.

You got to promise me you won't tell anyone about my plan, Ambrose says. Watch out for those birds, I says. They told Wilma about your bag of garbage, I bet. They got good ears, those ones. You got to sing that song so they can't hear. So they won't remember. You know that song?

No, say Ambrose. You better listen then, I says. Otherwise those birds will tell everyone what your plan is. So I show Ambrose the song and he sings it pretty good, that boy. And he borrows my shovel. My good shovel. And I don't see him for a long time. And I don't see Wilma either. And I don't tell Ambrose's plan.

But I know what happened.

But I can't tell.

I promised.

You can count on me.

Activities

1. In discussing contemporary Aboriginal literature, Thomas King has identified two frequently recurring themes: a sense of community and the oral tradition. How are these two themes reflected in "Magpies"? What other themes are central to this story?

2. With a partner, use a literary reference guide to develop working definitions for the terms *reliable narrator* and *unreliable narrator*. Prepare to write an analytical essay on narration in "Magpies" by developing a profile of the narrator. Consider from whose point of view the story is told. What information does the story provide about this narrator and about his or her relationship to characters and events? Create a thesis statement in which you take a position on whether this narrator is reliable or unreliable. When writing your essay, use definition and detailed evidence to support your thesis.

3. Work with a small group to present this story as readers' theatre. Identify the roles you will need to include and decide how you will incorporate the narrator's part. Explore various ways of staging the reading and of focusing audience attention on the speaker. Develop an audience reaction sheet. After the performance, write a group self-evaluation based on feedback from the audience, as well as your own analysis of your performance.

Another Viewpoint: Culture

It has been observed that the focus on good and evil that often appears in Western and other literatures is commonly replaced in Native literature with a focus on balance and harmony. Discuss this perspective in relation to "Magpies" and at least two other works by Aboriginal authors.

Dialogue, 1991, Nuwa Wamala Nnyanzi

The Winner

Barbara Kimenye

Barbara Kimenye was born in 1940, in Buganda, the former kingdom of East Africa on the north shore of Lake Victoria, now part of Uganda. In Africa, she worked as private secretary for the government of Buganda. She was also a newspaper journalist and columnist in Kenya. In 1974, she moved to London, England, and became a social worker. She is well known for her children's books and has published story collections dealing with the everyday lives of Ugandans. Many African writers, like Kimenye, choose to write in English in order to reach a wider audience. Others write only in African languages because they believe that their culture and values are best carried by their own language. What might some of the disadvantages and advantages be of writing in a "second" language?

When Pius Ndawula won the football pools, overnight he seemed to become the most popular man in Buganda. Hosts of relatives converged upon him from the four corners of the kingdom: cousins and nephews, nieces and uncles, of whose existence he had never before been aware, turned up in Kalasanda by the busload, together with crowds of individuals who, despite their downtrodden appearance, assured Pius that they and they alone were capable of seeing that his money was properly invested—preferably in their own particular businesses! Also lurking around Pius's unpretentious mud hut were newspaper reporters, slick young men weighed down with cameras and sporting loud checked caps or trilbies set at conspicuously jaunty angles, and serious young men from Radio Uganda who were anxious to record Pius's delight at his astonishing luck for the edification of the Uganda listening public.

The rest of Kalasanda were so taken by surprise that they could only call and briefly congratulate Pius before being elbowed out of the way by his more garrulous relations. All, that is to say, except Pius's greatest friend Salongo, the custodian of the Ssabalangira's tomb. He came and planted himself firmly in the house, and nobody attempted to move him. Almost blind, and very lame, he had tottered out with the aid of a stout stick. Just to see him arrive had caused a minor sensation in the village, for he hadn't left the tomb for years. But recognizing at last a chance to house Ssabalangira's remains in a state befitting his former glory made the slow, tortuous journey worthwhile to Salongo.

Nantondo hung about long enough to have her picture taken with Pius. Or rather, she managed to slip beside him just as the cameras clicked, and so it was that every Uganda newspaper, on the following day, carried a front-page photograph of "Mr. Pius Ndawula and his happy wife," a caption that caused Pius to shake with rage and threaten legal proceedings, but over which Nantondo gloated as she proudly showed it to everybody she visited.

"Tell us, Mr. Ndawula, what do you intend to do with all the money you have won…?"

"Tell us, Mr. Ndawula, how often have you completed pools coupons…?"

"Tell us…Tell us…Tell us…"

Pius's head was reeling under this bombardment of questions, and he was even more confused by Salongo's constant nudging and muttered advice to "Say nothing!" Nor did the relatives make things easier. Their persistent clamouring for his attention, and the way they kept shoving their children under his nose, made it impossible for him to think, let alone talk.

It isn't at all easy, when you have lived for sixty-five years in complete obscurity, to adjust yourself in a matter of hours to the role of a celebrity, and the strain was beginning to tell.

Behind the hut—Pius had no proper kitchen—gallons of tea were being boiled, whilst several of the female cousins were employed in ruthlessly hacking down the bunches of *matoke* from his meagre plantains to cook food for everybody. One woman—she had introduced herself as Cousin Sarah—discovered Pius's hidden store of banana beer, and dished it out to all and sundry as though it were her own. Pius had become very wary of Cousin Sarah. He didn't like the way in which she kept loudly remarking that he needed a woman about the place, and he was even more seriously alarmed when suddenly Salongo gave him a painful dig in the ribs and muttered, "You'll have to watch that one—she's a sticker!"

Everybody who came wanted to see the telegram that announced Pius's win. When it had arrived at the Ggombolola Headquarters—the postal address of everyone residing within a radius of fifteen miles—Musisi had brought it out personally, delighted to be the bearer of such good tidings. At Pius's request he had gone straightaway to tell Salongo, and then back to his office to send an acknowledgement on behalf of Pius to the pools firm, leaving the old man to dream rosy dreams. An extension of his small coffee *shamba,* a new roof on his house—or maybe an entirely new house—concrete blocks this time, with a veranda perhaps. Then there were hens. Salongo and he had always said there was money in hens these days, now that the women ate eggs and chicken; not that either of them agreed with the practice. Say what you liked, women who ate chicken and eggs were fairly asking to be infertile! That woman welfare officer who came around snooping occasionally tried to say it was all nonsense, that chicken meat and eggs made bigger and better babies. Well, they might look bigger and better, but nobody could deny that they were fewer! Which only goes to show.

But news spreads fast in Africa—perhaps the newspapers have contacts in the pools offices. Anyway, before the telegram had even reached Pius, announcements were appearing in the local newspapers, and Pius was still quietly lost in his private dreams when the first batch of visitors arrived. At first he was at a loss to understand what was happening. People he hadn't seen for years and only recognized with difficulty fell upon him with cries of joy. "Cousin Pius, the family are delighted!" "Cousin Pius, why have you not visited us all this time?"

Pius was pleased to see his nearest and dearest gathered around him. It warmed his old heart once more to find himself in the bosom of his family, and he welcomed them effusively. The second crowd to arrive were no less well received, but there was a marked coolness on the part of their forerunners.

However, as time had gone by and the flood of strange faces had gained momentum, Pius's *shamba* had come to resemble a political meeting. All to be seen from the door of the house was a turbulent sea of white *kanzus* and brilliant *busutis,* and the house itself was full of people and tobacco smoke.

The precious telegram was passed from hand to hand until it was reduced to a limp fragment of paper with the lettering partly obliterated: not that it mattered very much, for only a few members of the company could read English.

"Now, Mr. Ndawula, we are ready to take the recording." The speaker was a slight young man wearing a checked shirt. "I shall ask you a few questions, and you simply answer me in your normal voice." Pius looked at the leather box with its two revolving spools, and licked his lips. "Say nothing!" came a hoarse whisper from Salongo. The young man steadfastly ignored him, and went ahead in his best BBC manner. "Well, Mr. Ndawula, first of all let me congratulate you on your winning the pools. Would you like to tell our listeners what it feels like suddenly to find yourself rich?" There was an uncomfortable pause, during which Pius stared mesmerized at the racing spools and the young man tried frantically to span the gap by asking, "I mean, have you any plans for the future?" Pius swallowed audibly, and opened his mouth to say something, but shut it again when Salongo growled, "Tell him nothing!"

The young man snapped off the machine, shaking his head in exasperation. "Look here, sir, all I want you to do is to say something—I'm not asking you to make a speech! Now, I'll tell you what. I shall ask you again what it feels like suddenly to come into money, and you say something like 'It was a wonderful surprise, and naturally I feel very pleased'—and will you ask your friend not to interrupt! Got it? Okay, off we go!"

The machine was again switched on, and the man brightly put his question, "Now, Mr. Ndawula, what does it feel like to win the pools?"

Pius swallowed, then quickly chanted in a voice all off key, "It was a wonderful surprise and naturally I feel very happy and will you ask your friend not to interrupt!" The young man nearly wept. This happened to be his first assignment as a radio interviewer, and it looked like it would be his last. He switched off the machine and mourned his lustreless future, groaning. At that moment Cousin Sarah caught his eye. "Perhaps I can help you," she said. "I am Mr. Ndawula's cousin." She made this pronouncement in a manner that suggested Pius had no others. The young man brightened considerably. "Well, madam, if you could tell me something about Mr. Ndawula's plans, I would be most grateful." Cousin Sarah folded her arms across her imposing bosom, and when the machine again started up, she was off. Yes, Mr. Ndawula was very happy about the money. No, she didn't think he had any definite plans on how to spend it—with all these people about he didn't have time to think. Yes, Mr. Ndawula lived completely alone, but she was prepared to stay and look after him for as long as he needed her. Here a significant glance passed between the other women in the room, who clicked their teeth and let out long "Eeeeeeehs!" of incredulity. Yes, she believed she was Mr. Ndawula's nearest living relative by marriage…

Pius listened to her confident aplomb with growing horror, while Salongo frantically nudged him and whispered, "There! What did I tell you! That woman's a sticker!"

Around three in the afternoon, *matoke* and tea were served, the *matoke* on wide fresh plantain leaves, since Pius owned only three plates, and the tea in anything handy—tin cans, old jars, etc.—because he was short of cups too. Pius ate very little, but he was glad of the tea. He had shaken hands with so many people that his arm ached, and he was tired of the chatter and the comings and goings in his house of all these strangers. Most of all he was tired of Cousin Sarah, who insisted on treating him like an idiot invalid. She kept everybody else at bay, as far as she possibly could, and when one woman plonked a sticky fat baby on his lap, Cousin Sarah dragged the child away as though it were infectious. Naturally, a few cross words were exchanged between Sarah and the fond mother, but by this time Pius was past caring.

Yosefu Mukasa and Kibuka called in the early evening, when some of the relatives were departing with effusive promises to come again tomorrow. They were both alarmed at the weariness they saw on Pius's face. The old man looked utterly worn out, his skin grey and sickly. Also, they were a bit taken aback by the presence of Cousin Sarah, who pressed them to take tea and behaved in every respect as though she were mistress of the house. "I believe my late husband knew you very well, sir," she told Yosefu. "He used to be a Miruka chief in Buyaga County. His name was Kivumbi." "Ah, yes," Yosefu replied, "I remember Kivumbi very well indeed. We often hunted together. I was sorry to hear of his death. He was a good man." Cousin Sarah shrugged her shoulders. "Yes, he was a good man. But what the Lord giveth, He also taketh away." Thus was the late Kivumbi dismissed from the conversation.

Hearing all this enabled Pius to define the exact relationship between himself and Cousin Sarah, and even by Kiganda standards it was virtually nonexistent, for the late Kivumbi had been the stepson of one of Pius's cousins.

"Your stroke of luck seems to have exhausted you, Pius," Kibuka remarked, when he and Yosefu were seated on the rough wooden chairs brought forth by Cousin Sarah.

Salongo glared at the world in general and snarled, "Of course he is exhausted! Who wouldn't be with all these scavengers collected to pick his bones?" Pius hushed him as one would a child. "No, no, Salongo. It is quite natural that my family should gather round me at a time like this. Only I fear I am perhaps a little too old for all this excitement."

Salongo spat expertly through the open doorway, narrowly missing a group of guests who were preparing to bed down, and said, "That woman doesn't think he's too old. She's out to catch him. I've seen her type elsewhere!"

Yosefu's mouth quirked with amusement at the thought that "elsewhere" could only mean the Ssabalangira's tomb, which Salongo had guarded for the better part of his adult life. "Well, she's a fine woman," he remarked. "But see here, Pius," he went on, "don't be offended by my proposal, but wouldn't it be better if you came and stayed with us at Mutunda for tonight? Miriamu would love to have you, and you look as though you need a good night's rest, which you wouldn't get here—those relatives of yours outside are preparing a fire and are ready to dance the night away!"

"I think that's a wonderful idea!" said Cousin Sarah, bouncing in to remove the tea cups. "You go with Mr. Mukasa, Cousin Pius. The change will do you as much good as the rest. And don't worry about your home—I shall stay here and look after things." Pius hesitated. "Well, I think I shall be all right here—I don't like to give Miriamu any extra work…." Salongo muttered, "Go to Yosefu's. You don't want to be left alone in the house with that woman—there's no knowing what she might get up to…!" "I'll pack a few things for you, Pius," announced Cousin Sarah and bustled off before anything more could be said, pausing only long enough to give Salongo a look that was meant to wither him on the spot.

So Pius found himself being driven away to Mutunda in Yosefu's car, enjoying the pleasant sensation of not having to bother about a thing. Salongo too had been given a lift to as near the tomb as the car could travel, and his wizened old face was contorted into an irregular smile, for Pius had promised to help him build a new house for the Ssabalangira. For him the day had been well spent, despite Cousin Sarah.

Pius spent an enjoyable evening with the Mukasas. They had a well-cooked supper, followed by a glass of cold beer as they sat back and listened to the local news on the radio. Pius had so far relaxed as to tell the Mukasas modestly that he had been interviewed by Radio Uganda that morning, and when Radio Newsreel was announced they waited breathlessly to hear his voice. But instead of Pius, Cousin Sarah came booming over the air. Until that moment the old man had completely forgotten the incident of the tape recording. In fact, he had almost forgotten Cousin Sarah. Now it all came back to him with a shiver of apprehension. Salongo was right. That woman did mean business! It was a chilling thought. However, it didn't cause him to lose any sleep. He slept like a cherub, as if he hadn't a care in the world.

Because he looked so refreshed in the morning, Miriamu insisted on keeping him at Mutunda for another day. "I know you feel better, but after seeing you yesterday, I think a little holiday with us will do you good. Go home tomorrow, when the excitement has died down a bit," she advised.

Soon after lunch, as Pius was taking a nap in a chair on the veranda, Musisi drove up in the Land Rover, with Cousin Sarah by his side. Miriamu came out to greet them, barely disguising her curiosity about the formidable woman about whom she had heard so much. The two women sized each other up and decided to be friends.

Meanwhile, Musisi approached the old man. "Sit down, son." Pius waved him to a chair at his side. "Miriamu feeds me so well it's all I can do to keep awake."

"I am glad you are having a rest, sir." Musisi fumbled in the pocket of his jacket. "There is another telegram for you. Shall I read it?" The old man sat up expectantly and said, "If you'll be so kind."

Musisi first read the telegram in silence, then he looked at Pius and commented, "Well, sir, I'm afraid it isn't good news."

"Not good news? Has somebody died?"

Musisi smiled. "Well, no. It isn't really as bad as that. The thing is, the pools firm say that owing to an unfortunate oversight they omitted to add, in the first telegram, that the prize money is to be shared among three hundred other people."

Pius was stunned. Eventually he murmured, "Tell me, how much does that mean I shall get?"

"Three hundred into seventeen thousand pounds won't give you much over a thousand shillings."

To Musisi's astonishment, Pius sat back and chuckled. "More than a thousand shillings!" he said. "Why, that's a lot of money!"

"But it's not, when you expected so much more!"

"I agree. And yet, son, what would I have done with all those thousands of pounds? I am getting past the age when I need a lot."

Miriamu brought a mat onto the veranda and she and Cousin Sarah made themselves comfortable near the men. "What a disappointment!" cried Miriamu, but Cousin Sarah sniffed and said, "I agree with Cousin Pius. He wouldn't know what to do with seventeen thousand pounds, and the family would be hanging round his neck forevermore!"

At mention of Pius's family, Musisi frowned. "I should warn you, sir, those relatives of yours have made a terrific mess of your *shamba*—

your plantains have been stripped—and Mrs. Kivumbi here," nodding at Sarah, "was only just in time to prevent them digging up your sweet potatoes!"

"Yes, Cousin Pius," added Sarah. "It will take us some time to put the *shamba* back in order. They've trodden down a whole bed of young beans."

"Oh, dear," said Pius weakly. "This is dreadful news."

"Don't worry. They will soon disappear when I tell them there is no money, and then I shall send for a couple of my grandsons to come and help us do some replanting." Pius could not help but admire the way Sarah took things in her stride.

Musisi rose from his chair. "I'm afraid I can't stay any longer, so I will go now and help Cousin Sarah clear the crowd, and see you tomorrow to take you home." He and Sarah climbed back into the Land Rover and Sarah waved energetically until the vehicle was out of sight.

"Your cousin is a fine woman," Miriamu told Pius, before going indoors. Pius merely grunted, but for some odd reason he felt the remark to be a compliment to himself.

All was quiet at Pius's home when Musisi brought him home next day. He saw at once that his *shamba* was well nigh wrecked, but his drooping spirits quickly revived when Sarah placed a mug of steaming tea before him, and sat on a mat at his feet, explaining optimistically how matters could be remedied. Bit by bit he began telling her what he planned to do with the prize money, ending with, "Of course, I shan't be able to do everything now, especially since I promised Salongo something for the tomb."

Sarah poured some more tea and said, "Well, I think the roof should have priority. I noticed last night that there are several leaks. And whilst we're about it, it would be a good idea to build another room on and a small outside kitchen. Mud and wattle is cheap enough, and then the whole place can be plastered. You can still go ahead and extend your coffee. And as for hens, well, I have six good layers at home, as well as a fine cockerel. I'll bring them over!"

Pius looked at her in silence for a long time. She is a fine looking woman, he thought, and that blue *busuti* suits her. Nobody would ever take her for a grandmother—but why is she so anxious to throw herself at me?

"You sound as if you are planning to come and live here," he said at last, trying hard to sound casual.

Sarah turned to face him and replied, "Cousin Pius, I shall be very frank with you. Six months ago my youngest son got married and brought his wife to live with me. She's a very nice girl, but somehow I can't get used to having another woman in the house. My other son is in Kampala, and although I know I would be welcome there, he too has a wife, and three children, so if I went there I wouldn't be any better off. When I saw that bit about you in the paper, I suddenly remembered—although I don't expect you to—how you were at my wedding and so helpful to everybody. Well, I thought to myself, here is somebody who needs a good housekeeper, who needs somebody to keep the leeches off, now that he has come into money. I came along right away to take a look at you, and I can see I did the right thing. You do need me." She hesitated for a moment, and then said, "Only you might prefer to stay alone...I'm so used to having my own way, I never thought about that before."

Pius cleared his throat. "You're a very impetuous woman," was all he could find to say.

A week later, Pius wandered out to the tomb and found Salongo busily polishing the Ssabalangira's weapons. "I thought you were dead," growled the custodian, "it is so long since you came here—but then, this tomb thrives on neglect. Nobody cares that one of Buganda's greatest men lies here."

"I have been rather busy," murmured Pius. "But I didn't forget my promise to you. Here! I've brought you a hundred shillings, and I only wish it could have been more. At least it will buy a few cement blocks."

Salongo took the money and looked at it as if it were crawling with lice. Grudgingly he thanked Pius and then remarked, "Of course, you will find life more expensive now that you are keeping a woman in the house."

"I suppose Nantondo told you," Pius smiled sheepishly.

"Does it matter who told me?" the custodian replied. "Anyway, never say I didn't warn you. Next thing she'll want will be a ring marriage!"

Pius gave an uncertain laugh. "As a matter of fact, one of the reasons I came up here was to invite you to the wedding—it's next month."

Salongo carefully laid down the spear he was rubbing upon a piece of clean barkcloth and stared at his friend as if he had suddenly grown another head. "What a fool you are! And all this stems from your scribbling noughts and crosses on a bit of squared paper! I knew it would bring no good! At your age you ought to have more sense. Well, all I can advise is that you run while you still have the chance!"

For a moment Pius was full of misgivings. Was he, after all, behaving like a fool? Then he thought of Sarah, and the wonders she had worked with his house and his *shamba* in the short time they had been together. He felt reassured. "Well, I'm getting married, and I expect to see you at both the church and the reception, and if you don't appear, I shall want to know the reason why!" He was secretly delighted at the note of authority in his voice, and Salongo's face was the picture of astonishment. "All right," he mumbled, "I shall try and come. Before you go, cut a bunch of bananas to take back to your good lady, and there might be some cabbage ready at the back. I suppose I've got to hand it to her! She's the real winner!"

Notes

Buganda a state in southern Uganda

garrulous talkative in a tedious, rambling manner; from the Latin word *garrulus*, meaning "chatter"

Ssabalangira refers to any revered man in Uganda who is deceased

matoke a Ugandan food staple; cooked green bananas usually served with a meat sauce

kanzu a robe worn by some East African men

busuti a long cloak

shamba a garden with fruits and vegetables

aplomb confident composure or self-assurance

Activities

1. Choose several passages in the story that you found particularly engaging and explain in a few sentences why each appeals to you. Share your thoughts with the class and come up with a co-operative list of the positive features of "The Winner." Name other literary works you have read which have similar characteristics. If you disliked the story, be prepared to explain why.

2. Why do you think Kimenye chose to conclude the story with a scene between Pius and Salongo? In a group, make a list of other moments either within the story or beyond the story that could also serve as appropriate endings. Select an ending from your list which you think would be most effective and write it. Which ending do you prefer, yours or the author's? Explain.

3. Locate and read reviews of children's books in a number of newspapers and on the Internet, and analyze their content and style. Then find and read several children's books by either Barbara Kimenye or other writers of African origin. Write a review of one of these books, using the reviews you read as models.

Windows

Bernice Morgan

Bernice Morgan was born in St. John's, Newfoundland, in 1935. She is a writer of short stories, plays, and novels. Her novel *Random Passage* and its sequel, *Waiting for Time*, were made into a CBC television mini-series; a production photograph of the filming appears on page 641 of this anthology. A book of her short stories, *The Topography of Love*, was published in 2000. Morgan has also worked for many years in public relations, first with Memorial University of Newfoundland, and later with the Newfoundland Teachers Association. Morgan's fiction often depicts the plight of immigrant individuals and families who settled in Canada. What major challenges do immigrants face in a new country? What are some of the ways they deal with them?

One morning in late winter, Leah Levitawitz opened her eyes on the sure knowledge that she was dying. Dawn did not waken her, for dawn never came to this room, only a pale greenish light that slithered down from the roof of the old house and along the dripping mouldy wall of the warehouse next door. It must have been the cold that woke her; it seeped in around the sagging sills and loose clapboards, the damp cold of late winter that cut through the threadbare blankets and even penetrated Leah's old tweed coat.

Leah checked down the length of her thin body. "Strange," she thought, "I don't feel any worse than I did yesterday...how can I be so sure this is it?"

Brain, heart, arms and legs seemed to be functioning as usual—sluggish but still in working order. In a little while she would get up, dress and go, very slowly, down the rickety steps to the kitchen. But not yet. Leah could hear the screams of her grandchildren and the tired, peevish voice of her son's wife. Leah burrowed down, pulling the old coat up over her yellow-grey hair. She would wait, as she always did, until they had gone, maybe Ruth would go out too, then she could creep down and have her drop of tea in peace. Leah closed her eyes against the dingy green light of the room and set herself to wait.

To wait, and to think about this new knowledge of death that had come from somewhere in the night. This dying, it must have been going on for a long time, she realized. Strange that it hadn't come to her before to put a name to it! She'd always thought of death as something that pounced upon you when you were least expecting it—like it had pounced down on Mikail twenty years ago, shoving him off that little piece of steel and smashing him like an egg on the concrete. Dead…the papers said, or deceased—it sounded like one quick, single act, but it wasn't going to be, not for her anyway. For her death would not pounce but come creeping, creeping, inch by inch—like a cat creeping toward its prey.

Leah wondered when it had started—when Mikail died? Probably, but it was a long way off then. Now it felt much closer. She remembered waking on the morning after he died, waking and not knowing, and then, knowing—and the terrible emptiness. Yes that must have been the beginning.

But in those years she hadn't the time to notice, she'd been too busy, getting coal and firewood, mitts and shoes—all the things that had to somehow be gotten before little children turned into men and women. And the lying—Leah remembered all the lying she'd done, when you had no money you bartered in lies, and she'd lied to everyone. To the landlord, "The Welfare man was here and said he'd have this place condemned if you didn't fix that roof." To the grocer, "I'm expecting a cheque from my brother, it should have been here yesterday, in the meantime I'll have to charge one or two things." To the teachers, "Sam is such a careless boy…he lost his gym shoes on the way to school the first day…I'll get him another pair the first chance I get."

She'd even lied to the children, "The winter's almost over now, things are always easier in the summer. Maybe this year we can all go on a little vacation, to a farm maybe, wouldn't it be nice to go to a farm?"

They had never gone to the farm. Leah wondered if all her lies lay piled up somewhere waiting to be displayed at some day of reckoning. Well, she didn't care...they had been necessary. Thank God it was behind her, all five of the children were raised and none of them had ended up in jail like some she'd known. Jack was the worst off and married to a woman who would rather whine than work, there wasn't much chance of his ever being any richer.

"Why do I stay with them?" she asked herself the question for the thousandth time and for the thousandth time replied with the automatic answer, "Because they need my pension." Only this morning she forced herself to stop and admit there was another reason, another answer to why she slept in this miserable room and listened to Ruth's whining day after day.

Three years ago when she had been notified that her old apartment building was being demolished, Jack had said, "Better come over and stop with us, Ma." None of the others had asked her to come with them.

Leah knew she got on Ruth's nerves, look how she was always trying to get her out of the house..."Aw Ma, go on over and visit your friend Mrs. Palaskine, you haven't been over there once this year." Or, "Ma, for God's sake go out somewheres...let Jack drop ya off at the park and you can take your time comin' back."

Take your time; that was funny.

Half asleep now, Leah's thoughts slipped back to her own childhood on a farm in Estonia. Someone told her that Estonia didn't exist any more, but of course that was nonsense, a country didn't disappear. They might call it a different name but it was still the same country.

It had been cold there, too, but she and her sisters had slept in a bed built against the side of the chimney. Sometimes in the morning the bricks were still warm with the heat of yesterday's fires.

The farm had been poor. "I haven't made much progress," Leah mused, "born poor and dying poor." There had been a few years, first when she and Mikail were married, when she'd thought that they might make it, might get ahead enough to own something, even a piece of land perhaps. She hadn't missed the farm in those years, it was only later, later when all the hope was gone that she'd begun to lie awake remembering how beautiful Estonia had been. The pattern of green leaves against a blue sky, the amber glow of firelight on stone walls, fields of wheat and girls in red kerchiefs cutting it…if Estonia still existed, then those things must exist also. Canada was a big country, Leah knew, she'd heard it often on the radio. There were probably trees and open fields, rivers and hills in Canada too…but she'd never seen them.

Leah dozed, the flicker of leaves in sunshine making dream pictures inside her closed eyes.

A noise, like a cannon ripping a city apart, tore across her room, jerking her awake and sitting. The noise kept up, it filled her head, the room, the house, the world. Dear God—could this be death? Leah felt her heart pounding and even in the chill of the room, sweat beaded around her neck. Then the noise stopped for a minute and she heard men shouting and trucks…it wasn't what she'd thought.

"Oh Lord, how foolish am I?" Leah eased her thin legs over the edge of the bed and pushed her feet into sagging carpet slippers. By the time she'd reached the window the noise had started again, but of course she couldn't see anything, only the wet slimy walls of the old warehouse that she'd been looking at for three years. "Digging up the street, someone's pipes froze again more than likely!" Well, now that she was up she'd better get dressed. The room felt even colder. "Will I live to see the end of winter?" she wondered.

In the kitchen a naked bulb hung from a twisted black cord. The kitchen window also faced the warehouse and the bulb was kept burning all day. Its hard, yellow glare revealed every grease mark on the motley wallpaper, every chip in the rust-coloured sink, it shone unmercifully on Ruth's tired face and unkempt hair.

The two women did not talk. Leah shuffled about getting a cup of tea and toasting a slice of bread on a fork over the coal fire. One thing Ruth did, she made good bread. Leah sniffed with pleasure as the edges of the bread turned golden brown.

Ruth stood at the sink listlessly washing dishes, her head tilted toward the radio. Ruth filled her days with second-hand drama. Leah watched the younger woman shaking her head over some unwise decision the radio character had made. "They're more real to her than I am—than any of us are."

Then the radio sputtered and the sobbing voice of the forsaken heroine disappeared under a barrage of sound.

"Oh damn, now I'll never know how it comes out! It's that darn machine they're workin' the street with."

Radio listening was a necessary background for dish washing. Ruth dried her hands and untied her apron.

"Look Ma, I'm goin' down town, the kids won't be home to lunch— you fix yourself something and I'll be back around four."

Being careful not to let her pleasure show, Leah nodded and turned the toast over on the fork.

It took Ruth only a minute in front of the cracked mirror to slash a red line across her mouth and button her lint-covered black coat. She started to leave, then stuck her head in the kitchen door to ask, "Anything you want?"

Leah shook her head and grunted negatively. As if she'd let that nit-wit shop for her! But Ruth always asked. She enjoyed shopping and spread the necessary purchases of socks, shoes and underwear over as many trips to the stores as possible.

You'd hardly notice the noise once you got used to it. Leah carefully carried her tea and toast over to the stove and sat with her feet in the oven. The old rocker was the only thing in the house that she owned. Ruth said she was always tripping over it but Leah was glad she'd held onto it. Leah sipped her tea and rocked. She wished she had some knitting— maybe she should have told Ruth to get her wool and needles. She could knit a bright wool afghan for her bed...but no, it would take too long, too long to finish.

It was nice to sit here with the warm stove and the warm tea, if only the light wasn't so bright! Carefully Leah set the thick cup down on the back of the stove, she got up slowly and turned off the terrible light. There! That was so much better, how she hated that light! Now the kitchen was almost dark, the pleasant glow of the fire softened the harsh look of poverty.

The noise wasn't really so bad, much more bearable than the radio. Leah began thinking once more about death, turning the idea over, getting used to it. She rocked and dozed.

The crash of glass and an icy wind at her back woke her. The entire window had smashed in, frame and all. Leah stood facing the broken glass and waited for something else to happen…this time she was more curious than frightened. What in the world was going on out there?

Two men appeared in the window wearing those yellow hats that look like mixing bowls. They were young, frightened and embarrassed. Leah could hardly keep from smiling. A voice behind the two young men shouted, "What the Hell you two doin'?" An older man with a clip board in his hand appeared. The young men blushed and stammered something about the lever of the crane.

"Honest to God I don't know where they get the jokers they send down to me these days—how the Hell did the lever slip? The same if you'd killed this old dame here! Look Missus," the big man stuck his head in the broken window, "we'll be through here in about two hours. How about if we nail a piece of plywood to keep the weather out and then I'll have someone come over and fix the window?"

Leah nodded, the heads disappeared and a few minutes later the hole was covered with a sheet of wood. Leah sighed, sorry the excitement had ended so soon. She looked at the splinters of glass and wood on the floor and wondered if she'd sweep them up. No, it was really too much trouble, she decided. Leah gave the fire one poke and settled down in the rocker again.

It was nice and quite comfortable but this time Leah couldn't sleep—the noises outside kept intruding. What in the world were they doing anyway? The house shook and on the back of the stove her cup rattled. If this kept on the house would fall down around her ears. There would be a nice fast death! Leah decided she wouldn't really mind…the city would have to pay Jack and Ruth for all the things that got broken. Except her of course. There wouldn't be any need to pay for her.

What would she get herself for lunch? She wasn't hungry but it gave her something to think about. She'd seen Ruth stick a package of sausages out in the back porch. Leah was fond of sausage, maybe she'd fry a few, but no—they always gave her heartburn and besides she'd have a greasy pan to scrub. Maybe she'd get herself an egg—that young public health nurse who came by was always askin' her if she'd had an egg—she'd never liked eggs. She couldn't bear thinkin' about what they really were— ah well, she'd have an egg today, boiled, that way there'd be no pot to wash!

The fire seemed to be dying. She got up and took a look at it— might just as well burn those pieces of window frame. As Leah stuffed the rotten wood into the stove she listened. The noises outside seemed to be different, the pounding had stopped.

"Maybe I'll just take a nip out and see what they're doin'."

Then she remembered she'd left her coat upstairs on her bed. It was too much trouble to climb the steep steps. Leah was just about to settle down in her rocker again when she noticed Jack's old army parka hanging on the kitchen door. She pulled it on, it was big and bulky, the sleeves covered her hands and it hung down to her knees—but it was warm. Near the front door there was a pair of children's rubber boots. Leah sat on the bottom stair and pulled them on over her slippers— she'd always been proud of her little feet.

It wasn't really as cold as she'd expected. Leah hobbled around the corner of the house. She stopped in amazement. The corner lot next door was empty! Just one big empty space, not a sign of the old warehouse remained! Two tractors were smoothing over the black earth.

Leah stood and watched them and marvelled. "Now wasn't that something!" She looked at the house, at the plywood-covered kitchen window and at her own bedroom window above it. They would be able to see right down the street! Sunlight would come in. And look what they were doin' now. Leah watched as cranes gently lifted two trees and set them down into holes. There'd be grass too, no doubt, they'd be just like rich people, with a garden of their own. Maybe the city would plant flowers, tulips perhaps, yes, tulips first, then petunias and later big orange coloured chrysanthemums…and the leaves would turn on the trees…Leah sighed. Maybe she could make a little plot of her own over by the kitchen window—surely no one would mind that. Maybe the children could help her, they probably couldn't tell one flower from another, or maybe they could. She didn't really know much about her grandchildren.

Watching the men plant the trees and lost in thoughts of how the land ("the land" was what her father had always called any open space) would look when summer came, Leah didn't realize someone was speaking to her until the big man touched her sleeve.

"Look Missus—you the lady in that house—where we broke the window?"

Leah nodded.

"Well I've just written down the measurements of that window and two carpenters will be over to repair it later. I wonder if you can tell me what kind of window it was. Did it have small panes of glass or what?"

Leah remembered the windows in the farmhouse in Estonia, they'd opened out from the middle—lovely on a summer's day to unlatch your window and look out across the land!

Leah cleared her throat. "Well it was a very unusual window…"

The big man had never seen a window like it. Leah had to draw a picture of the window on his yellow paper.

"Well, well," he studied the sketch, "seems to me it was plainer than that…I haven't seen a window like that…not for forty years! We'd have to get it custom made—" He looked at the house again. "The other windows aren't like that." The man fixed a skeptical look at the old woman in the army parka. "You sure it was that kind of window?"

With all the dignity she could muster Leah stared right back at him.

"It certainly was, young man! I had it copied especially from my old home in Estonia."

The words came out strong and clear—much better than she had feared. The man blinked and nodded.

"And just make sure there's a little latch in the middle." Leah waved him off with a regal hand—it was the first lie she'd told in years; it gave her a heady feeling to know she could still do it so well.

Leah took one more long look at the trees, to make sure they were being properly planted, and turned back to the house—she thought she'd fry the sausages after all, what was a little heartburn for something you liked! After lunch she'd walk over to see her friend Mrs. Palaskine. Mrs. Palaskine always got all the free seed catalogues. They could talk about what to do with the land this year!

Activities

1. In a class discussion about "Windows," explore to what extent you think Morgan's gender influenced her depiction of the main character. Consider, as well, to what extent you think your gender affects your response to the character.

2. Consider the use of symbolism in this story by identifying one or more objects that Morgan uses symbolically in "Windows." Write a thesis statement in which you explain how the symbolic use of the object you have identified contributes to the overall theme of the story. Then write an analytical essay in which you use detailed examples to make connections and illustrate your thesis. Have a partner evaluate to what extent the examples in your essay provide evidence to support your viewpoint.

3. With the class, discuss the implications of Morgan's decision to write this story from the third-person point of view. Include in your discussion how the point of view affects the tone. Then, with a partner, select a page of the story and rewrite it from the first-person point of view. Compare what you have written with Morgan's original. Share your adaptation with the class, and discuss the advantages and disadvantages of using one point of view over the other.

Another Viewpoint: Society

Many writers have focused on older adults, the process of aging, and "ageism," which is discrimination based on age. As a class, recall stories, poems, or songs you have encountered about older people at the point in their life Shakespeare described as "the time of yellow leaf." Discuss some different perspectives you have garnered either from your readings or actual experience with older adults.

Easter at My Aunt's

Christopher Pratt

About the Visual   Christopher Pratt was born in St. John's, Newfoundland, in 1935, and still lives in the province. He studied fine art at the Glasgow School of Art in Scotland and at Mount Allison University in New Brunswick, where he worked with Alex Colville. Pratt works in numerous media, including oil paint, watercolour, silk-screening, lithography, and collage. He has been appointed both a companion and an officer of the Order of Canada. Pratt often depicts features of buildings in his work. Why might an artist choose to focus on everyday, constructed objects, such as a door or a set of stairs? Do you think some subjects are more valid than others as the focal point of an artist's work?

Activities

1. Draw a sketch or write a journal entry describing in detail a special scene you remember from your past. Include any objects, colours, sounds, or smells that set in motion a sequence of associative memories.

2. Christopher Pratt's first studies at university were in engineering. Examine closely the style of Pratt's lithograph. What makes this lithograph a work of art rather than an engineer's drawing?

1985, lithograph, 39.5 cm x 51 cm

War

Timothy Findley

Timothy Findley was born in Toronto, in 1930. He worked as an actor early in his career, appearing on stages in North America, including Stratford, as well as in Europe. He has written for television and the stage, and his novel *The Wars* won the Governor General's Award for Fiction in 1977. Another novel, *Not Wanted on the Voyage,* and his first work of non-fiction, *Inside Memory: Pages for a Writer's Notebook,* both won Canadian Authors Association Awards. Some of the dialogue in this story appears in the form of a dramatic work, in which each character speaks without any narrative context. What are some of the differences between the use of dialogue in a work of fiction and its use in a dramatic work?

That's my dad in the middle. We were just kids then, Bud on the right and me on the left. That was taken just before my dad went into the army.

Some day that was.

It was a Saturday, two years ago. August, 1940. I can remember I had to blow my nose just before that and I had to use my dad's hankie because mine had a worm in it that I was saving. I can't remember why; I mean, why I was saving that worm, but I can remember why I had to blow my nose, all right. That was because I'd had a long time crying. Not exactly because my dad was going away or anything—it was mostly because I'd done something.

I'll tell you what in a minute, but I just want to say this first. I was ten years old then and it was sort of the end of summer. When we went

back to school I was going into the fifth grade and that was pretty important, especially for me because I'd skipped grade four. Right now I can't
even remember grade five except that I didn't like it. I should have gone
to grade four. In grade five everyone was a genius and there was a boy
called Allan McKenzie.

Anyway, now that you know how old I was and what grade I was
into, I can tell you the rest.

It was the summer the war broke out and I went to stay with my
friend, Arthur Robertson. Looking back on it, Arthur seems a pretty
silly name for Arthur Robertson because he was so small. But he was a
nice kid and his dad had the most enormous summer cottage you've
ever seen. In Muskoka, too.

It was like those houses they have in the movies in Beverly Hills.
Windows a mile long—pine trees outside and then a lake and then a
red canoe tied up with a yellow rope. There was an Indian, too, who
sold little boxes made of birch-bark and porcupine quills. Arthur
Robertson and I used to sit in the red canoe and this Indian would take
us for a ride out to the raft and back. Then we'd go and tell Mrs.
Robertson or the cook or someone how nice he was and he'd stand
behind us and smile as though he didn't understand English and then
they'd have to buy a box from him. He certainly was smart, that Indian,
because it worked about four times. Then one day they caught on and
hid the canoe.

Anyway, that's the sort of thing we did. And we swam too, and I
remember a book that Arthur Robertson's nurse read to us. It was about
dogs.

Then I had to go away because I'd only been invited for two weeks.
I went on to this farm where the family took us every summer when
we were children. Bud was already there, and his friend, Teddy Hartley.

I didn't like Teddy Hartley. It was because he had a space between
his teeth and he used to spit through it. Once I saw him spit two-and-
a-half yards. Bud paced it out. And then he used to whistle through it,
too, that space, and it was the kind of whistling that nearly made your
ears bleed. That was what I didn't like. But it didn't really matter, because
he was Bud's friend, not mine.

So I went by train and Mr. and Mrs. Currie met me in their truck. It was their farm.

Mrs. Currie got me into the front with her while Mr. Currie put my stuff in the back.

"Your mum and dad aren't here, dear, but they'll be up tomorrow. Buddy is here—and his friend."

Grownups were always calling Bud "Buddy." It was all wrong.

I didn't care too much about my parents not being there, except that I'd brought them each one of those birch-bark boxes. Inside my mother's there was a set of red stones I'd picked out from where we swam. I thought maybe she'd make a necklace out of them. In my dad's there was an old golf ball, because he played golf. I guess you'd have to say I stole it, because I didn't tell anyone I had it—but it was just lying there on a shelf in Mr. Robertson's boathouse, and he never played golf. At least I never saw him.

I had these boxes on my lap because I'd thought my mum and dad would be there to meet me, but now that they weren't I put them into the glove compartment of the truck.

We drove to the farm.

Bud and Teddy were riding on the gate, and they waved when we drove past. I couldn't see too well because of the dust but I could hear them shouting. It was something about my dad. I didn't really hear exactly what it was they said, but Mrs. Currie went white as a sheet and said: "Be quiet," to Bud.

Then we were there and the truck stopped. We went inside.

And now—this is where it begins.

After supper, the evening I arrived at the Curries' farm, my brother Bud and his friend Teddy Hartley and I all sat on the front porch. In a hammock.

This is the conversation we had.

BUD: (to me) Are you all right? Did you have a good time at Arthur Robertson's place? Did you swim?

ME: (to Bud) Yes.

TEDDY HARTLEY: I've got a feeling I don't like Arthur Robertson. Do I know him?

BUD: Kid at school. Neil's age. (He said that as if it were dirty to be my age.)

TEDDY HARTLEY: Thin kid? Very small?

BUD: Thin and small—brainy type. Hey, Neil, have you seen Ted spit?

ME: Yes—I have.

TEDDY HARTLEY: When did you see me spit? (Indignant as hell) I never spat for you.

ME: Yes, you did. About three months ago. We were still in school. Bud—he did too, and you walked it out, too, didn't you?

BUD: I don't know.

TEDDY HARTLEY: I never spat for you yet! Never!

ME: Two yards and a half.

TEDDY HARTLEY: Can't have been me. I spit four.

ME: Four YARDS!!

TEDDY HARTLEY: Certainly.

BUD: Go ahead and show him. Over the rail.

TEDDY HARTLEY: (Standing up) Okay. Look, Neil…Now watch…Come on, WATCH!!

ME: All right—I'm watching. (Teddy Hartley spat. It was three yards-and-a-half by Bud's feet. I saw Bud mark it myself.)

BUD: Three yards and a half a foot.

TEDDY HARTLEY: Four yards. (Maybe his feet were smaller or something.)

BUD: Three-and-foot. Three and one foot. No, no. A *half*-a-one. Of a foot.

TEDDY HARTLEY: Four.

BUD: Three!

TEDDY HARTLEY: Four! Four! Four!

BUD: Three! One-two-three-and-a-half-a-foot!

TEDDY HARTLEY: My dad showed me. It's four! He showed me, and he knows. My dad knows. He's a mathematical teacher—yes, yes, yes, he showed me how to count a yard. I saw him do it. And he knows, my dad!!

BUD: You dad's a crazy man. It's three yards and a half a foot.

TEDDY HARTLEY: (All red in the face and screaming) You called my dad a nut! You called my dad a crazy-man-nut-meg! Take it back, you. Bud Cable, you take that back.

BUD: You dad is a matha-nut-ical nutmeg tree.

TEDDY HARTLEY: Then your dad's a…your dad's a…your dad's an Insane!

BUD: Our dad's joined the army.

•　•　•

That was how I found out.

They went on talking like that for a long time. I got up and left. I started talking to myself, which is a habit I have.

"Joined the army? Joined the army? Joined the ARMY! Our dad?"

Our dad was a salesman. I used to go to his office and watch him selling things over the phone sometimes. I always used to look for what it was, but I guess they didn't keep it around the office. Maybe they hid it somewhere. Maybe it was too expensive to just leave lying around. But whatever it was, I knew it was important, and so that was one thing that bothered me when Bud said about the army—because I knew that in the army they wouldn't let my dad sit and sell things over any old phone—because in the army you always went in a trench and got hurt or killed. I knew that because my dad had told me himself when my uncle died. My uncle was his brother in the first war, who got hit in his stomach and he died from it a long time afterwards. Long enough, anyway, for me to have known him. He was always in a big white bed, and he gave us candies from a glass jar. That was all I knew—except that it was because of being in the army that he died. His name was Uncle Frank.

So those were the first two things I thought of: my dad not being able to sell anything any more—and then Uncle Frank.

But then it really got bad, because I suddenly remembered that my dad had promised to teach me how to skate that year. He was going to make a rink too, in the back yard. But if he had to go off to some old trench in France, then he'd be too far away. Soldiers always went in trenches—and trenches were always in France. I remember that.

Well, I don't know. Maybe I just couldn't forgive him. He hadn't even told me. He didn't even write it in his letter that he'd sent me at Arthur Robertson's. But he'd told Bud—he'd told Bud, but I was the one he'd promised to show how to skate. And I'd had it all planned how I'd really surprise my dad and turn out to be a skating champion and everything, and now he wouldn't even be there to see.

All because he had to go and sit in some trench.

*   *   *

I don't know how I got there, but I ended up in the barn. I was in the hayloft and I didn't even hear them, I guess. They were looking all over the place for me, because it started to get dark.

I don't know whether you're afraid of the dark, but I'll tell you right now, I am. At least, I am if I have to move around in it. If I can just sit still, then I'm all right. At least, if you sit still you know where you are—but if you move around, then you don't know where you are. And that's awful. You never know what you're going to step on next and I always thought it would be a duck. I don't like ducks—especially in the dark or if you stepped on them.

Anyway, I was in that hayloft in the barn and I heard them calling out—"Neil, Neil"—and "Where are you?" But I made up my mind right then I wasn't going to answer. For one thing, if I did, then I'd have to go down to them in the dark—and maybe I'd step on something. And for another, I didn't really want to see anyone anyway.

It was then that I got this idea about my father. I thought that maybe if I stayed hidden for long enough, then he wouldn't join the army. Don't ask me why—right now I couldn't tell you that—but in those days it made sense. If I hid then he wouldn't go away. Maybe it would be because he'd stay looking for me or something.

The trouble was that my dad wasn't even there that night, and that meant that I either had to wait in the hayloft till he came the next day— or else that I had to go down now, and then hide again tomorrow. I decided to stay where I was because there were some ducks at the bottom of the ladder. I couldn't see them but I could tell they were there.

I stayed there all night. I slept most of the time. Every once in a while they'd wake me up by calling out "Neil! Neil!"—but I never answered.

I never knew a night that was so long, except maybe once when I was in the hospital. When I slept I seemed to sleep for a long time, but it never came to morning. They kept waking me up but it was never time.

Then it was.

I saw that morning through a hole in the roof of the hayloft. The sunlight came in through cracks between the boards and it was all dusty; the sunlight, I mean.

They were up pretty early that morning, even for farmers. There seemed to be a lot more people than I remembered—and there were two or three cars and a truck I'd never seen before, too. And I saw Mrs. Currie holding on to Bud with one hand and Teddy Hartley with the other. I remembered thinking, "If I was down there, how could she hold on to me if she's only got two hands and Bud and Teddy Hartley to look after?" And I thought that right then she must be pretty glad I wasn't around.

I wondered what they were all doing. Mr. Currie was standing in the middle of a lot of men and he kept pointing out the scenery around the farm. I imagined what he was saying. There was a big woods behind the house and a cherry and plum-tree orchard that would be good to point out to his friends. I could tell they were his friends from the way they were listening. What I couldn't figure out was why they were up so early—and why they had Bud and Teddy Hartley up, too.

Then there was a police car. I suppose it came from Orillia or somewhere. That was the biggest town near where the farm was. Orillia.

When the policemen got out of their car, they went up to Mr. Currie. There were four of them. They all talked for quite a long time and then everyone started going out in all directions. It looked to me as though Bud and Teddy Hartley wanted to go, too, but Mrs. Currie made them go in the house. She practically had to drag Bud. It looked as if he was crying and I wondered why he should do that.

Then one of the policemen came into the barn. He was all alone. I stayed very quiet, because I wasn't going to let anything keep me from going through with my plan about my dad. Not even a policeman.

He urinated against the wall inside the door. It was sort of funny, because he kept turning around to make sure no one saw him, and he didn't know I was there. Then he did up his pants and stood in the middle of the floor under the haylofts.

"Hey! Neil!"

That was the policeman.

He said it so suddenly that it scared me. I nearly fell off from where I was, it scared me so much. And I guess maybe he saw me, because he started right up the ladder at me.

"How did you know my name?"

I said that in a whisper.

"They told me."

"Oh."

"Have you been here all night?"

"Yes."

"Don't you realize that everyone has been looking for you all over the place? Nobody's even been to sleep."

That sort of frightened me—but it was all right, because he smiled when he said it.

Then he stuck his head out of this window that was there to let the air in (so that the barn wouldn't catch on fire)—and he yelled down, "He's all right—I've found him! He's up here."

And I said: "What did you go and do that for? Now you've ruined everything."

He smiled again and said, "I had to stop them all going off to look for you. Now,"—as he sat down beside me—"do you want to tell me what it is you're doing up here?"

"No."

I think that sort of set him back a couple of years, because he didn't say anything for a minute—except "Oh."

Then I thought maybe I had to have something to tell the others anyway, so I might as well make it up for him right now.

"I fell asleep," I said.

"When—last night?"

"Yes."

I looked at him. I wondered if I could trust a guy who did that against walls, when all you had to do was go in the house.

"Why did you come up here in the first place?" he said.

I decided I could trust him because I remembered once when I did the same thing. Against the wall.

So I told him.

"I want to hide on my dad," I said.

"Why do you want to do that? And besides, Mrs. Currie said your parents weren't even here."

"Yes, but he's coming today."

"But why hide on him? Don't you like him, or something?"

"Sure I do," I said.

I thought about it.

"But he's…he's…Do you know if it's true, my dad's joined the army?"

"I dunno. Maybe. There's a war on, you know."

"Well, that's why I hid."

But he laughed.

"Is that why you hid? Because of the war?"

"Because of my dad."

"You don't need to hide because of the war—the Germans aren't coming over here, you know."

"But it's not that. It's my dad." I could have told you he wouldn't understand.

I was trying to think of what to say next when Mrs. Currie came into the barn. She stood down below.

"Is he up there, officer? Is he all right?"

"Yes, ma'am, I've got him. He's fine."

"Neil dear, what happened? Why don't you come down and tell us what happened to you?"

Then I decided that I'd really go all out. I had to, because I could tell they weren't going to—it was just obvious that these people weren't going to understand me and take my story about my dad and the army and everything.

"Somebody chased me."

The policeman looked sort of shocked and I could hear Mrs. Currie take in her breath.

"Somebody chased you, eh?"

"Yes."

"Who?"

I had to think fast.

"Some man. But he's gone now."

I thought I'd better say he was gone, so that they wouldn't start worrying.

"Officer, why don't you bring him down here? Then we can talk."

"All right, ma'am. Come on, Neil, we'll go down and have some breakfast."

They didn't seem to believe me about that man I made up.

We went over to the ladder.

I looked down. A lot of hay stuck out so that I couldn't see the floor.

"Are there any ducks down there?"

"No, dear, you can come down—it's all right."

She was lying, though. There was a great big duck right next to her. I think it's awfully silly to tell a lie like that. I mean, if the duck is standing right there it doesn't even make sense, does it?

But I went down anyway and she made the duck go away.

When we went out, the policeman held my hand. His hand had some sweat on it but it was a nice hand, with hair on the back. I liked that. My dad didn't have that on his hand.

Then we ate breakfast with all those people who'd come to look for me. At least, *they* ate. I just sat.

After breakfast, Mr. and Mrs. Currie took me upstairs to the sitting-room. It was upstairs because the kitchen was in the cellar.

All I remember about that was a vase that had a potted plant in it. This vase was made of putty and into the putty Mrs. Currie had stuck all kinds of stones and pennies and old bits of glass and things. You could look at this for hours and never see the same kind of stone or glass twice. I don't remember the plant.

All I remember about what they said was that they told me I should never do it again. That routine.

Then they told me my mother and my dad would be up that day around lunch time.

What they were really sore about was losing their sleep, and then all those people coming. I was sorry about that—but you can't very well go down and make an announcement about it, so I didn't.

•   •   •

At twelve o'clock I went and sat in Mr. Currie's truck. It was in the barn. I took out those two boxes I'd put in the glove compartment and looked at them. I tried to figure out what my dad would do with an old box like that in the army. And he'd probably never play another game of golf as long as he lived. Not in the army, anyway. Maybe he'd use the box for his bullets or something.

Then I counted the red stones I was going to give my mother. I kept seeing them around her neck and how pretty they'd be. She had a dress they'd be just perfect with. Blue. The only thing I was worried about was how to get a hole in them so you could put them on a string. There wasn't much sense in having beads without a string—not if you were going to wear them, anyway—or your mother was.

And it was then that they came.

I heard their car drive up outside and I went and looked from behind the barn door. My father wasn't wearing a uniform yet like I'd thought he would be. I began to think maybe he really didn't want me to know about it. I mean, he hadn't written or anything, and now he was just wearing an old blazer and some grey pants. It made me remember.

I went back and sat down in the truck again. I didn't know what to do. I just sat there with those stones in my hand.

Then I heard someone shout, "Neil!"

I went and looked. Mr. and Mrs. Currie were standing with my parents by the car—and I saw Bud come running out of the house, and then Teddy Hartley. Teddy Hartley sort of hung back, though. He was the kind of person who's only polite if there are grownups around him.

He sure knew how to pull the wool over their eyes, because he'd even combed his hair. Wild-root-cream-oil-Charlie.

Then I noticed that they were talking very seriously and my mother put her hand above her eyes and looked around. I guess she was looking for me. Then my dad started toward the barn.

I went and hid behind the truck. I wasn't quite sure yet what I was going to do, but I certainly wasn't going to go up and throw my arms around his neck or anything.

"Neil. Are you in there, son?"

My dad spoke that very quietly. Then I heard the door being pushed open, and some chicken had to get out of the way, because I heard it making that awful noise chickens make when you surprise them doing something. They sure can get excited over nothing—chickens.

I took a quick look behind me. There was a door there that led into the part of the barn where the haylofts were and where I'd been all night. I decided to make a dash for it. But I had to ward off my father first—and so I threw that stone.

I suppose I'll have to admit that I meant to hit him. It wouldn't be much sense if I tried to fool you about that. I wanted to hit him because when I stood up behind the truck and saw him then I suddenly got mad. I thought about how he hadn't written me, or anything.

It hit him on the hand.

He turned right around because he wasn't sure what it was or where it came from. And before I ran, I just caught a glimpse of his face. He'd seen me and he sure looked peculiar. I guess that now I'll never forget his face and how he looked at me right then. I think it was that he looked as though he might cry or something. But I knew he wouldn't do that, because he never did.

Then I ran.

From the loft I watched them in the yard. My dad was rubbing his hands together and I guess maybe where I'd hit him it was pretty sore. My mother took off her handkerchief that she had round her neck and put it on his hand. Then I guess he'd told them what I'd done, because this time they all started toward the barn.

I didn't know what to do then. I counted out the stones I had left and there were about fifteen of them. There was the golf ball, too.

I didn't want to throw stones at all of them. I certainly didn't want to hit my mother—and I hoped that they wouldn't send her in first. I thought then how I'd be all right if they sent in Teddy Hartley first. I didn't mind the thought of throwing at him, I'll tell you that much.

But my dad came first.

I had a good view of where he came from. He came in through the part where the truck was parked, because I guess he thought I was still there. And then he came on into the part where I was now—in the hayloft.

He stood by the door.

"Neil."

I wasn't saying anything. I sat very still.

"Neil."

I could only just see his head and shoulders—the rest of him was hidden by the edge of the loft.

"Neil, aren't you even going to explain what you're angry about?"

I thought for a minute and then I didn't answer him after all. I looked at him, though. He looked worried.

"What do you want us to do?"

I sat still.

"Neil?"

Since I didn't answer, he started back out the door—I guess to talk to my mother or someone.

I hit his back with another stone. I had to make sure he knew I was there.

He turned around at me.

"Neil, what's the matter? I want to know what's the matter."

He almost fooled me, but not quite. I thought that perhaps he really didn't know for a minute—but after taking a look at him I decided that he did know, all right. I mean, there he was in that blue blazer and everything—just as if he hadn't joined the army at all.

So I threw again and this time it really hit him in the face.

He didn't do anything—he just stood there. It really scared me. Then my mother came in, but he made her go back.

I thought about my rink, and how I wouldn't have it. I thought about being in the fifth grade that year and how I'd skipped from grade three. And I thought about the Indian who'd sold those boxes that I had down in the truck.

"Neil—I'm going to come up."

You could tell he really would, too, from his voice.

I got the golf ball ready.

To get to me he had to disappear for a minute while he crossed under the loft and then when he climbed the ladder. I decided to change my place while he was out of sight. I began to think that was pretty clever and that maybe I'd be pretty good at that war stuff myself. Field Marshal Cable.

I put myself into a little trench of hay and piled some up in front of me. When my dad came up over the top of the ladder, he wouldn't even see me and then I'd have a good chance to aim at him.

The funny thing was that at that moment I'd forgotten why I was against him. I got so mixed up in all that Field Marshal stuff that I really forgot all about my dad and the army and everything. I was just trying to figure out how I could get him before he saw me—and that was all.

I got further down in the hay and then he was there.

He was out of breath and his face was all sweaty, and where I'd hit him there was blood. And then he put his hand with my mother's han-kie up to his face to wipe it. And he sort of bit it (the handkerchief). It was as if he was confused or something. I remember thinking he looked then just like I'd felt my face go when Bud had said our dad had joined the army. You know how you look around with your eyes from side to side as though maybe you'll find the answer to it somewhere near you? You never do find it, but you always look anyway, just in case.

Anyway, that's how he was just then, and it sort of threw me. I had that feeling again that maybe he didn't know what this was all about. But then, he had to know, didn't he? Because he'd done it.

I had the golf ball ready in my right hand and one of those stones in the other. He walked toward me.

I missed with the golf ball and got him with the stone.

And he fell down. He really fell down. He didn't say anything—he didn't even say "ouch," like I would have—he just fell down.

In the hay.

I didn't go out just yet. I sat and looked at him. And I listened. Nothing.

Do you know, there wasn't a sound in that whole place? It was as if everything had stopped because they knew what had happened.

My dad just lay there and we waited for what would happen next. It was me.

I mean, I made the first noise.

I said: "Dad?"

But nobody answered—not even my mother.

So I said it louder. "*Dad?*"

It was just as if they'd all gone away and left me with him, all alone.

He sure looked strange lying there—so quiet and everything. I didn't know what to do.

"Dad?"

I went over on my hands and knees.

Then suddenly they all came in. I just did what I thought of first. I guess it was because they scared me—coming like that when it was so quiet.

I got all the stones out of my pockets and threw them, one by one, as they came through the door. I stood up to do it. I saw them all running through the door, and I threw every stone, even at my mother.

And then I fell down. I fell down beside my dad and pushed him over on his back because he'd fallen on his stomach. It was like he was asleep.

They came up then and I don't remember much of that. Somebody picked me up, and there was the smell of perfume and my eyes hurt and I got something in my throat and nearly choked to death and I could hear a lot of talking. And somebody was whispering, too. And then I felt myself being carried down and there was the smell of oil and gasoline and some chickens had to be got out of the way again and then there was sunlight.

Then my mother just sat with me, and I guess I cried for a long time. In the cherry and plum-tree orchard—and she seemed to understand because she said that he would tell me all about it and that he hadn't written me because he didn't want to scare me when I was all alone at Arthur Robertson's.

And then Bud came.

My mother said that he should go away for a while. But he said: "I brought something" and she said: "What is it, then?" and now I remember where I got that worm in my handkerchief that I told you about.

It was from Bud.

He said to me that if I wanted to, he'd take me fishing on the lake just before the sun went down. He said that was a good time. And he gave me that worm because he'd found it.

So my mother took it and put it in my hankie and Bud looked at me for a minute and then went away.

The worst part was when I saw my dad again.

My mother took me to the place where he was sitting in the sun and we just watched each other for a long time.

Then he said: "Neil, your mother wants to take our picture because I'm going away tomorrow to Ottawa for a couple of weeks, and she thought I'd like a picture to take with me."

He lit a cigarette and then he said: "I would, too, you know, like that picture."

And I sort of said: "All right."

So they called to Bud, and my mother went to get her camera.

But before Bud came and before my mother got back, we were alone for about ten hours. It was awful.

I couldn't think of anything and I guess he couldn't, either. I had a good look at him, though.

He looked just like he does right there in that picture. You can see where the stone hit him on his right cheek—and the one that knocked him out is the one over the eye.

Right then the thing never got settled. Not in words, anyway. I was still thinking about that rink and everything—and my dad hadn't said anything about the army yet.

I wish I hadn't done it. Thrown those stones and everything. It wasn't his fault he had to go.

For another thing, I was sorry about the stones because I knew I wouldn't find any more like them—but I did throw them, and that's that.

They both got those little boxes, though—I made sure of that. And in one there was a string of red beads from Orillia and in the other there was a photograph.

There still is.

Notes

Muskoka a cottage and resort region in Ontario, approximately 200 km north of Toronto

Indian term originally used for First Nations peoples by European colonialists who thought they had landed in India when they arrived in North America. Today, a small number of First Nations do refer to themselves as Indians, but the most accurate term for Aboriginal people generally is First Nations, Native, or indigenous people.

Wild-root-cream-oil-Charlie a greasy cream that many young men used at the time to slick down unruly hair

Field Marshal traditionally, an officer of a very high rank in the British army

Activities

1. Reread the story, focusing specifically on the way in which Findley has captured the thoughts and feelings of a twelve-year-old boy who is looking back on events that happened when he was ten years old. Focus particularly on the explanations and interpretations that the narrator at the age of twelve offers for things he said and did at age ten. In what ways does the older version of the narrator understand more fully the significance of the events described in the story?

2. Find examples of vocabulary, expressions, and syntax in the story that are typical of a young person. What are some features of language that are used unconventionally to imitate the direct speech of a young person whose use of language is still developing?

3. At one point in his story, the narrator switches from normal narrative conventions to a dramatic version of a conversation held by the three boys. This part of the selection is set up more as a play than as a story. Explain how effectively this scene works as a piece of drama. Pick another episode in the story that would work well as a dramatic scene and rewrite it using the example provided by Findley as a model. Remember to make the dialogue specific to each character's personality. Prepare an oral or taped reading of your scene.

Another Viewpoint: Society

With a group of approximately six students, plan a symposium on the subject of war. Have each student select and read or view a work that focuses on war, such as the novel *All Quiet on the Western Front* (1929) by German author Erich Maria Remarque, paintings by Canadian designated "war artists" Frederick Varley or Molly Lamb Bobak, the non-fiction book *The Guns of August* (1962) by American author Barbara Tuchman, poetry by the British writer Wilfred Owen, or the American film *The Thin Red Line* (Fox Pictures, 2000). During your symposium, have each student articulate the impressions of and ideas about war evident in each text. Then explore some of the following questions: What characteristics are common to all wars, regardless of the era or location? How has war changed over the centuries? Is war today more dangerous than wars of previous eras? How does war affect the daily life of civil society? Can war ever be eradicated?

Peace and War

Moacyr Scliar

Translated by Tricia Feeney

Moacyr Scliar, born in 1937, is one of Brazil's most distinguished writers, and the most recognized voice of Brazilian-Jewish literature. He graduated from medical school and has written several short story collections, beginning with *The Carnival of the Animals,* in 1968. He writes in Portuguese, the official language of Brazil. Many of his stories have been translated into English and other languages. Scliar has been the recipient of many prizes, including the Guimaraes Rosa Prize. Scliar's recent novels focus on some of Brazil's famous historical figures. His work has been described as "magical and powerful." To what extent do you expect stories to be "magical" in the sense of taking you beyond the world and ideas that are familiar to you? How would you describe the relationship between fiction and reality in general?

I was late for the war; I had to take a taxi. A setback: with the recent fare increase, it was an unforeseen and unwelcome expense, a blow to my budget. Nevertheless, I arrived just in time to clock on, thereby avoiding greater problems. There was a long queue next to the clocking-on machine: I wasn't the only laggard. There was Walter, my trench colleague, grumbling: he'd had to take a taxi too. We were neighbours and we had entered the war almost at the same time. On the second Thursday of every month we caught the bus from the corner of the street, to take part in the hostilities.

"I'm fed up with this business," said Walter.

"So am I," I replied.

Sighing, we punched our cards and headed for the administration shed where the cloakroom had temporarily (more than fifteen years ago) been installed.

"Late today?" asked the youth in charge of the cloakroom.

We didn't bother to reply. We took the keys to our lockers. We quickly changed our clothes, putting on our old campaign uniforms, collected our rifles and ammunition (twenty cartridges) and made our way to the front line.

The setting for the conflict was open country, on the outskirts of the city. The battlefield was fenced off with barbed wire posted with signboards: WAR, KEEP OUT. An unnecessary warning: few people came there to that place of cottages and summer retreats.

We, the soldiers, occupied a trench almost two kilometres long. An enemy, whom we never saw, was about one kilometre away, also entrenched. The ground between the two trenches was strewn with debris: wrecked armoured cars and tanks mingled with the bones of horses, a reminder of a time when the struggle had been fierce. Now the conflict had entered a stable phase—a holding operation, in the words of our commander. Battles no longer occurred. The only piece of advice they gave us was not to get out of the trench. A problem for me: my younger son wanted an empty shell cartridge, which I had not been able to obtain. The boy kept asking for it; I could do nothing.

We went down into the trench, Walter and I. The place was not altogether uncomfortable. We had tables, chairs, a small stove, cooking utensils, not to mention a record-player and a portable TV. I suggested a game of cards.

"Later," he said. He was examining his rifle with a furrowed brow and an air of annoyance.

"This lousy thing doesn't work any more," he announced.

"Well," I said, "it's over fifteen years old, it's already given all it had to give." And I offered him my weapon. At that moment we heard a crack and the whine of a bullet over our heads.

"That was close," I said.

"Those idiots," grumbled Walter. "One of these days they'll end up hurting someone." He took my weapon, stood up and fired two shots into the air.

"Let that be a warning to you," he shouted, and sat down again. An orderly appeared, with a cordless telephone: "Your wife, Mr. Walter."

"The devil take her!" he exclaimed. "Even here she won't leave me in peace." He picked up the phone.

"Hello! Yes, it's me. I'm fine. Of course I'm fine. No, nothing's happened to me, I've already told you I'm fine. I know you get nervous, but there's no need. Everything's all right. I'm well wrapped up, it's not raining. Did you hear? Everything's fine. No need to apologize. I understand. Bye bye."

"What a pain that woman is," he said, handing the telephone back to the orderly. I said nothing. I too had a problem with my wife, but a different one: she didn't believe that we were at war. She suspected I spent the day in a motel. I would have liked to explain to her what sort of war this was, but to tell the truth I didn't know. No one did. It was a very confusing thing; so much so that a commission had been set up to study the situation. The chairman of the commission came to visit us from time to time, and complained about the car he'd been given for his tours of inspection: an old banger, according to him. For reasons of economy they refused to change it.

All was quiet on the front that morning; one of us fired a shot, those on the other side replied, and that was it. At midday they served lunch. Green salad, roast meat and Greek rice, followed by a tasteless pudding.

"This is getting worse and worse," complained Walter. The orderly asked him if he thought he was in a restaurant, or what. Walter didn't reply.

We lay down for our afternoon nap and slept peacefully. When we awoke, night was falling.

"I think I'll be off now," I said to Walter. He couldn't come with me: he was on duty that night. I went to the cloakroom, changed my clothes.

"How was the war?" the cheeky youth asked.

"Fine," I replied, "just fine." I called into admin to collect my cheque from a sour-faced official. I signed the three copies of the receipt. I got to the bus stop in plenty of time.

At home, my wife was waiting for me in her leotard. I'm ready, she said, drily. I went to the bedroom and put on my kit. We went into the study, climbed on to our ergometric bicycles.

"Where were we, then?" I asked.

"You never seem to know," she replied. She picked up the map, studied it for a moment and said: "Bisceglie, on the Adriatic coast."

We began to pedal furiously. Two hours later, when we stopped, we were near Molfetta, still on the Adriatic. We're hoping to do Italy in a year. After that, we'll see. I don't like to make long-term plans; because of the war, naturally, but even more because keeping the future unknown is a source of permanent excitement.

Notes

clock on to sign in to work

Bisceglie, Molfetta Italian towns on the Adriatic Sea

Activities

1. Write a short response to the story, focusing on your first reactions. If you were describing this story to a friend, what key points would you include? What connections can you make between this story and other works you have viewed or read?

2. In a group, discuss this story's meaning and theme. To what extent could this story be described as a parable? If you consider it to be a parable, what does the story represent? Be prepared to defend your interpretation by providing convincing evidence and sound reasoning.

3. Scliar provides a detailed description of the setting in which the conflict is taking place. Reread the story, recording specific descriptive details that contribute to vivid visual images. Use this information to create a visual representation of the setting using a medium of your choice. Compare your representation with those of other students. How did this activity enhance or change your interpretation of the story?

The Spirit of Haida Gwaii

Bill Reid

About the Visual   One of Canada's most renowned artists, Bill Reid was born in Victoria, British Columbia, in 1920 into the Haida First Nation. During his life, he received an impressive list of honours, including the Lifetime National Aboriginal Achievement Award. He died in 1998. *The Spirit of Haida Gwaii* is located in the Canadian Embassy in Washington, D.C. Reid said that his sculpture made no political or artistic statement: he only wanted to thank the mythical Haida figures, depicted in the canoe, who had given his life meaning. How might a political statement be different from an artistic one? In what ways might mythical figures contribute to a person's meaning of life?

Activities

1. As you view the photograph of *The Spirit of Haida Gwaii*, list every item you see, beginning with whatever first catches your eye. Without using any evaluative language, make your list of items as descriptive and detailed as possible, including the shapes, lines, and forms, and the position and juxtaposition of the sculpture's parts. Share your list with others in the class.

2. In *The Spirit of Haida Gwaii*, Reid has packed many figures into a confined space. This compression of energies is an underlying principle of Haida art. What mood or feeling does this "containment" produce? How might the impact of the piece change if the canoe were larger or if there were fewer passengers?

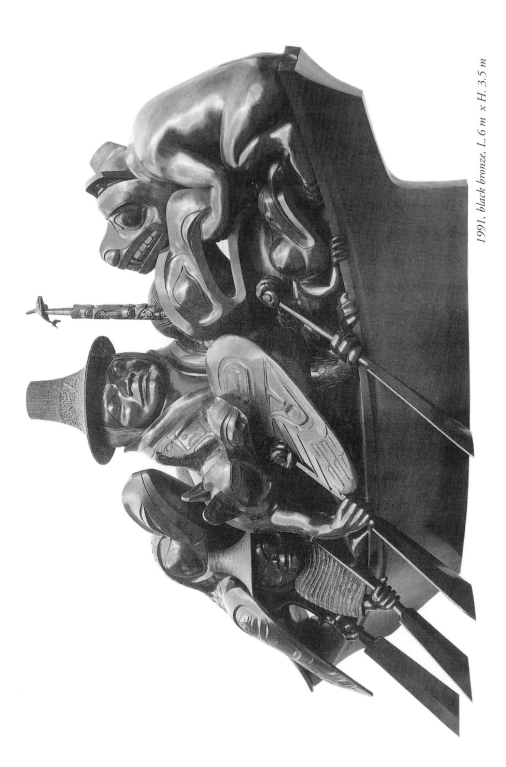

1991, black bronze, L. 6 m x H. 3.5 m

Mazes

Ursula K. Le Guin

Ursula K. Le Guin was born in Berkeley, California, in 1929. Her father was a renowned anthropologist and her mother a writer. She attended Harvard University and Columbia University. Her first published work appeared in 1962. Le Guin is celebrated primarily for her writing in the fields of science fiction and fantasy. Among her awards are five HUGOS, five Nebulas, and the National Book Award. Le Guin, who is also a poet and essayist, has said, "I don't write stories to make a point or push opinions. In fact, usually I write a story and only find out what I was thinking or telling...when I read it afterwards." What types of writing benefit from planning? Is there a type of writing that benefits from a stream-of-consciousness approach and, if so, why?

I have tried hard to use my wits and keep up my courage, but I know now that I will not be able to withstand the torture any longer. My perceptions of time are confused, but I think it has been several days since I realized I could no longer keep my emotions under aesthetic control, and now the physical breakdown is also nearly complete. I cannot accomplish any of the greater motions. I cannot speak. Breathing, in this heavy foreign air, grows more difficult. When the paralysis reaches my chest I shall die: probably tonight.

The alien's cruelty is refined, yet irrational. If it intended all along to starve me, why not simply withhold food? But instead of that it gave me plenty of food, mountains of food, all the greenbud leaves I could possibly want. Only they were not fresh. They had been picked; they were dead; the element that makes them digestible to us was gone, and one might as well eat gravel. Yet there they were, with all the scent and shape of greenbud, irresistible to my craving appetite. Not at first, of course. I told myself, I am not a child, to eat picked leaves! But the belly gets the better of the mind. After a while it seemed better to be chewing something, anything, that might still the pain and craving in the gut. So I ate, and ate, and starved. It is a relief, now, to be so weak I cannot eat.

The same elaborately perverse cruelty marks all its behaviour. And the worst thing of all is just the one I welcomed with such relief and delight at first: the maze. I was badly disoriented at first, after the trapping, being handled by a giant, being dropped into a prison; and this place around the prison is disorienting, spatially disquieting, the strange, smooth, curved wall-ceiling is of an alien substance and its lines are meaningless to me. So when I was taken up and put down, amidst all this strangeness, in a maze, a recognizable, even familiar maze, it was a moment of strength and hope after great distress. It seemed pretty clear that I had been put in the maze as a kind of test or investigation, that a fast approach toward communication was being attempted. I tried to co-operate in every way. But it was not possible to believe for very long that the creature's purpose was to achieve communication.

It is intelligent, highly intelligent, that is clear from a thousand evidences. We are both intelligent creatures, we are both maze-builders: surely it would be quite easy to learn to talk together! If that were what the alien wanted. But it is not. I do not know what kind of mazes it builds for itself. The ones it made for me were instruments of torture.

The mazes were, as I said, of basically familiar types, though the walls were of that foreign material much colder and smoother than packed clay. The alien left a pile of picked leaves in one extremity of each maze, I do not know why; it may be a ritual or superstition. The first maze it put me in was babyishly short and simple. Nothing expressive or even interesting could be worked out from it. The second, however, was a kind of simple version of the Ungated Affirmation, quite adequate for the reassuring outreaching statement I wanted to make. And the last, the long maze, with seven corridors and nineteen connections, lent itself surprisingly well to the Maluvian mode, and indeed to almost all the New Expressionist techniques. Adaptations had to be made to the alien spatial understanding, but a certain quality of creativity arose precisely from the adaptations. I worked hard at the problem of that maze, planning all night long, re-imagining the lines and spaces, the feints and pauses, the erratic, unfamiliar, and yet beautiful course of the True Run. Next day when I was placed in the long maze and the alien began to observe, I performed the Eighth Maluvian in its entirety.

It was not a polished performance. I was nervous, and the spatio-temporal parameters were only approximate. But the Eighth Maluvian survives the crudest performance in the poorest maze. The evolutions in the ninth encatenation, where the "cloud" theme recurs so strangely transposed into the ancient spiralling motif, are indestructibly beautiful. I have seen them performed by a very old person, so old and stiff-jointed that he could only suggest the movements, hint at them, a shadow-gesture, a dim reflection of the themes: and all who watched were inexpressibly moved. There is no nobler statement of our being. Performing, I myself was carried away by the power of the motions and forgot that I was a prisoner, forgot the alien eyes watching me; I transcended the errors of the maze and my own weakness, and danced the Eighth Maluvian as I have never danced it before.

When it was done, the alien picked me up and set me down in the first maze—the short one, the maze for little children who have not yet learned how to talk.

Was the humiliation deliberate? Now that it is all past, I see that there is no way to know. But it remains very hard to ascribe its behaviour to ignorance.

After all, it is not blind. It has eyes, recognizable eyes. They are enough like our eyes that it must see somewhat as we do. It has a mouth, four legs, can move bipedally, has grasping hands, etc.; for all its gigantism and strange looks, it seems less fundamentally different from us, physically, than a fish. And yet, fish school and dance and, in their own stupid way, communicate! The alien has never once attempted to talk with me. It has been with me, watched me, touched me, handled me, for days: but all its motions have been purposeful, not communicative. It is evidently a solitary creature, totally self-absorbed.

This would go far to explain its cruelty.

I noticed early that from time to time it would move its curious horizontal mouth in a series of fairly delicate, repetitive gestures, a little like someone eating. At first I thought it was jeering at me; then I wondered if it was trying to urge me to eat the indigestible fodder; then I wondered if it could be communicating *labially*. It seemed a limited and unhandy language for one so well provided with hands, feet, limbs, flexible spine, and all; but that would be like the creature's perversity, I thought. I studied its lip-motions and tried hard to imitate them. It did not respond. It stared at me briefly and then went away.

In fact, the only indubitable *response* I ever got from it was on a pitifully low level of interpersonal aesthetics. It was tormenting me with knob-pushing, as it did once a day. I had endured this grotesque routine pretty patiently for the first several days. If I pushed one knob I got a nasty sensation in my feet, if I pushed a second I got a nasty pellet of dried-up food, if I pushed a third I got nothing whatever. Obviously, to demonstrate my intelligence I was to push the third knob. But it appeared that my intelligence irritated my captor, because it removed the neutral knob after the second day. I could not imagine what it was trying to establish or accomplish, except the fact that I was its prisoner and a great deal smaller than it. When I tried to leave the knobs, it forced me physically to return. I must sit there pushing knobs for it, receiving punishment from one and mockery from the other. The deliberate outrageousness of the situation, the insufferable heaviness and thickness of this air, the feeling of being forever watched yet never understood, all combined to drive me into a condition for which we have no description at all. The nearest thing I can suggest is the last interlude of the Ten Gate Dream, when all the feintways are closed and the dance narrows in and in until it bursts terribly into the vertical. I cannot say what I felt, but it was a little like that. If I got my feet stung once more, or got pelted once more with a lump of rotten food, I would go vertical forever... I took the knobs off the wall (they came off with a sharp tug, like flowerbuds), laid them in the middle of the floor, and defecated on them.

The alien took me up at once and returned to my prison. It had got the message, and had acted on it. But how unbelievably primitive the message had had to be! And the next day, it put me back in the knob room, and there were the knobs as good as new, and I was to choose alternate punishments for its amusement… Until then I had told myself that the creature was alien, therefore incomprehensible and uncomprehending, perhaps not intelligent in the same manner as we, and so on. But since then I have known that, though all that may remain true, it is also unmistakably and grossly cruel.

When it put me into the baby maze yesterday, I could not move. The power of speech was all but gone (I am dancing this, of course, in my mind; "the best maze is the mind," the old proverb goes) and I simply crouched there, silent. After a while it took me out again, gently enough. There is the ultimate perversity of its behaviour: it has never once touched me cruelly.

It set me down in the prison, locked the gate, and filled up the trough with inedible food. Then it stood two-legged, looking at me for a while.

Its face is very mobile, but if it speaks with its face I cannot understand it, that is too foreign a language. And its body is always covered with bulky, binding mats, like an old widower who has taken the Vow of Silence. But I had become accustomed to its great size, and to the angular character of its limb-positions, which at first had seemed to be saying a steady stream of incoherent and mispronounced phrases, a horrible nonsense-dance like the motions of an imbecile, until I realized that they were strictly purposive movements. Now I saw something a little beyond that, in its position. There were no words, yet there was communication. I saw, as it stood watching me, a clear signification of angry sadness—as clear as the Sembrian Stance. There was the same lax immobility, the bentness, the assertion of defeat. Never a word came clear, and yet it told me that it was filled with resentment, pity, impatience, and frustration. It told me it was sick of torturing me, and wanted me to help it. I am sure I understood it. I tried to answer. I tried to say, "What is it you want of me? Only tell me what it is you want." But I was too weak to speak clearly, and it did not understand. It has never understood.

And now I have to die. No doubt it will come in to watch me die; but it will not understand the dance I dance in dying.

Notes

aesthetic related to beauty and good taste; from the Greek word *aisthetikos*, meaning "of sense perception"

perverse persistent in going against what is expected or considered to be right

feint a false movement intended to deceive the viewer; from the Old French *feindre*, meaning "to feign"

parameter a limit or boundary

motif a recurring element or theme in an artistic or literary work; originally a French word meaning "motive"

labially using the lips

indubitable unquestionable, without a doubt

feintways false passages or parts

Activities

1. In your journal, make a list of issues about human nature and interaction with alien beings that are raised in this story. What is your response to Le Guin's views on these subjects? Share your ideas with the class. After the discussion, make notes on aspects of speaking and listening which you find difficult. Then list strategies for improving your performance.

2. What does the narrator reveal about the captor? Reread the story, noting passages where the captor's behaviour and attitudes are described. How does the author's use of irony affect your response to these descriptions?

3. Why do you think Le Guin chose not to provide a physical description of the alien narrator in the story? Imagine that you have been given the task of creating an illustration for "Mazes." What medium and visual style will you choose? How can you balance the author's style with your need to represent the content? In a group, present and discuss your illustrations. Assess the choices you made in your illustration and consider how its impact might be strengthened.

Was It a Dream?

Guy de Maupassant

Translated by Marjorie Laurie

Guy de Maupassant is considered to be the greatest French writer of short stories. He was born in 1850 in Normandy, studied law in Paris, served in the army during the Franco-Prussian War, and worked as a civil servant. De Maupassant's productivity was remarkable: three hundred stories, six novels, three travel books, and one volume of verse. His writing is characterized by strong, naturalistic language and keen observations of human life. He died at the age of forty-three in Paris, in 1883. In your opinion, is tragic love or fulfilled love a better subject for a story? What examples of each type can you provide to explain your choice?

I had loved her madly!

Yesterday I returned to Paris, and when I saw my room again—our room, our bed, our furniture, everything that remains of the life of a human being after death—I was seized by such a violent attack of fresh grief that I felt like opening the window and throwing myself out into the street. I could not remain between these walls which had sheltered her, which retained a thousand atoms of her, of her skin and of her breath. I took up my hat to make my escape, and just as I reached the door I passed the large mirror in the hall, which she had put there so that she might look at herself every day from head to foot as she went out, from her little boots to her bonnet.

I stopped short in front of that looking glass in which she had so often been reflected—so often, so often, that it must have retained her reflection. I was standing there trembling, with my eyes fixed on the glass—on that flat, profound, empty glass—which had contained her entirely and had possessed her as much as I. I felt as if I loved that glass. I touched it; it was cold. Sorrowful mirror, burning mirror, horrible mirror, to make men suffer such torments! Happy is the man whose heart forgets everything that it has contained.

I went out without knowing it toward the cemetery. I found her simple grave, a white marble cross, with these few words:

<blockquote>She loved, was loved, and died.</blockquote>

She is there below. I sobbed with my forehead on the ground, and I stopped there for a long time. Then I saw it was getting dark, and a strange, mad wish, the wish of a despairing lover, seized me. I wished to pass the night in weeping on her grave. But I should be seen and driven out. How was I to manage? I was cunning and got up and began to roam that city of the dead. I walked and walked. How small this city is in comparison with the city in which we live. And yet how much more numerous the dead are than the living. We need high houses, wide streets, and much room. And for all the generations of the dead, there is scarcely anything. The earth takes them back. Adieu!

At the end of the cemetery, I was in its oldest part, where the crosses themselves are decayed. It is full of untended roses, of strong and dark cypress trees—a sad and beautiful garden.

I was perfectly alone. So I crouched under a green tree and hid myself amid the thick and sombre branches.

When it was quite dark, I left my refuge and began to walk softly. I wandered about for a long time, but could not find her tomb again. I went on with extended arms, knocking against the tombs with my hands, my feet, my knees, my chest, even with my head, without being able to find her. I groped about like a blind man; I felt the stones, the crosses, the iron railings, and the wreaths of faded flowers. I read the names with my fingers. I could not find her again!

There was no moon. What a night! I was horribly frightened in those narrow paths between two rows of graves. I sat down on one of them, for I could not walk any longer; my knees were so weak. I could hear my heart beat! And I heard something else as well. What? A confused, nameless noise. Was the noise in my head, in the impenetrable night, or beneath the mysterious earth? I looked all around me: I was paralyzed with terror, cold with fright, ready to shout out, ready to die.

Suddenly it seemed to me that the slab of marble on which I was sitting was moving. As if it were being raised. With a bound I sprang onto the neighbouring tomb, and I distinctly saw the stone which I had just quitted rise upright. Then the dead person appeared, pushing the stone back with its bent back. I saw it quite clearly, although the night was so dark. On the cross I could read:

> Here lies Jacques Olivant,
> who died at the age of fifty-one.
> He loved his family,
> was kind and honourable,
> and died in the grace of the Lord.

The dead man also read what was inscribed on the tombstone; then he picked up a stone off the path, a little, pointed stone, and began to scrape the letters carefully. He slowly effaced them, and with the hollows of his eyes he looked at the place where they had been engraved. Then, with the tip of the bone that had been his forefinger, he wrote in luminous letters:

> Here reposes Jacques Olivant,
> who died at the age of fifty-one.
> He hastened his father's death by his unkindness, as
> he wished to inherit his fortune;
> he tortured his wife,
> tormented his children,
> deceived his neighbours,
> robbed everyone he could,
> and died wretched.

When he had finished writing, the dead man stood motionless, looking at his work. On turning around, I saw that all the graves were open, that all the dead had emerged, and that all had effaced the lines inscribed on their gravestones by their relations, substituting the truth instead. And I saw that all had been tormentors of their neighbours—malicious, dishonest, hypocrites, liars, rogues; that they had stolen, deceived, performed every disgraceful, every abominable action, these good fathers, these faithful wives, these devoted sons, these chaste daughters, these honest tradesmen. They were all writing at the same time, on the threshold of their eternal abode, the truth, the terrible and the holy truth, of which everybody was ignorant, or pretended to be ignorant while they were alive.

I thought that *she* also must have written something on her tombstone; and now, running without any fear, I went toward her, sure that I should find her immediately. I recognized her at once without seeing her face, and on the marble cross where shortly before I had read:

She loved, was loved, and died.

I now saw:

Having gone out in the rain one day
in order to deceive her lover,
she caught cold and died.

It appears they found me at daybreak, lying on the grave, unconscious.

Activities

1. With a group, reflect on the different ways of interpreting the title of the story. Which one do you think best fits the story? What answer would you give to this interpretation of the title? Consider what the author's purpose might have been in choosing an ambiguous title. Keep notes during your discussion and share your ideas with the rest of the class.

2. Author Henry James wrote that de Maupassant's axiom seemed to be "that you produce the effect of truth better by painting people from the outside than from the inside." Consider how this statement applies to "Was It a Dream?" Discuss the notion of *truth* as it is depicted in the story.

3. Imagine the scene that might take place in this narrative when a police officer and a cemetery groundskeeper awaken the narrator in the morning. Work in groups of three to write and then act out this conversation for the class. Have your classmates assess your work in terms of how effectively you use dialogue to reveal character.

Another Viewpoint: Literary Modes and Forms

Guy de Maupassant is considered a key figure in the development of the short story as a literary form. Using a variety of primary and secondary sources, write a research essay on the history of the short story as a genre. Be sure to cite specific writers from a variety of cultures as examples.

No Great Mischief

Alistair MacLeod

Alistair MacLeod was born in North Battleford, Saskatchewan, in 1936. As a child, he moved with his family to Nova Scotia, and he has been linked with the landscape and the people of Cape Breton ever since. Known primarily as a writer of short fiction, MacLeod wrote his first novel, *No Great Mischief*, to great acclaim when he was in his sixties. It won the prestigious international IMPAC Award in 2001, as well as the Trillium Prize in 2000. MacLeod's fiction explores individual Maritimers against a timeless backdrop of universal human nature. Does all literature contain "universal messages"? Whether you agree or not, do you think a requirement of good fiction should be that it include a message or meaning that can be applied to all of humanity?

My twin sister and I were the youngest children in our family, and we were three on March 28 when it was decided that we would spend the night with our grandparents.

After he returned from naval service in the war, my father had applied for the position of lightkeeper on the island which seemed almost to float in the channel about a mile and half from the town which faced the sea. He had long been familiar with boats and the sea and, after passing the examination, was informed in a very formal letter that the job was his. He and my mother were overjoyed because it meant they would not have to go away, and the job reeked of security, which was what they wanted after the disruption of the years of war. The older generation was highly enthusiastic as well. "That island will stay there for a damn long time," said Grandpa appreciatively, although he later apparently sniffed, "Any fool can look after a lighthouse. It is not like being responsible for a *whole* hospital."

On the morning of March 28, which was the beginning of a weekend, my parents and their six children and their dog walked ashore across the ice. Their older sons, who were sixteen, fifteen, and fourteen, apparently took turns carrying my sister and me upon their shoulders, stopping every so often to take off their mitts and rub our faces so that our cheeks would not become so cold as to be frozen without our realizing it. Our father, accompanied by our brother Colin, who was eleven, walked ahead of us, testing the ice from time to time with a long pole, although there did not seem much need to do so for he had "bushed" the ice some two months earlier, meaning he had placed spruce trees upright in the snow and ice to serve as a sort of road guide for winter travellers.

During the coldest days of winter, the so-called "dog days," the ice became amazingly solid. It was a combination of drift ice from the region of the eastern Arctic and "made" ice which resulted from the freezing of the local channel. In extremely cold winters if the ice was smooth, it was possible to move freely from the island to the mainland and back again. One could walk, or skate, or fashion an iceboat which would skim and veer with cutting dangerous speed across the stinging surface. People would venture out on the ice with cars and trucks, and on one or two weekends there would be horse races to the delight of all. The sharpshod horses would pull light sleighs or even summer sulkies as they sped around yet another track staked out by temporary spruce. At the conclusion of their races, their owners would hurry to cover them with blankets as the perspiration on their coats began to turn to frost. They seemed almost, for a few brief moments, to be horses who had prematurely aged before the eyes of those who watched them, their coats of black and brown turning to a fragile white. White horses frozen on a field of ice and snow.

My parents welcomed the winter ice because it allowed them to do many practical things that were more difficult to accomplish in the summer. They could truck their supplies over the ice without the difficulty of first hauling everything to the wharf and then trying to load it on the boat which swayed below and then, after sporting it across to the island, having to hoist it up out of the boat to the wharf's cap and then again having to transport it up the cliff to the promontory where the lighthouse stood. They took coal and wood across in the winter, and walked and traded animals, leading them by their halters across the treacherous and temporary bridge.

Also in the winter their social life improved, as unexpected visitors crossed to see them, bringing rum and beer and fiddles and accordions. All of them staying up all night, singing songs and dancing and playing cards and telling stories, while out on the ice the seals moaned and cried and the ice itself thundered and snapped and sometimes groaned, forced by the pressures of the tides and currents, running unabated and unseen beneath the cold white surface. Sometimes the men would go outside to urinate and when they would return the others would ask, "*De chuala?*" "What did you hear?" "Nothing," they would say. "*Cha chuala sion.*" "Nothing, only the sound of the ice."

On March 28 there was a lot for my family to do. My older brothers were going to visit their cousins in the country—those who still lived in the old *Calum Ruadh* houses neighbouring the spot which my grandparents had left when they became people of the town. If they could get a ride they were going to spend the weekend there. Even if they could not get a ride, they were planning to walk, saying that ten miles on the inland sheltered roads would not be as cold as a mile and a half straight across the ice. My parents were planning to cash my father's cheque, which they hoped my grandparents had picked up at the post office, and my brother Colin was looking forward to his new parka, which my mother had shrewdly ordered from the Eaton's sale catalogue when such heavy winter garments were reduced by the coming promise of spring. He had been hoping for it since before Christmas. My sister and I were looking forward to the visit with our grandparents, who always made a great to-do about us and always told us how smart we were to make such a great journey from such a far and distant place. And the dog knew where she was going too, picking her way across the ice carefully and sometimes stopping to gnaw off the balls of snow and ice which formed between the delicate pads of her hardened paws.

Everything went well and the sun shone brightly as we journeyed forth together, walking first upon the ice so we could later walk upon the land.

In the late afternoon, the sun still shone, and there was no wind but it began to get very cold, the kind of deceptive cold that can fool those who confuse the shining of the winter sun with warmth. Relatives visiting my grandparents' house said that my brothers had arrived at their destination and would not be coming back until, perhaps, the next day.

My parents distributed their purchases into haversacks, which were always at my grandparents' house, and which they used for carrying supplies upon their backs. Because my parents' backs would be burdened and because my brothers were not there, it was decided that my sister and I would "spend the night" and that our brothers would take us back to the island when they returned. It was suggested that Colin also might stay, but he was insistent that he go, so that he might test the long-anticipated warmth of the new parka. When they left, the sun was still shining, although it had begun to decline, and they took two storm lanterns which might serve as lights or signs and signals for the last part of the trip. My mother carried one and Colin the other, while my father grasped the ice pole in his hand. When they set out, they first had to walk about a mile along the shore until they reached the appropriate place to "get on" the ice and then they started across, following the route of the spruce trees which my father had set out.

Everyone could see their three dark forms and the smaller one of the dog outlined upon the whiteness over which they travelled. By the time they were halfway across, it was dusk and out there on the ice they lit their lanterns, and that too was seen from the shore. And then they continued on their way. Then the lanterns seemed to waver and almost to dance wildly, and one described an arc in what was now the darkness and then was still. Grandpa watched for almost a minute to be sure of what he was seeing and then he shouted to my grandmother, "There is something wrong out on the ice. There is only one light and it is not moving."

My grandmother came quickly to the window. "Perhaps they stopped," she said. "Perhaps they're resting. Perhaps they had to adjust their packs. Perhaps they had to relieve themselves."

"But there is only one light," said Grandpa, "and it is not moving at all."

"Perhaps that's it," said Grandma hopefully. "The other light blew out and they're trying to get it started."

My sister and I were playing on the kitchen floor with Grandma's cutlery. We were playing "store," taking turns buying the spoons and knives and forks from each other with a supply of pennies from a jar Grandma kept in her lower cupboard for emergencies.

"The light is still not moving," said Grandpa and he began hurriedly to pull on his winter clothes and boots, even as the phone began ringing. "The light is not moving. The light is not moving," the voices said. "They're in trouble out on the ice."

And then the voices spoke in the hurriedness of exchange: "Take a rope." "Take some ice poles." "Take a blanket that we can use as a stretcher." "Take brandy." "We will meet you at the corner. Don't start across without us."

"I have just bought all his spoons and knives," said my sister proudly from the kitchen floor, "and I still have all these pennies left."

"Good for you," said Grandma. "A penny saved is a penny earned."

When they were partway to the shore, their lights picked up the dog's eyes, and she ran to Grandpa when he called to her in Gaelic, and she leaped up to his chest and his outstretched arms and licked his face even as he threw his mitts from his hands so he could bury them deep within the fur upon her back,

"She was coming to get us," he said. "They've gone under."

"Not under," someone said. "Perhaps down but not under."

"I think under," said Grandpa. "She was under, anyway. She's soaked to the spine. She's smart and she's a good swimmer and she's got a heavy, layered coat. If she just went down, she'd be down and up in a second but she's too wet for that. She must have gone down, and then the current carried her under the ice and she had to swim back to the hole to get herself back out."

They went out on the ice in single file, the string of their moving lights seeming almost like a kind of Christmas decoration; each light moving to the rhythm of the man who walked and carried it in his hand.

They followed the tracks and walked towards the light which remained permanent in the ice. As they neared it, they realized it was sitting on the ice, sitting upright by itself and not held by any hand. The tracks continued until they came to the open water, and then there were no more.

Years later, my sister and I were in Grade XI and the teacher was talking to the class about Wordsworth and, as an example, was reading to us from the poem entitled "Lucy Gray." When she came to the latter lines, both my sister and I started simultaneously and looked towards each other, as if in the old, but new to us, we had stumbled upon the familiar experience:

"They followed from the snowy bank
Those footmarks, one by one,
Into the middle of the plank;
And further there were none!"

"And further there were none!" But on March 28 we were tiring of our game of store and putting the cutlery away as our grandmother prepared to ready us for bed while glancing anxiously through the window.

Out on the ice the dog began to whine when they came near the open water, and the first men in the line lay on their stomachs, each holding the feet of the man before him, so that they might form a type of human chain with their weight distributed more evenly than if they remained standing. But it was of no use, for other than the light there was nothing, and the ice seemed solid right up to the edge of the dark and sloshing void.

There was nothing for the men to do but wonder. Beyond the crater, the rows of spruce trees marched on in ordered single file in much the same way that they led up to the spot of their interruption. It was thought that perhaps only one tree had gone down and under. The section of the ice that had gone was not large, but as my grandfather said, "It was more than big enough for us."

The tide was going out when they vanished, leaving nothing but a lantern—perhaps tossed on to the ice by a sinking hand and miraculously landing upright and continuing to glow, or perhaps, set down after its arc, wildly but carefully by a hand which sought to reach another.

The men performed a sort of vigil out on the ice, keeping the hole broken open with their ice poles and waiting for the tide to run its course. And in the early hours of the morning when the tide was in its change, my brother Colin surfaced in one of those half-expected uncertainties known only to those who watch the sea. The white fur hood of his parka broke the surface and the half-frozen men who were crouched like patient Inuit around the hole shouted to one another, and reached for him with their poles. They thought that he had not been a great distance under, or that his clothes had snagged beneath the ice; and they thought that, perhaps, since he was not bearing a backpack, he had not been so heavily burdened and, perhaps, the new material in his parka possessed flotation qualities that had buoyed him to the top. His eyes were open and the drawstrings of his hood were still neatly tied and tucked beside his throat in the familiar manner that my mother always used.

My parents were not found that day, or the next, or in the days or months that followed.

Notes

drift ice a piece of ice carried along by water currents

sulkies a two-wheeled, single-person vehicle pulled by a horse, which is used in trotting races

Calum Ruadh a Gaelic phrase meaning "the red Calum," which is the nickname for a character in the novel *No Great Mischief*, from which this excerpt is taken

Activities

1. What emotional response do you think the author intends his narrative to elicit from his audience? By what means does he invoke this emotional response in his readers? What lasting impression, if any, will you take away from this narrative?

2. MacLeod has said about his writing, "I like to give the impression that I am telling the story rather than writing the story." Reread the excerpt to see to what extent this statement applies to this excerpt from *No Great Mischief*. Locate at least three sentences or passages which have the feel of oral storytelling. Write two or three sentences explaining each of your choices. Share your ideas with your classmates and then discuss any advantages and disadvantages of this style of writing.

3. Imagine that this narrative will be read aloud on the radio and it is your job to select accompanying music. Locate three or more appropriate vocal or instrumental selections to be played as an introduction, interlude, and fade-out to the reading. Prepare a verbal pitch you would present to the producer of the program, explaining how your musical choices would contribute to the listeners' enjoyment and understanding of the narrative.

Another Viewpoint: Culture

Many prominent Canadian writers and literary critics, such as Margaret Atwood in her book *Survival: A Thematic Guide to Canadian Literature* (1972), have noted that a central preoccupation and symbol in Canadian texts has been survival. With the class, discuss different ways in which the concept of survival is manifested: What circumstances are people surviving? Then read Alistair Macleod's entire novel *No Great Mischief* and compare it with other instances in Canadian literature in which individuals survive—or do not survive—their circumstances. Have a group discussion on which characteristics of Canadian culture contribute to a focus on survival.

wrap-up
short fiction

1. Write a formal comparative essay in which you discuss the treatment of the same or a similar theme in two of the stories in this unit. Have a classmate review a complete draft of your essay to help you strengthen its content and improve its organization. Ask your classmate to evaluate such features of the draft as a clear thesis statement, logical connections between key ideas, and the reinforcement of arguments through the use of compelling evidence.

2. Identify two or three stories in this unit that you think have strong poetic qualities. Outline in a chart what those poetic qualities are and how the stories you have selected exemplify them. Present your thoughts to the class. In a panel discussion, compare your choice of stories and ideas with those of two other classmates who have participated in this activity. In your presentation and subsequent discussion, be sure to include and accurately use pertinent academic and theoretical concepts and language.

3. On your own or with a partner, choose a story in this unit that made a strong impression on you. Next, use the Internet to do research on how to form and run a reading group. Write a two- to three-page guide for creating a reading group to explore this story. In it, provide specific questions for a group discussion and include concise background on the author and his or her work as it relates to the questions you have devised. Use a desktop publishing program to write, format, and publish your guide, adding appropriate graphics to enhance your publication.

4. Work with a group to create a radio play script for characters from at least two of the stories in this unit. In discussing and preparing your script, assign roles within your group, such as a director, researchers to scan stories and recommend characters, actors to perform the radio play, and technicians to take charge of background music and sound effects. Audiotape your play and present it to the class. In a post-presentation discussion, elicit feedback from your classmates on the strengths of your performance and areas for improvement.

Contrasting, often opposing, cosmic and moral forces (such as light and dark, virtue and vice) are common in many mythological and belief systems. In Hindu mythology, Durga is one of the manifestations of the goddess Devi. A many-armed warrior seated on a tiger, Durga represents benevolence. Here, Durga battles the monster Mahisha, a colossal water-buffalo, representing the forces of malevolence.

Can you remember watching a movie or reading a story and thinking, "The same thing has happened to me"? Maybe an event in a book or film reminded you of an incident in the life of someone you know or of another story you have come across. Narratives, regardless of their literary forms or specific historical or cultural contexts, spring from themes or patterns that are universal. These themes and patterns—such as self-discovery, love, and the cycles of days and seasons—are known as *archetypes*. Archetypes are truthful, essential prototypes of characters or events that provide a blueprint for the individual experiences that make up real life. Archetypes can be considered a reflection of what has been called the *collective unconscious*, a shared body of knowledge, assumptions, and interpretations that an entire culture holds, sometimes without even being aware of it. An archetypal approach to literature reveals recurring patterns and themes in myths, folklore, literature, and art—even in cultures widely separated by time and space.

Some archetypes express the way in which individuals experience the world—in roles such as the hero, rebel, or star-crossed lover. Other archetypes explore the situations in which we find ourselves and the journeys we undertake—such as initiation, loss of innocence, or death of a loved one. Part of what gives literature its power and primacy is the way it attracts its reader by creating interest on multiple levels. When we immerse ourselves in texts, we experience these archetypal patterns, universal themes, and literary modes and consciously or unconsciously integrate them into our lives.

This In-Depth includes a variety of selections that highlight such archetypal patterns and concepts as duty, passage of seasons, and utopia. Excerpts from Northrop Frye's classic essay "The Archetypes of Literature" describe the archetypes and patterns prevalent in narratives. In an interview, Joseph Campbell talks about heroes in mythology. The short story "Araby" by James Joyce, with its quest motif, follows the structure of a medieval romance. The poem "Ode to the West Wind" by Percy Bysshe Shelley and "Utopian Dreams," a book review by Val Ross, contain many of the ideals about rebirth and new beginnings also associated with the literary mode of romance. As you explore this section, consider ways in which universal themes and patterns create ties and common understanding in communities and cultures that you know. (To find related activities on archetypal patterns and literary modes and forms, see the references in the Another Viewpoint Index on page 714.)

From The Archetypes of Literature

Northrop Frye

Canadian literary critic Northrop Frye was born in Sherbrooke, Quebec, in 1912, and he spent the formative years of his life in Moncton, New Brunswick. In the history of Canadian scholarship, Frye has emerged as perhaps the most prominent figure. From 1939 until his death in 1991, he was based at Victoria College, University of Toronto, where he taught English and served as an administrator. Frye's authoritative study of the poetry of William Blake, *Fearful Symmetry* (1947), is considered a classic critical work. His synopsis of the principles and techniques of literary criticism, *Anatomy of Criticism* (1957), was his first work to win him international prominence. He won the Governor General's Award for Nonfiction in 1986 for *Northrop Frye on Shakespeare*. In the following two excerpts from his essay "The Archetypes of Literature," first published in 1951, Frye lays out some of the broader categories and modes by which texts can be classified. In order to show how texts work, he concentrates on the recurrent structures that might be described as *natural*. In this essay, Frye wrote, "All literary genres are derived from the quest myth." What do you know about the quest myth? Based on your own reading experience, do you agree or disagree with Frye's comment, and why?

[Frye, in this first excerpt from "The Archetypes of Literature," outlines four phases in the cycles of the day, the year, and human life. The quest hero and "subordinate characters" in literature, in his view, are bounded by these phases. The main literary modes—romance, comedy, tragedy, and satire—also reflect these phases.]

1. The dawn, spring, and birth phase. Myths of the birth of the hero, of revival and resurrection, of creation and (because the four phases are a cycle) of the defeat of the powers of darkness, winter, and death. Subordinate characters: the father and the mother. The archetype of romance and of most dithyrambic and rhapsodic poetry.

2. The zenith, summer, and marriage or triumph phase. Myths of apotheosis, of the sacred marriage, and of entering into Paradise. Subordinate characters: the companion and the bride. The archetype of comedy, pastoral, and idyll.

3. The sunset, autumn, and death phase. Myths of fall, of the dying god, of violent death and sacrifice and of the isolation of the hero. Subordinate characters: the traitor and the siren. The archetype of tragedy and elegy.

4. The darkness, winter, and dissolution phase. Myths of the triumph of these powers; myths of floods and the return of chaos, of the defeat of the hero, and Götterdämmerung myths. Subordinate characters: the ogre and the witch. The archetype of satire.

[In this second excerpt, Frye identifies archetypal communities, images, and characters that spring from the comic and tragic "visions" of the world.]

1. In the comic vision the *human* world is a community, or a hero who represents the wish-fulfillment of the reader. The archetype of images of symposium, communion, order, friendship, and love. In the tragic vision the human world is a tyranny or anarchy, or an individual or isolated man, the

leader with his back to his followers, the bullying giant of romance, the deserted or betrayed hero. Marriage or some equivalent consummation belongs to the comic vision; the harlot, witch, and other varieties of Jung's "terrible mother" belongs to the tragic one. All divine, heroic, angelic, or other superhuman communities follow the human pattern.

2. In the comic vision the *animal* world is a community of domesticated animals, usually a flock of sheep, or a lamb, or one of the gentler birds, usually a dove. The archetype of pastoral images. In the tragic vision the animal world is seen in terms of beasts and birds of prey, wolves, vultures, serpents, dragons, and the like.

3. In the comic vision the *vegetable* world is a garden, grove, or park, or a tree of life, or a rose or lotus. The archetype of Arcadian images, such as that of Marvell's green world or of Shakespeare's forest comedies. In the tragic vision it is a sinister forest like the one in *Comus* or at the opening of the *Inferno,* or a heath or wilderness, or a tree of death.

4. In the comic vision the *mineral* world is a city, or one building or temple, or one stone, normally a glowing precious stone—in fact the whole comic series, especially the tree, can be conceived as luminous or fiery. The archetype of geometrical images: the "starlit dome" belongs here. In the tragic vision the mineral world is seen in terms of deserts, rocks, and ruins, or of sinister geometrical images like the cross.

5. In the comic vision the *unformed* world is a river, traditionally fourfold, which influenced the Renaissance image of the temperate body with its four humours. In the tragic vision this world usually becomes the sea, as the narrative myth of dissolution is so often a flood myth. The combination of the sea and beast images gives us the leviathan and similar water-monsters.

Notes

etiological having to do with the study of the cause, origin, or reason for something

dithyrambic an irregular or frenzied poetic expression; from the ancient Greek *dithurambos*, an impassioned hymn and dance held in honour of the god Dionysus

apotheosis glory, exaltation, ultimate achievement

Götterdämmerung myths narratives that deal with the turbulent end to an institution or a ruler's regime

Jung refers to Carl Jung (1875–1961). Originally a student of Sigmund Freud, this Swiss psychiatrist founded analytical psychology; Jung studied the links between myths, archetypes, and psychology, and he pioneered such concepts as "the collective unconscious."

Arcadian related to a pastoral paradise, the home of song-loving shepherds; in Greek mythology, Arcadia is the home of Pan, god of flocks and herds

Shakespeare's forest comedies refers to those romantic comedies by William Shakespeare, such as *A Midsummer Night's Dream* and *As You Like It*, in which characters move from the normal world of conflict and trouble into a "green world" in which these troubles are magically resolved

Marvell a reference to Andrew Marvell (1621–1678), an English metaphysical poet; his poems often contain have idyllic pastoral themes

starlit dome a reference to the following lines in the poem "Byzantium" by W.B. Yeats, in which he contrasts a spiritual, unchanging world with the ever-changing physical human world: "A startlit or moonlit dome disdains / All that man is, / All mere complexities, / The fury and mire of human veins."

four humours refers to what the Ancient Greeks believed were the four chief fluids of the body (blood, phlegm, yellow bile, and black bile) that were thought to determine a person's physical and mental qualities.

Comus a pastoral entertainment written by John Milton about the confrontation between good and evil

Inferno part one of three of *The Divine Comedy* by Italian poet Dante Alighieri (1265–1321), which is an allegorical journey through Hell.

leviathan a mythical, monstrous sea creature

There are common, or archetypal, traits in mythical figures revered by different cultures. This sculpture in the garden of the Versailles Palace in France depicts the figure of Diana from Roman mythology, who was goddess of the hunt and the protector of nature. The goddess Artemis in Ancient Greek mythology is identified with Diana. In Africa, in parts of Nigeria and Benin formerly known as Dahomey, people honoured a deity of the hunt named Age. To protect hunters, the Nago and Yoruba peoples of West Africa looked to Ogun, who corresponds with the deity Ogoun in the mythology of the Caribbean country of Haiti. For the Tlaxcalan indigenous people of Mexico, the god of hunting, Mixcoatl, took the form of a "cloud serpent."

The Hero's Adventure

Joseph Campbell with Bill Moyers

Joseph Campbell, an American writer on mythology and comparative religion, was born in New York City in 1904. Campbell received his master's degree in English and comparative literature from Columbia University in 1927 before pursuing post-graduate studies in Arthurian legends at the Universities of Paris and Munich. His predominant argument was that the world's mythologies, ritual practices, folk traditions, and major religions share certain symbolic themes, motifs, and patterns of behaviour. Campbell died in 1987. Bill Moyers was born in Oklahoma in 1934. He began his journalism career at age 16 as a cub reporter in Texas. During his thirty years in the media, Moyers has received numerous prizes, including over thirty Emmy Awards. Five of Moyers' books based on his television series have become best sellers, including *Joseph Campbell and the Power of Myth*, from which this interview excerpt is taken. Consider your definition of a hero and how it relates to Campbell's. How do his characteristics of a hero compare with your own? Based on Campbell's definition and criteria of heroes, what examples of heroes can you name?

Moyers: Why are there so many stories of the hero in mythology?

Campbell: Because that's what's worth writing about. Even in popular novels, the main character is a hero or heroine who has found or done something beyond the normal range of achievement and experience. A hero is someone who has given his or her life to something bigger than oneself.

Moyers: So in all of these cultures, whatever the local costume the hero might be wearing, what is the deed?

Campbell: Well, there are two types of deed. One is the physical deed, in which the hero performs a courageous act in battle or saves a life. The other kind is the spiritual deed, in which the hero learns to experience the supernormal range of human spiritual life and then comes back with a message.

The usual hero adventure begins with someone from whom something has been taken, or who feels there's something lacking in the normal experiences available or permitted to the members of his society. This person then takes off on a series of adventures beyond the ordinary, either to uncover what has been lost or to discover some life-giving elixir. It's usually a cycle, a going and a returning.

But the structure and something of the spiritual sense of this adventure can be seen already anticipated in the puberty or initiation rituals of early tribal societies, through which a child is compelled to give up its childhood and become an adult—to die, you might say, to its infantile personality and psyche and come back as a responsible adult. This is a fundamental psychological transformation that everyone has to undergo. We are in childhood in a condition of dependency under someone's protection and supervision for some fourteen to twenty-one years—and if you're going on for your Ph.D., this may continue to perhaps thirty-five. You are in no way a self-responsible, free agent, but an obedient dependent, expecting and receiving punishments and rewards. To evolve out of this position of psychological immaturity to the courage of self-responsibility and assurance requires a death and a resurrection. That's the basic motif of the universal hero's journey—leaving one condition and finding the source of life to bring you forth into a richer or mature condition.

Moyers: So even if we happen not to be heroes in the grand sense of redeeming society, we still have to take that journey inside ourselves spiritually and psychologically.

Campbell: That's right. Otto Rank in his important little book *The Myth of the Birth of the Hero* declares that everyone is a hero in birth, when he undergoes a tremendous psychological as well as physical transformation from the condition of a little water creature living in a realm of amniotic fluid into an air-breathing mammal which ultimately will be standing. That's an enormous transformation, and had it been consciously undertaken, it would have been, indeed, a heroic act. And there was a heroic act on the mother's part, as well, who had brought this all about.

Moyers: Then heroes are not all men?

Campbell: Oh, no. The male usually has the more conspicuous role, just because of the conditions of life. He is out there in the world, and the woman is in the home. But among the Aztecs, for example, who had a number of heavens to which people's souls would be assigned according to the conditions of their death, the heaven for warriors killed in battle was the same for mothers who died in childbirth. Giving birth is definitely a heroic deed, in that it is the giving over of oneself to the life of another.

Moyers: Don't you think we've lost that truth in this society of ours, where it's deemed more heroic to go out into the world and make a lot of money than it is to raise children?

Campbell: Making money gets more advertisement. You know the old saying: if a dog bites a man, that's not a story, but if a man bites a dog, you've got a story there. So the thing that happens and happens and happens, no matter how heroic it may be, is not news. Motherhood has lost its novelty, you might say.

Moyers: That's a wonderful image, though—the mother as hero.

Campbell: It has always seemed so to me. That's something I learned from reading these myths.

Moyers: It's a journey—you have to move out of the known, conventional safety of your life to undertake this.

Campbell: You have to be transformed from a maiden to a mother. That's a big change, involving many dangers.

Moyers: And when you come back from your journey, with the child, you've brought something for the world.

Campbell: Not only that, you've got a life job ahead of you. Otto Rank makes the point that there is a world of people who think that their heroic act in being born qualifies them for the respect and support of their whole community.

Moyers: But there's still a journey to be taken after that.

Campbell: There's a large journey to be taken, of many trials.

Moyers: What's the significance of the trials, and tests, and ordeals of the hero?

Campbell: If you want to put it in terms of intentions, the trials are designed to see to it that the intending hero should be really a hero. Is he really a match for this task? Can he overcome the dangers? Does he have the courage, the knowledge, the capacity, to enable him to serve?

•　•　•

Campbell: If you realize what the real problem is—losing yourself, giving yourself to some higher end, or to another—you realize that this itself is the ultimate trial. When we quit thinking primarily about ourselves and our own self-preservation, we undergo a truly heroic transformation of consciousness.

And what all the myths have to deal with is transformations of consciousness of one kind or another. You have been thinking one way, you now have to think a different way.

Moyers: How is consciousness transformed?

Campbell: Either by the trials themselves or by illuminating revelations. Trials and revelations are what it's all about.

Moyers: Isn't there a moment of redemption in all of these stories? The woman is saved from the dragon, the city is spared from obliteration, the hero is snatched from danger in the nick of time.

Campbell: Well, yes. There would be no hero deed unless there were an achievement. We can have the hero who fails, but he's usually represented as a kind of clown, someone pretending to more than he can achieve.

.   .   .

Moyers: Does your study of mythology lead you to conclude that a single human quest, a standard pattern of human aspiration and thought, constitutes for all humankind something that we have in common, whether we lived a million years ago or will live a thousand years from now?

Campbell: There's a certain type of myth which one might call the vision quest, going in quest of a boon, a vision, which has the same form in every mythology. That is the thing that I tried to present in the first book I wrote, *The Hero with a Thousand Faces*. All these different mythologies give us the same essential quest. You leave the world that you're in and go into a depth or into a distance or up to a height. There you come to what was missing in your consciousness in the world you formerly inhabited. Then comes the problem either of staying with that, and letting the world drop off, or returning with that boon and trying to hold on to it as you move back into your social world again. That's not an easy thing to do.

Moyers: So the hero goes *for* something, he doesn't just go along for the ride, he's not simply an adventurer?

Campbell: There are both kinds of heroes, some that choose to undertake the journey and some that don't. In one kind of adventure, the hero sets out responsibly and intentionally to perform the deed. For instance, Odysseus' son Telemachus was told by Athena, "Go find your father." That father quest is a major hero adventure for young people. That is the adventure of finding what your career is, what your nature is, what your source is. You undertake that intentionally. Or there is the legend of the Sumerian sky goddess, Inanna, who descended into the underworld and underwent death to bring her beloved back to life.

Then there are adventures into which you are thrown—for example, being drafted into the army. You didn't intend it, but you're in now.

You've undergone a death and resurrection, you've put on a uniform, and you're another creature.

One kind of hero that often appears in Celtic myths is the princely hunter, who has followed the lure of a deer into a range of forest that he has never been in before. The animal there undergoes a transformation, becoming the Queen of the Faerie Hills, or something of that kind. This is a type of adventure in which the hero has no idea what he is doing but suddenly finds himself in a transformed realm.

Moyers: Is the adventurer who takes that kind of trip a hero in the mythological sense?

Campbell: Yes, because he is always ready for it. In these stories, the adventure that the hero is ready for is the one he gets. The adventure is symbolically a manifestation of his character. Even the landscape and the conditions of the environment match his readiness.

Notes

elixir a substance or medicine thought to have the power to cure all ills or to provide a person with eternal life

Aztecs an Aboriginal people traditionally from central Mexico and noted for their rich civilization

Odysseus a mythical Greek hero who was the king of Ithaca and leader of the Greeks in the Trojan War; he returned home after ten years of wandering

Telemachus in Greek mythology, son of Odysseus and Penelope who helped kill Penelope's suitors

Athena the Greek goddess of wisdom, warfare, and the practical arts

Sumerian a reference to a fourth millennium BCE civilization based in Mesopotamia, between the Tigris and Euphrates rivers, in today's Iraq

Ode to the West Wind

Percy Bysshe Shelley

Born in 1792, Percy Bysshe Shelley was a poet whose work represented the sense of freedom, individualism, and search for truth and
beauty that characterized the Romantic Movement in English life and
literature. He was married to Mary Wollstonecraft Godwin, who later,
as Mary Shelley, wrote the novel *Frankenstein*. In 1818, Shelley and
his spouse settled permanently in Italy, where many of his most
famous poems were written. In 1822, just before his thirtieth birthday, Shelley drowned in a storm while sailing the Mediterranean.
Nature, for Romantic poets such as Shelley and Coleridge, contains
forces that speak powerfully to fundamental aspects of human experience. What are some of the forces in nature that resonate in this
way? Which forces are a powerful inspiration for poets with whom
you are familiar? In what ways are you aware of and feel the power
of the natural world?

I

O wild West Wind, thou breath of Autumn's being,
Thou, from whose unseen presence the leaves dead
Are driven, like ghosts from an enchanter fleeing,

Yellow, and black, and pale, and hectic red,
Pestilence-stricken multitudes: O Thou,
Who chariotest to their dark wintry bed

The winged seeds, where they lie cold and low,
Each like a corpse within its grave, until
Thine azure sister of the Spring shall blow

Her clarion o'er the dreaming earth, and fill
(Driving sweet buds like flocks to feed in air)
With living hues and odours plain and hill:

Wild Spirit, which art moving everywhere;
Destroyer and Preserver; hear, O hear!

II

Thou on whose stream, 'mid the steep sky's commotion,
Loose clouds like Earth's decaying leaves are shed,
Shook from the tangled boughs of Heaven and Ocean,

Angels of rain and lightning: there are spread
On the blue surface of thine aery surge,
Like the bright hair uplifted from the head

Of some fierce Maenad, even from the dim verge
Of the horizon to the zenith's height,
The locks of the approaching storm. Thou Dirge

Of the dying year, to which this closing night
Will be the dome of a vast sepulchre,
Vaulted with all thy congregated might

Of vapours, from whose solid atmosphere
Black rain and fire and hail will burst: O hear!

III

Thou who didst waken from his summer dreams
The blue Mediterranean, where he lay,
Lulled by the coil of his chrystalline streams,

Beside a pumice isle in Baiæ's bay,
And saw in sleep old palaces and towers
Quivering within the wave's intenser day,

All overgrown with azure moss and flowers
So sweet, the sense faints picturing them! Thou
For whose path the Atlantic's level powers

Cleave themselves into chasms, while far below
The sea-blooms and the oozy woods which wear
The sapless foliage of the ocean, know

Thy voice, and suddenly grow grey with fear,
And tremble and despoil themselves: O hear!

IV

If I were a dead leaf thou mightest bear;
If I were a swift cloud to fly with thee;
A wave to pant beneath thy power, and share

The impulse of thy strength, only less free
Than thou, O Uncontrollable! If even
I were as in my boyhood, and could be

The comrade of thy wanderings over Heaven,
As then, when to outstrip thy skiey speed
Scarce seemed a vision; I would ne'er have striven

As thus with thee in prayer in my sore need.
Oh! lift me as a wave, a leaf, a cloud!
I fall upon the thorns of life! I bleed!

A heavy weight of hours has chained and bowed
One too like thee: tameless, and swift, and proud.

V

Make me thy lyre, even as the forest is:
What if my leaves are falling like its own!
The tumult of thy mighty harmonies

Will take from both a deep, autumnal tone,
Sweet though in sadness. Be thou, Spirit fierce,
My spirit! Be thou me, impetuous one!

Drive my dead thoughts over the universe
Like withered leaves to quicken a new birth!
And, by the incantation of this verse,

Scatter, as from an unextinguished hearth
Ashes and sparks, my words among mankind!
Be through my lips to unawakened Earth

The trumpet of a prophecy! O Wind,
If Winter comes, can Spring be far behind?

Notes

hectic feverish

Thine azure…Spring Here, Shelley refers to the springtime's reviving wind.

clarion in this instance, a high-pitched trumpet; an Old French word originating from the medieval Latin word *clario*, meaning "clear"

angels in this instance, means messengers or harbingers

Maenad a female devoted to the worship of Dionysus (also known as Bacchus), the Greek god of wine and vegetation

vapours clouds

chrystalline streams the currents that flow into the Mediterranean Sea

pumice isle an island formed from porous volcanic stone

Baiæ's bay the site west of Naples, Italy, where villas were erected by Roman emperors

lyre in this instance, the Aeolian lyre, or wind harp, that responds to the wind with musical chords; a common Romantic image for the response of the human mind to the forces of nature

trumpet of a prophecy an allusion to the last trumpet of the apocalypse as described in the Book of Revelation in the Bible

Araby

from Dubliners

James Joyce

A major figure in twentieth-century literature, James Joyce was born in Dublin, Ireland, in 1882. After the age of twenty, Joyce spent nearly his entire life away from Ireland, but he never stopped writing about his homeland. His first book, *Dubliners* (1907), was followed by his experimental masterpieces *Portrait of the Artist as a Young Man* (1916), *Ulysses* (1922), and *Finnegans Wake* (1939). He died in 1941. It has been observed that Joyce's narratives—no matter how daring in their use of literary forms—remain grounded in universal themes and patterns. How might you go about identifying such themes and patterns in a modern work? How would what you have discovered affect your reading of the work?

North Richmond Street, being blind, was a quiet street except at the hour when the Christian Brothers' School set the boys free. An uninhabited house of two storeys stood at the blind end, detached from its neighbours in a square ground. The other houses of the street, conscious of decent lives within them, gazed at one another with brown imperturbable faces.

The former tenant of our house, a priest, had died in the back drawing-room. Air, musty from having been long enclosed, hung in all the rooms, and the waste room behind the kitchen was littered with old useless papers. Among these I found a few paper-covered books, the pages of which were curled and damp: *The Abbot,* by Walter Scott,

The Devout Communicant and *The Memoirs of Vidocq*. I liked the last best because its leaves were yellow. The wild garden behind the house contained a central apple-tree and a few straggling bushes under one of which I found the late tenant's rusty bicycle-pump. He had been a very charitable priest; in his will he had left all his money to institutions and the furniture of his house to his sister.

When the short days of winter came dusk fell before we had well eaten our dinners. When we met in the street the houses had grown sombre. The space of sky above us was the colour of ever-changing violet and towards it the lamps of the street lifted their feeble lanterns. The cold air stung us and we played till our bodies glowed. Our shouts echoed in the silent street. The career of our play brought us through the dark muddy lanes behind the houses where we ran the gantlet of the rough tribes from the cottages, to the back doors of the dark dripping gardens where odours arose from the ashpits, to the dark odorous stables where a coachman smoothed and combed the horse or shook music from the buckled harness. When we returned to the street light from the kitchen windows had filled the areas. If my uncle was seen turning the corner we hid in the shadow until we had seen him safely housed. Or if Mangan's sister came out on the doorstep to call her brother in to his tea we watched her from our shadow peer up and down the street. We waited to see whether she would remain or go in and, if she remained, we left our shadow and walked up to Mangan's steps resignedly. She was waiting for us, her figure defined by the light from the half-opened door. Her brother always teased her before he obeyed and I stood by the railings looking at her. Her dress swung as she moved her body and the soft rope of her hair tossed from side to side.

Every morning I lay on the floor in the front parlour watching her door. The blind was pulled down to within an inch of the sash so that I could not be seen. When she came out on the doorstep my heart leaped. I ran to the hall, seized my books and followed her. I kept her brown figure always in my eye and, when we came near the point at which our ways diverged, I quickened my pace and passed her. This happened morning after morning. I had never spoken to her, except for a few casual words, and yet her name was like a summons to all my foolish blood.

Her image accompanied me even in places the most hostile to romance. On Saturday evenings when my aunt went marketing I had to go to carry some of the parcels. We walked through the flaring streets, jostled by drunken men and bargaining women, amid the curses of labourers, the shrill litanies of shop-boys who stood on guard by the barrels of pigs' cheeks, the nasal chanting of street-singers, who sang a *come-all-you* about O'Donovan Rossa, or a ballad about the troubles in our native land. These noises converged in a single sensation of life for me: I imagined that I bore my chalice safely through a throng of foes. Her name sprang to my lips at moments in strange prayers and praises which I myself did not understand. My eyes were often full of tears (I could not tell why) and at times a flood from my heart seemed to pour itself out into my bosom. I thought little of the future. I did not know whether I would ever speak to her or not or, if I spoke to her, how I could tell her of my confused adoration. But my body was like a harp and her words and gestures were like fingers running upon the wires.

One evening I went into the back drawing-room in which the priest had died. It was a dark rainy evening and there was no sound in the house. Through one of the broken panes I heard the rain impinge upon the earth, the fine incessant needles of water playing in the sodden beds. Some distant lamp or lighted window gleamed below me. I was thankful that I could see so little. All my senses seemed to desire to veil themselves and, feeling that I was about to slip from them, I pressed the palms of my hands together until they trembled, murmuring: *O love! O love!* many times.

At last she spoke to me. When she addressed the first words to me I was so confused that I did not know what to answer. She asked me was I going to *Araby*. I forgot whether I answered yes or no. It would be a splendid bazaar, she said; she would love to go.

—And why can't you? I asked.

While she spoke she turned a silver bracelet round and round her wrist. She could not go, she said, because there would be a retreat that week in her convent. Her brother and two other boys were fighting for their caps and I was alone at the railings. She held one of the spikes, bowing her head towards me. The light from the lamp opposite our door caught the white curve of her neck, lit up her hair that rested there and, falling, lit up the hand upon the railing. It fell over one side of her dress and caught the white border of a petticoat, just visible as she stood at ease.

—It's well for you, she said.

—If I go, I said, I will bring you something.

What innumerable follies laid waste my waking and sleeping thoughts after that evening! I wished to annihilate the tedious intervening days. I chafed against the work of school. At night in my bedroom and by day in the classroom her image came between me and the page I strove to read. The syllables of the word *Araby* were called to me through the silence in which my soul luxuriated and cast an Eastern enchantment over me. I asked for leave to go to the bazaar on Saturday night. My aunt was surprised and hoped it was not some Freemason affair. I answered few questions in class. I watched my master's face pass from amiability to sternness; he hoped I was not beginning to idle. I could not call my wandering thoughts together. I had hardly any patience with the serious work of life which, now that it stood between me and my desire, seemed to me child's play, ugly monotonous child's play.

On Saturday morning I reminded my uncle that I wished to go to the bazaar in the evening. He was fussing at the hallstand, looking for the hat-brush, and answered me curtly:

—Yes, boy, I know.

As he was in the hall I could not go into the front parlour and lie at the window. I left the house in bad humour and walked slowly towards the school. The air was pitilessly raw and already my heart misgave me.

When I came home to dinner my uncle had not yet been home. Still it was early. I sat staring at the clock for some time and, when its ticking began to irritate me, I left the room. I mounted the staircase and gained the upper part of the house. The high cold empty gloomy rooms liberated me and I went from room to room singing. From the front window I saw my companions playing below in the street. Their cries reached me weakened and indistinct and, leaning my forehead against the cool glass, I looked over at the dark house where she lived. I may have stood there for an hour, seeing nothing but the brown-clad figure cast by my imagination, touched discreetly by the lamplight at the curved neck, at the hand upon the railings and at the border below the dress.

When I came downstairs again I found Mrs Mercer sitting at the fire. She was an old garrulous woman, a pawnbroker's widow, who collected used stamps for some pious purpose. I had to endure the gossip of the tea-table. The meal was prolonged beyond an hour and still my uncle did not come. Mrs Mercer stood up to go: she was sorry she couldn't wait any longer, but it was after eight o'clock and she did not like to be out late, as the night air was bad for her. When she had gone I began to walk up and down the room, clenching my fists. My aunt said:

—I'm afraid you may put off your bazaar for this night of Our Lord.

At nine o'clock I heard my uncle's latchkey in the hall-door. I heard him talking to himself and heard the hall-stand rocking when it had received the weight of his overcoat. I could interpret these signs. When he was midway through his dinner I asked him to give me the money to go to the bazaar. He had forgotten.

—The people are in bed and after their first sleep now, he said.

I did not smile. My aunt said to him energetically:

—Can't you give him the money and let him go? You've kept him late enough as it is.

My uncle said he was very sorry he had forgotten. He said he believed in the old saying: *All work and no play makes Jack a dull boy.* He asked me where I was going and, when I had told him a second time, he asked me did I know *The Arab's Farewell to His Steed.* When I left the kitchen he was about to recite the opening lines of the piece to my aunt.

I held a florin tightly in my hand as I strode down Buckingham Street towards the station. The sight of the streets thronged with buyers and glaring with gas recalled to me the purpose of my journey. I took my seat in a third-class carriage of a deserted train. After an intolerable delay the train moved out of the station slowly. It crept onward among ruinous houses and over the twinkling river. At Westland Row Station a crowd of people pressed to the carriage doors; but the porters moved them back, saying that it was a special train for the bazaar. I remained alone in the bare carriage. In a few minutes the train drew up beside an improvised wooden platform. I passed out on to the road and saw by the lighted dial of a clock that it was ten minutes to ten. In front of me was a large building which displayed the magical name.

I could not find any sixpenny entrance and, fearing that the bazaar would be closed, I passed in quickly through a turnstile, handing a shilling to a weary-looking man. I found myself in a big hall girdled at half its height by a gallery. Nearly all the stalls were closed and the greater part of the hall was in darkness. I recognized a silence like that which pervades a church after a service. I walked into the centre of the bazaar timidly. A few people were gathered about the stalls which were still open. Before a curtain, over which the words *Café Chantant* were written in coloured lamps, two men were counting money on a salver. I listened to the fall of the coins.

Remembering with difficulty why I had come I went over to one of the stalls and examined porcelain vases and flowered tea-sets. At the door of the stall a young lady was talking and laughing with two young gentlemen. I remarked their English accents and listened vaguely to their conversation.

—O, I never said such a thing!

—O, but you did!

—O, but I didn't!

—Didn't she say that?

—Yes. I heard her.

—O, there's a…fib!

Observing me the young lady came over and asked me did I wish to buy anything. The tone of her voice was not encouraging; she seemed to have spoken to me out of a sense of duty. I looked humbly at the great jars that stood like eastern guards at either side of the dark entrance to the stall and murmured:

—No, thank you.

The young lady changed the position of one of the vases and went back to the two young men. They began to talk of the same subject. Once or twice the young lady glanced at me over her shoulder.

I lingered before her stall, though I knew my stay was useless, to make my interest in her wares seem the more real. Then I turned away slowly and walked down the middle of the bazaar. I allowed the two pennies to fall against the sixpence in my pocket. I heard a voice call from one end of the gallery that the light was out. The upper part of the hall was now completely dark.

Gazing up into the darkness I saw myself as a creature driven and derided by vanity; and my eyes burned with anguish and anger.

Notes

blind a dead-end street

The Abbot, The Devout Communicant, The Memoirs of Vidocq respectively, a popular historical romance by Sir Walter Scott, a Roman Catholic religious manual, and the memoirs of the chief of the French detective force

Mangan the surname of the Irish poet James Clarence Mangan, who was much admired by James Joyce

litanies prayers consisting of supplications by the Christian clergy and fixed responses by the congregation; from the medieval Latin word *letania*, meaning "entreaty"

come-all-you about O'Donovan Rossa a topical song that began "Come all you gallant Irishmen..." about the popular Irish leader Jeremiah O'Donovan (1831–1915), who was jailed by the British for inciting rebellion

the troubles the long-standing conflict in Northern Ireland between the Irish Catholics and the Irish Protestants; the latter are supported by the British armed forces

chalice the cup in which the wine of the Christian Eucharist is consecrated; from the Latin word *calix*, meaning "cup"

Freemason a Protestant fraternal organization that is unpopular with Irish Catholics

The Arab's Farewell to His Steed a popular sentimental poem by Caroline Norton

salver a tray for serving food or beverages; from the Spanish *salvar*, meaning "to save" or alternately "to taste food to detect poison"

Utopian Dreams

Val Ross

Val Ross was born in London, Ontario, in 1950. She worked at *Maclean's* magazine from 1979 to 1987, completing her tenure there as arts editor. For much of the 1990s, she covered books and magazines as a publishing editor at *The Globe and Mail*. In "Utopian Dreams," Ross reviews John Carey's *The Faber Book of Utopias,* a collection of utopian visions from across eras and cultures. What do you think causes people to experience dreams of utopia? What historical figures can you think of who have had views of a utopian society? What historical and world events resulted from these views or from other people trying to put into practice the utopian views of these people?

A worm gnaws at the blueprint of almost every social scheme that sets out to maximize human potential and human happiness. That worm—sometimes it destroys the entire blueprint—is the question of responsibility for Utopian dirt. Countless hippie communes came apart a generation ago in squabbles over who would clean the john and wash the encrusted dinner dishes.

In Plato's *The Republic* and Thomas More's *Utopia,* the dirty work is handled by slaves—one of the many reasons why those pioneering utopian thinkers' plans have dated so badly. In Aldous Huxley's dystopian *Brave New World* (1934), state hatcheries breed workers called "Deltas" who are stupid enough to accept scutwork happily. Alas, Huxley's hatcheries inflict terrible collateral damage on such concepts as motherhood, individual love, and human dignity. In Kurt Vonnegut's *Player Piano* (1952), machines do almost everything—leaving the human population unemployed, feeling useless, and prone to substance abuse, family breakdown, and violence.

This 1929 British poster uses a medical procedure of the time as a metaphor for what the Conservative and Unionist Party promised to do for constituents. Known as sun-ray treatment, a person would sit under an ultra-violet lamp to receive "artificial sunlight." This was thought to help everything from tuberculosis and allergies to skin ulcers and hair loss. The poster, with its promises of a glowing future, couples centuries-old utopian themes with techniques of modern political propaganda.

Those who invent schemes to promote human happiness must sooner or later wade into the offal matter of dirty work. But few have come up with solutions that neither oppress one segment of the population nor dislocate the role of useful work in human society. Of the 101 writers from Plato to Vonnegut anthologized in the fascinating, provocative, and idiosyncratic new *Faber Book of Utopias*, one of the few to have mused fruitfully on this issue is the French utopian writer Charles Fourier (1772–1837).

In Fourier's communal, egalitarian communities—groups of precisely 1,620 people he called Phalanxes—he dreamed that everyone would achieve happiness by doing only the jobs they were most suited to. Fourier imagined that people who rejoiced in heavy exertion (the "industrial athletes") would go off to build canals while more reflective souls would head for the looms and beehives.

It would be no different when it came to cleaning latrines; Fourier reasoned that the filthiest jobs would be done by those people who actually enjoy mucking around in filth—children, especially little boys. He proposed organizing these latrine cleaners into "a kind of half-savage legion" known as "Little Hordes." Each Little Horde would have its own slang, its own uniforms, and its own dwarf ponies to ride upon. Hauling poop would be a grand game.

Fourier's utopia is one of the more amiable visions in *The Faber Book of Utopias*, an inventory of more than 2,000 years of imaginary societies, broken dreams, strange hopes, and cautionary tales. Editor John Carey, author of *The Intellectuals and the Masses* and Merton Professor of English at Oxford, opens with an anonymous Egyptian, circa 1500 BCE, conjuring up "an island of the spirit, full of every good thing," and ranges through dreamers as varied as Ovid, Robert Owen, and Hitler.

The term "Utopia," invented by More in 1516, means "no place." As Carey notes, that makes his a book of nowheres. And that's a good thing. Many of the visions meant to be positive (eu-topian, as in euphoric) are instead actively repugnant.

Pious sadism informs the vision of the early Christian Tertullian, who imagined Heaven as a place where he would be eternally entertained by the torture of infidels; Hitler's utopian dream was of a Ukraine populated only by Teutonic races. "To count as a utopia, an imaginary place must be an expression of desire," Carey writes. But because our fellow humans have such dark desires, one of his book's clearest messages is that one person's utopia is another's dystopia.

Each vision reflects the anxieties of its age. Carey's earliest selections are fixated on food; they are about lands of eternal spring and fruitful abundance. Plato, Plutarch, Tacitus, and the utopias of 2,000 years ago are of societies (the Republic, the Germanic, and the Spartan) that are admirable because of their rigorous promotion of virtuous males.

Dreamers from the Renaissance on ponder how to organize society so as to minimize desires associated with wealth (More and Voltaire both invent worlds where gold is so common that no one covets it). By the early 20th century, dystopias abound, suggesting that world war sapped the optimism of the dreaming classes. More recent inventors of utopias regain a hopeful practicality.

One is the upbeat Michio Kaku, professor of theoretical physics at City University of New York. Kaku predicts that within the next couple of centuries, ubiquitous computers will give us smart homes, smart cars, and smart refrigerators, all monitoring and responding to our needs. ("Rather like living inside a Disney movie," Carey writes in his introductory note to Kaku, "where inanimate objects offer advice and crack jokes.")

Carey's witty and learned introductions—or justifications—for each selection are among the book's best and most informative passages. His introduction to the writings of H.G. Wells makes no effort to conceal his disgust at Wells' racism (he disdained "black, brown, yellow and dirty-white" peoples) and his embrace of eugenics. In *Anticipations* (1901), Wells wrote that the über-men of his "New Republic" would not be squeamish about "the merciful obliteration of weak and silly and pointless things"—notions that Carey terms "chilling."

While appalled by secular utopias from the likes of Wells and Hitler, Carey likewise has little enthusiasm for religious utopias. He hasn't bothered to include St. Augustine or selections from communities such as the Shakers. Instead, he has made room for some peripheral (if enjoyable) material from English literature such as Rupert Brooke's poem *Heaven*, which imagines a fishy utopia of "paradisal grubs, unfading moths, immortal flies," and Joseph Conrad's version of merchant navy life as paradise (a selection from *Youth*).

I'm not sure what Brooke and Conrad are doing in here. But I have no problem with a passage from Julian Barnes' *A History of the World in 10 1/2 Chapters*, in which the narrator goes to Heaven, eats a perfect bacon-and-egg breakfast, and learns that everything is available in Heaven, including God, *if one wants it to be*. This selection is delicious and ultimately terrifying.

Perhaps the editor's idiosyncratic choices for his book are precisely the point. Carey defines utopia as a place of desire, so it is only fitting that his anthology of utopias consists of whatever he desired to put in.

I thank him for including Oscar Wilde. Wilde's not as imaginative as Fourier when it comes to apportioning ugly jobs. ("Man is made for something better than disturbing dirt. All work of that kind should be done by a machine.") But he is very clear about the point of utopias. "A map of the world that does not include Utopia is not even worth glancing at, for it leaves out the one country at which Humanity is always landing," Wilde wrote in 1891. "And when Humanity lands there it looks out, and, seeing a better country, sets sail. Progress is the realization of Utopias."

Notes

egalitarian the belief in human equality with respect to one's social, economic, and political rights and privileges

Tertullian a Carthaginian theologian (circa 160–230 CE) who formed his own separate sect within the Christian church

Teutonic of or relating to the Germanic peoples

eugenics the highly controversial study of the attempt to hereditarily "improve" the human race by controlled, selective breeding

St. Augustine Aurelius Augustine (354–430 CE) is considered to be one of the most prominent Roman Catholic priests in history. His book *Confessions* is a classic of Christian theology.

Shakers an American religious sect which believed in the coming of an ideal society and which practised celibacy and lived a very disciplined communal lifestyle; popularly known today for their furniture and household design

Universal Themes and Patterns: Activities

1. With a partner, choose a universal theme or archetypal pattern and create a list of works of literature, movies, television programs, songs, videos, comics, magazines, illustrations, and advertisements that make use of your chosen theme or pattern. Then use text, sound, illustrations, photographs, and other visual images to create a multimedia presentation showing the enduring presence and impact of this universal theme or archetypal pattern in society.

2. In Northrop Frye's analysis of the literary mode of romance, he examines how romance reflects the phases of spring and birth. The romantic mode generally deals with such topics as humanity's quest for an ideal; the desire to return to nature; and the search for truth, beauty, goodness, and a better world. In a class presentation, outline and discuss how recurrent images, individual words, phrases, and figurative expressions in "Ode to the West Wind" and "Utopian Dreams" reflect the essentials and ideals of romance as outlined by Frye.

3. With a partner, do research to create a working definition of the term *dystopia*. Then locate and view a film that deals with either a utopian vision, such as *Animal Farm* (Turner Network Television, 2000), or a dystopian vision such as *1984* (Virgin Productions, 1984) or *Fahrenheit 451* (Image Entertainment, 2000). Write a review of the film for a mass-circulation newspaper audience. Include in your review the following features: a synopsis of the plot (without spoiling the ending); an explanation of how the film reflects a universal theme or archetypal pattern; and an evaluation of the effectiveness and quality of its cinematic techniques and their impact on viewers. Exchange draft reviews with a partner and ask for suggestions to improve your style and content.

4. Both Northrop Frye and Joseph Campbell emphasize the importance of the quest theme in literature. Does the importance of this feature extend to non-western literature? Choose a culture that is non-western, such as North American Aboriginal or South Asian. Then research a variety of primary and secondary print and non-print sources to determine the main characteristics of its oral and written literature. Write a formal essay in which you discuss the extent to which the quest theme applies to the literature of this culture. Be sure to integrate researched information into your essay, such as quotations from secondary sources.

2 essays, articles, and media

The contemplation of things as they are, without substitution or imposture, without error or confusion, is in itself a nobler thing than a whole harvest of invention.

— *Francis Bacon*

If you want a slice of life, look out the window. An artist has to look out that window, isolate one or two suggestive things, and embroider them together with poetry and fabrication, to create a revelation.

— *Barbara Kingsolver*

Portrait of the Essay as a Warm Body

Cynthia Ozick

Cynthia Ozick was born in New York in 1928. A writer of fiction, non-fiction, and drama, she has received numerous literary awards, including Guggenheim and National Endowment for the Arts fellowships. She has written several collections of essays, including *Quarrel and Quantary,* published in 2000. "Portrait of the Essay as a Warm Body" first appeared in *The Atlantic Monthly,* then became the introduction to *Best American Essays of 1998.* Ozick has said, "All good stories are honest and most good essays are not." What makes a good essay? What purposes and audiences do you associate with essays? In what ways can forms of non-fiction, such as essays and memoirs, be considered "literature"?

An essay is a thing of the imagination. If there is information in an essay, it is by-the-by, and if there is an opinion in it, you need not trust it for the long run. A genuine essay has no educational, polemical, or sociopolitical use; it is the movement of a free mind at play. Though it is written in prose, it is closer in kind to poetry than to any other form. Like a poem, a genuine essay is made out of language and character and mood and temperament and pluck and chance.

And if I speak of a genuine essay, it is because fakes abound. Here the old-fashioned term poetaster may apply, if only obliquely. As the poetaster is to the poet—a lesser aspirant—so the article is to the essay:

a look-alike knock-off guaranteed not to wear well. An article is gossip. An essay is reflection and insight. An article has the temporary advantage of social heat—what's hot out there right now. An essay's heat is interior. An article is timely, topical, engaged in the issues and personalities of the moment; it is likely to be stale within the month. In five years it will have acquired the quaint aura of a rotary phone. An article is Siamese-twinned to its date of birth. An essay defies its date of birth, and ours too.

A small historical experiment. Who are the classical essayists who come at once to mind? Montaigne, obviously. Among the nineteenth-century English masters, the long row of Hazlitt, Lamb, De Quincey, Stevenson, Carlyle, Ruskin, Newman, Martineau, Arnold. Of the Americans, Emerson. It may be argued that nowadays these are read only by specialists and literature majors, and by the latter only when they are compelled to. However accurate the claim, it is irrelevant to the experiment, which has to do with beginnings and their disclosures. Here, then, are some introductory passages:

> One of the pleasantest things in the world is going on a journey; but I like to go by myself. I can enjoy society in a room; but out of doors, nature is company enough for me. I am then never less alone than when alone.
> —William Hazlitt, "On Going on a Journey"

> To go into solitude, a man needs to retire as much from his chamber as from society. I am not solitary whilst I read and write, though nobody is with me. But if a man would be alone, let him look at the stars.
> —Ralph Waldo Emerson, "Nature"

> The human species, according to the best theory I can form of it, is composed of two distinct races, the men who borrow, and the men who lend.
> —Charles Lamb, "The Two Races of Men"

The future of poetry is immense, because in poetry, where it is worthy of its high destinies, our race, as times goes on, will find an ever and surer stay. There is not a creed which is not shaken, not an accredited dogma which is not shown to be questionable, not a received tradition which does not threaten to dissolve…. But for poetry, the idea is everything; the rest is a world of illusion, of divine illusion.

—Matthew Arnold, "The Study of Poetry"

The changes wrought by death are in themselves so sharp and final, and so terrible and melancholy in their consequences, that the thing stands alone in man's experience, and has no parallel upon earth. It outdoes all other accidents because it is the last of them. Sometimes it leaps suddenly upon its victims, like a Thug; sometimes it lays a regular siege and creeps upon their citadel during a score of years. And when the business is done, there is a sore havoc made in other people's lives, and a pin knocked out by which many subsidiary friendships hung together.

—Robert Louis Stevenson, "Aes Triplex"

It is recorded of some people, as of Alexander the Great, that their sweat, in consequence of some rare and extraordinary constitution, emitted a sweet odor, the cause of which Plutarch and others investigated. But the nature of most bodies is the opposite, and at their best they are free from smell. Even the purest breath has nothing more excellent than to be without offensive odor, like that of very healthy children.

— Michel de Montaigne, "Of Smells"

What might such a little anthology of opening sentences reveal? First, that language differs from one era to the next: there are touches of archaism here, if only in punctuation and cadence. Second, that splendid minds may contradict each other (outdoors, Hazlitt never feels alone; Emerson urges the opposite). Third, that the theme of an essay can be anything under the sun, however trivial (the smell of sweat) or crushing (the thought that we must die). Fourth, that the essay is a consistently recognizable and venerable—or call it ancient—form. In English: Addison and Steele in the eighteenth century, Bacon and Browne in the seventeenth, Lyly in the sixteenth, Bede in the seventh. And what of the biblical Koheleth—Ecclesiastes—who may be the oldest essayist reflecting on one of the oldest subjects: world-weariness?

So the essay is ancient and various: but this is a commonplace. There is something else, and it is more striking yet—the essay's power. By "power" I mean precisely the capacity to do what force always does: coerce assent. Never mind that the shape and intent of any essay is against coercion or suasion, or that the essay neither proposes nor purposes to get you to think like its author. A genuine essay is not a doctrinaire tract or a propaganda effort or a broadside. Thomas Paine's "Common Sense" and Émile Zola's "J'Accuse" are heroic landmark writings; but to call them essays, though they may resemble the form, is to misunderstand. The essay is not meant for the barricades; it is a stroll through someone's mazy mind. All the same, the essay turns out to be a force for agreement. It co-opts agreement; it courts agreement; it seduces agreement. For the brief hour we give to it, we are sure to fall into surrender and conviction. And this will occur even if we are intrinsically roused to resistance.

To illustrate: I may not be persuaded by Emersonianism as an ideology, but Emerson—his voice, his language, his music—persuades me. When we look for superlatives, not for nothing do we speak of "commanding" or "compelling" prose. If I am a skeptical rationalist or an advanced biochemist, I may regard (or discard) the idea of the soul as no better than a puff of warm vapour. But here is Emerson on the soul: "When it breathes through [man's] intellect, it is genius; when it breathes through his will, it is virtue; when it flows through his affection, it is love." And then—well, I am in thrall, I am possessed; I believe.

The novel has its own claims on surrender. It suspends our participation in the society we ordinarily live in, so that—for the time we are reading—we forget it utterly. But the essay does not allow us to forget our usual sensations and opinions; it does something even more potent: it makes us deny them. The authority of a masterly essayist—the authority of sublime language and intimate observation—is absolute. When I am with Hazlitt, I know no greater companion than nature. When I am with Emerson, I know no greater solitude than nature.

And what is most odd about the essay's power to lure us into its lair is how it goes about this work. We feel it when a political journalist comes after us with a point of view—we feel it the way the cat is wary of the dog. A polemic is a herald, complete with feathered hat and trumpet. A tract can be a trap. A magazine article generally has the scent of so-much-per-word. What is certain is that all of these are more or less in the position of a lepidopterist with his net: they mean to catch and skewer. They are focused on prey—i.e., us. The genuine essay, by contrast, never thinks of us; the genuine essay may be the most self-centred (the politer word would be subjective) arena for human thought ever devised.

Or else, though still not having you and me in mind (unless as an exemplum of common folly), it is not self-centred at all. When I was a child, I discovered in the public library a book that enchanted me then, and the idea of which has enchanted me for life. I have no recollection either of the title or of the writer—and anyhow very young readers rarely take note of authors; stories are simply and magically *there*. The characters included, as I remember them, three or four children and a delightful relation who is a storyteller, and the scheme was this: each child calls out a story element—most often an object—and the storyteller gathers up whatever is supplied (blue boots, a river, a fairy, a pencil box) and makes out of these random, unlikely, and disparate offerings a tale both logical and surprising. An essay, it seems to me, may be similarly constructed— if so deliberate a term applies. The essayist, let us say, unexpectedly stumbles over a pair of old blue boots in a corner of the garage, and this reminds her of when she last wore them—twenty years ago, on a trip to Paris, where on the banks of the Seine she stopped to watch an old fellow sketching, with a box of coloured pencils at his side. The pencil wiggling over his sheet is a greyish pink, which reflects the threads of sunset pulling westward in the sky, like the reins of a fairy cart…and so on. The mind meanders, slipping from one impression to another, from reality to memory to dreamscape and back again.

In the same way Montaigne, in our sample, when contemplating the unpleasantness of sweat, ends with the pure breath of children. Or Stevenson, starting out with mortality, speaks first of ambush, then of war, and finally of a displaced pin. No one is freer than the essayist—free to leap out in any direction, to hop from thought to thought, to begin with the finish and finish with the middle, or to eschew beginning and end and keep only a middle. The marvel of it is that out of this apparent causelessness, out of this scattering of idiosyncratic seeing and telling, a coherent world is made. It is coherent because, after all, an essayist must be an artist, and every artist, whatever the means, arrives at a sound and singular imaginative frame—or call it, on a minor scale, a cosmogony.

And it is into this frame, this work of art, that we tumble like tar babies, and are held fast. What holds us there? The authority of a voice, yes; the pleasure—sometimes the anxiety—of a new idea, an untried angle, a snatch of reminiscence, bliss displayed or shock conveyed. An essay can be the product of intellect or memory, lightheartedness or gloom, well-being or disgruntlement. But always there is a certain quietude, on occasion a kind of detachment. Rage and revenge, I think, belong to fiction. The essay is cooler than that. Because it so often engages in acts of memory, and despite its gladder or more antic incarnations, the essay is by and large a serene or melancholic form. It mimics that low electric hum, sometimes rising to resemble actual speech, that all human beings carry inside their heads—a vibration, garrulous if somewhat indistinct, that never leaves us while we wake. It is the hum of perpetual noticing: the configuration of someone's eyelid or tooth, the veins on a hand, a wisp of string caught on a twig, some words your fourth-grade teacher said, so long ago, about the rain, the look of an awning, a sidewalk, a bit of cheese left on a plate. All day long this inescapable hum drums on, recalling one thing and another, and pointing out this and this and this. Legend has it that Titus, emperor of Rome, went mad because of the buzzing of a gnat that made its home in his ear; and presumably the gnat, flying out into the great world and then returning to her nest, whispered what she had seen and felt and learned there. But an essayist is more resourceful than an emperor, and can be relieved of this interior noise, if only for the time it takes to record its murmurings. To seize the hum and set it down for others to hear is the essayist's genius.

It is a genius bound to leisure, and even to luxury, if luxury is measured in hours. The essay's limits can be found in its own reflective nature. Poems have been wrested from the inferno of catastrophe or war, and battlefield letters too: these are the spontaneous bursts and burnings that danger excites. But the meditative temperateness of an essay requires a desk and a chair, a musing and a mooning, a connection to a civilized surround; even when the subject itself is a wilderness of lions and tigers, mulling is the way of it. An essay is a fireside thing, not a conflagration or a safari.

This may be why, when we ask who the essayists are, it turns out—though novelists may now and then write essays—that true essayists rarely write novels. Essayists are a species of metaphysician: they are inquisitive—also analytic—about the least grain of being. Novelists go about the strenuous business of marrying and burying their people, or else they send them to sea, or to Africa, or (at the least) out of town. Essayists in their stillness ponder love and death. It is probably an illusion that men are essayists more often than women (especially since women's essays have in the past frequently assumed the form of unpublished correspondence). And here I should, I suppose, add a note about maleness and femaleness as a literary issue—what is popularly termed "gender," as if men and women were French or German tables and sofas. I *should* add such a note; it is the fashion, or, rather, the current expectation or obligation—but there is nothing to say about any of it. Essays are written by men. Essays are written by women. That is the long and the short of it. John Updike, in a genially confident discourse on maleness ("The Disposable Rocket"), takes the view—though he admits to admixture—that the "male sense of space must differ from that of the female, who has such an interesting, active, and significant inner space. The space that interests men is outer." Except, let it be observed, when men write essays: since it is only inner space—interesting, active, significant—that can conceive and nourish the contemplative essay. The "ideal female body," Updike adds, "curves around the centres of repose," and no phrase could better describe the shape of the ideal essay—yet women are no fitter as essayists than men. In promoting the felt salience of sex, Updike nevertheless drives home an essayist's point. Essays, unlike novels, emerge from the sensations of the self. Fiction creeps into foreign bodies; the novelist can inhabit not only a sex not his own, but also beetles and noses and hunger artists and nomads and beasts; while the essay is, as we say, personal.

And here is an irony. Though I have been intent on distinguishing the marrow of the essay from the marrow of fiction, I confess I have been trying all along, in a subliminal way, to speak of the essay as if it—or she—were a character in a novel or a play: moody, fickle, given on a whim to changing her clothes, or the subject; sometimes obstinate, with a mind of her own; or hazy and light; never predictable. I mean for her to be dressed—and addressed—as we would Becky Sharp, or Ophelia, or Elizabeth Bennet, or Mrs. Ramsay, or Mrs. Wilcox, or even Hester Prynne. Put it that it is pointless to say (as I have done repeatedly, disliking it every moment) "the essay," "an essay." The essay—an essay—is not an abstraction; she may have recognizable contours, but she is highly coloured and individuated; she is not a type. She is too fluid, too elusive, to be a category. She may be bold, she may be diffident, she may rely on beauty, or on cleverness, on eros or exotica. Whatever her story, she is the protagonist, the secret self's personification. When we knock on her door, she opens to us, she is a presence in the doorway, she leads us from room to room; then why should we not call her "she"? She may be privately indifferent to us, but she is anything but unwelcoming. Above all, she is not a hidden principle or a thesis or a construct: she is *there*, a living voice. She takes us in.

Notes

poetaster a paltry or inferior poet

lepidopterist a person who studies or collects butterflies

cosmogony in the strictest sense, an explanation, study, or model of the origin of the universe; here, a reference to an artist providing a coherent, imaginative universe in his or her works

tar babies in this instance, a difficult problem, especially one that is only aggravated by attempts to solve it; specifically, an allusion to the book *Brer Rabbit* by J.C. Harris (1848–1908), in which this phrase had a controversial and derogatory meaning

admixture a combination, especially of disparate elements

Becky Sharp, Ophelia, Elizabeth Bennet, Mrs. Ramsay, Mrs. Wilcox, Hester Prynne female characters from the following well-known literary works, respectively: *Vanity Fair* by William Thackeray, *Hamlet* by William Shakespeare, *Pride and Prejudice* by Jane Austen, *To the Lighthouse* by Virginia Woolf, *Howard's End* by E.M. Forster, and *The Scarlet Letter* by Nathaniel Hawthorne

Activities

1. Comment on the effectiveness of the title. To what extent does it engage the reader's interest? How well does it reflect the approach and theme of the essay? How effectively does Ozick use personification in the title to convey her theme?

2. Reread the essay, paying particular attention to the rhythm and cadence of the language. Choose two paragraphs that seem particularly effective and analyze the syntax. How does Ozick use techniques such as parallelism, repetition, variations in sentence length and type, inverted syntax, and sentence fragments to create particular effects?

3. Ozick has strong views about the nature and purpose of an essay. Think about a specific type of literature, art, music, sport, or other activity that is important to you. Write a personal essay on this subject with a clearly stated thesis, and use some of the techniques and stylistic devices of Ozick's essay. You may want to title your work, "Portrait of __ as __." In revising your essay, pay particular attention to your syntax. Then invite a peer editor to comment on your sentence variety and your use of techniques such as subordination, parallelism, and repetition.

Ka-Ching!

Margaret Atwood

Internationally acclaimed author Margaret Atwood was born in Ottawa, Ontario, in 1939. She received a bachelor's degree from the University of Toronto in 1961 and a master's degree from Harvard University in 1962. Since the mid-1960s, Atwood has received continuous critical acclaim for more than thirty books of fiction, poetry, essays, literary criticism, and children's literature. She is the recipient of dozens of awards, including most of the major literary prizes in Canada, as well as many from around the world, including the British Booker Prize in 2000 for her novel *The Blind Assassin*. Atwood is known for her careful craftsmanship, her precision with language, her erudition, and her stinging wit. In "Ka-Ching!" Atwood wittily describes her first job. What was your first job? What did you learn from it? Which skills required for that job are necessary for all your future jobs?

I'll pass over the mini-jobs of adolescence—the summer-camp stints that were more like getting paid for having fun. I'll pass over, too, the self-created pin-money generators—the puppet shows put on for kids at office Christmas parties, the serigraph posters turned out on the ping-pong table—and turn to my first real job. By "real job," I mean one that had nothing to do with friends of my parents or parents of my friends but was obtained in the adult manner, by looking through the ads in newspapers and going in to be interviewed—one for which I was entirely unsuited, and that I wouldn't have done except for the money. I was surprised when I got it, underpaid while doing it, and frustrated in the performance of it, and these qualities have remained linked, for me, to the ominous word "job."

The year was 1962, the place was Toronto. It was summer, and I was faced with the necessity of earning the difference between my scholarship for the next year and what it would cost me to live. The job was in the coffee shop of a small hotel on Avenue Road; it is now in the process of being torn down, but at that time it was a clean, well-lighted place, with booths along one side and a counter—possibly marble—down the other. The booths were served by a waitressing pro who lipsticked outside the lines, and who thought I was a mutant. My job would be serving things at the counter—coffee I would pour, toast I would create from bread, milkshakes I would whip up in the obstetrical stainless-steel device provided. ("Easy as pie," I was told.) I would also be running the customers' money through the cash register—an opaque machine with buttons to be pushed, little drawers that shot in and out, and a neurotic system of locks.

I said I had never worked a cash register before. This delighted the manager, a plump, unctuous character out of some novel I hadn't yet read. He said the cash register, too, was easy as pie, and I would catch on to it in no time, as I was a smart girl with an M.A. He said I should go and get myself a white dress.

I didn't know what he meant by "white dress." I bought the first thing I could find on sale, a nylon afternoon number with daisies appliquéd onto the bodice. The waitress told me this would not do: I needed a dress like her *uniform*. ("How dense can you be?" I overheard her saying.) I got the uniform, but I had to go through the first day in my nylon daisies.

This first humiliation set the tone. The coffee was easy enough—I just had to keep the Bunn filled—and the milkshakes were possible; few people wanted them anyway. The sandwiches and deep-fried shrimp were made at the back: all I had to do was order them over the intercom and bin the leftovers.

But the cash register was perverse. Its drawers would pop open for no reason, or it would ring eerily when I swore I was nowhere near it; or it would lock itself shut, and the queue of customers waiting to pay would lengthen and scowl as I wrestled and sweated. I kept expecting to be fired for incompetence, but the manager chortled more than ever. Occasionally, he would bring some man in a suit to view me. "She's got an M.A.," he would say, in a proud but pitying voice, and the two of them would stare at me and shake their heads.

An ex-boyfriend discovered my place of employment, and would also come to stare and shake his head, ordering a single coffee, taking an hour to drink it, leaving me a sardonic nickel tip. The Greek short-order cook decided I would be the perfect up-front woman for the restaurant he wanted to open: he would marry me and do the cooking, I would speak English to the clientele and work—was he mad?—the cash register. He divulged his bank balance, and demanded to meet my father so the two of them could close the deal. When I declined, he took to phoning me over the intercom to whisper blandishments, and to plying me with deep-fried shrimp. A girl as scrawny as myself, he pointed out, was unlikely to get such a good offer again.

Then the Shriners hit town, took over the hotel, and began calling for buckets of ice, or for doctors because they'd had heart attacks: too much tricycle-riding in the hot sun was felling them in herds. I couldn't handle the responsibility, the cash register had betrayed me once too often, and the short-order cook was beginning to sing Frank Sinatra songs to me. I gave notice.

Only when I'd quit did the manager reveal his true stratagem: they'd wanted someone as inept as me because they suspected their real cashier of skimming the accounts, a procedure I was obviously too ignorant to ever figure out. "Too stunned," as the waitress put it. She was on the cashier's side, and had me fingered as a stoolie all along.

Notes

serigraph a print made by the process of silk-screening, a stencil method in which a design is imposed on a screen of silk or other fine mesh material. Blank areas are coated with an impermeable substance and ink is forced through the mesh onto the printing surface.

ominous menacing; something related to an omen foreshadowing trouble

obstetrical related to the branch of medicine dealing with childbirth

unctuous characterized by exaggerated or insincere earnestness; something that feels oily or soapy when touched, greasy

appliquéd fabric that has been stitched onto another fabric as an ornament

perverse determinedly going against what is right; wayward or difficult to get along with

sardonic mocking, bitter, or scornful

blandishments cajoling, flattering compliments

stratagem a method that is formulated and executed to achieve a specific goal; originally referred to as a trick devised to deceive the enemy

stoolie a person acting as a decoy or informer, such as one who is a spy for the police; sometimes referred to as a "stool pigeon"

Activities

1. List all of the details that Atwood reveals about herself in the essay, from both the perspective of her past and her perspective at the time she wrote this essay. What, according to Atwood, are her strengths and weaknesses? Which are stated overtly and which are implied? How can you tell that Atwood is looking back with some nostalgia at a past experience?

2. With a partner, use the glossary in this anthology and other reference tools to create a working definition of the term *irony*. Then reread the essay and identify each time Atwood uses irony in this essay. Have a class discussion in which you explore questions such as the following: What is the tone of this essay and in which ways has the author's use of irony contributed to it? Is there a relationship between Atwood's subject matter in this essay and her decision to use irony? What are the differences between irony, satire, and parody? Are any elements of satire or parody used in this essay?

3. With a partner, use the Internet to identify and do research on any specific field of study in a master's degree program at a university. Then choose a job that is unrelated to this field of study and do research on that occupation. With your partner, write a comedic script for two people in which a master's program student does not have the appropriate skills to fulfill the job requirements. With your partner, act out your script to a group and invite their feedback on what elements of the script and the performance enhance the humour of your production.

Afternoon of an American Boy

E.B. White

Elwyn Brooks White was born in Mount Vernon, New York, in 1899. He is best known as a humourist and commentator on contemporary culture. After working on a newspaper, he became a contributing editor of the weekly magazine *The New Yorker*, writing the column "The Talk of the Town." White also wrote poetry and two children's books which have become classics: *Charlotte's Web* (1942) and *Stuart Little* (1945). He died in 1985. One critic wrote that "E.B. White is able to draw attention, in particular, to those ordinary or transitory things and imbue them with new meanings." In "Afternoon of an American Boy," he recollects his first date. What feelings do you have about dating? What anxieties do you have about first dates? What amusing possibilities do first dates hold?

When I was in my teens, I lived in Mount Vernon, in the same block with J. Parnell Thomas, who grew up to become chairman of the House Committee on Un-American Activities. I lived on the corner of Summit and East Sidney, at No. 101 Summit Avenue, and Parnell lived four or five doors north of us on the same side of the avenue, in the house the Diefendorfs used to live in.

Parnell was not a playmate of mine, as he was a few years older, but I used to greet him as he walked by our house on his way to and from the depot. He was a good-looking young man, rather quiet and shy. Seeing him, I would call "Hello, Parnell!" and he would smile and say "Hello, Elwyn!" and walk on. Once I remember dashing out of our yard on roller skates and executing a rink turn in front of Parnell, to show off, and he said, "Well! Quite an artist, aren't you?" I remember the words. I was delighted at praise from an older man and sped away along the flagstone sidewalk, dodging the cracks I knew so well.

The thing that made Parnell a special man in my eyes in those days was not his handsome appearance and friendly manner but his sister. Her name was Eileen. She was my age and she was a quiet, nice-looking girl. She never came over to my yard to play, and I never went over there, and, considering that we lived so near each other, we were remarkably uncommunicative; nevertheless, she was the girl I singled out, at one point, to be of special interest to me. Being of special interest to me involved practically nothing on a girl's part—it simply meant that she was under constant surveillance. On my own part, it meant that I suffered an astonishing disintegration when I walked by her house, from embarrassment, fright, and the knowledge that I was in enchanted territory.

In the matter of girls, I was different from most boys of my age. I admired girls a lot, but they terrified me. I did not feel that I possessed the peculiar gifts or accomplishments that girls liked in their male companions—the ability to dance, to play football, to cut up a bit in public, to smoke, and to make small talk. I couldn't do any of these things successfully, and seldom tried. Instead, I stuck with the accomplishments I was sure of: I rode my bicycle sitting backward on the handle bars, I made up poems, I played selections from "Aïda" on the piano. In winter, I tended goal in the hockey games on the frozen pond in the Dell. None of these tricks counted much with girls. In the four years I was in the Mount Vernon High School, I never went to a school dance and I never took a girl to a drugstore for a soda or to the Westchester Playhouse or to Proctor's. I wanted to do these things but did not have the nerve. What I finally did manage to do, however, and what is the subject of this memoir, was far brassier, far gaudier. As an exhibit of teenage courage and ineptitude, it never fails to amaze me in retrospect. I am not even sure it wasn't un-American.

My bashfulness and backwardness annoyed my older sister very much, and at about the period of which I am writing she began making strong efforts to stir me up. She was convinced that I was in a rut, socially, and she found me a drag in her own social life, which was brisk. She kept trying to throw me with girls, but I always bounced. And whenever she saw a chance she would start the phonograph and grab me, and we would go charging around the parlour in the toils of the one-step, she gripping me as in a death struggle, and I hurling her finally away from me through greater strength. I was a skinny kid but my muscles were hard, and it would have taken an unusually powerful woman to have held me long in the attitude of the dance.

One day, through a set of circumstances I have forgotten, my sister managed to work me into an afternoon engagement she had with some others in New York. To me, at that time, New York was a wonderland largely unexplored. I had been to the Hippodrome a couple of times with my father, and to the Hudson-Fulton Celebration, and to a few matinees, but New York, except as a setting for extravaganzas, was unknown. My sister had heard tales of tea-dancing at the Plaza Hotel. She and a girlfriend of hers and another fellow and myself went there to give it a try. The expedition struck me as a slick piece of arrangement on her part. I was the junior member of the group and had been roped in, I imagine to give symmetry to the occasion. Or perhaps Mother had forbidden my sister to go at all unless another member of the family was along. Whether I was there for symmetry or for decency I can't really remember, but I was there.

The spectacle was a revelation to me. However repulsive the idea of dancing was, I was filled with amazement at the setup. Here were tables where a fellow could sit so close to the dance floor that he was practically on it. And you could order cinnamon toast and from the safety of your chair observe girls and men in close embrace, singing along, the music playing while you ate the toast, and the dancers so near to you that they almost brushed the things off your table as they jogged by. I was impressed. Dancing or no dancing, this was certainly high life, and I knew I was witnessing a scene miles and miles ahead of anything that took place in Mount Vernon. I had never seen anything like it, and a ferment must have begun working in me that afternoon.

Incredible as it seems to me now, I formed the idea of asking Parnell's sister Eileen to accompany me to a tea dance at the Plaza. The plan shaped up in my mind as an expedition of unparalleled worldliness, calculated to stun even the most blasé girl. The fact that I didn't know how to dance must have been a powerful deterrent, but not powerful enough to stop me. As I look back on the affair, it's hard to credit my own memory, and I sometimes wonder if, in fact, the whole business isn't some dream that has gradually gained the status of actuality. A boy with any sense, wishing to become better acquainted with a girl who was "of special interest," would have cut out for himself a more modest assignment to start with—a soda date or a movie date—something within reasonable limits. Not me. I apparently became obsessed with the notion of taking Eileen to the Plaza and not to any darned old drugstore. I had learned the location of the Plaza, and just knowing how to get to it gave me a feeling of confidence. I had learned about cinnamon toast, so I felt able to cope with the waiter when he came along. And I banked heavily on the general splendour of the surroundings and the extreme sophistication of the function to carry the day, I guess.

I was three days getting up nerve to make the phone call. Meantime, I worked out everything in the greatest detail. I heeled myself with a safe amount of money. I looked up trains. I overhauled my clothes and assembled an outfit I believed would meet the test. Then, one night at six o'clock, when Mother and Father went downstairs to dinner, I lingered upstairs and entered the big closet off my bedroom where the wall phone was. There I stood for several minutes, trembling, my hand on the receiver, which hung upside down on the hook. (In our family, the receiver always hung upside down, with the big end up.)

I had rehearsed my first line and my second line. I planned to say, "Hello, can I please speak to Eileen?" Then, when she came to the phone, I planned to say, "Hello, Eileen, this is Elwyn White." From there on, I figured I could ad-lib it.

At last, I picked up the receiver and gave the number. As I had suspected, Eileen's mother answered.

"Can I please speak to Eileen?" I asked, in a low troubled voice.

"Just a minute," said her mother. Then, on second thought, she asked, "Who is it, please?"

"It's Elwyn," I said.

She left the phone, and after quite a while Eileen's voice said "Hello, Elwyn." This threw my second line out of whack, but I stuck to it doggedly.

"Hello, Eileen, this is Elwyn White," I said.

In no time at all I laid the proposition before her. She seemed dazed and asked me to wait a minute. I assume she went into a huddle with her mother. Finally, she said yes, she would like to go tea-dancing with me at the Plaza, and I said fine, I would call for her at quarter past three on Thursday afternoon, or whatever afternoon it was—I've forgotten.

I do not know now, and of course did not know then, just how great was the mental and physical torture Eileen went through that day, but the incident stacks up as a sort of unintentional un-American activity, for which I was solely responsible. It all went off as scheduled: the stately walk to the depot; the solemn train ride, during which we sat staring shyly into the seat in front of us; the difficult walk from Grand Central across Forty-second to Fifth, with pedestrians clipping us and cutting in between us; the bus ride to Fifty-ninth Street; then the Plaza itself, and the cinnamon toast, and the music, and the excitement. The thundering quality of the occasion must have delivered a mental shock to me, deadening my recollection, for I have only the dimmest memory of leading Eileen onto the dance floor to execute two or three unspeakable rounds, in which I vainly tried to adapt my violent sister-and-brother wrestling act into something graceful and appropriate. It must have been awful. And at six o'clock, emerging, I gave no thought to any further entertainment, such as dinner in town. I simply herded Eileen back all the long, dreary way to Mount Vernon and deposited her, a few minutes after seven, on an empty stomach, at her home. Even if I had attempted to dine her, I don't believe it would have been possible; the emotional strain of the afternoon had caused me to perspire uninterruptedly, and any restaurant would have been justified in rejecting me solely on the ground that I was too moist.

Over the intervening years (all thirty-five of them), I've often felt guilty about my afternoon at the Plaza, and a few years ago, during Parnell's investigation of writers, my feeling sometimes took the form of a guilt sequence in which I imagined myself on the stand, in the committee room, being questioned. It went something like this:

PARNELL: Have you ever written for the screen, Mr. White?

ME: No, sir.

PARNELL: Have you ever been, or are you now, a member of the Screen Writers' Guild?

ME: No, sir.

PARNELL: Have you ever been, or are you now, a member of the Communist Party?

ME: No, sir.

Then, in this imaginary guilt sequence of mine, Parnell digs deep and comes up with the big question, calculated to throw me.

PARNELL: Do you recall an afternoon, along about the middle of the second decade of this century, when you took my sister to the Plaza Hotel for tea under the grossly misleading and false pretext that you knew how to dance?

And as my reply comes weakly, "Yes, sir," I hear the murmur run through the committee room and see reporters bending over their notebooks, scribbling hard. In my dread, I am again seated with Eileen at the edge of the dance floor, frightened, stunned, and happy—in my ears the intoxicating drumbeat of the dance, in my throat the dry, bittersweet taste of cinnamon.

I don't know about the guilt, really. I guess a good many girls might say that an excursion such as the one I conducted Eileen on belongs in the un-American category. But there must be millions of aging males now slipping into their anecdotage, who recall their Willie Baxter period with affection, and who remember some similar journey into ineptitude, in that precious, brief moment in life before love's pages, through constant reference, had become dog-eared, and before its narrative, through sheer competence, had lost the first, wild sense of derring-do.

Notes

Aïda a popular nineteenth-century opera by Italian composer Giuseppe Verdi (1813–1901)

Hippodrome a sports arena used for horse shows

blasé exhibiting detachment due to a cynical worldliness

anecdotage the telling of anecdotes, which are accounts of interesting or humorous events; in this instance, a pun on the word "dotage"

Willie Baxter a character in *Seventeen,* an American novel popular in the 1940s, by Booth Tarkington. Baxter was a teenager determined to persuade everyone, including himself, that he was an authentic, full-grown man.

derring-do daring or reckless action

Activities

1. Reread "Afternoon of an American Boy" and find all the references White makes to being "American" or "un-American." What does he mean when he uses the term "un-American"? What underlying comment is he making?

2. White's writing style has been described in the following way: "educated vocabulary, evocative phrasing, specific images, embedded insights, and unexpected wording." Find examples from this essay to support each description. Share your findings with a group.

3. Interview several people of both genders, including peers and adults, about their recollections of first dates. Use this information to write an analysis of the experience of first dates in which you draw on the experiences of E.B. White, your interviewees, and yourself.

A Place to Stand On

Margaret Laurence

Margaret Laurence was born in Neepawa, Manitoba, in 1926. After studying English literature at Winnipeg's United College, she worked as a reporter for the *Winnipeg Citizen*. She lived the beginning of her adult life in England and Africa, eventually settling in Lakefield, Ontario. Laurence is best known for her Manawaka series of books which includes *The Stone Angel* (1964) and *The Diviners* (1974). She also published children's stories, essays, and memoirs. Laurence received many honours, including two Governor General's Literary Awards for Fiction. She was also a fervent social activist. She died in 1987. Laurence's experiences of growing up in Manitoba and living in Africa are important elements in her writing. To what extent do you think place is important in fiction? In what ways have the places where you grew up influenced your development?

> *The creative writer perceives his world once and for all in childhood and adolescence, and his whole career is an effort to illustrate his private world in terms of the great public world we all share.*
>
> —*Graham Greene*, Collected Essays

I believe that Graham Greene is right in this statement. It does not mean that the individual does not change after adolescence. On the contrary, it underlines the necessity for change. For the writer, one way of discovering oneself, of changing from the patterns of childhood and adolescence to those of adulthood, is through the explorations inherent in the writing itself. In the case of a great many writers, this exploration at some point—and perhaps at all points—involves an attempt to understand one's background and one's past, sometimes even a more distant past which one has not personally experienced.

This sort of exploration can be clearly seen in the works of contemporary African writers, many of whom recreate their people's past in novels and plays in order to recover a sense of themselves, an identity and a feeling of value from which they were separated by two or three generations of colonialism and missionizing. They have found it necessary, in other words, to come to terms with their ancestors and their gods in order to be able to accept the past and be at peace with the dead, without being stifled or threatened by that past.

Oddly enough, it was only several years ago, when I began doing some research into contemporary Nigerian writing and its background, that I began to see how much my own writing had followed the same pattern—the attempt to assimilate the past, partly in order to be freed from it, partly in order to try to understand myself and perhaps others of my generation, through seeing where we had come from.

I was fortunate in going to Africa when I did—in my early twenties—because for some years I was so fascinated by the African scene that I was prevented from writing an autobiographical first novel. I don't say there is anything wrong in autobiographical novels, but it would not have been the right thing for me—my view of the prairie town from which I had come was still too prejudiced and distorted by closeness. I had to get farther away from it before I could begin to see it. Also, as it turned out ultimately, the kind of novel which I can best handle is one in which the fictional characters are very definitely *themselves*, not me, the kind of novel in which I can feel a deep sense of connection with the main character without a total identification which for me would prevent a necessary distancing.

I always knew that one day I would have to stop writing about Africa and go back to my own people, my own place of belonging, but when I began to do this, I was extremely nervous about the outcome. I did not consciously choose any particular time in history, or any particular characters. The reverse seemed to be true. The character of Hagar in *The Stone Angel* seemed almost to choose me. Later, though, I recognized that in some way, not at all consciously understood by me at the time, I had had to begin approaching my background and my past through my grandparents' generation, the generation of pioneers of Scots-Presbyterian origin, who had been among the first to people the town I called Manawaka. This was where my own roots began. Other past generations of my father's family had lived in Scotland, but for me, my people's real past—my own real past—was not connected except distantly with Scotland; indeed, this was true for Hagar as well, for she was born in Manawaka.

The name Manawaka is an invented one, but it had been in my mind since I was about seventeen or eighteen, when I first began to think about writing something set in a prairie town. Manawaka is not my hometown of Neepawa—it has elements of Neepawa, especially in some of the descriptions of places, such as the cemetery on the hill or the Wachakwa valley through which ran the small brown river which was the river of my childhood. In almost every way, however, Manawaka was not so much any one prairie town as an amalgam of many prairie towns. Most of all, I like to think, it is simply itself, a town of the mind, my own private world, as Graham Greene says, which one hopes will ultimately relate to the outer world which we all share.

When one thinks of the influence of a place on one's writing, two aspects come to mind. First, the physical presence of the place itself—its geography, its appearance. Second, the people. For me, the second aspect of environment is the most important, although in everything I have written which is set in Canada, whether or not actually set in Manitoba, somewhere some of my memories of the physical appearance of the prairies come in. I had, as a child and as an adolescent, ambiguous feelings about the prairies. I still have them, although they no longer bother me. I wanted then to get out of the small town and go far away, and yet I felt the protectiveness of that atmosphere, too. I felt the loneliness and the isolation of the land itself, and yet I always considered southern Manitoba to be very beautiful, and I still do. I doubt if I will ever live there again, but those poplar bluffs and the blackness of that soil and the way in which the sky is open from one side of the horizon to the other—these are things I will carry inside my skull for as long as I live, with the vividness of recall that only our first home can have for us.

Nevertheless, the people were more important than the place. Hagar in *The Stone Angel* was not drawn from life, but she incorporates many of the qualities of my grandparents' generation. Her speech is their speech, and her gods their gods. I think I never recognized until I wrote that novel just how mixed my own feelings were toward that whole generation of pioneers—how difficult they were to live with, how authoritarian, how unbending, how afraid to show love, many of them, and how willing to show anger. And yet, they had inhabited a wilderness and made it fruitful. They were, in the end, great survivors, and for that I love and value them.

The final exploration of this aspect of my background came when I wrote—over the past six or seven years—*A Bird in the House,* a number of short stories set in Manawaka and based upon my childhood and my childhood family, the only semi-autobiographical fiction I have ever written. I did not realize until I had finished the final story in the series how much all these stories are dominated by the figure of my maternal grandfather, who came of Irish Protestant stock. Perhaps it was through writing these stories that I finally came to see my grandfather not only as the repressive authoritarian figure from my childhood, but also as a boy who had to leave school in Ontario when he was about twelve, after his father's death, and who as a young man went to Manitoba by sternwheeler and walked the fifty miles from Winnipeg to Portage la Prairie, where he settled for some years before moving to Neepawa. He was a very hard man in many ways, but he had had a very hard life. I don't think I knew any of this, really knew it, until I had finished those stories. I don't think I ever knew, either, until that moment how much I owed to him. One sentence, near the end of the final story, may show what I mean: "I had feared and fought the old man, yet he proclaimed himself in my veins."

My writing, then, has been my own attempt to come to terms with the past. I see this process as the gradual one of freeing oneself from the stultifying aspect of the past, while at the same time beginning to see its true value—which, in the case of my own people (by which I mean the total community, not just my particular family), was a determination to survive against whatever odds.

The theme of survival—not just physical survival, but the preservation of some human dignity and in the end some human warmth and ability to reach out and touch others—this is, I have come to think, an almost inevitable theme for a writer such as I, who came from a Scots-Irish background of stern values and hard work and puritanism, and who grew up during the drought and depression of the thirties and then the war.

This theme runs through two of my novels other than *The Stone Angel* (in which it is, of course, the dominant theme). In *A Jest of God* and *The Fire-Dwellers*, both Rachel and Stacey are in their very different ways threatened by the past and by the various inadequacies each feels in herself. In the end, and again in their very different ways and out of their very different dilemmas, each finds within herself an ability to survive—not just to go on living, but to change and to move into new areas of life. Neither book is optimistic. Optimism in this world seems impossible to me. But in each novel there is some hope, and that is a different thing entirely.

If Graham Greene is right—as I think he is—in his belief that a writer's career is "an effort to illustrate his private world in terms of the great public world we all share," then I think it is understandable that so much of my writing relates to the kind of prairie town in which I was born and in which I first began to be aware of myself. Writing, for me, has to be set firmly in some soil, some place, some outer and inner territory which might be described in anthropological terms as "cultural background." But I do not believe that this kind of writing needs therefore to be parochial. If Hagar in *The Stone Angel* has any meaning, it is the same as that of an old woman anywhere, having to deal with the reality of dying. On the other hand, she is not an old woman anywhere. She is very much a person who belongs in the same kind of prairie Scots-Presbyterian background as I do, and it was, of course, people like Hagar who created that background, with all its flaws and its strengths. In a poem entitled *Roblin Mills, Circa 1842,* Al Purdy said:

> They had their being once
> and left a place to stand on

They did indeed, and this is the place we are standing on, for better and for worse.

I remember saying once, three or four years ago, that I felt I had written myself out of that prairie town. I know better now. My future writing may not be set in that town—and indeed, my novel, *The Fire-Dwellers,* was set in Vancouver. I may not always write fiction set in Canada. But somewhere, perhaps in the memories of some characters, Manawaka will probably always be there, simply because whatever I am was shaped and formed in that sort of place, and my way of seeing, however much it may have changed over the years, remains in some enduring way that of a small-town prairie person.

Notes

Graham Greene renowned English novelist (1904–1991), who explored social and moral issues in novels often set in foreign countries

research into contemporary Nigerian writing a reference to *Long Drums and Cannons* (1968), Laurence's study of Nigerian literature

Roblin Mills, circa 1842 a reference to Al Purdy's poem about a pioneer settlement near Belleville in southern Ontario

Activities

1. In this essay, Laurence discusses the role of place in writing. She suggests that, for her, place has two characteristics: the physical environment and the people who inhabit it. Explain the ways in which Laurence felt ambivalent about the prairie community in which she grew up and about the people who lived there. Compare her feelings about people and places from her past with your own experience.

2. Prepare an analysis of the structure Laurence uses in this essay. Begin by selecting five major paragraphs. For each, reread the opening sentence. What is the main topic of the paragraph? What details in the paragraph support and develop the topic? How are the topics of individual paragraphs connected to the main topic and thesis of her paper?

3. In this essay, Margaret Laurence refers to several of the books she has written. Make a list in your journal of each title and record what she tells her readers about each book in this essay. Locate and read one of the books and prepare a book review of it. Focus your review on Laurence's use of physical space and the people who inhabit it.

Another Viewpoint: Society

The early part of Laurence's career was spent in Africa. Several of her early books were set in Africa or dealt with African issues. In this essay, Laurence suggests that, in her view, contemporary African writers "recreate their people's past in novels and plays in order to recover a sense of themselves, an identity and a feeling of value from which they were separated by two or three generations of colonialism and missionizing." Find an example of contemporary African fiction and assess to what extent Laurence's observation is accurate.

Chameleons and Codas

Patricia Conrad

Patricia Conrad lives in Calgary, Alberta. In this selection, Conrad chronicles her experiences growing up as a child of hearing-impaired parents. In our society, we are aware that sometimes hearing-impaired people are treated insensitively, whether intentionally or not, by the hearing world. What are some examples of insensitivity to which the children of deaf adults might be subjected? What strategies do you think could help facilitate respect between the non-hearing and the hearing worlds?

What I know of life and people, I learned as I juggled two worlds and two languages. As a hearing daughter born to deaf parents in rural Alberta, I lived at the crossroads of two cultures, a foreigner on the fringes of both. I had the ability to hear, so how could I understand the deaf experience? Yet I was never truly "hearing" either; a piece of my heart remained staunchly "deaf." So I became a chameleon, changing my colour as I shifted from one world to the other.

Sound had little meaning for Mom and Dad; he had been deaf since birth and she lost her hearing at the age of six because of illness. Their world was visual, not auditory, their conversations signed rather than spoken. Their language (American Sign Language, or ASL) became ours too; we "talked" with our hands and "listened" with our eyes. My siblings and I, all hearing, had licence to shout, sing, or yodel at will. No one told us to be quiet. We lived near a busy highway, with semi-trailer trucks roaring by at all hours. My parents were oblivious to the din, and we kids were so used to it we just tuned it out. My siblings and I squabbled without parental intervention, and learned the hard way to resolve our conflicts—with little finesse, alas; usually it boiled down to who yelled the loudest or gave up first.

Although sound was meaningless, sight and touch were vital to my parents. Vibration got us kids in trouble more than once. We dared not race down the stairway while Dad was napping; the shudder of the floor woke him instantly.

Like most deaf folk, my parents relied on visual and tactile cues to get each other's attention, stomping on the floor or flicking the light switch. We kids did the same, or else tapped a shoulder. We learned early that such deaf cultural norms are taboo in the hearing world. Foot-stomping is too loud, light-flashing too rude, and touching people (even a shoulder tap) too intimate.

At school, I excelled in my classes because it seemed the hearing thing to do, and besides, didn't it prove my parents' aptitude for raising us? I was a social dud but impressed my teachers.

Only when my two worlds collided did my chameleon soul falter, for how can one be two colours at once? Whenever my parents signed in public, curious onlookers stared, fascinated by their splendid expressions and fluttering hands. I grew fiercely protective, scowling at the oglers or blocking their view. I like to think I terrorized the bejesus out of some, though I cannot say for certain they noticed me at all.

Before the days of professional interpreters, TTYs (telephones with print displays), and enlightened attitudes, my siblings and I talked for our parents, relayed phone messages, and became their communication link to the hearing world. I took on the task of enlightening the insensitive, although results were variable. Many had not learned the "yelling the loudest or giving up first" method of conflict resolution. Others were not as bent on their own enlightenment as I was.

"Hey, is your mom deaf and dumb?" a classmate asked me once. Resisting the urge to respond in kind ("Hey, did your mom raise you to be hearing and thoughtless?"), I shot back: "She's deaf, but she's not dumb!" Hardly eloquent, but it addled him enough that he backed off.

My father, too, was saddled with "disabled" and "handicapped" stereotypes. "Can your daddy *drive*?" a stranger asked, incredulous, as Dad and I strode toward our car one day. It perplexed me when adults knew so little. (I was chest-high to my father and a half-dozen years shy of driving age. Just who did this guy think was about to take the wheel?) "Yes," I blurted, an answer so profound it surely bowled him over.

Indeed, my parents' disability was not their deafness, but people's attitudes toward it. At home, and with deaf friends (or anyone who used ASL), they conversed easily and fluently. With others, they wrote notes; both my parents carried notepads and pens everywhere. Dad especially was a master of mime, and would act out anything, even at the risk of looking ridiculous.

"Was it different, having deaf parents?" people ask. Different than what? It was the only life I knew, as normal to me as anyone else's is to them—and as precious.

Good parenting doesn't require functional ears; nor does good loving. We had plenty of both. Daddy was a farmer, a sociable fellow who loved teasing and rambunctious play with his kids. Mom was more shy and more reserved around people, but I adored her; she was the most unselfish being I ever knew. Mama's single-minded goal in life was to raise us well and release us to the world equipped with all we'd need, plus a healthy dose of common sense. She succeeded admirably.

As I grew into adulthood, I fretted that I would one day be forced to choose between my two worlds, and what good is a chameleon with only one colour? So I opted for careers that would keep me in both: teaching deaf students, freelance interpreting, and teaching interpreter trainees.

Today adults like me are labelled CODAs, an acronym for "children of deaf adults." But I prefer the deeper meaning of the word coda: an independent, concluding musical passage. Even a diehard chameleon yearns to one day find her own niche, and combine the best of both worlds into a multicoloured melody that is hers alone.

What I learned of life and people, chameleons and codas, I gained from two diverse communities. Growing up with deaf parents taught me resiliency, compassion in the face of ignorance, and the value of human diversity. In viewing the world from more than one angle, I learned to cherish my parents' gift to me: fluency in two languages, understanding of two cultures, access to two worlds—and the tools to create an independent coda with my own unique rhythm.

Now, if you'll excuse me, I believe my music's playing…

Activities

1. The author says, "Indeed, my parents' disability was not their deafness, but people's attitudes toward it." In a small group, identify and discuss what you think Conrad's purpose is in writing this selection. What led you to your conclusions? How effectively do you think Conrad has achieved her purpose for writing? Share your group's ideas with other groups in the class.

2. The author refers to herself as a chameleon and a coda. Review the essay to identify each occurrence of the two metaphors. What is the effect of her use of each metaphor? How does her use of these two metaphors relate to her main idea or theme?

3. Hearing-impaired people and their friends and families use ways other than voice to communicate with each other. Use the Internet and other sources to conduct some research about American/International sign language, handspeak, finger spelling, and any other forms of communication used by hearing-impaired people. Prepare the text for a radio or television broadcast in which you describe the key features of these non-verbal communication systems.

Another Viewpoint: Society

Consider the following statement by the author: "I learned to cherish my parents' gift to me: fluency in two languages, understanding of two cultures, access to two worlds." If possible, contact some people in your community who are the children or siblings of hearing-impaired adults and interview them about whether Conrad's statement reflects their experiences. What are some of the characteristics of the culture of hearing-impaired people and their children? How is it different from that of people in the hearing world? Compare your findings with those of other students who conducted interviews.

Elegy in Stone

Steven Heighton

Steven Heighton was born in Toronto, Ontario, in 1961. Heighton studied at Queen's University in Kingston, Ontario, the city he subsequently made his home. He is a writer of poetry, essays, and fiction. Heighton was awarded the Gerald Lampert Prize and received a gold medal for fiction at the National Magazine Awards. His book of poems *The Ecstasy of Skeptics* (1995) was a finalist for the Governor General's Literary Award. In this selection, Heighton describes his visit to the war memorial at Vimy Ridge in France. Consider the war memorial in your community or another one you have visited. What objects, words, and other features are included in this memorial? If you were designing a war memorial, which features would you include and which would you leave out? What impact would you expect these features to have on visitors to the memorial?

Vimy Ridge, April 1992

The park's entrance—a border crossing, really—was modest enough: a small sign you could easily miss if you were driving past. But we were on foot. And though it turned out to be a much longer walk than we'd expected, it was a good place to walk, the fields along the road billowing with mustard, wheat, and poppies, the oaks and maples fragrant with new growth. We could be in Canada, I thought—then remembered that, for official purposes, we were.

The wind as we neared the ridge grew chilly, the sky grey.

Before long the road passed through a forest of natural growth and entered an old plantation of white pines, thick and towering, a spacious colonnade receding in the gloom. Fences appeared along the road, then signs warning us not to walk among the trees where sheep foraged above grassed-in trenches, shell holes, unexploded mines. In the blue-green, stained-glass light of the forest, the near-silence was eerie, solemn, as in the cathedral at Arras.

Finally we heard voices, saw a file of parked cars ahead through the trees, and came out at the main exhibit site of the park, some distance below the monument that crowns Vimy Ridge. Here, in 1917, from a line of trenches now preserved in concrete and filled daily with French tourists, the Canadian troops had launched their attack. Preserved like-wise is the first obstacle they had met: the front-line German trench, barely a grenade's throw away. This whites-of-their-eyes proximity sur-prised us and made stories of verbal fraternization between the lines—of back and forth banter in broken English and German—all the more plausible, and poignant.

A few years after the end of the First World War the government of France gave Canada a sizable chunk of the cratered, barren terrain around Vimy Ridge, where 20,000 Canadians fell before the ridge was finally taken on 12 April 1917. Today many Canadian visitors to France pass the memorial park en route to Arras or Lille without realizing the site is officially a small piece of Canada. Though "plot" might be a better word, for although the trenches where Canadian and Allied soldiers lived and died during their siege have healed over, the fields are scarred with ceme-teries and the woodlots filled with unmarked graves.

We'd arrived the night before in nearby Arras, finding a hotel and visiting the town's medieval cathedral. The hotel manager had elabo-rately regretted that we hadn't come two weeks earlier, on Easter Monday, when French President François Mitterrand, and Prime Minister Brian Mulroney and a handful of Vimy veterans had arrived for the seventy-fifth anniversary of the ridge's fall. I told the manager that I'd read about the ceremony back home, but felt the park was probably best experienced without the crowds and fanfare of an official visit. I could have said more but didn't trust my French enough to try explaining how disturbed

I'd been by photographs of those heads of state and their aides beaming glibly among the hunched veterans, whose nation-building sacrifice was clearly far from the politicians' minds.

Nation-building sacrifice sounds far too much like the kind of pious, pushy rhetoric I've learned to mistrust and fear, yet for years the bloody achievement of the Canadians on Vimy Ridge did stand, like the ridge itself, as a landmark, a high point around which the idea of a distinct Canadian identity could form.

"*C'est magnifique,*" the manager told us when we explained we wanted to go. "*Magnifique.*"

At the park's main exhibit site we went into a small, undistinguished brick building to see about a tour of the tunnel system under the trenches. The young guides, in Parks Canada uniforms, explained that we'd just missed the tour and unfortunately would have to wait for the next. But as we turned and went outside to confer, they must have noticed the small Canadian flag sewn onto my backpack, because one of them came out after us and beckoned us toward the tunnels. "You should have told us you're Canadian," he said with a soft Manitoba-French accent. "We don't get all that many."

The low-ceilinged, labyrinthine "subways"—where men ate and slept before the attack and couriers ran with their messages and sappers set charges under the German lines—have been carefully restored, but more or less unembellished. The impression, as above in the trenches, was sobering. I was relieved that this sad, clammy underworld had not been brightened up into some gaudy monument to Our Glorious Past; I was relieved that it still looked, and felt, like a tomb. It reminded me of the tunnels of the besieged Huguenots under the cathedral in Arras.

It was good to get back up into the daylight. We agreed to meet Mario and the other guides for a beer that night in town.

We followed the road up the last part of the ridge to the monument, wind blowing over the bare fields in a steady barrage. Seventy-five years before, the Canadians had advanced at dawn through driving sleet and snow, and now, nearing the exposed crown of the ridge, we could see how weather of that intensity must be quite common. The monument stands atop Hill 145, the Canadians' final objective and the highest point for miles around—but on the morning of the attack it must have been invisible through the snow and the timed barrage behind which the men were advancing.

Before the hilltop and the monument came in sight I'd felt uneasy, recalling the many monuments I had seen that stylized or made over the true face of war so as to safeguard an ideology, to comply with aesthetic conventions, or to make life easier for the recruiters of future wars. But as we neared the monument—two enormous white limestone pillars that meet at the base to form a kind of elongated U—I was impressed. And, as before, relieved. I'd first become anxious when the hotel keeper had told us to expect something "magnifique," but now I saw that in a sense he was right, for here was something magnificent in its simplicity, its solemnity, its understatement. And brilliant in its implication, because the pillars did not quite form a triumphant V, as you might expect, but a shape uncannily resembling the sights mounted on machine guns of the First World War—the kind that claimed tens of thousands of Canadian lives in the war and several thousand on the morning of the attack.

I don't believe such resemblances can be assigned to chance. An artist's hand is always guided in large part by the subconscious. I don't know whether the architect of the Vimy monument was ever asked about his intentions, conscious or subconscious, but in a sense they're no longer the point; unlike so many other old monuments, Walter Seymour Allward's is strikingly modern because of the way it surpasses, or second-guesses, all conventional intent.

We drew closer. Our feeling that this monolith was more a cenotaph, a vast elegy in stone instead of petrified hot air, grew stronger. And with it a feeling of pride. But a kind of pride very different, I think, from the tribal, intolerant swagger so many monuments have been built to inspire. A shy pride in our country's awkwardness at blowing its own horn—because sooner or later every country that does blow its own horn, with flamboyance, starts looking for somebody else to outblow. A pride in our reluctance—our seeming inability—to canonize brave, scared, betrayed adolescents as bearded heroes of mythic dimension, larger than life. Unreal.

And the monument is a cenotaph: we find its base inscribed with the names of the 11,285 Canadians whose final resting place is unknown. Blown to pieces. Lost in the mud, or buried anonymously in the graveyards below the ridge. The parade of names marches on and on, a kind of elegy whose heartbreaking syllables are English- and French-Canadian, Ojibway, Ukrainian, Dutch, German, Italian, Japanese…

Many are the names of our own distant relations.

The figures carved on and around the monument, though dated in style, are not blowing trumpets or beating breasts or drums. They seem instead to grieve. We round the monument and the Douai Plain fans out below us: another figure, much larger, cloaked, stands apart at the edge of the monument overlooking the plain. Behind her a sparsely worded inscription, in English and French, tells of the ridge's fall.

The figure, we will learn later that night, is Canada, "mourning her lost sons."

Tonight in Arras we'll learn other things as well from the Canadian guides we meet for a beer. That the whole park is planted with shrubs and trees from Canada. That 11,285 pines were planted after the war for every lost man whose name appears on the monument. That the prime minister's Easter visit was indeed a grand and lavish affair—everything the monument itself is not—but that the old soldiers on display carried themselves with dignity and a quiet, inconspicuous pride. And it's that feeling we end up coming back to toward the end of the night when the drinks have made us a bit more open and, I suppose, sentimental. Because we learn that these young expatriates have all felt just as we have about the austerity of the Vimy monument—and, by implication, the Canadian tendency to downplay the "heroism" of our achievements, to refuse to idealize, poeticize, and thus censor an obscene, man-made reality.

Or am I wrong to offer Canada these drunken toasts on a virtue that's largely a matter of historical and political necessity? Perhaps what I'm trying to say is that Canadians are lucky to have been spared, so far, that sense of collective power combined with intense tribal identity that makes every imperial nation so arrogant, competitive, and brutal. And as our friends guide us back to our hotel, I wonder if Canadians will ever stop berating themselves for not believing—as too many other nations have believed, and keep on believing—that they're better than others, that they're the chosen, the elect, the Greatest Nation on Earth, with God on their side.

"Make sure to let people back home know about the memorial," Mario calls out as we enter our hotel. And I reflect that a visit to the monument and the many battlefields around it might help convince some Canadians that there are worse things than uncertainty and understatement.

And if the monument doesn't convince them, or the battlefields, then surely the graveyards will. In the park or within walking distance lie thirty cemeteries where the remains of over 7,000 Canadians are buried. They are peaceful places, conscientiously tended. Flowers bloom over every grave. Many are poppies. The paint on the crosses is fresh, a dazzling white in the April sun. Here, no doubt, many of the boys whose names appear on the monument are actually buried, beneath long files of anonymous crosses, or stones ranked like chairs in a vast, deserted cathedral. Another endless parade, this time of the nameless—though here and there we do find stones inscribed with a name, an age. David Mahon, 1901–1917. IN MEMORY OF OUR DEAR AND ONLY CHILD.

We recite the words aloud, but this time the feeling they inspire has little to do with pride. The huge limestone gunsight looms above us on the ridge as we enter yet another aisle, and read, yet again:

A SOLDIER OF THE GREAT WAR

A Canadian Regiment

Known Unto God

Notes

Huguenots French Protestants who, during the sixteenth and seventeenth centuries, were in frequent conflict with French Catholics. Because of continued persecution, many Huguenots immigrated to foreign countries, including Canada; from a combination of the Old High German word *eid*, meaning "oath" and *ginōz*, meaning "companion"

Activities

1. The Battle of Vimy Ridge has been described as a defining moment in Canadian history. What did you learn from this essay about the battle itself, Canada's role in it, and the significance of the battle for Canada and its allies?

2. Steven Heighton wrote this essay when he was a young man. In what ways might this essay have been different in style and content if it had been written by someone older? Include examples from the essay to support your interpretation.

3. Interview someone who has experienced war first-hand. Use the results of your interview and those of other students in the class to prepare a commemorative booklet that could be used on Remembrance Day. Help edit each other's writing by focusing on elements of style that make the experiences as vivid as possible for the readers.

Another Viewpoint: Archetypal Patterns

In his essay, Heighton makes the observation that "an artist's hand is always guided in large part by the subconscious." This statement is an expression of the psychoanalytic approach to art and literature that emphasizes the role of the unconscious in the creative process. Take a second look at the essay. To what extent do you think Heighton's own unconscious influenced the style and content of this essay? Provide evidence from the text to support your observations.

The Death of the Moth

Virginia Woolf

Virginia Woolf, one of the most important writers of the twentieth century, was born in London, England, in 1882. Woolf received little formal education. However, she had an inquiring mind and educated herself by reading from her father's library. After his death, she moved to the London neighbourhood known as Bloomsbury and was part of a brilliant circle of writers and intellectuals known as the Bloomsbury Group. Woolf's best-known novels include *Mrs. Dalloway* (1925) and *To the Lighthouse* (1927). Together with her husband, Leonard Woolf, she established and ran Hogarth Press, which published some of the most innovative literature of the day. Virginia Woolf died in 1941. In some religious or ethical systems, the death of a creature such as a moth is considered to be as significant as the death of a person. What is your response to this idea?

Moths that fly by day are not properly to be called moths; they do not excite that pleasant sense of dark autumn nights and ivy-blossom which the commonest yellow-underwing asleep in the shadow of the curtain never fails to rouse in us. They are hybrid creatures, neither gay like butterflies nor sombre like their own species. Nevertheless the present specimen, with his narrow hay-coloured wings, fringed with a tassel of the same colour, seemed to be content with life. It was a pleasant morning, mid-September, mild, benignant, yet with a keener breath than that of the summer months. The plow was already scoring the field opposite

◄ *Virginia Woolf, 1902, George Charles Beresford*

the window, and where the share had been, the earth was pressed flat and gleamed with moisture. Such vigour came rolling in from the fields and the down beyond that it was difficult to keep the eyes strictly turned upon the book. The rooks too were keeping one of their annual festivities; soaring round the treetops until it looked as if a vast net with thousands of black knots in it had been cast up into the air; which, after a few moments, sank slowly down upon the trees until every twig seemed to have a knot at the end of it. Then, suddenly, the net would be thrown into the air again in a wider circle this time, with the utmost clamour and vociferation, as though to be thrown into the air and settle slowly down upon the treetops were a tremendously exciting experience.

The same energy which inspired the rooks, the ploughmen, the horses, and even, it seemed, the lean bare-backed downs, sent the moth fluttering from side to side of his square of the windowpane. One could not help watching him. One was, indeed, conscious of a queer feeling of pity for him. The possibilities of pleasure seemed that morning so enormous and so various that to have only a moth's part in life, and a day moth's at that, appeared a hard fate, and his zest in enjoying his meagre opportunities to the full, pathetic. He flew vigorously to one corner of his compartment, and, after waiting there a second, flew across to the other. What remained for him but to fly to a third corner and then to a fourth? That was all he could do, in spite of the size of the downs, the width of the sky, the far-off smoke of houses, and the romantic voice, now and then, of a steamer out at sea. What he could do he did. Watching him, it seemed as if a fibre, very thin but pure, of the enormous energy of the world had been thrust into his frail and diminutive body. As often as he crossed the pane, I could fancy that a thread of vital light became visible. He was little or nothing but life.

Yet, because he was so small, and so simple a form of the energy that was rolling in at the open window and driving its way through so many narrow and intricate corridors in my own brain and in those of other human beings, there was something marvellous as well as pathetic about him. It was as if someone had taken a tiny bead of pure life and decking it as lightly as possible with down and feathers, had set it dancing and zigzagging to show us the true nature of life. Thus displayed one could not get over the strangeness of it. One is apt to forget all about life, seeing it humped and bossed and garnished and cumbered so that it has to move with the greatest circumspection and dignity. Again, the thought of all that life might have been had he been born in any other shape caused one to view his simple activities with a kind of pity.

After a time, tired by his dancing apparently, he settled on the window ledge in the sun, and, the queer spectacle being at an end, I forgot about him. Then, looking up, my eye was caught by him. He was trying to resume his dancing, but seemed either so stiff or so awkward that he could only flutter to the bottom of the windowpane; and when he tried to fly across it he failed. Being intent on other matters I watched these futile attempts for a time without thinking, unconsciously waiting for him to resume his flight, as one waits for a machine, that has stopped momentarily, to start again without considering the reason of its failure. After perhaps a seventh attempt he slipped from the wooden ledge and fell, fluttering his wings, on to his back on the windowsill. The helplessness of his attitude roused me. It flashed upon me that he was in difficulties; he could no longer raise himself; his legs struggled vainly. But, as I stretched out a pencil, meaning to help him to right himself, it came over me that the failure and awkwardness were the approach of death. I laid the pencil down again.

The legs agitated themselves once more. I looked as if for the enemy against which he struggled. I looked out of doors. What had happened there? Presumably it was midday, and work in the fields had stopped. Stillness and quiet had replaced the previous animation. The birds had taken themselves off to feed in the brooks. The horses stood still. Yet the power was there all the same, massed outside, indifferent, impersonal, not attending to anything in particular. Somehow it was opposed to the little hay-coloured moth. It was useless to try to do anything. One could only watch the extraordinary efforts made by those tiny legs against an oncoming doom which could, had it chosen, have submerged an entire city, not merely a city, but masses of human beings; nothing, I knew, had any chance against death. Nevertheless after a pause of exhaustion the legs fluttered again. It was superb, this last protest, and so frantic that he succeeded at last in righting himself. One's sympathies, of course, were all on the side of life. Also, when there was nobody to care or to know, this gigantic effort on the part of an insignificant little moth, against a power of such magnitude, to retain what no one else valued or desired to keep, moved one strangely. Again, somehow, one saw life, a pure bead. I lifted the pencil again, useless though I knew it to be. But even as I did so, the unmistakable tokens of death showed themselves. The body relaxed, and instantly grew stiff. The struggle was over. The insignificant little creature now knew death. As I looked at the dead moth, this minute wayside triumph of so great a force over so mean an antagonist filled me with wonder. Just as life had been strange a few minutes before, so death was now as strange. The moth having righted himself now lay most decently and uncomplainingly composed. O yes, he seemed to say, death is stronger than I am.

Notes

benignant mild and serene

share in this instance, the blade of a plough

down in this instance, an undulating, treeless upland

rooks European and Asiatic crows with a hoarse chirp

vociferation loud, insistent, unpleasant noise

bossed embossed, ornamented

garnished decorated, embellished

cumbered hindered, burdened

circumspection cautiousness, prudence

wayside along the way

mean in this instance, unimposing or insignificant

Activities

1. According to the American philosopher and essayist Henry David Thoreau, "There is no such thing as pure *objective* observation. For your observation to be interesting—to be significant—it must be *subjective.*" Discuss "The Death of the Moth" in terms of this quotation. In what sense, if any, would you say that this essay is significant to you? Explain.

2. State in your own words the thesis of this essay. Create an outline or diagram showing how the essay is structured. How is time used in this essay? How does the author move back and forth between the external world and a reflective contemplation of it?

3. On the Internet or at your library, locate a copy of Virginia Woolf's *Monday or Tuesday,* a book of early short stories representative of the *stream-of-consciousness* style of writing. Scan the book to find a story that interests you and read it. Then write an essay analyzing the use and effectiveness of stream-of-consciousness.

Another Viewpoint: Critical Approaches

Using the Internet and other resources, research the Bloomsbury Group to which Virginia Woolf belonged. Who were the other members of the group and for which works are they best known? What were the commonalities in their approach to life and literature? Present the results of your investigation in a research essay or class presentation.

Guy Lafleur

Ken Dryden

Ken Dryden was born in Islington, Ontario, in 1947. During the 1970s, he was the all-star goaltender with the Montreal Canadiens. In his rookie year, Dryden won the Calder Trophy; he also won the Vezina Trophy five times as the league's top goaltender. He sat out the 1974–75 NHL season to finish his law degree. A member of both the Hockey and the Sports halls of fame, Dryden has continued to find success as a lawyer, writer, sports commentator, lecturer, consultant, and, most recently, as the president and general manager of the Toronto Maple Leafs. He is the author of several books, including *The Game* (1983), which was nominated for a Governor General's Literary Award. What is it about professional athletes that appeals to us? Some people think that it is important for well-known athletes to act as role models in their personal conduct, while others argue that we should simply judge them on their athletic ability. What is your opinion?

The Forum is disturbingly empty: just a few players sit quietly cocooned away in a dressing room; twenty-five or thirty staff work in distant upstairs offices; throughout the rest of its vast insides a few dozen men are busy washing, painting, fixing, tidying things up. There is one other person. Entering the corridor to the dressing room, I hear muffled, reverberating sounds from the ice, and before I can see who it is, I know it's Lafleur. Like a kid on a backyard rink, he skates by himself many

◀ *Guy Lafleur*

minutes before anyone joins him, shooting pucks easily off the boards, watching them rebound, moving skates and gloved hands wherever his inventive instincts direct them to go. Here, far from the expedience of a game, away from defenders and linemates who shackle him to their banal predictability, alone with his virtuoso skills, it is his time to create.

The Italians have a phrase, *inventa la partita.* Translated, it means to "invent the game." A phrase often used by soccer coaches and journalists, it is now, more often than not, used as a lament. For in watching modern players with polished but plastic skills, they wonder at the passing of soccer *genius*—Pelé, di Stefano, Puskas—players whose minds and bodies in not so rare moments created something unfound in coaching manuals, a new and continuously changing game for others to aspire to.

It is a loss they explain many ways. In the name of team play, there is no time or place for individual virtuosity, they say; it is a game now taken over by coaches, by technocrats and autocrats who empty players' minds to control their bodies, reprogramming them with X's and O's, driving them to greater *efficiency* and *work rate,* to move *systems* faster, to move games faster, until achieving mindless pace. Others fix blame more on the other side: on smothering defences played with the same technical sophistication, efficiency, and work rate, but in the nature of defence, easier to play. Still others argue it is the professional sports culture itself which says that games are not won on good plays, but by others' mistakes, where the safe and sure survive, and the creative and not-so-sure may not.

But a few link it to a different kind of cultural change, the loss of what they call "street soccer": the mindless hours spent with a ball next to your feet, walking with it as if with a family pet, to school, to a store, or anywhere, playing with it, learning new things about it and about yourself, in time, as with any good companion, developing an *understanding.* In a much less busy time undivided by TV, rock music, or the clutter of modern lessons, it was a child's diversion from having nothing else to do. And, appearances to the contrary, it was creative diversion. But now, with more to do, and with a sophisticated, competitive society pressing on the younger and younger the need for training and skills, its time has run out. Soccer has moved away from the streets and playgrounds to soccer fields, from impromptu games to uniforms and referees, from any time to specific, scheduled time; it has become an *activity* like anything else, organized and maximized, done right or not at all. It has become something to be taught and learned, then tested in games; the answer at the back of the book, the one and only answer. So other time, time not spent with teams in practices or games, deemed wasteful and inefficient, has become time not spent at soccer.

Recently, in Hungary, a survey was conducted asking soccer players from 1910 to the present how much each practised a day. The answer, on a gradually shrinking scale, was three hours early in the century to eight minutes a day today. Though long memories can forget, and inflate what they don't forget, if the absolute figures are doubtful, the point is nonetheless valid. Today, except in the barrios of Latin America, in parts of Africa and Asia, "street soccer" is dead, and many would argue that with it has gone much of soccer's creative opportunity.

When Guy Lafleur was five years old, his father built a small rink in the backyard of their home in Thurso, Quebec. After school and on weekends, the rink was crowded with Lafleur and his friends, but on weekdays, rushing through lunch before returning to school, it was his alone for half an hour or more. A few years later, anxious for more ice time, on Saturday and Sunday mornings he would sneak in the back door of the local arena, finding his way unseen through the engine room, under the seats, and onto the ice. There, from 7:30 until just before the manager awakened about 11, he played alone; then quickly left. Though he was soon discovered, as the manager was also coach of his team, Lafleur was allowed to continue, by himself, and then a few years later with some of his friends.

There is nothing unique to this story; only its details differ from many others like it. But because it's about Lafleur it is notable. At the time, there were thousands like him across Canada on other noon-hour rinks, in other local arenas, doing the same. It was when he got older and nothing changed that his story became special. For as others in the whirl of more games, more practices, more off-ice diversions, more travel, and everything else gave up solitary time as boring and unnecessary, Lafleur did not. When he moved to Quebec City at fourteen to play for the Remparts, the ice at the big Colisée was unavailable at other times, so he began arriving early for the team's 6 p.m. practices, going on the ice at 5, more than thirty minutes before any of his teammates joined him. Now, many years later, the story unchanged, it seems more and more remarkable to us. In clichéd observation some would say it is a case of the great and dedicated superstar who is first on the ice, last off. But he is not. When practice ends, Lafleur leaves, and ten or twelve others remain behind, skating and shooting with Ruel. But every day we're in Montreal, at 11 a.m., an hour before Bowman steps from the dressing room as signal for practice to begin, Lafleur goes onto the ice with a bucket of pucks to be alone.

Not long ago, thinking of the generations of Canadians who learned hockey on rivers and ponds, I collected my skates and with two friends drove up the Gatineau River north of Ottawa. We didn't know it at the time, but the ice conditions we found were rare, duplicated only a few times the previous decade. The combination of a sudden thaw and freezing rain in the days before had melted winter-high snow, and with temperatures dropping rapidly overnight, the river was left with miles of smooth glare ice. Growing up in the suburbs of a large city, I had played on a river only once before, and then as a goalie. On this day, I came to the Gatineau to find what a river of ice and a solitary feeling might mean to a game.

We spread ourselves rinks apart, breaking into river-wide openings for passes that sometimes connected, and other times sent us hundreds of feet after what we had missed. Against the wind or with it, the sun glaring in our eyes or at our backs, we skated for more than three hours, periodically tired, continuously renewed. The next day I went back again, this time alone. Before I got bored with myself an hour or two later, with no one watching and nothing to distract me, loose and daring, joyously free, I tried things I had never tried before, my hands and feet discovering new patterns and directions, and came away feeling as if something was finally clear.

The Canadian game of hockey was weaned on long northern winters uncluttered by things to do. It grew up on ponds and rivers, in big open spaces, unorganized, often solitary, only occasionally moved into arenas for practices or games. In recent generations, that has changed. Canadians have moved from farms and towns to cities and suburbs; they've discovered skis, snowmobiles, and southern vacations; they've civilized winter and moved it indoors. A game we once played on rivers and ponds, later on streets and driveways and in backyards, we now play in arenas, in full team uniform, with coaches and referees, or to an ever-increasing extent we don't play at all. For, once a game is organized, unorganized games seem a wasteful use of time; and once a game moves indoors, it won't move outdoors again. Hockey has become suburbanized, and as part of our suburban middle-class culture, it has changed.

Put in uniform at six or seven, by the time a boy reaches the NHL, he is a veteran of close to 1,000 games—30-minute games, later 32-, then 45-, finally 60-minute games, played more than twice a week, more than seventy times a year between late September and late March. It is more games from a younger age, over a longer season than ever before. But it is less hockey than ever before. For, every time a twelve-year-old boy plays a 30-minute game, sharing the ice with teammates, he plays only about ten minutes. And ten minutes a game, anticipated and prepared for all day, travelled to and from, dressed and undressed for, means ten minutes of hockey a day, more than two days a week, more than seventy days a hockey season. And every day that a twelve-year-old plays only ten minutes, he doesn't play two hours on a backyard rink, or longer on school or playground rinks during weekends and holidays.

It all has to do with the way we look at free time. Constantly preoccupied with time and keeping ourselves busy (we have come to answer the ritual question "How are you?" with what we apparently equate with good health, "Busy"), we treat non-school, non-sleeping, or non-eating time, unbudgeted free time, with suspicion and no little fear. For, while it may offer opportunity to learn and do new things, we worry that the time we once spent reading, kicking a ball, or mindlessly coddling a puck might be used destructively, in front of TV, or "getting into trouble" in endless ways. So we organize free time, scheduling it into lessons—ballet, piano, French—into organizations, teams, and clubs, fragmenting it into impossible-to-be-bored segments, creating in ourselves a mental metabolism geared to moving on, making free time distinctly unfree.

It is in free time that the special player develops, not in the competitive experience of games, in hour-long practices once a week, in mechanical devotion to packaged, processed, coaching-manual, hockey-school skills. For while skills are necessary, setting out as they do the limits of anything, more is needed to transform those skills into something special. Mostly it is time—unencumbered, unhurried, time of a different quality, more time, time to find wrong answers to find a few that are right; time to find your own right answers; time for skills to be practised to set higher limits, to settle and assimilate and become fully and completely yours, to organize and combine with other skills comfortably and easily in some uniquely personal way, then to be set loose, trusted, to find new instinctive directions to take, to create.

But without such time a player is like a student cramming for exams. His skills are like answers memorized by his body, specific, limited to what is expected, random and separate, with no overviews to organize and bring them together. And for those times when more is demanded, when new unexpected circumstances come up, when answers are asked for things you've never learned, when you must intuit and piece together what you already know to find new answers, memorizing isn't enough. It's the difference between knowledge and understanding, between a super-achiever and a wise old man. And it's the difference between a modern suburban player and a player like Lafleur.

For a special player has spent time with his game. On backyard rinks, in local arenas, in time alone and with others, time without short-cuts, he has seen many things, he has done many things, he has *experienced* the game. He understands it. There is *scope* and *culture* in his game. He is not a born player. What he has is not a gift, random and other-worldly, and unearned. There is surely something in his genetic makeup that allows him to be great, but just as surely there are others like him who fall short. He is, instead, *a natural.*

"Muscle memory" is a phrase physiologists sometimes use. It means that for many movements we make, our muscles move with no message from the brain telling them to move, that stored in the muscles is a learned capacity to move a certain way, and, given stimulus from the spinal cord, they move that way. We see a note on a sheet of music, our fingers move; no thought, no direction, and because one step of the transaction is eliminated—the information-message loop through the brain—we move faster as well.

When first learning a game, a player thinks through every step of what he's doing, needing to direct his body the way he wants it to go. With practice, with repetition, movements get memorized, speeding up, growing surer, gradually becoming part of the muscle's memory. The great player, having seen and done more things, more different and personal things, has in his muscles the memory of more notes, more combinations and patterns of notes, played in more different ways. Faced with a situation, his body responds. Faced with something more, something new, it finds an answer he didn't know was there. He *invents the game.*

Listen to a great player describe what he does. Ask Lafleur or Orr, ask Reggie Jackson or Julius Erving what makes them special, and you will get back something frustratingly unrewarding. They are inarticulate jocks, we decide, but in fact they can know no better than we do. For ask yourself how you walk, how your fingers move on a piano keyboard, how you do any number of things you have made routine, and you will know why. Stepping outside yourself you can think about it and decide what *must* happen, but you possess no inside story, no great insight unavailable to those who watch. Such movement comes literally from your body, bypassing your brain, leaving few subjective hints behind. Your legs, your fingers move, that's all you know. So if you want to know what makes Orr or Lafleur special, watch their bodies, fluent and articulate, let them explain. They know.

When I watch a modern suburban player, I feel the same as I do when I hear Donnie Osmond or René Simard sing a love song. I hear a skilful voice, I see closed eyes and pleading outstretched fingers, but I hear and see only fourteen-year-old boys who can't tell me anything.

Hockey has left the river and will never return. But like the "street," like an "ivory tower," the river is less a physical place than an *attitude,* a metaphor for unstructured, unorganized time alone. And if the game no longer needs the place, it needs the attitude. It is the rare player like Lafleur who reminds us.

Notes

Pelé, di Stefano, Puskas refers to three star soccer players of the twentieth century: the Brazilian "Pelé" whose real name is Edson Arantes do Nascimento; the Argentinian Alfredo di Stefano; and the Hungarian Ferenc Puskas

Bobby Orr a hockey defenceman, born in Parry Sound, Ontario, in 1948, who spent his career with the Boston Bruins

Reggie Jackson Pennsylvania-born star baseball player for the Oakland Athletics and the New York Yankees; nicknamed "Mr. October" for his tremendous performances in numerous World Series championships

Julius Erving a star basketball player with the New York Knicks during the 1970s

René Simard Québécois singer who began his career as a child soprano and became a well-known Canadian pop singer in the 1970s

Activities

1. According to Dryden, a major "cultural change" in recent years has resulted in the loss of the special environment that nurtured the growth of athletes such as Guy Lafleur. What features of Canadian culture and hockey culture fostered the development of Lafleur? What has changed in how athletes are developed in today's society? Based on your experience as a sports player or spectator, do you agree with Dryden's assessment?

2. In your notebook, write down the topic of each paragraph in this selection. Then organize the entries in your list into three to five major categories. What do you notice about the organizational pattern that Dryden uses in his profile of Guy Lafleur? How has he connected the various elements into a coherent, unified whole? How does the organization of the essay contribute to Dryden's theme and the persuasiveness of his argument?

3. With a group, use Dryden's profile to prepare a list of elements for an effective biographical sketch. Then watch a television program or film based on the biography of a famous person. Using the criteria you developed, assess the quality of the biography. Prepare a brief report on the effectiveness of the format, structure, and style used in the biography.

My Mother's Blue Bowl

Alice Walker

Alice Walker was born in Georgia in 1944. She studied at Spellman College in Georgia and Sarah Lawrence College in New York. A passionate social activist in the American civil rights movement, Walker has taught literature and women's studies at various American universities. In 1974, Walker received the prestigious Guggenheim Fellowship. In 1983, her novel *The Color Purple* won the Pulitzer Prize and the American Book Award. Walker's writing often draws on her experiences growing up as an African-American in the South. What fiction and non-fiction selections have you read that create powerful pictures of the author's childhood? To what extent do you draw on your own childhood memories when you are generating ideas for a piece of writing?

Visitors to my house are often served food—soup, potatoes, rice—in a large blue stoneware bowl, noticeably chipped at the rim. It is perhaps the most precious thing I own. It was given to me by my mother in her last healthy days. The days before a massive stroke laid her low and left her almost speechless. Those days when to visit her was to be drawn into a serene cocoon of memories and present-day musings and to rest there, in temporary retreat from the rest of the world, as if still an infant, nodding and secure at her breast.

For much of her life my mother longed, passionately longed, for a decent house. One with a yard that did not have to be cleared with an axe.

One with a roof that kept out the rain. One with floors that you could not fall through. She longed for a beautiful house of wood or stone. Or of red brick, like the houses her many sisters and their husbands had. When I was thirteen she found such a house. Green-shuttered, white-walled. Breezy. With a lawn and a hedge and giant pecan trees. A porch swing. There her gardens flourished in spite of the shade, as did her youngest daughter, for whom she sacrificed her life doing hard labour in someone else's house, in order to afford peace and prettiness for her child, to whose grateful embrace she returned each night.

But, curiously, the minute I left home, at seventeen, to attend college, she abandoned the dream house and moved into the projects. Into a small, tight apartment of few breezes, in which I was never to feel comfortable, but that she declared suited her "to a T." I took solace in the fact that it was at least hugged by spacious lawn on one side, and by forest, out the back door, and that its isolated position at the end of the street meant she would have a measure of privacy.

Her move into the projects—the best housing poor black people in the South ever had, she would occasionally declare, even as my father struggled to adjust to the cramped rooms and hard, unforgiving qualities of brick—was, I now understand, a step in the direction of divestiture, lightening her load, permitting her worldly possessions to dwindle in significance and, well before she herself would turn to spirit, roll away from her.

She owned little, in fact. A bed, a dresser, some chairs. A set of living-room furniture. A set of kitchen furniture. A bed and wardrobe (given to her years before, when I was a teenager, by one of her more prosperous sisters). Her flowers: everywhere, inside the house and outside. Planted in anything she managed to get her green hands on, including old suitcases and abandoned shoes. She recycled everything, effortlessly. And gradually she had only a small amount of stuff—mostly stuff her children gave her: nightgowns, perfume, a microwave—to recycle or to use.

Each time I visited her I marvelled at the modesty of her desires. She appeared to have hardly any, beyond a thirst for a Pepsi-Cola or a hunger for a piece of fried chicken or fish. On every visit I noticed that more and more of what I remembered of her possessions seemed to be missing. One day I commented on this.

Taking a deep breath, sighing, and following both with a beaming big smile, which lit up her face, the room, and my heart, she said: Yes, it's all going. I don't need it anymore. If there's anything you want, take it when you leave; it might not be here when you come back.

The dishes my mother and father used daily had come from my house; I had sent them years before when I moved from Mississippi to New York. Neither the plates nor the silver matched entirely, but it was all beautiful in her eyes. There were numerous paper items, used in the microwave, and stacks of plastic plates and cups, used by the scores of children from the neighbourhood who continued throughout her life to come and go. But there was nothing there for me to want.

One day, however, looking for a jar into which to pour leftover iced tea, I found myself probing deep into the wilderness of the overstuffed, airless pantry. Into the land of the old-fashioned, the outmoded, the outdated. The humble and the obsolete. There was a smoothing iron, a churn. A butter press. And two large bowls.

One was cream and rose with a blue stripe. The other was a deep, vivid blue.

May I have this bowl, Mama, I asked, looking at her and at the blue bowl with delight.

You can have both of them, she said, barely acknowledging them, and continuing to put leftover food away.

I held the bowls on my lap for the rest of the evening, while she watched a TV program about cops and criminals that I found too horrifying to follow.

Before leaving the room I kissed her on the forehead and asked if I could get anything for her from the kitchen; then I went off to bed. The striped bowl I placed on a chair beside the door, so I could look at it from where I lay. The blue bowl I placed in the bed with me.

In giving me these gifts, my mother had done a number of astonishing things, in her typically offhand way. She had taught me a lesson about letting go of possessions—easily, without emphasis or regret— and she had given me a symbol of what she herself represented in my life.

For the blue bowl especially was a cauldron of memories. Of cold, harsh, wintry days, when my brothers and sister and I trudged home from school burdened down by the silence and frigidity of our long trek from the main road, down the hill to our shabby-looking house. More rundown than any of our classmates' houses. In winter my mother's riotous flowers would be absent, and the shack stood revealed for what it was. A grey, decaying, too small barrack meant to house the itinerant tenant workers on a prosperous white man's farm.

Slogging through sleet and wind to the sagging front door, thankful that our house was too far from the road to be seen clearly from the school bus, I always felt a wave of embarrassment and misery. But then I would open the door. And there inside would be my mother's winter flowers: a glowing fire in the fireplace, colourful handmade quilts on all our beds, paintings and drawings of flowers and fruits and, yes, of Jesus, given to her by who knows whom—and, most of all, there in the centre of the rough-hewn table, which in the tiny kitchen almost touched the rusty wood-burning stove, stood the big blue bowl, full of whatever was the most tasty thing on earth.

There was my mother herself. Glowing. Her teeth sparkling. Her eyes twinkling. As if she lived in a castle and her favourite princes and princesses had just dropped by to visit.

The blue bowl stood there, seemingly full forever, no matter how deeply or rapaciously we dipped, as if it had no bottom. And she dipped up soup. Dipped up lima beans. Dipped up stew. Forked out potatoes. Spooned out rice and peas and corn. And in the light and warmth that was *Her*, we dined.

Thank you, Mama.

Activities

1. Write a response to this essay by recording your initial impressions of the text. Then make connections between this essay and objects or relationships in your own life. Compare your responses with those of your classmates. To what extent did your own experiences, values, and perspectives influence your interpretation?

2. Choose a passage of approximately five to eight sentences that strikes you as particularly powerful. Analyze each sentence, considering its length and whether its type is simple, compound, complex, fragment, or run-on. Write a short passage on a topic of your choice in which you mimic the sentences you analyzed. Share your insights and conclusions about Walker's use of syntax in a class or group discussion.

3. Write an autobiographical essay in which you reflect on an object, place, or activity that symbolizes an important relationship with someone in your life. In developing your essay, use Walker's essay as a model in weaving together exposition, description, and narration in order to convey the nature and importance of the relationship. Invite a partner to react to the structure and style of your first draft. Then revise your essay to strengthen the organization and deepen the impact of the language.

Another Viewpoint: Society

Alice Walker identifies the American writers Flannery O'Connor and Zora Neale Hurston as key influences on her writing. Research the connections among these three women writers from the American South. To what extent did the society of the American South in the twentieth century contribute to these writers' visions?

Migrant Mother

Dorothea Lange

About the Visual   Dorothea Lange was born in Hoboken, New Jersey, in 1895. After high school, she decided to train as a photographer, despite never having used a camera before. She began her professional career in 1918 when she opened a portrait studio in San Francisco. By the 1930s, however, Lange took her camera to the streets to record the plight of people of the Depression era. In 1935, she was hired by the Farm Security Administration (FSA); her task was to document families leaving their devastated farms in the dust bowl of the American Midwest in a migration to California in search of work. Lange died in 1965. She called the camera "an instrument that teaches people to see without a camera." What might she have meant by this statement? To what extent is the statement paradoxical?

Activities

1. This photograph was taken in the United States during the Great Depression. Record your initial response to the photograph—your thoughts, feelings, questions, and associations. Share your response with the class and note the similarities and differences in your classmates' reactions. How do you account for them?

2. Discuss how the perspective, scale, and composition of this photograph contribute to its impact. Consider, for example, how the following changes would affect the picture: increasing or decreasing the distance between the camera and the subject, showing more of the background or only the face of the mother, or taking the picture from a lower or a higher angle.

1936, black-and-white print

Two Heads, *15th or 16th century, Leonardo da Vinci*

Of Youth and Age

Francis Bacon

Sir Francis Bacon was born in London, England, in 1561, and died in 1626. He studied law at Cambridge University, travelled through Europe, and returned to England to serve in the English court. Bacon made significant contributions to Renaissance thought and culture through his scientific and political writings, especially *The Advancement of Learning* and the *Novum Organum* (New Instrument of Learning). In the latter, he emphasized the importance of what has become the modern scientific method. Often called the first English essayist, Bacon wrote with wit and style about such diverse topics as marriage, truth, education, travel, beauty, revenge, riches, and friendship. What are some of the outstanding characteristics of the young and the old? Why are young people often in conflict with their elders? What can the two groups learn from each other?

A man that is young in years may be old in hours, if he have lost no time. But that happeneth rarely. Generally, youth is like the first cogitations, not so wise as the second. For there is a youth in thoughts as well as in ages. And yet the invention of young men is more lively than that of old, and imaginations stream into their minds better, and as it were more divinely. Natures that have much heat, and great and violent desires and perturbations, are not ripe for action till they have passed the meridian of their years: as it was with Julius Caesar, and Septimius Severus. Of the latter of whom it is said, *Juventutem egit erroribus, imo furoribus, plenam,* and yet he was the ablest emperor, almost, of all the list. But reposed natures may do well in youth. As it is seen in Augustus Caesar, Cosmus,

Duke of Florence, Gaston de Foix, and others. On the other side, heat and vivacity in age is an excellent composition for business. Young men are fitter to invent than to judge, fitter for execution than for counsel, and fitter for new projects than for settled business. For the experience of age, in things that fall within the compass of it, directeth them, but in new things abuseth them. The errors of young men are the ruin of business; but the errors of aged men amount but to this, that more might have been done, or sooner. Young men, in the conduct and manage of actions, embrace more than they can hold; stir more than they can quiet; fly to the end, without consideration of the means and degrees; pursue some few principles which they have chanced upon absurdly; care not to innovate, which draws unknown inconveniences; use extreme remedies at first; and, that which doubleth all errors, will not acknowledge or retract them; like an unready horse that will neither stop nor turn. Men of age object too much, consult too long, adventure too little, repent too soon, and seldom drive business home to the full period, but content themselves with a mediocrity of success. Certainly it is good to compound employments of both; for that will be good for the present, because the virtues of either age may correct the defects of both; and good for succession, that young men may be learners while men in age are actors; and, lastly, good for extern accidents, because authority followeth old men, and favour and popularity youth. But for the moral part, perhaps youth will have the preeminence, as age hath for the politic. A certain rabbin, upon the text, *Your young men shall see visions, and your old men shall dream dreams,* inferreth that young men are admitted nearer to God than old, because vision is a clearer revelation than a dream. And certainly, the more a man drinketh of the world, the more it intoxicateth; and age doth profit rather in the powers of understanding than in the virtues of the will and affections. There be some have an over-early ripeness in their years, which fadeth betimes. These are, first, such as have brittle wits, the edge whereof is soon turned; such as was Hermogenes the rhetorician, whose books are exceeding subtle, who afterward waxed stupid. A second sort is of those that have some natural dispositions which have better grace in youth than in age, such as is a fluent and luxuriant speech, which becomes youth well, but not age: so Tully saith of Hortensius, *Idem manebat, neque idem docebat.* The third is of such as take too high a strain at the first, and are magnanimous more than tract of years can uphold. As was Scipio Africanus, of whom Livy saith in effect, *Ultima primis cedebant.*

Notes

Juventutem egit erroribus, imo furoribus, plenam from *The Life of Severus* by the Roman writer Spartianus; translated from the Latin as "He passed a youth full of folly, or rather of madness"

Cosmus, Duke of Florence refers to the historical figure Cosimo de'Medici

Gaston de Foix King Louis XII of France's nephew, who died at the battle of Ravenna in 1512

Hermogenes Greek rhetorician of the second century CE, who is said to have lost his memory at the age of twenty-five

Tully refers to the Roman philosopher and orator Cicero, who lived in the first century BCE

Hortensius Roman orator, at one time a rival of Cicero

Idem manebat, neque idem docebat translated from the Latin as "He remained the same when the same style no longer became him"

tract in this instance, length

Scipio Africanus Roman general who died in 183 BCE. According to some historians, Scipio was more suited to war than to the peaceful times of his later years.

Ultima primis cedebant translated from the Latin as "His last actions were not equal to his first"

Activities

1. In your notebook, make two lists. One list should feature the characteristics of "youth," according to Bacon, and the other the characteristics of "age." Beside each characteristic, mark whether you agree or disagree. Compare your responses with those of others in the class. Have a small group or whole class debate on the advantages and disadvantages of both youth and age.

2. Bacon did not divide his essays into paragraphs. Using what you know about the principles of paragraph organization, divide "Of Youth and Age" into paragraphs. In a small group, compare and discuss the reasons for your decisions. With the group, try to come to a consensus about the placement of paragraph divisions and present your decisions to the class.

3. Many of the references that Bacon uses in this essay may be obscure to the modern reader. The notes following the essay provide information on the sources cited by Bacon. Check these sources and evaluate the extent to which the allusions enrich or obscure the meaning of Bacon's essay for contemporary readers.

Another Viewpoint: Critical Approaches

Sir Francis Bacon was an important political and cultural figure in the era known as the Renaissance in Europe. Do research about the Renaissance and Bacon's life. Write an essay in which you explain how the circumstances and values of the Renaissance period might have influenced Bacon as he was writing this essay.

Why I Write

George Orwell

Generally considered to be one of the major essayists of the twentieth century, George Orwell was born Eric Arthur Blair in 1903 in what
was then British-ruled India. He was educated in England and, after
graduation, served in Burma with the Indian Imperial Police. Among
his best-known works are *Burmese Days*, the story of his police
career; *Homage to Catalonia,* a record of his involvement in the
Spanish Civil War; *Animal Farm*, an allegory about the failure of
Russian socialism under Stalin; and *Nineteen Eighty-Four* (1948), his
portrayal of life under totalitarian rule in the future. Orwell died in
1950. In this essay, Orwell tells his readers that a writer's "subject matter will be determined by the age he lives in." What do you think he
means by this? Do you agree with him? Why or why not? What are
some of the major issues that affect writers today?

From a very early age, perhaps the age of five or six, I knew that when I
grew up I should be a writer. Between the ages of about seventeen and
twenty-four I tried to abandon this idea, but I did so with the consciousness that I was outraging my true nature and that sooner or later
I should have to settle down and write books.

I was the middle child of three, but there was a gap of five years on
either side, and I barely saw my father before I was eight. For this and
other reasons I was somewhat lonely, and I soon developed disagreeable
mannerisms which made me unpopular throughout my schooldays.
I had the lonely child's habit of making up stories and holding conversations with imaginary persons, and I think from the very start my

literary ambitions were mixed up with the feeling of being isolated and undervalued. I knew that I had a facility with words and a power of facing unpleasant facts, and I felt that this created a sort of private world in which I could get my own back for my failure in everyday life. Nevertheless the volume of serious—i.e. seriously intended—writing which I produced all through my childhood and boyhood would not amount to half a dozen pages. I wrote my first poem at the age of four or five, my mother taking it down to dictation. I cannot remember anything about it except that it was about a tiger and the tiger had 'chair-like teeth'—a good enough phrase, but I fancy the poem was a plagiarism of Blake's 'Tiger, Tiger'. At eleven when the war of 1914–18 broke out, I wrote a patriotic poem which was printed in the local newspaper, as was another, two years later, on the death of Kitchener. From time to time, when I was a bit older, I wrote bad and usually unfinished 'nature poems' in the Georgian style. I also, about twice, attempted a short story which was a ghastly failure. That was the total of the would-be serious work that I actually set down on paper during all those years.

However, throughout this time I did in a sense engage in literary activities. To begin with there was the made-to-order stuff which I produced quickly, easily and without much pleasure to myself. Apart from school work, I wrote *vers d'occasion*, semi-comic poems which I could turn out at what now seems to me astonishing speed—at fourteen I wrote a whole rhyming play, in imitation of Aristophanes, in about a week—and helped to edit school magazines, both printed and in manuscript. These magazines were the most pitiful burlesque stuff that you could imagine, and I took far less trouble with them than I now would with the cheapest journalism. But side by side with all this, for fifteen years or more, I was carrying out a literary exercise of a quite different kind: this was the making up of a continuous 'story' about myself, a sort of diary existing only in the mind. I believe this is a common habit of children and adolescents. As a very small child I used to imagine that I was, say, Robin Hood, and picture myself as the hero of thrilling adventures, but quite soon my 'story' ceased to be narcissistic in a crude way and became more and more a mere description of what I was doing and the things I saw. For minutes at a time this kind of thing would be running through my head: 'He pushed the door open and entered the room. A yellow beam of sunlight, filtering through the muslin curtains, slanted on to the table, where a matchbox, half open, lay beside the inkpot. With his right hand in his pocket he moved across to the window. Down in the street a tortoiseshell cat was chasing a dead leaf,' etc., etc. This habit continued till I was about twenty-five, right through my non-literary years. Although I had to search, and did search, for the right words, I seemed to be making this descriptive effort almost against my will, under a kind of compulsion from outside. The 'story' must, I suppose, have reflected the styles of the various writers I admired at different ages, but so far as I remember it always had the same meticulous descriptive quality.

When I was about sixteen I suddenly discovered the joy of mere words, i.e. the sounds and associations of words. The lines from *Paradise Lost*—

> So hee with difficulty and labour hard
> Moved on: with difficulty and labour hee,

which do not now seem to me so very wonderful, sent shivers down my backbone; and the spelling 'hee' for 'he' was an added pleasure. As for the need to describe things, I knew all about it already. So it is clear what kind of books I wanted to write, in so far as I could be said to want to write books at that time, I wanted to write enormous naturalistic novels with unhappy endings, full of detailed descriptions and arresting similes, and also full of purple passages in which words were used partly for the sake of their sound. And in fact my first completed novel, *Burmese Days*, which I wrote when I was thirty but projected much earlier, is rather that kind of book.

I give all this background information because I do not think one can assess a writer's motives without knowing something of his early development. His subject matter will be determined by the age he lives in—at least this is true in tumultuous, revolutionary ages like our own—but before he ever begins to write he will have acquired an emotional attitude from which he will never completely escape. It is his job, no doubt, to discipline his temperament and avoid getting stuck at some immature stage, or in some perverse mood: but if he escapes from his early influences altogether, he will have killed his impulse to write. Putting aside the need to earn a living, I think there are four great motives for writing, at any rate for writing prose. They exist in different degrees in every writer, and in any one writer the proportions will vary from time to time, according to the atmosphere in which he is living. They are:

(i) *Sheer egoism.* Desire to seem clever, to be talked about, to be remembered after death, to get your own back on grown-ups who snubbed you in childhood, etc., etc. It is humbug to pretend that this is not a motive, and a strong one. Writers share this characteristic with scientists, artists, politicians, lawyers, soldiers, successful business men—in short, with the whole top crust of humanity. The great mass of human beings are not acutely selfish. After the age of about thirty they abandon individual ambition—in many cases, indeed, they almost abandon the sense of being individuals at all—and live chiefly for others, or are simply smothered under drudgery. But there is also the minority of gifted, wilful people who are determined to live their own lives to the end, and writers belong in this class. Serious writers, I should say, are on the whole more vain and self-centred than journalists, though less interested in money.

(ii) *Aesthetic enthusiasm.* Perception of beauty in the external world, or, on the other hand, in words and their right arrangement. Pleasure in the impact of one sound on another, in the firmness of good prose or the rhythm of a good story. Desire to share an experience which one feels is valuable and ought not to be missed. The aesthetic motive is very feeble in a lot of writers, but even a pamphleteer or a writer of text-books will have pet words and phrases which appeal to him for non-utilitarian reasons; or he may feel strongly about typography, width of margins, etc. Above the level of a railway guide, no book is quite free from aesthetic considerations.

(iii) *Historical impulse.* Desire to see things as they are, to find out true facts and store them up for the use of posterity.

(iv) *Political purpose*—using the word 'political' in the widest possible sense. Desire to push the world in a certain direction, to alter other people's idea of the kind of society that they should strive after. Once again, no book is genuinely free from political bias. The opinion that art should have nothing to do with politics is itself a political attitude.

It can be seen how these various impulses must war against one another, and how they must fluctuate from person to person and from time to time. By nature—taking your 'nature' to be the state you have attained when you are first adult—I am a person in whom the first three motives would outweigh the fourth. In a peaceful age I might have written ornate or merely descriptive books, and might have remained almost unaware of my political loyalties. As it is I have been forced into becoming a sort of pamphleteer. First I spent five years in an unsuitable profession (the Indian Imperial Police, in Burma), and then I underwent poverty and the sense of failure. This increased my natural hatred of authority and made me for the first time fully aware of the existence of the working classes, and the job in Burma had given me some understanding of the nature of imperialism: but these experiences were not enough to give me an accurate political orientation. Then came Hitler, the Spanish civil war, etc. By the end of 1935 I had still failed to reach a firm decision. I remember a little poem that I wrote at that date, expressing my dilemma:

A happy vicar I might have been
Two hundred years ago
To preach upon eternal doom
And watch my walnuts grow;

But born, alas, in an evil time,
I missed that pleasant haven,
For the hair has grown on my upper lip
And the clergy are all clean-shaven.

And later still the times were good,
We were so easy to please,
We rocked our troubled thoughts to sleep
On the bosoms of the trees.

All ignorant we dared to own
The joys we now dissemble;
The greenfinch on the apple bough
Could make my enemies tremble.

But girls' bellies and apricots,
Roach in a shaded stream,
Horses, ducks in flight at dawn,
All these are a dream.

It is forbidden to dream again;
We maim our joys or hide them;
Horses are made of chromium steel
And little fat men shall ride them.

I am the worm who never turned,
The eunuch without a harem;
Between the priest and the commissar
I walk like Eugene Aram;

And the commissar is telling my fortune
While the radio plays,
But the priest has promised an Austin Seven,
For Duggie always pays.

I dreamed I dwelt in marble halls,
And woke to find it true;
I wasn't born for an age like this;
Was Smith? Was Jones? Were you?

The Spanish war and other events in 1936–7 turned the scale and thereafter I knew where I stood. Every line of serious work that I have written since 1936 has been written, directly or indirectly, *against*
totalitarianism and *for* democratic socialism, as I understand it. It seems
to me nonsense, in a period like our own, to think that one can avoid

writing of such subjects. Everyone writes of them in one guise or another. It is simply a question of which side one takes and what approach one follows. And the more one is conscious of one's political bias, the more chance one has of acting politically without sacrificing one's aesthetic and intellectual integrity.

What I have most wanted to do throughout the past ten years is to make political writing into an art. My starting point is always a feeling of partisanship, a sense of injustice. When I sit down to write a book, I do not say to myself, 'I am going to produce a work of art'. I write it because there is some lie that I want to expose, some fact to which I want to draw attention, and my initial concern is to get a hearing. But I could not do the work of writing a book, or even a long magazine article, if it were not also an aesthetic experience. Anyone who cares to examine my work will see that even when it is downright propaganda it contains much that a full-time politician would consider irrelevant. I am not able, and I do not want, completely to abandon the world-view that I acquired in childhood. So long as I remain alive and well I shall continue to feel strongly about prose style, to love the surface of the earth, and to take pleasure in solid objects and scraps of useless information. It is no use trying to suppress that side of myself. The job is to reconcile my ingrained likes and dislikes with the essentially public, non-individual activities that this age forces on all of us.

It is not easy. It raises problems of construction and of language, and it raises in a new way the problem of truthfulness. Let me give just one example of the cruder kind of difficulty that arises. My book about the Spanish Civil War, *Homage to Catalonia,* is, of course, a frankly political book, but in the main it is written with a certain detachment and regard for form. I did try very hard in it to tell the whole truth without violating my literary instincts. But among other things it contains a long chapter full of newspaper quotations and the like, defending the Trotskyists who were accused of plotting with Franco. Clearly such a chapter, which after a year or two would lose its interest for any ordinary reader, must ruin the book. A critic whom I respect read me a lecture about it. 'Why did you put in all that stuff?' he said. 'You've turned what might have been a good book into journalism.' I happened to know, what very few people in England had been allowed to know, that innocent men were being falsely accused. If I had not been angry about that I should never have written the book.

In one form or another this problem comes up again. The problem of language is subtler and would take too long to discuss. I will only say that of late years I have tried to write less picturesquely and more exactly. In any case I find that by the time you have perfected any style of writing, you have always outgrown it. *Animal Farm* was the first book in which I tried, with full consciousness of what I was doing, to fuse political purpose and artistic purpose into one whole. I have not written a novel for seven years, but I hope to write another fairly soon. It is bound to be a failure, every book is a failure, but I do know with some clarity what kind of book I want to write.

Looking back through the last page or two, I see that I have made it appear as though my motives in writing were wholly public-spirited. I don't want to leave that as the final impression. All writers are vain, selfish, and lazy, and at the very bottom of their motives there lies a mystery. Writing a book is a horrible, exhausting struggle, like a long bout of some painful illness. One would never undertake such a thing if one were not driven on by some demon whom one can neither resist nor understand. For all one knows that demon is simply the same instinct that makes a baby squall for attention. And yet it is also true that one can write nothing readable unless one constantly struggles to efface one's own personality. Good prose is like a window pane. I cannot say with certainty which of my motives are the strongest, but I know which of them deserve to be followed. And looking back through my work, I see that it is invariably where I lacked a *political* purpose that I wrote lifeless books and was betrayed into purple passages, sentences without meaning, decorative adjectives and humbug generally.

Notes

Kitchener Lord Kitchener, much decorated and honoured British administrator and soldier, famous for campaigns in Egypt and South Africa

Vers d'occasion public poetry inspired by historically or socially significant events

Spanish Civil War In 1936, a group of generals, led by Francisco Franco and supported by fascist governments in Italy and Germany, revolted against Republican government forces. Despite popular support by people from many different nationalities who came to Spain to fight with Republicans against fascism, Franco became the dictator of a totalitarian Spanish state in 1939.

Activities

1. In this analytical essay, George Orwell explains his development as a writer. The author discusses key stages in his personal and professional life and the characteristics of his writing at each stage. In your notebook, describe the characteristics of the stages discussed by Orwell, as well as the personal, political, and historical events that influenced him at each stage.

2. The essay is organized chronologically. Prepare a timeline for Orwell's biography, based on the information provided in the article. Include events from both Orwell's personal life and contemporary historical events. Within the existing chronological structure, what other organizational patterns does Orwell use? Use your timeline to make a schematic plan, incorporating the major topics and subtopics found in Orwell's essay. Assess the effectiveness of the combination of various organizational structures used by Orwell in this essay.

3. Write your own analytical, autobiographical essay using Orwell's as a model. Begin by creating a personal timeline of key dates and events in your life. Using on-line or published yearbooks, write down important historical, political, and cultural events that parallel those in your life. Weave the personal and historical events together as Orwell has done in this essay.

Another Viewpoint: Critical Approaches

Orwell suggests in this essay that it is difficult for a writer to separate himself or herself from the political, historical, and cultural context in which a novel or any work of art is created. Some literary critics agree with this view. Others suggest that a work of art should be treated as a self-contained object and that we do not need to go outside of the text to understand it. What do you think would be Orwell's reply to such critics? Which side do you think is correct? Use examples from your own reading to support your argument.

The Not-So-Deadly Sin

Barbara Kingsolver

Barbara Kingsolver was born in Kentucky in 1955. At university in Indiana, she studied both science and creative writing and, after graduation, she worked as a science writer at the University of Arizona. Her articles have been published in many journals. She is also a well-known fiction writer, especially for the international best-seller *The Poisonwood Bible*. To Kingsolver, writing is in part a form of political activism. She has written that in her twenties she "began to understand how a person could write about the problems of the world in a compelling and beautiful way." She has said that writing should "improve on" real life. To what extent do you think that writing can reflect real life? How can writing improve on real life? Are some forms of writing better at depicting real life and others better at improving it? If so, why?

Write a non-fiction book, and be prepared for the legion of readers who are going to doubt your facts. But write a novel, and get ready for the world to assume every word is true.

Whenever I am queried about my fiction, if people want to know something in particular they nearly always want to know the same thing: How much is autobiographical? Did it all really happen, in exactly that way? Was my childhood like that? Which character is me? Commonly people don't ask, they just assume. I get letters of sympathy for the loss of my sister (the heroine of one of my novels lost her sister) and my father (ditto, same novel). Since one of my characters adopted a Cherokee child, I get advice about cross-cultural adoptions. And so on.

My sister and parents are alive and well, thanks. I don't have an adopted child. The mute waif named Turtle who appears in two of my novels is the polar opposite of my own Camille—a sunny, blonde child who spoke her first word at eight months and hasn't stopped talking since. At the time I invented Turtle, I had no child at all. Mine came later, and I didn't find her in a car, as happened in *The Bean Trees*. Mine was harder to produce. I never use my own family and friends as the basis of fictional characters, mainly because I would like them to remain my family and friends. And secondarily, because I believe the purpose of art is not to photocopy life but distill it, learn from it, improve on it, embroider tiny distinct pieces of it into something insightful and entirely new. As Marc Chagall said, "Great art picks up where nature ends."

I know, in real life, many fascinating people; every one of them has limits on what she or he can be talked into. Most, in fact, will ask for my recommendations on their love lives or vacation plans, then reliably do the opposite. When I'm writing a story, I can't mess around with that kind of free spirit. I need characters I can count on to do what I say—take on a foundling baby rather than call the police; fall in love with my self-effacing heroine rather than the sturdy, good-looking divorcée down the street; pursue a passion for cockfighting, then give it all up at a lover's request; die for honour; own up to guilt. What's more, they must do it all *convincingly*. That means they have to be carrying in their psyches all the right motives—the exact combination of past experiences that will lead them to their appointment with my contrived epiphany. Trying to graft a plot onto the real-life history of anyone I actually know, including myself, would be as fruitless as lashing a citrus branch onto the trunk of an apple tree. It would look improbable. It would wither and die. Better to plant a seed in the good dirt of imagination. Grow a whole story from scratch.

Most people readily acknowledge the difference between life and art. Why, then, do so many artists keep answering the same question again and again? No, none of those characters is me. It's not my life, I made it up. Yes, *all of it!* Strangers' assumptions about deaths in my family and the like, odd as this might seem, have caused us some genuine pain. How I wish my art could stand apart from us, carrying no more suggestions about my private life than the work of, say, a stonemason or a tree surgeon. I was raised to be polite, but sometimes I'm inclined to get cranky and bark about this: Give us writers a little credit, will you? We're not just keeping a diary here, we're inventing! Why can't you believe we're capable of making up a story from scratch? Of stringing together a long, elaborate *lie*, for heaven's sake?

When it's put that way, it dawns on me that this may be the snag—the part about lying. In the book-jacket photos I look like a decent girl, and decent girls don't lie. That social axiom runs deep, possibly deeper than any other. The first important moral value we teach our children, after "don't hit your sister," is the difference between fantasy and truth. Trying to pass off one for the other is a punishable infraction, and a lesson that sticks for life. Whether or not we are perfectly honest in adulthood, we *should* be, and we know that on a visceral level. So visceral, in fact, a machine measuring heart rate and palm perspiration can fairly reliably detect a lie. We don't even have to think about it. Our hearts know.

So I suppose I should be relieved when people presume my stories are built around a wholesome veracity. They're saying, in effect, "You don't *look* like a sociopath." And it's true, I'm not; I pay my taxes and don't litter. Track down any grade-school teacher who knew me in childhood and she'll swear I was a goodie two-shoes even back then.

But ask my mother, and she'll tell you I always had a little trouble with the boundaries of truth. As the aerospace engineers say, I pushed the envelope. As a small child I gave my family regular updates on the white horse wearing a hat that lived in the closet. When I was slightly older, family vacations offered me the delightful opportunity to hang out alone in campground restrooms, intimating to strangers that I came from a foreign country and didn't comprehend English, or plumbing. When I got old enough to use public transportation by myself, my sport was to entertain other passengers with melodramatic personal histories that occurred to me on the spot. I was a nineteen-year-old cello virtuoso running away from my dreadful seventy-year-old husband; or I had a brain tumour, and was determined to see every state in the union by Greyhound in the remaining two months of my life; or I was a French anthropologist working with a team that had just uncovered the real cradle of human origins in a surprising but as-yet-undisclosable location. Oh, how my fellow passengers' eyes would light up. People two rows ahead of me would put down their paperbacks, sling an elbow over the back of the seat, and ride all the rest of the way to Indianapolis backward, asking questions. I probably registered an increased heart rate and sweaty palms, but I couldn't stop myself. I strove for new heights in perjury, trying to see how absurd a yarn I could spin before some matron would finally frown at me over her specs and say, "Now really, dear."

No one ever did. I concluded that people want pretty desperately to be entertained, especially on long bus rides through flat midwestern cornfields.

For me, it was more than a pastime. It was the fulfillment of my own longing to reach through the fences that circumscribed my young life, and taste other pastures. Through my tales I discovered not exactly myself but all the selves I might have been—the ones I feared, the ones I hoped for, and the ones I'd never know. None of them was me. Each of them was a beckoning path into the woods of what might have been.

Eventually I found a socially acceptable outlet for my depravity. Now I spend hours each day, year after year, sitting at my desk with a wicked smirk on my face, making up whopping, four-hundred-page lies. Oh, what a life.

I do want to state for the record that I no longer have any inclination toward real dishonesty; I don't bear false witness to strangers or to friends. And I check my laces obsessively when serving the journalist's or essayist's trade. So my mother isn't to blame—she did, evidently, teach me to know true from false. I gather I was just born with an excess of story, the way another poor child might come into this world with extra fingers on each hand. My imagination had more figment in it than my life could contain, so some of it leaked out here and there. As I've matured, I've learned to control the damage.

I don't believe I'm extraordinary on this account. Every one of us, I think, is born with an excess of story. Listen quietly to a group of toddlers at play: the lies will swarm around their heads, thick as a tribe of bright butterflies, flickering gracefully from one child to another, until they notice a grown-up has come into the room—and in a sudden rush of wings the lies will vanish into air.

A little bit sad, isn't it? If you look it up, you'll find lying was never registered as one of the seven deadly sins. (Pride—an anemic sin if you ask me—is on that list, and so is gluttony, and of all things, sloth. But not lying.) Yet, in the age of evidence and reason, it has gotten such a very bad name. When so many smart, lively people keep insisting to me that all my stories must be true, I begin to suspect they can't quite get their minds around the notion of pure fabrication.

I want to tell them: Stop a minute, right where you are. Relax your shoulders, shake your head and spine like a dog shaking off cold water. Tell that imperious voice in your head to be still, then close your eyes, and tap the well. Find the lie you are longing to tell. It's in there. When you manage to wrestle that first one out, a whole flood may gush out behind it. Take them up in your hands, drink their clarity, write them down in a secret book. Tell them to your children behind the golden door of "Once upon a time." Choose one chair at your dinner table, give it to a different family member each night, and declare it "the liar's seat."

Or take a long bus trip through the cornfields. You may find a new career.

Notes

Marc Chagall a renowned Russian painter (1889–1985) noted for his dream-like, fanciful imagery; his influences included Jewish mysticism and the art-work of the French Post-Impressionists and Picasso

seven deadly sins a reference to the most severe sins according to the Judeo-Christian tradition as documented in the Bible, identified as pride, avarice, lust, anger, sloth, gluttony, and envy

Activities

1. In this essay, although Kingsolver calls stories "lies" and "fabrications," in what sense are fictional narratives "true"? What reasons does Kingsolver give for people's fascination with stories? If stories are lies, what is their purpose? Have a class discussion in which you identify some of the truths in fictional stories you have read.

2. Find what you think is Kingsolver's thesis statement for this essay. Explain how Kingsolver uses personal anecdotes, humour, emotional appeal, and logical reasoning to make her arguments convincing to the reader. Write an alternative thesis statement that captures the subject of the essay and Kingsolver's tone.

3. Use Kingsolver's suggestion about declaring a chair as a "liar's seat" for a class improvisation activity. Take turns or ask for volunteers to sit in the "liar's seat." Open the flood gates of your imagination and begin to tell a fictional "chain" story. On a pre-arranged signal, have different students assume the "liar's seat" and take up the story where the previous narrator left off. Use some of the lies that Kingsolver told to fellow passengers on the bus as story starters.

Call of the Weird

Drew Hayden Taylor

Drew Hayden Taylor was born at the Curve Lake Reserve near Peterborough, Ontario, in 1962. Taylor is a writer of non-fiction, fiction, plays, and television and film scripts. His plays have received numerous awards, including the Chalmers Award. Taylor has written that "storytelling, in my opinion, should always be a mysterious process; otherwise there goes much of the fun. If we know where the stories come from, then the journey to where they end might seem a little less magical." In this essay, Taylor explores cultural assumptions and misunderstandings. Can you think of a time when someone made inaccurate assumptions about your cultural background? What are some of the dangers of making assumptions about others based on their background?

When I first read the job description for the position of Artistic Director of Native Earth Performing Arts, Toronto's only professional Native theatre company, I don't remember coming across any paragraph or subsection anywhere on the page requiring me to become the "oracle of the Aboriginal trivia."

On any given day, questions of unusual and frequently surreal nature are posed to me and the other intelligent, though often puzzled, members of the office. The number of times I've seen heads, with telephones attached, shaking in amazement, makes me wonder about the logical processes of people's minds.

We are a theatre company. That is what we do. We produce plays by and about Native people. Check it out, it's in our mandate. We'll fax it to you if you don't believe us. The majority of questions that Bell Canada sends our way are not within our realm of expertise. While one of our functions as a theatre company is to educate the public, that does not mean one at a time, about obscure issues, while our other work waits. We have lives too, you know.

Our beleaguered office staff has put together a collection of some of the more…interesting…inquiries to come through our office in recent months.

I'm trying to find Sam Ke-something or other. I really don't know how to pronounce his last name. Do you know where I can find him? Or, *I'm trying to locate a Bob Whitecloud of the Sioux tribe in the States. I heard he might be in Canada. Can you tell me how to get in touch with him?*

It's a little known fact that Native Earth Performing Arts is the focal point for all Native people in North America. The one million or so people claiming some sort of Aboriginal ancestry all pass through our doors at one point or another. That's why we have to replace our carpets at least four times a year.

Do all the seats face the stage?

I guess you can call us slaves to conformity. We did try having the seats face the back of the theatre but audience reaction, shall we say, was not that favourable.

Hi, I'm wondering if you can help me. I'm to locate an Apache wedding prayer.

I checked. Sorry, no Apaches in our office, married or not. I did however manage to find a Mohawk secret handshake.

I'm with a casting company for a movie. I'm looking for a Native man, tall and lean with long dark hair and presence. Preferably he should be in his early 30s. And yes, he has to look very striking.

Yeah, most of the women in my office are looking for him too. What do you want me to do about it? The line starts behind them.

I'm phoning from Edinburgh, Scotland. I'm doing research on Native people in the 1930s. Can you send me information?

There were none. I have it on good authority all Native people were killed off in the late 1800s. But in the latter part of this century, due to an overabundance of bureaucrats in Ottawa, the federal government decided to create a new department to employ these people. So the Department of Indian Affairs was created with no Indians. Through secret DNA experiments, a new race of Native people was created at a clandestine location known as…Algonquin Park.

I'm Herman —— from Germany. I'm looking for people of the Bear clan. My last name means bear in German. Do you know any or can you help me find the Bear clan?

Sorry, we have yet to update our database and cross-reference our membership, actors, directors, stage managers, and others by clan affiliation. We're awaiting the software to come out for Windows.

We're an organization of men against men who commit violence against women. We want to know if you guys could provide any ceremonies or spiritual things of that nature that would help us with healing and matters like that.

While that is a noble cause, we are not "Ceremonies 'R' Us," or "have medicine pouch, will travel."

Do you know where I can get my hands on some Inuit throat singers?

As a Native organization, we do not condone violence against the Inuit.

In all fairness and honesty, we do try to be as polite and helpful as possible, and pass callers on to the appropriate organizations. But we are in the business of making art, not making a Native trivial pursuit game. But it makes me wonder if the Mirvishes ever get calls asking, "There's this Jewish song I keep hearing. Hava-something. You wouldn't happen to know the full title and who sang it, would you?"

Notes

Native Earth Performing Arts an arts organization based in Toronto that produces and promotes Aboriginal theatrical works

Mirvishes the father and son team of Ed and David Mirvish, businessmen who have been influential in the development and presentation of theatre in Canada and who own the Royal Alexandra Theatre, among others, in Toronto

Activities

1. Have a class discussion on the title of this essay. To what work of literature does it allude? Explain the purpose of the literary allusion in the title and how Taylor's title prepares us for the content, style, and tone of the essay.

2. Use the glossary in this anthology and other reference tools to review the meaning of the term *irony*. Prepare to write an analytical essay by finding examples of irony in Taylor's essay. Create a thesis statement in which you explain the impact of Taylor's use of irony on his audience. When writing your essay, use the method of *cause and effect* to explore and assess how Taylor uses this literary device to instruct his readers and persuade them to change their attitudes.

3. Working with a partner, pick one of the questions and answers from Taylor's essay and use it as the basis for a humorous improvised skit. In your skit, reconstruct the entire conversation that could have taken place. Record your skit or perform it for another pair. Afterward, have the pair evaluate how successful both the content and the style of your skit were in using humour to inform, entertain, and educate.

Another Viewpoint: Culture

Discuss whether or not you think this type of irony would be appropriate if it had been written by someone with a non-Native background. Do research into the issue of voice appropriation. Then participate in a class discussion in which you explore and analyze the arguments that form the basis of this issue.

A Modest Proposal

For Preventing the Children of Poor People in Ireland from Being a Burden to Their Parents or Country, and for Making Them Beneficial to the Public

Jonathan Swift

Jonathan Swift, one of the most renowned satirists in world literature, is best known for his novel *Gulliver's Travels*. Although he spent a great deal of his life in England, Swift was born in Ireland in 1667, where he died in 1745. He was an Anglican priest, but often chastised the Church for religious complacency. Though Swift began by writing poetry, he turned increasingly to satire and social commentary, frequently about the plight of the Irish, who were experiencing extreme poverty and famine. What responsibility do writers have to comment on social issues and injustices? To what extent can they affect public opinion and government policy? Why do you think writers are often among the first people imprisoned by totalitarian regimes?

It is a melancholy object to those who walk through this great town or travel in the country, when they see the streets, the roads, and cabin doors, crowded with beggars of the female sex, followed by three, four, or six children, all in rags and importuning every passenger for an alms. These mothers, instead of being able to work for their honest livelihood, are forced to employ all their time in strolling to beg sustenance for their helpless infants, who, as they grow up, either turn thieves for want of work, or leave their dear native country to fight for the Pretender in Spain, or sell themselves to the Barbadoes.

I think it is agreed by all parties that this prodigious number of children in the arms, or on the backs, or at the heels of their mothers, and frequently of their fathers, is in the present deplorable state of the kingdom a very great additional grievance; and therefore whoever could find out a fair, cheap, and easy method of making these children sound, useful members of the commonwealth would deserve so well of the public as to have his statue set up for a preserver of the nation.

But my intention is very far from being confined to provide only for the children of professed beggars; it is of a much greater extent, and shall take in the whole number of infants at a certain age who are born of parents in effect as little able to support them as those who demand our charity in the streets.

As to my own part, having turned my thoughts for many years upon this important subject, and maturely weighed the several schemes of other projectors, I have always found them grossly mistaken in their computation. It is true, a child just dropped from its dam may be supported by her milk for a solar year, with little other nourishment; at most not above the value of two shillings, which the mother may certainly get, or the value in scraps, by her lawful occupation of begging; and it is exactly at one year old that I propose to provide for them in such a manner as instead of being a charge upon their parents or the parish, or wanting food and raiment for the rest of their lives, they shall on the contrary contribute to the feeding, and partly to the clothing, of many thousands....

The number of souls in this kingdom being usually reckoned one million and a half, of these I calculate there may be about two hundred thousand couple whose wives are breeders; from which number I subtract thirty thousand couples who are able to maintain their own children, although I apprehend there cannot be so many under the present distresses of the kingdom; but this being granted, there will remain an hundred and seventy thousand breeders. I again subtract fifty thousand for those women who miscarry, or whose children die by accident or disease within the year. There only remain an hundred and twenty thousand children of poor parents annually born. The question therefore is, how this number shall be reared and provided for, which, as I have already said, under the present situation of affairs, is utterly impossible by all the methods hitherto proposed. For we can neither employ them in handicraft or agriculture; we neither build houses (I mean in the country) nor cultivate land. They can very seldom pick up a livelihood by stealing till they arrive at six years old, except where they are of towardly parts; although I confess they learn the rudiments much earlier, during which time they can however be looked upon only as probationers, as I have been informed by a principal gentleman in the county of Cavan, who protested to me that he never knew above one or two instances under the ages of six, even in a part of the kingdom so renowned for the quickest proficiency in that art.

I am assured by our merchants that a boy or a girl before twelve years old is no salable commodity; and even when they come to this age they will not yield above three pounds, or three pounds and half a crown at most on the Exchange; which cannot turn to account either to the parents or the kingdom, the charge of nutriment and rags having been at least four times that value.

I shall now therefore humbly propose my own thoughts, which I hope will not be liable to the least objection.

I have been assured by a very knowing American of my acquaintance in London, that a young healthy child well nursed is at a year old a most delicious, nourishing, and wholesome food, whether stewed, roasted, baked, or boiled; and I make no doubt that it will equally serve in a fricassee or a ragout.

I do therefore humbly offer it to public consideration that of the hundred and twenty thousand children, already computed, twenty thousand may be reserved for breed, whereof only one fourth part to be males, which is more than we allow to sheep, black cattle, or swine; and my reason is that these children are seldom the fruits of marriage, a circumstance not much regarded by our savages, therefore one male will be sufficient to serve four females. That the remaining hundred thousand may at a year old be offered in sale to the persons of quality and fortune through the kingdom, always advising the mother to let them suck plentifully in the last month, so as to render them plump and fat for a good table. A child will make two dishes at an entertainment for friends;

and when the family dines alone, the fore or hind quarter will make a reasonable dish, and seasoned with a little pepper or salt will be very good boiled on the fourth day, especially in winter.

I have reckoned upon a medium that a child just born will weigh twelve pounds, and in a solar year if tolerably nursed increaseth to twenty-eight pounds.

I grant this food will be somewhat dear, and therefore very proper for landlords, who, as they have already devoured most of the parents, seem to have the best title to the children.

Infant's flesh will be in season throughout the year, but more plentiful in March, and a little before and after. For we are told by a grave author, an eminent French physician, that fish being a prolific diet, there are more children born in Roman Catholic countries about nine months after Lent than at any other season; therefore, reckoning a year after Lent, the markets will be more glutted than usual, because the number of popish infants is at least three to one in this kingdom; and therefore it will have one other collateral advantage, by lessening the number of Papists among us.

I have already computed the charge of nursing a beggar's child (in which list I reckon all cottagers, labourers, and four fifths of the farmers) to be about two shillings per annum, rags included; and I believe no gentleman would repine to give ten shillings for the carcass of a good fat child, which, as I have said, will make four dishes of excellent nutritive meat, when he hath only some particular friend or his own family to dine with him. Thus the squire will learn to be a good landlord, and grow popular among the tenants; the mother will have eight shillings net profit, and be fit for the work till she produces another child.

Those who are more thrifty (as I must confess the times require) may flay the carcass; the skin of which artificially dressed will make admirable gloves for ladies, and summer boots for fine gentlemen.

As to our city of Dublin, shambles may be appointed for this purpose in the most convenient parts of it, and butchers we may be assured will not be wanting; although I rather recommend buying the children alive, and dressing them hot from the knife as we do roasting pigs.

A very worthy person, a true lover of his country, and whose virtues I highly esteem, was lately pleased in discoursing on this matter to offer a refinement upon my scheme. He said that many gentlemen of this kingdom, having of late destroyed their deer, he conceived that the want of venison might be well supplied by the bodies of young lads and maidens, not exceeding fourteen years of age nor under twelve, so great a number of both sexes in every county being now ready to starve for want of work and service; and these to be disposed of by their parents, if alive, or otherwise by their nearest relations. But with due deference to so excellent a friend and so deserving a patriot, I cannot be altogether in his sentiments; for as to the males, my American acquaintance assured me from frequent experience that their flesh was generally tough and lean, like that of our schoolboys, by continual exercise, and their taste disagreeable; and to fatten them would not answer the charge. Then as to the females, it would, I think with humble submission, be a loss to the public, because they soon would become breeders themselves; and besides, it is not improbable that some scrupulous people might be apt to censure such a practice (although indeed very unjustly) as a little bordering upon cruelty; which I confess, hath always been with me the strongest objection against any project, how well soever intended.

But in order to justify my friend, he confessed that this expedient was put into his head by the famous Psalmanazar, a native of the island Formosa, who came from thence to London above twenty years ago, and in conversation told my friend that in his country when any young person happened to be put to death, the executioner sold the carcass to persons of quality as a prime dainty; and that in his time the body of a plump girl of fifteen, who was crucified for an attempt to poison the emperor, was sold to his Imperial Majesty's prime minister of state, and other great mandarins of the court, in joints from the gibbet, at four hundred crowns. Neither indeed can I deny that if the same use were made of several plump young girls in this town, who without one single groat to their fortunes cannot stir abroad without a chair, and appear at the playhouse and assemblies in foreign fineries which they never will pay for, the kingdom would not be the worse.

Some persons of a desponding spirit are in great concern about that vast number of poor people who are aged, diseased, or maimed, and I have been desired to employ my thoughts what course may be taken to ease the nation of so grievous an encumbrance. But I am not in the least pain upon that matter, because it is very well known that they are every day dying and rotting by cold and famine, and filth and vermin, as fast as can be reasonably expected. And as to the younger labourers, they are now in almost as hopeful a condition. They cannot get work, and consequently pine away for want of nourishment to a degree that if at any time they are accidentally hired to common labour, they have not strength to perform it; and thus the country and themselves are happily delivered from the evils to come.

I have too long digressed, and therefore shall return to my subject. I think the advantages by the proposal which I have made are obvious and many, as well as of the highest importance.

For first, as I have already observed, it would greatly lessen the number of Papists, with whom we are yearly overrun, being the principal breeders of the nation as well as our most dangerous enemies; and who stay at home on purpose to deliver the kingdom to the Pretender, hoping to take their advantage by the absence of so many good Protestants, who have chosen rather to leave their country than stay at home and pay tithes against their conscience to an Episcopal curate.

Secondly, the poorer tenants will have something valuable of their own, which by law may be made liable to distress, and help to pay their landlord's rent, their corn and cattle being already seized and money a thing unknown.

Thirdly, whereas the maintenance of an hundred thousand children, from two years old and upwards, cannot be computed at less than ten shillings a piece per annum, the nation's stock will be thereby increased fifty thousand pounds per annum, besides the profit of a new dish introduced to the tables of all gentlemen of fortune in the kingdom who have any refinement in taste. And the money will circulate among ourselves, the goods being entirely of our own growth and manufacture.

Fourthly, the constant breeders, besides the gain of eight shillings sterling per annum by the sale of their children, will be rid of the charge of maintaining them after the first year.

Fifthly, this food would likewise bring great custom to taverns, where the vintners will certainly be so prudent as to procure the best receipts for dressing it to perfection, and consequently have their houses frequented by all the fine gentlemen, who justly value themselves upon their knowledge in good eating; and a skilful cook, who understands how to oblige his guests, will contrive to make it as expensive as they please.

Sixthly, this would be a great inducement to marriage, which all wise nations have either encouraged by rewards or enforced by laws and penalties. It would increase the care and tenderness of mothers toward their children, when they were sure of a settlement for life to the poor babes, provided in some sort by the public, to their annual profit instead of expense. We should see an honest emulation among the married women, which of them could bring the fattest child to the market. Men would become as fond of their wives during the time of their pregnancy as they are now of their mares in foal, their cows in calf, or sows when they are ready to farrow; nor offer to beat or kick them (as is too frequent a practice) for fear of a miscarriage.

Many other advantages might be enumerated. For instance, the addition of some thousand carcasses in our exportation of barrelled beef, the propagation of swine's flesh, and improvement in the art of making good bacon, so much wanted among us by the great destruction of pigs, too frequent at our tables, which are no way comparable in taste or magnificence to a well-grown, fat, yearling child, which roasted whole will make a considerable figure at a lord mayor's feast or any other public entertainment. But this and many others I omit, being studious of brevity.

Supposing that one thousand families in this city would be constant customers for infants' flesh, besides others who might have it at merry meetings, particularly weddings and christenings, I compute that Dublin would take off annually about twenty thousand carcasses, and the rest of the kingdom (where probably they will be sold somewhat cheaper) the remaining eighty thousand.

I can think of no one objection that will probably be raised against this proposal, unless it should be urged that the number of people will be thereby much lessened in the kingdom. This I freely own, and it was indeed one principal design in offering it to the world. I desire the reader will observe, that I calculate my remedy for this one individual kingdom of Ireland and for no other that ever was, is, or I think ever can be upon earth. Therefore let no man talk to me of other expedients: of taxing our absentees at five shillings a pound: of using neither clothes nor household furniture except what is of our own growth and manufacture: of utterly rejecting the materials and instruments that promote foreign luxury: of curing the expensiveness of pride, vanity, idleness, and gaming in our women: of introducing a vein of parsimony, prudence, and temperance: of learning to love our country, in the want of which we differ even from Laplanders and the inhabitants of Topinamboo: of quitting our animosities and factions,… of being a little cautious not to sell our country and conscience for nothing: of teaching landlords to have at least one degree of mercy toward their tenants: lastly, of putting a spirit of honesty, industry, and skill into our shopkeepers; who, if a resolution could now be taken to buy only our native goods, would immediately unite to cheat and exact upon us in the price, the measure, and the goodness, nor could ever yet be brought to make one fair proposal of just dealing, though often and earnestly invited to it.

Therefore I repeat, let no man talk to me of these and the like expedients, till he hath at least some glimpse of hope that there will ever be some hearty and sincere attempt to put them in practice.

But as to myself, having been wearied out for many years with offering vain, idle, visionary thoughts, and at length utterly despairing of success, I fortunately fell upon this proposal, which, as it is wholly new, so it hath something solid and real, of no expense and little trouble, full in our own power, and whereby we can incur no danger in disobliging

England. For this kind of commodity will not bear exportation, the flesh being of too tender a consistence to admit a long continuance in salt, although perhaps I could name a country which would be glad to eat up our whole nation without it.

After all, I am not so violently bent upon my own opinion as to reject any offer proposed by wise men, which shall be found equally innocent, cheap, easy, and effectual. But before something of that kind shall be advanced in contradiction to my scheme, and offering a better, I desire the author or authors will be pleased maturely to consider two points. First, as things now stand, how they will be able to find food and raiment for an hundred thousand useless mouths and backs. And secondly, there being a round million of creatures in human figure throughout this kingdom, whose sole subsistence put into a common stock would leave them in debt two millions of pounds sterling, adding those who are beggars by profession to the bulk of farmers, cottagers, and labourers, with their wives and children who are beggars in effect; I desire those politicians who dislike my overture, and may perhaps be so bold to attempt an answer, that they will first ask the parents of these mortals whether they would not at this day think it a great happiness to have been sold for food at a year old in the manner I prescribe, and thereby have avoided such a perpetual sense of misfortunes as they have since gone through by the oppression of landlords, the impossibility of paying rent without money or trade, the want of common sustenance, with neither house nor clothes to cover them from the inclemencies of the weather, and the most inevitable prospect of entailing the like or greater miseries upon their breed forever.

I profess, in the sincerity of my heart, that I have not the least personal interest in endeavouring to promote this necessary work, having no other motive than the public good of my country, by advancing our trade, providing for infants, relieving the poor, and giving some pleasure to the rich. I have no children by which I can propose to get a single penny; the youngest being nine years old, and my wife past childbearing.

Notes

the Pretender in Spain James Stuart, son of James I, who claimed the English throne in 1688, but was unsuccessful and continued to live in exile in Spain. A Roman Catholic, he was supported by the Scottish and Irish.

sell themselves to the Barbadoes work as indentured servants in the Caribbean, especially the island of Barbados

raiment clothing

apprehend understand

towardly parts advanced readiness to learn

probationers in training to be thieves

popish, Papists Roman Catholics

cottagers tenant farmers

repine to be discontented

artificially in this instance, skilfully

shambles slaughterhouses

Psalmanazar George Psalmanazar (circa 1679–1763) was an English literary imposter whose real name is not known. Born and educated in France, he was able without detection to invent a complete "Formosan" language and teach this language at Oxford University. In 1706, he was forced to repudiate his claims.

mandarins high public officials; from the Sanskrit word *mantrin*, meaning "counsellor"

gibbet gallows where people were hanged; from the Old French word *gibet*, a diminutive of the word *gibe*, meaning "club"

groat small sum of money

Papists...deliver the kingdom to the Pretender Most Roman Catholics supported James Stuart in his struggle to become king of England.

custom in this instance, business

receipts a synonym for the word *recipes*

Activities

1. In point form, outline the speaker's "modest proposal" and several reasons presented to support it. Then record your personal reactions: How did you react when you first realized what is being proposed? At what point did you realize that the proposal is satirical?

2. Swift's essay "A Modest Proposal" is carefully structured in its beginning (paragraphs 1–7), middle (paragraphs 8–19), and end (paragraphs 20–37). Read the essay and outline the following: which aspects of his topic Swift presents in each section; the methods of development Swift uses to make his argument; and the inclusion of Swift's personal motives and values. Share your observations in a small group.

3. Write your own "modest proposal" to draw attention to a current injustice, cruelty, or folly. After you have completed a first draft, revise your draft to make sure that your thesis is clearly stated and developed, and to enhance the effectiveness of your style.

Another Viewpoint: Literary Modes and Forms

Satire is designed to expose human weaknesses and follies, often with the purpose of stimulating intellectual and social reform. Satirists look at the disparity between the ideal and the reality of individuals, institutions, or practices. In an analytical essay, explore which injustices Swift is denouncing, which particular elements of satire are evident, and which "ideal" conditions Swift is hoping to achieve by his proposal.

Tower of Babel, 1928, M.C. Escher

Get Beyond Babel

Ken Wiwa

Ken Wiwa was born in Lagos, Nigeria, in 1968. Educated in England, Wiwa became a journalist. He was thrust into the spotlight when his father, Ken Saro-Wiwa, was arrested and sentenced to death in Nigeria for his efforts to protect human rights and the environment. Though the son had previously distanced himself from his father's political activities, he led the public campaign to save his father's life. Despite worldwide outcry, Ken Saro-Wiwa was executed in 1995. Today, Ken Wiwa lives and writes in Toronto. In 2000, he published a memoir, *In the Shadow of a Saint: A Son's Journey to Understand His Father's Legacy.* Many individuals and organizations work to protect our physical environment. Threats to our cultural environments also exist. How can a culture be threatened? Do you think we should have the same level of concern for endangered languages and cultures as we do for endangered species?

Earlier this week I received compelling evidence that I am doomed to extinction. According to figures released by the Worldwatch Institute, half of the world's 6,800 languages face annihilation; that's because they are spoken by fewer than 2,500 people. Here in Canada, only three of 50 aboriginal languages may survive the coming cultural Armageddon. Lurking in the reaction to this news, I suspect, is the fear that we will end up speaking English in some monocultural flatland called "Disney."

There is an impassioned school of thought that says that unless we take active steps to preserve our "cultural diversity"—read "languages"—the human race is in danger. When we lose a language, these doomsday prophets say, we lose its knowledge base and worldview; this, they assure us, impoverishes us all.

As a member of an indigenous people, and as someone actively concerned about the fate of my culture, I used to subscribe to this view. I'd soak up the arguments of philologists and writers I admired warning about the implications of losing our languages. I bought all these arguments. Then I started examining my own community's experience.

I am Ogoni. We number an estimated 500,000, and speak six mutually unintelligible dialects—languages, by now—on an overpopulated but fertile floodplain in southern Nigeria. The Ogoni languages and culture are threatened by Nigeria's socioeconomic realities. Our environment has been compromised by aggressive and irresponsible oil exploration. Unemployment, inadequate health care, and neglect by the country's rulers have ripped out my community's heart.

The young, the energetic, and the ambitious have no option but to leave in search of better opportunities. The community is left in the care of the old and the infirm. A whole generation of Ogoni is growing up elsewhere, speaking English, forgetting our languages, exiled from our villages and our traditions. When the elders die, they take our traditions, our folk tales, our myths, our history, and our cultural memories with them. As we say in Africa, "When an old man dies it is like a library has been burned down."

Which is why I started looking into Ogoni history, thinking about my language, trying to shoehorn our myths and folk tales into a compelling story to keep them alive for another generation. But the more I study our history, especially the way our culture and our language has evolved, the more I suspect that those of us who have set out with the intention of reviving a culture by fixing it in time and space may actually be doing more harm than good.

Take the development of my language. According to one of our creation myths, the original Ogoni settlement was at a place called Nama. Here the first Ogoni people cleared the surrounding forest, left one tree standing, and established our roots. Over time our community grew, and people migrated westward into the rain forests until there were 128 villages in Ogoni. Because these settlements were isolated, the language altered subtly. If you go to Ogoni today you can still hear the effects. In the eastern villages we speak a different dialect from the villages on the western fringes.

The point I am making here is that language is in constant flux. To fix it in a particular time and place is to arrest the movement and vitality that shape a language's evolution. The more I examine the way my language has evolved, the more I believe that the best a language can do in response is to go with the flow. As far as I know, no Ogoni language has a word for "computer," but we do say *faa-bu-yon* (car of the sky)— or airplane.

Unless we make a huge effort to open up the language and the culture to embrace our experience of contact with other cultures and the modem world, we will always be vulnerable. To say that is not to diminish the past or our culture, but to acknowledge a simple truth: indigenous peoples must not turn inward and cling to nostalgia for sustenance. Though we look back, we must always go forward.

For me, that's the great poetic insight in Gabriel García Márquez's novel, *One Hundred Years of Solitude.* The community of Macondo begins amid vibrant energy, but ossifies into a parochialism trapped in a cycle of self-repeating prophecies that refuse to embrace or even acknowledge the passage of time. When Marquez delivers his verdict on Macondo (races condemned to 100 years of solitude do not get a second chance), it seems to me to be a warning to all the language curators and conservationists working to preserve our cultures in some cultural museum.

It is a warning that the guardians of the French language, the Académie française, might heed. Once French was the international language of the world; thanks to the Académie's fastidious custody, it is becoming inflexible. English, on the other hand, has rarely been as neurotic about its purity. Most English words are borrowed from other languages; little Anglo-Saxon survives. Only an incurable romantic would attempt to revive Old English for general use. No, English has evolved, absorbed, and adapted. Open to foreign influence, it borrows unashamedly. That's why English has more than 500,000 words in its vocabulary, while French has little more than 100,000.

For me the rise and pre-eminence of English is an example to all cultures about how a language survives and thrives. When Julius Caesar invaded Britain 2,000 years ago, English did not exist. Fifteen hundred years later, Shakespeare had a potential audience of only five million English-speakers. Over the next 400 years, English would come to be spoken by more than one billion people. According to *The Story of English* (by Robert McCrum and Robert MacNeil), English is now "more widely scattered, more widely spoken than any other language has ever been."

Thanks to its versatility, shameless habit of appropriation, and the violence and aggression of its people, English is now the *lingua franca* of the world. What is more remarkable is that despite its mongrel nature, the English worldview has persisted. Through all the mutations and adaptations it has still managed to service and protect a small island's place in the world.

The English people and the English language have survived by picking up influences and adapting words from dead languages, like Latin and ancient Greek, and grafting elements from their worldviews, religions, and philosophies onto the English trunk.

English is both a lesson and an obstacle to the development of other languages and cultures. Which is why it strikes me that to lament the death of languages and to prescribe a solution that freezes language in time is to condemn a culture and a language to certain extinction.

If cultural diversity is so vital to our survival as a race, we must understand how languages work over time. After all, it only took English 400 years to achieve its current status. Who is to say that in another 500 years English will not go the same way as Greek, Latin, or French? There is one more lesson that leaps out from my reading of the story of English. It is this: languages and cultures don't die—they just get absorbed into something else.

Notes

Babel a biblical city where construction of a tower ended when builders could not understand each other's language

Worldwatch Institute a non-profit public policy research organization that collects and analyzes cross-disciplinary information about global environmental issues

Armageddon a huge battle resulting in the total defeat of one side; a reference, in the New Testament, to a battle between good and evil before the day of judgment; from the Hebrew words *har megiddon*, meaning "the hill of Megiddo"

Académie française a French literary academy whose mission is to "protect the purity" of the French language.

lingua franca any combination of languages which two people who do not speak the same language use to communicate with each other; refers, specifically, to a mixture of Italian, French, Greek, Turkish, Arabic, and other languages formerly spoken on the eastern Mediterranean coast

Activities

1. Write an informal response to this essay, in which you describe and react to its context. Consider questions such as the following: From what social and cultural perspective or context is Wiwa writing? How does your social and cultural perspective affect your reaction to his essay?

2. Meet in groups of three to analyze and discuss the organization and persuasive strategies Wiwa uses. Assign each person one of the following sections of the essay: paragraphs 1–6, 7–11, or 12–16. Have each person make a chart that documents his or her paragraphs' topic, purpose, rhetorical devices, and persuasive strategies. Meet to share and discuss your analyses. As a group, evaluate the effectiveness of the organization and persuasive strategies Wiwa has used.

3. Do research to identify other views and data related to the issue of endangered languages in Canada and elsewhere. Organize a class debate on one of the following resolutions: a) Endangered languages should be preserved; b) Preserving a language is not an essential part of preserving a culture. Invite feedback on the effectiveness of the arguments presented.

The Death of History Is Bunk

Patrick Watson

Patrick Watson was born in Toronto in 1929. He has worked as an actor, producer, director, and writer. He has hosted such documentary television programs as *This Hour Has Seven Days*, *The Watson Report*, *Live from the Lincoln Center* and *The Canadians*. His *Witness to Yesterday* television series featured encounters with great figures from the past. From 1989 to 1994, he was the chairman of the CBC. In 1998, he was appointed to the position of commissioning editor for History Television. Some people are concerned about the extent to which people are familiar with the history of their own country. Do you think Canadians and citizens from other countries know enough about Canadian history? What stands out in your memory about the Canadian history you have studied in school? What do you think are the best ways to teach Canadian history?

It is fashionable to deplore the fact that few Canadian schools teach Canadian history. The hand-wringers whimper that young Canadians don't know about Canada's first prime minister, or the date of Confederation, or the meaning of Vimy Ridge.

The assumption is that naming events and memorizing dates make for good citizenship and a wise life. Garbage! If the disappearance of history from high-school curriculums means that the kind of classes I suffered as a kid are gone for good, then bravo. The new generations have been spared the mind-paralyzing waste we were forced to endure, copying from the blackboard lists of dates, of battles, of kings and other dignitaries, of the passing of legislation. If we could reproduce those vacuous details in a quiz, we passed—we had "done history."

But such an approach has not disappeared from the minds of those who write books about who killed Canadian history. In 2000, author Rudyard Griffiths wrote in the *Globe and Mail* that history means "defining events."

"To deny students…a coherent education in the history of Canada is to shut them out of the National Conversation," he wrote. If readers are unable to equate the Charlottetown Conference with Confederation, "they are ill-equipped to gauge the veracity of the claim that Charlottetown was, indeed, a defining moment."

Hello? I cannot equate the Charlottetown Conference with Confederation! And if anybody tells me they can I will soon lose interest in them as conversational partners.

It is a thin theory of history that "equates" a conference with the complex and endless activities that flow therefrom. The Canadian Confederation got a name and some marching orders at Charlottetown, yes. But would it not be more enlightening to know that was done in the salons and backrooms and bedrooms and dining rooms and rectories and bars where the real thinking and compromises took place—before and after being brought to the long table in the big room with the high, arched windows?

To think that Charlottetown defined Confederation is to leave out a catalogue of later events of massive impact, such as the genocide of the European Jews, the Russian Revolution, the telephone, rural electrification, Marquis wheat, urban tramways, free public schools, Italian restaurants, American movies, and television. These are only a few transforming forces that have spoken more to the texture of the civil society we are trying to build than did one conference, however much a crossroads, a century and a third ago.

There are, of course, moments that change our compass bearing sufficiently that we can determine a measure of definition in them. But the Canadians who continuously reshape our society are the class president who sticks up for a principle, the poet or novelist, designer, painter, candidate for town council, fundraiser, creative restaurateur, or the comic who says, "The separatist movement is the glue that holds Canada together." These people remake our nation not by redefining Canada, but by tinkering with it.

That's what writer Evan Solomon says makes us what we are: our tinkering. The Americans like to define. They started with a Declaration of Independence and followed with a Bill of Rights and a Constitution. So now when things go wrong, they scratch their historical heads and ask, "What did the Founding Fathers intend?"

Canadians don't do that. We say, "Well, the old buggy won't run on these new roads with those worn tires; let's see if we can figure out a better way." We are not overwhelmed by guilt or a sense of failure when it's time to fix things.

History contains, but is not made up of great events, defining moments, crucial institutions. History, like art and music, begins locally and grows outward as its students grow in their capacity to look at a larger world. The first historical question is, "Mommy, where did I come from?" In a sense it is the only important question. The exploration of history is a rewarding activity only if it produces meaning out of the chaos of experience. Then, if we find meaning that we can share with others, we become engaged with those others. That engagement will be the beginning of citizenship. Citizenship does not begin with preachings about defining moments, whether Charlottetown or John A. Macdonald or Vimy Ridge.

Travelling the country to the heritage fairs that have emerged from the Heritage Project of Charles Bronfman's CRB Foundation, I have seen Canadian children come back from a foray into the local community, their eyes glistening with the joy of having discovered meaning by doing local history.

In a small city in the B.C. interior I met a 12-year-old girl who, curious about her French surname, tracked it back through the generations. She found not only a lot of ancient photographs and clippings, but ultimately the actual parchment that carried the signature of the Sovereign, appointing her great-great-great-grandfather as the first French-speaking judge of the superior court of Quebec. Do I have to spell out what that search meant in terms of history? Of meaning? Of engagement with her society? And of pride and satisfaction in the completion of a self-initiated search? She owns that piece of history. She knows, existentially, what doing history means and that it is not memorizing the dates of battles or the names of prime ministers.

At the Summerside heritage fair, two 11-year-olds wondered aloud to each other what all those old rusted bits of farm machinery were that lay half-buried in the fence rows—"Hey, Dad, what is that stuff?" Dad didn't know. So they asked some elderly farmers. One of these found an old Massey-Harris catalogue. Another had a friend with a front-end loader who agreed to lift some of this stuff out of the ground so they could see it better. And with that kind of help, those two boys put together a display in a hangar at the old Summerside base of part of the past of Prince Edward Island that nobody else knew.

Perhaps some day a girl in Kelowna or a couple of boys in Summerside will want to fit some of the things they have learned into a larger context. Perhaps they will stumble, in a novel or a play or a book or a film, over the fact that Canada refused asylum to refugees from the Holocaust, and that changing that attitude radically changed the country. Perhaps their inquiries will go elsewhere: to the reason why a certain stream runs red and murky, not clear and sweet; or to the puzzle behind a group who demand that a certain prayer be made formally part of the school day, or what a man meant about the state and the bedrooms of the nation.

But however far their inquiries go, no amount of classroom time, or fretting about the legacy of Charlottetown, can approach what those kids discovered when they found a meaningful answer to an apparently trivial question.

So if we genuinely care about how history impinges upon citizenship (that is, our collective search for a civil society), let us fret less about what is catalogued in the curriculum, and more about how to stimulate the young inquiring mind.

There is a hunger for narrative about our past. History Television here in Canada has had a steady growth in viewership in its four years of life, 64 per cent last year alone. Those heritage fairs, which began in Winnipeg eight years ago with a few hundred kids, last year found more than 100,000 young Canadians doing research projects and writing playlets and producing historical videos. Across Canada, playwrights are attracting enthusiastic audiences to history on the stage, much of it very local in setting, if not in significance.

Hollywood continues to love movies on historical subjects; they win Oscars and other international awards. Millions of kids are playing historical computer games. CTV's broadcast of *Nuremberg* this month averaged two million viewers a night. Even CBC Television, as committed to ratings and the sale of advertising as any other aggressive network, has committed tens of millions of dollars and some 30 hours of documentary television to its *Canada: A People's History.*

History isn't dead; we are making it every day, and it is making us.

Notes

Vimy Ridge battle fought from April 9–14, 1917, during World War I, in which 3,598 Canadians were killed. It was the first time that Canadians attacked as a united group. Despite the large number of casualties, they swept the German soldiers off the ridge and their success created a strong sense of achievement and national pride.

Charlottetown Conference Held in September 1864, this conference set Confederation in motion. The Maritime legislatures had planned the conference to discuss a union of the Maritime provinces, but representatives from the rest of Canada asked to attend. There delegates agreed on an outline for what would become the new country of Canada.

Marquis wheat a hybrid variety of wheat produced by Canadians Percy and Charles Saunders at the end of the nineteenth century. Its early maturation greatly extended the area where wheat could be grown.

Activities

1. In this essay, Patrick Watson holds a strong position on the teaching of history. In your notebook, describe what kind of teacher you think Watson would make. Would you like to be a student in his class? What is your response to the types of learning activities he suggests?

2. In a three-column chart, prepare an analysis of the techniques that Watson uses to persuade his readers. In the first column, list the techniques Watson uses to appeal to reason, emotion, authority, and to ethics, beliefs, values. In the second column, write an example of each technique from the essay. In the third column, write a sentence of your own that illustrates effective use of the technique. Then list each fact or example he uses to illustrate his argument.

3. Patrick Watson has served as the commissioning editor for History Television. In this capacity, the commissioning editor receives submissions and makes decisions about the kinds of programs that will be broadcast on this specialty channel. In small groups, brainstorm some ideas that you think would make effective and interesting programming for History Television. Include suggestions that would have particular appeal for high-school students of history. You may want to send your best ideas via e-mail to a history television channel.

Wanderers by Choice

Eva Hoffman

Eva Hoffman was born in Krakow, Poland, in 1945, the child of Holocaust survivors. When she was thirteen, the family immigrated to Vancouver. At age nineteen, Hoffman moved to the United States and eventually became an editor and writer for the *New York Times*. She has written widely on political and cultural subjects and has received many grants and awards, including a Guggenheim Fellowship. Think of someone you know who has travelled extensively. What are the benefits and the challenges of travel? Would you ever consider living in another country? If so, what appeals to you about this prospect? What challenges might you face?

Exile was once the worst punishment. Now it's a glamorous adventure.

Since Adam and Eve left the Garden of Eden, is there anyone who does not, in some way, feel like an exile? We feel ejected from our first homes and landscapes, from our first romance, from our authentic self. An ideal sense of belonging, of attuning with others and ourselves, eludes us.

Historically, the symbolic meaning and experience of exile have changed. In medieval Europe, it was the worst punishment possible, because people's identities were defined by their role and place in society. This implied a highly charged concept of home—although home did not necessarily mean birthplace. For medieval clerics, it was the city that housed the papal seat. Jews nurtured a powerful idea of home that existed on two levels: the real communities they inhabited and "Israel," which became an imaginative centre from which they derived their essential identity.

In recent years, great shifts in the political and social landscape have affected the very notion of exile. Cross-cultural movement has become the norm, which means that leaving one's native country is not as dramatic or traumatic as it used to be. The ease of travel and communication, combined with the looser borders, gives rise to endless criss-crossing streams of wanderers and guest workers, nomadic adventurers and international drifters. Many are driven by harsh circumstance, but the element of choice is there for most.

People who leave the former Soviet Union nowadays are likely to be economic migrants or Mafia tax dodgers rather than dissidents expelled by ruthless state power. One Bengali village has a tradition of long migrations: many men leave for years or even decades, but always intend to return. They are not powerless victims of globalization; smart young men choose different countries for the economic advantages they offer. Almost all go back, a bit richer and more important in the eyes of their fellow villagers.

The *Herald Tribune* recently characterized the increasing number of American expatriates in Europe: "They are the Americans abroad, and their number is soaring in a time when travel is unblinkingly routine, communications easy and instant, and telecommuting a serious option. They are abroad in a world where they can watch the Super Bowl live from a Moscow sports bar or send an e-mail from an Internet café in Prague."

We all recognize these basic features of our new, fast-changing social landscape. Whether or not we have left, we know how easy it is to leave. We know that we live in a global village, although the village is virtual indeed—dependent not on locality but on the detachment of knowledge, action, information, and identity from a specific place. We have become less spacebound.

Exile used to be considered difficult. It involves dislocation, disorientation, self-division. But today we have come to value exactly those qualities of experience that exile demands—uncertainty, displacement, fragmented identity. Within this framework, exile becomes sexy and glamorous. Nomadism and diasporism have become fashionable terms in intellectual debate. Not only actual exile is at stake, but also how we situate ourselves in the world.

My emigration took place during the Cold War, though not in the worst Stalinist years. I happened to be a young, unwilling emigrant, yanked from my happy childhood. I felt the loss of my first homeland acutely, fuelled by the sense that this departure was irrevocable. Poland was suddenly unreachable, and I felt as if I were being taken out of life itself.

Like so many emigrants, I was in effect without language. To lose an internal language is to slide into an inarticulate darkness where we become alien to ourselves; to lose the ability to describe the world is to render the world a bit less vivid. It takes time before a new language begins to inhabit us deeply, to enter the fabric of our psyches and express who we are.

As with language, so with culture: how much incoherence we risk if we fall out of its matrix. We know that cultures differ in customs, food, religions, social arrangements. What takes longer to understand is that each culture has subliminal values and beliefs. They inform our most intimate assumptions and perceptions, our sense of beauty, of acceptable distances between people, or notions of pleasure and pain. On that fundamental level, a culture gives form and focus to our mental and emotional lives. We are nothing more—or less—than an encoded memory of our heritage.

Real dislocation, the loss of all familiar external and internal parameters, is not glamorous or cool. It is an upheaval in the deep material of the self.

Exile, however, gives perspective, making every emigrant an anthropologist and relativist. To have a deep experience of two cultures is to know that no culture is absolute, to discover that the seemingly natural aspects of our identities and social reality can be arranged, shaped, or articulated in another way. Biculturalism has its pleasures—the relish of sharpened insight, the savviness of skepticism—and they can become addictive.

These virtues have serious defects. The addiction may be too seductive; as a psychological choice, being in exile may become not only too arduous but also too easy. The exile lives in a story in which one's past becomes radically different from the present. The lost homeland, sequestered in the imagination as a mythic, static realm, can be idealized or demonized, or become a space of projections and fantasies.

In our habitually diasporic and nomadic world, the playing field has changed. When all borders are crossable and all boundaries permeable, it is harder to imagine an idyllic realm or a permanent enemy. This situation is initially confusing, yet its merits are easily discernible. We move not only between places but also between cultures with grace and ease. We are less shocked by prevailing assumptions, less prone to absolute assertions. The literature of this new nomadism, represented by Salman Rushdie, is full of multiple cultural references colliding and colluding in robust, vital play. This is a vision of exile as comedy rather than despair.

But I wonder if, in our world of easy come, easy go, of sliding among places and meanings without alighting on any of them for very long, we don't lose an internal focus and certain strengths that come from gathering experiences and accumulating understanding, from placing ourselves squarely where we are and living in a shared framework. I wonder if, in trying to exist in barely perceivable spaces, or conceiving of experience as movement between discrete dots on a horizontal map, we don't risk what the novelist Milan Kundera calls "the unbearable lightness of being." It is the illness that comes upon unanchored people, those who travel perpetually to new moments and sensations and to whom no internal feeling is more important than another.

Among nomads, exile loses its charge because there is no place from which one can be expelled, no powerful notion of home. Indeed, now we are less likely to say that all fiction is homesickness than to say that all homesickness is fiction—that home never was what it was cracked up to be, the haven of safety and affection we imagine. Instead, we conceive of home mostly as a site of enclosure and closure, of narrow-mindedness and nationalism. There are two kinds of homes: the home of our childhood and origin, which is a given, and the home of our adulthood, which is achieved only through hard-earned, patient choice, the labour of understanding and gradual arrival.

In a parable about the founder of the Jewish Hasidic movement, thieves tell the Baal Shem Tov about a network of underground corridors that leads directly from Poland to Palestine and offer to take him there. With great difficulty, they walk through the tunnels more than halfway to their destination. Then, suddenly, the Baal Shem Tov sees before him "a flaming sword, turning this way and that," and decides to turn back.

On one level this parable shows the Baal Shem Tov's ambivalence about going to Palestine. On another, its unconscious, compressed message may be that we can't steal into paradise, or take a shortcut to the tree of life. Of course, the parable also suggests something about the fear of approaching our object of desire and finding ourselves in paradise—which may then turn out to be an ordinary garden, needing weeding, tilling, and watering.

To be sure, it takes long, strenuous work to find terrain of safety or significance or love. And it may often be easier to live in exile with a fantasy of paradise than to suffer the ambiguities and compromises of cultivating actual, earthly places. And yet, if we do not create home structures for ourselves, we risk exile that we do not even recognize as banishment. And, paradoxically, if we do not acknowledge the possibility and pain of expulsion, then we will not know that somewhere a tree of life—if we labour hard enough to approach it—can yield fruits of meaning after all.

Notes

clerics members of the clergy, such as priests or ministers

papal seat the residence of the Pope of the Roman Catholic Church, located in Rome, Italy

diasporism dispersal of people away from their homeland; from the Greek words *dia*, meaning "through," and *speirein*, meaning "to scatter or sow"

Cold War the struggle for power and prestige between the Western powers and the Communist bloc from the end of World War II to about 1990

Stalinist policies associated with Joseph Stalin, the leader of the Soviet Union from 1924 to 1953; marked by terror and authoritarianism

psyches in this instance, souls

matrix the object or place where something originates; from the Latin word *mater*, meaning "mother"

sequestered isolated, set apart

colluding conspiring or plotting with others

Milan Kundera a renowned novelist, born in Czechoslovakia, who settled in France for political reasons and had his Czech citizenship revoked by the Communist regime

Jewish Hasidic movement Founded in Poland in the eighteenth century, this branch of Judaism stresses joyous religious expression through song and dance.

Baal Shem Tov in Hebrew, the Master of the Good Name; the name given to the founder of the modern Hasidic movement, Israel ben Eliezer, whose life was the subject of many tales

Activities

1. Write a letter to the editor of a hypothetical magazine in which this article might appear. Before you begin, select a number of magazines and study the content and style of their letters to the editor. Using these letters as a model for your own, express your response to the author's ideas.

2. Discuss the rhetorical strategies the author employs in "Wanderers by Choice." Identify, for example, the effective use of narrative, description, analogy, and cause and effect. With a partner, reread some recent pieces of your own writing and consider how incorporating these strategies would strengthen your work.

3. Recall a time when you experienced some of the thoughts and emotions the author describes in this essay. Write a narrative essay in which you explore this incident in your life. How did your experience change your understanding of yourself or of the world? Read your work aloud in order to ensure that your punctuation contributes to the clarity of your text.

Peace, Technology, and the Role of Ordinary People

Ursula Franklin

Ursula Franklin was born in Munich, Germany, in 1921. She studied at the Technical University of Berlin in Germany and did postdoctoral work at the University of Toronto. Franklin is a world-renowned expert in the structure of metals and alloys. She pioneered the development of archaeometry, the science of applying the modern techniques of materials analysis to archaeology. In 1984, Franklin became the first woman to be named a full university professor at the University of Toronto. Franklin has helped to develop Canadian science policy through the Science Council of Canada and the Natural Sciences and Engineering Research Council of Canada. She has worked tirelessly to educate scientists and society on the impact of technology upon our quality of life and our survival. Her many honours include a Governor General's Award in 1991 and Companion of the Order of Canada in 1992. In this speech, she outlines the transformation of war from the time of the Cold War to what she believes is now a war for global market power. What does peace mean to you? What conditions must exist in order for world peace to exist?

What I would like to do tonight is to look at what has happened to the concerns about peace and science since 1989 when John and Lois Dove so tragically left us. I want to do it by looking at the three corners that encompass this field of concern: one is peace, the second is technology, and the third is the role of ordinary people in the search for peace.

In 1989 it looked as if our concerns for peace were coming to some resolution. It looked as if there might be peace because the end of the Cold War appeared to be in sight; the quest for peace in some way was going to be, if not completely successful, at least substantially advanced.

The general quest for peace can be seen as the set of questions that makes us think: how do we get from here to a world in which there is, to use a term that Kenneth Boulding favoured, stable peace?

We know that peace means the presence of justice, and the absence of fear, as well as the absence of war—war both as a threat and as a reality. It appeared in 1989 that there might be a chance to get closer to that goal of stable peace. Our dream of getting there seemed closer to realization.

The peace we pray and work for is not a commodity, but the consequence of a just ordering of society. Thus there are essential political, human, and economic components that make peace possible. What would become possible through stable peace is the prevalence of justice, compassion, and fairness and with it the absence of fear.

Unfortunately, the sphere of our own reality has changed very drastically since 1989, mostly for the worse, even though our activities in the quest for peace have not diminished. The global political realities have changed in a very strange way. All who had hoped that, with the end of the Cold War, some of the developments that we had pressed for would come to pass were deeply saddened by the turn of events.

There had been, for instance, the expectation that money that used to be spent on the arms race would become available to meet human needs. In other words, there was the hope for a peace dividend. We expected there would be more money for teaching and research, for arresting environmental deterioration, for building institutions of peace and international co-operation. Once the burden of the arms race would be lightened or lifted, we thought, a very different set of priorities for the use of public funds would emerge. Why did this not happen? The end of the Cold War did not rechannel resources into peace, the environment, or unmet human needs. Instead of the promised peace dividend, we got a displacement of war, rather than an abolition of war. The displacement of war occurred essentially on two levels. On the first level, war as the old shooting reality is still painfully present in Bosnia, Chechnya, and many other places in the world.

But in addition to the replacement of the threat of war between the big powers by war among smaller states, we have witnessed another form of the displacement of war: its displacement into the economic sphere. As part of these developments we have seen significant transmutations of the social institution of war. War has been updated with a set of modern instruments to assist in the struggle for global commercial hegemony.

Economic competition and conflict have taken on the very characteristics of active, slaughtering warfare—from propaganda and scapegoating to the loss of lives, displacement of populations, and the destruction of natural and built environments. These events put the peace movement again in the position of having to struggle against the arrogance and ignorance of power, against impending destruction, occupation, and conquest.

Instead of enjoying a peace dividend, we see in our own country cutbacks and layoffs. We see neglect and degradation of scholarship, of the civil environment, and of nature. The so-called job crisis, the automation of work and human tasks, is on the most profound level a war against people. The new policies of rationalization and globalization of alliances and trade agreements are part and parcel of the type of threat system that the peace movement has tried to expose and fight at least for the past four decades.

In spite of the end of the Cold War, neither the mentality nor the practitioners of the threat system have disappeared. On the contrary, the threat system is growing internationally and nationally. What we have seen at the end of the Cold War was not, as one might have hoped for in 1989, a decrease in the incidence of war. What happened, I hold, is that war has been transposed into another key.

Just as music can be transposed into another key, I would like to put to you the thought that war, in addition to its continuing presence in terms of armed struggle and the preparation for armed conflict (complete with arms sales and attendant profits) has undergone a social and political transposition into a new key. We, as peace people, need to understand, explain, and confront the new transposition, the new mutation of the social institution of war.

At this point you well may ask: How come? What happened? Surely, with the end of the Cold War, the justification and the stated reason for an arms race ended (remember, there was an evil empire, justifying everything from Star Wars to stealth bombers). Why did the major world power not convert to peace? Why did the co-operative and constructive developments we had hoped for not come about? In order to come to grips with these questions, let us reflect for a moment on the nature of the transposition of war into a new key and on the new instruments that are now playing the old tunes.

First, anyone wanting to make war needs an enemy. In the new war context one may ask: Who is the enemy? Where is the enemy? In looking for an answer, it will be necessary to give some special attention to the recent manifestation of modern technologies. Let's start with a definition of technology. From my point of view, technology is best defined as practice, i.e., "the way things are done around here."

Current practice, of course, includes machines and devices, computers and every form of network and machinery. Yet all these instrumentalities are embedded in something larger, which is why I find helpful the definition of technology as "the way things are done around here." Clearly, the way things are done today is not necessarily the way things were done in the past nor the way things will be done in the future. Thus this definition of technology lets us keep determinism and fatalism at bay.

Citizen advocacy has often involved discussions of technology, critiques of the way things were done—as well as what was being done. Technological changes have frequently brought groups within society face to face with the need to influence decision-making and regulations in areas that suddenly affected everyone's daily lives—be it the testing of nuclear weapons, the pollution of air or water, or the depiction of violence on television. The subject and thrust of citizen interventions can be a sensitive barometer indicating incipient changes in social and political relationships.

What then should be the themes of citizen interventions in the mid-'90s, particularly those involving the work for peace? I am convinced that it is necessary to refocus the citizens' perspectives and priorities as well as to scrutinize the role technology played in the transition from the Cold War world to the present post–Cold War relations.

In the Massey Lectures on "The Real World of Technology" I tried to illustrate the relationships between the development of military technologies and economic policies of national governments. I said then that there are two distinct tasks for any state that wishes to use military production as an infrastructure for the advancement of technology and employment: (1) the state has to assure the flow of money to the military-industrial complex, and (2) the state has to assure at the same time the ongoing presence of an enemy who can justify massive outlays of public funds for research, development, and procurement of instruments and infrastructures of "defence."

The designated enemy must warrant the development of the most advanced technological devices. The enemy must be cunning, threatening, and just barely beatable by novel, truly ingenious, and heroic technologies. And I added then (it was 1989) that it will be interesting to see how Western "defence" infrastructures respond to the possibility that internal changes in the Soviet Union could eliminate its role as the designated enemy.

I ventured the thought that the social and political needs for an enemy might be so deeply entrenched in the real world of technology, as we know it, that new enemies would have to appear relatively speedily, so that the existing technological power structure could be maintained. Even then I was afraid that there could be a turning inward of the war machine. One has to remember that, after all, the enemy does not have to be the government or the citizens of a foreign state. There is a lot of scope, as well as historical precedence, for pursuing the enemy within.

Unfortunately, it seems that this turning inward of the war machine was what happened when "the evil empire" collapsed. The West's technological infrastructures were not dismantled but continued to be used. Their new use, I would suggest to you, is a new form of war (i.e., the transposition I spoke about earlier) that is now called globalization and global competition.

In other words, the technological tools of control and conquest are now serving their old functions in a new key, thus creating a new form of war. The new battlefields are "the markets," though not pleasant local markets like the St. Lawrence Market or the Kensington Market, where real people sell and buy, chat, and get to know each other.

The new markets are the stock and currency markets, the faceless markets of electronic transactions. The responses of these markets have become significant indicators of the supposed well-being of people and nations. How the stock and money markets react to elections and referenda appears to be much more meaningful to governments than the so-called will of the people. It is, of course, not new that wars are being fought for access to resources, for the enhancement of commerce and trade. What is new, in terms of the transmutation of war itself, is that the battlefields are no longer territorial. There is no physical ground involved that may be "ours" or "theirs."

What the technologies of forty years of war-making have achieved is to make territory immaterial, just as intercontinental ballistic missiles have made national boundaries immaterial and neutrality irrelevant. The development that we witness now is an internally consistent extension of the extraterritoriality in modern weapons developments.

The full arsenal of the publicly financed technologies of war—from operations research to computer systems, from satellites to space communications and integrated networks—has become the instrument of a new transposed war for global commercial power.

You may well ask, "If what we experience today is indeed a war without national boundaries and defined territories, who is the enemy? Where is the enemy?"

Let me give you my response first, and then my arguments—which you may or may not consider valid. In the war of global competition the enemy are people—not the people, meaning a particular class, group, or nationality, but all those people who look at community, at work, at nature, and at other human beings as sources of meaning and interaction and not as commodities.

Whatever cannot be merely bought and sold, whatever cannot be expressed in terms of money and gain/loss transactions, stands in the way of "the market" and is enemy territory to be occupied, transformed, and conquered. Whatever work can be done by machines or devices, will be done by machines or devices, rather than by people, who become surplus; they have to be "laid off"—put aside like dirty dishes, sent away to someone else—the nightmare of ethnic cleansing in a technological transposition.

Let me now restate my interpretation of the current scene, because I would like to come to the third strand of my argument: the question of the role of ordinary people. I hold that in the new form of transposed war there is no longer a clear distinction between "them" and "us"—a distinction that passports might define. The new enemy territory that is being attacked is the territory of non-market forces and its inhabitants.

It is every area that is informed by concerns other than the market considerations of buying and selling and profiting. The new battlefields are in those territories, physical as well as mental, that are the home of the common good, of art, of friendship and scholarship, of whatever is held in common and cannot be cut up into private parcels of property. This realm and those who care for it contain the main targets and enemies of the new war.

It may be that I am wrong in my interpretation and I would be most happy if this were so. Yet I feel compelled to make this argument and urge you to talk about these thoughts. It is imperative that we not close our eyes to what is going on in our country and in many other countries.

From a historical peace perspective we are in the middle of a market-driven war on the common good. Wherever human beings see themselves neither as buyers nor sellers, as customers nor clients, but feel that their values, their vitality, and their sustenance comes out of a collectivity of interests, a community of shared experiences, their lives may be under attack. The attack can be subtle or neighbourly. It is not always clear and overt. Yet for the peace movement, this face of war must become as unacceptable as the old face of war.

When we began the work for peace as the Voice of Women we tried to speak to women across the globe about the future of all our children. We must now speak about the new war in the same manner. We must ask each other: what about the common good, the care of the environment? What kind of work will there be for our children? What is happening to the human community? In what way can we make cause with other ordinary people of this world in a concerted resistance against the new war?

You may ask how we can refocus the new peace approach, when many of the old problems are still so much with us. There are still nuclear weapons and their testing, land mines, arms sales, and weapons development.

The new developments, however, are so much embedded in the old, both technologically and politically, that both can and should be addressed together. We need to analyze as clearly as possible the market ideology as war, identify its destructiveness as well as its immorality, and protest its practice by our country and with our money.

Surely, the commandment "thou shall not kill" does not apply only to those who use guns or bombs. Peace is a most pressing issue to engage all of us who wish to use Camus' words—to be neither victim nor executioner.

Notes

John and Lois Dove so tragically left us John Dove was a professor of chemistry at the University of Toronto, and his wife Lois Dove was an accomplished biochemist; they were also committed peace activists. When they were killed in an automobile accident in Botswana, their friends and colleagues established an annual event in their honour at University College, University of Toronto.

Cold War from 1945 to 1990, the state of tension and military rivalry between the United States and the USSR, which stopped short of full-scale war

Kenneth Boulding (1910–1993) a renowned American economist and social scientist who worried about humanity's ability to survive the challenges of the modern world

transmutations transformations

hegemony the dominance of one state over others; from the Greek word *hēgēmon*, meaning "leader"

globalization the process of making something worldwide in scope or application

determinism the philosophical belief that every act, event, and decision is the result of antecedents that are independent of human will

fatalism the belief that events in the world are predetermined and unalterable

incipient beginning to exist or to appear

Massey Lectures Each year, CBC Radio and Massey College in Toronto invite one of the world's leading thinkers to deliver five one-hour talks, on a subject of current interest, at the University of Toronto. In 1989, Ursula Franklin spoke on "The Real World of Technology."

ballistic missile a projectile that takes on a free-falling flight path after an internally guided, self-powered ascent

ethnic cleansing the removal of an ethnic group from a society by expulsion or killing

Camus Albert Camus (1913–1960), a French existentialist who won the Nobel Prize for literature in 1957

Activities

1. Reread Franklin's speech and compare and contrast her message with your own experiences and beliefs. Use your findings to create a thesis statement for a personal essay that will explain in which ways you agree and in which ways you disagree with the ideas Franklin presents. When writing your essay, use detailed examples to illustrate the similarities and differences between Franklin's point of view and your own. Include an explanation of the ways in which you questioned Franklin's assertions and reasoning, rather than simply accepting the ideas you read.

2. Ursula Franklin draws an analogy between war and music. Identify, explain, and evaluate her use of this analogy in making her point. Is the analogy developed well enough to have a significant effect on the reader? How does her analogy support the thesis of her speech?

3. In this speech, delivered by Franklin in 1996, she proposes that the "new" war that has evolved since the Cold War is the war for global commercial power. She says the enemy of globalization comprises "those people who look at community, at work, at nature, and at other human beings as sources of meaning and interaction and not as commodities." Work in a group to do research on globalization in the twenty-first century. To what extent does her argument apply to key world events that have occurred since 1996? Are there ways in which her argument no longer applies or have events since 1996 further bolstered her point of view? Share your ideas in a class discussion.

Another Viewpoint: History

Locate some reference materials on the Cold War and do research into this time in world history. What countries were involved in the Cold War? What conditions created the Cold War? What conditions emerged as a result of it? What literary works reflect the Cold War and in what ways do they do so? How did this historical event affect other countries that were not directly involved? How and why did the Cold War finally come to an end?

Slide to Entropy

Kathleen Winter

Kathleen Winter was born in Corbridge, England, in 1960, and immigrated with her family to Newfoundland at the age of eight. Winter is a researcher and writer whose poetry, short stories, and essays have been published in numerous Canadian periodicals. Her novella *Where Is Mario?* was published in 1987 and her personal journal, *The Necklace of Occasional Dreams*, appeared in 1996. Winter writes a weekly column entitled "Portraits" in the St. John's newspaper *The Telegram*, in which she comments on life as she observes it in the city's streets, workplaces, and houses. "Slide to Entropy" provides readers with a humorous account of the writer's change in lifestyle in middle age. What prevents people from eating nutritionally sound foods all of the time? Why might people's eating habits either improve or deteriorate during the course of their lives?

I don't know how long I've been railing against entropy. It could be since an Australian clairvoyant—the youth hostels were full of them in my travelling days—took one look at me and pronounced I'd end up spending all my time reading trash pulp fiction.

Oh no, my dear, I said inwardly. You will find me continuing my studies with Beaudelaire, with Anaïs Nin and Katherine Mansfield. Perhaps with luck I might even move on to de Maupassant and Shakespeare. I kept my guard up, not only against pulp novels, but against all that goes with them. Lounging around eating family packs of cheesies watching daytime soaps, ending up at bingo instead of yoga, forgetting to buy soy milk and putting Carnation in your tea…. All of a sudden, though, last week my guard came down.

West Indies sarong

It started in Dominion, where I go because they have wholewheat couscous and organic brown rice cereal. My hand bypassed these staples my family loves to see me come home with, and it grabbed canned chili with meatballs and a club-sized pack of white English muffins and a bottle of mustard pickles.

I was just in the store to get away from my kids for a while, not really to buy groceries. I do that sometimes to look at exotic peppers from the West Indies and imagine myself there in a sarong. This time I looked at cans, cans, cans and thought, imagine, you have only to scoot the can opener around them and you have ravioli or Alphagettis without peeling a thing.

At the checkout I did not leaf through Country Living or the antiques magazines but went straight for a two-inch thick No. 1 best-seller with embossed red foil letters, and I bought it.

Two days later and 39 pages into a bunch of stereotyped characters who I'm enjoying very much, I blame our last camping trip. My friend said I could read any book I wanted in her cabin. Over the detective novels and Archie comics I chose a murder mystery featuring a writerly old woman sleuth. It was the thin edge of the wedge. Beaudelaire and brown rice, you are finished.

Every day I discover more advantages to letting down my guard. You cannot read Beaudelaire if you have youngsters hanging off you and jumping on you and demanding glasses of milk and new things to put in their bookbags. But you can do these things and read a No. 1 best-seller. God knows, maybe one can do these things and write one—isn't that a thought. But that's getting too ambitious. That's raising the old guard. Better to let it stay down and just enjoy. Enjoyment is what the slide to entropy is all about, and why hadn't I figured it out before?

Fake cheese dip

Because I had not read the choice of TV programs one can get with a satellite dish, I have now. My husband, coincidentally, brought the flyer home the day I found out about crackers that come with their own little vat of fake cheese dip. Until now, the only thing we've watched with our brown rice has been the news on the one channel we get.

Life is suddenly careening toward entropy and I like it. This is middle age. This is mellowing out. This is the time my children cry out, "Mommy, what's got into you? You're getting to be so much fun."

Fun? Uh-oh, what's that? The anti-entropy alert slides up the back of my head and I come to my senses and boil a pot of rice. I tell myself we can eat it with fresh legumes in a sauce of herbs from the kitchen garden, but I am lying. I know I'm going to open up that can of meatball chili and eat it while I peruse the channel combinations to see if we can get one that has Martha Stewart, "Beverly Hillbillies" reruns, and "Days of Our Lives" in succession on a weekday afternoon...

Notes

entropy the scientific term for an inevitable and steady deterioration of a system; a transformation

clairvoyant a person who can purportedly see what cannot be perceived by the senses, such as events in distant places or events in the future; from the French words *clair*, meaning "clear," and *voir*, meaning "to see"

Charles Beaudelaire (1821–1868) a French Romantic poet

Anaïs Nin (1903–1977) an American author best known for her diaries

Katherine Mansfield (1828–1923) New Zealand's most renowned writer of fiction

Guy de Maupassant (1850–1893) considered to be the greatest French short story writer

Carnation the brand name of a type of canned, evaporated milk

Dominion the brand name of a chain of supermarkets throughout Canada

Activities

1. Use the glossary in this anthology, a dictionary, and other reference tools to create working definitions of the terms *mood* and *tone*. What are the differences between these two concepts? With a partner, discuss whether the tone and mood of this piece are the same or different and why. What feelings do the tone and mood of the piece evoke in you?

2. Write a few well-developed paragraphs in which you answer the following questions: Why does Winter use humour in this selection? What techniques of humour does she use? How does humour contribute to what her purpose might be in writing the piece? What is her thesis? Under what circumstances would you choose to use humour to make a point?

3. Create a single-frame cartoon or a multiple-frame cartoon strip to illustrate Winter's point. Make sure that you maintain her theme and tone. Share your completed cartoon with a classmate and ask for feedback on how effectively you reflected the theme and tone of Winter's work. Based on the feedback you receive, make any revisions you think will improve your cartoon's effectiveness.

Paradise, a Poet, and Promised Land

George Elliott Clarke

George Elliott Clarke was born in the Black Loyalist community of Windsor Plains, Nova Scotia, in 1960 and grew up in Halifax. A poet, journalist, and political activist, Clarke is a seventh generation Africadian. He earned his B.A. from the University of Waterloo, an M.A. from Dalhousie University, and a Ph.D. in English from Queen's University. His poetry, written in a lyrical style, intentionally alludes to his Black Loyalist heritage. In 1998, Clarke received the esteemed Portia White Prize for what has been called his "influential and resounding Maritime voice," and in 2001 he won the Governor General's Literary Award for *Execution Poems*. This article explores Clarke's understanding of a "sense of place" and "promised land." What place would you consider to be your paradise, your promised land? On what land do you "feel whole"?

Postcard images of Nova Scotia accent either the granite slag-heap coastline of Peggy's Cove or Cape Breton's cliff-hugging Cabot Trail. But when I was a "coloured" kid growing up in Halifax's rough-and-tumble North End (all pavement and smashed glass and malice-eyed cops and pink-faced drunks), I felt immeasurably blessed. I knew that, 40 minutes away by car, bus, or train, there was a grassy apple-blossomed paradise, the "Gateway to the Annapolis Valley," the town of Windsor. Just southeast of it was Three Mile Plains, a black Eden where my mother's parents lived.

Three Mile Plains is also—ecumenically—"Five Mile Plains" and "Windsor Plains." Not flat, it's several loping kilometres of rolling slope upon which folks farm, raise cows and horses, and allow hay to explode skyward.

My mother's people—American slaves liberated by the British during the War of 1812—arrived in coastal Nova Scotia in 1813. A generation later, they moved inland, perhaps to join a larger black community, to Three Mile Plains. There, blacks were granted too little land—deliberately—to become farmers. So they toiled in gypsum quarries and in white people's homes to eke out livings. Some of them, including my maternal relatives, intermarried with the Mi'kmaq. They also erected a church, Windsor Plains (African) United Baptist, and attended the segregated (until 1956) one-room Three Mile Plains School.

Acadia University reported in 1965 that most Three Mile Plains adults had only an elementary-school education. However, my mother, Geraldine Elizabeth Johnson, graduated from teachers' college and my father, Bill Clarke, is a self-taught polymath, so when I was born in 1960 (my mother matching my initials to her own), they ensured that I received the best public education available.

My formal schooling was gilded by visits to unpaved Green Street, which bisects Three Mile Plains, and my grandparents' two-storey, white wooden house—with ocean-sounding conch-shell doorstops and a veranda—and what seemed an expansive, dandelioned, and willow-treed sloping front lawn. I loved their antique wood stove and the smells of burning wood crackling in the blue dawns and the Sunday supper riches from their garden: carrots, cucumbers, lettuce, cabbage, potatoes. They even had a pear tree and a crabapple tree. The cheek-by-jowl woods, approached via tall fields of hay, sprouted trickily thorny blackberry and raspberry bushes along their fringe and brandished hazelnut bushes among pine, birch, spruce, alder, and maple trees. A footpath plunged and twisted through the woods down to the iron tracks that bore freight and passengers through the valley, the train horns blaring *whoo, whoo* as they trundled past us, leaving a fragrant—to a child—whiff of diesel fuel in the air.

I was a bookish boy. I thrilled to know that the Mi'kmaq deity, Glooscap, presided over Blomidon—only some 30 km west—and that Henry Wadsworth Longfellow's tragic Acadian heroine, Evangeline, had wept, Ruth-like, amid the "unalien" marsh of Grand Pré. I adored a memorial at Hantsport to William Hall, the third Canadian—and first black—to win the Victoria Cross. I knew that English Canada's first great writer, Thomas Chandler Haliburton, had lived near Windsor's Shakespeareanly named Avon River. For me, the intense, infernal beauty of Three Mile Plains and the Annapolis Valley is a fount of emotional history and heart-startling poetry: "Arcadia." I'd begun to craft poetry—unmusicked "songs"—when I was 15, and Three Mile Plains was their locus. The day I became incontrovertibly, irremediably a poet was February 12, 1977, my 17th birthday, when my mother and I drove to Three Mile Plains on a sunny, frigid, snowy morning. That day, as I trudged up and down hilly, white-dusted Green Street, I drafted in my head a poem, my first attempt to sing a black *and* Nova Scotian—an *Africadian*—consciousness. With my breath hanging clear in front of me, I claimed my Afro-Mi'kmaq heritage. I was standing on land that has always made *us* feel whole.

When my mother passed away last August, my two brothers and I inherited her Three Mile Plains property. Walking there, I feel as though I'm traversing a little northern fragment of Africa. Promised land.

Notes

Eden the first home of Adam and Eve in the Old Testament of the Bible

War of 1812 a war declared by the United States against Great Britain in June 1812. The United States attacked Upper and Lower Canadas, incorrectly assuming that the settlers who lived there would readily secede to the Americans. At the end of 1814, British and American negotiators agreed to return to the status quo of 1811.

Mi'kmaq the First Nation people centred primarily in Nova Scotia, New Brunswick, Prince Edward Island, and the Gaspé Peninsula of Québec

Henry Wadsworth Longfellow an American writer (1824–1884) best known for his narrative poem *Evangeline: A Tale of Acadie* (1847)

Victoria Cross a bronze Maltese cross given by Canada and Britain as their highest military award

Activities

1. Listen carefully as your teacher or a classmate performs an oral reading of this selection. Allow the author's words to create images in your mind. Afterward, share with your class your most vivid mental pictures. Discuss how Clarke uses details, words, phrases, and writing techniques to create strong imagery for his readers.

2. Discuss with a partner what you consider to be the mood of "Paradise, a Poet, and Promised Land" and discuss ways in which Clarke formulates this mood. Consider what an opposite mood to Clarke's would be. With a partner, create a collage that reflects the mood of the article and a second collage that reflects the opposite mood. Consider how you can use composition in your collages to further emphasize each mood. After completing your collages, share them with your classmates. Can they identify the mood you intended in each collage?

3. Write a personal essay about an important association you have with a particular place. Make your writing powerful by including the following in your personal essay: a subjective, first-person point of view; a unifying mood; personal anecdotes and flashbacks; strong imagery and vivid sensory details; and stylistic devices such as parallelism, repetition, and varied sentence lengths. Share your essay with a group of classmates. Ask them to comment on how you used descriptive details to evoke a sense of place.

Another Viewpoint: History

Although the American slaves who came to Canada were liberated by the British during the War of 1812, they still encountered discrimination and differential treatment. Clarke mentions one example of how blacks were granted land, but too little of it to become viable farmers. With a group of your classmates, complete some research on the discriminatory social and economic conditions faced by Africadians in the Maritimes in the years following the War of 1812 to the present time. Present a summary of your research in the form of an illustrated timeline.

Hockey Night in Port Hawkesbury

Lynn Coady

Lynn Coady was born in Sydney, Nova Scotia, in 1970. She was adopted into a large Cape Breton family and raised in Port Hawkesbury and the Margaree Valley of Nova Scotia. Coady writes novels, plays, screenplays, and short stories, as well as non-fiction. Her novel *Strange Heaven* was nominated for the Governor General's Literary Award and won Coady the Canadian Authors Association/Air Canada Award for the most promising writer in Canada. It is a *coming-of-age* novel that reveals how growing up in any culture is universally difficult. Think of some coming-of-age novels, stories, or movies that you are familiar with. What difficult aspects of growing up are dealt with in these narratives? In your opinion, how realistic are these accounts and to what extent do they reflect your own experiences? Why do you think this genre is so popular?

My hometown's hockey team was called the Port Hawkesbury Pirates. Their colours were maroon and white and they had a fierce pirate's-head eyepatch emblazoned in the centre of their jerseys. Their greatest rivals were the Antigonish Bulldogs. I remember one particular playoff where the entire town was mobilized against the mainland village of Antigonish. My dad owned the Dairy Queen, and used its towering sign to denigrate everything about our neighbours on the other side of the causeway. *Ho ho Shebo,* he used to have up there, to the befuddlement of tourists looking for a deal on Brazier Burgers. Shebo was the name of the opposing team's coach. It was a chant the town liked to use whenever our team was ahead. Another day it was *Port Hawkesbury Pirates versus the Antigonish Poodles*. I thought that up. Dad was tickled, and thrilled me by enshrining it beneath the DQ logo for a whole two weeks.

I went to the big game with my dad. I was attired in a Port Hawkesbury Pirates jacket zipped up over a Pirates jersey. Perched on my head was a Pirates cap. Clutched in my hand, a Go Pirates pennant. I loved everything about that night. Listening to Dad holler the most eloquent of personal insults at the nefarious Shebo, the guffaws of the surrounding adults. A woman swaddled head to toe in fox-fur cursing a blue streak like I had never heard. The hard benches. My brother's hand-me-down long johns bunching underneath my clothes. The insane excitement all around me such as I had never experienced in that town before or after.

But I can't relate to you a single thing about the actual game. Because I didn't understand a goddamn thing that was going on. When the crowd screamed, I screamed. When the crowd booed, I booed. When the crowd threatened to disembowel the referee, I too became a mindless, homicidal maniac. I was having the time of my life. But when the actual game was going on, and the crowd sat in rapt awe, this is approximately what was going on in my head:

Guy skating, guy skating, guy skating. Another guy. Skate, skate, skate. Guy from other team. Skate, skate. Who has it now?

Oh. Fat guy. Skating, skating…

There you have, summed up, my eternally ambivalent relationship with the game of hockey and everything it represents. And it represents a lot, let's not kid ourselves. To grow up anywhere in small-town Canada is to grow up with the conviction that hockey is, if not the only thing that matters, one of the things that definitely matters most. In memories of my family, my town, my youth, hockey is always front and centre. My dad coached, and my two older brothers played. Hockey-related pictures, trophies, plaques galore adorn my parents' home.

As a teenager, I was not permitted to be off in my room "sulking" when a Leafs game was on. It was a sacred time that I was expected to participate in, like when we said the rosary. Dad and the boys would eat chips with dip, drink pop, yell and bounce up and down in their seats. My mother would commandeer the couch and sneak in little naps between goals and intermission, when she would play Ron McLean to Dad's Don Cherry. A Toronto game is the only thing I have ever seen my father stay up past 11 for. I would sit at the very back of the living room with a selection of magazines on the table beside me.

You think I am not aware of what I sound like: Miss Priss, brimming with lofty notions and a hearty disdain for anything involving protective cups. "Really, faw-tha, another Leafs game? Can't you see I'm reading Joyce? If only we had an alternative cinema, I'd be so out of here." But it's not true. I was an adolescent, remember, and even more than screening the occasional Fassbinder film, what I really wanted was to fit in. Hockey wasn't merely my dad's trip. It was everybody's. People spoke hockey, do you see? It was like a club, or a religion, and if you understood it, everybody else could understand you. You made sense to them. You fit.

Here are some terms and expressions I don't understand to this day.

Blue line.

Sudden death.

De-*fense*! De-*fense*! (I know what the word means, but why do people yell it over and over again?)

And what's with the octopi?

I have alternated my whole life from a fierce resentment of hockey to a wistful longing I can't quite put my finger on. The resentment is simple enough. It comes from having the overriding importance of hockey burned into me my entire life while at the same time understanding that someone like me (female) should never expect to have anything to do with such a vastly significant phenomenon. It comes from the fact that were I to admit this to any of my brothers they would assume I had not received enough oxygen to my brain as a baby.

So off I went into the world of books and English departments, where nary a taint of hockey fever could be felt—or so I thought. (Bill Gaston's newest novel is about a former pro-hockey player who becomes an English undergrad. The comedy writes itself.) Imagine my chagrin when I discovered that my own patron saint of Maritime Lit despised such stuffy havens for precisely the reason I sought them out. In *Hockey Dreams*, a veritable hymn to the gods of the rink, David Adams Richards tells of a variety of literary snotties who think it terribly impish to root for the Russians because "Wayne Gretzky's just so Canadian." Then there is the woman from Penguin Books who becomes awfully confused when Richards and a Czech writer strike up an animated conversation about the (Pittsburgh) Penguins. That would be me, I can't help but think. Desperately veering the conversation toward Kafka, praying no one discovered my pathetic ignorance about what really mattered—who made the big save, who got the most assists.

But what confounds me even more is how much I relate to this book. I understand, whether I want to or not. It is not so much the games Richards is remembering, but the way his friends floated in their oversized jerseys, the smell of wet wool, sub-zero Saturdays gathered around *Hockey Night in Canada*. The feeling. Throughout the book, Richards struggles to explain the unexplainable, the mystery of hockey. There are those who understand and those who will never understand, he intimates. I know what he means, because I am both.

So that wistful longing makes sense, I suppose, when I look back on that Pirates versus Bulldogs game. I grew up with the understanding that hockey was all-important, hockey players were gods, and to be a hockey fan was to enter into some kind of enchanted circle that bestowed instant community and good fellowship upon you. That's what I was feeling that night. I was sitting on the Port Hawkesbury side of the rink, *our* rink, screaming for *our* team, on behalf of *our* town. I was 12 years old, sexually invisible, my days of artsy alienation far off in the inconceivable future. For a moment, I belonged. Because of hockey.

Notes

Ron McLean, Don Cherry Canadian television hockey commentators

Joyce James Joyce (1882–1941), the groundbreaking Irish writer whose works include the novels *Ulysses* (1922) and *Finnegans Wake* (1939)

Fassbinder Rainer Werner Fassbinder (1945–1982), a German film director-writer

Bill Gaston award-winning Canadian author of novels, short fiction, and poetry

chagrin feeling of humiliation based on miscalculation or failure

David Adams Richards leading Maritime writer (born in 1950) whose prizes include the Governor General's Literary Award for his novel *Nights Below Station Street*

Kafka Franz Kafka (1883–1924), a Czech writer whose work centred on the problematic existence of humanity in the modern era

Activities

1. Lynn Coady describes her relationship with the game of hockey as "ambivalent." Trace how this ambivalence is documented in the article. What thoughts and feelings about hockey did the article provoke in you? Did the article provide you with any insights into why hockey can be so important to life in a small community?

2. For what kind of audience has this article been written? What assumptions do you think Coady makes regarding her readers' ages, educational and cultural backgrounds, values and attitudes, and knowledge about hockey? How does her language and syntax reflect her relationship with her audience?

3. Write a personal essay in which you explore an aspect of yourself that sets you apart from other members of your family. Begin your essay with an episode that clearly illustrates the issue you will be examining. Speculate on how this "difference" might affect your future relationship with various family members. Make a recording of yourself reading your essay. Listen to it to determine whether you have maintained a consistent tone and style throughout. Make any necessary revisions to improve the effectiveness of your written essay.

The Sixth Flight

Chantal Tranchemontagne

Chantal Tranchemontagne was born in Cornwall, Ontario, in 1973. As a child, her parents taught her that travel, exploration, and adventure were the keys to a well-rounded education. She received a B.A. from the University of Guelph in Ontario. She then drove across Canada with friends, after which she moved on a monthly basis throughout western Canada, working in a variety of jobs, including as a construction worker, restaurant server, stonemason, and librarian's assistant. Tranchemontagne received a graduate diploma in journalism from Concordia University in Montreal, where she currently works as a freelance writer. Why do you think the idea of human-powered flight has fascinated people for so many centuries? Do you think there will be a time in the near future when individual flying machines will come into use? Consider how the automobile changed the world and speculate on the ramifications of such flying machines.

The birdman emerged from the river, his wetsuit glistening in the early evening sun. He caught me by surprise, but I wasn't averse to a little company, as I'd only recently brought my rusty '82 Toyota pickup to a shuddering halt after a two-year post-university circumnavigation of Alberta and British Columbia. I was just about as beat up and burnt out as my truck, and had begun squatting on the Birkenhead River, just outside of the Mt. Currie Reserve in the Coastal Mountains, 40 kilometres north of Whistler. I had rigged a 10-metre square tarp as a roof,

◀ *Hanging from the rafters, Chantal Tranchemontagne practises turning manoeuvres*

and set up an apartment: my tent became a cozy bedroom; a lugged-in couch swathed in mosquito netting made a fine living room; a stone firepit with cooking grills functioned as a kitchen; and a solar shower perched precariously in a tree provided the final luxury—hot water, on sunny days at least. It wasn't Frank Lloyd Wright, but my simple dwelling came with a river view and a skylight that filled each night with more stars than a city dweller would see in a lifetime.

Homestead in place, I made plans to explore the region by foot, raft, bike, and maybe even skis. The last thing I expected was an aerial view of my adopted habitat, but a chance encounter with Jim the Birdman changed all that.

It seemed I had chosen a prime spot for finding warm uprisings of air—the phenomena that drove human fliers wild with delight. Despite his watery entrance, the Birdman was first and foremost a paraglider. I offered him a beer, and my education in the philosophy, history, mechanics, meteorology, and gadgetry of paragliding began almost immediately. Thermals are critical for keeping the rectangular parachute aloft, but almost as crucial was getting the chute and equipment up high enough to launch. I thought that behind the Birdman's friendliness was my charming personality. I took it in stride when I found out he was just a guy looking for a ride.

And of course he wasn't alone. Paragliding is relatively new. Just a decade ago, only five or so pioneers soared above the steep, treed valleys of the Mackenzie Basin. I arrived in the middle of a mini-boom in the sport. Up to 40 paragliders roamed the logging access roads looking for a lift to one of several launch sites around the valley, most located in old clearcuts.

That summer, I became a chauffeur for Jim, his paragliding cronies, and their gear. My limousine was an abused 4x4, cab window smashed by a windblown tree, body scratched and torn from windfall, and chassis dented by boulders on rough lumber roads. On my first fare, I wrestled the steering wheel, my foot constantly slipping off the clutch. After 30 minutes of violent bouncing and rocking, we reached the end of the road. By then, I was so sore and stiff that I was more than ready to rediscover the beauty of hiking.

We walked down a steep trail to the launch site, a 20-square-metre forest clearing that had been raked and meticulously scoured to remove any debris that could snag a paraglider line. Three windsocks blew high in second-growth fir trees and several pieces of flagging tape flapped haphazardly from twigs stuck in the ground and out of the way. They were sacrosanct: these wind indicators determined the pilots' fate.

During these jarring rides and long waits in mountain meadows, my enlightenment continued. I learned that paragliders delicately juggle many variables. There's only one constant—what goes up, must come down—but how far, when, and where are decided by Mother Nature.

At night I would retreat to the tranquillity of my isolated campsite, but my charges knew to find me every morning enjoying a Montreal-style bagel at the Pony Espresso coffee house in Pemberton. I wasn't the only one to watch and learn. Newer pilots, fresh from paragliding school at Whistler or drawn here from Vancouver or abroad, showed up at launch sites to watch experienced pilots take off.

I got used to the technical banter on the weather, especially as we waited on mountainsides for a gust of wind. To lift the wing, just the right amount of breeze is required. Optimism permeated the hours whiled away playing hacky sack. I soon realized that the fliers' eagerness consisted of 90 per cent hope. Still, the remaining ingredient—the 10 per cent of actual meteorological knowledge—was essential. I learned that cold creeping shadows on the south side of the valley pushed warm winds up the north ridge to where we sat at the Mackenzie launch site. These wondrous updrafts were the invitation to take off into smooth, buoyant air.

I realized that to survive the summer without destroying my back, I would have to learn to fly off this mountain, otherwise I would remain the designated driver. I watched as Jim and his cohorts set up and laid out the wing. All joking and small talk ceased as they checked strings for tangles, pulled on the bulky harness, and clipped into the glider. Like a newborn gosling I was imprinted with the first thing I saw: Safety is paramount, check and double-check every detail before takeoff.

The takeoffs were a sight unto themselves. The pilots would run down a slight slope, straining against the harness to lift the wing out of the dirt. The running was almost Monty Pythonesque as the chute arched and lifted slowly behind them. Just as they disappeared below the brim of the hill, the wind caught the paragliders and lifted them miraculously off their feet.

All Earth-like encumbrances disappeared. Each paraglider became a human bird. Every successful launch contained the same miracle of freedom. And every drive down the launch road reaffirmed my conviction. I must begin to fly.

The weeks passed, and I lived, ate, and slept to the soothing gurgle of the Birkenhead River. I met new people, often from different parts of the globe. I climbed crags from Squamish to the Swiss Cheese Wall in Whistler and kayaked the lively Birk in my own backyard. Even the dreaded drive up to the Mackenzie launch was made tolerable as I gradually came to assist in more launches. I was no sucker for punishment; I knew I was getting a free education, one that might cost top dollar at a school. But what really kept me keen was wanting to get a taste of what the posse of pilots were obsessed with—flying with the birds. "Zenlike," they said. "A natural high." "Nothing is the same after you've been to 3,000 metres." My new-found friends would try, but fail, to nail the right description. I wasn't the obsessive type, but I knew that before the fall pulled me back East to work and school, I would have to try to launch.

I observed the surefire signs of flight addiction in others. I saw the excitement of first-time pilots on their early flights, the awe as their skills grew, and finally the obsession and addiction with the paragliding high. At this stage, another clue to their obsession was the gadgetry. The truly addicted spent small fortunes on radios, variometers (which show speed, ascent, and altitude), and Global Positioning Systems.

One bright morning I was getting ready to hike to a nearby peak when the Birdman showed up. By this time I could read the signs of a great flying day. Morning sun, puffy cumulus clouds, light wind. "Will you drive us to the launch?" The trip up was getting old, but Jim knew how to push the right buttons. "A couple of more times," he egged me on, "and you'll be able to soar with the birds, too." We clambered into the 4x4.

Today, I fly high. My first five attempts were unspectacular, but I did manage to get off the ground, at least. First a 60-metre scramble, then I tried a few short jaunts from the 500-metre Mackenzie launch. These flights were tense, scary, and thrilling affairs. On the morning of my sixth flight, a late August breeze brought hints of summer's demise. Our ride was via helicopter to the launch—south-facing and on the same range as Mackenzie. We congregated at Pemberton Helicopters at 10:00 a.m., and met with local pilot, John Goats. The 15-minute flight was a treat—no hiking or back-wrenching ride—just a motorized bird's-eye view of peaks and patchwork fields. We circled above turquoise Tenquille Lake and dropped into an alpine meadow blanketed with flowering white and purple lupines. The helicopter slid away, leaving us gulping in fresh, cool mountain air.

We tied flagging tape to twigs to serve as primitive wind meters. All signs indicated a beautiful day. The wind was blowing gently up-slope and the sun was beaming onto the cliffs below, creating rock-released thermals. Earlier in the summer I had seen paragliders play above these cliffs, now it was my turn. If my first five tries had taught me anything, it was not to be too scared to enjoy the view. Still, I was a little frightened. But mostly, I was excited.

My friend Ty laid out his wing. He performed his safety check, tested his radio, and with a final wave, he was off, hooting and hollering with glee above us. My little brother was visiting, and was to try a tandem flight with Robert, a charismatic pilot and the owner of Whistler Paragliding. They went next, and I snapped some photos to send back to our mom. The duo started running. The takeoff looked a little awkward, what with both of them tethered together. But once they were in the air, they looked comfortable.

After a few more launches by more experienced pilots, it was finally my turn. I was still more excited than nervous, but kept my butterflies in check by mentally going through the launching motions. After my safety check, I looked back at Jim for the signal. The wind picked up slightly and I started to run, straining to get my wing off the ground. There were 37 cells to inflate on my paraglider, and each seemed to be working extra hard to pull me back. I felt the wing swinging to the right and tried to bring it back to centre. It didn't work. Instead of risking a serious accident, I pulled down on the steering toggles and flared the wing back to the ground. It dragged me a few feet through the dirt but that, even with the inconvenience of setting up again, was small compared with a crash and a hospital stay. I bunched up the wing and walked back uphill. Jim reassured me that aborting was the right move. I reset, ran, and this time the launch was perfect.

There is a common misconception that paragliders are extreme athletes or worse, crazy thrill-seekers. But suspended above the Mackenzie Basin, I could only think it was everyone else who was crazy for not trying this at least once. The ground was speckled with barns that looked like tiny Lego blocks. The grand, glacial Lillooet River looked like a stream. But the mountains looked ever so huge. I circled to gain attitude, then headed out toward the valley and caught thermals that lifted me 150 metres, like an elevator. From this height I could see the Miller Creek Glacier, Mount Overseer, and the Pemberton ice cap. The air was smooth and the nervousness from my previous flights was gone: it was time to play. Again I caught a thermal: higher, further, faster. Without realizing it I had moved from excitement to awe. Although this was longer than I had ever flown, I couldn't even consider landing. I was having too much fun.

Forty glorious minutes later, 40 kilometres away from the launch site, and from a height of 1,700 metres, I began to descend. I targeted a farmer's field to land in—no growing crops, no cattle, no freshly plowed fields, just a nice, safe, grassy field.

Despite the perfect landing zone, I was still concerned. An old, beat up, black Chevy truck was creeping its way along a dirt road on the perimeter of the field. Some landowners are known to chase off paragliders, or worse, demand payment in the form of a case of beer. Although Pemberton residents are mostly friendly, more than one flyer has a story to say about a rough welcome. For now, however, there was no time for distractions. I focused on my well-choreographed routine: stand up in the harness, flare the wing to slow down, and when the feet touch the ground, run like hell.

It should have been simple, but I miscalculated the wind direction and landed with it behind me. I was going faster than I'd hoped. My legs couldn't keep up with the wing, and instead of a gentle landing, my feet planted hard, my knees buckled, and I became intimate with good old B.C. soil. After a few seconds of mild shock, I extracted my face from the ground, dirty but unharmed.

I was staring at a pair of worn boots less than a foot away from where I lay. I stood up quickly, expecting a reprimand. The man introduced himself as Grandpa Ronayne, a potato farmer whose family had been in the Pemberton Valley since the late 1800s. His overalls were permanently stained with dirt (not unlike my face), his straw hat held together by duct tape. But instead of a scolding, his wrinkled face broke into a smile, and soon he was talking weather like only a farmer can. "And what about that turkey vulture," he asked. I looked at him quizzically and he lifted his finger to the sky. There, above us, a large, red-headed bird was soaring, wings stretched out, unmoving. "He's been stalking you for a while," said Grandpa Ronayne.

From the earliest times, humans have strived to soar with the birds. I, too, had dreamt about flying alongside a majestic eagle. A vulture would have to do, I thought. In fact, my dream had come true on my first real flight, but I had been too busy enjoying the view to realize it. Suddenly, it seemed easier to understand why some people get obsessed with paragliding.

Notes

squatting in this instance, occupying land without the permission of the owner

Frank Lloyd Wright American architect (1869–1959) who revolutionized building design and techniques

paraglider a non-motorized, foot-launched inflatable wing constructed of rip-stop nylon from which the pilot is suspended in a sitting position by Kevlar lines

thermals rising currents of warm air

chassis the supporting frame of an automobile

sacrosanct sacred or holy

Monty Pythonesque referring to the "silly walks" performed by members of the British comedy troupe Monty Python's Flying Circus

Global Positioning System a network of satellites emitting precisely timed signals which a receiver anywhere on Earth can use to fix its exact position

rock-released thermals bubbles of hot air (created when rocks are heated by the sun), which rise through the surrounding air

Birkenhead River, Mt. Currie Reserve, Coastal Mountains, Whistler, Mackenzie Basin, Pemberton, Squamish, Swiss Cheese Wall, Tenquille Lake, Lillooet River, Miller Creek Glacier, Mount Overseer locations in southwestern British Columbia

Activities

1. Why do you think people engage in highly risky activities, such as paragliding, mountain climbing, or sky diving? Do extreme sports like these appeal to you? What insights did you gain from this article about the author's reasons for taking up paragliding and how the experience affected her?

2. In a group, study a number of feature articles in magazines, making note of the elements they contain. Then skim "The Sixth Flight," making notes on design features you would incorporate into a fully-formatted design of this article. With the group, come to a consensus on such decisions as the following: the choice and placement of colour; typeface; type size; visuals; and pull-quotes. Create a deck for the article and use paper to create a rough layout of your design. Present your layout to another group.

3. Locate and read the poem "High Flight," written in September 1941 by John Gillespie Magee Jr., a nineteen-year-old Spitfire pilot who was training to serve in World War II with the Royal Canadian Air Force. Paraphrase the experiences and emotions Magee describes. Discuss the relationship between the poet's response to the experience of flight and those of Chantal Tranchemontagne and her acquaintances. How do the historical era and circumstances in which these accounts were written explain the differences in style and spiritual perspective?

Buying Your Next Synthesizer

Amin Bhatia

Composer Amin Bhatia was born in London, England, in 1961. He immigrated to Canada and now lives in Toronto. Bhatia has been writing, recording, and programming music for twenty years. Bhatia has said that he originally wanted to work with an orchestra, but pragmatism led him to the synthesizer. Because early synthesizers could only play one note at a time, Bhatia was forced to learn how each instrument of the orchestra worked in order to simulate and record it properly. He now uses real instruments in his writing, but his days with a Roland sequencer and a Minimoog have given him insight into arranging and orchestration for real players. He scores music for film and television, as well as doing sound design for clients such as MuchMusic. "Buying Your Next Synthesizer" is an example of an expository article which explains how a buyer can "audition" a new synthesizer. What kinds of research do you engage in before purchasing an electronic item? What kinds of information sources are available to consumers for this research? How much influence do first-hand accounts or testimonials have in your purchasing decisions?

In response to phone calls and e-mails I've had from other musicians in the community I've put together a short guide to help you when you buy your next synthesizer.

I must begin with the bad news that it's going to take you weeks, not hours, to get up and running. Yes, it is amazing technology, and yes, it claims to make you a star overnight. But if you've bought that new synthesizer on the belief that you'll be making music with an instant orchestra within a few hours, then sit down and have a good cry now. As wonderful as this technology is, there are very few brochures or salespeople that have the guts to tell you that it's going to take some time to get it right!

Think about how many years it takes to master an acoustic instrument. A synthesizer studio is a group of instruments, each one with a whole new set of freedoms and restrictions. The freedom is that any instrument is capable of hundreds of unique and exciting sounds. The restriction is that the technical and sonic structure of each synthesizer has nothing in common with another one. You'll have to learn each synthesizer in your studio, one at a time before you can take it into battle on your next project. If this were a live player that you'd never heard of, would you trust him or her with a solo at your next recording date without even an audition? Same thing.

And yes you should read the manual, no matter how badly it's written. It's your only clue to what the manufacturers were thinking when they built the thing. When you open the box, take the manual out first and read through it somewhere else, ideally over a weekend. Then when you come back, you'll have a peripheral idea of its workings as well as a general idea of where to find something in the manual.

In getting to know your new instrument you have to start with its existing sounds. A major fallacy is the instrument's display that tells you what sound you are playing. Unlike looking at a real player who holds an oboe in his hands, the synth patch display that says "oboe" is no guarantee that you're going to hear a convincing simulation. Synth technology is a combination of waveforms or digital data programmed by technicians and while some are amazing, some are downright awful. One might dial up "English horn" or even "bagpipe" and come up with an oboe sound that actually sounds more convincing.

So, ignore the display and use your ear. Go through your new synthesizer patch by patch and make note of the sounds that truly inspire you. Play with each sound for a long time (have your MIDI sequencer running to capture that musical idea too) and try the sound in different registers and different dynamics. Also decide where it would be placed in an ensemble situation. Is it a distant sound, akin to muted strings? Or a small but pointed solo sound that would perform the same function of a flute double for violins? Any ensemble skills you have, whether orchestrating or playing in a band, are valuable here. Thinking in terms of layers now will help you blend these instruments later.

Now rename your sound. Give it a practical name that relates to its timbre, e.g., "metallic piano" or "breathy flute." Patch names like "Itz Kool" or "Angela's Pad" serve no useful purpose and you should rename these patches to something more useful. If your synthesizer has ROM presets only (non-rewritable memory) then you won't be able to rewrite the patches. In this case use a notepad or a database to log your favourite sounds and their memory location.

This auditioning exercise is crucial because it allows you to get to know the personality of the instrument and helps you instinctively write for it. This also allows you to give the instrument your own unique trademark since you've chosen the sounds that appeal to you. Just as in acoustic writing, it's not the sound, but how you blend that sound with others, that will make or break a good arrangement. In time you'll start editing patch parameters and actually change and create new sounds.

After the above exercise you can then consider taking your new synth into battle with the rest of your toys and tricks on your next gig. Don't do it before. How many times have we had a friend call us over to "check this out," only to be greeted with malfunctions and "that's funny, it never did that before…Oh I know…nope that's not it…just give me a minute…"

Time is precious. Use it and your new gear well.

Notes

synthesizer an electronic instrument, often played with a keyboard, combining simple waveforms to produce more complex sounds

acoustic an instrument that does not feature electronically modified sound

sonic of or relating to audible sound

peripheral relating to an outside boundary or outer surface

oboe a slender woodwind instrument that uses a double reed to produce a humming sound similar to that of a bagpipe

MIDI sequencer a standard for representing sound in a form that a computer can understand

timbre the distinctive tone of an instrument

Activities

1. In a group, discuss what you know about how synthesizers work. How is each track of a synthesizer different from a "real" player of the instrument it recreates? What are the advantages and disadvantages of using synthesizers to perform music? With which performers or bands who use synthesizers are you familiar? What makes a musician a good synthesizer performer? Access print and non-print resources to flesh out your understanding of this modern musical instrument.

2. Bhatia identifies several ideas for getting started with a new synthesizer. With a partner, review the article to identify all the tips he suggests. Create a checklist of tips. Then review the career section of a number of newspapers to acquaint yourself with the format and language used in employment ads. Use your checklist to write a job advertisement for a synthesizer salesperson.

3. Choose a topic on which you could give advice. It might be on how to make something, or how to write something, or how to perform a particular skill. Make notes on the stages you go through to complete the activity, including any problems that might be encountered during the process. Then write an expository article about your topic using process analysis to help you organize and explain the stages. Exchange work with a classmate and evaluate the article's clarity and coherence. Make any revisions your partner suggests that will improve the organization and effectiveness of your piece.

A Chat with Al Purdy

Kate Climenhage

Kate Climenhage was born in Brockville, Ontario, in 1976, and grew up in the neighbouring town of Orono. She received a bachelor's degree in literature from the University of Guelph in 2000. Climenhage, who is both a writer and a photographer, was still a teenager when she was asked by *IN2PRINT* magazine to conduct this interview with Canadian poet Al Purdy. Born in Wooler, Ontario, in 1918, Al Purdy is one of Canada's most respected poets. Although known primarily as a poet, Purdy wrote radio and television plays, book reviews, travel essays, and magazine articles. Purdy, who won two Governor General's Literary Awards for Poetry, died in 2000. Kate Climenhage had the opportunity to interview one of her childhood idols. If you could interview a person of your choice, who would it be and why? What approach would you take in the interview and what would you hope to learn?

Who were the first poets you read?

I was in first year of high school and it was the poetry we were taught then—Bliss Carmen, Charles G.D. Roberts—the Canadian poets. You know, the usual array.

I was rather taken with Bliss Carmen at the time—something I should be ashamed to admit now (laugh) but I'm not. I can still remember some of them. "Make me over Mother April when the sap begins to stir." They were rhyming and metric and very different from mine.

Many years later I was hypnotized by Dylan Thomas. I imitated Dylan Thomas for a long time. D.H. Lawrence was probably the strongest influence of anybody. Strangely enough, Lawrence is not paid much attention as a poet but only as a novelist or an essayist. *Lady Chatterley's Lover* was so sensational that it takes away attention from his poems. As far as I'm concerned, his poems are groundbreaking.

There have been other influences of course.

I think Layton influenced me: he loosened the language up quite a bit. Other than that there were no people who ever took me in hand and said, "You write like this." Some people do have those exemplars or teachers, mentors.

Do you think that's a good thing?

I don't know. From my own experience, I think you can learn all you want to from books and from your own curiosity—if you want, if you're really interested. To read a fine poem, a really good poem, is to learn something. It's to learn what the guy or the woman who wrote it knew when they wrote it. You can see the tricks that are used. You see everything else about that writer because he put it in that poem. I've done that and learned from other people. And, of course, you learn from life itself.

Do you think that starting out metrically and in a tight form helped you to develop?

Well, I think that a little stupidity helps a great deal. When you start out writing poems, the reason you write is you think, "Look at me, Ma, how great I am, how wonderful I am." You want to show off. I did the same thing and I thought it was wonderful. After a while I came to the conclusion that it wasn't so wonderful. You come to a kind of a plateau in your life, and you look at what you've done and it ain't so hot. So, you look for other exemplars, other models if you like, and you find 'em and then you move again. You can, anyway. I did. And I kept doing it. I kept moving. So, I don't think it ever ends because you never stop, at least as long as you're not quite senile, you keep on going.

Metred forms are very tough to break away from—you get too much in the habit. I wrote in metre for years as in my first published book: "I saw the milkweed float away, to curtsy, climb and hover, and seek among the crowded hills, another warmer lover." Well, that's crap.

Free verse is much harder than metric. If you write in metrics, the metre makes you remember. It's much harder to write something that is not metred and rhymed. I've got passages without metre or rhyme that I think are better than anything—*And women with such a glow it makes their background vanish.* That's one of them. You get these lines in your mind. If you're writing in rhyme you're trying to fit them in to make them rhyme. You use inversions, you revert the normal sequence of grammar.

Well, you can see the way I feel but if you want to write in metre, why you go ahead and write in metre. But the thing is you've got to say something and it's not so easy. You'd think it's easy; it's easy to write anything down but to make it mean something is something else.

What kind of discipline does it take to be a writer?

Oh God, I don't know. I have no idea. I wrote when I was interested in something. I never did sit down to write poems every day at a certain time. I think that's pretty silly. You write when you have something in your mind that says *this is a poem.* You're on the lookout for something. Your mind knows when you come to something that will make a poem. I knew an Australian poet who said that a poet should stay stupid— that was his way of phrasing it.

Keep your mind open. For instance, within the last five years, I had four or five people die that I knew quite well. In fact I was very fond of them; they were friends, or more than friends. I thought about the things about them that would make a poem and I just wrote the poem. That's the last poem I've written. It's just sort of an elegy for them, if you like.

I heard you reading at the Albion Hotel in Guelph, Ontario. You said something like, "I know no one here knows any of my stuff so I'm just going to read what I want." I was wondering if you actually think that of the younger generation or if it was just tongue-in-cheek…

When you go to a town that you've not read at before you take it for granted that people have never heard you read and that you're not very familiar to them. I always like that but it's always a challenge. I think it's a lot of fun to get up there before an audience and get them, uh, let's say, eating out of the palm of your hand (laughs). You know you're a stranger to most of them and I think it's a lot of fun. It's an ego trip of course: I used to deny that I liked it because I didn't like the idea of an ego trip. But I don't mind a bit, it's fun.

I'm not afflicted with nerves. At the so-called tribute at Harbourfront [1996 Toronto Harbourfront International Reading Series] it got me. I recited "Necropsy of Love," just about the only poem of mine I can remember. All those people applauding and I felt quite emotional. This affected my voice adversely. Very difficult to read when it affects your voice like that.

What advice would you give to young writers?

When I was a writer-in-residence at University of Western Ontario there were a lot of people come in and all they wanted was to be told that their stuff was good. I asked one of them—I remember particularly— "What do you read?" He said he didn't read; he didn't want to be influenced. That is absolute crap because that's what you *do* want to be—you want to be influenced. There's nobody who's going to stop you from writing poems. It isn't a matter of making a decision—I am now going to be a poet. I'm going to write. You wanna write, you write. *Who's stopping you?* Your mother's not going to stop you. She's glad to get you out of her hair.

People ask, "Should I give up everything else to write great poems?" The only answer I can give them is there's nobody stopping you. It isn't even a matter of decision. I do believe that if you're writing prose and you intend to write a novel it is very difficult if you're working at some job. But poems? Lord, I wrote all the time I worked in factories. No matter what you're doing you can write poems.

If I had to give anybody any advice it would be never go into a business with your in-laws.

Notes

Bliss Carman and Sir Charles G.D. Roberts Carman (1861–1929) and Roberts (1860–1943) were two of a group of Canadian poets known as the Confederation Poets who wrote lyrical romantic verse inspired by the Canadian landscape. Also included in the group were Archibald Lampman (1861–1899) and Duncan Campbell Scott (1862–1947).

Activities

1. In a small group, discuss the following questions: Why did Purdy write? How did Purdy's writing change over the course of his career? How does this interview reveal qualities about Purdy both as a person and as a writer?

2. The title of this selection, "A Chat with Al Purdy," suggests an informal, casual tone. Look again at the language used by Purdy in answering the questions. What particular elements are typical of oral speech? Refer to specific words, phrases, aspects of grammar, syntax, and usage to prove that the language is conversational rather than formal. Next, find at least one example of each of the following: sentence fragments, interjections, unconventional usage, colloquial language, slang, unconventional spelling, contractions, and run-on sentences. Use your examples to draw conclusions about the differences between oral language and written language.

3. In the interview, Purdy names poets who influenced his development as a writer: Bliss Carman, Charles G.D. Roberts, Dylan Thomas, D.H. Lawrence, and Irving Layton. Research at least one poem by each of these poets. Then locate and read more of Purdy's poetry and write an analytical essay in which you identify similarities in the content and style of the work of these six poets. Be sure to include evidence from the poems in your analysis.

Ours by Design

Alison Blackduck

Alison Blackduck was born in Inuvik, Northwest Territories, in 1975. In 2000, Blackduck completed her undergraduate degree in communication studies at Concordia University. While still at university, she began writing freelance articles. She became a reporter for the *Nunatsiaq News* in Iqaluit, Nunavut, and worked at the CBC North's Inuvik bureau. Blackduck's writing has appeared in such publications as the *Globe and Mail*, the *Gazette*, and *Up Here* magazine, and she is a regular columnist for the *Toronto Star*. Blackduck wrote this article because, as she said, "The amauti, a symbol of traditional Inuit garment design, is being threatened with exploitation. Inuit are seeking a way to protect it as intellectual property. They're hoping to clear the way for other indigenous groups as they go." A very complex, controversial issue in our contemporary world is how we protect cultures, while at the same time creating an atmosphere for them to co-exist. Under what circumstances should we accommodate transformations to culture? What are some of the ways we, as a society, can reconcile the need to recognize, respect, and protect cultures with the need to accept the inevitable adaptations of cultures?

Robbie Watt credits the amauti—the jacket-like garment most Inuit women use to carry their infants and toddlers—for making him the person he is today.

◄ *Young Mother Skipping, 1992, Mary Pudlat*

"It was my home, it was my bed," says Watt, president of Avataq Cultural Institute, an organization mandated to protect and promote Inuit culture in Nunavik (Northern Quebec).

"The amauti was my everything; I didn't want to be anywhere else... It's the same for all Inuit, male and female."

In a way, his recollections of an infancy spent snuggled in the warmth and security of his mother's amauti is an expression of his gratitude toward Inuit women for their integral contribution to Inuit identity. It's also an acknowledgement of the debt all Inuit owe to women for their ingenuity and hard work.

Watt is in Rankin Inlet, Nunavut, for a workshop hosted by Pauktuutit, the Inuit women's association which represents all Inuit women living in Canada. The workshop's focus is to develop a strategy to protect the intellectual property of the Inuit people at a regional, national, and international level. The participants also hope other indigenous people will benefit from their work.

"No other organization is doing what we're doing—not the AFN [the Assembly of First Nations], not the Métis National Council. They're looking at us as pioneering this work," says Veronica Dewar, president of Pauktuutit.

The people who have travelled from across Nunavut and Nunavik for this workshop are using the amauti design as a test case. They feel the design has been threatened in recent years by non-Inuit commercial interests. If the women can find a way to protect this unique Inuit innovation from being exploited for mass profit without their permission, they should be able to apply it to other Inuit designs, like the kayak, or commodities such as Inuit knowledge of the therapeutic benefits of particular plants, herbs, and flowers. Writers and artists are covered by copyright, inventors apply for patents, companies have trademarks—surely a people can protect their collective knowledge.

"So much of our Inuit culture needs protecting," says Rankin Inlet's Bernadette Dean, social development coordinator for the Kivalliq Inuit Association. "Look at what countries around the world have done with the kayak," she continues. "To my knowledge, not one red penny has been given to the Inuit...to me, it's a form of exploitation."

In October 1999, the New York fashion designer Donna Karan sent her global design director, Bonnie Young, to several western Arctic communities to purchase items such as handmade seal-skin clothing, beaded jackets, and knitted fur clothing. The purpose was to gather things Karan could use to help inspire her Fall 2000 collection.

Young reportedly bought a tuilli—a beaded amauti—from Pangnirtung, kamiks, fur garments, and garments knitted from musk-ox hair at a store in Yellowknife. Was Karan planning to acknowledge the source of her inspiration? Nobody knows. Despite calls from numerous Canadian reporters, neither Karan nor Young would comment publicly on the buying trip.

The lack of acknowledgement for use of another's ideas is the problem. Those ideas are called intellectual property, ideas that are new and result from human creativity and entrepreneurship. Knowledge wasn't considered a commodity until the invention of the printing press in the fifteenth century, says Barry Mandelker, who holds a master of laws in intellectual property. With the advent of mass-produced books like the Bible, and pamphlets printed and sold by publishers, the general public began perceiving abstract knowledge as having a concrete monetary value.

Even then, the concept of the right to protect and to profit from one's ideas didn't arise immediately. "Shakespeare and Milton didn't have copyright," Mandelker says. "The first [intellectual property] legislation in the world wasn't enacted until 1710—the Statute of Anne, which was named after the British monarch of the day."

Almost two centuries passed before international lawmakers legislated the Berne Convention for the Protection of Literary and Artistic Works, in 1886. Its aim was to advance capitalistic ideals like the pre-eminence of individual rights over collective rights, stimulate market growth through promoting and rewarding human innovation, and spur industrial competition.

The Berne Convention, which has been revised several times, wasn't only about money. Peoples' demands for effective intellectual property legislation were also based on then-radical notions of rights and fairness, and ensuring that people and their work were managed in a fair and just manner by authorities and their fellow citizens. These notions were born of a time marked indelibly by the French and American revolutions, and the American Bill of Rights, whose first amendment protects freedom of speech and of the press.

Today, protection of intellectual property is used mostly for economic gain and influence. "Major corporations file and receive thousands of patents every year," says Mandelker. "Often it's not about protecting new innovations, it's about protecting their market position and intimidating their competitors."

But the economic gain and influence offered by such laws are what many indigenous people are seeking. It would give them some measure of control over what's left of their cultural identity after centuries of colonization displaced them from their traditional lands and alienated them, leading to widespread poverty and few means to access economic opportunity.

Intellectual property rights for indigenous peoples is a hot topic around the world these days. In Canada, Mandelker and another intellectual property specialist were hired just a year ago by the federal government, Mandelker as a copyright policy analyst and the other with Industry Canada. It's a move they say reflects the increasing interest in and awareness of the conundrums surrounding intellectual property, which is still a relatively new legal concept.

In Canada, a 1999 government publication called Intellectual Property and Aboriginal People stipulates that to be protected, intellectual property "must be new, novel, original, or distinctive." The paper acknowledges these criteria can be tricky to determine, and indicates that intellectual property must have "utility," be "fixed," or be "used" in order to be protected.

The paper also describes the mechanisms in place to protect those ideas. Patents protect new technological products and processes. Copyrights protect original literary, artistic, dramatic, or musical works and computer software when they are expressed or fixed in a material form. Industrial designs protect the shape, pattern, or ornamentation applied to a manufactured product. Trademarks safeguard words, symbols, or pictures used to distinguish goods or services of an individual or organization from those of others in the marketplace. None of these lasts forever except the trademark, as long as the trademark holder renews it every 15 years.

These avenues of protection, however, don't quite fit the concept of protecting the intellectual property of a people. Pauktuutit, the Inuit women's association, has discovered this through four years of trying to find a way to protect the amauti design on behalf of Inuit women.

Pauktuutit has applied established international intellectual property legislation and it's trying to be creative with newer legislation like the United Nations Convention on Biological Diversity. The convention wasn't intended to protect intellectual property: its focus was to protect global biodiversity, conserve the environment, and ensure benefits arising from the use of genetic resources are shared fairly. But the wording of one of its articles has led many indigenous people to argue that section protects not only their knowledge of their environment but also their culture.

On the whole, however, Pauktuutit finds the existing legislation and mechanisms too time-specific and too narrow in scope. Copyright, for example, remains in effect only until 50 years after the death of the producer, at which time the work enters the public domain. This means anybody can use it without acknowledging the original producer or paving royalties for its use. That's not good enough, says Pauktuutit's Dewar. She says Inuit want their ideas and innovations to be protected in perpetuity for all Inuit, not just a few individuals or those represented by certain organizations.

The other constraint of current legislation is its narrow scope. Intellectual property protection applies to individual producers or organizations, and what's considered worthy of protection by international treaties like the Berne Convention is limited.

Where does the amauti fit in the existing legal framework?

Inuit have been using the amauti design for generations, so the design is neither original nor new. Even if it were discovered who developed that first amauti, Inuit have used the design for so long that legal experts would likely categorize it as belonging in the public domain. The same problem may apply to the kayak design, which has long been insinuated into the global cultural mainstream through mass production. Since it has been used for many generations, is it too considered "public domain"?

Of all available options—trademark, copyright, patent among them—Pauktuutit has concluded that an Inuit trademark is probably best-suited for identifying the physical manifestation of Inuit ideas. Robbie Watt of the Avataq Cultural Institute agrees trademark protection could work. However, he says, it should be amended in form and content to reflect the cultural reality of not only Inuit but other indigenous people, too. He suggests a Cultural Property, or CP, symbol similar to the ™ used to distinguish trademarks.

"We've come to a stumbling block," Watt said at the workshop. "Legally, we need a definition, but if all we want is meaningful recognition of our creations, maybe a special trademark would work."

A CP or other trademark would identify all products created by and through the application of indigenous peoples' knowledge. The Canadian government has employed a similar strategy for more than 30 years with its trademarked igloo design to identify "Canadian Eskimo art." However, that strategy is out of date, say intellectual property specialists like Mandelker. Besides, the igloo trademark doesn't apply to all indigenous people. Pauktuutit's directors want to design a solution that's inclusive.

How do Inuit women at the grassroots define the issue? Sewers like Rhoda Karetak of Arviat, Susan Avingaq from Igloolik, and Kugluktuk's Alice Anablak say that if an Inuk makes an anorak emblazoned with a copyrighted logo like the Toronto Maple Leaf insignia for her child, that's an acceptable use of another entity's design.

If the woman then decides to mass-produce the anoraks and sell them for profit, however, that's a problem. It would lead undoubtedly to National Hockey League lawyers sending her cease-and-desist orders and threatening a lawsuit if she didn't comply. In other words, the women believe that personal use inspired by another's knowledge is acceptable. Exploiting that knowledge for commercial gain is not.

World leaders are listening to what indigenous people have to say about the lack of legal protection their knowledge receives. "I just returned from an international UN conference on protecting traditional knowledge and folklore," Mandelker says. "Right now, every nation in the world is working on this."

Interest in indigenous peoples' views has as much to do with the fact that intellectual property protection as a whole has emerged as a hot topic in legal, government, and social justice circles over the past few years. But Article 8 (j) of the United Nations' Convention on Biological Diversity, which went into effect in 1993, is shining the spotlight on this particular issue.

This article states the traditional knowledge of indigenous people should be used only with the approval of the holders of such knowledge, and only if they also profit from the application of their knowledge. It also stipulates that each signatory must respect, promote, and preserve the traditional knowledge and activities of indigenous people and local communities.

However, the protection the article offers is limited at best. The Convention on Biological Diversity wasn't created as intellectual property legislation. However, says copyright expert Mandelker, "Once the treaty was ratified, indigenous people who were worried about the misappropriation of their knowledge focused on that aspect of the relationship between intellectual property rights and traditional knowledge."

One of the convention's objectives was to address emerging issues like genetic information and biotechnology. The United Nations wanted to ensure the fair and equitable distribution of benefits arising from the use of genetic resources, including acknowledging the source of genetic material and sharing benefits with that source.

One interesting development is that the treaty is now being associated with everything from cutting-edge technology—such as genetic sequencing—to age-old technology such as traditional Inuit clothing designs that are a reflection of cultural expression.

For the Inuit in the midst of the intellectual property discussion, finding a creative way to protect the amauti design as intellectual property is a priority. For people like Robbie Watt, the amauti is bound inextricably with Inuit identity. For people such as Pauktuutit president Veronica Dewar, international recognition of Inuit intellectual property is a human right.

"Our crafts are being exploited," Dewar says. "Inuit are real, we have feelings, and our knowledge is ours."

Notes

indigenous refers to those parts of nature, such as particular plants, animals, or ethnicities of people, in a specific region that originated in that region; from the Latin word *indigena*, meaning "native"

integral significant part of something that cannot be taken away from the whole; something required for completeness

collective referring to a group as one entity

misappropriation to take something from someone that is rightfully that person's, or to use it wrongly, as in exploitation

Activities

1. Have a class discussion in which you explore the following questions: What are some of the purposes of copyright laws? What is meant by "intellectual property" and "public domain"? What are today's trademarks, copyrights, and patents each designed to protect? What procedures might be required to protect the traditional arts of indigenous peoples from exploitation?

2. In a small group, select six to eight sequential paragraphs in this article. In a chart entitled "facts," list every fact that appears in the passage you have chosen. In a second chart entitled "opinions," list every opinion that appears in the passage. Beside each item in your "facts" list, make notes in point form on how credible each fact is and what makes it either credible or not. Beside each item in your "opinions" list, make notes in point form on how persuasive each opinion is to you, and how surrounding information influences whether or not it is persuasive. Present your information to the class and elicit feedback on your conclusions.

3. Working in small groups, select an Aboriginal community and do research on some of its inventions and practices. Choose one invention or practice and outline requirements you would have if you were creating a cultural property trademark for this item or practice. Develop a rationale and a defence of your proposal. Present your proposal to the class and get feedback on the thoroughness and persuasiveness of your argument.

Another Viewpoint: Society

With a group, identify an important technology-related copyright issue. State the issue in the form of a resolution for a class debate. Conduct the debate, videotaping it if possible to help identify strengths and areas for improvement in your presentation.

Look What I Found

About the Visual   Marian Henley was born in Dallas, Texas, in 1954. She has been a full-time cartoonist since her weekly comic strip "Maxine!" debuted in 1981. Other cartoons by Henley have appeared in publications such as *MAD* magazine. She published her first book, *Maxine!*, in 1987. In 1989, she produced and starred in three short live-action videos based on "Maxine!" which have appeared on MTV. She also published a short fiction book called *Smile* in 1991. *Laughing Gas*, a twenty-year collection of "Maxine!" strips, appeared in May 2002. What subjects can be more effectively illustrated in a cartoon than in writing? Why do you think comic strips aimed at children are sometimes more appealing than standard books? How are cartoons aimed at adults different from those intended for children?

Activities

1. Put yourself in this picture by imagining the beach environment where these two characters are situated. In a journal entry, write what you might notice in this type of setting. List all the sensory details, both beautiful and messy, that you can imagine finding on a beach.

2. Consider the gender of each character. Do you think that Henley has engaged in any gender stereotyping in this cartoon? Why or why not? With a partner, create six to eight more frames for this cartoon. In your cartoon, maintain and extend the characterizations of the two people that Henley has created. Then post your cartoons in the classroom and discuss with your partner the similarities and differences among your classmates' work.

1989

Landscape with the Fall of Icarus

About the Visual   Pieter Brueghel, who historians believe lived from 1525 to 1569, was a Flemish painter who worked most of his life in what is now Belgium. After being apprenticed to a leading artist in the city of Antwerp, he travelled to Italy to continue his studies. In his work, he celebrated peasant life and also produced paintings on religious and mythological themes. This painting focuses on a Greek legend, in which Daedalus and his son Icarus escape from the island of Crete using wings of wax and bird feathers. Icarus disregards his father's warning not to fly too close to the sun; his wings melt and he falls into the sea and drowns. Why do you think artists over the centuries have been moved to paint and sculpt so many works based on mythological and religious themes? To what extent do you think these subjects might continue to occupy artists in centuries to come?

Activities

1. What does the portrayal of Icarus in the painting tell you about Brueghel's feelings toward Icarus? If you were an artist, which moment in the story of Icarus and Daedalus would you represent in a painting? Explain your choice.

2. One critic has suggested that the perspective of the painting—looking at the landscape and action from above—indicates that the audience is sharing Daedalus' horrified vision of the tragedy rather than observing an objective portrayal of the scene. Explain whether or not you agree. How does the painting's perspective, or angle of view, affect your understanding of the picture and your emotional response to it?

c. 1558, oil on canvas, mounted on wood, 73.5 cm x 112 cm

About the Visual   Hiroshige Utagawa was born in the city of Edo, now Tokyo, in 1797. Hiroshige won recognition as a landscape artist, especially for the two print series *One Hundred Famous Views of Edo* and *Fifty-three Stations of the Tokaido*, which are considered his masterpieces. It has been said of Hiroshige that "he captured, in a poetic, gentle way that all could understand, the ordinary person's experience of the Japanese landscape...." He died in 1858. What main features of any society are typically expressed in its most popular art form? Why do you think that the art of different cultures is so varied? Do you believe that these differences are more pronounced today than they were one or two centuries ago or that the differences have diminished? Why?

Activities

1. *Shower at Ohashi Bridge* is considered one of the most outstanding of Hiroshige's landscape works. Choose three elements of this picture that you think contribute most to this assessment of the work. Write several sentences about each element and then share your thoughts with the class. After your discussion, consider how your classmates' ideas contributed to your appreciation of the work.

2. *Shower at Ohashi Bridge* is part of Hiroshige's series *One Hundred Famous Views of Edo.* With the class, brainstorm a list of famous views or settings in the community where you live. Choose one of the views on your list and create a painting or drawing of it in the style of Hiroshige. Present your work to a group of classmates and explain the stylistic and content choices you made.

19th century, nishiki-e print ▶

SHOWER AT OHASHI BRIDGE | 369

The Poetry of Earth and Sky

Photographer Courtney Milne was born in Saskatoon, Saskatchewan, in 1943. Milne received formal training in photography and has two master's degrees, one in psychology and the other in journalism and mass communication. Since 1975, he has been a freelance photographer, concentrating on nature and landscape. Milne has taken over 420,000 exposures in over thirty-five countries across seven continents. Ormond Mitchell, son of W.O. Mitchell, was born in Edmonton, Alberta, in 1943. His spouse, Barbara Mitchell, was born in Saskatoon in 1944. They both grew up in High River, Alberta. They lived in western Canada before moving to England, where each received a doctorate degree in English literature. Both teach at Trent University in Peterborough, Ontario. Do you believe that the landscape in which people grow up influences their personality and how they view the world? Why or why not? To what degree, if any, does the landscape of your community influence your life?

Notes

litmus literally, a blue powder derived from lichens used in paper form as a test for chemical acidity or basicity; in this instance, used metaphorically to mean investigating or experimenting; from the Old Norse words *litr*, meaning "colour" or "dye," and *mosi*, meaning "moss" or "bog"

minimalist related to a movement of abstract art, consisting of simple geometric forms

wolf willow a North American shrub found especially on the prairies

Activities

1. In the last sentence of the essay, the authors describe W.O. Mitchell's skill in appealing to his readers' senses, particularly the sense of sight. Do you think there is any contradiction in illustrating Mitchell's words with photographs? Why or why not?

2. Choose three photographs from this essay in which pattern is an important element. Explain how the focus on pattern enhances the impact of each photograph. Take your own photographs in which you emphasize the patterns you discover in both the natural and constructed environment.

Photography by Courtney Milne
Text by Ormond Mitchell and Barbara Mitchell

The Poetry of Earth and Sky

Half a century after the writing of Who Has Seen the Wind,
Courtney Milne's images capture the timeless elements
of W.O. Mitchell's prose: the drama of cloudscape, the
seasonal extremes, the promise of harvest, the geometry
of land and sky

W.O. Mitchell was born in 1914 in Weyburn, Saskatchewan. As a child, he absorbed the wide spaces of the prairie, its dramatic shifts of light and shadow, its straight lines, and its salient signs of life and death. For the rest of his life, he was marked by this landscape, emotionally and even, it seemed, physically. His face was as transparently expressive as a field of wheat, bright and mobile in the wind, but as easily transformed by the shadow of the clouds. His tousled hair always looked as wild as the prairie grasses. One of his school chums described him as having "no side." What he meant was that W.O. had a guilelessness that invited immediate friendship, an openness as wide as the prairie itself. There was nothing restrained about him; he was down-to-earth and irreverent. But he also had a darker streak—a profound sense of mortality and the passing of things taught to him early on the prairies.

Now and as a child I walked out here to ultimate emptiness, and gazed to no sight destination at all. Here was the
melodramatic part of the earth's skin that had stained me
during my litmus years, fixing my inner and outer perspective, dictating the terms of the fragile identity contract I
would have with myself for the rest of my life.

—*How I Spent My Summer Holidays*

"It's going to storm, Sammy," shouted Brian.

A tumbleweed bounding past the boy and the old man

caught itself against the strands of the fence, then,

released, went rolling on its way. An unnatural dusk that

had grown over the whole prairie made Brian strain his

eyes to see through the spreading darkness of dust licked up by the wind in its course across the land. His ears were filled with the sound of the wind, singing fierce and lost and lonely, rising and rising again, shearing high and higher still, singing vibrance in a void forever and forever wild.

— *Who Has Seen the Wind*

Who Has Seen the Wind opens with one of the most recognizable lines in Canadian literature: "Here was the least common denominator of nature, the skeleton requirements simply, of land and sky—Saskatchewan prairie." The mathematical metaphor not only catches the visual image of a landscape reduced to the bare minimum of sky, horizonline, and land, it also suggests the skeletal destiny of humans. The novel depicts Brian's quest for answers to the basic, "skeleton" questions about birth and death. Visually precise and metaphorically suggestive though it is to Canadian eyes, this first line of the novel was considered dull and boring by W.O.'s American editor. When asked to remove it, W.O. argued that it expressed the "bareness of the prairie itself" and that it must stay in. There was, he thought, a distinction to be made between bareness and dullness. What W.O. saw was that the ultimate emptiness of the prairie was also melodramatic.

And for sensitive eyes and ears, there is variety in the seasonal changes to prairie, in its cloudscapes, in its wind voices. W.O.'s sensibility, his philosophy of being, his aesthetics were all informed by this minimalist landscape, which trained him to look closely and to listen acutely. In *Who Has Seen the Wind*, he celebrates prairie landscape in rich, lyrical prose and explores the growth of this way of seeing in his child protagonist, Brian. He called the prairie, and later the foothills, his "grass

tower": "I had a grass tower childhood in the Saskatchewan prairies. Now I value the opportunity to stand still, to stare, to listen. You can do these things well in a grass tower. The listening is particularly important to a writer."

Looking up at sky and looking down at earth, "you're in a world," says the kid in *Jake and the Kid*, and "she's your own world." As a young boy, W.O., along with his friends, had the whole prairie around Weyburn as their world, their grass tower.

They hunted gophers, dug caves, and swam in the Souris River—more a slow-moving creek with cattails spearing its mud banks—or

skated on it in winter. The prairie sharpened his senses, and his prose is rich with what he called sensuous fragments: the "stitching sound of grasshoppers," the "faint honey scent of wolf willow," the "escargot taste and smell" of the Souris, the meadowlark's "sudden bright notes splintering stillness." Even the no sound of a hot mid-August noon is captured: "She was kind of numb out there, like the prairie bumped its funny bone." Like Joseph Conrad, one of his literary heroes, W.O. believed that the writer must appeal to his readers' senses, must strive through image and rhythm to make us touch, hear, smell, taste—above all, to make us "see" our world.

Canada: A Virtual History

Journalist Ray Conlogue was born in Toronto in 1949. Conlogue received a bachelor's degree in English literature and a master's degree in drama from the University of Toronto. From 1980 to 1991, he was the theatre critic for the *Globe and Mail*. Conlogue won a National Newspaper Award for theatre criticism in 1986. This newspaper feature article describes a television production about Canadian history. In what ways do you think filmed productions of historical periods should be realistic? What kinds of "poetic licence" do you think writers and directors can take when recreating a historical drama?

Notes

Iroquois term that refers to a confederation of five Aboriginal nations that originally inhabited the northern part of New York State

Captain James Cook explorer, navigator, and map-maker who charted part of the Gaspé and helped prepare the map that enabled James Wolfe's armada to navigate the St. Lawrence River

Plains of Abraham the site of the battle for Quebec in September 1759 between the British forces led by James Wolfe and the French forces led by Montcalm, both of whom were mortally wounded in the battle

Louis Riel (1844–1885) Métis leader, founder of Manitoba, and the central figure in the Northwest Rebellion

Montagnais Aboriginal people living in the eastern and northern portions of the Quebec-Labrador peninsula

Activities

1. In one column of a chart, describe three visuals referred to in the article. Beside each description, explain how it was created. Assess the effectiveness of the techniques for the viewer.

2. Analyze the characteristics of a newspaper feature article, using this selection as a model. Then assess the effectiveness of this article using the criteria you have developed. Focus on the use of elements such as the following: a "hook" at the beginning to capture the reader's interest, the use of a journalist's "W5H" (Who, What, Where, When, Why, and How), detailed examples, background information, and interviews with experts.

Canada:
A virtual history

CBC had a relatively paltry $25 million to bring the story of our nation to life, writes **Ray Conlogue**, so it used some ambitious digital magic to take us back in time

"**M**ake the meteorite warmer and slower, please!"

This, if you can believe Steve Dutcheshen, was a typical director's request to CBC-TV's special-effects department during the creation of *Canada: A People's History*. Four new episodes of the 16-part, $25-million series are airing this month and producer Mark Starowicz has given the go-ahead to show how the magic was done.

The first half of the series, running from prehistory through early settlement and up to Confederation, is mostly about the prephotographic era. To get visuals of the British fleet attacking Quebec in 1763, or of Iroquois torturing French missionaries, it was necessary to generate the images by a variety of clever techniques. One involved filming actors climbing stepladders, then shrinking down the footage so they could "seem" to be working the sails on a 5-foot museum model of a warship. Another called on computers to create a huge village of native teepees out of film footage of a single teepee "which, on top of it all, was too narrow," says Roger Hupman, an effects director. "We had to make it twice as wide, which means each teepee has the same wrinkles twice."

Not to mention slowing down a meteorite, changing daytime footage of a steam locomotive to night-time, and, says Dutcheshen, "my favourite instruction of all: 'Keep the French bodies, the heads haven't arrived yet.'"

How to recreate the past with special-effects computers

The challenge: Create the illusion that British ships are attacking Quebec. **Step 1:** A five-foot-long model is filmed in various positions against a neutral backdrop, making it easy for artists to remove the background later.

Step 2: Current footage of Quebec City is altered to remove any buildings constructed after the attack of 1759, such as the landmark Chateau Frontenac, from the skyline. Clouds are added for dramatic effect.

Step 3: Superimpose various ship shots on the background to create the illusion of many vessels. Artists change colour of ships to fit background and add reflections and shadows.

Now, this may seem unnecessarily complicated to those who have kept up with developments in Hollywood. When the producers of *Titanic* wanted to recreate the doomed liner racing through the ocean, they built their own museum-quality "model" (14 metres, the length of many houses), and then used prototype high-power computers to create an ocean for it to slice through— binary point by binary point— likewise calling up the throngs of passengers from the cyber-ether.

But the *Titanic* team had 100 million bucks (U.S.), and the CBC didn't. Although the 30-hour series's $25-million (Cdn) budget had the usual right-wing critics choking in indignation (waste of taxpayers' dollars, splut, splut), it works out to less than $1-million per hour—about what the average U.S. sitcom costs.

That had consequences. Take eighteenth-century warships, for example. Even with a bank of shiny new effects computers, the CBC simply didn't have the gigabytes, or the time, to generate an image of a warship. The Royal Ontario Museum kindly let them film a magnificent, fully detailed 5-foot model of a period British battleship, which the new computers were then able to duplicate many times over (the whole British fleet bearing down on Quebec in the summer of 1759 is in fact the same ship, promiscuously cloned).

"And," says series executive producer Mark Starowicz, "when you have a close-up of a prow cutting through water with a crew hanging off the bow, the ship you see is actually the Endeavour." A CBC crew captured footage of the working replica of Capt. James Cook's ship (based in Sydney, Australia) off the North American east coast.

By such devious devices was a vanished world recreated. And yet, despite his exacting passion for accuracy, and the knowledge that video clips from the series would be "freeze-framed in Canadian classrooms" for decades to come, Starowicz knew that compromises would have to be made.

"Take the battle of the Plains of Abraham," he says. "In the real event, the muskets sounded like popcorn popping and there was so much smoke the soldiers couldn't even find the battle after the third volley." A far cry from the clear vistas of soldiers on the TV screen, and the satisfying thunder of musket volleys.

Starowicz considers it a triumph that CBC spent as much on current-generation graphic compositing computers as it did. And, remembering all the jibes he endured about how young viewers would not be interested in "musty" history, it is an additional sweet pleasure that "the graphic compositing department is full of kids with green hair."

One of them, a twentysomething named Jennifer Vuckovic (who has, as it happens, alarmingly jet-black hair), was responsible for creating the celebratory ball which marked the signing of the British North America Act in 1867. "It's what I call rotoscope hell," she says, recalling that the director of photography who oversaw the original filming of a small group of actors dancing in period costume, "didn't realize we'd need a middle layer of dancers to fill the historic ballroom we were using."

The trick here is that the costumed actors were filmed against a

A rope trick that didn't work

The challenge: Have sailors climb ropes on ships to make static model boats look more realistic.
The problem: Actors in costume were shot against a neutral background climbing ladders to simulate the effect of climbing ropes. However, when these images were shrunk and superimposed on the ship footage, the effect was unconvincing and was dropped.

neutral background in Toronto, and later superimposed on the historic ballroom located in Prince Edward Island. Fair enough—it saves travel expenses—but why not just film a whole lot of actors in the first place? "The costumes cost a fortune," replies Vuckovic.

Instead, she created the "middle layer" of dancers out of the existing footage, picking one here, one there, shrinking them to the appropriate size, and setting them spinning in the background of dancers who are—are you still with me?—themselves. "But they're rearranged and smaller, and we're real sure that nobody has noticed," says Vuckovic. The feat, however, required her to sit in front of a rotoscope camera for two weeks, rolling the film backward and forward a few frames at a time until the job was done. "It's worse than carpal tunnel syndrome," she says morosely, before rushing off to meet friends at a club.

Dutcheshen, a Manitoba native who studied fine arts in Winnipeg

And filling the ballroom with dancers

The challenge: Create a ballroom full of dancers with a limited number of actors wearing expensive costumes.

Step 1: Film many sequences of a small group of dancers in various positions in front of a neutral backdrop, some in the foreground, some in the background.

and design at the Ontario College of Art, feels that much of his team's work was about pictorial design. Actors supposedly dining on a train were actually shot in a studio, with footage of country-side racing past being projected on a train-window cut-out behind them. The result looked miserably fake until Dutcheshen's team created reflections of the actors' faces and wineglasses in the window glass. "As a fine artist, I found a lot of it came down to painting skills. I had to know which details would make it look real."

And it was with a pang that I learned that the Confederation-era locomotive steaming off toward the horizon in one episode was in fact lifted from the 1974 CBC series *The National Dream*. The locomotive was originally shot moving through rocky Ontario countryside by day, and Roger Hupman demonstrates the painfully tricky business of generating a new setting for it—the

Step 2: Combine the various sequences digitally. If viewers look closely, they can see the same actors in different parts of the room at the same time.

Prairies by night—as demanded by the script. Why not just shoot such a train again? Here's the answer that causes the pang: "*The National Dream* was shot when such a train could be found."

The team is rightly proud that it managed to weave material from so many sources, in so many media—real and virtual—into a convincing on-screen result. And their commitment to historic truth was obsessive. In a War of 1812 scene they realized that a U.S. general had been filmed in a brick fort at a time when forts were actually wooden palisades. It wasn't hard to computer-brush in a wooden palisade, but there were gaps between the logs where you should have seen the general's brass buttons.

"So we put them in, and it's pretty good," says Dutcheshen, "except that when he moves, his buttons don't."

But you didn't notice, did you? Not the first time, anyway.

Getting it right

At the other extreme from computer leg-erdemain is the rock-solid reality of what is called "materials history." In *Canada: A People's History*, the Native war paint was made from coloured clay and the chiefs' armour from plaited reeds, exactly as they would have been centuries ago. "The reed armour looks bizarre," says Peter Twist, "but it worked against arrows."

Twist, an engineer by training, became a builder of museum displays and Parks Canada installations out of a passion for history. Asked by CBC to help out on one episode of *A People's History*, he soon became a fixture. He was the one who found out what caps and badges were worn by the Midland battalion which fought Louis Riel, and that the French cannoneers on the Plains of Abraham wore red coats. He fully expected to see them stuck in blue coats, like the French infantry, in order to avoid confusion with the red coats of the British, "but to my amazement the CBC was absolutely rigorous about his-torical accuracy." This contrasts with U.S. films he's worked on where the "histor-ical sensitivity is laughable."

In Ontario-based episodes, Twist also advised on Native history, which some-times caused friction with Natives cer-tain they knew their culture better than he did. "But a lot of Natives' impressions of their culture have been corrupted by Buffalo Bill shows and so on," says Twist. "So I'd have to say, 'No, you [your ances-tors] didn't dress like that, they dressed like this.'"

He emphasizes that most Natives who participated "built up trust in us; they liked what was happening."

In the Quebec shoots, Native adviser Marco Bacon, a Montagnais from Lac Saint-Jean, was in charge of historic accuracy. Not surprisingly, he sees the issue differently. White advisers, he says, find it hard to accept "when we try to validate things through oral tradition. And it's true that many of our rituals were condemned and people were afraid to practise them. But they remembered them and told their children. That's why a Native can disagree with a historian. The historian presumes, but the Native can feel in his bones whether something is right or not."

Bacon worked for many years as a film actor, playing Native roles that were "more folklore than authentic. I found if I was going to argue with a director, I needed authoritative facts to change his manner of seeing things." He became a self-taught researcher, and willingly used any European documents he could find. Today he laments the paucity of docu-mentation of his own people, the Montagnais. "They weren't taken back to Europe like the Iroquois."

Bacon and Twist both agree that there were dark spots where no infor-mation exists, and here it was neces-sary to guess. "You try not to overdo it, or imagine too much," says Bacon.

"We'd take a best guess," says Twist. "A film isn't like a book, you can't leave a black box. When guessing, we'd go with the mundane."

And both agree that the world hasn't necessarily caught up with what the CBC was trying to do. Some U.S. reviewers, says Twist, "were horrified by our sympathetic treatment of the Natives. They didn't like it that we quoted, say, an American who survived a native massacre of his shipmates and wrote that Americans like him had it coming to them. One of the things I liked about this series was that we could not change a word or sentence of an original document."

Anna Husarska was born and raised in Warsaw, Poland, studied in France, and now uses New York as her home base. She has worked as a journalist and translator since 1979, contributing to publications such as *The Buenos Aires Herald*, *The New Republic*, *The New Yorker*, *The Washington Post*, and *The Wall Street Journal*. Husarska's facility for languages—she writes in five languages, speaks six languages fluently, and has working knowledge of three additional languages—has been invaluable in her work. Husarska has covered civil wars and other conflicts in Central America, Central Europe, the Middle East, and Southeast Asia. In this selection, Husarska explains how she prepares for her assignments. What challenges—to their mobility, research and communications capabilities, ethics, and psyche—do journalists reporting on conflicts in other countries have to deal with? What do you imagine would be the rewards of such work?

Notes

infrastructure the system of public works in a country, such as telephone and train service

flak jacket a bullet-proof jacket worn in a war zone

fonctionnaire de l'aventure a government official or civil servant

Activities

1. To many people, working as a foreign correspondent is an appealing job involving travel and adventure. Write a short report explaining how the information in this annotated graphic might influence a person's understanding of this career. Look up each of the places and nationalities listed within it and cite specific information from the selection to support your ideas. In your conclusion, reflect on your own suitability for and your interest in this kind of work.

2. Construct a character analysis of Anna Husarska, using information from "Unzipped." In your analysis, consider what she says as well as the tone she creates. How might her attitudes have been formed by the situations in which she has worked over the years? Ask a classmate to read your work and provide feedback on how you might rephrase passages or combine sentences to improve the clarity of your writing.

Unzipped

What's inside the travel bag of a foreign
correspondent on the go?

After I get the call, I start pack-
ing and turn on the short-
wave radio to find out who
hates whom where I am heading, and
perhaps the reason why they kill each
other. To communicate from countries
with inefficient infrastructures, I take
my satellite phone [1]; the problem is,
if the security police are efficient they'll
confiscate it.

I take a whole bunch of plug
adapters [2] and a good pair of alligator

Maps, country surveys, and posters of war criminals come in handy [7]. I write in notebooks [8] that fit in my back pocket and last for six months—if my handwriting's not too big and the war not too intensive. I carry CDs [9] with dictionaries and encyclopedias—they make my copy look intelligent. And of course, a book [10], perhaps about a former conflict, just for a change?

The basic survival kit is really simple: compass, Mag-Lite, Swiss Army knife, Leatherman all-purpose tool [11]. Cash [12] is crucial—most countries-at-war don't take credit cards—and I stuff it in a variety of places; in Somalia, $2,000 cash cushioned each of my running shoes.

A black, 100 per cent polyester skirt [13] that never wrinkles goes on every trip. For Muslim (or potentially Muslim) countries I always have a head scarf [14].

As for toiletries: reduce, reduce, reduce, which means small, concentrated quantities of shampoo, washing powder, and cream [15]. I take *chancletas* [16], the awful flip-flops that I bought in Tajikistan. They are the only thing that G. (the man who waits for my return) really insists I wear—he fears an infection. I fear for other things that I'll catch and often put a flak jacket in my backpack. And always, always some coffee [17], Cuban if possible, for a kick-start before facing more atrocities—another day at the office for what my friend calls *fonctionnaire de l'aventure*.

clips [3] so I can plug in wherever I am. And of course I include my laptop [4], whose hard drive is the closest thing to home.

I need credentials, business cards, and clippings of previous coverage [5]. I usually take a big sign stating my profession [6], but I am not sure it keeps the snipers away.

The Humpback of Notre Dame

About the Visual   Between 1993 and 1998, the Government of Newfoundland and Labrador's Department of Tourism, Culture and Recreation conceived and initiated an award-winning advertising campaign to entice visitors to the province. This "Imagine That" campaign grew to eight print advertisements, including the ad depicted here, posters, billboards, television commercials, and a postcard mail campaign. These advertisements were circulated throughout Canada and numerous other countries. The campaign had a forty per cent *conversion rate*, meaning that forty per cent of the people who saw the advertisements and then called to inquire actually visited the province. Not calculated in the conversion rate were those people who saw the ad and went to the province without calling. This advertisement contains not just a reference to a site on the northeast coast of Newfoundland, Notre Dame Bay, but a literary allusion as well. What are the purpose and contribution of literary allusions? If a viewer or reader is not aware of the allusion, is the impact of the phrase lost? Why or why not?

Activities

1. In a class discussion, share information and impressions of various provinces you have visited in Canada. If you have never visited Newfoundland and Labrador, would the advertisement "The Humpback of Notre Dame" entice you to visit there? Why or why not? What is the main impression of Newfoundland and Labrador you get from the advertisement? Does the ad successfully appeal to your wishes, attitudes, values, or lifestyle?

2. The first purpose of print advertisements is to catch and hold viewers' eyes and attention. In an essay, explore to what extent this advertisement uses the following attention-grabbing techniques in either illustration or text: a catchy title or headline; hyperbole and tongue-in-cheek humour; parallel structure and repetition; juxtaposition; symbolism; size, style, and placement of typeface or font.

Notre Dame Bay, where whales and icebergs cross paths.

Ten-thousand-year-old
icebergs drift south.
Humpbacks migrate north.
This is the place where
their paths cross.

The humpback
of Notre Dame.

Two of nature's leviathans.
Two wonders of the world.
They say you can't see
the icebergs for whales.

NEWFOUNDLAND
& LABRADOR
www.gov.nf.ca/tourism/

Morty Mania

Judy Waytiuk was born in Winnipeg, Manitoba, in 1950. For over thirty years, Waytiuk has worked as a reporter, commentator, documentarian, producer, and anchor in the media of newspaper, radio, and television. From 1987 to 1994, she was head of television news and current affairs programming for Global Television's Winnipeg affiliate. Her articles have appeared in publications including *Chatelaine* and the *National Post*. In "Morty Mania," she profiles Manitoba's very successful MTS advertising campaign. In what ways have specific advertisements influenced your view of a particular product or service? Can you think of ads that had a negative impact on you, rather than the intended positive one? If so, what was it about those ads that repelled you?

Notes

anthropomorphism attributing human characteristics to animals or inanimate objects, or personality to an animal or a god; from the Greek words *anthrōpos*, meaning "human being," and *morphē*, meaning "form"

self-deprecating refers to humorously negative remarks a person has made about herself or himself

Huns generally, a disparaging term referring to barbarous, uncivilized people; historically, refers to members of a nomadic, pastoral people who invaded Europe in the fourth and fifth centuries CE and were defeated in 455 CE

Activities

1. In a two-column chart, list on the left all the advertising campaigns you remember that were appealing to you. On the right, list all of the advertising campaigns you remember because they were ridiculous or offensive to you. Below, list the features of these advertisements that made them either appealing or offensive. Compare your list with that of a partner to see which, if any, features appear on both lists. Discuss reasons for your choices.

2. In small groups, analyze the features of the two advertisements depicted here, considering the target audience and the need to which the ad is appealing; the product or service being promoted; design elements such as use of colour, typeface, and layout; and the underlying values that are espoused through the ads.

morty
mania

Judy Waytiuk

how Manitoba's

MTS turned a

lovable bison

into a pop-cult

phenomenon that

ranks among the

top 1 per cent in

ad recall

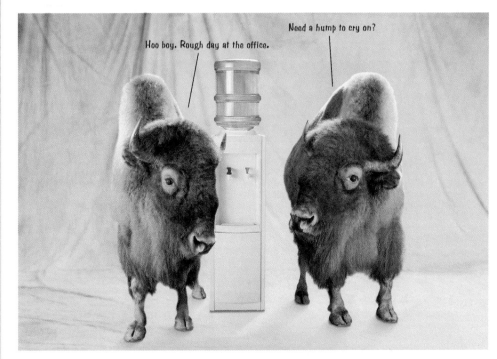

THE MOST RELIABLE SUPPORT IN MANITOBA.

With MTS, all your business needs are backed up with an incomparable level of support and service. From local, long distance and wireless, to high-speed Internet, telephone systems, equipment and data applications, we have technicians province-wide to ensure your business never misses a beat. To speak to someone who knows what they're talking about, call your MTS sales representative or 225-5687 (CALLMTS) toll-free today.

mts.mb.ca

MTS BUSINESS
All your needs. In one place.

MTS

Morty the Manitoba Telecom Services bison and his wry, shaggy friends and relations have stolen the hearts of Manitobans even more effectively than Molson's Joe and his "I AM Canadian" rant fired up Canadians a year ago. Joe was a one-spot wonder, while the MTS campaign, now into its second year, has turned into a Manitoba mania.

The developers of the campaign say it took luck, a maintenance man, creative brilliance, and agonizing corporate rethinking—

"THE MAINTENANCE GUY DISCREETLY SUGGESTED THAT THE BISON MIGHT BE A MORE APPROPRIATE ANIMAL."

without which none of the other factors would have come into play. So was it worth it to MTS?

Jack Riediger, the telco's Winnipeg-based advertising and marketing services manager, never dreamed a campaign could do this well. "We're benchmarking this stuff against things like the 'I AM Canadian' campaign," he says. "Our overall advertising recall is well over 80 per cent, and that's very high. Last quarter we said the problem is we'll never be able to improve on it, and it just keeps getting better."

Paul Millen, senior vice-president at Ipsos-ASI in Toronto, an advertising research company, offers further figures to show just how remarkably well this campaign is working. "In overall recall, we track over 1,500 campaigns in Canada, and this is in the top 1 per cent," he says. "We work with most of the major advertisers across the country, and this is one of the most successful campaigns I've ever been associated with."

Manitobans traded MTS bison paper cut-out Christmas tree ornaments as gifts last year. Bison Beanie Babies are hot items. Kids wanted bison costumes at Halloween, and they trade bison knock-knock jokes while waiting at bus stops. At the Fort Whyte Nature Centre outside Winnipeg, a flyer advertising a lecture series on bison leads off "Contrary to the popular television commercials, today's bison do not talk, laugh, wear sweaters, or surf the Internet."

Bison are this province's animal symbol. They're everywhere—stuffed in museums, bronze-sculpted in the legislature, painted on the province's crest and flag, served on restaurant menus, and alive and kicking in herds in parks and nature centres.

And anthropomorphism has always been "a popular and effective vehicle—Spuds Mackenzie, the Hamm's bear, Exxon and Esso with their tiger in your tank, Qantas and the koala bear," points

WHY GO ANYWHERE ELSE?

With MTS, all your business needs are at one source. From local, long distance and wireless, to high-speed Internet, telephone systems, equipment and data applications, MTS can accommodate any size business. And with incomparable service availability, you know you're getting the support your business can rely on. To see what we can do for you, call your MTS sales representative or 225-5687 (CALLMTS) toll-free today.

MTS BUSINESS
All your needs. In one place.

mts.mb.ca

MTS

out Rob Warren, director of the Asper Centre for Entrepreneurship at the University of Manitoba. "People like animals, especially animals that are somehow warm and cuddly. And even though bison are big animals, they look very docile and huggable."

Aside from MTS, only Ensis Growth Fund, a Manitoba government-sponsored investment fund, has used bison in an ad campaign—as a thundering backdrop herd on a projection screen while the CEO drones on about growth opportunities.

"Kids want bison costumes at Halloween, and they trade bison jokes while waiting at bus stops."

"It's not creative at all," sniffs Warren, who thinks part of the reason for MTS's success is that, for a heady change, "here's somebody standing up with one of our major symbols, and making something of it. Manitobans are usually so self-deprecating, and this is a direct descendant of the Joe 'I AM Canadian' thing, on a local level." Besides, he adds, the MTS campaign is by far the best-executed, most creative stuff in a market where the advertising humour benchmark is Nick Hill, discount furniture baron, "talking about number-one son leaving the sofa-making machine on too long."

Morty arrived on the scene in October 1999, with a spot selling long-distance services. Manitobans ran to their TV sets when Morty bellowed "WHAT?" in response to another bison yelling "We stampede AT TWO!" "Gesundheit," the monosyllabic Morty finally shouted back—a tad irritably.

Manitoba chuckled, and fell in love.

Since then, Morty's been seen painted with a stylized fluorescent red lightning streak while bopping (in a dignified manner) to a vaguely heavy-metal guitar riff. That spot sold high-speed Internet service. Cellphones wearing tiny bison horns promote the company's cellular service, as do "backup bison" twitching their skinny tails, in perfect digitized unison, to the beat of a white-bread Motown bison soloist singing "My mamma tol' me, yuh bettuh shop around."

Simon Cameron, VP associate creative director at Cossette Communication-Marketing in Vancouver, hatched the campaign with associate CD John Edmonds. "When a new ad comes on television, viewers will call someone in from the kitchen to see it," observes Cameron. "People are actively waiting for the next execution to appear." Cossette has churned out more than three dozen bison TV playlets in the last 16 months, and they remain Manitoba's hottest ads.

"IT'S NOT ABOUT A LOGO OR AN AD— IT'S ABOUT THE EXPERIENCE ONE HAS WITH A PARTICULAR BRAND."

MTS is understandably delighted, but how'd it happen? Cameron thinks "it's one of those things where there are so many small, tiny reasons why it works. I think, in broad strokes, that having the freedom to use humour in the message goes a long way."

The humour is deft, and is the first reason cited by both observers and creators for the campaign's popularity. But the real root of its success lies in the reasons that this warm, funny bent was finally chosen by a company with a long tradition of straight-up slice-of-life advertising.

MTS had been a provincial Crown corporation for most of its history. In the late '90s, the company went public at the same time deregulation opened the floodgates to hard-nosed, aggressive competition. MTS president and CEO Bill Fraser was trying to pull diverse corporate segments together into a clean whole as he ran defence against invading telco Huns.

The public, meanwhile, viewed MTS as conservative, stuffy, stodgy,

and old—a deadly reputation when young people form the bulk of the burgeoning market for newfangled forms of communication, MTS's major business-growth areas.

On the upside, says Riediger, it was considered "homegrown. We could be trusted. People felt we were part of the family, and a secure supplier."

Impact Research, Cossette Communications Group's research arm, did a marketing audit inside and outside the company, while Peter Drummond, managing director of Geyser Branding, also in Montreal, steered the MTS reinvention project from the strategic perspective. Reinvention, says Drummond, "takes incredible vision, incredible commitment from the top. Sometimes it requires organizational change, behavioural change, reorganization across a number of sectors. Not all companies can go as deep as we're talking about, but it's a matter of trying to close the gap as much as possible."

He's talking about the gap between what the company is and how it perceives itself—and what the public sees through ads and experiences through direct contact. "Look at all the great brands out there, whether Disney, Harley-Davidson, or Virgin. They consider the brand an integral part of the experience," Drummond points out. "It's not about a logo, it's not about an ad, but it's about the experience that one has with that brand."

At the same time, MTS had strained its existing agency beyond capacity. "We literally were choking the last agency we had, [the Winnipeg office of] Palmer Jarvis," says Riediger. "We would throw a couple of campaigns at them and deadlines would start falling, and we just had so much volume to do. And there wasn't any agency [in Manitoba] that was any bigger."

Besides, although MTS spends more than 70 per cent of its ad budget inside the province, Manitoba is not a creative genius hotbed. "Let's face it," Riediger says, "if you're a top creative talent, you're going to be looking in bigger markets to be working." So a new agency, the Vancouver office of Cossette, came on the scene just as MTS realized "we were taking ourselves far too seriously in our advertising."

In their Vancouver office in mid-1999, Cameron and Edmonds had settled on prairie dogs as the new MTS symbol, and were kicking around potential creative. "The maintenance guy, who's from Winnipeg, was doing something in our office," recalls Cameron. "Once he got interested in what we were doing, he discreetly suggested the bison might be a more appropriate animal."

Hmmm, the two thought. "It's just such a deeply entrenched icon that it was almost too obvious," says Edmonds now. There were some at MTS who worried "talking bison might be seen as goofy, and we didn't want to be perceived as goofy," Riediger remembers. But the chance was taken, and brand linkage has been "hugely successful. You see a bison, you know it's MTS. There's no question. Pretty much all the dimensions have strengthened: people's regard for the brand, do we have the best advertising, will we compete successfully in the future?"

As for where Morty and all his

bison buddies go next, "if we manage this thing carefully, I can't imagine it taking a downturn in the near future. Where we take it next, I'm not really too concerned about that," says Riediger. "We determine what the message has to be, then let the creative guys tell us whether the creative platform can take the message. And we haven't run across anything yet that the creative platform couldn't support."

Still, there is one fly in the ointment. "People are remembering the commercial but not the product," Warren observes.

He's right, and MTS knows it. Riediger wants better product recall. "The challenge in the campaign is to make sure the creative doesn't overpower the message," he says. "For the most, we're either at norms or slightly above norms." And, concedes Millen, product recall "is an area we've targeted as a priority for improvement."

Exactly how MTS will do so hasn't been figured out yet. But Morty's chewing on the problem...

Daniel Wood was born in Newton, Massachusetts, in 1943. He moved to Canada in 1969, as a conscientious objector to the Vietnam War, and has been based in Vancouver ever since. Both a writer and a photographer, Wood is the author of over fifteen books and scores of magazine articles for which he has received dozens of awards. For more than twenty years, he has taught writing at the University of British Columbia and Simon Fraser University. "The Monkey's Paw" explores highly complex and controversial issues about scientific subjects. When exploring a scientific subject, for which qualities do you look to give you confidence about the validity of information? Why is it so important that information be as complete as possible and not simply correct? What occurs when facts are accurate, but critical information is missing from an argument?

Notes

nature-versus-nurture dichotomy two mutually exclusive theories of the origin of human behaviour, one holding that behaviour is innate (nature), the other that behaviour is learned (nurture)

paradigm a philosophical or theoretical framework on which ideas are based

epidemiology the branch of medicine that deals with the control of disease; from the Greek words *epidēmia*, meaning "prevalence of disease," and *logos*, meaning "speech" or "reason"

spectre an image that haunts the mind

mitigate to lessen the effect of something

cryptology the deciphering of messages written in code; from the Greek words *kruptos*, meaning "hidden," and *logos*, meaning "speech" or "reason"

Brave New World a satirical novel by Aldous Huxley, which paints a grim picture of a future in which human embryos are grown in bottles and conditioned to collectivism and passivity

eugenics the highly controversial belief that the human race can be "improved" by selective breeding

determinism the belief that human action is not free, but determined by preceding events or natural laws

proclivities tendencies toward particular actions or habits

tabula rasa a term in psychology suggesting that humans are born as "blank slates" and are completely shaped by their environment; from the Latin, meaning "blank slate"

Human Genome Project an effort to identify all thirty thousand or more genes in human DNA and to deal with issues related to human genetics

sword of Damocles a symbol of anxiety; from the Greek legend in which Damocles, a fourth-century BCE courtier, praised the happiness of Dionysus, the ruler of Syracuse. Dionysus then hung a sword by a single hair and had it dangle over Damocles' head to symbolize the precariousness of happiness.

IMF abbreviation for International Monetary Fund, an agency of the United Nations that purchases foreign currencies in order to discharge international debt and stabilize exchange rates

terra incognita from the Latin, meaning "unknown territory"

Activities

1. In the course of this article, the author and the people he interviews pose many controversial questions. Choose the question that interests you the most and explore your thoughts on it in a journal entry. Share and discuss your ideas with your classmates.

2. The title of the article alludes to the classic story "The Monkey's Paw" by W.W. Jacobs, as well as to the Laurie Anderson song "Monkey's Paw." Use the Internet to obtain copies of these works. Write an essay in which you examine the thematic links between the article, the story, and the song. Reflect on Wood's purpose in choosing this title.

3. In his conclusion, the author implies that he believes cloning human beings is a less serious action than manipulating human genes. As a class, discuss these issues and frame a resolution for a debate. Do research to locate facts and knowledgeable opinions to support the position you take on the resolution. After the debate, assess your performance as a speaker and consider how you might work to improve your skills for future debates.

Daniel Wood

The Monkey's Paw

The scientific study of twins is

revealing fascinating links

between genes and human

behaviour. In this hall of mirrors,

the reflections are becoming

increasingly disturbing.

As the morning sun clears the highest branches of the elms in Twinsburg, Ohio, it reveals an utterly bizarre scene, for snaking beneath the trees in the town square are lines of perfectly matched sets of twins, triplets, and quadruplets—some 2,660 sets of them in all—each set dressed exactly alike. A stranger catches me gawking and whispers, "It's like Noah's Ark!" There are overweight twins dressed as Holstein cows, blond triplets in geometric-print micro-minis, bonneted baby quadruplets in comically elongated strollers. The head of each line converges on a cluster of bunting-wrapped fire engines, impatient baton twirlers, crepe-draped floats, fez-topped Shriners, and roving television cameras. It's impossible not to stare. It's impossible not to smile.

Here, for example, are identical twins Doug and Phil Malm,

41, of Moscow, Idaho, who met identical twins Jena and Jill, 31, at the Twinsburg Twins Days Festival in 1991, proposed to them on the festival stage in 1992, were married on the same stage in 1993, and have since spent, they tell me, every single day together, all four living in the same house, sharing bank accounts and holidays and toiletries. Here are bachelors John and Bill Reiff, 68, riding a rusty tandem bicycle and sporting Minnesota Twins baseball caps. They are looking, they say, for some twins to marry. Here are the Holland twins, Margaret and Louise, who have dressed alike—unfailingly—for 90 years. Here are identical twins Patti Carter and Carmen Smith, 38, from Windsor, Ontario, who developed their own language as youngsters and today wear matching pink toe and fingernail polish. "There's no line between us," says Patti. "We understand what each other thinks and why we're thinking it."

At 9:15 a.m., the fire engines begin wailing, a latter-day Noah shouts into his megaphone, and the lines go marching two by two up Ravenna Road, heading for the Twins Days' festivities. The road is lined with thousands of grin-ning onlookers, among them dozens of scientists and researchers who have come to Twinsburg to study twins. Twins are a unique example of genetic inheritance—they can tell us which characteristics are learned and which are part of our genetic code. Researchers have known this for a century, but what the new generation of scientists is discovering has turned everything previously thought about human psychology and behaviour on its head.

On the wall of Tony Vernon's office at the University of Western Ontario, in London, are a half-dozen photos of previous Twinsburg celebrants, including one of 2,800 matched pairs staring up at the camera with the words "Where's Waldo?" scrawled across their faces. Vernon, a 48-year-old professor of psychology, is one of scores of twins researchers worldwide who are investigating the strange realm of behavioural genetics. Based on his study of 500 twin sets, he is asking a very controversial question: How do our genes determine our behaviour?

Most mammals can produce dizygotic, or fraternal, twins, which are the result of the simultaneous fertilization of two different eggs.

Twins research has removed the old dichotomy between nature and nurture. It's not a dichotomy — it's both.

As do any pair of siblings, fraternal twins share 50 per cent of their genes. Humans and armadillos, however, also have the ability to produce monozygotic twins, one fertilized egg splitting into identical halves at a very early stage of development. Monozygotic twins are, in fact, natural clones, identical down to their genes.

In the past two decades, twins studies have become hugely popular. The Scandinavians have massive twins registers that go back generations. In England, the United States, Australia, and Canada, there are several ongoing studies involving almost 50,000 sets of twins.

Vernon compares fraternal and identical twins in two ways. First, since identical twins are 100 per cent the same, any differences in their responses to Vernon's questions about their behaviour point to areas least affected by genetic encoding. Analyses of his survey reveal clear patterns of high or low genetic influence. Second, by comparing responses from identical twins with those from fraternal twins, he can assess which characteristics are inherited and which are environmental— the old nature-versus-nurture dichotomy. A decade ago, behavioural psychologists thought all behaviour was the result of learned responses to specific childhood experiences. Not any more.

"The old idea that behaviour is all nurturing is gone," says Vernon. "It's a paradigm change. There's not a single personality characteristic that doesn't show some genetic basis."

Every twins researcher is finding the same thing, he says: political views, alcoholism, marital choices, altruism, religious beliefs, attitudes toward sex—everything, even intelligence quotient (IQ), can be an inherited trait. "Want a smart, blond, blue-eyed, Aryan kid?" asks Vernon. He pauses to make sure his words have sunk in and then sighs. "The ramifications are enormous. With cloning increasingly easy, we'll have the means to change human evolution."

Halfway around the planet from London, 48-year-old Nick Martin, a professor of genetic epidemiology at Brisbane's Queensland Institute of Medical Research, sits atop one of the world's largest twins registries: 27,000 pairs of Australian twins. Since he's been collecting data for 20 years and comparing the survey results from a pool of 7,000 sets of adults, he can statistically assess with accuracy the genetic versus the non-genetic influences affecting human intelligence and personality traits.

In an early study, Martin showed that 80 per cent of the variation in IQ among twins was genetic. The results scared him. "Twenty years ago," he says, "to even breathe IQ and genes in the same sentence was to invite a raging controversy. You'd be called a Nazi. The nature/nurture question was no joke. But we found so many things that were genetically influenced, it was getting boring: we wanted to find something that wasn't genetic. Surely, we thought,

social attitudes were completely determined by culture."

To test the hypothesis that 100 per cent of our social attitudes is the result of nurturing, Martin and his associates looked at twins' attitudes toward capital punishment, divorce, voting, sexual attraction, and religion. To their astonishment, they found that on average, only 50 per cent of the variation in those attitudes is determined by culture: the other 50 per cent is genetic. They also found that 65 per cent of the variation in predisposition to alcoholism in both men and women is genetically heritable. Even more surprising, they found virtually no correlation between family environment and the development of children's behaviour. It is as though parenting hardly matters.

Martin is well aware of the profound implications of what he's saying. He knows that the spectre of eugenics and racism and ethnic purity lurks behind his findings, but he reassures me that the direction of modern research is simply to locate places in the 70,000-gene human genetic code that influence disease, depression, or addiction in order to better understand the interaction of genes and the environment. The goal, he assures me, is to develop new therapies, new drugs (drug companies are avidly funding twins research), and new microsurgical techniques to mitigate or eliminate the detrimental genetic defects, not to open the door to genetic manipulation.

In North America, the number of multiple births is increasing exponentially, largely due to the widespread use of fertility drugs. Since 1973, the rate that women are having twins has doubled and the level of greater-numbered multiple births has increased sevenfold.

I feel uneasy, however. Today it may be merely cryptology—decoding the secret genetic messages—but what about the future? What about altering people's behaviour or IQ? Martin's research confounds deeply held views about the malleability of human nature, the role of society in improving disadvantaged people's lives, as well as religious and ethical notions of free will and equality.

"Where's this twins research leading?" I ask.

"People see *Brave New World* scenarios," he says. "Critics are afraid we're going to turn humans into frogs. I'm not going to pooh-pooh that: there are big ethical challenges ahead. But the '60s idea that there's an equality baseline in humans is wrong. There's no such thing as equality. We're affected by genetic variation. Why shouldn't people triumph over genetic adversity? If you're short, you can wear high heels. And if enough people want blond, blue-eyed babies, what's the danger?"

Part of the answer lies in looking at how science got to the point of considering the genetic manipulation of human beings. It is a curious detour in the path of this story, for the road back in the mirror world of twins is as convoluted as the road ahead.

Twins research began 125 years ago, when British scientist Francis Galton, a cousin of Charles Darwin, founded behavioural genetics with his work on the role heredity plays in intelligence, personality, and class. He invented the word *eugenics*, from the Greek word for "well-born," to propose a solution to the problems, as he saw them then, of reproduction among the unfit, the colonial underclass, and the mentally handicapped: control their reproductivity. By the turn of the century, many socialists and early feminists, including a

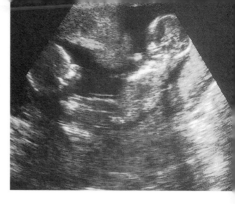

Amazingly, identical twins reared apart are *more* likely to share major life events than are identical twins reared together.

number of prominent Canadians, were avowed supporters of eugenics. They believed that the betterment of civilization would be brought about by enforced family planning, selective sterilization, and the state regulation of reproductive rights. By the 1930s, several Canadian provinces and more than half the American states had eugenics laws.

By then, however, the centre for twins research was Frankfurt, Germany, and the man in charge was Dr. Josef Mengele. Within a few years, Mengele and his assistants were patrolling the station platform at Auschwitz, shouting "Twins? Twins?" to the disembarking prisoners, hoping to make use of Jewish twins in his research into the genetics of creating a master race. He gathered 3,000 twins at Auschwitz, first cloistering them as human guinea pigs before systematically destroying them. Only 157 of the twins survived.

For the next decade, behavioural genetics and twins studies more or less ceased, tainted by the association with the Holocaust. In their place rose a belief in environmental determinism led by Harvard University psychologist B.F. Skinner, who argued that it was conditioning—nurture—that shaped human destiny. With good education and progressive legislation, Skinner argued, the constraints of poverty or class could be erased. People would be able to realize their nascent potential. Undesirable inherited traits could be conditioned out, socially acceptable ones conditioned in.

Then University of Minnesota psychologist Thomas Bouchard, now 61, began looking at the genetics of twins behaviour. Amid accusations of being a Nazi sympathizer, Bouchard pointed back toward genes, toward nature, as the determining factor in human personality. The pendulum had begun to swing again.

Bouchard's interest in genetic heritability had begun 19 years earlier, after his chance encounter with Jim Springer and Jim Lewis, both then 39 and both from Ohio. They were the rarest of twins and most prized by researchers: identical twins who had been separated at birth, were raised in different families, and had grown to adulthood completely unaware of each other's existence. Their nature was the same, but their nurturing was not. What Bouchard learned from them, and from the 135 sets of raised-apart twins he went on to study, opened the lid to a genetic Pandora's box.

When Jim Lewis finally found his twin brother, Jim Springer, after years of searching through court records, he knew their unwed mother had put them up for adoption shortly after giving birth. When the two first met, Lewis describes it as "like looking into a mirror." For starters, both had the same first name. They were physically identical. But when they got talking, the similarities were astounding. Both had childhood dogs named Toy. Both had been nail-biters and fretful sleepers. Both had migraines. Both had married first wives named Linda, second wives named Betty. Lewis named his first son James Allen; Springer named his James Alan. For years, they both had taken holidays on the same Florida beach. They both drank Miller Lite, smoked Salem cigarettes, loved stock car racing, disliked baseball, left regular love notes to their wives, made doll furniture in their basements, and had added circular white benches around the trees in their backyards.

When Bouchard ran them through what has become his standard 50 hours of testing—involving a 15,000-item questionnaire series, physical measurements, psychiatric interviews, and videotaping—the "Jim Twins" became even more bizarre. Their IQs, habits, facial expressions, brainwaves, heartbeats, and handwriting were nearly identical. As Jim Lewis puts it, "In all the tests we took, it looked like one person had taken them twice."

Bouchard was staggered. His findings contradicted his own most fundamental belief as a social psychologist: that almost all psychological traits were environmentally shaped. For further research, he established the Minnesota Center for Twin and

Adoption Research—where else but in the Twin Cities of Minneapolis and St. Paul—and the project soon collected data on 8,000 sets of twins. He now knows that in many traits, identical twins raised apart are as alike as those raised together. In fact, identical twins, unlike fraternal twins, become more identical over time.

Bouchard's twins tests show that genetic factors account for 66 per cent of the variance in intelligence, 60 per cent for heritability of social attitudes, and 50 per cent for religiosity and personality.

What everyone finds incomprehensible is that studies of identical pairs like the Jim twins also show that twins reared apart are more likely to share major life events than are identical twins reared together. The twins for whom Twinsburg, Ohio, was named, for example, lived apart but died on the same day from the same illness at the age of 57. Since events have no DNA, such twin events are inexplicable. The only explanation that fits is a source of much scientific discussion: human experience may actually be shaped by genetic proclivities. In other words, nature and nurture are linked forces, shaping each other.

"How this happens, we don't know!" booms Bouchard. "We haven't the vaguest idea! We don't know how genes assemble the brain or how the brain assembles experiences."

My own brain boggles: can the mind assemble experiences in such a way as to influence their outcome?

Every discussion I have with identical twins in Twinsburg suggests that they aren't quite like the rest of us. Although most twins don't dress alike except at Twinsburg and don't share the same home like the Malms, they do testify to a depth of connectedness that as a single, I find hard to fathom. Take the Windsor, Ontario, twins, Patti Carter and Carmen Smith. Their twinness, they tell me, is a source of immense security. Although they have different jobs and different weights, they are each other's best friend, they talk on the telephone at least once a day, and they take their holidays together. Others, such as the identical Richmond twins from Aurora, Illinois, have no identity outside their twinness. At the Twinsburg Wiener Roast (two hot dogs, two bags of potato chips, and a package of twin Hostess Twinkies each), LaVelda and LaVona, 65, tell me that they dated 13 sets of twins before finding identical twins Arthur and Alwin Richmond in 1973. At their wedding, most of the bridesmaids, the organists, and the wedding-cake figurines were all twins. There were 30 more sets among the guests. To celebrate the marriage, they went to their first Twinsburg Twins Days together. The four then lived in the same house, sharing everything from meals to toothpaste. And, Alwin tells me, the three have "struggled" since the death of Arthur 11 years ago. "Losing an identical twin," he says, "is like losing half yourself." As he speaks, he is wearing a metre-high Egyptian-style headpiece covered with scores of photographs of the two couples.

Twinning varies widely from race to race. On average, only 6 pairs of twins per 1,000 births occur in Japan, 20 per 1,000 in North America, and 45 per 1,000 in Nigeria. The Yoruba tribe of Nigeria, who eat estrogen-rich yams, average 90 sets of twins per 1,000, the highest rate on earth.

Once Bouchard published his findings, others, seeing the implications of his research, wanted Twinsburg twins for their own studies, and before long, behavioural geneticists, clinical psychologists, and medical researchers were flocking annually to Ohio, soliciting volunteers and mailing out surveys to thousands of far-flung twins.

When John Livesley, a University of British Columbia (UBC) professor of psychiatry, heard about Bouchard's work, he realized that twins would be invaluable in finding the root causes of certain personality pathologies: such things as depression, phobias, compulsions, and violence. "Twins," he says, "are nature's perfect experiment. Twins research can define the architecture of personality. We're looking at the basis of human nature."

Working with psychologist Kerry Jang, Livesley is studying the questionnaire results from more than 1,000 sets of Canadian twins, who responded to 3,000 statements, such as: "I like to squash flies." "Frightening thoughts sometimes come into my head." "I follow the same route when I go someplace." As he runs through the statistical tabulations for me, showing the heritability in percentages of various components that define a behaviour such as callousness, his voice becomes animated.

"Look at this!" he keeps repeating, pointing to anomalies in the figures. "This is very exciting!"

He explains, for example, that the figures show certain elements of callous, psychopathic behaviour are strongly genetic and therefore not amenable to traditional clinical treatment. They are, to use the old saying, bred in the bone. But other aspects of callousness—those that show a low genetic heritability—appear to be affected primarily by environmental forces and are therefore more likely to respond to therapy.

Overall, like other twins research, the UBC Twin Project has found that 50 per cent of personality is genetic (nature) and 50 per cent is environmental (nurture). But the genetic components of many types of behaviours vary. Phobias, for

example, display a 20 per cent heritability; nicotine addiction shows a 70 per cent heritability.

It is clear from these figures that in many areas, people have a genetic proclivity toward certain behaviours. These are not inevitable, but they are inclinations that may be heightened or diminished by surrounding events. "Your personality," says Livesley, "alters the way you see the world. If you're an optimist, you see the world through rose-coloured glasses. If you're a pessimist, it's grey. Genetics shapes the environment you select, and it shapes the way you perceive it."

It also appears that some elements of personality vary between the sexes. In the UBC sample, compulsiveness, suspicion, and violence showed a strong heritability in males, but not in females. Submissiveness was heritable only among females. Furthermore, some elements of personality—modesty, self-discipline—appeared to be entirely the result of nurturing.

"People used to quote [English philosopher John] Locke," says Livesley. "The brain is a *tabula rasa*. But clearly, it's not." What emerges from these findings is that the brain is a slate that comes with writing scribbled all over it. "We used to think we could change those basic traits. We can't. We know now the basic personality is fixed. What twins research has done is remove the old dichotomy between nature and nurture. It's not a dichotomy; it's both."

This is a refrain I hear repeated

again and again. Gradually I find myself succumbing to the barrage of data from dozens of twins research projects around the world. Stockholm, Minneapolis, Brisbane, Vancouver, London, Twinsburg…for every human behaviour, the heritability statistics are remarkable. Something geneticist Kenneth Kendler tells me sets my mind reeling. Kendler is one of the researchers working with the data of the Virginia 30,000, a massive American study involving 7,000 pairs of twins and their families.

"Heritability is only the beginning for understanding humans," he says. "We're on the coast of a huge, unknown continent, and we've found the mouths of some rivers. We've only started to chart the geography of human behaviour and intelligence."

Kendler notes that by the year 2003, the Human Genome Project will have identified the entire 70,000-gene human genetic code. "Then," he says. "Then!" His voice rises, his finger points to the ceiling, but he doesn't finish the sentence. In the ensuing silence, I imagine a genetic sword of Damocles hanging over the heads of twenty-first-century humankind. I know that once we have identified every gene in the code, it is a small step to choosing which ones we want in our body or our family or our country and which ones we don't.

"Is that what you mean?" I ask Kendler.

"Talk to Plomin," he says.

That's what they all tell me. Robert Plomin is the genial deputy director of the Kings College Social Genetics and Developmental Psychiatry Research Centre in London, England. He has been investigating twins for medical research since the early 1970s. He tells me that molecular genetics used to concentrate on finding which chromosome is associated with each of the 1,000 single-gene disorders, such as cystic fibrosis, which affect only 2 per cent of humankind, and has begun to explore the complex, multiple-gene field of human behaviour. Metaphorically speaking, he is switching his attention from single stars to whole constellations. Plomin's goal is to bridge 1980s behavioural genetics twins research with twenty-first-century molecular genetics. We have the technology. And he has focused on that dangerous bugaboo, intelligence.

In particular, the genetics of IQ.

With data from 15,000 pairs of British twins, Plomin has found a 75 per cent correlation between genes and early childhood language development disorders. After correlating that with studies of American 13-year-olds—kids with identifiable, genius-level IQs and kids with average IQs—he has found the precise sites, the "genetic markers," as he calls them, that show a difference between high and average IQ. Each of the three chromosomes, he explains, may account for only a 2 per cent increase in IQ. There are many more to be found. But he will find them. Soon.

"Intelligence is not one thing," he says, "not one gene. It's not like catching a whale. It's more like catching little fish, one by one. IQ is the sum of a lot of behaviours. In three to five years," he goes on, echoing Kendler's words, "we'll be postgenomic. We'll have the human genetic code down. At that point, we'll have to figure out exactly how the different genes affect IQ."

Plomin, too, talks mainly about using this information to develop better treatments for disorders. His voice is calm and rational.

> "We're on the coast of a huge, unknown continent, and we've only started to chart the geography of human behaviour and intelligence."

Nonetheless, I find myself wondering if I'm just naive, or whether someone, somewhere, won't soon be exploring pathways that humans can take to enhance intelligence genetically.

On the Internet, for example, there is a Web site called Future Generations. Whoever maintains it admits that it is politically incorrect in its mission statement: 1. Intelligence is highly heritable; 2. The least intelligent are having the most children worldwide; and 3. Without reversing this trend, civilization will decline.

The future, it seems, could begin very soon to resemble the past. The difference between enforced sterilization, as preached in the 1930s, and whole populations rendered genetically asexual is, after all, essentially technological. My guide to that possible future is Charles Crawford, an evolutionary psychologist at British Columbia's Simon Fraser University. He's a legendary synthesizer and visionary and, it seems somehow appropriate to me, is legally blind. His mind encompasses several million years of human behaviour, from modern primate research to Neanderthal studies to the development of civilizations to twentieth-century behavioural genetics research. And he believes that current twins studies are a watershed event.

"With Bouchard, with the Jim twins," he says, "it's bizarre, almost frightening. We don't understand what it means. Livesley and Jang at UBC say the same thing: the power of genes. We're floundering because it's all so astounding."

"What about Plomin?" I ask.

"Plomin's work raises the issue of eugenics," says Crawford. "It takes us back a hundred years. In evolution, the message is always: nothing comes free. We're wealthy now in North America and Europe; we can afford to be kind.

But in 25, 50 years? When our society's in decline, and we're going to the IMF for bailouts? When the Chinese are doing well? Then the issues the twins projects are beginning to raise may come back to haunt us. Do we abort babies with gene X or Y or Z?"

Crawford shrugs. "That's when we'll have to come to terms with some fundamental questions," he says. "I'm glad I'll be dead by then."

At Chasers, a crowded nightclub just outside Twinsburg, Ohio, the Twins Days parade, the wiener roast, the look-alike competitions, the talent show, the T-shirt sales, and even the scientific testing are history. I'm sitting with 250 sets of identically dressed twins, all of them drinking and dancing. The music is loud, the voices are raised, and the ambience is dim. Two by two, male twins are putting the hustle on female twins. It seems as if everyone has safely boarded Noah's Ark and is doing exactly what the Boss intended. Except me: the doomed dodo. Phil Malm sees my hang-dog expression and shouts in my ear, "It's a place where you feel out of place."

The world record for the number of children produced by one woman goes to an eighteenth-century Russian who had 16 pairs of twins, 7 sets of triplets, and 4 sets of quadruplets. Altogether, she had 69 children.

I nod. I do. The song that comes to my mind is Laurie Anderson's "Monkey's Paw": *But Nature's got rules / and Nature's got laws, / And if you cross her look out! / It's the monkey's paw.*

The words seem eerily apt in light of what I've learned about twins research. We are at the threshold of a new world. What will happen when we have charted the entire geography of human behaviour and intelligence? Will we take the small step from cloning sheep to cloning human beings? Or the bigger step from removing a gene responsible for a genetic disorder to inserting one that makes us more intelligent or vote a certain way? The continent rising before us is almost entirely *terra incognita*, marked in my mind by the snaking twin helix of DNA and the traditional cartographer's warning: Here be dragons.

Restoring Life on the Edge

Chris Rose was born in Vancouver, British Columbia, in 1950. He is a reporter with the *Vancouver Sun* newspaper. This article highlights the Living By Water project, which aims to rejuvenate shorelines by changing people's attitudes about how to maintain their shoreline properties. Newspapers and other information sources are filled with daily reports on environmental issues. How do you assess these reports? In order to judge their importance and reliability, what kinds of questions do you ask yourself as you read or view these reports?

Notes

riparian of, on, or relating to the banks of a natural body or course of water

roughshod treat with brutal force; from the practice in which horses are shod with horseshoes that have projecting nails or points to prevent slipping

covenants binding agreements

septic refers to a sewage disposal system in which waste is decomposed by an aerobic bacteria

epiphany an understanding or perception of something through a sudden intuitive realization

biodiversity biological variety

Activities

1. Before reading the article, what were your views about the ideal shoreline and waterfront property? To what extent did your views change as a result of reading this selection? Why did your views either change or remain the same?

2. This article contains very specific, illuminating detail. With a partner, reread the article and in your notebook write down every sentence that is general rather than specific. Read these sentences in sequence and compare the style, tone, and impact of the new passage with the original article. Then choose an environmental topic of particular interest to you. With your partner, write down any general ideas about it that you can think of. Do research to locate specific details about your topic and use them to write your own expository article.

Restoring life on the edge

Chris Rose

From a small Interior lake to the Strait of Georgia, the Living by Water project aims to rejuvenate shorelines by changing attitudes and allowing nature another chance.

GARDOM LAKE—At first glance, the waterfront here seems unkempt. Rotting logs are scattered about, vegetation grows close to the shoreline, the tiny beach is hidden in the reeds, and the floating dock isn't much wider than a city sidewalk.

There is no concrete boat launch, no asphalt parking lot, no homes crammed against the water's edge, and no perfectly manicured lawn so often associated with the good life, and those lucky enough to own riparian properties.

But that's just fine with Sarah Kipp and Clive Callaway, owners of this property on a spring-fed lake 541 m above sea level. They eagerly predict the untidy beauty of natural vegetation and a reclaimed shoreline teeming with animal life are a sign of good things to come.

Their property—complete with bulrushes, cattails, duck down, mud, and a rich collage of decomposing foliage—is at the forefront of a new campaign to restore shorelines and help heal the environment.

UNSPOILED: Sarah Kipp on a part of the Gardom Lake shoreline that has been left natural. Photo: Ian Smith, Vancouver Sun

Kipp and Callaway note that a generous buffer zone of plants between the houses and the shore helps cleanse the air and filter the water—some of which will eventually make its way 480 km southwest to Vancouver via Shuswap Lake, the South Thompson, and the Fraser River.

As Kipp says, in reference to the estimated 2.6 million people living near the Strait of Georgia, "we all live downstream of something."

And that "something" is what

Kipp and Callaway are trying to change.

They contend that few waterfront dwellers realize how they are degrading their piece of shoreline—along with their emotional and financial investment—by allowing unchecked urban attitudes to run roughshod over nature.

"Together we make a huge impact," says Callaway, adding that watching their waterfront become healthy again has taken on spiritual overtones.

"We love to look at it, we love to hear it, we love to experience it. Every Canadian who's spent time by the water's edge would probably agree with us. It's an exciting place, it's alive, it's vibrant."

"We see the shoreline as a ribbon of life."

That's where their non-profit Living By Water Project, with its gentle philosophy of heightened environmental awareness, comes in.

Kipp, who has a master of arts degree specializing in geography from the University of Alberta, and Callaway, who has a master of environmental design degree from the University of Calgary, bought a seasonal fishing lodge here on 4.5 hectares when they decided to leave the big city 12 years ago.

"We had a dream to change our lifestyle—to live in semi-wilderness, out of the rat race—and do something useful for the environment," Callaway, 55, says.

He and Kipp, 49, became entranced by Gardom Lake, situated on a rolling height of land between the Shuswap and the Okanagan, and 17 km southeast of Salmon Arm.

"It is so special," he adds. "We've just come to love living on the edge."

For about eight years they tried to run the lodge, which had a number of cabins on it, as an environment teaching centre but it increasingly became difficult to raise money, sustain the workload, and operate it year-round.

They eventually sold off some of their property and voluntarily put "conservation covenants" on the remaining three hectares to protect the natural features of the shoreline. Except for the small communal wharf and tiny beach shared by the seven owners, no other development along the 185 m of communal shoreline was allowed.

Little by little, by trial and error, Kipp and Callaway accumulated a wealth of knowledge about their shoreline.

They learned everything they never wanted to know about septic systems, water tables, setbacks, infiltration, evaporation. They were told that the elegant European willows planted decades ago along their portion of the lake should be replaced with native willows and dogwoods, which let more light onto the shore, which in turn provides a healthier habitat for fish, birds, insects, and turtles.

They began to realize that humans—even well-meaning humans—can cause as much damage to the environment as greedy industry and nearsighted government policy. They learned that bulrushes eat heavy metals, and that wild grasses are more beneficial than an attractive lawn. They were shocked to understand that "non-point source pollution" was a scientific way of saying that all

sorts of tiny, non-traceable human excesses can account for a problem of gigantic proportions.

The epiphany they experienced suggested waterfront dwellers quit trying to triumph over nature and instead live in harmony with the plants and animals that naturally gravitate to shorelines.

"Basically we see the shoreline as a ribbon of life," said Callaway, noting Environment Canada describes riparian areas as one of the most productive ecological zones on Earth.

Three years ago, armed with freshly acquired insights, Kipp and Callaway decided that if they could be re-educated about their little bit of paradise, so could others.

They came up with the idea of the Living By Water Project, which they hope will make people reassess how they mistreat shorelines on rivers, lakes, wetlands, and the ocean, negatively affecting water quality and degrading wildlife habitat.

Calling the project "a new fashion statement," Callaway says he and Kipp want it to become as pervasive in the next decade as recycling's blue box campaign has become since it began in the 1980s.

Their first big break came when they approached the Federation of B.C. Naturalists to help in fundraising. Deciding the idea of promoting a healthier waterfront lifestyle would appeal to ordinary citizens, the federation signed on, and became the lead partner for the project.

Tiny, non-traceable human excesses can account for a problem of gigantic proportions.

Federation president Anne Murray said her 5,500-member organization became involved two years ago because the project's message helps promote biodiversity from the edges of small Interior lakes to shorelines surrounding the Strait of Georgia.

"How waterfront residents behave with their little bit of property can add up to great results," Murray, a Delta resident, said. "Everybody gets worked up about forests [but] people don't always think of shorelines."

She noted that while riparian zones are incredibly important habitat, they are also extremely vulnerable—especially because so many people try to tame nature instead of allowing it to flourish.

Murray added shorelines and their rich nutrients have to be protected because that is where so much of the food chain begins.

"It's both a ribbon of life and a nursery of life. I think we're only just beginning to understand that as a society."

Some of Kipp and Callaway's research has already been implemented by the Adams Lake Indian Band near Chase because of concerns about unprecedented development on Shuswap Lake and declining water quality.

Greg Witzky, fisheries manager for the 600-member band, said Kipp and Callaway were recently hired to talk to non-Native lakeshore leaseholders about how to reverse shoreline degradation.

"We learned a lot of people wanted to protect the foreshore but they didn't know how to go about it," Witzky recalled. "People were really responsive in a positive manner. They wanted more information on how to protect their little shoreline."

As a result of that response, Witzky said, the band has since presented about 1,700 non-Natives who own land along Shuswap Lake with information packages on how to better protect the foreshore for fish habitat.

"If the fish are healthy, you can pretty well say that the whole lake is healthy too," Witzky said, adding what goes into the water near Chase eventually makes its way downstream to the coast.

Callaway says similar organizations in all the other provinces are now involved in the project, and he hopes the three territories will soon be included.

A major component of the project, which will be unveiled across Canada over the next two years, is a handbook about B.C. waterfront-living that Callaway and Kipp are now completing. It is expected to be published in the spring of 2000.

Editions dealing with other regions of the country, also written by Callaway and Kipp, will follow. Callaway expects about 125,000 copies of the handbook will be sold nationally in the next five years.

At least 5,000 copies of the 128-page book—titled *On the Living Edge*—will initially be printed. The handbook is full of tips designed to help first-time buyers of waterfront property and people who already reside along a shoreline.

The tips include choosing the proper type of detergent to use in the home and explanations about why not to cut the lawn too close to the edge of the water. There is also information on how to replant a natural shoreline and make sure the septic system is working properly.

The untidy beauty of natural vegetation is a sign of good things to come.

Coastal dwellers with access to a sewer system can learn how to deflect water running off roads and driveways into little ponds to reduce erosion and help keep pollutants out of the ocean. Other sections address hobby farmers and boaters.

Subsidized by five key sponsors, the book will likely cost about $6. The project has about 30 sponsors across Canada ranging from public and private foundations to various government departments.

More than $600,000 has already been raised nationally— about one-third from millennium funds. Callaway estimates an equal amount has been raised through donated time. He, Kipp, and two assistants are now working full time on the project and receiving funding managed by the federation of naturalists.

The project will be formally launched in Vancouver toward the end of January.

In addition to the book, the project will promote next September as "shoreline celebration and restoration month" and use artists, scientists, and community volunteers to bring attention to waterfront protection.

The project will also host a national children's poster competition in February, a touring theatre production in B.C. in August, and an instructional video by the end of next year. There are also plans for a travelling exhibition to demonstrate the values and functions of shorelines and a home-site visitation program will likely begin in B.C. next fall.

Callaway says it is important people realize that altering their shorelines isn't always expensive or difficult. Most changes to existing properties can be brought about incrementally, he said, while new developments can be planned with nature in mind before any building is started.

"It can be very, very simple— it's as simple as leaving it alone. They can be complicated but in many, many cases very simple actions can result in great improvements. So much of it is about changing habit and behaviour."

wrap-up
essays,
articles,
and media

1. Choose an essay in this unit that focuses on a problem affecting one or more people. Reread it carefully in preparation for writing an analytical essay about the problem addressed. Research what your audience needs to know about your subject. In your essay, clearly identify the problem, explain how it affects people, and outline the steps to your solution. Remain objective in your approach. Have a classmate read a draft of your essay and comment on its logic, clarity, and objectivity. Make any necessary revisions.

2. Create a glossary of academic and technical terms that appear in selections in this unit. For each of your entries, provide a precise, clear definition of the word or term and a sample sentence that includes it, both in your own words; a detailed outline of its origins and roots; and the page number in the anthology where it appears. Include a bibliography of the sources to which you referred in creating your glossary.

3. Develop a plan for a Web site that would provide information related to a topic of interest triggered by a selection in this unit. Think about how you will organize and synthesize your information. Your site plan should cover the purpose of your site, an annotated table of contents, a flowchart that illustrates the internal and external links you will include, a description of the navigation bar, and a list and brief description of visuals that will appear. As appropriate, provide rough sketches of the features of the site as part of your plan.

4. Work with a partner. After looking at several travel brochures or travel-related CD-ROMs, develop a checklist of criteria for developing an effective travel brochure or multimedia travel presentation. Use your checklist to help you create a brochure or multimedia presentation that will make people want to visit one of the settings depicted in a selection from this unit. Locate effective photographs and other visuals and arrange the visuals and the text into an order that makes sense. Review and revise your draft or multimedia script. Use a word-processing or desktop publishing program to create your brochure or deliver your multimedia presentation to the class.

In the morning, it might be a radio alarm clock that wakes you up. Then, perhaps you head to the computer to check your e-mail or to go to a favourite site. You may grab the remote to check out today's weather on television. Later, you wander into the kitchen to get some breakfast and find that a family member has the section of the newspaper that you want. Face-to-face communication is about to begin. Now take yourself back to humanity's early days, when the only form of communication was face-to-face. Through conversation, story-telling, and song, humans shared news or gossip, learned or taught a skill, and made a friend or an enemy. From then to now, methods of communication have expanded exponentially by means of print and electronic sources. Throughout history, those people who have communicated skilfully, decoded messages, and manipulated information in all its various forms have had social power. That is why contemporary theories of literacy go beyond the ability to read and write and include such concepts as *visual literacy* and *media literacy*. Your fluency in each medium—how well you understand such components as its internal language, its codes, conventions, formats, production requirements, and economic realities—as well as the ability to create your own media products allows you, as media expert Paolo Friere has said, to "read the world."

This In-Depth will offer insights about media both through its content and its various forms. Marshall McLuhan's "Aphorisms" touches on a range of topics and kick-starts your explorations. An essay by Neil Postman challenges you to deconstruct television and print news. A newspaper article by Ann Rees looks at on-line, *virtual* classrooms. A radio script by Bob Elliott and Ray Goulding takes a comic look at television news production. And a poem by Kenneth J. Harvey touches on a more personal connection between the specific medium of television and a person. As you gain a stronger understanding of the media that permeate our lives, you will have the insight and power to make the media work for you.

Aphorisms

Marshall McLuhan

A pioneer who revolutionized communications theory, Herbert Marshall McLuhan was born in Edmonton, Alberta, in 1911. As a professor of English at the University of Toronto, his seminal studies of the effects of mass media on thought and behaviour brought him international fame in the 1960s. His books include *Understanding Media* (1964). He died in 1980. McLuhan's aphorisms have been described as catchy, succinct, and deceptively simple. What is the purpose of an aphorism? Are there universal characteristics of aphorisms? If so, what are they?

My father decided in the sixties that he would try as much as he could to present his ideas in an aphoristic style. Aphorisms, as Francis Bacon said, are incomplete, a bit like cartoons. They are not filled-out essay writing that is highly compressed. The aphorism is a poetic form that calls for a lot of participation on the part of the reader. You have to chew on an aphorism and work with it for a while before you understand it fully. A good aphorism could keep you busy for a week—kicking it around, playing with it, exploring it, taking it apart to see what you can get out of it. And applying it here, there, and everywhere. My father deliberately chose this form of statement because he wanted to teach, not tell or entertain. He said, "For instruction, you use incomplete knowledge so people can fill things in—they can round it out and fill it in with their own experience." If what you want to do is simply to tell people something, then by all means spell it out in the connected essay. But if you want to teach, you don't do that. There's no participation in just telling: that's simply for consumers—they sit there and swallow it, or not. But the aphoristic style gives you the opportunity to get a dialogue going, to engage people in the process of discovery.

—Eric McLuhan

I don't explain—I explore.

Unlike previous environmental changes, the electric media constitute a total and near instantaneous transformation of culture, values, and attitudes.

Under instant circuitry, nothing is remote in time or in space. It's now.

Since the telegraph and radio the globe has contracted, spatially, into a single large village. Tribalism is our only resource since the electromagnetic discovery.

In the eighties, as we transfer our whole being to the
data bank, privacy will become
a ghost or echo of its former
self and what remains of community will disappear.

**Everybody at the speed of light tends to
become a nobody.**

The three-year-old standing
up in his playpen in front of
the TV sees as much of the
adult world as anybody.

In the electric age the connection in narrative and art is
omitted, as in the telegraph press. There is no storyline
in modern art or news—just a dateline. There is no past
or future, just an inclusive present.

At present, TV is a service only during a crisis.

PEOPLE NEVER REMEMBER BUT THE
COMPUTER NEVER FORGETS.

The News

Neil Postman

Neil Postman is a communications theorist, critic, educator, and essayist who was born in New York City. He received his doctorate from Columbia University. Postman has taught at New York University for over three decades, where he has served as the chair of Media Ecology and of the Department of Communication, Arts, and Sciences. This department focuses on how symbols are organized to convey meaning, how communication affects cultural institutions, and how new media affects education. He is the author of more than a dozen books, including *Amusing Ourselves to Death: Public Discourse in the Age of Show Business* (1986) and *Building a Bridge to the Eighteenth Century: Ideas from the Past that Can Improve Our Future* (1999). What are some of the differences between print, radio, and television news? Do you think that one medium is better suited to reporting on the news than others? Why or why not?

The whole problem with news on television comes down to this: all the words uttered in an hour of news coverage could be printed on one page of a newspaper. And the world cannot be understood in one page. Of course, there is a compensation: television offers pictures, and the pictures move. It is often said that moving pictures are a kind of language in themselves, and there is a good deal of truth in this. But the language of pictures differs radically from oral and written language, and the differences are crucial for understanding television news.

To begin with, the grammar of pictures is weak in communicating past-ness and present-ness. When terrorists want to prove to the world that their kidnap victims are still alive, they photograph them holding a copy of a recent newspaper. The dateline on the newspaper provides the proof that the photograph was taken on or after that date. Without the help of the written word, film and videotape cannot portray temporal dimensions with any precision. Consider a film clip showing an aircraft carrier at sea. One might be able to identify the ship as Soviet or American, but there would be no way of telling where in the world the carrier was, where it was headed, or when the pictures were taken. It is only through language—words spoken over the pictures or reproduced in them—that the image of the aircraft carrier takes on meaning as a portrayal of a specific event.

Still, it is possible to enjoy the image of the carrier for its own sake. One might find the hugeness of the vessel interesting; it signifies military power on the move. There is a certain drama in watching the planes come in at high speeds and skid to a stop on the deck. Suppose the ship were burning: that would be even more interesting. This leads to a second point about the language of pictures. The grammar of moving pictures favours images that change. That is why violence and destruction find their way onto television so often. When something is destroyed violently its constitution is altered in a highly visible way: hence the entrancing power of fire. Fire gives visual form to the ideas of consumption, disappearance, death—the thing which is burned is actually taken away by fire. It is at this very basic level that fires make a good subject for television news. Something was here, now it's gone, and the change is recorded on film.

Earthquakes and typhoons have the same power: before the viewer's eyes the world is taken apart. If a television viewer has relatives in Mexico City and an earthquake occurs there, then she may take an interest in the images of destruction as a report from a specific place and time. That is, she may look to television news for information about an important event. But film of an earthquake can still be interesting if the viewer cares nothing about the event itself. Which is only to say that there is another way of participating in the news—as a spectator who desires to be entertained. Actually to see buildings topple is exciting, no matter where the buildings are. The world turns to dust before our eyes.

Those who produce television news in America know that their medium favours images that move. That is why they despise "talking heads," people who simply appear in front of a camera and speak. When talking heads appear on television, there is nothing to record or document, no change in process. In the cinema the situation is somewhat different. On a movie screen, close-ups of a good actor speaking dramatically can sometimes be interesting to watch. When Clint Eastwood narrows his eyes and challenges his rival to shoot first, the spectator sees the cool rage of the Eastwood character take visual form, and the narrowing of the eyes is dramatic. But much of the effect of this small movement depends on the size of the movie screen and the darkness of the theatre, which make Eastwood and his every action "larger than life."

The television screen is smaller than life. It occupies about 15 per cent of the viewer's visual field (compared to about 70 per cent for the movie screen). It is not set in a darkened theatre closed off from the world but in the viewer's ordinary living space. This means that visual changes must be more extreme and more dramatic to be interesting on television. A narrowing of the eyes will not do. A car crash, an earthquake, a burning factory are much better.

With these principles in mind, let us examine more closely the structure of a typical newscast. In America, almost all news shows begin with music, the tone of which suggests important events about to unfold. (Beethoven's Fifth Symphony would be entirely appropriate.) The music is very important, for it equates the news with various forms of drama and ritual—the opera, for example, or a wedding procession—in which musical themes underscore the meaning of the event. Music takes us immediately into the realm of the symbolic, a world that is not to be taken literally. After all, when events unfold in the real world, they do so without musical accompaniment. More symbolism follows. The sound of teletype machines can be heard in the studio, not because it is impossible to screen this noise out, but because the sound is a kind of music in itself. It tells us that data are pouring in from all corners of the globe, a sensation reinforced by the world map in the background (or clocks noting the time on different continents).

Already, then, before a single news item is introduced, a great deal has been communicated. We know that we are in the presence of a symbolic event, a form of theatre in which the day's events are to be dramatized. This theatre takes the entire globe as its subject, although it may look at the world from the perspective of a single nation. A certain tension is present, like the atmosphere in a theatre just before the curtain goes up. The tension is represented by the music, the staccato beat of the teletype machines, and the sight of news-workers scurrying around typing reports and answering phones. As a technical matter, it would be no problem to build a set in which the newsroom staff remained off camera, invisible to the viewer, but an important theatrical effect would be lost. By being busy on camera, the workers help communicate urgency about the events at hand, which it is suggested are changing so rapidly that constant revision of the news is necessary.

The staff in the background also helps signal the importance of the person in the centre, the anchorman (or -woman) "in command" of both the staff and the news. The anchorman plays the role of host. He welcomes us to the newscast and welcomes us back from the different locations we visit during filmed reports. His voice, appearance, and manner establish the mood of the broadcast. It would be unthinkable for the anchor to be ugly, or a nervous sort who could not complete a sentence. Viewers must be able to believe in the anchor as a person of authority and skill, a person who would not panic in a crisis—someone to trust.

This belief is based not on knowledge of the anchorman's character or achievements as a journalist, but on his presentation of self while on the air. Does he look the part of a trusted man? Does he speak firmly and clearly? Does he have a warm smile? Does he project confidence without seeming arrogant? The value the anchor must communicate above all else is control. He must be in control of himself, his voice, his emotions. He must know what is coming next in the broadcast, and he must move smoothly and confidently from segment to segment. Again, it would be unthinkable for the anchor to break down and weep over a story, or laugh uncontrollably on camera, no matter how "human" these responses may be.

Many other features of the newscast help the anchor to establish the impression of control. These are usually equated with professionalism in broadcasting. They include such things as graphics that tell the viewer what is being shown, or maps and charts that suddenly appear on the screen and disappear on cue, or the orderly progression from story to story, starting with the most important events first. They also include the absence of gaps or "dead time" during the broadcast, even the simple fact that the news starts and ends at a certain hour. These common features are thought of as purely technical matters, which a professional crew handles as a matter of course. But they are also symbols of a dominant theme of television news: the imposition of an orderly world—called "the news"—upon the disorderly flow of events.

While the form of a news broadcast emphasizes tidiness and control, its content can best be described as chaotic. Because time is so precious on television, because the nature of the medium favours dynamic visual images, and because the pressures of a commercial structure require the news to hold its audience above all else, there is rarely any attempt to explain issues in depth or place events in their proper context. The news moves nervously from a warehouse fire to a court decision, from a guerrilla war to a World Cup match, the quality of the film often determining the length of the story. Certain stories show up only because they offer dramatic pictures. Bleachers collapse in South America: hundreds of people are crushed—a perfect television news story, for the cameras can record the face of disaster in all its anguish. Back in Washington, a new budget is approved by Congress. Here there is nothing to photograph because a budget is not a physical event; it is a document full of language and numbers. So the producers of the news will show a photo of the document itself, focusing on the cover where it says: "Budget of the United States of America." Or sometimes they will send a camera crew to the government printing plant where copies of the budget are produced. That evening, while the contents of the budget are summarized by a voice-over, the viewer sees stacks of documents being loaded into boxes at the government printing plant. Then a few of the budget's more important provisions will be flashed on the screen in written form, but this is such a time-consuming process—using television as a printed page—that the producers keep it to a minimum. In short, the budget is not televisable, and for that reason its time on the news must be brief. The bleacher collapse will get more minutes that evening.

With priorities of this sort, it is almost impossible for the news to offer an adequate account of important events. Indeed, it is the trivial event that is often best suited for television coverage. This is such a commonplace that no one even bothers to challenge it. Walter Cronkite, a revered figure in television and anchorman of the CBS Evening News for many years, has acknowledged several times that television cannot be relied on to inform the citizens of a democratic nation. Unless they also read newspapers and magazines, television viewers are helpless to understand their world, Cronkite has said. No one at CBS has ever disagreed with his conclusion, other than to say, "We do the best we can."

Of course, it is a tendency of journalism in general to concentrate on the surface of events rather than underlying conditions; this is as true for the newspaper as it is for the newscast. But several features of television undermine whatever efforts journalists may make to give sense to the world. One is that a television broadcast is a series of events that occur in sequence, and the sequence is the same for all viewers. This is not true for a newspaper page, which displays many items simultaneously, allowing readers to choose the order in which they read them. If a newspaper reader wants only a summary of the latest tax bill, he can read the headline and the first paragraph of an article, and if he wants more, he can keep reading. In a sense, then, everyone reads a different newspaper, for no two readers will read (or ignore) the same items.

But all television viewers see the same broadcast. They have no choices. A report is either in the broadcast or out, which means that anything which is of narrow interest is unlikely to be included. As NBC News executive Reuven Frank once explained:

> A newspaper, for example, can easily afford to print an item of conceivable interest to only a fraction of its readers. A television news program must be put together with the assumption that each item will be of some interest to everyone that watches. Every time a newspaper includes a feature, which will attract a specialized group, it can assume it is adding at least a little bit to its circulation. To the degree a

television news program includes an item of this sort...it must assume that its audience will diminish.

The need to "include everyone," an identifying feature of commercial television in all its forms, prevents journalists from offering lengthy or complex explanations, or from tracing the sequence of events leading up to today's headlines. One of the ironies of political life in modern democracies is that many problems which concern the "general welfare" are of interest only to specialized groups. Arms control, for example, is an issue that literally concerns everyone in the world, and yet the language of arms control and the complexity of the subject are so daunting that only a minority of people can actually follow the issue from week to week and month to month. If it wants to act responsibly, a newspaper can at least make available more information about arms control than most people want. But commercial television cannot afford to do so.

This illustrates an important point in the psychology of television's appeal. Many of the items in newspapers and magazines are not, in a strict sense, demanded by a majority of readers. They are there because some readers *might* be interested or because the editors think their readers *should* be interested. On commercial television, "might" and "should" are not the relevant words. The producers attempt to make sure that "each item will be of some interest to everyone that watches," as Reuven Frank put it. What this means is that a newspaper or magazine can challenge its audience in a way that television cannot. Print media have the luxury of suggesting or inviting interest, whereas television must always concern itself with conforming to existing interests. In a way, television is more strictly responsive to the demands of its huge audience. But there is one demand it cannot meet: the desire to be challenged, to be told "this is worth attending to," to be surprised by what one thought would not be of interest.

Another severe limitation on television is time. There is simply not enough of it. The evening news programs at CBS, NBC, and ABC all run for thirty minutes, eight of which are taken up by commercials. No one believes that twenty-two minutes for the day's news is adequate. For years news executives at ABC, NBC, and CBS have suggested that the news be expanded to one hour. But by tradition the half-hour after the national evening news is given over to the hundreds of local affiliate stations around the country to use as they see fit. They have found it a very profitable time to broadcast game shows or half-hour situation comedies, and they are reluctant to give up the income they derive from these programs.

The evening news produced by the three networks is profitable for both the networks and the local stations. The local stations are paid a fee by the network to broadcast the network news, and they profit from this fee since the news—produced by the network—costs them nothing. It is likely that they would also make money from a one-hour newscast, but not as much, they judge, as they do from the game shows and comedies they now schedule.

The result is that the evening news must try to do what cannot reasonably be done: give a decent account of the day's events in twenty-two minutes. What the viewer gets instead is a series of impressions, many of them purely visual, most of them unconnected to each other or to any sense of a history unfolding. Taken together, they suggest a world that is fundamentally ungovernable, where events do not arise out of historical conditions but rather explode from the heavens in a series of disasters that suggest a permanent state of crisis. It is this crisis—highly visual, ahistorical, and unsolvable—which the evening news presents as theatre every evening.

The audience for this theatre is offered a contradictory pair of re-sponses. On the one hand, it is reassured by the smooth presentation of the news itself, especially the firm voice and steady gaze of the trusty anchorman. Newscasts frequently end with a "human-interest story," often with a sentimental or comic touch. Example: a little girl in Chicago writes Gorbachev a letter, and he answers her, saying that he and President Reagan are trying to work out their differences. This item reassures view-ers that all is well, leaders are in command, we can still communicate with each other, and so on. But—and now we come to the other hand—the rest of the broadcast has told a different story. It has shown the au-dience a world that is out of control and incomprehensible, full of violence, disaster, and suffering. Whatever authority the anchorman may project through his steady manner is undermined by the terror inspired by the news itself.

This is where television news is at its most radical—not in giving publicity to radical causes, but in producing the impression of an ungovernable world. And it produces this impression not because the people who work in television are leftists or anarchists. The anarchy in television news is a direct result of the commercial structure of broadcasting, which introduces into news judgments a single-mindedness more powerful than any ideology: the overwhelming need to keep people watching.

Notes

Beethoven's Fifth Symphony a triumphant instrumental piece of music written by Ludwig van Beethoven (1770–1827), often recognized for its suspenseful "da-da-da-dum" opening

teletype machines electromechanical typewriters that transmit and receive messages coded in electrical signals carried by telegraph or telephone wires. These machines have become virtually obsolete since the onset of the use of the Internet and fax machines in the 1980s.

Congress the national legislative body of the United States, composed of the Senate and the House of Representatives

Gorbachev Mikhail Gorbachev, born in 1931, was the general secretary of the USSR's Communist Party (1985–1991) and the Soviet Union's president (1989–1991).

President Reagan Ronald Reagan, born in 1911, was the fortieth president of the United States, serving two terms from 1981 to 1989.

leftists believers and supporters of the ideology of the political left, which usually advocates liberal or radical measures to effect egalitarian change

anarchists proponents of anarchy, the absence of all forms of government. More generally, anarchy refers to political disorder or the absence of a cohesive principle.

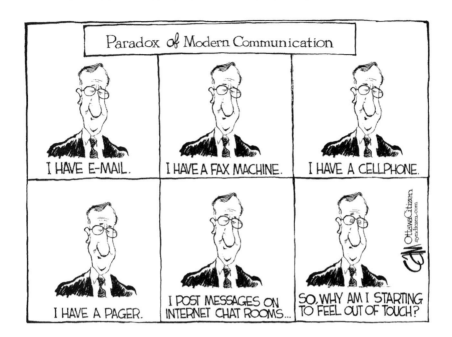

Paradox of Modern Communication

I HAVE E-MAIL.

I HAVE A FAX MACHINE.

I HAVE A CELLPHONE.

I HAVE A PAGER.

I POST MESSAGES ON INTERNET CHAT ROOMS...

SO, WHY AM I STARTING TO FEEL OUT OF TOUCH?

Learning Without Lectures

Ann Rees

Ann Rees was born in Cardiff, Wales, in 1952. She immigrated to Canada with her family at the age of five, moving to Cold Lake, Alberta. She has lived in many communities in Saskatchewan, Alberta, and British Columbia. For over two decades, Rees has been an investigative journalist in Vancouver with the *Province* newspaper, where she focuses on special projects and longer, in-depth investigations. Rees has said that, in terms of the journalist's "W5H" (Who, What, When, Where, Why, and How), her work is most focused on the "why" part. This article appeared in the *Province* on June 6, 2001. How does Rees' use of language reflect the timeliness of newpapers? How does the information she provides suit the needs of the target audience?

Tammy Mooney is on the cutting edge of education in B.C.'s first high-tech university.

The 33-year-old enrolled in the first class at the two-year-old Technical University of B.C. in Surrey.

"It is a risk and a challenge, but I have no regrets whatsoever," said Mooney, who is working toward a bachelor of science degree in management and technology.

What makes Tech B.C. so different is that there are no traditional lectures.

Students are required to read the lecture material on-line.

"We don't listen to our professor talk," said Mooney, who is also student council president.

In many ways the courses are similar to a traditional correspondence course, but with a significant difference.

Students have regular tutorials with their professors and fellow students in which they discuss what they have read and "fill in the gaps" in their understanding of the material.

"It requires a lot of self-discipline and time-management," said Mooney, who already holds an e-commerce certificate.

But the computer labs, which the professors attend, are "very interactive and we ask a lot of questions." Students also have access to professors during office hours and by e-mail and phone.

Chat rooms are also a popular venue for students working on the many teamwork assignments.

Mooney would like professors to participate in some of the chat rooms so that instruction can be more immediately interactive.

"There is always a lag time with e-mail," she said.

Math is the only course students believe would benefit from traditional live or videotaped instruction, rather than being taught through on-line instruction.

"We found, as students, that anything that is mathematics-based, you need to watch your professor as they are going through the examples in math," said Mooney. "Streaming video would work fine."

Tech B.C.'s enrolment is scheduled to double this fall from 200 to 400 students, who will be housed in temporary quarters at Surrey Place Mall.

By the time a permanent facility is completed in 2003, enrolment will be 1,600, according to Jane Fee, associate vice-president of Tech B.C.

She believes the entirely on-line—as opposed to lecture-based—approach to teaching is a first in North America.

Which is why Tech B.C. refers to its students as learners.

"Basically, the old notion of a teacher is someone who imparts education and a student as someone who receives it," Fee explained. "A learner is someone who is more actively involved in the process."

The on-line program frees professors from lecture time to allow more time with the learners.

"Most of the time, when the students are in a situation where they are with a faculty member, it is relatively small groups compared [with] what you would find elsewhere," said Fee.

The labs tend to comprise groups of four to 12 students.

Tech B.C. will introduce third-year courses this fall and a fourth year next fall.

At the end of four years, students will graduate with a bachelor of science in information technology, management and technology or interactive arts.

The university will offer a master's and Ph.D. this fall.

The university is well equipped with up-to-date computer equipment, but since students do much of their work at home, they also require up-to-date home computers, said Mooney.

King Zog's Birthday

Bob Elliott and Ray Goulding

Bob Elliott and Ray Goulding teamed up in 1946 at the radio station WHDH in Boston, Massachusetts, where Elliott had a morning show and Goulding read the news. From their radio program, *Matinee with Bob and Ray*, they turned to writing television scripts and screenplays and created a Broadway show, *The Two and Only*. In the late 1970s, their radio program was revived on National Public Radio. As humourists, they are best known for their memorable characters. What makes a protest rally memorable or newsworthy? What are some examples of recent protests that you have seen on television newscasts? What were the issues and how did the demonstrators show their opinions?

BOB: It's been said that some news might never occur if there were no microphones or television cameras to cover it; that events are often staged by pressure groups just to get some free air time. Editors can't know in advance whether a story is going to be real news—or just a media event. That was our problem when we handed out this assignment to reporter Artie Schermerhorn…

SCHERMERHORN: Here outside Oakdale Park we're awaiting the big protest rally that Albanian monarchists have scheduled for King Zog's birthday. This gentleman is one of the demonstrators…

DEMONSTRATOR: I don't think I should say anything before the others get here. Could you come back later?

SCHERMERHORN: No, I'm sorry. Your people were supposed to be staging a huge demonstration here an hour ago.

DEMONSTRATOR: Well, the others are coming over from Jersey in Bruno's Datsun. And you know us Albanians. We're always late.

SCHERMERHORN: Well, at least, tell us the purpose of this big protest you plan to stage—once the others get here.

DEMONSTRATOR: We're all of Albanian descent. And every year, we get together on King Zog's birthday and reminisce about the good old times.

SCHERMERHORN: And then you stage a demonstration in favour of restoring the monarchy. Is that it?

DEMONSTRATOR: No. Then we usually play pinochle. But this year we decided to try for some TV coverage. Only the guy in your newsroom said he wouldn't send a film crew out just to show us playing pinochle.

SCHERMERHORN: You really don't need to go into…

DEMONSTRATOR: He said it would only be visual if we got the whole mob together with picket signs. Then maybe the police would come and we'd have a pitched battle and…

SCHERMERHORN: Did our editor know that your whole membership could get into one car when he suggested that?

DEMONSTRATOR: I don't believe any specific numbers were mentioned—no.

SCHERMERHORN: I see. Well, now that you've gotten us down here, would you please pick up your sign and walk around with it?

DEMONSTRATOR: I'd feel kind of foolish doing it alone. Couldn't we wait till we're on the air?

SCHERMERHORN: We're on the air, fellah.

DEMONSTRATOR: Oh, gosh. This is a real shame. Without the other guys here it may look like our group doesn't have much popular support.

SCHERMERHORN: I imagine it may look that way!

DEMONSTRATOR: Could you position your cameraman farther over, so I'll seem like a bigger crowd? You know, like the others are all standing behind me?

SCHERMERHORN: Look, Buster—I had a choice of two assignments today. And the one I turned down was a big ecology rally.

DEMONSTRATOR: Well, I wouldn't worry. Those people demonstrate at least once a week.

SCHERMERHORN: But today they were having Robert Redford. He was scheduled to do a sit-in next to a barrel of toxic chemical waste.

DEMONSTRATOR: I'm afraid you're a little naive. I hear they always promise Robert Redford—but he usually doesn't even know about it.

SCHERMERHORN: Well, his name still draws a crowd. But I passed it up for you.

DEMONSTRATOR: And you won't be sorry. After all, there's nothing visual about a sit-in. For TV, you want people moving around. *(He picks up sign and starts walking in a small circle)* Up the monarchy! Albania for Albanians! Long live the monarchy!

SCHERMERHORN: And there you have it—the action at this moment from the potentially explosive rally at Oakdale Park. Now this is Artie Schermerhorn sending it back to our studio.

Notes

King Zog Ahmed Bey Zogu (1895–1961), a politician who was Albania's premier (1922–1924), its president (1925–1928), and king (1928–1939). When Italy invaded Albania in 1939, Zog went into exile and later abdicated the throne (1946).

Jersey a nickname for New Jersey, a state in the United States on the Hudson River where it feeds into the Atlantic Ocean; its northern part is across the river from Manhattan and the Bronx in New York City

pinochle a card game played by two to four persons using a special deck of forty-eight cards

Robert Redford an American movie actor and director, born in 1937, whose watershed role was in *Butch Cassidy and the Sundance Kid* (1969). He starred in films such as *All the President's Men* (1976) and *Out of Africa* (1986).

almost visible

Kenneth J. Harvey

Kenneth J. Harvey was born in St. John's, Newfoundland, in 1962, and has lived in that province for much of his life. He writes poetry, fiction, and essays and has published thirteen books. Harvey was nominated for the Commonwealth Writers Prize and the Chapters/Books in Canada First Novel Award. His opinion pieces have appeared in newspapers across Canada. He is the founder of the ReLit Awards, which honours books produced by independent literary publishers in Canada. Harvey has been writer-in-residence at the University of New Brunswick and at Memorial University in Newfoundland. He has said, "I wrote 'almost visible' many years ago. In fact, I couldn't have been much older than a grade twelve student at the time." What is your relationship to television? What role does television play in your life?

almost visible

he was almost
visible
thin
pale
fading
in and out
of conversation
speech;
an irregular
flickering
(a loose connection)
his eyes
folding
half-shut
moving
like the current
of a timeless
tv
a ghost
of neon
blinking
in and out
of dreams
holding himself
between words
and then slipping
fading
almost visible

Media on Media: Activities

1. When Marshall McLuhan first spoke of a single *global village*—in which time and space disappear and everyone, regardless of physical location, is connected simultaneously through electronic media—the Internet was used only by the military and academics and the Web did not even exist. Make a multimedia presentation in which you explore how the Web fulfills McLuhan's vision of a global village.

2. Locate a videotape of a television news program from ten or more years ago. Carefully watch it, as well as a current television news program. Write a commentary for a radio broadcast in which you compare the two news samples, offering reasons for the ways in which TV news has either changed or stayed the same. Make sure that you have a clearly stated thesis and that you use a comparative report structure to pique the interest of your listeners.

3. Imagine that you have just voted in your first federal or provincial election. In the weeks preceding the election, you researched the candidates, parties, and issues, but you find that the media does not answer all your questions and, at times, provides biased coverage. Set yourself the task of helping thirteen- to sixteen-year-olds read and view the news critically, identify bias, and recognize the differences between explicit and implicit messages. In a group, plan, script, and tape a video to achieve this goal. Keep an ongoing diary of choices you make during the production process to help you assess your overall effectiveness.

4. In a group, research and evaluate possibilities for post-secondary education provided by technology, such as Internet distance-learning or instructional videos. Analyze the various options for technological learning you discover by defining each option and considering its applications and implications. Be sure to evaluate these options in light of your experiences at school and your goals for the future. As a group, present your findings in one of two ways: as an oral or multimedia presentation with a well-developed thesis; or as a dramatic or comic presentation based on a prepared script.

Arguments and persuasion are all around us. We find them in television commercials, billboards, radio spots, Internet screens, company logos, and letters to the editor. They exist in places as diverse as television commentaries, resumés, telemarketing calls, designer labels, flyers, annual reports, political speeches, and T-shirts. When we use the word *argument*, we often mean a quarrel or dispute. The term *persuasion* may bring to mind an infomercial's attempt to manipulate us into buying something we don't need. In fact, the ability to develop and sustain thoughtful arguments—and to use those arguments to persuade people to take action—is essential not only to our academic career, but to our working and personal lives as well.

Let's say that a classmate has an opinion about something and wants to formulate an argument. She creates her argument by proving her point of view through the *choice* and *arrangement* of ideas, evidence, and language. The main purpose of her argument is not necessarily to change others' opinions, but to lay out a detailed position. Once she has determined her thesis, she supports it by presenting numerous credible facts, anecdotes, and up-to-date statistics to convince her audience of the validity of her thesis. To help strengthen her argument, she can use an organizing principle such as classification, comparison and contrast, or cause and effect. She also needs to be able to anticipate and refute potential counter-arguments. She must avoid potential bias and ensure that her argument is not distorted by any personal prejudices she may hold on the topic. As she thinks through her argument, she may find that discussing it and writing about it will help her to make her argument more precise.

Persuasion takes argumentation one step further. It uses an argument as the basis for urging people to alter their thinking or behaviour. Generally, persuasion reflects an emotional commitment on the part of the writer, artist, or speaker and appeals to the audience's human needs, emotions, and values.

This In-Depth introduces you to what Aristotle had to say about the techniques of persuasion. You will also read a newspaper editorial that examines the issue of privacy of information. Three opinion pieces are offered exploring one issue: the sale of a natural resource. And you'll read a poem that presents an argument about poetry. As you read through this section, remember that the ability to reflect deeply on an issue and to successfully articulate thoughts in oral or written forms is an invaluable skill. (For related selections, turn to the argumentative and persuasive essays section on pages 283–322 of this anthology.)

Effective Persuasion

from Rhetoric

Aristotle

Translated by W. Rhys Roberts

Renowned philosopher and scholar Aristotle was born in Stagirus, Greece, in 384 BCE. In 367 BCE, he went to Athens to study at Plato's academy. There, he served as the tutor of Alexander the Great and founded the famed Lyceum school. Aristotle's teachings cover a vast array of subjects, including logic, ethics, biology, physics, psychology, astronomy, rhetoric, poetry, and politics. As a philosopher, scholar, and scientist, Aristotle has had an extensive and profound influence on many fields of study. The following excerpts are from *Rhetoric*, his study of the art and technique of eloquence. In this text, he argues for the middle ground between two conflicting contemporary positions, one supporting the importance of content, the other the importance of style. Aristotle believed in the importance of both. How are these two elements different from each other? In what ways are both elements important?

...we must be able to employ persuasion, just as strict reasoning can be employed, on opposite sides of a question, not in order that we may in practice employ it in both ways (for we must not make people believe what is wrong), but in order that we may see clearly what the facts are, and that, if another man argues unfairly, we on our part may be able to confute him. —*from Book 1, Part 1*

A statement is persuasive and credible either because it is directly self-evident or because it appears to be proved from other statements that are so. In either case it is persuasive because there is somebody whom it persuades. —*from Book 1, Part 2*

Of the modes of persuasion furnished by the spoken word there are three kinds. The first kind depends on the personal character of the speaker; the second on putting the audience into a certain frame of mind; the third on the proof, or apparent proof, provided by the words of the speech itself. Persuasion is achieved by the speaker's personal character when the speech is so spoken as to make us think him credible. We believe good men more fully and more readily than others: this is true generally whatever the question is, and absolutely true where exact certainty is impossible and opinions are divided. This kind of persuasion, like the others, should be achieved by what the speaker says, not by what people think of this character before he begins to speak. It is not true, as some writers assume in their treatises on rhetoric, that the personal goodness revealed by the speaker contributes nothing to his power of persuasion; on the contrary, his character may almost be called the most effective means of persuasion he possesses. Secondly, persuasion may come through the hearers, when the speech stirs their emotions. Our judgments when we are pleased and friendly are not the same as when we are pained and hostile. It is toward producing these effects, as we maintain, that present-day writers on rhetoric direct the whole of their efforts…. Thirdly, persuasion is effected through the speech itself when we have proved a truth or an apparent truth by means of the persuasive arguments suitable to the case in question.

There are, then, these three means of effecting persuasion. The man who is to be in command of them must, it is clear, be able (1) to reason logically, (2) to understand human character and goodness in their various forms, and (3) to understand the emotions—that is, to name them and describe them, to know their causes and the way in which they are excited…. —*from Book 1, Part 2*

Notes

rhetoric the study of the art of effective speaking and writing; in this case, also the title of Aristotle's study of the effective use of oral and written language. In contemporary culture, the term *rhetoric* has developed a negative connotation through the implication that rhetoric is the artificial, even misleading, use of language.

Giant Database Is Ripe for Abuse

Edmonton Journal

This editorial appeared in the *Edmonton Journal* on May 18, 2000. It was written in response to the release of an annual report by Bruce Phillips, the federal privacy commissioner at the time. In his report, Phillips warns about the potential abuse of a huge database, called the Longitudinal Labour Force File, which was continuously compiled and maintained by Human Resources Development Canada (HRDC), a department of the federal government. The writer of the editorial echoes Phillips' concern and argues in favour of immediate action to ensure the privacy of Canadian citizens. Subsequent to Phillips' report, the database was dismantled by Jane Stewart, federal minister responsible for the HRDC. Are you worried about the potential abuse of the accumulation of personal information in computer databases and, if so, why? Who might be especially concerned about this practice and who might promote it?

Just because you're paranoid doesn't mean the government hasn't compiled a detailed dossier of personal information about you in its computers.

In fact, Human Resources Development Canada has dossiers on almost 34 million Canadians all in one single, huge database—quite a feat considering there are only 30 million people in this country. But because HRDC never purges the database, it has accumulated files on the dead as well as the living.

In his latest report to government, federal privacy commissioner Bruce Phillips not only points out the surprising existence of this database—despite assurances from previous privacy commissioners that no such single information bank existed—but he also highlights the deep concerns it raises for the privacy of Canadians.

The HRDC database contains information gleaned from a wide range of other federal departments—information from tax returns, which are supposed to be used only by Canada Customs and Revenue, details of social and income security programs from Health and Welfare Canada, information on unemployment insurance and employment programs from Employment and Immigration, to name just a few. And HRDC, in its continuing quest to compile still more information, is considering expanding the database to include further details about student loans, pensions, and old age security.

The information is used primarily for research and program analysis, a benign enough purpose. It may be turned over to provincial governments or to private sector firms or universities under research contracts to government.

Such a huge stockpile of personal information has clear benefits for bureaucrats and researchers, who undoubtedly have no malevolent intent. Nonetheless, the potential for breach of privacy, whether through unintentional error or outside infiltration, is disturbing.

As Phillips points out, the sheer volume of information alone—up to 2,000 elements on a single individual—is cause for concern, particularly when the vast majority of Canadians don't know this information is being collected about them, or cross-referenced with other personal details. There are few legal restrictions on how the information is used, unlike at Statistics Canada, for example, which operates under strict legislation. And the files are never purged. "Without an end, the temptation is to subject everyone to unrelenting information surveillance," Phillips says.

The simple existence of a single, huge database leaves it ripe for abuse. Who knows what some future government or individual might deem beneficial to extract from this mountain of information? Phillips raises the spectre of information being used to make decisions or predictions about individuals, or being retrieved in an unforeseen way, such as by ethnic origin or disability.

Perhaps most disturbing, though, is the department's apparent lack of interest in addressing these privacy issues. Phillips' office first raised the concerns almost two years ago, but HRDC officials have been slow to respond. While they have addressed some of the security issues, they have been less willing to tackle the privacy concerns.

Certainly there are benefits to having an extensive research database to mine, but they do not outweigh the potential risks to individual privacy.

While we cannot turn back the technological clock to a pre-computer, pre-Internet age when access to such information would have been far more limited, we can put safeguards in place to protect its privacy.

These could include separating the information into a number of different databases, as Phillips recommends, and establishing strict rules on the kind of information collected and the way in which it is used.

Let's Stop Being Hysterical, Shall We, and Start Selling Water to Those Who Need It

Lee Morrison

Lee Morrison was born in Vidora, Saskatchewan, in 1932. A former member of parliament, he is a geological engineer who has worked in the mining industry for a variety of companies. Since retiring from politics, he has written for a range of publications, including the *Calgary Sun, Regina Leader Post, Ottawa Citizen, Calgary Herald,* and *Toronto Star.* He currently resides in Eastend, Saskatchewan. This opinion piece was originally published in *Report,* a news magazine. As the title suggests, Morrison takes a controversial position on the issue of selling our water. Before reading the selection, what suppositions can you make about its content and tone from its title? Do you think this title is effective for an opinion piece? Why or why not?

There are encouraging signs that the dog-in-the-manger nationalism barring Canadian bulk water exports may slowly be giving way to common sense. The Liberal government of Newfoundland is poised to permit sales from Gisborne Lake on the island's south shore, and Jean Chrétien is sending mixed but somewhat favourable signals about the federal position.

In spite of furious howling by the xenophobic Council of Canadians and its NDP political arm, and tut-tutting by the increasingly politically correct Canadian Alliance, there is a reasonable chance that this previously unmentionable subject will soon receive serious consideration.

With 0.5% of the world's population, Canada is blessed with 20% of the earth's fresh water, including 9% of the renewable supply. We mismanage it, pollute it, and waste it, but won't even consider exporting it to eager buyers in the U.S., Asia, and the Middle East. A lot of nonsense has been written about water being too precious to sell—the very blood in the veins of Mother Earth, etc. Certainly, it is one of life's necessities, but so is the food that we buy and sell every day. Food, lumber, and bulk water are all renewable resources, but we export only the first two, because water is somehow "sacred." Meanwhile, we merrily dispose of precious, non-renewable natural gas. When it's gone, our lives will be much less comfortable, but we'll still have 20 times the water we need. Oh joy!

There are three possible ways to export water: on a small scale, in bottles, which we do now; by sea, in supertankers, which has quite recently become economically feasible; and by massive inter-basin transfers via systems of canals and pipelines that are technically possible, but too astronomically costly and environmentally questionable to merit serious consideration.

There is a myth that Canada would be "obliged" under the North American Free Trade Agreement (NAFTA) to permit inter-basin transfers if any bulk water exports were allowed, but nothing in the agreement inhibits the rights of provinces to manage their resources. NAFTA requires only that domestic and foreign entrepreneurs be treated equally and that contracts be honoured. Provinces would continue to decide what water could be tapped, at what rate, under what conditions, and for what price—just as they do now with oil.

Proponents of a total export ban tend to damage their credibility by resorting to exaggerated propaganda and misrepresentation. In 1998, Ontario issued a permit to a private company to ship water from Lake Superior to Asia. After a protest orchestrated by the Council of Canadians, the permit was cancelled. The council, in a fundraising letter headed "They're coming to take our water," proclaimed, "This country came within a whisker of selling as much as 600 million litres of our precious water each year." Oh my. It left unexplained that this is less than one-eighth of 1% of the amount that Lake Superior loses to evaporation on one hot summer's day, or about one-fifth of what the greater

Chicago area daily draws from Lake Michigan. Nonetheless, the letter probably raised a wad of money from the gullible.

Much has been made of the fact that only 1% of Great Lakes water is renewed annually. That equates to 121 cubic kilometres of new water in Lake Superior alone; enough to fill about 600,000 very large tankers which, tied bow to stern, would encircle the earth five times. In a recent press release, Alliance deputy House Leader Cheryl Gallant raised alarm about the Great Lakes question. Like most MPs, her grasp of mathematics is apparently limited to counting the votes that may be gained by appealing to public prejudice and misinformation.

In any event, shipping Great Lakes water, in even modest quantities, isn't an attractive proposition. Ontarians drink the stuff, but its quality isn't great, so why ship it halfway around the world? Besides, the very large tankers needed to make shipment economically attractive can't pass through the canal system from the sea. Finally, it is boundary water, which raises legal questions.

The provinces with the brightest prospects for selling water are Newfoundland and British Columbia. Both have easily accessible unpolluted sources, with no jurisdictional problems.

In British Columbia, 1.3 billion cubic metres of fresh water (enough to fill seven thousand 200,000 ton tankers) reaches the sea every day. There are dozens of streams from which water of exceptionally high quality could be loaded into tankers for shipment anywhere in the world, especially to southern California.

How much could fresh, clean, easily accessible water be worth? I pay almost 1/5 of a cent per litre for the foul-tasting discharge from my household taps. Sparkling mountain water should be worth substantially more, but instead of encouraging market development, British Columbia has banned large-scale exports. Meanwhile, neighbouring Alaska has granted a long-term export licence to a Canadian company negotiating possible sales to far-away Singapore.

Ultimately, the price of bulk water will be determined, as it should be, by competition among suppliers and by the benchmark price of desalinated water, which is currently about 1/4 to 1/3 cent per litre. Desalination, however, has its shortcomings. The product is generally inferior to fresh water, and a desalination plant, unlike a supertanker, can't be economically used only during a drought and sent elsewhere when water is plentiful. The town of Santa Barbara, California, learned that economic lesson the hard way in the 1990s.

With aggressive private sector marketing, British Columbia and Newfoundland could ultimately earn billions of dollars in royalties by exporting tiny fractions of their liquid wealth. The petty obstructiveness of those who would rather see it all spill into the sea than sell a little to those who need it is not only mean-spirited, it is masochistic. By spitefully refusing to market an abundant renewable resource, they deprive Canadians of economic benefits far into the future. It's time to grow up.

Notes

dog-in-the-manger a person who selfishly withholds from others something useless to himself; from "The Fable of the Dog" (one of *Aesop's Fables*) in which the dog prevents an ox from eating hay which he himself does not want

Council of Canadians a public interest group founded in 1985, dedicated to the development of policies that encourage Canadian economic, political, social, and cultural sovereignty

North American Free Trade Agreement (NAFTA) a trade and investment liberalization arrangement signed by Canada, the United States, and Mexico; it came into effect on January 1, 1994, and extended and superseded the Canada–United States Free Trade Agreement of 1989

desalination the process of removing salt from sea water

Our Water Sovereignty Is at Risk

Eric Reguly

Eric Reguly was born in Vancouver, British Columbia, in 1957. He earned a B.A. in English and French literature and a master's degree in journalism from the University of Western Ontario. Reguly's many articles have been published in a range of publications, including the London *Times*, the *Financial Post* in New York and London, the *Financial Times* of Canada, *Alberta Report* magazine, and the *London (Ontario) Free Press*. He has also served as host for "ROB-TV" (Report on Business Television). The following opinion piece was originally published in the *Globe and Mail* where he regularly comments on a variety of issues in his column "To the Point." This piece presents a point of view opposite to the one written by Lee Morrison, which precedes it. When examining two sides of an issue in two separate texts, what similarities might you expect? What kinds of differences in the two texts might you encounter?

A CBC documentary called *Captured Rain*, broadcast in December 2000, examined the emotionally charged issue of bulk water exports and left little doubt that the United States eventually will get as much Canadian water as it wants. The documentary didn't elicit an iota of interest among the ruling Liberals and was barely mentioned in the press.

A week later, the U.S. Interior Department published the results of an extensive, two-year study on the effects of global warming on water. Among other things, it warned of vanishing mountain snowpacks and a hotter and drier South. It too was widely ignored, even though the Interior Department is hardly a partisan observer of climate change.

Add the conclusions of the CBC documentary to the conclusions of the U.S. government report and you've got a scenario that, you would think, would nudge Canadian bulk water exports back on to the political agenda. But no. Water exports were a hot topic last year, when a U.S. company sued the federal government for water it agreed to buy but never got. This year, water, except for the Walkerton tragedy, received about as much publicity as Canadian mutton exports to Kazakhstan. There is no federal-provincial water accord. Bill C-15, the legislation that would have amended the International Boundary Waters Treaty Act to prohibit the bulk removal of boundary waters (notably the Great Lakes) is dead. There is no national ban on bulk water exports. Canada's environment minister, David Anderson, showed early promise but has been a dud on water, the one resource that most Canadians seem willing to protect.

Water could go the way of so many of Canada's resources and industries. Not so many years ago, light manufacturing, such as appliance making, was a big Canadian industry. It has all but disappeared. In the 1980s, Canada gave up any notion of energy sovereignty when it signed the free-trade agreement with the United States. Canadian water sovereignty may be next, if it hasn't gone already.

The American case for importing water grows by the day. In the U.S. Southwest, especially California, lack of water is cited as the biggest impediment to the state's economic growth. The current power crisis in California and the Northwest is partly a result of the shortage of water needed to power hydroelectric generators. Groundwater supplies in the Midwest, where much of the world's grain is produced, are at critically short levels. Population growth in the Sun Belt states is putting enormous pressure on existing supplies. There are millions of pools to fill, lawns to water, and cars to wash. The demand for water from thirsty states and countries is so great that the governors of the eight Great Lakes states this month called for a binding agreement with Canada by 2004 to protect the lakes from excessive withdrawals.

The water issue came to the forefront last year when two export schemes came to national attention. The first came from California's Sun Belt Water, which wanted to import water by tanker from British

Columbia to moisten the southern California landscape. The plan failed when the B.C. government slapped a moratorium on bulk water exports. Sun Belt retaliated by suing Ottawa for $10.5-billion under NAFTA's investment provisions, on the grounds that provinces are not allowed to halt the free trade of goods. The second came from Nova Group, which somehow secured an Ontario licence to siphon water from Lake Superior and export it by tanker to Asia. When the news broke, everyone from Canadian nationalists to governors of the Great Lakes states went berserk and the licence was revoked.

Threats to Canadian water would not exist if Canadian politicians specifically excluded water from NAFTA's trade list. It wasn't, which means there is little doubt that bulk water exports, once they start, will become a commercial good whose international sale comes under NAFTA protection. One possible way around this is to use environmental law to make water invulnerable to trade challenges. This too hasn't happened.

In the end, of course, it's all about business. As long as the United States is willing to pay for Canadian water, ways probably will be found to provide it. But until an environmentally sound export structure is found, why open the floodgates and take the risk that they can't be closed? Better yet, why not impose a national bulk water export ban and force industry to come to water instead of the other way around? Think of the jobs it would create as water becomes scarcer and scarcer in the United States and factories move north.

Notes

U.S. Interior Department refers to the U.S. Department of the Interior, which is the United States federal government's principal conservation agency. Its mandate is to serve as a steward for the approximately 437 million acres of public lands in the United States and for the natural and cultural resources connected with these lands.

Walkerton tragedy In May 2000, in the town of Walkerton, Ontario, a number of residents became ill and some died, as a result of deadly E. coli bacteria that contaminated the town's water supply.

Kazakhstan a country in central Asia

free-trade agreement a bilateral free-trade deal between Canada and the United States, enacted on January 1989 after almost three years of negotiations

Great Lake states refers to the eight states in the United States which touch on the Great Lakes: Illinois, Indiana, Michigan, Minnesota, New York, Ohio, Pennsylvania, and Wisconsin

NAFTA acronym for the North American Free Trade Agreement, a trade and investment liberalization arrangement signed by Canada, the United States, and Mexico; it came into effect on January 1, 1994, and extended and superseded the Canada–United States Free Trade Agreement of 1989

From Water

Marq de Villiers

Marq de Villiers was born in Bloemfontein, South Africa, in 1940. He currently resides in Lunenberg, Nova Scotia. A former editor and publisher of *Toronto Life*, he is currently the editorial director for *Where Magazine International*. *Water*, from which the following updated afterword was taken, was first published in Canada and won the 1998 Governor General's Literary Award for Nonfiction. It has since been published widely in other countries and translated into nine languages. He has published several other books on exploration, history, politics, and travel. His latest book, *Sahara* (to be published in 2002), is about the natural history of the Sahara region. In this selection, de Villiers considers both sides of the argument on the issue of the sale of water. What tone appeals to you when you are reading or listening to an argumentative essay? Do you believe certain tones are more effective in an argument than others, or does it depend on the subject matter and purpose of the piece? Why?

I'd always considered the export debate to be ludicrous, and in the last year or so most of the applications for corporate export licences have quietly faded from view. This is partly because of the politics, of course. Brian Tobin in Newfoundland robustly declared himself categorically against any water exports; Ottawa followed suit with a more equivocal ban. But politics wasn't the real reason. The exporting of water, in reality, simply made no business sense. The only real customers for Canadian water are the southern Californians and the arid states of the Colorado basin down to High Plains, Texas; the most optimistic business projections for delivering water to customers came in at about $2 a ton, and that figure depended on a number of more or less implausible assumptions. Set that against the fact that in August 1999 Tampa Bay Water in Florida announced it had hired a consortium to build a new reverse-osmosis desal plant that would produce 25 million gallons of fresh water a day, at a declared cost of 45 cents a ton. At second glance, the economics didn't seem quite as rosy—over the life of the plant, the water would cost better than $2 a ton, but this is still better than most other sources. The economics were possible because Tampa Bay is less naturally saline than the Gulf of Mexico and because the plant would be built next door to a major power plant that would supply it with cheap electricity. Nevertheless, the price was such that it attracted a delegation from Singapore, which was planning a 36-million-gallons-a-day plant—at an average cost of nearly $8 a ton. It simply reinforced what I had been telling interviewers for the better part of a year: if I had any money to invest (a vain hope), I'd sink it into desal research and not into the illusory business of exporting water.

As for privatization…the anti-corporatist lobby groups were vociferous in their opposition to turning any water delivery or purification systems over to private enterprise: bafflingly, their main argument seemed to be that since water was part of the global commons it should therefore not "belong" to anyone, which rather missed the point that it was the delivery of the commodity, not the commodity itself, that was at issue. The other argument revolved around pricing, and there were dozens of stories circulating that private water companies had boosted prices beyond the reach of the poor and had even cut off some of the truly indigent altogether. Most of these stories proved, on examination, to be false. In this all-or-nothing debate, the notion that public authorities could suitably regulate private companies seems hardly to have emerged. It's true there were problems, but the real argument, in most of the world without adequate water, was not whether the rich would benefit from private water supplies but whether there would be any water deliveries at all: strapped Third World governments were in no position to repair their crumbling infrastructure or to extend it to the relentlessly expanding slums in the new megacities. I have made the point, in the past, that even studies by NGOs suspicious of private enterprise had found baseless the notion that ending water subsidies would boost prices beyond the reach of the poor. And then a World Water Forum in The Hague early in 2000 declared forthrightly, and correctly, that without privatization, water matters would get steadily worse. It was, the meeting said, privatization or nothing, and the ideological debate was therefore, at this stage, pointless.

Some people have told me that they found an incongruity between my gloomy recounting of the world's water woes, and my "relatively" optimistic final chapter. Yet I continue to believe that, serious as the world's water problems are, they are not without solution. There is enough water for everyone; we just need the political will and therefore the money to do what we already know needs to be done. For example, in Boston, among other places, proper pricing has forced through conservationist measures with relatively little pain; proper use of market forces and a true cost-accounting of polluters (so that they can therefore pay their real share of the necessary cleanup) are not pie-in-the-sky economics but sensible business practice.

My environmentalist friends also distrust my reliance on technology; among many of them there is an almost Luddite suspicion of technological solutions. I, on the other hand, think sophisticated engineering can be usefully combined with a conservationist ethic to provide solutions that can be arrived at in no other way. It's true, as some have pointed out, that were we to provide cheap and energy-efficient desalination of seawater, one of the net results would be to encourage even more growth in places where, ecologically speaking, it shouldn't happen, such as in the deserts of the southwestern United States. This is the same argument that has brought home to traffic engineers that adding a lane to a freeway never alleviated traffic congestion, but only encourages more cars onto the roads. So in a way, I agree. But I never said that water woes can be solved in isolation from other human-caused problems.

It all, in the end, comes back to the engine that drives all environmental problems—the astonishing growth in human populations. Meanwhile, people are dying of contaminated water. If engineers can save them, they should be enabled to do so.

For Canada, which is so water-rich, what is the proper course? What, in this welter of conflicting assumptions and rapidly changing hydrological realities, should a Canadian water policy seek to achieve?

In my view, all water policy-making should follow three imperatives:

- Water should be priced to mandate thrifty use (that is, it should be priced for conservation).
- Water users should be obligated to maintain the water that passes through their systems in as pristine a state as possible and should be penalized for not doing so.
- Unsustainable withdrawals from water systems should be prohibited.

All three of these have practical implications for Canadian users of water and, if they are used to govern bulk sales of water to others, will allow those sales to do the minimum amount of damage—and at the same time neatly bypass NAFTA's Chapter 11, which seeks to prevent nations differentiating between domestic and foreign investors—the notion that you can't sell at one price to the locals and at another to foreigners.

Even if Canada has plenty of water, it makes no sense to waste it. There are hundreds of communities in Canada that still don't meter water usage. The town in which I now live, Lunenburg in Nova Scotia, charges a flat annual rate and allows me to use as much as I please. It is no surprise that communities where water is measured and charged for use less water than those that don't. The Americans can be worse than we can, but sometimes they're better, too.

As I've said above, the idea that this penalizes the poor and makes manufacturing more expensive is wrong. American industrial users use much less water than Chinese ones, for example, because their technology is more advanced, and so charging more for water in the end has the beneficial result of winnowing out older and less efficient factories. And as for the poor…in most countries it is the rich who benefit from the current subsidies, since they use more water and are more likely to be connected to the grid in the first place.

And there is no reason why there has to be a single-tier pricing system. For example, I would suggest a three-tier system similar to the one in the south of France. This could consist of a very low price (yes, a subsidized price) for basic human uses like sanitation and drinking. Fifty litres per person per day is usually sufficient for these purposes. After that, charge more for uses that include, say, watering the garden. And charge the earth if someone wants to fill a swimming pool. Apart from the obvious advantages such a system would have on consumption habits, there is a peripheral benefit: for Canadians, it would have a substantial inhibiting effect on foreign bulk sales.

Why? Obviously, the Americans have enough water for basic sanitation and for simple household uses; therefore, any water they import could—should—be charged at the highest rate, perfectly legitimately, under NAFTA. Call it, say, $6 a ton. At that price, only a few very desperate customers would buy, and the amount of water being shifted would be minimal. Alternatively, if the country decides it wants a small water export industry, adjust the pricing accordingly. It's important to note that this is not a tax or a subsidy or a fee but a price—this is free marketeering at work. We, the nominal "owners" of the water, would simply be charging customers what they would be willing to pay.

The second policy imperative is to insist that water users leave the water they use in as pristine a state as they found it. That is, either don't change the water, or pay for its restoration. This has several benefits. It will focus public perception on the parlous state of our waterways. It will force industry to be more technologically sophisticated—or pay the price. And it will, at last, help to regulate agricultural uses of pesticides and herbicides.

Industry, of course, will squeal. They will maintain that the added costs would be ruinous to their competitiveness. They will seek to label the charge a "tax" when it is nothing of the sort. We should pay no attention to this. The argument has the same weight as the notion a hundred years ago that forbidding the use of child labour would drive businesses into bankruptcy. Ignore it.

The third necessary component of a national water policy is a flat-out prohibition of unsustainable withdrawals from drainage basins, and of unsustainable transfers from one basin to another. Of course, definitions of what is "sustainable" will sustain the lawyers for years to come, but the policy is nevertheless right. It will effectively put an end to the grandiose notions that have so stimulated visionary engineers over the years (the notion, for example, to turn Hudson Bay into a fresh water lake and divert its rivers southwards).

Megaprojects aren't the only reason to prohibit water transfers. We also need them to prevent the small-scale draining of wetlands and "swamps" and floodplains for "development," changes that damage water tables and exaggerate natural hazards such as floods or droughts. Such a prohibition would help us remember what water is, a substance fundamental to human life and society. We all need to be reminded, from time to time, of the deeper implications of that ecologists' motto that "we're all downstream."

Notes

Brian Tobin Born in Newfoundland, Tobin became a federal member of parliament in 1980, at the age of 26. In 1996, he resigned to become the premier of Newfoundland, an office he held until 2000, when he returned to federal politics to become a cabinet minister in the Liberal party's majority government.

reverse-osmosis desal the movement of fresh water through a semi-permeable membrane when pressure is applied to a solution (such as seawater) on one side of it

indigent impoverished, destitute

Third World a term referring to developing countries; originally coined in the context of the United States as the "First World" and the Soviet Union as the "Second World"; currently considered pejorative because it implies developing countries are less important than developed countries

NGOs the abbreviation for non-governmental agencies; generally refers to an agency which provides a social service, but is neither created nor funded by a government

The Hague refers to The Hague Tribunal, an international institution, founded in the Netherlands in 1899, which judges international legal cases and proposes nominees to the International Court of Justice

Luddite originally, referred to a member of a group of workers who engaged in riots (1811–1816), destroying machinery that threatened to eliminate jobs; in contemporary usage, refers to any person who shuns technology and believes that society is better off without its reliance on technology

pristine in this instance, remaining free from dirt or bacteria; clean

NAFTA acronym for the North American Free Trade Agreement, a trade and investment liberalization arrangement signed by Canada, the United States, and Mexico; it came into effect on January 1, 1994, and extended and superseded the Canada–United States Free Trade Agreement of 1989

wetlands a lowland area, such as a marsh or swamp, that is saturated with moisture and contains a delicate ecosystem

floodplains plains bordering a river that are made up of soil deposited by flooding

Poetry

Marianne Moore

Marianne Moore was born near St. Louis, Missouri, in 1887, and educated at Bryn Mawr College in Pennsylvania. After graduation, she taught business at Carlisle Indian School, worked as a librarian in New York, and edited *The Dial*, a poetry magazine. Her early poems attracted serious attention. T.S. Eliot described her poems as "part of the body of endurable poetry written in our time." Another of her contemporaries, Randall Jarrell, described her poetry as having "the lacy mathematical extravagance of a snowflake." In 1951, her *Collected Poems* won all the top prizes for that year: the National Book Award, the Bollinger Prize, and the Pulitzer Prize. She died in 1972. The following poem begins with a rather surprising comment about poetry, but continues with some thoughtful insights into the nature of poetry. What do you think is the value of poetry? Which poems have been particularly meaningful to you?

I, too, dislike it: there are things that are important beyond all this fiddle.
  Reading it, however, with a perfect contempt for it, one discovers in
  it after all, a place for the genuine.
    Hands that can grasp, eyes
    that can dilate, hair that can rise
      if it must, these things are important not because a

high-sounding interpretation can be put upon them but because they are
  useful. When they become so derivative as to become unintelligible,
  the same thing may be said for all of us, that we
    do not admire what
    we cannot understand: the bat
      holding on upside down or in quest of something to

eat, elephants pushing, a wild horse taking a roll, a tireless wolf under
   a tree, the immovable critic twitching his skin like a horse that feels
        a flea, the base-
  ball fan, the statistician—
    nor is it valid
      to discriminate against "business documents and

schoolbooks"; all these phenomena are important. One must make a
        distinction
   however: when dragged into prominence by half poets, the result is
        not poetry,
  nor till the poets among us can be
    "literalists of
    the imagination"—above
      insolence and triviality and can present

for inspection, "imaginary gardens with real toads in them," shall we have
  it. In the meantime, if you demand on the one hand,
   the raw material of poetry in
    all its rawness and
    that which is on the other hand
      genuine, then you are interested in poetry.

Notes

"business documents and schoolbooks" Moore, herself, provided a note
for this reference in the poem. She quotes from a section from the diary
of the Russian writer Leo Tolstoy (1828–1910), in which he considers the
difference between poetry and prose: "Where the boundary between prose
and poetry lies, I shall never be able to understand. The question is raised in
manuals of style, yet the answer to it lies beyond me. Poetry is verse: prose
is not verse. Or else poetry is everything with the exception of business
documents and school books."

"literalists of the imagination" Here, Moore refers to a passage from the
book *Ideas of Good and Evil* (1903) by the English writer W.B. Yeats
(1865–1939), in which he talks about the deficiencies of the Romantic poet

William Blake (1757–1827): "The limitation of his view was from the very intensity of his vision; he was a too literal realist of imagination, as others are of nature; and because he believed that the figures seen by the mind's eye, when exalted by inspiration, were 'eternal existences,' symbols of divine essences, he hated every grace of style that obscured their lineaments."

Argument and Persuasion: Activities

1. Write an argumentative essay in which you present your position on the issue of the sale of water by Canada to other countries. Use the selections in this unit as your sources. Be sure to include a clearly stated thesis, an effective organizational structure, well-reasoned and persuasive arguments, convincing supporting information, a thoughtful conclusion, and accurate documentation.

2. On your own or with a partner, locate a sample of two or three print or Internet newsletters published by special interest groups. Analyze the various techniques used in the newsletters to make the groups' arguments and to persuade readers. In your analysis, consider features or elements such as methods of development (for example, cause and effect); use of rhetorical devices (for example, analogy); and the actual design or layout of the newsletter (for example, use of boldface and highlighted quotations). Present your analysis orally or in a written report to the class, using graphic organizers and visual aids as appropriate.

3. Choose a topic of urgent local, provincial, or national interest for a formal class debate. Working with a group, formulate a resolution for the debate, choose two teams, and appoint a moderator and two judges. Ensure that all participants are clear on their respective roles and on the criteria and procedural rules for a formal debate. At the end of the debate, the judges, in consultation with the moderator, will make an oral presentation to the class, identifying the strengths and weaknesses of each team's arguments.

4. Work with a group to prepare a documentary video on an issue related to the topic of water. As sources, use the selections provided in this unit, as well as material available in your school resource centre and through the Internet. In your production, demonstrate the ways in which video can be used to argue a position and persuade viewers of the need to take action. During the production process, keep ongoing notes on your choices to help you reflect on and increase the effectiveness of your process and final product.

3 poetry

I wrote when I was interested in something, I never did sit down to write poems at a certain time. I think that's pretty silly. You write when you have something in your mind that says "this is a poem."

— *Al Purdy*

Writing for me is a puzzle, the working out of a puzzle. I have to find the right word, the right line, the right sentence all the time.

— *Dionne Brand*

Engineers' Corner

Wendy Cope

Wendy Cope, who was born in Erith, Kent, England, in 1945, is known for her humorous poetry. "Engineers' Corner" is from her book *Making Cocoa for Kingsley Amis* (1986), in which she includes parodies of writers she admires. Cope, who studied literature at Oxford University, contends that humorous poetry can convey a serious message: "I believe that a humorous poem can also be 'serious,' deeply felt, and say something that matters." She has received numerous awards, including the American Academy of Arts and Letters Award for Light Verse in 1995. How do countries decide which of their citizens should be honoured with statues and other commemorative hallmarks, such as stamps or holidays? How important are writers and artists to their countries? What other groups might deserve special honours and why?

Engineers' Corner

Why isn't there an Engineers' Corner in Westminster Abbey? In Britain we've always made more fuss of a ballad than a blueprint.... How many schoolchildren dream of becoming great engineers?
— Advertisement placed in The Times *by the Engineering Council*

We make more fuss of ballads than of blueprints—
That's why so many poets end up rich,
While engineers scrape by in cheerless garrets.
Who needs a bridge or dam? Who needs a ditch?

Whereas the person who can write a sonnet
Has got it made. It's always been the way,
For everybody knows that we need poems
And everybody reads them every day.

Yes, life is hard if you choose engineering—
You're sure to need another job as well;   10
You'll have to plan your projects in the evenings
Instead of going out. It must be hell.

While well-heeled poets ride around in Daimlers,
You'll burn the midnight oil to earn a crust,
With no hope of a statue in the Abbey,
With no hope, even, of a modest bust.

No wonder small boys dream of writing couplets
And spurn the bike, the lorry and the train.
There's far too much encouragement for poets—
That's why this country's going down the drain.   20

Notes

Westminster Abbey a cathedral in London, England, built between 1045 and approximately 1400 CE in the English gothic style. It is where the monarchs of the United Kingdom are crowned and is the burial place of the country's leading poets, in a section called "Poets' Corner."

The Times a newspaper based in London, England

Daimler a type of luxury car

bust a sculpture of a person's head, shoulders, and chest

Activities

1. Reread the advertisement at the beginning of this poem, in which the British Engineering Council conducts a campaign to bring public attention to the contributions of engineers and to recruit young people into the profession. With a partner, consider the explicit or literal meaning of the advertisement. Next consider what implicit message it conveys. To what extent do you agree with the implicit message?

2. Do research to create a working definition of the term *verbal irony*. Then create a two-column chart. In one column, summarize the literal meaning of each stanza. In the second column, record the key idea you believe Cope intends to convey in each stanza. Create a thesis statement for an analytical essay in which you explore and evaluate Cope's use of verbal irony. In your essay, contrast the differences between the literal and the intended meaning, speculate on Cope's purpose, and evaluate how effectively Cope has achieved her purpose.

Is the Pathetic Fallacy True?

Elizabeth Brewster

Elizabeth Brewster was born in Chipman, New Brunswick, in 1922. She has lived in Ontario, Alberta, British Columbia, Saskatchewan, England, and the United States. From 1972 until her retirement in 1992, she taught in the Department of English at the University of Saskatchewan. Brewster has been the recipient of numerous prizes for her poetry and has been awarded several honorary degrees. She is the author of twenty-two books—poetry, short stories, and novels— as well as being a founding member of the literary journal *Fiddlehead* and a lifetime member of the League of Canadian Poets. Based on your own experience, how would you explain the phrase "a sense of wonder"? Why do you think this sense either increases or decreases as you grow older?

Is the Pathetic Fallacy True?

When I was a child
the stones were living.
Hot under my hand, they felt like flesh,
and sands slipped through my fingers
with a caress.

Yes, everything was alive:

the clumsy, roaring wind
stepped on the flounced pink dress
of the apple-tree,
tearing it to shreds   10

the puffed cheeks of clouds

the brook with its pebbled tongue
and the hoarse old grave old sea
its gravelly song

and earth itself
a brown warm girl
turning and tanning in the sun.

All false, all wrong,
somebody told me:
Winds are not lovers,   20
clumsy or gentle.
There's no blood
in stones,
no tears in water.

Nevertheless
sometimes lately when I touch a chair or table
I think I feel atoms stir
under my fingers

and at night in dreams I hear
the small remote voices of grains of dust   30
or the inaudible whispers of stars

as they will speak to me some time
when I lie with the living grass above me
and the wind my old lover
singing me to sleep

and to wake

Notes

pathetic fallacy the act of attributing human emotions or characteristics
to inanimate objects or to nature

Activities

1. Elizabeth Brewster begins her poem by asking a question in the title.
Paraphrase the title "Is the Pathetic Fallacy True?" restating the poet's central question in your own words. With a classmate, discuss how the poem
relates to your paraphrase of its title.

2. In a class presentation, explore the relationship in "Is the Pathetic Fallacy
True?" between Brewster's use of personification and her focus on the
topic of the pathetic fallacy.

EVENING

Mary Cassatt

About the Visual   Mary Cassatt was born in 1844, in Allegheny City, Pennsylvania, now part of Pittsburgh. She attended the Pennsylvania Academy of Fine Arts and later continued her studies in Europe. In 1874, she settled in Paris, where she came under the influence of the French painter Edgar Degas, who invited her to join the Impressionist group of artists. Cassatt adopted the Impressionist technique of applying paint rapidly from a bright palette. An exhibition of Japanese prints inspired her to begin printmaking. She also practised the art of etching. What characteristics, if any, do poetry and visual works of art have in common? How does your response to works of art compare with your response to poetry?

Activities

1. Cassatt has been praised for her ability to create "the joyous quietude, the tranquil simplicity of an interior." Discuss the impact of *Evening* in terms of this statement. Record your response to the works in your journal and then share responses in a small group.

2. Mary Cassatt's work often expresses the bond between women and their children. The models who sat for *Evening* were Cassatt's own mother and sister. By what means does Cassatt articulate the close relationship between her adult sister and her mother in this work? In your answer, consider factors such as composition and the use of lighting.

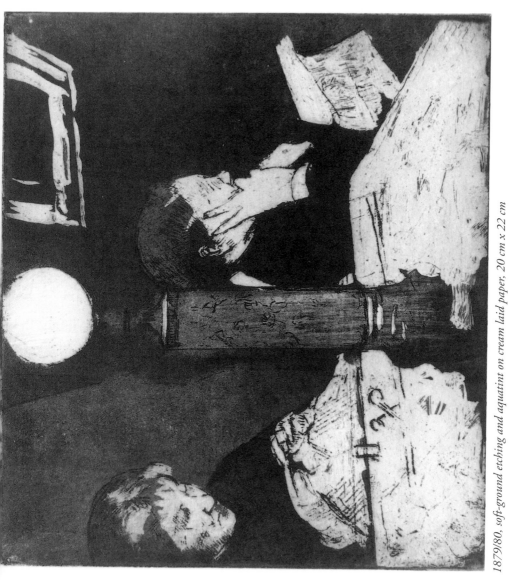

1879/80, soft-ground etching and aquatint on cream laid paper, 20 cm x 22 cm

Birch Bark

Michael Ondaatje

Canadian novelist, poet, and filmmaker Michael Ondaatje was born in Sri Lanka (then known as Ceylon) in 1943. After studying in England, Ondaatje immigrated to Canada in 1962; today he lives in Toronto. Ondaatje, who published his first book of poetry in 1967, has received two Governor General's Literary Awards for poetry. In 1992, he received the prestigious Booker Prize for his novel *The English Patient,* subsequently made into an Academy Award-winning film. Recent books include *Handwriting,* a book of poetry, and *Anil's Ghost,* a novel set in Sri Lanka that was co-winner of the Giller Prize in 2000. Ondaatje's work—which often blends fact and fiction, poetry and prose, and personal and political issues—is characterized by strong images. He has said that his writing is less influenced by books than by other art forms, such as music and painting. In what ways do other art forms influence your writings? Would art forms primarily influence your creative writing, or might they have an impact on your non-fiction writing as well?

Birch Bark

(for George Whalley)

An hour after the storm on Birch Lake
the island bristles. Rock. Leaves still falling.
At this time, in the hour after lightning
we release the canoes.
Silence of water
purer than the silence of rock.
A paddle touches itself. We move
over blind mercury, feel the muscle
within the river, the blade
weave in dark water.   10

Now each casual word is precisely chosen
passed from bow to stern, as if
leaning back to pass a canteen.
There are echoes, repercussions of water.
We are in absolute landscape,
among names that fold in onto themselves.

To circle the island means witnessing
the blue grey dust of a heron
released out of the trees.
So the dialogue slides   20
nothing more than friendship
an old song we break into
not needing all the words.

We are past naming the country.
The reflections are never there
without us, without the exhaustion
of water and trees after storm.

Notes

George Whalley a Canadian literary critic, translator, and author of books, including *Poetic Process* (1973)

Birch Lake a lake in northern Ontario, approximately 100 km north of Red Lake, partially accessible only by bush plane. The area is a ruggedly beautiful terrain of lakes and timberland.

mercury a liquid metallic chemical compound, known colloquially as quicksilver. The chemical symbol for mercury (Hg) is derived from the Greek word *hydrargyros*, meaning "water silver."

Activities

1. The author uses the five senses to communicate his experiences in this poem. Create a five-column chart, labelling each column with one of the senses. In your chart, list every word or image in the poem that falls into one of your five categories. In a small group, compare your findings. Have a class discussion by answering questions such as: Which sense did the author evoke most often in this poem? Which sensory detail do you find most effective and why? In what ways would the poem be different if it evoked only one of the senses?

2. Like many poems, the meaning of "Birch Bark" appears to exist on several levels—literal and figurative, conscious and unconscious. The different levels of meaning are partially created through Ondaatje's use of personification. In a small group, list every instance of personification that occurs in the poem. Have a group discussion on the following: To what extent does this poem explore the relationship between humans and nature? To what extent is it about the nature of friendship? With your group, use chart paper to create a graphic organizer such as a Venn diagram to document some of the poem's themes. Under each general theme that you list, provide images or phrases from the poem that contribute to that theme. Share your findings with the class.

vancouver–courtenay–calgary

George Bowering

Born in the Okanagan Valley of British Columbia in 1935, George Bowering has made the landscape and people of western Canada a major focus of his poetry and fiction. He has published dozens of books and taught at universities in Alberta, Quebec, and British Columbia. Bowering once said, "When I started writing, I wanted mainly to be a sports writer who 'committed poetry' from time to time." A major figure in contemporary Canadian literature, Bowering has won two Governor General's Awards, one in 1969 for poetry, the other in 1980 for fiction. One critic wrote that "Bowering calls on the language and cadence of common speech; a witty sense of play animates his vision in all his poetic works." What places have had the most impact on you as an individual? What features of the landscape were particularly important to you as a child, and why? In what ways did the people who lived there influence you?

vancouver–courtenay–calgary

The ocean
is the last thing
to think of
leaving Vancouver

to the Island
offshore up to Sunshine
Coast where shells
sprout out of the water

like eggs in chicken nests
pluckt, eaten all
in an hour.
A thing taken

for granted this time
of year. But
think: next year
we will live across

the Rockies: earth
will be the largest concern.
A thin trickle of water
cuts thru cow country mud.

Shrimp sells for
three dollars a pound;
sunshine is dry with
wide white mountain clouds.

The plains
are ever present
to the eye
looking back, smooth as water.

Notes

Sunshine Coast refers to an 86 km stretch of mainland coast that begins just north of Vancouver in British Columbia

Activities

1. In this poem, Bowering uses words and phrases to evoke strong emotions about places on opposite sides of the Rocky Mountains. For the narrator, what emotions are associated with the places described in the poem? Which place do you think the narrator prefers? Use specific references to the poem to support your response.

2. Early in his career, Bowering was strongly influenced by developments in modern American poetry that used plain, concrete language, avoiding abstraction and the excessive use of similes and metaphors. Examine the language Bowering uses in this poem and assess the extent to which it exhibits these characteristics while still evoking powerful feelings. What parts of speech are predominant in the poem? Why do you think the poet has chosen these parts of speech?

Prairie Flight

Dorothy Livesay

Dorothy Livesay was born in Winnipeg, Manitoba, in 1909. Livesay's father was a journalist and author who was the first general manager of the Canadian Press. Her mother was a poet of distinction and a translator of poetry from Ukrainian into English. Livesay attended the University of British Columbia, the University of Toronto, and the Sorbonne in Paris. Livesay lived at various times in British Columbia, New Brunswick, and Alberta. She was a founding member of the League of Canadian Poets and won numerous awards for her poetry, including two Governor General's Awards, in 1944 and in 1947. Livesay became an officer of the Order of Canada in 1987. She died in 1996. Livesay's early poetry deals with issues of women's rights and international peace, as well as the plight of the aged. Her later poems tend to reflect more personal and intimate emotions and reflections. Do you prefer poetry that is highly personal or poetry that deals with contemporary issues? Do you think one of these approaches is more valuable than the other? If so, why?

Prairie Flight

In Canada
no need for abstract painters.
Farmers have shaped
with their hands, their boots, their horses' hooves
last, with tractors
a bright geometry imposed
on buffalo bones

Staring at land
only for wheat and hay
with the curled rivers and lakes
sore thumbs
right in their way
those silent carvers of the land
send messages they never see.

Activities

1. Have a class discussion about how Livesay uses free verse to fuse the form and the meaning of her poem. In your discussion, refer to the poem's speech-like rhythm, the natural, easy-flowing word order, the variations of line length according to the importance of ideas, and the control of shorter and longer pauses.

2. Livesay ends her first stanza with the lines "a bright geometry imposed / on buffalo bones." In several paragraphs, discuss the effectiveness of these lines in terms of their descriptive power, their use of alliteration, and the historical context to which they refer.

Fern Hill

Dylan Thomas

Dylan Thomas was born in Swansea, Wales, in 1914. The son of an English schoolmaster, Thomas never learned the Welsh language. At the age of twenty, he moved to London and published his first collection of poems. During his lifetime, Thomas produced books of poetry, essays, stories, radio plays, and film scripts. Thomas' poetry, which was influenced by the intricate patterns of sound and meaning of the English poet Gerard Manley Hopkins, was seen as a reaction against the classicism of the poet W.H. Auden. An international literary star during his lifetime, he died in 1953. Thomas' passion, his arresting imagery, and his bold experiments with language have ensured him a permanent place in the pantheon of best-loved twentieth-century poets. Would you say that the majority of poets espouse an optimistic or a pessimistic view of life? To what extent do you think this attitude reflects the attitude of the general public?

Fern Hill

Now as I was young and easy under the apple boughs
About the lilting house and happy as the grass was green,
   The night above the dingle starry,
    Time let me hail and climb
   Golden in the heydays of his eyes,
And honoured among wagons I was prince of the apple towns
And once below a time I lordly had the trees and leaves
    Trail with daisies and barley
  Down the rivers of the windfall light.

And as I was green and carefree, famous among the barns   10
About the happy yard and singing as the farm was home,
   In the sun that is young once only,
    Time let me play and be
   Golden in the mercy of his means,
And green and golden I was huntsman and herdsman, the calves
Sang to my horn, the foxes on the hills barked clear and cold,
    And the sabbath rang slowly
  In the pebbles of the holy streams.

All the sun long it was running, it was lovely, the hay
Fields high as the house, the tunes from the chimneys, it was air   20
   And playing, lovely and watery
    And fire green as grass.
   And nightly under the simple stars
As I rode to sleep the owls were bearing the farm away,
All the moon long I heard, blessed among stables, the nightjars
  Flying with the ricks, and the horses
   Flashing into the dark.

And then to awake, and the farm, like a wanderer white
With the dew, come back, the cock on his shoulder: it was all
  Shining, it was Adam and maiden,   30
    The sky gathered again
  And the sun grew round that very day.
So it must have been after the birth of the simple light
In the first, spinning place, the spellbound horses walking warm
  Out of the whinnying green stable
    On to the fields of praise.

And honoured among foxes and pheasants by the gay house
Under the new made clouds and happy as the heart was long,
  In the sun born over and over,
    I ran my heedless ways,   40
  My wishes raced through the house high hay
And nothing I cared, at my sky blue trades, that time allows
In all his tuneful turning so few and such morning songs
  Before the children green and golden
    Follow him out of grace,

Nothing I cared, in the lamb white days, that time would take me
Up to the swallow thronged loft by the shadow of my hand,
  In the moon that is always rising,
    Nor that riding to sleep
  I should hear him fly with the high fields   50
And wake to the farm forever fled from the childless land.
Oh as I was young and easy in the mercy of his means,
    Time held me green and dying
  Though I sang in my chains like the sea.

Notes

Fern Hill the farm of Ann Jones, Dylan Thomas' aunt, where he spent his summer holidays as a boy

dingle a small, wooded valley; from the Middle English *dell*, meaning a hollow

hail to call out an enthusiastic greeting

heydays the period of one's life in which one experiences the greatest vigour or prosperity; possibly of Germanic origin, perhaps from the low German *heidi* or *heida*, an exclamation of joy

windfall a fruit brought down by the wind

night-jars medium-sized nocturnal birds such as whippoorwills or nighthawks; also called goatsuckers

ricks stacks of hay in the open air

Adam and maiden Adam and Eve in the Garden of Eden as described in the Book of Genesis in the Bible

Activities

1. Do you think that Dylan Thomas' purpose in writing this poem was celebratory or cautionary? Based on your response, how would you express either its celebratory or cautionary view of time? To what extent do the poet's ideas fit in with your own experiences and observations?

2. How would you describe the predominant tone in the first stanza of "Fern Hill"? Contrast this with the tone of the last three lines of the poem. Go through the poem stanza by stanza, identifying words and images that foreshadow the emotional closure which Thomas voices at the end. Do you think the poet has managed to successfully integrate the innocent joy of the child with the mature resignation of the adult, without invalidating either one? Explain.

AMIRI BARAKA

C. Daniel Dawson

About the Visual   The subject of this portrait is the writer Amiri Baraka, born LeRoi Jones in 1934. Baraka was educated at Howard University and became part of the 1950s "beat" scene in New York's Greenwich Village. The assassination of activist Malcolm X in 1965 led Baraka to distance himself from white culture. He dropped his Western name and adopted black nationalist views, which he later abandoned for Marxism. Today Baraka continues his work as a writer, speaker, and activist for African-American causes. The photographer of this portrait, C. Daniel Dawson, was born in 1944 and studied at Columbia University. Dawson is an award-winning African-American photographer and filmmaker. Why do you think an intentional portrait of a person might reveal either more or less than a candid snapshot of the same person?

Activities

1. Write a poem in which you respond to some aspect of this photograph. For example, you might focus on its mood, its subject, the emotion you discover within the photograph, or the emotion it elicits from you. Have a partner read a polished version of your poem to provide feedback on the consistency of your tone. Make revisions to strengthen your work. Share your poem with the class.

2. According to the American photographer Robert Llewellyn, "Every photograph you make is a self-portrait." What do you think the portrait of Amiri Baraka reveals about C. Daniel Dawson? Consider the choices Dawson made in terms of subject, props, mood, medium, lighting, and composition.

c. 1970, gelatin silver print ▶

The Committee to
Upgrade Celestial Signs

Kurt Brown

Kurt Brown was born in Brooklyn, New York, in 1944. He attended the University of Connecticut. For many years, he lived in Aspen, Colorado, where he founded the Aspen Writers' Conference. Brown has edited several books of poetry, and he published his own first collection, *Return of the Prodigals*, in 1999. Why do you think people are fascinated by the patterns that stars form in the night sky? What human impulse caused the ancient Greeks and other civilizations to connect these patterns to their myths and heroes?

The Committee to Upgrade Celestial Signs

> meets once a year
> > to re-evaluate old myths
> > > that spangle heaven:
> > Taurus,   Draco,
> Perseus,
> > Boötes…
> outdated in their Greek shining.

Quickly renamed,
        they are reconfigured into modern shapes
          —cluster by cluster—
      Guitaris Major,   Double Arches,
    Empire State Building,
           Bottle of Coke…
Each fall,
     the firmament glitters like a new marquee,
      a hit parade of celebrities
          to correspond
   with the season's upcoming shows:
    where Cepheus glittered—
        the visage of an actress
           shines;
  Libra morphs into the body
       of a reigning hunk;
   the Pleiades burn all night—
        divas in a female rock group.
Trained over centuries
     to forget the past
entire populations suffer
      from cultural
        amnesia
      catalyzed by constant change—
"This is NOW!"
     a favorite bumper sticker shouts,
  and
    "Welcome to the Interactive Cosmos!"
Constellations rise and fall,
      brief as ads
        that flash across the blank screen
         of heaven.

Computers work around the clock
          to thread stars
               into relevant patterns
    while last year's icons
        fade
           like the memory
    Of someone's face
        before cosmetic surgery.
At last
      the Committee votes on current choices,
            having sifted
     through a copious Printout
         of Possible Skies:
Hands go up around the table
          as they nod and smile—
    with the stroke of a finger
         the Zodiac is realigned
    against the infinite blackness behind the stars.

Notes

Taurus, Draco, Perseus, Boötes, Cepheus, Libra, Pleiades constellations of stars, named after figures in Greek mythology

Activities

1. Make a list of key characteristics of contemporary life that Brown highlights in this poem. Choose three that you feel are key to the poem. Around each concept, cluster relevant words and phrases from the poem and form your own associations around each concept. In small groups, compare your clusters and create a statement about the meaning and theme of the poem.

2. Write an essay in which you analyze and assess the style of the poem based on its diction, syntax, and literary devices. Consider the effect of these choices on such elements as tone and theme, and evaluate the impact of these choices.

The Heroes You Had as a Girl

Bronwen Wallace

Bronwen Wallace was a poet, short story writer, essayist, and film-maker. She was born in 1945 in Kingston, Ontario. She attended Queen's University, then moved to Windsor where she became a social activist, focusing on issues concerning the working class and women. After seven years, she moved back to Kingston, where she taught at St. Lawrence College and Queen's University and made documentary films. Wallace received the National Magazine Award, the Pat Lowther Award, and the Du Maurier Award for Poetry. Wallace died in 1989. Who comes to mind when you consider the heroes you had when you were a child? What might those heroes reveal about you at that time? Who are some of your heroes today and what qualities do they have in common with your earlier heroes?

The Heroes You Had as a Girl

The heroes you had as a girl
were always three grades ahead of you
taller than the boys in your own class
taller even than your brothers
and the layers of muscle ripening
under their thin shirts their jeans
made your palms itch
for something you didn't know how to explain
but wanted to   sitting with your girlfriends
in the hot dry grass   10
at the edge of the parking-lot
where all day Saturday they worked on their cars
hunched over the greasy mysteries of their engines
occasionally raising their heads
their eyes flicking
to where you were included
as part of the landscape

Sundays they practised more dangerous manoeuvres
till your eyes stung with the smell
of oil and burning rubber   20
and once they built arches of flaming
orange crates   you remember them spinning
through the air when one car missed
remember the screams that burned your throat
before you realized no-one was hurt
your voices fluttering like foolish birds
on the wild currents of their laughter

and now twenty years later the hero
who drove that car returns as unexpectedly
as the memory and just as out of place   30
you watch him study a display of bathroom fixtures
in the hardware department of Simpsons-Sears
he's grown fat and balding
and you think how easy it would be
to walk right over tap him
on the shoulder say *hello*
remember me   and if he didn't
you could laugh it off
at least you've kept your figure
that's not what stops you now   40
though something does
and as he walks away
you can feel the dry grass biting
the backs of your legs   the uncomfortable
angle of your knees as you sat just so
practising your own dangerous manoeuvres
not being noticed   not noticing
the other girls   forgetting their names
the shapes of their faces reddening in the sun
(though you remember those burning arches   50
your throat tightening again around those foolish screams,
you think you could explain it now
and that's what stops you
knowing you want nothing less
than for him to turn
peel off his shirt to show you
burn scars on his chest
and in the sullen landscape of his eyes
you want the faces of those girls
your own among them burning   60
brighter than any fire

Activities

1. In a letter, Bronwen Wallace once expressed concern that women's writing was often discounted as "personal" rather than "universal." Consider to whom this poem is addressed. Why do you think Wallace chose to use the second-person point of view? Meet with a small group to discuss whether this is a poem about human experience or one woman's personal story. Try to come to consensus on your conclusions. Report to the class, providing evidence for your interpretation.

2. With a group, present a readers' theatre performance of the poem. Decide what meaning you want to convey to your listeners and explore various ways of reading in order to create the effects you want. After your performance, write an independent analysis of what you learned about the meaning and style of the poem through your reading.

Another Viewpoint: Critical Approaches

Gender criticism examines how gender identity influences both the creation and the reception of literary works. In your view, to what extent, if any, do male and female writers differ in their choice of subject or in their perspective? Formulate a thesis to explain whether you think that women are more likely to create works that interest other women and whether the same can be said of men. When you read or view a story, to what extent are you aware of the gender of the author? In what ways might your gender influence the way in which you read a work of literature?

foremother

Lillian Bouzane

Lillian Bouzane was born in Little Bay NDB, Newfoundland, in 1932. A writer of fiction, non-fiction, and poetry, she has received many literary prizes, including Government of Newfoundland and Labrador Arts and Letters Awards for both fiction and non-fiction. In 1999, she published *In the Hands of the Living God*, a novel that recounts the story of John Cabot, and his discovery of Newfoundland, through the eyes of his wife, Mathye Cabot of Venice. The novel is written in the form of letters and diary entries. "Foremother" recounts selected events from the life of the narrator's great-grandmother. How is life different for women today than for their great-grandmothers? When you think of women in Canada in the 1800s, what images come to mind?

foremother

my great-grandmother watched her husband
wash overboard
in a Labrador gale
just one more fishing skipper lost
in the Strait of Belle Isle
nobody noticed

she was a grieving woman
until the merchant at Quirpon
moved to short-change her by fifty quintal
on the fish from their last voyage
with a scorn she bothered to show
she ordered the catch reloaded
took the wheel herself
and set her course for the next harbour
where she sold it at a neat profit

steeling her nerve
she raised her flag to full staff
and sailed into her home port
the priest came to see her
to admonish and comfort
she gave him good whiskey
with a glint in her eye
that said "don't meddle with me"
he didn't

each year thereafter
she made two voyages to the Labrador Coast
spring and summer
hired for hands only bedlamer boys
kept her name clear
took one trip to Boston each year
left the children behind
with orders to say to the neighbours
"don't meddle with my mother's good name"
they obeyed her

when she was fifty
and had fourteen schooners in her name
she married again
a man half her age
she made him her bookkeeper/bartender
he was good at both
she got ten winters out of him
she said so herself

once she sailed her flagship
to Montreal to buy a dress
her only purchase
when the Duke's son came
to plant a tree
and settle other matters of State
she danced the night through with him
at the government ball
he walked her down to the harbour
they sat on her quarter-deck 'til dawn
drinking port and singing bawdy songs
it was said he asked her to marry him
it was said she turned him down
she already had more ships than he

before the bank crash of 1894
she liquidated her assets
bought gold
lived another ten years to be ninety
to the consternation of her sons
and the delight of her daughters
who loved her
and got her money
they passed it on to my mother
who educated my five sisters and me
with what was left of it

40

50

60

I, her offspring, thrice removed
write this poem in praise of her
and tell only half I know   70

Notes

Strait of Belle Isle a body of water separating the island of Newfoundland
from Labrador

fifty quintal approximately 2,300 kg; from the Old French word *quintal* and
the medieval Latin word *quintalen*; originally from the Arabic word *qintār*

thrice removed three generations later

Activities

1. Choose a scene from this poem that is particularly rich in descriptive
details, and represent it in a visual form, such as a sketch, web, map, or
word cluster. Use a line from the poem as a caption. Compare your choice
and representation with those of other students. Which scenes were most
often chosen and why?

2. Analyze and assess the effectiveness of the free-verse form that Bouzane
has chosen for this poem. Next, consider how Bouzane has created imagery
and to what effect she has used repetition. Be prepared to explain and support your analysis in a class discussion.

Another Viewpoint: Critical Approaches

In a small group, use dictionaries, other reference materials, and the Internet
to research the term *feminism*, and try to reach consensus on a working
definition of this term. Once you have refined your definition, have a class discussion on whether this poem is or is not a "feminist" poem.

To You Who Would Wage War Against Me

Kateri Akiwenzie Damm

Born in Toronto in 1965, Kateri Akiwenzie Damm is of mixed Chippewa and Ojibwe ancestry. Akiwenzie Damm received a master's degree in English literature from the University of Ottawa. She credits her grandmother with providing her with the inspiration to become a writer. Akiwenzie Damm, who has published numerous collections of poetry, is deeply committed to promoting the work of indigenous writers, not only from Canada but other countries as well. In 1999, she established NiSHin Productions, an indigenous performing arts production company. More recently she has lived and worked on the Camp Croker Reserve on the Saugeen Peninsula near Wiarton, Ontario. This poem explores a relationship. When you interact with someone, how do you try to figure out what that person is really thinking and feeling? How might a person try to hide his or her true thoughts and feelings from you?

To You Who Would Wage War Against Me

I.

there are many lines
you have not traced on my palms
still
you think you know me

when i speak
you nod knowingly
as if
you've already read my mind
and are only politely acknowledging
the confirmation of my spoken words   10

II.

but you cannot possibly know
what i've been contemplating
these days

my head is full of blood
but you show no fear
and i do not trust my hands
which feel to me like stones

you do not cower when i approach
though i am like a runaway train
and i can hear your voice   20
cool and steady
while my brain screams profanities
into the air around your ears

our past has given you no reason
to be afraid
but still i am surprised you cannot see
the danger burning brightly in my eyes
the fire i am struggling to control

III.

as i sit stewing in the kitchen's false
light
with tears my daughter
comes to me
frightened by what she cannot see
afraid tonight to sleep

i hold her in my arms
singing soft words of comfort
feeling her heart quickly
beating against my chest
knowing before i can think
that i have forgotten us
for our stupid little war

knowing in the incandescent light
that anger will never move me
as delicately as she has moved me this
night

Notes

incandescent   artificial light produced by a hot, glowing filament

Activities

1. The title of the poem refers to a nameless "you" and "me." Look closely at the poem for clues about the personalities of the two people referred to by the pronouns in the title. By reading between the lines, what can you conclude about the personalities of the two individuals, the conflict between them, and how they react to each other? Be sure to support your observations with references to the poem.

2. The poem deals with two powerful contrasting emotions, anger and love. What words and images does the writer use to convey the intensity of these emotions? What is the significance of the narrator's observation that "anger will never move me / as delicately as she has moved me this / night"? In the end, why does the narrator's concern and love for her daughter move her more than anger? In general, which of the two emotions do you think is stronger? Explain your choice.

Another Viewpoint: Culture

Consider the extent to which Akiwenzie Damm's cultural background adds another possible level of meaning to this poem. Is it culturally significant that the "you" and "me" remain unidentified? Who else could be referred to by these generic pronouns? Use the Internet to research information on Kateri Akiwenzie Damm. Then, in an analytical essay, use what you discover about the author as the basis for your interpretation of the poem.

I, Icarus

Alden Nowlan

Alden Nowlan was born in Windsor, Nova Scotia, in 1933. A remark-ably prolific writer, he published twenty-four books. Although his formal education ended at grade five, Nowlan became a successful journalist, story writer, playwright, and novelist. In 1967, he was the recipient of the Governor General's Award for his book *Bread, Wine and Salt*. Throughout his career, Nowlan gained notoriety for fic-tionalizing his own life. About his writing, he said, "I write for the same reason that I'm six-feet three-inches tall: I can't do anything about it." One critic wrote that Nowlan's work is "rich in regional sensibility and in affection for ordinary people, but connected—by Nowlan's intelligence, temperament, and reading—to a literary world far beyond folk culture." Nowlan became well known for this ability to combine the views of ordinary people and events with a sense of the mystery of life. To what extent do you think literature deals with the mysteries of human life?

I, Icarus

There was a time when I could fly. I swear it.
Perhaps, if I think hard for a moment, I can even tell you the year.
My room was on the ground floor at the rear of the house.
My bed faced a window.
Night after night I lay on my bed and willed myself to fly.
It was hard work, I can tell you.
Sometimes I lay perfectly still for an hour before I felt
      my body rising from the bed.
I rose slowly, slowly until I floated three or four feet
      above the floor.
Then, with a kind of swimming motion, I propelled myself
      toward the window.
Outside, I rose higher and higher, above the pasture fence,
      above the clothesline, above the dark, haunted trees
      beyond the pasture.
And, all the time, I heard the music of flutes.
It seemed the wind made this music.
And sometimes there were voices singing.

Notes

Icarus refers to the story of Daedalus and Icarus. According to this Greek legend, Daedalus was the architect of the elaborate labyrinth that housed the Minotaur in Crete. Daedalus helped the hero Theseus escape from the labyrinth after he had been imprisoned there by the king of Crete. As punishment, Daedalus and his son, Icarus, were themselves placed in the labyrinth. Determined to escape, Daedalus made a pair of wings for himself and one for his son. Before taking off, Daedalus cautioned his son about flying too close to the sun, but Icarus disobeyed his father. The heat of the sun melted the wax that held the feathers together and Icarus dropped into the sea and drowned.

Activities

1. Reread the poem, looking specifically at the words and images Nowlan uses to describe the experience of flight. Why does he say that willing himself to fly was "hard work"? Why is his flight limited to "three or four feet above the floor" at first? How and why does the nature of his flight change once he leaves the house? Why are the trees below him "dark" and "haunted"? How do you explain the music he hears?

2. In literature, the source of an allusion—a direct or indirect reference in one work to another work or to a historical person or event—is often mythological or religious. Use reference materials to investigate the links in this poem to Icarus and to Aeolian harps. How does the allusion to Icarus enhance the experience described by the narrator? How does the allusion to Aeolian harps enrich the meaning of the last three lines of the poem? Can you detect other allusions in the poem?

Another Viewpoint: Archetypal Patterns

Many human situations, such as the idealism or rebelliousness of youth, are inherently similar and can be analyzed as archetypes. The psychologist Carl Jung suggested that the meaning of the Icarus myth is related to the idealism of youth, which often leads to over-confidence. He warns us that "the human ego can be exalted to experience godlike attributes, but only at the cost of over-reaching itself and falling to disaster." In a well-developed paragraph, consider the extent to which Jung's observation is demonstrated in Nowlan's poem.

Musée des Beaux Arts

W.H. Auden

Wystan Hugh Auden was born in 1907, in York, England. Auden was interested primarily in science and at first intended to be a mining engineer, but by 1922 he had discovered his vocation as a poet. His first volume of poetry was published in 1930. The brilliance and originality of his work brought him a wide readership and much praise from critics. As well as writing poetry, Auden collaborated on plays and on travel books that focused on countries such as China and Iceland. He also wrote opera libretti, working with renowned twentieth-century composers including Benjamin Britten and Igor Stravinsky. In his works, he addressed social, political, and religious issues. In 1939, he moved to the United States, where he won the Pulitzer Prize for *The Age of Anxiety* in 1948. Auden eventually returned to England, where he died in 1973. "Musée des Beaux Arts" is a poem Auden wrote in response to a painting by Pieter Brueghel entitled *Landscape with the Fall of Icarus*, which appears on page 367 of this anthology. The poem explores how humans react when disasters occur to others. When you see news reports of wars and natural disasters, to what extent do you feel a sense of personal obligation toward the people involved? How active a role do you think Canada should take in solving problems in other countries?

Musée des Beaux Arts

About suffering they were never wrong,
The Old Masters: how well they understood
Its human position; how it takes place
While someone else is eating or opening a window or just walking
    dully along;
How, when the aged are reverently, passionately waiting
For the miraculous birth, there always must be
Children who did not specially want it to happen, skating
On a pond at the edge of the wood:
They never forgot
That even the dreadful martyrdom must run its course   10
Anyhow in a corner, some untidy spot
Where the dogs go on with their doggy life and the torturer's horse
Scratches its innocent behind on a tree.

In Brueghel's Icarus, for instance: how everything turns away
Quite leisurely from the disaster; the ploughman may
Have heard the splash, the forsaken cry,
But for him it was not an important failure; the sun shone
As it had to on the white legs disappearing into the green
Water; and the expensive delicate ship that must have seen
Something amazing, a boy falling out of the sky,   20
Had somewhere to get to and sailed calmly on.

Notes

Musée des Beaux Arts an art museum in Brussels, Belgium, where Brueghel's *Landscape with the Fall of Icarus* can be found

Old Masters distinguished European painters of the fifteenth through seventeenth centuries whose works have become recognized as masterpieces. Among the Old Masters are Botticelli, Da Vinci, Michelangelo, Raphael, Titian, Bosch, Holbein, Brueghel, El Greco, Rubens, Velázquez, and Rembrandt.

miraculous birth the birth of Christ to the Virgin Mary and her husband Joseph, as recorded in the New Testament of the Bible

dreadful martyrdom the death of Christ on the cross. In Christianity, Christ is believed to have sacrificed himself to save humanity.

Brueghel Pieter Brueghel the Elder, a Flemish painter of the sixteenth century noted for landscapes and scenes in the lives of ordinary people; also spelled Bruegel and Breughel

Icarus In the Greek legend, Daedalus and his son Icarus escape from the island of Crete using wings of wax and bird feathers. Icarus disregards his father's warning not to fly too close to the sun; his wings melt and he falls into the sea.

Activities

1. In the legend of Icarus and Daedalus, as told by the Roman poet Ovid (43 BCE–17 CE), the plowman, the shepherd, and the angler witnessed with amazement the fall of Icarus from the sky. How is Auden's poem a meditation on the difference between the original story and Brueghel's version of it? In general, what do you think influences varied interpretations of an event?

2. Auden combines allusions to Christianity and Greek mythology in this poem. Discuss the connections he makes between the "miraculous birth," "the dreadful martyrdom," and the story of Icarus and Daedalus. How do these allusions contribute to an understanding of the poem?

People on the Bridge

Wislawa Szymborska

Translated by Joanna Trzeciak

Wislawa Szymborska was born in Konik, Poland, in 1923. In 1952, she joined the Communist Party, but later repudiated her membership and disclaimed the work she published during her tenure in the Party. Szymborska, whose poetry has been translated into many languages, has written only 200 poems, in part because she discards much of what she writes. She received the Nobel Prize in Literature in 1996. In her acceptance speech, Szymborska said, "Inspiration is not the exclusive privilege of poets or artists generally. Inspiration visits all those who've consciously chosen their calling and do their job with love and imagination. Difficulties and setbacks never quell their curiosity." This poem was inspired by a Japanese print, *Sudden Shower at Ohashi Bridge* by Hiroshige Utagawa, which appears on page 369 of this anthology. When you look at a print or a painting, to what extent do you speculate about the story behind the picture or the fate of the people who are illustrated? Are you more inclined to project yourself into the scene or to view it with detached objectivity?

People on the Bridge

Strange planet and strange people on it.
They yield to time, but don't want to recognize time.
They have their ways of expressing resistance.
They make pictures such as this:

Nothing remarkable at first glance.
One can see water,
one riverbank,
a narrow boat strenuously moving upstream,
a bridge over the water,
and people on the bridge.

They are clearly picking up the pace,
as rain starts lashing down from a dark cloud.

The point is, nothing happens further.
The cloud changes neither shape nor color.
The rain neither subsides nor surges.
The boat moves without moving.
The people on the bridge run
exactly where they ran before.

It is hard to get by without commentary:
This is not at all an innocent picture.
Time's been stopped here,
its laws no longer consulted.
It's been denied impact on the course of events,
disregarded and dishonored.

Thanks to a rebel,
one Hiroshige Utagawa
(a being who, by the way,
passed away, as is proper, long ago),
time stumbled and fell.

Perhaps it is merely a prank without much meaning,
a whim on the scale of just a few galaxies,
but just in case,
let's add what happens next:

For generations it has been considered in good taste
to hold this painting in high esteem,
to praise it and be greatly moved by it.

For some, even that is not enough.
They hear the patter of rain,
feel the chill of raindrops on necks and shoulders,
they look at the bridge and the people on it   40
as if they saw themselves there,
in that never-ending race
along the endless road, to be traveled for eternity
and they have the audacity to believe
that it is real.

Notes

Hiroshige Utagawa a Japanese artist (1797–1858) from the Edo period in
Japan

Activities

1. Paraphrase each stanza of the poem. Then write a response in which
you react to the theme and ideas of the poem. Comment on connections you
made to your own experiences or to other literary works.

2. Use an authoritative literary reference guide to locate and record definitions of *poetry* and *prose*. Create a two-column chart, labelled "poetic
characteristics" and "prose characteristics." Analyze the poem carefully,
recording in the appropriate columns the features that are poetic and those
that are prosaic. Then create a thesis statement in which you state how
effectively these two characteristics work together to create a unified poem.

Another Viewpoint: Literary Modes and Forms

Both this poem and "Musée des Beaux Arts" by W.H. Auden, which appears
on page 518 of this anthology, can be classified as reflective verse. Reflective
literature often poses essential questions, searches for universal truths, and
expresses profound themes regarding humanity's existence. Discuss in
which ways each of these poems is reflective, and to what extent the way
in which each poem relates to a specific work of art contributes to its reflective nature.

Progress

Emma LaRocque

Emma LaRocque was born in 1941 in Big Bay, Alberta. A Métis by birth, she is currently a professor of Native Studies at the University of Manitoba. LaRocque began publishing essays, social commentaries, and research articles in 1971. She describes herself as a "closet poet" and has published only a handful of poems in literary journals and collections. LaRocque has said, "Writing is the art of bringing to birth the human condition in thought form." She has reflected optimistically on the struggle of Native women writers, saying, "To be a Native writer of some consciousness is to be in a lonely place. Happily, our isolation is about to come apart at the seams." When you think of "progress," what words, ideas, and images come to mind? To what extent are these associations positive and optimistic? Which negative aspects of progress are of concern to you?

Progress

Earth poet
So busy
weaving
      magic
into words

so busy
placing
      patterns
quilting
      stars
so busy
making
      the sun
dance
so busy
singing
      your songs
in circles
so busy
tipping
      moons
in dreams

Earth poet
so busy
touching
      the land
scape
mad modern man
must make me
look at
cold steel spires
stealing earth and sun
      dance.

Activities

1. In a group, discuss the significance of the poem's title. What "progress" is represented in the poem? How does the repetition of the words "so busy" relate to the title? How does the title contribute to the meaning of the poem? Try to reach consensus on these questions and justify your answers in a class discussion.

2. Free verse uses the simple rhythms of everyday speech. Poet W.H. Auden said that a poet needs an "infallible ear" to determine where the lines should end. Enter the text of the poem into a word-processing file and experiment with different line lengths and breaks. How effective are LaRocque's original choices? How does the form of this poem help to convey the meaning? Did you find another line arrangement you preferred?

Summer Night

Langston Hughes

Langston Hughes was born in Joplin, Missouri, in 1902, and grew up there and in Illinois. After high school, he briefly attended university and travelled to Mexico, Europe, and Africa, before completing his studies. In 1924, he moved to Harlem in New York City, where he became a key figure in the "Harlem Renaissance" cultural movement. A prolific writer, Hughes wrote poetry, humorous sketches, social-protest essays, children's books, short story collections, novels, and twenty plays. He is best known for his portrayals of African-American life in the United States, as well as his connection to the world of jazz and blues music, which influenced his writing. Hughes received many awards, including Guggenheim and Rosenwald Fellowships. He died in 1967. What specific memories do you associate with summer nights? In what ways do the physical aspects of summer, in the country or city, contribute to a particular memory you have?

Summer Night

The sounds
Of the Harlem night
Drop one by one into stillness.
The last player-piano is closed.
The last victrola ceases with the
"Jazz Boy Blues."
The last crying baby sleeps
And the night becomes
Still as a whispering heartbeat.
I toss   10
Without rest in the darkness,
Weary as the tired night,
My soul
Empty as the silence,
Empty with a vague,
Aching emptiness,
Desiring,
Needing someone,
Something.

I toss without rest   20
In the darkness
Until the new dawn,
Wan and pale,
Descends like a white mist
Into the court-yard.

Notes

player-piano a piano that is fitted with an apparatus that allows it to play songs automatically by pulling down the required keys from the inside, giving the appearance of a "phantom" player

victrola a record player manufactured in the 1920s

Activities

1. Read the poem aloud with a partner, paying particular attention to the sounds and images. What mood does the poem convey? What images stand out in your mind? How do the line breaks and the language of the poem help to create these effects?

2. Langston Hughes is often called the "jazz poet." Do research into the jazz of the 1920s. Next, on the Internet, locate an early jazz recording, preferably from the 1920s or 1930s. Alternate listening to the recording with rereading the poem. After you have listened to the music several times, create a Venn diagram or write an essay comparing Hughes' poem to the jazz music you heard.

Another Viewpoint: Critical Approaches

Biographical criticism explores how knowledge of an author's life and background can illuminate our understanding of her or his writing. One literary critic has written that "Hughes refused to differentiate between his personal experience and the common experience of black America." Research biographical information on Langston Hughes. Consider to what extent you think "Summer Night" is a poem of black America. In a literary research essay, explain whether your interpretation of Hughes' poems is enhanced by connecting Hughes' life with the life he wrote about in his poetry. Make sure that your interpretation includes a carefully formulated and clearly stated thesis.

The Love Song of J. Alfred Prufrock

T.S. Eliot

A major figure in twentieth-century literature, T.S. Eliot was born in St. Louis, Missouri, in 1888. He earned a master's degree from Harvard University, then studied literature and philosophy in France and Germany. He eventually settled in England shortly after the outbreak of World War I, where he came under the influence of the poet Ezra Pound, who assisted in the publication of Eliot's work. In 1922, he published his poem "The Wasteland," generally considered one of the most influential poetic works of the twentieth century. In addition to poetry, Eliot wrote numerous successful plays and works of literary criticism. His book of light verse *Old Possum's Book of Practical Cats* was turned into the immensely popular musical *Cats* by Andrew Lloyd Webber. Eliot, who died in 1965, helped create the modernist style of blending references to the classics with mundane realism, and expressing this blend in majestic language which seems to mock the subject. "The Love Song of J. Alfred Prufrock" was written while Eliot was still a college student at Harvard and is often considered the first modernist poem. What are some of the subjects you would expect a college or university student to write about? What do you think would be a typical student's attitude to these subjects?

◀ *Les Escaliers de Montmartre, 1936, Gilberte Brassai*

The Love Song of J. Alfred Prufrock

S'io credesse che mia risposta fosse
A persona che mai tornasse al mondo,
Questa fiamma staria senza piu scosse.
Ma perciocche giammai di questo fondo
Non torno vivo alcun, s'i'odo il vero,
Senza tema d'infamia ti rispondo.

Let us go then, you and I,
When the evening is spread out against the sky
Like a patient etherized upon a table;
Let us go, through certain half-deserted streets,
The muttering retreats
Of restless nights in one-night cheap hotels
And sawdust restaurants with oyster shells:
Streets that follow like a tedious argument
Of insidious intent
To lead you to an overwhelming question…   10
Oh, do not ask, "What is it?"
Let us go and make our visit.

In the room the women come and go
Talking of Michelangelo.

The yellow fog that rubs its back upon the windowpanes,
The yellow smoke that rubs its muzzle on the windowpanes
Licked its tongue into the corners of the evening,
Lingered upon the pools that stand in drains,
Let fall upon its back the soot that falls from chimneys,
Slipped by the terrace, made a sudden leap,   20
And seeing that it was a soft October night,
Curled once about the house, and fell asleep.

And indeed there will be time
For the yellow smoke that slides along the street,
Rubbing its back upon the windowpanes;
There will be time, there will be time
To prepare a face to meet the faces that you meet;
There will be time to murder and create,
And time for all the works and days of hands
That lift and drop a question on your plate;   30
Time for you and time for me,
And time yet for a hundred indecisions,
And for a hundred visions and revisions,
Before the taking of a toast and tea.

   In the room the women come and go
Talking of Michelangelo.

   And indeed there will be time
To wonder, "Do I dare?" and, "Do I dare?"
Time to turn back and descend the stair,
With a bald spot in the middle of my hair—   40
(They will say: "How his hair is growing thin!")
My morning coat, my collar mounting firmly to the chin,
My necktie rich and modest, but asserted by a simple pin—
(They will say: "But how his arms and legs are thin!")
Do I dare
Disturb the universe?
In a minute there is time
For decisions and revisions which a minute will reverse.

   For I have known them all already, known them all—
Have known the evenings, mornings, afternoons,   50
I have measured out my life with coffee spoons;
I know the voices dying with a dying fall
Beneath the music from a farther room.
   So how should I presume?

And I have known the eyes already, known them all—
The eyes that fix you in a formulated phrase,
And when I am formulated, sprawling on a pin,
When I am pinned and wriggling on the wall,
Then how should I begin
To spit out all the butt-ends of my days and ways?   60
    And how should I presume?

    And I have known the arms already, known them all—
Arms that are braceleted and white and bare
(But in the lamplight, downed with light brown hair!)
Is it perfume from a dress
That makes me so digress?
Arms that lie along a table, or wrap about a shawl.
    And should I then presume?
    And how should I begin?

           . . .

    Shall I say, I have gone at dusk through narrow streets   70
And watched the smoke that rises from the pipes
Of lonely men in shirt-sleeves, leaning out of windows?…

    I should have been a pair of ragged claws
Scuttling across the floors of silent seas.

           . . .

    And the afternoon, the evening, sleeps so peacefully!
Smoothed by long fingers,
Asleep…tired…or it malingers,
Stretched on the floor, here beside you and me.
Should I, after tea and cakes and ices,
Have the strength to force the moment to its crisis?   80
But though I have wept and fasted, wept and prayed,
Though I have seen my head (grown slightly bald)
      brought in upon a platter,

I am no prophet—and here's no great matter;
I have seen the moment of my greatness flicker,
And I have seen the eternal Footman hold my coat, and snicker,
And in short, I was afraid.

    And would it have been worth it, after all,
After the cups, the marmalade, the tea,
Among the porcelain, among some talk of you and me,
Would it have been worth while,   90
To have bitten off the matter with a smile,
To have squeezed the universe into a ball
To roll it toward some overwhelming question,
To say: "I am Lazarus, come from the dead,
Come back to tell you all, I shall tell you all"—
If one, settling a pillow by her head,
        Should say: "That is not what I meant at all.
        That is not it, at all."

    And would it have been worth it, after all,
Would it have been worth while,   100
After the sunsets and the dooryards and the sprinkled streets,
After the novels, after the teacups, after the skirts that trail along the
        floor—
And this, and so much more?—
It is impossible to say just what I mean!
But as if a magic lantern threw the nerves in patterns on a screen:
Would it have been worth while
If one, settling a pillow or throwing off a shawl,
And turning toward the window, should say:
        "That is not it at all,
        That is not what I meant, at all."   110

                    . . .

No! I am not Prince Hamlet, nor was meant to be;
Am an attendant lord, one that will do
To swell a progress, start a scene or two,
Advise the prince; no doubt, an easy tool,
Deferential, glad to be of use,
Politic, cautious, and meticulous;
Full of high sentence, but a bit obtuse;
At times, indeed, almost ridiculous—
Almost, at times, the Fool.

    I grow old…I grow old… 120
I shall wear the bottoms of my trousers rolled.

    Shall I part my hair behind? Do I dare to eat a peach?
I shall wear white flannel trousers, and walk upon the beach.
I have heard the mermaids singing, each to each.

I do not think that they will sing to me.

I have seen them riding seaward on the waves
Combing the white hair of the waves blown back
When the wind blows the water white and black.

We have lingered in the chambers of the sea
By sea-girls wreathed with seaweed red and brown 130
Till human voices wake us, and we drown.

Notes

S'io credesse...ti rispondo This Italian epigraph is a quotation from *The Inferno* by the Italian writer Dante Alighieri (1265–1321). It is translated into English as: "If I thought that my reply would be to one who would ever return to the world, this flame would stay without further movement; but, since no one has ever returned alive from this depth, if what I hear is true, I answer without fear of infamy" (*Inferno*, 27, lines 61–66). Here, Guido da Montefeltro, enclosed in the flames of hell for being a false counsellor during his life on Earth, tells Dante about the shame of his evil life, because he believes that Dante, like all damned souls, will never return to Earth to report it.

And indeed there will be time a reference to a line from Andrew Marvell's poem "To His Coy Mistress": "Had we but world enough, and time..."

And time for all the works and days of hands a reference to "Works and Days," a poem about the farming year by Hesiod, Greek poet of the eighth century BCE

I know the voices dying with a dying fall a reference to a line in Duke Orsino's speech in Shakespeare's *Twelfth Night* (1.1.4): "That strain again! It had a dying fall"

I should have been a pair of ragged claws a reference to Hamlet's comment to Polonius: "For you yourself, sir, should be old as I am, if, like a crab, you could go backward" (2.2.205–6)

Though I have seen my head (grown slightly bald) brought in upon a platter a reference to the biblical story of John the Baptist in Mark 6.17–28 and Matthew 14.3–11

To have squeezed the universe into a ball a reference to part of Marvell's poem "To His Coy Mistress": "Let us roll all our strength and all / Our sweetness up into one ball, / and tear our pleasures with rough strife / Thorough the iron gates of life"

"I am Lazarus, come from the dead" a reference to the biblical story of Lazarus in Luke 16.19–31 and John 11.1–44

Almost, at times, the Fool a reference from Elizabethan drama to the role of the fool, who functions both as a clown and as a teacher of his social superiors

I have heard the mermaids singing a reference to a line in John Donne's poem "Go and Catch a Falling Star": "Teach me to hear mermaids singing," considered an impossibility

Activities

1. The poem is written in the form of a dramatic monologue that presents the thoughts and feelings of a single character. What do you learn about J. Alfred Prufrock from his monologue? What are his likes, dislikes, concerns, fears, and anxieties? How does he relate to others? What kind of person do you think he is?

2. When first published, this poem was the source of much bewilderment. Reasons for this confusion included Eliot's deliberate elimination of the connectives and transitions between passages, his frequent allusions to other works of literature, and his extremely ironic tone. In groups, analyze and assess Eliot's use of these features in the poem.

Another Viewpoint: Critical Approaches

On the Internet and elsewhere, research the terms *modernism* and *postmodernism* as they apply to literature. When did the terms first appear and how were they used? Are they still used in the same way? What literary works from a variety of countries reflect these concepts and how do they do so? Present the results of your research in a class presentation or as a research essay.

Afternoons & Coffeespoons

Brad Roberts of The Crash Test Dummies

Since 1988, Brad Roberts has been the lead singer and songwriter of the Canadian band The Crash Test Dummies. Roberts was born in Winnipeg, Manitoba, in 1964. He was studying for a master's degree in literature and philosophy when he left the University of Winnipeg to form his band. The release of their first album, *The Ghosts That Haunt Me* (1991), produced the hit "Superman's Song." This international success was followed by the best-selling album *God Shuffled His Feet* (1993), which included the hit "Mmm, Mmm, Mmm" as well as the song "Afternoons & Coffeespoons." In reviewing this album, a music critic in the *Globe and Mail* wrote, "Roberts' voice, a resonant baritone, sets him apart from most pop singers, [as do] his equally distinctive songs, which dare to address substantial ideas with penetrating wit." Notable awards for the band include a Juno in 1991 for Group of the Year and three U.S. Grammy Awards, including Best New Artist. What is your impression of the music and words of the songs you have heard by The Crash Test Dummies? What makes the songs different from those of typical rock bands?

Afternoons & Coffeespoons

There's a breeze that makes my breathing not so easy
I've had my lungs checked out with X rays
I've smelled the hospital hallways

Someday I'll have a disappearing hairline
Someday I'll wear pyjamas in the daytime

Times when the day is like a play by Sartre
When it seems a bookburning's in perfect order—
I gave the doctor my description
I tried to stick to my prescriptions

Someday I'll have a disappearing hairline   10
Someday I'll wear pyjamas in the daytime

Afternoons will be measured out
Measured out, measured with
Coffeespoons and T.S. Eliot

Maybe if I could do a play-by-playback
I could change the test results that I will get back
I've watched the summer evenings pass by
I've heard the rattle in my bronchi...

Someday I'll have a disappearing hairline
Someday I'll wear pyjamas in the daytime   20

Afternoons will be measured out
Measured out, measured with
Coffeespoons and T.S. Eliot

Notes

Sartre a reference to Jean-Paul Sartre (1905–1980), the French novelist, playwright, essayist, and leader of the philosophical movement known as *existentialism*

Activities

1. Look closely at the lyrics of "Afternoons & Coffeespoons." Identify those words and phrases that allude to "The Love Song of J. Alfred Prufrock." What do you think Roberts is trying to say about existence? How do the references to Eliot's poem reinforce his thoughts and feelings? In what ways are Roberts' lyrics similar in style to Eliot's poem? In what ways do Roberts' lyrics speak to a contemporary audience?

2. Like Eliot, Roberts makes use of striking and unusual images. Analyze and explain some of the similes and metaphors that you find in the lyrics. Assess how well you think they capture the songwriter's meaning.

The River

Derek Walcott

Derek Walcott was born on the island of St. Lucia in 1930. Considered by many to be the most important Caribbean poet and dramatist writing in English, he was awarded the Nobel Prize in Literature in 1992. Walcott has published over twenty volumes of poetry and more than twenty-five plays. As a writer, his primary aim has been to create literature that remains true to Caribbean life and traditions. A dominant theme in his work is the region's fusion of indigenous, African, Asian, and European cultures. To what extent do you think literature should be closely connected to the region and culture in which it was created? What obligation do writers have to deal with the important issues of their time and native place?

The River

was one, once;
reduced by circumstance
the Council tends it. Once

it could roar through town,
foul-mouthed, brown-muscled, brazenly
drunk, a raucous country-bookie,

but lately it has grown
too footloose for this settlement
of shacks, rechristened a city;

its strength wasted on gutters,
it never understood the age,
what progress meant,

so its clear, brown integument
shrivelled, its tongue stutters
through the official language,

it surrenders its gutturals
to the stern, stone Victorian bridge;
reclaimed, it dies a little

daily, it crawls towards a sea
curdled with oil-slick, its force
thins like the peasantry,

it idles like those resinous
wrinkled woodsmen, the country
reek still on them, hoarse

with municipal argument,
who, falling suddenly silent
on wire-bright afternoons, reflect

on mornings when a torrent
roared down their gorges, and
no one gave a damn what the words meant.

Notes

country-bookie eastern and southern Caribbean dialect term for "country bumpkin"

integument a natural covering, such as skin, rind, or husk

gutturals sounds or letters produced in the throat

stern Victorian bridge a reference to a bridge that crosses the river, likely built in the architectural style of Victorian England

resinous like a resin, a sticky substance formed in and oozing from trees

Activities

1. In this poem, Walcott personifies the river of the past and of the present, using contrasting words and images. With a partner, explore the significance of this contrast. What do you think has caused the changes between the past and the present? What impact do the changes have on the reader? How does the poet feel about these changes?

2. In his acceptance speech for the Nobel Prize, Walcott discussed the similarity between the culture of the Caribbean islands and the process of making poems: "Antillean art is this restoration of our shattered histories, our shards of vocabulary, our archipelago becoming a synonym for pieces broken off the original content. And this is the exact process of making poetry, or what should be called not its 'making' but its remaking." In what ways has Walcott demonstrated this process of "remaking" in both the content and style of "The River"?

Another Viewpoint: Society

Consider this viewpoint: "Poems about nature always express a concern, at times only implicit, about the state of the natural environment." Choose two or three poems about nature. To what extent do you think the writers of these poems are expressing a concern about the environment? To what extent do you think they are using nature as a backdrop to express ideas about human experience?

grammar poem

Rita Wong

Rita Wong was born in 1968 in Calgary, Alberta, where she grew up. She has worked as an archivist, a teacher of English as a second language, and a coordinator for the Alberta/Northwest Territories Network of Immigrant Women. Her writing has appeared in many literary magazines and in an anthology entitled *monkeypuzzle* (1998). Wong was the recipient of the 1998 Asian Canadian Writers' Workshop Emerging Writer Award for Poetry. In 2002, she received her doctoral degree from Simon Fraser University. Many people equate grammar with a dull, frustrating discipline. What is your working definition of *grammar* and what do you predict about a poem entitled "grammar poem"? What qualities of grammar have the potential to make it an interesting subject?

grammar poem

write around the absence, she said, show
its existence
demonstrate
its contours
how it
tastes
where
its edges
fall
hard
on my stuttering tongue, how its tones &
pictograms get flattened out by the
steamroller of the english language,

this is
the sound of
my chinese tongue
whispering: nei tou
gnaw ma? *no*
tones can
survive this
alphabet

live
half-submerged
in the salty home of
my mother tongue,
shallows

its etymology of
assimilation
tramples budding
memory into sawdusty
stereotypes, regimented capitals,
arrogant nouns & more nouns,
punctuated by subservient descriptors.
grammar is the dust on the streets waiting to be washed off
by immigrant cleaners or blown into your eyes by the wind. grammar
is the invisible net in the air, holding your words in place. grammar,
like wealth, belongs in the hands of the people who produce it.

Notes

tones different pitches used in a tonal language in which one word can be expressed several ways to mean very different things

pictograms written words presented as characters or graphics, such as those used in the Cantonese, Mandarin, and Japanese languages; alternatively, hieroglyphics used in the ancient Egyptian language. These are all in contrast to languages, such as Phoenician, Latin, and English, which use an alphabet.

etymology the origin and history of a word or of words, often presented in dictionaries, between the pronunciation and the definition of a word; from the Greek words *etumon*, meaning "the true sense of a word," and *logia*, meaning "study of or dealing with"

assimilation the process of taking over and incorporating into its own

Activities

1. With a partner, take turns reading the poem aloud. As you read, tell your partner what you are thinking as your eyes follow the words. Afterward, discuss how this "think-aloud" exercise gave you insight into your reading. Discuss any sections that were confusing to you. Share your insights with another pair by asking three questions about the poem.

2. In a group, copy out all the metaphors for language that you find in the poem. Have a class discussion on the use of these metaphors in the poem. Then choose a literary technique that interests you, such as personification or irony, and create your own shape poem.

Another Viewpoint: Critical Approaches

Post-colonial literary theory examines issues of imperialism and nationality. Do research into the meaning of the terms *post-colonial* and *imperialism*. What messages do you find in "grammar poem" that could be considered post-colonial? Explain whether or not you agree with the messages you have identified. Then, in a brief critical analysis, select four consecutive lines and analyze them from the perspective of the "politics" of language.

Hua Mu-lan, 1995, Lu Yanguang

Mu-lan

Anonymous

Translated by Hans H. Frankel

Folk ballads are narrative poems that have been orally transmitted among ordinary people, either through recitation or song. "Mu-lan," also known as "The Ballad of Mu-lan," was composed between 500 and 600 CE and tells a story set during a military campaign between Mu-lan's people, the Hsien-pi of what is now northern China, and their enemies, the nomadic Jou-jan. The poem would have been written down by a member of the court or the literati. The original Chinese poem comprises sixty-two lines, each of which consists generally of five Chinese "characters," or written symbols. This original poem was written in the form of Chinese poetry known as "yüeh-fu." This form was derived from folk songs, which usually were narrative poems accompanied by music. The poem was expanded into a novel near the end of China's late Ming Dynasty (1368–1644 CE). What kinds of stories get told in your own family year after year? Which of your family stories have been passed down from previous generations? How do you explain your family's interest in these stories?

Mu-lan

Tsiek tsiek and again *tsiek tsiek,*
Mu-lan weaves, facing the door.
You don't hear the shuttle's sound,
You only hear Daughter's sighs.
They ask Daughter who's in her heart,
They ask Daughter who's on her mind.
"No one is in Daughter's heart,
No one is on Daughter's mind.
Last night I saw the draft posters,
The Khan is calling many troops,   10
The army list is in twelve scrolls,
On every scroll there's Father's name.
Father has no grown-up son,
Mu-lan has no elder brother.
I want to buy a saddle and horse,
And serve in the army in Father's place."

In the East Market she buys a spirited horse,
In the West Market she buys a saddle,
In the South Market she buys a bridle,
In the North Market she buys a long whip.   20
At dawn she takes leave of Father and Mother,
In the evening camps on the Yellow River's bank.
She doesn't hear the sound of Father and Mother calling,
She only hears the Yellow River's flowing water cry *tsien tsien.*

At dawn she takes leave of the Yellow River,
In the evening she arrives at Black Mountain.
She doesn't hear the sound of Father and Mother calling,
She only hears Mount Yen's nomad horses cry *tsiu tsiu.*
She goes ten thousand miles on the business of war,
She crosses passes and mountains like flying.   30
Northern gusts carry the rattle of army pots,

Chilly light shines on iron armor.
Generals die in a hundred battles,
Stout soldiers return after ten years.

On her return she sees the Son of Heaven,
The Son of Heaven sits in the Splendid Hall.
He gives out promotions in twelve ranks
And prizes of a hundred thousand and more.
The Khan asks her what she desires.
"Mu-lan has no use for a minister's post.   40
I wish to ride a swift mount
To take me back to my home."

When Father and Mother hear Daughter is coming
They go outside the wall to meet her, leaning on each other.
When Younger Sister hears Elder Sister is coming
She fixes her rouge, facing the door.
When Little Brother hears Elder Sister is coming
He whets the knife, quick quick, for pig and sheep.
"I open the door to my east chamber,
I sit on my couch in the west room,   50
I take off my wartime gown
And put on my old-time clothes."
Facing the window she fixes her cloudlike hair,
Hanging up a mirror she dabs on yellow flower-powder.
She goes out the door and sees her comrades.
Her comrades are all amazed and perplexed.
Traveling together for twelve years
They didn't know Mu-lan was a girl.
"The he-hare's feet go hop and skip,
The she-hare's eyes are muddled and fuddled.   60
Two hares running side by side close to the ground,
How can they tell if I am he or she?"

Notes

Khan the provincial lord

Yellow River the second largest river in China, nearly 5,000 km long

Mount Yen's nomad horses the enemy cavalry

stout brave, bold, strong

Splendid Hall the most important temple of the ancient Chinese rulers

Son of Heaven the Emperor

yellow flower-powder yellow make-up, commonly used by nomadic women of Northern China to powder their foreheads

Activities

1. Mu-lan's military exploits are merely hinted at in the poem. Do you think this omission is meant to stimulate the reader to imagine the details of the battles? Or does it suggest that the essence of the poem lies elsewhere? Discuss your response to the poem in terms of its content and focus.

2. The Chinese version of "Mu-lan" has neither punctuation nor personal pronouns. The division of the poem into verses is also at the translator's discretion. With this in mind, enter the text of "Mu-lan" into a word-processing file and experiment with punctuation, pronouns, and verse divisions until you have a version that expresses the poem as you'd like it to be read. Exchange and discuss alternative versions in a group.

From

Beowulf

Anonymous

Translated by Seamus Heaney

Composed at some point between the eighth and tenth centuries CE, *Beowulf* is the oldest surviving poem written in Old English, a linguistic predecessor of modern English. An epic poem of more than 3,000 lines, *Beowulf* contains fictional (and probably some factual) events that occurred in the sixth century CE in the Germanic regions of Northern Europe. *Beowulf* is the story of the exploits and character of a renowned Scandinavian warrior and hero who travels across the sea to the land of the Danes to help the Danish King Hrothgar rid his country of a monster called Grendel. After battles with Grendel and Grendel's mother, Beowulf returns to his homeland, Geatland, where he rules as king for fifty years. The section below occurs before Beowulf's battle with Grendel. It is taken from a 1999 translation by Seamus Heaney, an Irish poet born in 1939 in Northern Ireland. Heaney is the recipient of numerous awards, including the Nobel Prize in Literature in 1995 and the Whitbread Book of the Year Award for this translation of *Beowulf*. What comes to mind when you read or hear the word *hero*? In what ways is a hero today similar to one from the distant past?

Beowulf and the Dragon, 1932, *Rockwell Kent*

From Beowulf

When he heard about Grendel, Hygelac's thane
was on home ground, over in Geatland.
There was no one else like him alive.
In his day, he was the mightiest man on earth,
high-born and powerful. He ordered a boat
that would ply the waves. He announced his plan:
to sail the swan's road and search out that king,
the famous prince who needed defenders.
Nobody tried to keep him from going,
no elder denied him, dear as he was to them.   10
Instead, they inspected omens and spurred
his ambition to go, whilst he moved about
like the leader he was, enlisting men,
the best he could find; with fourteen others
the warrior boarded the boat as captain,
a canny pilot along coast and currents.
Time went by, the boat was on water,
in close under the cliffs.
Men climbed eagerly up the gangplank,
sand churned in surf, warriors loaded   20
a cargo of weapons, shining war-gear
in the vessel's hold, then heaved out,
away with a will in their wood-weathered ship.
Over the waves, with the wind behind her
and foam at her neck, she flew like a bird
until her curved prow had covered the distance
and on the following day, at the due hour,
those seafarers sighted land,
sunlit cliffs, sheer crags
and looming headlands, the landfall they sought.   30

It was the end of their voyage and the Geats vaulted
over the side, out on to the sand,
and moored their ship. There was a clash of mail
and a thresh of gear. They thanked God
for that easy crossing on a calm sea.

When the watchman on the wall, the Shieldings' lookout
whose job it was to guard the sea-cliffs,
saw shields glittering on the gangplank
and battle-equipment being unloaded
he had to find out who and what   40
the arrivals were. So he rode to the shore,
this horseman of Hrothgar's, and challenged them
in formal terms, flourishing his spear:

"What kind of men are you who arrive
rigged out for combat in coats of mail,
sailing here over the sea-lanes
in your steep-hulled boat? I have been stationed
as lookout on this coast for a long time.
My job is to watch the waves for raiders,
any danger to the Danish shore.   50
Never before has a force under arms
disembarked so openly—not bothering to ask
if the sentries allowed them safe passage
or the clan had consented. Nor have I seen
a mightier man-at-arms on this earth
than the one standing here: unless I am mistaken,
he is truly noble. This is no mere
hanger-on in a hero's armour.
So now, before you fare inland
as interlopers, I have to be informed   60
about who you are and where you hail from.
Outsiders from across the water,
I say it again: the sooner you tell
where you come from and why, the better."

The leader of the troop unlocked his word-hoard;
the distinguished one delivered this answer:
"We belong by birth to the Geat people
and owe allegiance to Lord Hygelac.
In his day, my father was a famous man,
a noble warrior-lord named Ecgtheow.   70
He outlasted many a long winter
and went on his way. All over the world
men wise in counsel continue to remember him.
We come in good faith to find your lord
and nation's shield, the son of Halfdane.
Give us the right advice and direction.
We have arrived here on a great errand
to the lord of the Danes, and I believe therefore
there should be nothing hidden or withheld between us.
So tell us if what we have heard is true   80
about this threat, whatever it is,
this danger abroad in the dark nights,
this corpse-maker mongering death
in the Shieldings' country. I come to proffer
my wholehearted help and counsel.
I can show the wise Hrothgar a way
to defeat his enemy and find respite—
if any respite is to reach him, ever.
I can calm the turmoil and terror in his mind.
Otherwise, he must endure woes   90
and live with grief for as long as his hall
stands at the horizon, on its high ground."

Undaunted, sitting astride his horse,
the coast-guard answered, "Anyone with gumption
and a sharp mind will take the measure
of two things: what's said and what's done.

I believe what you have told me: that you are a troop
loyal to our king. So come ahead
with your arms and your gear, and I will guide you.
What's more, I'll order my own comrades   100
on their word of honour to watch your boat
down there on the strand—keep her safe
in her fresh tar, until the time comes
for her curved prow to preen on the waves
and bear this hero back to Geatland.
May one so valiant and venturesome
come unharmed through the clash of battle."

Notes

Beowulf the son of King Hygelac's sister. Foremost among the Geat warriors, Beowulf hears the story of Grendel from a sea captain who visits King Hygelac's hall.

Grendel a night stalker, the "Death shadow," a troll-like creature who makes his lair among the sea inlets and coastal marshes. This monster, who hates all humans and all joy, hears the music and laughter from King Hrothgar's mead hall and comes each night, killing the best of the King's thanes. No sword could cut this monster's hide. No Danish champion could be found with the strength to subdue this creature.

Hygelac King of the Geats, uncle to Beowulf

Geatland a geographic area; in modern times southern Sweden

swan's road this phrase means "the sea"; it is an example of the Old English and Old Norse poetic technique known as a "kenning," in which a compound word is used instead of a single noun to mean one thing: other examples are "oar-steed" for a ship and "whale's road" for the sea

Shieldings the Danes

Hrothgar a great warrior and king of the Danes

Ecgtheow Beowulf's father. As a young man, Ecgtheow was embroiled in a blood feud and killed a man. He and his young wife had to leave Geatland and found a loyal friend in the Danish King Hrothgar. Beowulf was born at the Danish Court. It was King Hrothgar who paid compensation to the family of the man Ecgtheow had killed, thus allowing Ecgtheow and his family to return to Geatland. When Beowulf, as a young man, heard of King Hrothgar's trouble with the monster Grendel, he felt an obligation to help this friend and repay his father's debt to the Danish king.

Halfdane King Hrothgar's father

Hrothgar's hall the great mead hall of Hrothgar. The hall was called Heorot, the Hart, because great antlers of a stag graced its gable. The size and magnificence of the hall were known far and wide. Ironically, instead of a place of joy and celebrations, the great hall became a place of terror because of Grendel's attacks.

Activities

1. What impression of Beowulf are you left with after reading this exerpt? In a journal entry, describe the warrior by referring to what others say about him and what he himself says in the passage. In your entry, consider what you were able to predict about the Anglo-Saxon ideal of a hero. Does Beowulf seem like a war-monger or a peace-maker?

2. Find a definition of epic poetry and discuss some of the elements and characteristics of that form evident in this excerpt from *Beowulf*. Describe what you were able to predict from this passage in terms of the themes in *Beowulf* that pertain to all epic poems.

Another Viewpoint: Society

The events in *Beowulf* could be compared with current strife-torn political situations. Complete some research on contemporary wars, their causes, and their aftermaths. Is there some universal message that endures in this epic poem to address the feuding and anguish that exist in many areas of the world today? Present the findings of your research as a multimedia presentation to your class.

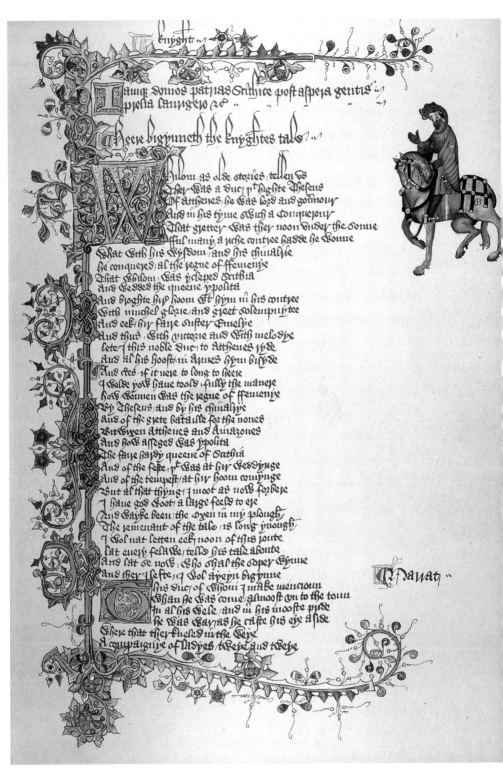

Ellesmere manuscript, c. 1410

From

The Canterbury Tales: General Prologue

Geoffrey Chaucer

Translated into modern English by Nevill Coghill

Geoffrey Chaucer, the most important writer of Middle English, is believed to have been born in London, England, circa 1340. At the age of seventeen, he became a page at court and was associated with the royal household for the rest of his life, both as a business person and a poet. In 1359, Chaucer served in the English army during its invasion of France, where he was captured and held for ransom. He was given a life pension in 1367 and went on diplomatic missions to France and Italy. On one trip to Italy, he discovered the works of Dante, Boccaccio, and Petrarch, which greatly influenced his own writing. Chaucer worked on his masterpiece *The Canterbury Tales* from 1387 until his death in 1400. He was buried in the Poets' Corner of Westminster Abbey, where a monument was erected to him in 1555. *The Canterbury Tales*, which comprises 17,000 lines, consists of stories told by pilgrims travelling to the shrine of Saint Thomas Becket in Canterbury Cathedral. In this excerpt, Chaucer's original Middle English text appears on the left-hand pages, with the modern English translation on the facing, right-hand pages. It is interesting to note that, starting at line 57, each Middle English line of verse cannot necessarily be translated into one line in modern English; therefore, the remaining lines of this excerpt do not have a one-to-one correspondence. What other "on-the-road" narratives have you come across in print or on the screen? What elements do these narratives share? How are these elements used to achieve specific effects on the reader or viewer?

From The Canterbury Tales: General Prologue

Middle English

Here bygynneth the Book of the Tales of Caunterbury.

    Whan that Aprill with his shoures soote
The droghte of March hath perced to the roote,
And bathed every veyne in swich licour
Of which vertu engendred is the flour;
Whan Zephirus eek with his sweete breeth
Inspired hath in every holt and heeth
The tendre croppes, and the yonge sonne
Hath in the Ram his halfe cours yronne,
And smale foweles maken melodye,
That slepen al the nyght with open eye—   10
So priketh hem nature in hir corages—
Thanne longen folk to goon on pilgrimages,
And palmeres for to seken straunge strondes,
To ferne halwes, kowthe in sondry londes;
And specially from every shires ende
Of Engelond to Caunterbury they wende,
The hooly blisful martir for to seke
That hem hath holpen whan that they were seeke.
    Bifil that in that seson on a day
In Southwerk at the Tabard as I lay   20
Redy to wenden on my pilgrymage
To Caunterbury with ful devout corage,
At nyght was come into that hostelrye
Wel nyne and twenty in a compaignye
Of sondry folk, by aventure yfalle
In felaweship, and pilgrimes were they alle,
That toward Caunterbury wolden ryde.
The chambres and the stables weren wyde,
And wel we weren esed atte beste.

Here begins the Book of the Tales of Canterbury. Modern
English

    When in April the sweet showers fall
And pierce the drought of March to the root, and all
The veins are bathed in liquor of such power
As brings about the engendering of the flower,
When also Zephyrus with his sweet breath
Exhales an air in every grove and heath
Upon the tender shoots, and the young sun
His half-course in the sign of the Ram has run
And the small fowl are making melody
That sleep away the night with open eye   10
(So nature pricks them and their heart engages)
Then people long to go on pilgrimages
And palmers long to seek the stranger strands
Of far-off saints, hallowed in sundry lands,
And specially, from every shire's end
Of England, down to Canterbury they wend
To seek the holy blissful martyr, quick
To give his help to them when they were sick.
    It happened in that season that one day
In Southwark, at The Tabard, as I lay   20
Ready to go on pilgrimage and start
For Canterbury, most devout at heart,
At night there came into that hostelry
Some nine and twenty in a company
Of sundry folk happening then to fall
In fellowship, and they were pilgrims all
That towards Canterbury meant to ride.
The rooms and stables of the inn were wide;
They made us easy, all was of the best.

And shortly, whan the sonne was to reste, 30
So hadde I spoken with hem everichon
That I was of hir felaweship anon,
And made forward erly for to ryse,
To take oure wey ther as I yow devyse.
    But nathelees, whil I have tyme and space,
Er that I ferther in this tale pace,
Me thynketh it acordaunt to resoun
To telle yow al the condicioun
Of ech of hem, so as it semed me,
And whiche they weren, and of what degree, 40
And eek in what array that they were inne;
And at a knyght than wol I first bigynne.

THE KNYGHT

    A KNYGHT ther was, and that a worthy man,
That fro the tyme that he first bigan
To riden out, he loved chivalrie,
Trouthe and honour, fredom and curteisie.
Ful worthy was he in his lordes werre,
And therto hadde he riden, no man ferre,
As wel in cristendom as in hethenesse,
And evere honoured for his worthynesse. 50
    At Alisaundre he was whan it was wonne.
Ful ofte tyme he hadde the bord bigonne
Aboven alle nacions in Pruce.
In Lettow hadde he reysed and in Ruce,
No Cristen man so ofte of his degree.
In Gernade at the seege eek hadde he be
Of Algezir, and riden in Belmarye.
At Lyeys was he and at Satalye,
Whan they were wonne; and in the Grete See
At many a noble armee hadde he be. 60

And, briefly, when the sun had gone to rest,
I'd spoken to them all upon the trip
And was soon one with them in fellowship,
Pledged to rise early and to take the way
To Canterbury, as you heard me say.

    But none the less, while I have time and space,
Before my story takes a further pace,
It seems a reasonable thing to say
What their condition was, the full array
Of each of them, as it appeared to me,
According to profession and degree,   40
And what apparel they were riding in;
And at a Knight I therefore will begin.

THE KNIGHT

    There was a Knight, a most distinguished man,
Who from the day on which he first began
To ride abroad had followed chivalry,
Truth, honour, generousness and courtesy.
He had done nobly in his sovereign's war
And ridden into battle, no man more,
As well in Christian as in heathen places,
And ever honoured for his noble graces.   50
When we took Alexandria, he was there.
He often sat at table in the chair
Of honour, above all nations, when in Prussia.
In Lithuania he had ridden, and Russia,
No Christian man so often, of his rank.
When, in Granada, Algeciras sank
Under assault, he had been there, and in
North Africa, raiding Benamarin;
In Anatolia he had been as well
And fought when Ayas and Attalia fell,   60

At mortal batailles hadde he been fiftene,
And foughten for oure feith at Tramyssene
In lystes thries, and ay slayn his foo.
This ilke worthy knyght hadde been also
Somtyme with the lord of Palatye
Agayn another hethen in Turkye;
And everemoore he hadde a sovereyn prys.
And though that he were worthy, he was wys,
And of his port as meeke as is a mayde.
He nevere yet no vileynye ne sayde 70
In al his lyf unto no maner wight.
He was a verray, parfit gentil knyght.
    But for to tellen yow of his array,
His hors weren goode, but he was nat gay.
Of fustian he wered a gypoun
Al bismotered with his habergeoun,
For he was late ycome from his viage,
And wente for to doon his pilgrymage.

For all along the Mediterranean coast
He had embarked with many a noble host.
In fifteen mortal battles he had been
And jousted for our faith at Tramissene
Thrice in the lists, and always killed his man.
This same distinguished knight had led the van
Once with the Bey of Balat, doing work
For him against another heathen Turk;
He was of sovereign value in all eyes.
And though so much distinguished, he was wise   70
And in his bearing modest as a maid.
He never yet a boorish thing had said
In all his life to any, come what might;
He was a true, a perfect gentle-knight.
  Speaking of his equipment, he possessed
Fine horses, but he was not gaily dressed.
He wore a fustian tunic stained and dark
With smudges where his armour had left mark;
Just home from service, he had joined our ranks
To do his pilgrimage and render thanks.   80

Notes

liquor a potent liquid

engendering bringing about; giving rise to

Zephyrus the god or personification of the West Wind in classical mythology

heath a flat, open area of wasteland

Ram the astrological sign of Aries

pricks awakens, incites

palmers pilgrims returning from the Holy Land, wearing a cross of palm branches

stranger strands foreign shores

sundry various; from the Old English word *syndrig*, meaning "separate"

shire a group of counties in England, such as Devonshire and Hampshire

wend go, travel

the holy, blissful martyr Saint Thomas Becket, an English bishop who was murdered and buried in Canterbury Cathedral

Southwark a town across from London on the Thames River

The Tabard the Tabard Inn

array clothing

degree social rank

Alexandria a city in northern Egypt, captured by Christians in 1365

Prussia an area of northeastern Europe, conquered by the Teutonic Knights in the thirteenth century

Granada a state in Spain

Algeciras a city in Granada, Spain

Benamarin a Moorish kingdom in North Africa

Anatolia the Asian part of Turkey

Ayas, Attalia cities in Asia Minor, captured by the Crusaders in 1361 and 1367, respectively

Tramissene a Moorish kingdom in North Africa

Bey of Balat the lord of a city in Asia Minor

sovereign great

fustian made of sturdy cotton and linen fabric; originally referring to cloth from El Fostat, a district of Cairo, Egypt

Activities

1. Reread the first eleven lines of the poem and discuss them in a group. What might Chaucer's reasons have been for writing opening lines filled with references common to love lyrics of his time? What symbolic parallel between spring awakening and setting off on a pilgrimage might the author be suggesting? How do these lines "set up" what follows?

2. Discuss Chaucer's method of characterizing the Knight. What does Chaucer's description reveal about his own values and the values of his society? Given the historical context of this work and its courtly audience, why is it not surprising that the author focuses on the "full array" of the pilgrims, their "profession and degree, / And what apparel they were riding in"?

Another Viewpoint: Literary Modes and Forms

Geoffrey Chaucer wrote his works at the end of the medieval era. In small groups, choose a medieval romance, such as one of the King Arthur legends, the story of Tristan and Isolde (with various spellings such as Isolt and Isolde), or the story of Sir Gawain and the Green Knight, and complete some research on it. Find out some background information. Present your findings to the class, outlining the key characteristics of your text. Then discuss with the class the following: in what way was the medieval romance well suited to the medieval era? What variations on these romances do we find in contemporary literature?

Sonnet 116

William Shakespeare

William Shakespeare was born in 1564 in Stratford-upon-Avon, England. Shakespeare's 154 sonnets, which were printed in 1609, were probably written in the 1590s. They are considered the most personal works by Shakespeare, who died on his birthday in 1616, at the age of fifty-two. Why do you think that love is the most celebrated emotion in poetry, song, and story? Does the majority of literature with which you are familiar present a realistic or an idealized picture of love?

Sonnet 116

Let me not to the marriage of true minds
Admit impediments; love is not love
Which alters when it alteration finds,
Or bends with the remover to remove.
O no, it is an ever-fixed mark
That looks on tempests and is never shaken;
It is the star to every wand'ring bark,
Whose worth's unknown, although his highth be taken.
Love's not Time's fool, though rosy lips and cheeks
Within his bending sickle's compass come;
Love alters not with his brief hours and weeks,
But bears it out even to the edge of doom.
    If this be error and upon me proved,
    I never writ, nor no man ever loved.

Notes

impediments in this instance, bars or hindrances to a legal marriage

the remover one who changes his mind or position

ever-fixed mark a mark on land used by mariners to fix their position at sea; for example, a church steeple or high cliff

the star in this instance, the North Star

wand'ring bark a ship or boat that has lost its way

highth be taken measuring the elevation of stars above the horizon for purposes of navigation

fool plaything; alternatively, a court jester

sickle an implement consisting of a curved metal blade attached to a short wooden handle. Death is often portrayed as carrying a sickle.

compass the circular range of a sickle, cutting down grass

bears survives

doom death or Judgment Day

upon against

Activities

1. Shakespeare often uses the couplet at the end of a sonnet to summarize the ideas he has developed in the preceding twelve lines. Is this true of "Sonnet 116"? If not, what do you think is the function of this couplet in relation to the rest of the sonnet?

2. Go through the sonnet, making note of all the verbs, adjectives, and nouns that are repeated two or more times. (If the same root word is used, count it as a repetition.) Consider what other synonyms could have been used. Why, in each case, do you think Shakespeare chose to repeat the same word? Assess how this study of the sonnet's diction has contributed to your understanding of the poet's style.

Another Viewpoint: Literary Modes and Forms

Research the poetic form known as the *sonnet*, investigating the characteristics of the Italian (Petrarchan) and the English (Shakespearean) sonnet. Comment on the rhyme, rhythm, and structure of each form. Then demonstrate how Shakespeare's use of the conventional structure and organization of the English sonnet contributes to the theme and the coherence of "Sonnet 116."

A Poison Tree

William Blake

About the Visual   William Blake was born in 1757, in London, England. Although he received little formal education, he became an avid reader of Latin and Greek classical literature and the Bible. As a fifteen-year-old, Blake was apprenticed to an engraver and later set up his own engraving business. Blake engraved his poems on illustrated backgrounds, so that they looked like handwriting rather than type. He died in 1827. This poem is about anger. How well are you able to hide your feelings when you are angry? To what extent do you think that it is better to express rather than repress feelings such as anger? What do you think are acceptable and unacceptable methods of expressing anger?

Activities

1. In virtually every culture, trees have symbolic significance. With the class, make a list of everything you can think of that a tree might symbolize. In a discussion, explore which of these symbols have positive associations and which have negative ones.

2. Read the poem aloud several times, considering how the form of this poem enhances the meaning. Describe the following features, giving specific examples and reasons for how they affect your interpretation and reaction to the poem: rhyme scheme, rhythm and metre, organization into stanzas, language, and syntax.

1794, copperplate engraving, 16 x 14 cm ▶

A POISON TREE.

I was angry with my friend;
I told my wrath, my wrath did end.
I was angry with my foe:
I told it not. my wrath did grow.

And I waterd it in fears,
Night & morning with my tears;
And I sunned it with smiles,
And with soft deceitful wiles.

And it grew both day and night,
Till it bore an apple bright.
And my foe beheld it shine,
And he knew that it was mine.

And into my garden stole,
When the night had veild the pole;
In the morning glad I see;
My foe outstretchd beneath the tree.

The Watersnakes Appear, 1877, Gustave Doré

The Rime of the Ancient Mariner

Samuel Taylor Coleridge

Poet, critic, and philosopher Samuel Taylor Coleridge was born in 1772. Although he was a brilliant scholar, he dropped out of university and joined the cavalry. By 1797, Coleridge had become a close friend of William Wordsworth, with whom he published *Lyrical Ballads*, in which "The Rime of the Ancient Mariner" first appeared. This collection of poetry is generally considered the beginning of the English Romantic Movement. Later, Coleridge published *Biographia Literaria*, the most significant book of criticism of its time. He died in London in 1834. How important is it to consider people's intentions when judging their acts? Why does or doesn't it matter whether someone behaves maliciously or thoughtlessly, if the consequences are the same?

The Rime of the Ancient Mariner

Facile credo, plures esse Naturas invisibiles quam visibiles in rerum universitate. Sed horum omnium familiam quis nobis enarrabit? et gradus et cognationes et discrimina et singulorum munera? Quid agunt? quae loca habitant? Horum rerum notitiam semper ambivit ingenium humanum, nunquam attigit. Juvat, interea, non diffiteor, quandoque in animo, tanquam in tabula, majoris et melioris mundi imaginem contemplari: ne mens assuefacta hodiernae vitae minutiis se contrahat nimis, et tota subsidat in pusillas cogitationes. Sed veritati interea invigilandum est, modusque servandus, ut certa ab incertis, diem a nocte, distinguamus. (T. Burnet, *Archaeol. Phil.*)

ARGUMENT

How a ship, having first sailed to the Equator, was driven by storms to the cold Country towards the South Pole; how the Ancient Mariner cruelly and in contempt of the laws of hospitality killed a Seabird and how he was followed by many and strange Judgments: and in what manner he came back to his own Country.

PART I

An ancient Mariner meeteth three Gallants bidden to a wedding feast, and detaineth one.

It is an ancient Mariner,
And he stoppeth one of three.
—"By thy long gray beard and glittering eye,
Now wherefore stopp'st thou me?

The Bridegroom's doors are opened wide,
And I am next of kin;
The guests are met, the feast is set:
May'st hear the merry din."

He holds him with his skinny hand,
"There was a ship," quoth he.   10
"Hold off! unhand me, graybeard loon!"
Eftsoons his hand dropt he.

He holds him with his glittering eye—
The Wedding-Guest stood still,
And listens like a three years' child:
The Mariner hath his will.

The Wedding-Guest sat on a stone;
He cannot choose but hear;
And thus spake on that ancient man,
The bright-eyed Mariner.   20

"The ship was cheered, the harbour cleared,
Merrily did we drop
Below the kirk, below the hill,
Below the lighthouse top.

The Sun came up upon the left,
Out of the sea came he!
And he shone bright, and on the right
Went down into the sea.

Higher and higher every day,
Till over the mast at noon—"   30
The Wedding-Guest here beat his breast,
For he heard the loud bassoon.

The bride hath paced into the hall,
Red as a rose is she;
Nodding their heads before her goes
The merry minstrelsy.

The Wedding-Guest he beat his breast,
Yet he cannot choose but hear;
And thus spake on that ancient man,
The bright-eyed Mariner.   40

"And now the STORM-BLAST came, and he
Was tyrannous and strong;
He struck with his o'ertaking wings,
And chased us south along.

With sloping masts and dipping prow,
As who pursued with yell and blow
Still treads the shadow of his foe,
And forward bends his head,
The ship drove fast, loud roared the blast,
And southward aye we fled.   50

And now there came both mist and snow,
And it grew wondrous cold:
And ice, mast-high, came floating by,
As green as emerald.

And through the drifts the snowy clifts
Did send a dismal sheen:
Nor shapes of men nor beasts we ken—
The ice was all between.

The ice was here, the ice was there,
The ice was all around: 60
It cracked and growled, and roared and howled,
Like noises in a swound!

At length did cross an Albatross,
Thorough the fog it came;
As if it had been a Christian soul,
We hailed it in God's name.

It ate the food it ne'er had eat,
And round and round it flew.
The ice did split with a thunder-fit;
The helmsman steered us through! 70

And a good south wind sprung up behind;
The Albatross did follow,
And every day, for food or play,
Came to the mariners' hollo!

In mist or cloud, on mast or shroud,
It perched for vespers nine;
Whiles all the night, through fog-smoke white,
Glimmered the white Moon-shine."

"God save thee, ancient Mariner!
From the fiends, that plague thee thus!— 80
Why look'st thou so?"—With my cross-bow
I shot the ALBATROSS.

PART II

The Sun now rose upon the right:
Out of the sea came he,
Still hid in mist, and on the left
Went down into the sea.

And the good south wind still blew behind,
But no sweet bird did follow,
Nor any day for food or play
Came to the mariners' hollo! 90

His shipmates cry out against the ancient Mariner for killing the bird of good luck.

And I had done a hellish thing,
And it would work 'em woe:
For all averred, I had killed the bird
That made the breeze to blow.
Ah wretch! said they, the bird to slay,
That made the breeze to blow!

But when the fog cleared off, they justify the same, and thus make themselves accomplices in the crime.

Nor dim nor red, like God's own head,
The glorious Sun uprist:
Then all averred, I had killed the bird
That brought the fog and mist.   100
'Twas right, said they, such birds to slay,
That bring the fog and mist.

The fair breeze continues; the ship enters the Pacific Ocean, and sails northward, even till it reaches the Line.

The fair breeze blew, the white foam flew,
The furrow followed free;
We were the first that ever burst
Into that silent sea.

The ship hath been suddenly becalmed.

Down dropped the breeze, the sails dropped down,
'Twas sad as sad could be;
And we did speak only to break
The silence of the sea!   110

All in a hot and copper sky,
The bloody Sun, at noon,
Right up above the mast did stand,
No bigger than the Moon.

Day after day, day after day,
We stuck, nor breath nor motion;
As idle as a painted ship
Upon a painted ocean.

And the Albatross
begins to be avenged.

Water, water, everywhere,
And all the boards did shrink;   120
Water, water, everywhere,
Nor any drop to drink.

The very deep did rot: O Christ!
That ever this should be!
Yea, slimy things did crawl with legs
Upon the slimy sea.

About, about, in reel and rout
The death-fires danced at night;
The water, like a witch's oils,
Burnt green, and blue and white.   130

A Spirit had followed
them; one of the
invisible inhabitants of
this planet, neither
departed souls nor
angels; concerning
whom the learned Jew,
Josephus, and the
Platonic
Constantinopolitan,
Michael Psellus, may
be consulted. They are
very numerous, and
there is no climate or
element without one
or more.

And some in dreams assurèd were
Of the Spirit that plagued us so;
Nine fathom deep he had followed us
From the land of mist and snow.

And every tongue, through utter drought,
Was withered at the root;
We could not speak, no more than if
We had been choked with soot.

The shipmates, in their
sore distress, would
fain throw the whole
guilt on the ancient
Mariner: in sign
whereof they hang the
dead sea bird round his
neck.

Ah! well-a-day! what evil looks
Had I from old and young!   140
Instead of the cross, the Albatross
About my neck was hung.

Part III

There passed a weary time. Each throat
Was parched, and glazed each eye.
A weary time! a weary time!
How glazed each weary eye,

The ancient Mariner beholdeth a sign in the element afar off.

When looking westward, I beheld
A something in the sky.

At first it seemed a little speck,
And then it seemed a mist; 150
It moved and moved, and took at last
A certain shape, I wist.

A speck, a mist, a shape, I wist!
And still it neared and neared:
As if it dodged a water-sprite,
It plunged and tacked and veered.

At its nearer approach, it seemeth him to be a ship; and at a dear ransom he freeth his speech from the bonds of thirst.

With throats unslaked, with black lips baked,
We could nor laugh nor wail;
Through utter drought all dumb we stood!
I bit my arm, I sucked the blood, 160
And cried, A sail! a sail!

With throats unslaked, with black lips baked,
Agape they heard me call:

A flash of joy;

Gramercy! they for joy did grin,
And all at once their breath drew in,
As they were drinking all.

And horror follows. For can it be a ship that comes onward without wind or tide?

See! see! (I cried) she tacks no more!
Hither to work us weal;
Without a breeze, without a tide,
She steadies with upright keel! 170

The western wave was all aflame.
The day was well nigh done!
Almost upon the western wave
Rested the broad bright Sun;
When that strange shape drove suddenly
Betwixt us and the Sun.

It seemeth him but the skeleton of a ship.

And straight the Sun was flecked with bars,
(Heaven's Mother send us grace!)
As if through a dungeon-grate he peered
With broad and burning face.   180

And its ribs are seen as bars on the face of the setting Sun.

Alas! (thought I, and my heart beat loud)
How fast she nears and nears!
Are those *her* sails that glance in the Sun,
Like restless gossameres?

The Specter-Woman and her Deathmate, and no other on board the skeleton ship.

Are those *her* ribs through which the Sun
Did peer, as through a grate?
And is that Woman all her crew?
Is that a DEATH? and are there two?
Is DEATH that woman's mate?

Like vessel, like crew!

Her lips were red, *her* looks were free,   190
Her locks were yellow as gold:
Her skin was as white as leprosy,
The Night-mare LIFE-IN-DEATH was she,
Who thicks man's blood with cold.

Death and Life-in-Death have diced for the ship's crew, and she (the latter) winneth the ancient Mariner.

The naked hulk alongside came,
And the twain were casting dice;
"The game is done! I've won! I've won!"
Quoth she, and whistles thrice.

No twilight within the
courts of the Sun.

The Sun's rim dips; the stars rush out:
At one stride comes the dark; 200
With far-heard whisper, o'er the sea,
Off shot the spectre-bark.

At the rising of the
Moon,

We listened and looked sideways up!
Fear at my heart, as at a cup,
My life-blood seemed to sip!
The stars were dim, and thick the night,
The steersman's face by his lamp gleamed white;
From the sails the dew did drip—
Till clomb above the eastern bar
The hornèd Moon, with one bright star 210
Within the nether tip.

One after another,

One after one, by the star-dogged Moon,
Too quick for groan or sigh,
Each turned his face with a ghastly pang,
And cursed me with his eye.

His shipmates drop
down dead.

Four times fifty living men,
(And I heard nor sigh nor groan)
With heavy thump, a lifeless lump,
They dropped down one by one.

But Life-in-Death
begins her work on the
ancient Mariner.

The souls did from their bodies fly— 220
They fled to bliss or woe!
And every soul, it passed me by,
Like the whizz of my cross-bow!

Part IV

The Wedding-Guest
feareth that a Spirit is
talking to him;

"I fear thee, ancient Mariner!
I fear thy skinny hand!
And thou art long, and lank, and brown,
As is the ribbed sea-sand.

I fear thee and thy glittering eye,
And thy skinny hand, so brown."—
Fear not, fear not, thou Wedding-Guest!   230
This body dropped not down.

Alone, alone, all, all alone,
Alone on a wide wide sea!
And never a saint took pity on
My soul in agony.

The many men, so beautiful!
And they all dead did lie:
And a thousand thousand slimy things
Lived on; and so did I.

I looked upon the rotting sea,   240
And drew my eyes away;
I looked upon the rotting deck,
And there the dead men lay.

I looked to heaven, and tried to pray;
But or ever a prayer had gushed,
A wicked whisper came, and made
My heart as dry as dust.

I closed my lids, and kept them close,
And the balls like pulses beat;
For the sky and the sea, and the sea and the sky   250
Lay like a load on my weary eye,
And the dead were at my feet.

The cold sweat melted from their limbs,
Nor rot nor reek did they:
The look with which they looked on me
Had never passed away.

But the ancient Mariner assureth him of his bodily life, and proceedeth to relate his horrible penance.

He despiseth the creatures of the calm,

And envieth that they should live, and so many lie dead.

But the curse liveth for him in the eye of the dead men.

An orphan's curse would drag to hell
A spirit from on high;
But oh! more horrible than that
Is the curse in a dead man's eye!   260
Seven days, seven nights, I saw that curse,
And yet I could not die.

In his loneliness and
fixedness he yearneth
towards the journeying
Moon, and the stars
that still sojourn, yet
still move onward; and
everywhere the blue
sky belongs to them,
and is their appointed
rest, and their native
country and their own
natural homes,
which they enter
unannounced, as lords
that are certainly
expected and yet there
is a silent joy at their
arrival.

The moving Moon went up the sky,
And no where did abide:
Softly she was going up,
And a star or two beside—

Her beams bemocked the sultry main,
Like April hoar-frost spread;
But where the ship's huge shadow lay,
The charmèd water burnt alway   270
A still and awful red.

By the light of the
Moon he beholdeth
God's creatures of the
great calm.

Beyond the shadow of the ship,
I watched the watersnakes:
They moved in tracks of shining white,
And when they reared, the elfish light
Fell off in hoary flakes.

Within the shadow of the ship
I watched their rich attire:
Blue, glossy green, and velvet black,
They coiled and swam; and every track   280
Was a flash of golden fire.

Their beauty and their
happiness.

O happy living things! no tongue
Their beauty might declare:
A spring of love gushed from my heart,

He blesseth them in
his heart.

And I blessed them unaware:
Sure my kind saint took pity on me,
And I blessed them unaware.

The spell begins to break.

The self-same moment I could pray;
And from my neck so free
The Albatross fell off, and sank   290
Like lead into the sea.

PART V

Oh sleep! it is a gentle thing,
Beloved from pole to pole!
To Mary Queen the praise be given!
She sent the gentle sleep from Heaven,
That slid into my soul.

By grace of the holy Mother, the ancient Mariner is refreshed with rain

The silly buckets on the deck,
That had so long remained,
I dreamt that they were filled with dew;
And when I awoke, it rained.   300

My lips were wet, my throat was cold,
My garments all were dank;
Sure I had drunken in my dreams,
And still my body drank.

I moved, and could not feel my limbs:
I was so light—almost
I thought that I had died in sleep,
And was a blessèd ghost.

He heareth sounds and seeth strange sights and commotions in the sky and the element.

And soon I heard a roaring wind:
It did not come anear;   310
But with its sound it shook the sails,
That were so thin and sere.

The upper air burst into life!
And a hundred fire-flags sheen,
To and fro they were hurried about!
And to and fro, and in and out,
The wan stars danced between.

And the coming wind did roar more loud,
And the sails did sigh like sedge;
And the rain poured down from one black cloud; 320
The Moon was at its edge.

The thick black cloud was cleft, and still
The Moon was at its side:
Like waters shot from some high crag,
The lightning fell with never a jag,
A river steep and wide.

The bodies of the
ship's crew are
inspirited, and the ship
moves on;

The loud wind never reached the ship,
Yet now the ship moved on!
Beneath the lightning and the Moon
The dead men gave a groan.   330

They groaned, they stirred, they all uprose,
Nor spake, nor moved their eyes;
It had been strange, even in a dream,
To have seen those dead men rise.

The helmsman steered, the ship moved on;
Yet never a breeze up-blew;
The mariners all 'gan work the ropes,
Where they were wont to do;
They raised their limbs like lifeless tools—
We were a ghastly crew.   340

The body of my brother's son
Stood by me, knee to knee:
The body and I pulled at one rope,
But he said nought to me.

But not by the souls of the men, nor by demons of earth or middle air, but by a blessed troop of angelic spirits, sent down by the invocation of the guardian saint.

"I fear thee, ancient Mariner!"
Be calm, thou Wedding-Guest!
'Twas not those souls that fled in pain,
Which to their corses came again,
But a troop of spirits blest:

For when it dawned—they dropped their arms,   350
And clustered round the mast;
Sweet sounds rose slowly through their mouths,
And from their bodies passed.

Around, around, flew each sweet sound,
Then darted to the Sun;
Slowly the sounds came back again,
Now mixed, now one by one.

Sometimes a-dropping from the sky
I heard the sky-lark sing;
Sometimes all little birds that are,   360
How they seemed to fill the sea and air
With their sweet jargoning!

And now 'twas like all instruments,
Now like a lonely flute;
And now it is an angel's song,
That makes the heavens be mute.

It ceased; yet still the sails made on
A pleasant noise till noon,
A noise like of a hidden brook
In the leafy month of June,   370
That to the sleeping woods all night
Singeth a quiet tune.

Till noon we quietly sailed on,
Yet never a breeze did breathe:
Slowly and smoothly went the ship,
Moved onward from beneath.

The lonesome Spirit from the South Pole carries on the ship as far as the Line, in obedience to the angelic troop, but still requireth vengeance.

Under the keel nine fathom deep,
From the land of mist and snow,
The spirit slid: and it was he
That made the ship to go.   380
The sails at noon left off their tune,
And the ship stood still also.

The Sun, right up above the mast,
Had fixed her to the ocean:
But in a minute she 'gan stir,
With a short uneasy motion—
Backwards and forwards half her length
With a short uneasy motion.

Then like a pawing horse let go,
She made a sudden bound: 390
It flung the blood into my head,
And I fell down in a swound.

The Polar Spirit's fellow demons, the invisible inhabitants of the element, take part in his wrong; and two of them relate, one to the other, that penance long and heavy for the ancient Mariner hath been accorded to the Polar Spirit, who returneth southward.

How long in that same fit I lay,
I have not to declare;
But ere my living life returned,
I heard and in my soul discerned
Two voices in the air.

"Is it he?" quoth one, "Is this the man?
By him who died on cross,
With his cruel bow he laid full low   400
The harmless Albatross.

The spirit who bideth by himself
In the land of mist and snow,
He loved the bird that loved the man
Who shot him with his bow."

The other was a softer voice,
As soft as honeydew:
Quoth he, "The man hath penance done,
And penance more will do."

Part VI

FIRST VOICE
"But tell me, tell me! speak again,   410
Thy soft response renewing—
What makes that ship drive on so fast?
What is the ocean doing?"

SECOND VOICE
"Still as a slave before his lord,
The ocean hath no blast;
His great bright eye most silently
Up to the Moon is cast—

If he may know which way to go;
For she guides him smooth or grim.
See, brother, see! how graciously   420
She looketh down on him."

The Mariner hath
been cast into a trance;
for the angelic power
causeth the vessel to
drive northward faster
than human life could
endure.

FIRST VOICE
"But why drives on that ship so fast,
Without or wave or wind?"

SECOND VOICE
"The air is cut away before,
And closes from behind.

Fly, brother, fly! more high, more high!
Or we shall be belated:
For slow and slow that ship will go,
When the Mariner's trance is abated."

The supernatural
motion is retarded; the
Mariner awakes, and
his penance begins
anew.

I woke, and we were sailing on   430
As in a gentle weather:
'Twas night, calm night, the moon was high;
The dead men stood together.

All stood together on the deck,
For a charnel-dungeon fitter:
All fixed on me their stony eyes,
That in the Moon did glitter.

The pang, the curse, with which they died,
Had never passed away:
I could not draw my eyes from theirs,   440
Nor turn them up to pray.

The curse is finally
expiated.

And now this spell was snapped: once more
I viewed the ocean green,
And looked far forth, yet little saw
Of what had else been seen—

Like one, that on a lonesome road
Doth walk in fear and dread,
And having once turned round walks on,
And turns no more his head;
Because he knows, a frightful fiend   450
Doth close behind him tread.

But soon there breathed a wind on me,
Nor sound nor motion made:
Its path was not upon the sea,
In ripple or in shade.

It raised my hair, it fanned my cheek
Like a meadow-gale of spring—
It mingled strangely with my fears,
Yet it felt like a welcoming.

Swiftly, swiftly flew the ship,   460
Yet she sailed softly too:
Sweetly, sweetly blew the breeze—
On me alone it blew.

Oh! dream of joy! is this indeed
The lighthouse top I see?
Is this the hill? is this the kirk?
Is this mine own countree?

We drifted o'er the harbour bar,
And I with sobs did pray—
O let me be awake, my God!   470
Or let me sleep alway.

The harbour bay was clear as glass,
So smoothly it was strewn!
And on the bay, the moonlight lay,
And the shadow of the Moon.

The rock shone bright, the kirk no less,
That stands above the rock:
The moonlight steeped in silentness
The steady weathercock.

And the bay was white with silent light,   480
Till rising from the same,
Full many shapes, that shadows were,
In crimson colours came.

And appear in their own forms of light.

A little distance from the prow
Those crimson shadows were:
I turned my eyes upon the deck—
Oh, Christ! what saw I there!

Each corse lay flat, lifeless and flat,
And, by the holy rood!
A man all light, a seraph man,   490
On every corse there stood.

This seraph band, each waved his hand:
It was a heavenly sight!
They stood as signals to the land,
Each one a lovely light;

This seraph band, each waved his hand,
No voice did they impart—
No voice; but oh! the silence sank
Like music on my heart.

But soon I heard the dash of oars,   500
I heard the Pilot's cheer;
My head was turned perforce away
And I saw a boat appear.

The Pilot and the Pilot's boy,
I heard them coming fast:
Dear Lord in Heaven! it was a joy
The dead men could not blast.

I saw a third—I heard his voice:
It is the Hermit good!
He singeth loud his godly hymns   510
That he makes in the wood.
He'll shrieve my soul, he'll wash away
The Albatross's blood.

Part VII

The Hermit of the
Wood,

This Hermit good lives in that wood
Which slopes down to the sea.
How loudly his sweet voice he rears!
He loves to talk with marineres
That come from a far countree.

He kneels at morn, and noon, and eve—
He hath a cushion plump: 520
It is the moss that wholly hides
The rotted old oak-stump.

The skiff-boat neared: I heard them talk,
"Why, this is strange, I trow!
Where are those lights so many and fair,
That signal made but now?"

Approacheth the ship
with wonder.

"Strange, by my faith!" the Hermit said—
"And they answered not our cheer!
The planks looked warped! and see those sails,
How thin they are and sere!   530
I never saw aught like to them,
Unless perchance it were

Brown skeletons of leaves that lag
My forest-brook along;
When the ivy tod is heavy with snow,
And the owlet whoops to the wolf below,
That eats the she-wolf's young."

"Dear Lord! it hath a fiendish look,"
(The Pilot made reply)
"I am a-feared"—"Push on, push on!"   540
Said the Hermit cheerily.

The boat came closer to the ship,
But I nor spake nor stirred;
The boat came close beneath the ship,
And straight a sound was heard.

Under the water it rumbled on,
Still louder and more dread:
It reached the ship, it split the bay;
The ship went down like lead.

Stunned by that loud and dreadful sound,   550
Which sky and ocean smote,
Like one that hath been seven days drowned
My body lay afloat;
But swift as dreams, myself I found
Within the Pilot's boat.

Upon the whirl, where sank the ship,
The boat spun round and round;
And all was still, save that the hill
Was telling of the sound.

I moved my lips—the Pilot shrieked   560
And fell down in a fit;
The holy Hermit raised his eyes,
And prayed where he did sit.

I took the oars: the Pilot's boy,
Who now doth crazy go,
Laughed loud and long, and all the while
His eyes went to and fro.
"Ha! ha!" quoth he, "full plain I see,
The Devil knows how to row."

And now, all in my own countree,   570
I stood on the firm land!
The Hermit stepped forth from the boat,
And scarcely he could stand.

The ancient Mariner earnestly entreateth the Hermit to shrieve him; and the penance of life falls on him.

"O shrieve me, shrieve me, holy man!"
The Hermit crossed his brow.
"Say quick," quoth he, "I bid thee say—
What manner of man art thou?"

Forthwith this frame of mine was wrenched
With a woeful agony,
Which forced me to begin my tale;   580
And then it left me free.

And ever and anon throughout his future life an agony constraineth him to travel from land to land;

Since then, at an uncertain hour,
That agony returns:
And till my ghastly tale is told,
This heart within me burns.

I pass, like night, from land to land;
I have strange power of speech;
That moment that his face I see,
I know the man that must hear me:
To him my tale I teach.   590

What loud uproar bursts from that door!
The wedding-guests are there:
But in the garden-bower the bride
And bride-maids singing are:
And hark the little vesper bell,
Which biddeth me to prayer!

O Wedding-Guest! this soul hath been
Alone on a wide wide sea:
So lonely 'twas, that God himself
Scarce seemèd there to be.   600

O sweeter than the marriage feast,
'Tis sweeter far to me,
To walk together to the kirk
With a goodly company!—

To walk together to the kirk,
And all together pray,
While each to his great Father bends,
Old men, and babes, and loving friends
And youths and maidens gay!

And to teach, by his own example, love and reverence to all things that God made and loveth.

Farewell, farewell! but this I tell   610
To thee, thou Wedding-Guest!
He prayeth well, who loveth well
Both man and bird and beast.

He prayeth best, who loveth best
All things both great and small;
For the dear God who loveth us,
He made and loveth all.

The Mariner, whose eye is bright,
Whose beard with age is hoar,
Is gone: and now the Wedding-Guest   620
Turned from the bridegroom's door.

He went like one that hath been stunned,
And is of sense forlorn:
A sadder and a wiser man,
He rose the morrow morn.

Notes

Facile credo... "I readily believe that there are more invisible than visible Natures in the universe. But who will explain for us the family of all these beings, and the ranks and relations and distinguishing features and functions of each? What do they do? What places do they inhabit? The human mind has always sought the knowledge of these things, but never attained it. Meanwhile I do not deny that it is helpful sometimes to contemplate in the mind, as on a tablet, the image of a greater and better world, lest the intellect, habituated to the petty things of daily life, narrow itself and sink wholly into trivial thoughts. But at the same time we must be watchful for the truth and keep a sense of proportion, so that we may distinguish the certain from the uncertain, day from night." Adapted by Coleridge from Thomas Burnet, *Archaeologiae Philosophicae* (1692)

eftsoons a straight path

kirk a church

swound swoon

uprist arose

wist knew; from the Old English *witan*

gramercy an expression meaning "great thanks"; from the French phrase *grand-merci*

weal benefit; from the Old English word *wela*

hoary grey or white

silly lowly, harmless

sheen shone

sedge rush-like plants that grow around lakes and streams

corses corpses

jargoning warbling

rood the Christian cross; from the Old English word *rod*

shrieve to set free from sin; from the Old English word *scrifan*, meaning "to impose as a penance"; originally from the Latin word *scribere*, meaning "to write"

tod a bushy clump

crossed his brow refers to gesticulating to make the sign of the Christian cross

Activities

1. Divide a page into three columns. On your first reading of the poem, pause at the end of each section to paraphrase, question, and react. In the first column, write a point-form summary of the section; in the second, record at least two questions about the events, ideas, and language; and in the third, note your reaction to the section. Discuss your notes with a partner.

2. "The Rime of the Ancient Mariner" is a ballad, the oldest form of poetry. Choose three or four verses of the poem that are particularly appealing to your ear and analyze the rhyme scheme, metre, and stanzas. Write a short parody that follows the same form. Share your parodies, considering the following questions: How does the form of the poem enhance the meaning? What features of the form and style of this poem make it easy to memorize short excerpts? Why do you think this poem is one of the most quoted and parodied poems in the English language?

Another Viewpoint: History

During the eighteenth century, the British Empire expanded, as British explorers colonized other countries and merchants engaged in the slave trade. The British public was fascinated by tales of perilous voyages and exotic discoveries. Keeping this context in mind, reread the poem as a story of unfortunate exploration, paying particular attention to the geographical and topographical description. How does Coleridge depict travel and exploration? What might the ghost ship symbolize?

O Can You Leave Your Native Land?

Susanna Moodie

Susanna Moodie was born in 1803, in Suffolk, England, into an afflu-ent family. When her father died in 1818, Moodie and her sisters began to write books for children and romantic novels, in part to earn money. In 1832, she and her husband immigrated to Canada along with her sister, Catharine Parr Trail. Moodie's stories of pio-neer life near Cobourg, Ontario, including *Roughing It in the Bush* (1852) and *Life in the Clearings* (1854), provided a realistic reflection of wilderness living in stark contrast to the glowing reports usually given to potential immigrants to Canada by English land agents. This poem, which explores the topic of immigration to Canada, was writ-ten as song lyrics. Moodie has been commended for her fascination with differences in character, her considerable psychological insight, and a generous measure of wit and playfulness in her writing. Have you or your parents or friends immigrated to Canada from another country? If so, what were the first impressions of this country? What were some of the difficulties encountered and how were they dealt with?

O Can You Leave Your Native Land?

(For Music.)

O can you leave your native land,
      An exile's bride to be;
Your mother's home and cheerful hearth
      To tempt the main with me—
Across the wide and stormy sea
      To trace our foaming track,
And know the wave that heaves us on
      Will never bear us back?

And can you in Canadian wood
      With me the harvest bind,   10
Nor feel one lingering sad regret
      For all you leave behind!
Can those dear hands, unused to toil,
      The woodman's wants supply,
Nor shrink beneath the chilly blast
      When wintry storms are nigh?

Amid the shades of forests dark,
      Our loved isle will appear
An Eden, whose delicious bloom
      Will make the wild more drear—   20
And you in solitude will weep
      O'er scenes belov'd in vain,
And pine away your life to view
      Once more your native plain!

Then pause, dear girl, ere those fond lips
    Your wanderer's fate decide;
My spirit spurns the selfish wish—
    You must not be my bride—
But oh, that smile—those tearful eyes
    My firmer purpose move—   30
Our hearts are one—and we will dare
    All perils thus to love.

Activities

1. From whose point of view is this poem written and to whom is it addressed? How does the narrator describe life in the "Canadian wood"? How does this description contrast with that of life in the "native land"?

2. Reread the poem with a particular focus on the language used by the author. Make a list of words, phrases, and spellings that are typical of nineteenth-century language and style. Rewrite the poem using contemporary language and idioms.

Another Viewpoint: Culture

Margaret Atwood wrote a book of poetry in response to Moodie's writing; she called it *The Journals of Susanna Moodie*. In the afterword, Atwood makes the following observation: "What struck me most about [Susanna Moodie's] personality was the way in which it reflects many of the obsessions still with us." Consider the extent to which this poem contains some of the same "obsessions" that contemporary Canadians experience.

Dover Beach

Matthew Arnold

Born in 1822, Matthew Arnold was a major figure in Victorian England. Educated at Oxford University, he later had a great impact on the English education system as an inspector of schools. He was also a professor at Oxford, where he became a well-known literary critic who believed that objective literary criticism was essential to the welfare of a nation. Like many of his contemporaries, he struggled with the growing tension between science and religion during his era, which contributed to a sense of pessimism and spiritual isolation within his culture. Arnold died in 1888. To what extent do scenes in nature, such as an ocean, a forest, or a flock of birds, prompt you to reflect on your own life situation? What scenes are most likely to create a reflective mood for you and why?

◀ *Cliffs of Dover*

Dover Beach

The sea is calm tonight.
The tide is full, the moon lies fair
Upon the straits—on the French coast the light
Gleams and is gone; the cliffs of England stand,
Glimmering and vast, out in the tranquil bay.
Come to the window, sweet is the night air!
Only, from the long line of spray
Where the sea meets the moon-blanched land,
Listen! you hear the grating roar
Of pebbles which the waves draw back, and fling,   10
At their return, up the high strand,
Begin, and cease, and then again begin,
With tremulous cadence slow, and bring
The eternal note of sadness in.

Sophocles long ago
Heard it on the Aegean, and it brought
Into his mind the turbid ebb and flow
Of human misery; we
Find also in the sound a thought,
Hearing it by this distant northern sea.   20

The Sea of Faith
Was once, too, at the full, and round earth's shore
Lay like the folds of a bright girdle furled.
But now I only hear
Its melancholy, long, withdrawing roar,
Retreating, to the breath
Of the night wind, down the vast edges drear
And naked shingles of the world.

Ah, love, let us be true
To one another! for the world, which seems
30
To lie before us like a land of dreams,
So various, so beautiful, so new,
Hath really neither joy, nor love, nor light,
Nor certitude, nor peace, nor help for pain;
And we are here as on a darkling plain
Swept with confused alarms of struggle and flight,
Where ignorant armies clash by night.

Notes

Sophocles long ago heard it on the Aegean Sophocles (495–406 BCE) wrote about the powerlessness of human beings against fate. Two of his best-known tragic figures are Antigone and Oedipus. Some critics see a direct parallel between this poem and lines 583 to 591 of Sophocles' play *Antigone*.

shingles beaches covered with pebbles or small stones

Activities

1. What view of the world is depicted in this poem by Matthew Arnold? Which feelings is Arnold exploring? How does his view compare with your feelings and ideas about the future?

2. "Dover Beach" is a dramatic monologue. How does this form contribute to the poem's mood and theme? Try revising the poem to eliminate the first- and second-person references. How does this change the impact of the poem? Compare and justify your answers in a small group, challenging and building on each other's ideas.

Another Viewpoint: History

Some critics approach literature by stressing the relationship of literature to its historical period. To a great extent, "Dover Beach" reflects the intellectual and social world of the Victorian era. Conduct some research on the tension between science and religion during the Victorian period of English history. Use this information to set this poem in a historical context. Then discuss in what ways placing a text in its context can either enhance or distort the understanding of a literary work.

Because I Could Not Stop for Death—

Emily Dickinson

Emily Dickinson was born in 1830 in Amherst, Massachusetts. As a young adult, she began to withdraw from the world. By her forties, she refused to leave her house altogether, though she was an avid letter-writer. Dickinson wrote poetry beginning in her childhood and, after her death in 1886, nearly 2,000 poems were found in her house. The years of Dickinson's greatest poetic output, about 800 poems, coincided with the American Civil War. In terms of her use of metre, her major influences were the English hymn writer Isaac Watts, William Shakespeare, and the King James Version of the Bible. Critic Carl Van Doren wrote that Emily Dickinson "did not so much cut her poems to the bone as leave them as they were, without adding the customary flesh. Her work approaches poetry's irreducible minimum, which is poetry's immortal part." Initially regarded as an eccentric minor voice, Dickinson is recognized today as one of America's greatest poets. What is appealing or unappealing about minimalist poetry? With which other minimalist poets are you familiar and how do their works compare with Dickinson's?

Because I Could Not Stop for Death—

Because I could not stop for Death—
He kindly stopped for me—
The Carriage held but just Ourselves—
And Immortality.

We slowly drove—He knew no haste
And I had put away
My labor and my leisure too,
For His Civility—

We passed the School, where Children strove
At Recess—in the Ring—   10
We passed the Fields of Gazing Grain—
We passed the Setting Sun—

Or rather—He passed Us—
The Dews drew quivering and chill—
For only Gossamer, my Gown—
My Tippet—only Tulle—

We paused before a House that seemed
A Swelling of the Ground—
The Roof was scarcely visible—
The Cornice—in the Ground—   20

Since then—'tis Centuries—and yet
Feels shorter than the Day
I first surmised the Horses Heads
Were toward Eternity—

Notes

gossamer light, insubstantial fabric; alternatively, filmy substance like cobwebs

tippet a woman's cape or wrap

tulle sheer material often used for veils

cornice the molded, projecting horizontal piece which crowns the top of an architectural composition

surmised inferred

Activities

1. Consider the following possibilities: Is Dickinson's primary intent in this poem to give expression to the hope for immortality or to describe the experience of living with the knowledge of death? Do you have another interpretation of the poet's purpose? Support your idea with references to the poem. What is your response to the poem's central theme?

2. One critic has identified the tone of the poem as "sad thoughtfulness, languor, and repressed terror." What passages do you think led to this evaluation? What other words would you use to describe the tone? Which elements of diction contribute to the tone?

Another Viewpoint: Archetypal Patterns

Analyze the archetypal patterns of birth, time, and death in Emily Dickinson's poem and compare your findings with the treatment of these patterns in Dylan Thomas' "Fern Hill" on page 494 of this anthology. Use your analyses to write a comparative essay in which you focus on the dominant recurring images in each poem.

wrap-up
poetry

1. Choose a poem from this unit to read aloud or tape-record for a small group. Write an introduction to the poem in which you provide a rationale for your choice, including what impressed you most about the poem and how you think it gains meaning by being read aloud and listened to. Rehearse reading your introduction and the poem. Present it to the group and elicit feedback about the persuasiveness of your rationale and the effectiveness of your reading.

2. In a small group, select the three poems in this unit that you think most effectively link an abstract concept with a concrete image. In a four-column chart (using the headings "Title," "Concept," "Concrete Image," and "Technique," respectively), record details about your choices. Then select three other written or visual forms, such as a short story, film, or advertisement. As a group, do research to track down one example of each form you selected in which an abstract concept is linked with a concrete image. Add these examples to your chart. Present your results to the class for discussion.

3. Poetry in the twentieth century was noted for a number of *movements*, particular approaches to writing verse that shared common techniques and conceptual frameworks. Using print and non-print resources, research one of these movements. Write a formal essay in which you describe and analyze the main ideas and characteristics of the movement, using specific examples from your research and, if applicable, from this anthology. As you revise your work, pay particular attention to clarity of expression, the effectiveness of your style, and the proper citation and integration of researched information.

4. Suppose that you and a group of your classmates want to start a student poetry magazine at your school. With your group, plan a proposal that will convince school administrators to allow you to publish this magazine and to allocate start-up funds for your endeavour. Brainstorm with your group to identify the focus and goal of your magazine and write a concise statement of purpose. Research the costs associated with your project to demonstrate that you have carefully considered all facets of your proposal. Itemize the costs in order to justify the expenses needed to produce the magazine. Use a word-processing and spreadsheet program to produce your final proposal.

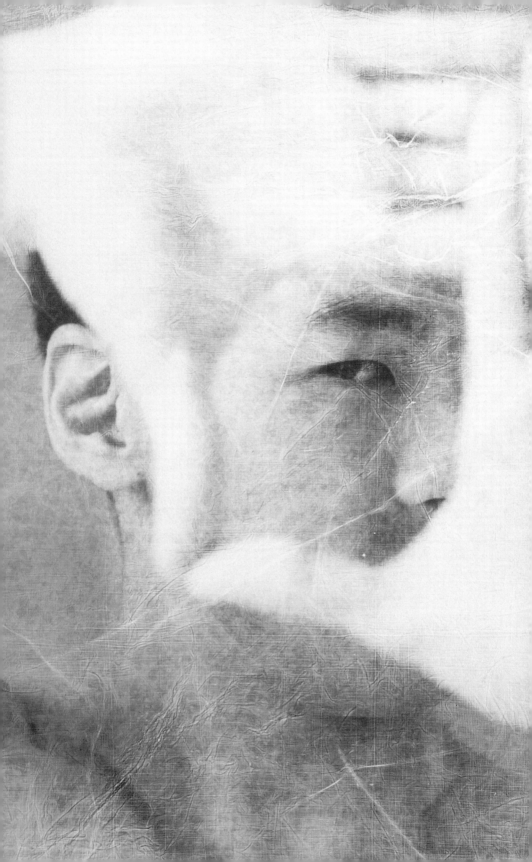

4 drama

Drama should have for its subject a single action, whole and complete, with a beginning, a middle, and an end. It will thus resemble a living organism in all its unity, and produce the pleasure proper to it.

— *Aristotle*

When you work in the theatre there's a special joy and wonder when you see all the parts that make up a play come together with an audience to create an event of transcendence. It's a kind of miracle.

— *Sharon Pollock*

A Marriage Proposal

Anton Chekhov

Translated by Theodore Hoffman

Anton Chekhov was born in Taganrog, Russia, in 1860, the grandson of a serf. Chekhov attended medical school in Moscow. By the time he began practising medicine in 1894, he was already publishing short stories and humorous sketches. He published his first play, *Ivanov,* in 1887. From then until his death in 1904, he wrote an impressive body of stories and plays, while continuing to work as a doctor. Chekhov is often described as a *realist*. His writing portrays tragicomic characteristics of ordinary people and events. He emphasizes internal drama, characterization, and mood, rather than plot. He once commented, "Any idiot can face a crisis; it is this day-to-day living that wears you out." To what extent do you agree with Chekhov's comment that daily life is more challenging than a crisis? Do you prefer literature and entertainment that deals with small events in people's lives or with larger-than-life characters engaged in enormous struggles? Why?

Characters

CHUBUKOV—*a wealthy, middle-aged gentleman who owns an estate in nineteenth-century Russia*

NATALIA—*his daughter, an unmarried woman ready to take a husband*

LOMOV—*a neighbour gentleman, a neurotic bachelor of thirty-five*

(CHUBUKOV's *mansion—the living room.* LOMOV *enters, formally dressed in evening jacket, white gloves, top hat. He is nervous from the start.)*

CHUBUKOV: *(Rising)* Well, look who's here! Ivan Vassilevitch! *(Shakes his hand warmly)* What a surprise, old man! How are you?

LOMOV: Oh, not too bad. And you?

CHUBUKOV: Oh, we manage, we manage. Do sit down, please. You know, you've been neglecting your neighbours, my dear fellow. It's been ages. Say, why the formal dress? Tails, gloves, and so forth. Where's the funeral, my boy? Where are you headed?

LOMOV: Oh, nowhere. I mean, here; just to see you, my dear Stepan Stepanovitch.

CHUBUKOV: Then why the full dress, old boy? It's not New Year's, and so forth.

LOMOV: Well, you see, it's like this. I have come here, my dear Stepan Stepanovitch, to bother you with a request. More than once, or twice, or more than that, it has been my privilege to apply to you for assistance in things, and you've always, well, responded. I mean, well, you have. Yes. Excuse me, I'm getting all mixed up. May I have a glass of water, my dear Stepan Stepanovitch? *(Drinks)*

CHUBUKOV: *(Aside)* Wants to borrow some money. Not a chance! *(Aloud)* What can I do for you my dear friend?

LOMOV:	Well, you see, my dear Stepanitch…Excuse me, I mean Stepan my Dearovitch…No, I mean, I get all confused, as you can see. To make a long story short, you're the only one who can help me. Of course, I don't deserve it, and there's no reason why I should expect you to, and all that.
CHUBUKOV:	Stop beating around the bush! Out with it!
LOMOV:	In just a minute. I mean, now, right now. The truth is, I have come to ask the hand…I mean, your daughter, Natalia Stepanovna, I, I want to marry her!
CHUBUKOV:	*(Overjoyed)* Great heavens! Ivan Vassilevitch! Say it again!
LOMOV:	I have come humbly to ask for the hand…
CHUBUKOV:	*(Interrupting)* You're a prince! I'm overwhelmed, delighted, and so forth. Yes, indeed, and all that!

(Hugs and kisses LOMOV*)*

This is just what I've been hoping for. It's my fondest dream come true. *(Sheds a tear)* And, you know, I've always looked upon you, my boy, as if you were my own son. May God grant to both of you His Mercy and His Love, and so forth. Oh, I have been wishing for this…But why am I being so idiotic? It's just that I'm off my rocker with joy, my boy! Completely off my rocker! Oh, with all my soul I'm…I'll go get Natalia, and so forth.

LOMOV:	*(Deeply moved)* Dear Stepan Stepanovitch, do you think she'll agree?
CHUBUKOV:	Why, of course, old friend. Great heavens! As if she wouldn't! Why she's crazy for you! Good God! Like a lovesick cat, and so forth. Be right back. *(Leaves)*

LOMOV:	God, it's cold. I'm gooseflesh all over, as if I had to take a test. But the main thing is, to make up my mind, and keep it that way. I mean, if I take time out to think, or if I hesitate, or talk about it, or have ideals, or wait for real love, well, I'll just never get married! Brrrr, it's cold! Natalia Stepanovna is an excellent housekeeper. She's not too bad looking. She's had a good education. What more could I ask? Nothing. I'm so nervous, my ears are buzzing. *(Drinks)* Besides, I've just got to get married. I'm thirty-five already. It's sort of a critical age. I've got to settle down and lead a regular life. I mean, I'm always getting palpitations, and I'm nervous, and I get upset so easy. Look, my lips are quivering, and my eyebrow's twitching. The worst thing is the night. Sleeping. I get into bed, doze off, and, suddenly, something inside me jumps. First my head snaps, and then my shoulder blade, and I roll out of bed like a lunatic and try to walk it off. Then I try to go back to sleep, but, as soon as I do, something jumps again! Twenty times a night, sometimes…

*(*NATALIA STEPANOVNA *enters)*

NATALIA:	Oh, it's only you. All Papa said was: "Go inside, there's a merchant come to collect his goods." How do you do, Ivan Vassilevitch?
LOMOV:	How do you do, dear Natalia Stepanovna?
NATALIA:	Excuse my apron, and not being dressed. We're shelling peas. You haven't been around lately. Oh, do sit down. *(They do)* Would you like some lunch?
LOMOV:	No thanks, I had some.

NATALIA:	Well, then smoke if you want. *(He doesn't)* The weather's nice today...but yesterday, it was so wet the workmen couldn't get a thing done. Have you got much hay in? I felt so greedy I had a whole field done, but now I'm not sure I was right. With the rain it could rot, couldn't it? I should have waited. But why are you so dressed up? Is there a dance or something? Of course, I must say you look splendid, but...Well, tell me, why are you so dressed up?
LOMOV:	*(Excited)* Well, you see, my dear Natalia Stepanovna, the truth is, I made up my mind to ask you to...well, to, listen to me. Of course, it'll probably surprise you and even maybe make you angry, but...*(Aside)* God, it's cold in here!
NATALIA:	Why, what do you mean? *(A pause)* Well?
LOMOV:	I'll try to get it over with. I mean, you know, my dear Natalia Stepanovna that I've known, since childhood, even, known, and had the privilege of knowing, your family. My late aunt, and her husband, who, as you know, left me my estate, they always had the greatest respect for your father and your late mother. The Lomovs and the Chubukovs have always been very friendly, you might even say affectionate. And, of course, you know, our land borders on each other's. My Oxen Meadows touch your birch grove...
NATALIA:	I hate to interrupt you, my dear Ivan Vassilevitch, but you said: "my Oxen Meadows." Do you really think they're yours?
LOMOV:	Why of course they're mine.
NATALIA:	What do you mean? The Oxen Meadows are ours, not yours!

LOMOV:	Oh, no, my dear Natalia Stepanovna, they're mine.
NATALIA:	Well, this is the first I've heard about it! Where did you get that idea?
LOMOV:	Where? Why, I mean the Oxen Meadows that are wedged between your birches and the marsh.
NATALIA:	Yes, of course, they're ours.
LOMOV:	Oh, no, you're wrong, my dear Natalia Stepanovna, they're mine.
NATALIA:	Now, come, Ivan Vassilevitch! How long have they been yours?
LOMOV:	How long? Why, as long as I can remember!
NATALIA:	Well, really, you can't expect me to believe that!
LOMOV:	But, you can see for yourself in the deed, my dear Natalia Stepanovna. Of course, there was once a dispute about them, but everyone knows they're mine now. There's nothing to argue about. There was a time when my aunt's grandmother let your father's grandfather's peasants use the land, but they were supposed to bake bricks for her in return. Naturally, after a few years they began to act as if they owned it, but the real truth is…
NATALIA:	That has nothing to do with the case! Both my grandfather and my great-grandfather said that their land went as far as the marsh, which means that the Meadows are ours! There's nothing whatever to argue about. It's foolish.
LOMOV:	But I can show you the deed, Natalia Stepanovna.
NATALIA:	You're just making fun of me…Great Heavens! Here we have the land for hundreds of years, and suddenly you try to tell us it isn't ours. What's wrong with you,

Ivan Vassilevitch? Those meadows aren't even fifteen acres, and they're not worth three hundred rubles, but I just can't stand unfairness! I just can't stand unfairness!

LOMOV: But, you must listen to me. Your father's grandfather's peasants, as I've already tried to tell you, they were supposed to bake bricks for my aunt's grandmother. And my aunt's grandmother, why, she wanted to be nice to them...

NATALIA: It's just nonsense, this whole business about aunts and grandfathers and grandmothers. The Meadows are ours! That's all there is to it!

LOMOV: They're mine!

NATALIA: Ours! You can go on talking for two days, and you can put on fifteen evening coats and twenty pairs of gloves, but I tell you they're ours, ours, ours!

LOMOV: Natalia Stepanovna, I don't want the Meadows! I'm just acting on principle. If you want, I'll give them to you.

NATALIA: I'll give them to *you*! Because they're ours! And that's all there is to it! And if I may say so, your behaviour, my dear Ivan Vassilevitch, is very strange. Until now, we've always considered you a good neighbour, even a friend. After all, last year we lent you our threshing machine, even though it meant putting off our own threshing until November. And here you are treating us like a pack of gypsies. Giving me my own land, indeed! Really! Why that's not being a good neighbour. It's sheer impudence, that's what it is...

LOMOV: Oh, so you think I'm just a land-grabber? My dear lady, I've never grabbed anybody's land in my whole life, and no one's going to accuse me of doing it now!

(Quickly walks over to the pitcher and drinks some more water)
The Oxen Meadows are mine!

NATALIA:	That's a lie. They're ours!
LOMOV:	Mine!
NATALIA:	A lie! I'll prove it. I'll send my mowers out there today!
LOMOV:	What?
NATALIA:	My mowers will mow it today!
LOMOV:	I'll kick them out!
NATALIA:	You just dare!
LOMOV:	*(Clutching his heart)* The Oxen Meadows are mine! Do you understand? Mine!
NATALIA:	Please don't shout! You can shout all you want in your own house, but here I must ask you to control yourself.
LOMOV:	If my heart wasn't palpitating the way it is, if my insides weren't jumping like mad, I wouldn't talk to you so calmly. *(Yelling)* The Oxen Meadows are mine!
NATALIA:	Ours!
LOMOV:	Mine!
NATALIA:	Ours!
LOMOV:	Mine!

(Enter CHUBUKOV)

CHUBUKOV:	What's going on? Why all the shouting?
NATALIA:	Papa, will you please inform this gentleman who owns the Oxen Meadows, he or we?
CHUBUKOV:	*(To LOMOV)* Why, they're ours, old fellow.

LOMOV:	But how can they be yours, my dear Stepan Stepanovitch? Be fair. Perhaps my aunt's grandmother did let your grandfather's peasants work the land, and maybe they did get so used to it that they acted as if it was their own, but...
CHUBUKOV:	Oh, no, no...my dear boy. You forget something. The reason the peasants didn't pay your aunt's grandmother, and so forth, was that the land was disputed, even then. Since then it's been settled. Why, everyone knows it's ours.
LOMOV:	I can prove it's mine.
CHUBUKOV:	You can't prove a thing, old boy.
LOMOV:	Yes I can!
CHUBUKOV:	My dear lad, why yell like that? Yelling doesn't prove a thing. Look, I'm not after anything of yours, just as I don't intend to give up anything of mine. Why should I? Besides, if you're going to keep arguing about it, I'd just as soon give the land to the peasants, so there!
LOMOV:	There's nothing! Where do you get the right to give away someone else's property?
CHUBUKOV:	I certainly ought to know if I have the right or not. And you had better realize it, because, my dear young man, I am not used to being spoken to in that tone of voice, and so forth. Besides which, my dear young man, I am twice as old as you are, and I ask you to speak to me without getting yourself into such a tizzy, and so forth!
LOMOV:	Do you think I'm a fool? First you call my property yours, and then you expect me to keep calm and polite! Good neighbours don't act like that, my dear Stepan Stepanovitch. You're no neighbour, you're a land grabber!

CHUBUKOV:	What was that? What did you say?
NATALIA:	Papa, send the mowers out to the meadows at once!
CHUBUKOV:	What did you say, sir?
NATALIA:	The Oxen Meadows are ours, and we'll never give them up, never, never, never, never!
LOMOV:	We'll see about that. I'll go to court. I'll show you!
CHUBUKOV:	Go to court? Well, go to court, and so forth! I know you, just waiting for a chance to go to court, and so forth. You pettifogging shyster, you! All of your family is like that. The whole bunch of them!
LOMOV:	You leave my family out of this! The Lomovs have always been honourable, upstanding people, and not a one of them was ever tried for embezzlement, like your grandfather was.
CHUBUKOV:	The Lomovs are a pack of lunatics, the whole bunch of them!
NATALIA:	The whole bunch!
CHUBUKOV:	Your grandfather was a drunkard, and what about your other aunt, the one who ran away with the architect? And so forth.
NATALIA:	And so forth!
LOMOV:	Your mother was a hunchback! *(Clutches at his heart)* Oh, I've got a stitch in my side…My head's whirling…Help! Water!
CHUBUKOV:	Your father was a rum-soaked gambler.
NATALIA:	And your aunt was queen of the scandalmongers!
LOMOV:	My left foot's paralyzed. You're a plotter…Oh, my heart. It's an open secret that in the last elections you brib…I'm seeing stars! Where's my hat?

NATALIA:	It's a low, mean, spiteful…
CHUBUKOV:	And you're a two-faced, malicious schemer!
LOMOV:	Here's my hat…Oh, my heart…Where's the door? How do I get out of here?…Oh, I think I'm going to die…My foot's numb. *(Goes)*
CHUBUKOV:	*(Following him)* And don't you ever set foot in my house again!
NATALIA:	Go to court, indeed! We'll see about that!

(LOMOV staggers out)

CHUBUKOV:	The devil with him! *(Gets a drink, walks back and forth excited)*
NATALIA:	What a rascal! How can you trust your neighbours after an incident like that?
CHUBUKOV:	The villain! The scarecrow!
NATALIA:	He's a monster! First he tries to steal our land, and then he has the nerve to yell at you.
CHUBUKOV:	Yes, and that turnip, that stupid rooster, has the gall to make a proposal. Some proposal!
NATALIA:	What proposal?
CHUBUKOV:	Why, he came to propose to you.
NATALIA:	To propose? To me? Why didn't you tell me before?
CHUBUKOV:	So he gets all dressed up in his formal clothes. That stuffed sausage, that dried-up cabbage!
NATALIA:	To propose to me? Ohhhh! *(Falls into a chair and starts wailing)* Bring him back! Back! Go get him! Bring him back! Ohhhh!
CHUBUKOV:	Bring who back?
NATALIA:	Hurry up, hurry up! I'm sick. Get him! *(Complete hysterics)*

CHUBUKOV:	What for? *(To her)* What's the matter with you? *(Clutches his head)* Oh, what a fool I am! I'll shoot myself! I'll hang myself! I ruined her chances!
NATALIA:	I'm dying. Get him!
CHUBUKOV:	All right, all right, right away! Only don't yell! *(He runs out)*
NATALIA:	What are they doing to me? Get him! Bring him back! Bring him back!

(A pause. CHUBUKOV runs in)

CHUBUKOV:	He's coming, and so forth, the snake. Oof! You talk to him. I'm not in the mood.
NATALIA:	*(Wailing)* Bring him back! Bring him back!
CHUBUKOV:	*(Yelling)* I told you, he's coming! Oh Lord, what agony to be the father of a grown-up daughter. I'll cut my throat some day, I swear I will. *(To her)* We cursed him, we insulted him, abused him, kicked him out, and now…because you, you…
NATALIA:	Me? It was all your fault!
CHUBUKOV:	My fault? What do you mean my fau…?

(LOMOV appears in the doorway)

Talk to him yourself!

(Goes out. LOMOV enters, exhausted)

LOMOV:	What palpitations! My heart! And my foot's absolutely asleep. Something keeps giving me a stitch in the side…
NATALIA:	You must forgive us, Ivan Vassilevitch. We all got too excited. I remember now. The Oxen Meadows are yours.
LOMOV:	My heart's beating something awful. My Meadows. My eyebrows, they're both twitching!

NATALIA:	Yes, the Meadows are all yours, yes, yours. Do sit down. *(They sit)* We were wrong, of course.
LOMOV:	I argued on principle. My land isn't worth so much to me, but the principle...
NATALIA:	Oh, yes, of course, the principle, that's what counts. But let's change the subject.
LOMOV:	Besides, I have evidence. You see, my aunt's grandmother let your father's grandfather's peasants use the land...
NATALIA:	Yes, yes, yes, but forget all that. *(Aside)* I wish I knew how to get him going. *(Aloud)* Are you going to start hunting soon?
LOMOV:	After the harvest I'll try for grouse. But oh, my dear Natalia Stepanovna, have you heard about the bad luck I've had? You know my dog, Guess? He's gone lame.
NATALIA:	What a pity. Why?
LOMOV:	I don't know. He must have twisted his leg, or got in a fight, or something. *(Sighs)* My best dog, to say nothing of the cost. I paid Mironov 125 rubles for him.
NATALIA:	That was too high, Ivan Vassilevitch.
LOMOV:	I think it was quite cheap. He's a first-class dog.
NATALIA:	Why Papa only paid eighty-five rubles for Squeezer, and he's much better than Guess.
LOMOV:	Squeezer better than Guess! What an idea! *(Laughs)* Squeezer better than Guess!
NATALIA:	Of course he's better. He may still be too young but on points and pedigree, he's a better dog even than any Volchanetsky owns.
LOMOV:	Excuse me, Natalia Stepanovna, but you're forgetting he's overshot, and overshot dogs are bad hunters.

NATALIA:	Oh, so he's overshot, is he? Well this is the first time I've heard about it.
LOMOV:	Believe me, his lower jaw is shorter than his upper.
NATALIA:	You've measured them?
LOMOV:	Yes. He's all right for pointing, but if you want him to retrieve…
NATALIA:	In the first place, our Squeezer is a thoroughbred, the son of Harness and Chisel, while your mutt doesn't even have a pedigree. He's as old and worn out as a pedlar's horse.
LOMOV:	He may be old, but I wouldn't take five Squeezers for him. How can you argue? Guess is a dog, Squeezer's a laugh. Anyone you can name has a dog like Squeezer hanging around somewhere. They're under every bush. If he only cost twenty-five rubles you got cheated.
NATALIA:	The devil is in you today, Ivan Vassilevitch! You want to contradict everything. First you pretend the Oxen Meadows are yours, and now you say Guess is better than Squeezer. People should say what they really mean, and you know Squeezer is a hundred times better than Guess. Why say he isn't?
LOMOV:	So, you think I'm a fool or a blind man, Natalia Stepanovna! Once and for all, Squeezer is overshot!
NATALIA:	He is not!
LOMOV:	He is so!
NATALIA:	He is not!
LOMOV:	Why shout, my dear lady?
NATALIA:	Why talk such nonsense? It's terrible. Your Guess is old enough to be buried, and you compare him with Squeezer!

LOMOV:	I'm sorry, I can't go on. My heart...it's palpitating!
NATALIA:	I've always noticed that the hunters who argue most don't know a thing.
LOMOV:	Please! Be quiet a moment. My heart's falling apart... *(Shouts)* Shut up!
NATALIA:	I'm not going to shut up until you admit that Squeezer's a hundred times better than Guess.
LOMOV:	A hundred times worse! His head...My eyes... shoulder...
NATALIA:	Guess is half-dead already!
LOMOV:	*(Weeping)* Shut up! My heart's exploding!
NATALIA:	I won't shut up!

(CHUBUKOV comes in)

CHUBUKOV:	What's the trouble now?
NATALIA:	Papa, will you please tell us which is the better dog, his Guess or our Squeezer?
LOMOV:	Stepan Stepanovitch, I implore you to tell me just one thing. Is your Squeezer overshot or not? Yes or no?
CHUBUKOV:	Well what if he is? He's still the best dog in the neighbourhood, and so forth.
LOMOV:	Oh, but isn't my dog, Guess, better? Really?
CHUBUKOV:	Don't get yourself so fraught up, old man. Of course, your dog has his good points—thoroughbred, firm on his feet, well-sprung ribs, and so forth. But, my dear fellow, you've got to admit he has two defects; he's old and he's short in the muzzle.
LOMOV:	Short in the muzzle? Oh, my heart! Let's look at the facts! On the Marusinsky hunt my dog ran neck and neck with the Count's, while Squeezer was a mile behind them...

CHUBUKOV:	That's because the Count's groom hit him with a whip.
LOMOV:	And he was right, too! We were fox hunting; what was your dog chasing sheep for?
CHUBUKOV:	That's a lie! Look, I'm going to lose my temper… *(Controlling himself)* my dear friend, so let's stop arguing, for that reason alone. You're only arguing because we're all jealous of somebody else's dog. Who can help it? As soon as you realize some dog is better than yours, in this case our dog, you start in with this and that, and the next thing you know—pure jealousy! I remember the whole business.
LOMOV:	I remember too!
CHUBUKOV:	*(Mimicking)* "I remember too!" What do you remember?
LOMOV:	My heart…my foot's asleep…I can't…
NATALIA:	*(Mimicking)* "My heart…my foot's asleep." What kind of a hunter are you? You should be hunting cockroaches in the kitchen, not foxes. "My heart!"
CHUBUKOV:	Yes, what kind of a hunter are you anyway? You should be sitting at home with your palpitations, not tracking down animals. You don't hunt anyhow. You just go out to argue with people and interfere with their dogs, and so forth. For God's sake, let's change the subject before I lose my temper. Anyway, you're just not a hunter.
LOMOV:	But you, you're a hunter? Ha! You only go hunting to get in good with the Count, and to plot, and intrigue, and scheme…Oh, my heart! You're a schemer, that's what!
CHUBUKOV:	What's that? Me a schemer? *(Shouting)* Shut up!
LOMOV:	A schemer!
CHUBUKOV:	You infant! You puppy!
LOMOV:	You old rat! You hawk!

CHUBUKOV: You shut up, or I'll shoot you down like a partridge! You idiot!

LOMOV: Everyone knows that—oh, my heart—that your wife used to beat you…Oh, my feet…my head…I'm seeing stars…I'm going to faint! *(He drops into an armchair)* Quick, a doctor! *(Faints)*

CHUBUKOV: *(Going on, oblivious)* Baby! Weakling! Idiot! I'm getting sick. *(Drinks water)* Me! I'm sick!

NATALIA: What kind of a hunter are you? You can't even sit on a horse! *(To her father)* Papa, what's the matter with him? Look, Papa! *(Screaming)* Ivan Vassilevitch! He's dead.

CHUBUKOV: I'm choking, I can't breathe…Give me air.

NATALIA: He's dead! *(Pulling* LOMOV's *sleeve)* Ivan Vassilevitch! Ivan Vassilevitch! What have you done to me? He's dead!

(She falls into an armchair. Screaming hysterically)
A doctor! A doctor! A doctor!

CHUBUKOV: Ohhhh…What's the matter? What happened?

NATALIA: *(Wailing)* He's dead! He's dead!

CHUBUKOV: Who's dead? *(Looks at* LOMOV*)* My God, he is! Quick! Water! A doctor!

(Puts glass to LOMOV's *lips)*
Here, drink this! Can't drink it—he must be dead, and so forth…Oh what a miserable life! Why don't I shoot myself? I should have cut my throat long ago! What am I waiting for? Give me a knife! Give me a pistol!

*(*LOMOV *stirs)*
Look, he's coming to. Here, drink some water. That's it.

LOMOV: I'm seeing stars…misty…Where am I?

CHUBUKOV:	Just you hurry up and get married, and then the devil with you! She accepted.

(Puts LOMOV's *hand in* NATALIA's*)*

	She accepts and so forth! I give you my blessing, and so forth! Only leave me in peace!
LOMOV:	*(Getting up)* Huh? What? Who?
CHUBUKOV:	She accepts! Well! Kiss her, damn you!
NATALIA:	He's alive! Yes, yes, I accept.
CHUBUKOV:	Kiss each other!
LOMOV:	Huh? Kiss? Kiss who? *(They kiss)* That's nice. I mean, excuse me, what happened? Oh, now I get it…my heart…those stars…I'm very happy, Natalia Stepanovna. *(Kisses her hand)* My foot's asleep.
NATALIA:	I…I'm happy too.
CHUBUKOV:	What a load off my shoulders! Whew!
NATALIA:	Well, now maybe you'll admit that Squeezer is better than Guess?
LOMOV:	Worse!
NATALIA:	Better!
CHUBUKOV:	What a way to enter matrimonial bliss! Let's have some champagne!
LOMOV:	He's worse!
NATALIA:	Better! Better, better, better, better!
CHUBUKOV:	*(Trying to shout her down)* Champagne! Bring some champagne! Champagne! Champagne!

Notes

formal dress, full dress clothing for either gender that is considered suitable for a formal occasion

tails short for a tailcoat, which is a formal man's jacket with an elongated back

gooseflesh a person's skin that has become rough, like that of a plucked goose, from cold or fright

lunatic an extremely foolish person; originally used as a derogatory term for a person who suffers from severe mental illness

rubles the standard monetary unit in Russia, divided into a hundred kopeks; from the Russian word *rublĭ*, meaning a "piece" cut from a silver bar

threshing machine the machine used for the process of beating out or separating grains or seeds from the stalk or another part of a plant, such as husks from cobs of corn

pack of gypsies in modern times, has come to refer to people who are inclined to a nomadic, unconventional way of life; originally referred to a nomadic ethnic group who migrated to Europe from northern India in the fourteenth century and who were persecuted in subsequent centuries for being "foreigners" outside the community

pettifogging quibbling over trivia

shyster a person who uses unethical, unscrupulous business practices

embezzlement someone who takes for one's own use such valuables as money in violation of a trust

hunchback an antiquated, derogatory term for a person whose back is hunched due to an abnormal curvature of the upper spine

devil in this instance, refers to a wicked person

Activities

1. In the style of a newspaper advice columnist, write short letters of advice to each of the three main characters in this play. Briefly summarize each character's "problem." Then outline a course of action that will help each character resolve the conflict and achieve his or her goals. Shape the content, style, and tone of your advice according to the context of a farming community in nineteenth-century Russia.

2. Choose a character in the play to analyze. Reread the play carefully and, in a character web or outline, record key characteristics and supporting evidence. Meet with two other students who have analyzed the same character to compare and discuss your notes. Choose one member of your group to be the "actor," while the other two serve as acting coaches. Discuss how the character should look, sound, and act. Have the actor practise reading her or his lines, while the coaches offer advice and support. As a class, present a dramatic reading of the play with actors from various groups taking turns in the roles. After the reading, discuss as a class: How were various actors' interpretations of the same character similar and different? What advice would the class offer an actor preparing for each of the roles?

3. Chekhov wrote this play in 1888. With a partner, consider Chekhov's purpose in writing this play and who his audience might have been. Discuss such questions as the following: What are you able to infer about audiences of his time? What does the play reveal about audience expectations for gender roles in 1888? How might Chekhov have wanted his audience to react? Does the play have a message or purpose other than to amuse the audience? What strategies did he use to engage the audience and to accomplish his purpose? Formulate a thesis statement that puts forward your interpretation of Chekhov's audience and his purpose. Select and organize examples from the play to support your thesis and incorporate them into an analytical essay.

SET DESIGN FOR
The Foreigner

Karen Schulz Gropman

About the Visual   Karen Schulz Gropman was born in Racine, Wisconsin, in 1951. She began her career as a theatrical set decorator and has been the art director on many feature films, including *The Cider House Rules* (1999) and *The Shipping News* (2001). Schulz Gropman designed this set for Larry Shue's play *The Foreigner* for the Astor Place Theatre in New York. The very small stage and auditorium of this theatre explain the odd shape and angles of her ground plan. When this production moved to a theatre in Chicago, Schulz Gropman had to adapt the set to accommodate that stage's wide thrust. Can you think of an unconventional space in your community that would be an interesting place in which to produce a play? If so, what play would you stage and why?

Activities

1. Look at the photograph of the set; then examine the ground plan. To what extent does referring to the photograph of the set help you to decipher the ground plan? Identify the similarities and the differences between the two.

2. In a group, obtain a number of plays and locate the descriptions of the stage setting at the beginning of the first scene. Read aloud and discuss the settings to familiarize yourself with their content and form. Then, together as a group, select a short story that you think would lend itself to being dramatized. Work by yourself to write a description of the stage setting. Discuss your ideas with the group.

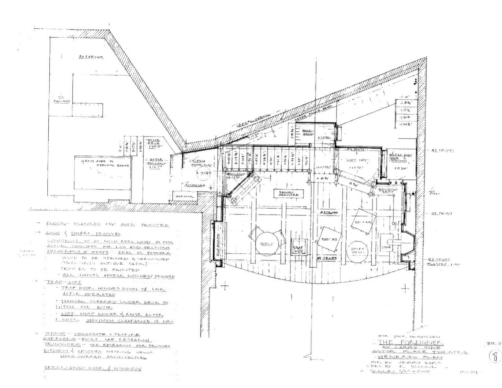

BATHROOM

JR BALCONY

CROSS OVER TO DRESSING ROOMS

STAIR DECK +3'9½"

ACTOR BALCONY +12'7"

→ FLOORS - PLANKED +¾" AGED PAINTED

→ LOGS & TIMBER TRUSSES

CONSTRUCT ½" AS MUCH REAL WOOD IN FORM
ACTUAL SAWWORK FOR LOG END SECTIONS
RANDOM FLRS & POSTS REAL AS POSSIBLE
  WOOD TO BE STAINED & VARNISHED
  (WALNUT?) ANTIQUE SATIN)
  TRUSSES TO BE PAINTED
  - ALL JOINTS APPEAR NOTCHED/PEGGED

→ TRAP - LIFT
  · TRAP DOOR HINGES DOWN W/ LOCK
    ACTOR OPERATED
  · TUNNEL CLEARED UNDER DECK TO
    DITCH FOR ACTOR
  · LIFT MUST LOWER & RAISE ACTOR
    & LOCK. MAXIMUM CLEARANCE IS NEC.

→ STONE - HOMASOTE + TEXTURE
  CASTBOARD - BUILT PER RESEARCH
  IRONWORK - SEE RESEARCH FOR TEXTURE
  KITCHEN & UPSTAIRS MASKING WALLS
  HARD COATED ARCHITECTURAL

  DETAIL-AWAY DOOR & WINDOW

FOR JACK HANNIGAN
THE FOREIGNER
BY LARRY SHUE
ACTORS PLACE THEATRE
GENERAL PLAN
DIR. BY JEFFREY ZAKS
SCEN. BY R. SCHULZ
SCALE: 1/2" = 1'-0"

(1)

From

Acoose: Man Standing Above Ground

Janice Acoose and Brenda Zeman

Janice Acoose was born in Broadview, Saskatchewan, in 1954. Her father was a member of the Saulteaux First Nation on the Sakimay Reserve and her mother was a Métis from Marival. She is also the granddaughter of the renowned runner Paul Acoose. She received a doctorate in English literature from the University of Saskatchewan. Acoose is a professor of indigenous literature, a distinguished scholar, journalist, scriptwriter, and producer. She was Saskatchewan's first Native Affairs columnist for the *Saskatoon Star Phoenix*. Brenda Zeman was born in Saskatoon, Saskatchewan, in 1951. She received a bachelor of science degree in anthropology from McMaster University in Ontario. Zeman received a teacher's certificate in 1977 from the University of Toronto, where she was a professional track-and-field athlete with the Toronto Tigers. She earned a master's degree in cultural anthropology from California State University at Long Beach. Zeman has said, "Athletes make good actors, because both professions excel at performance. In fact, I don't perceive many differences between sport and art." Both Acoose and Zeman have talked about writing as a mission. Do you believe that writers have the power to change the world in any way? Do they have a responsibility to do so? What kinds of writers do you think are the most influential? If you were to become a professional writer, what genre of writing would you pursue?

JANICE: Running has always been a tradition in my family. It was thoughts of my mooshum that inspired me as I first played with the idea of becoming a runner myself. Finally one day I thought, Janice Acoose, you are the granddaughter of Paul Acoose, one of the great long-distance runners, so what are you doing? Get out there and run. It's in your blood! *(Street sounds, birds. She begins to run.)*

I remember that first morning I went out to run. It was a warm day in March. The last of winter's cold was disappearing. It reminded me of another such morning a long time ago, the first time I met my mooshum. *(Street cross-fades to sound of powwow drums, singing.)* My dad told us we were going to the reserve to a powwow. You know, coming from the city, the only knowledge I had of my people were images I had seen in movies, rough and wild-looking creatures. When we drove through the gate I saw a number of tents set up. There were children and dogs running about. Almost immediately my dad's face broke out in a wide grin. And then I saw this man coming toward us. The sound of bells tinkled from his moccasins as they softly struck the ground. His face was painted up and he wore a bonnet of feathers. "Grandfather?" I said. And I remember him replying, "Noosisim, I'm your mooshum. You call me mooshum." *(Street traffic, running, come up again.)*

My memories were interrupted by city traffic that squeezed me to the outer limits of the road, like I was an intruder. So I turned around and started jogging toward open country.

My mooshum always hated cars. He would never ride in them. He walked everywhere.

I remember the first time I discovered he was a runner. A moonyaw, or a whiteman, had come out to the reserve to paint his picture. I asked him why that man was there. He motioned for me to sit down beside him and then he began to tell me his story. He talked about his father, Old Samuel Acoose, and his grandfather, Quewich, both famous runners. He told me of places he had raced in, places that seemed like they were on the other side of the world, like Madison Square Garden in New York City, Vancouver and Winnipeg. As he talked, the age disappeared and he looked strong and proud.

I reminded myself that I have a long way to go to achieve the kind of inner strength he had, and I turned and headed for home. As I ran I thought of how he must have felt when he returned home from racing. He was a hero, a world-class runner. But on the reserve, every aspect of his life was controlled by an Indian Agent.

My mooshum was a proud man, rich in the knowledge of his culture, yet prohibited by law from carrying on the traditions of his grandfathers. I can still hear him proudly speaking of the rain dance and the joy he felt as a grass dancer. But I also remember the Sunday ritual, when he would worship the Christian god. Rather than hold his head high in pride as he did when he spoke of the rain dance, he hung his head as he entered the house of worship.

Anger came over me as I remembered the way he was treated. But almost as soon as it came, it was gone.

I thought of the years when I watched my grandparents grow old. My kookum bedridden with illness, my mooshum always by her side. When she slept, he would sit with us kids, him in the middle and us all around. He told us then about the strengths and the beliefs of our people, the Saulteaux. He tried to teach us our language and instill values within us by telling us stories. I remember one thing he told me, "Never throw your hair away when you comb it." He said your hair is your strength. He reached into his pocket and showed me a little white bear. He told me he kept his and my kookum's hair and always wrapped it around the white bear. This always kept them safe. Then he put it back in the pocket closest to his heart.

My kookum and mooshum were two unique spirits. Their home on the reserve was a special meeting place for all my cousins, aunts and uncles. That special feeling isn't there anymore.

As I got to the last part of my run I slowed down to a walk, so I could cool down. Because of all the running, my legs were numb and my feet felt as though they weren't touching the ground! It was then I finally *really* understood my grandfather's name—Acoose, "Man Standing Above Ground."

Notes

mooshum grandfather

noosisim granddaughter

Madison Square Garden a sports and entertainment complex in New York City

Indian Agent historically, the representative of the government who lived on First Nations reserves and was in charge of many aspects of reserve life

rain dance a dance that honours rain and its importance to the nation

grass dancer a dancer whose job is to flatten the grass in the arena before a powwow; the "grass" also refers to the braids of sweetgrass tied to the dancer's belt.

kookum grandmother

Saulteaux a branch of the Ojibwa First Nation that lives in western Ontario and eastern Manitoba

Activities

1. What was your response to the voice and character of the speaker, Janice? To what extent do you think the identity of Janice, the monologuist, overlaps with Janice Acoose, the playwright, and Janice Acoose, the granddaughter of Paul Acoose? To what extent do Acoose's three roles lend authenticity to the work? What else do you think the playwrights might have had in mind when they made this choice of speaker?

2. Examine the structure of this monologue. How is it organized? Consider how the playwrights have balanced elements from the past and the present; dialogue and narrative; reflection and description. How has the content of the speech been shaped by its dramatic purpose?

3. Dramatize the life of a historical character, friend, or family member in a short radio play. You may want to obtain a copy of a complete, one-act radio play to use as a model for your own work. Prepare a taped performance of your play and present it to a group. Invite feedback on how effectively you employed the technical tools of radio drama, such as sound effects, music, and narrative bridges, to strengthen your play's impact.

FILM LOCATION FOR Random Passage

CBC Television

Random Passage is a CBC television film based on two novels by Bernice Morgan, whose story "Windows" appears on pages 109–117 of this anthology. This film, set in the early nineteenth century and shot in 2000, depicts the life of fictional character Mary Bundle from her indenture in England to her new pioneer life in St. John's and Cape Random, Newfoundland. In the photograph, the film's director, John N. Smith, who is seated, watches as a camera operator films a scene in which a boat in the distance slowly approaches the shores of Cape Random. If you were selecting locations for a film, what requirements would you have for an indoor set and for an outdoor set? Are there features of a location that are essential for all film sets, regardless of subject matter?

Activities

1. Still photography captures a moment in time. What are some of the elements this photograph reveals about the moment in time in which it was taken? Are you able to surmise anything about the atmosphere of the film set from this photograph? If someone looked at this photograph a hundred years from now, which features would reflect the culture and the era in which this film was created?

2. Consider what role in the filmmaking process the woman seated in the foreground of the photograph might have. Then, adopting the tone of a professional person in her work environment, write, present, and evaluate a dramatic monologue in the voice of this woman.

2000, black-and-white print ▶

Stop!

Donna Lewis

Donna Lewis was born in Winnipeg, Manitoba, in 1963 and grew up in nearby Sperling. She received a bachelor's degree from the University of Manitoba in 1984. Lewis is a film and stage actor and a playwright. She taught acting at the Manitoba Theatre for Young People, and has been a teacher of English as a Second Language and of yoga. Lewis has also collaborated on the writing of plays, including *How Do You Do?* which was produced by the Prairie Theatre Alliance of Manitoba. In *Stop!* Lewis uses humour to explore the practice of meditation. When a writer explores a subject in a humorous way, do you think the main purpose is to "make fun of" the subject, or can there be other reasons for doing so? If so, what are some of the results achieved by taking a lighter approach to a subject?

Characters

A Meditator

Three Actors: ONE, TWO, THREE, personifying thoughts.

Setting

An empty stage.

(A MEDITATOR *sits on stage listening to a meditation tape.)*

TAPED VOICE: The idea of meditation is to quiet the mind… To bring about a stillness, a peaceful state, free from the confusion of your constant daily thoughts. Sit quietly and comfortably. Breathe deeply… Relax and breathe… Thoughts will come marching in.

(Enter ONE, TWO, THREE. *They stand just behind the* MEDITATOR *who expresses facially and physically what they are saying at times, while at other times is rather perplexed by what is being said.)*

But don't let them control you. After all, who's in the driver's seat?

*(*MEDITATOR *points to self questioningly.)*

You are! Now relax. And pay attention to your breath.

*(*MEDITATOR *takes a deep breath. Throughout the play, the actors can use deep breathing where appropriate for laughs or poignancy.)*

ONE: I hope I'm not offending anyone.

THREE: Buy breath mints, toothpaste, chewing gum. Eat less garlic.

ONE: It's just that sometimes it's like I'm rotting inside. As if the food just goes into my gut and just sits there.

THREE: Have that looked at.

ONE: What do they give you for rotting insides anyway? He'll probably tell me the rotting thing is all in my mind…just some crazy thought. Maybe he'll give me one of those pills that just has sugar in it. What do you call those again?

THREE: Pla-ce-bo, Latin for "I shall please."

ONE: They can give you pills to fix anything. They have this chemical called digitalis. I hear it regulates your heartbeat. It makes your heart normal.

Two:	Boomboomboomboomboomboomboomboom. Boomboom… Boomboom… Boomboom.
One:	Nowadays you have to do this—*(Makes quotation sign with hands.)*—when you say the word "normal." And then you have to say "if there is such a thing."
Three:	Normal is a relative term.
Two:	My relative's dog had a heart murmur. It had this extra part to its heartbeat. Kinda like boom boom chh. Boom boom chh. She said it didn't affect him except that he would never be able to fly. I mean in an airplane, the "normal" way.
One:	Before you go getting a dog, they say you really should be able to take care of your houseplants. Then, when you can manage the plants and the pets, then you are ready to have a baby.
Three:	Water the plants. Feed the dog. Have a baby.
Two:	I remember when I was a baby.
One:	I'm sure babies can see what you are like inside. I've noticed that some babies really seem to like me. They smile and laugh.

(Two smiles and laughs.)
> But then there are other babies who really don't like me at all. In fact whenever I am near them, they start screaming.

(Two screams. Meditator covers ears.)
> What if I had one of those babies. One that didn't like me. One that hated me. It'd be awful.

Three:	It is unfair to bring a child into this world. Water the plants. Feed the dog. Eat a healthy breakfast.
One:	I caught a glimpse of myself in the toaster this morning. Scary.

THREE:	Breakfast—the most important meal of the day. Start the day off right!
ONE:	My face looked all distorted in the front of the toaster. The top of my head lined up perfectly with the top of the toaster. Toast, toast, toast, I'm thinking about toast. Then all of a sudden the toast comes popping out of the toaster just like it was popping out of the top of my head. My thoughts came right out of my head. Pow! A couple of Tylenol and back to bed.
TWO:	I remember when I was little. I used to stare into the big stainless steel tea kettle. It was round, so whatever was close up to the round, protruding part looked really big, but whatever was further away looked really small. I'd stand back and put my hand out in front, right near the kettle, and my hand would be gigantic and the rest of me would be miniature and I'd say in a deep voice, "Stop!"
THREE:	*(Sings.)* "Stop in the name of love, before you break my heart."
TWO:	It was a lot of fun until I burned my hand on the boiling kettle. I feel like my hand can remember that last "stop!"
THREE:	*(Sings.)* "Think it o–o–ver."
ONE:	If only my palm reader were able to speak English. He studies my hand and then looks up at me and says, "Afraid, so afraid. Why? Why so afraid?" Then he says, "You are so so lucky."
THREE:	Buy a lottery ticket. Mail *Reader's Digest* Sweepstakes. Say a prayer to Saint Jude, patron saint of hopeless causes. Be more positive.
ONE:	So was it like this, "You are *so so* lucky!" or "You are so-so lucky"? *(Makes a hand gesture meaning "sort of.")* Hmmm.

THREE:	*(Sings.)* "Think it o–o–ver. Think it o–o–ver."
TWO:	Our family's pretty lucky. When I was a baby, a world traveller came to work for my dad at harvest time and one night he snuck away in the middle of the night without taking one of his suitcases. He didn't say anything—if he'd be back for it, or what was in it or anything… The suitcase…filled with treasures from the Orient?… Or dirty socks and underwear?
ONE:	So lucky. So so lucky. So-so lucky.
TWO:	The suitcase has always been there, ever since I can remember and nobody's looked inside. It isn't even locked. I snapped the latch open one day but it had this safety catch that kept it from flying open. I wanted to see what was inside but some deep voice in me said "stop." What if I brought bad luck to my family?
THREE:	*(Sings softly.)* "Stop before you tear us apart. Think it o–o–ver."
TWO:	Still, you gotta wonder what's in there—what you're missing… Now it's kept up in the attic.
THREE:	Out of sight, out of mind.
ONE:	That time the door-to-door vacuum salesman vacuumed my head in a demonstration, man, did that machine pick up a lot of dirt. My guests and I could not believe the dust and lint that was sucked from my head.
THREE:	Cleanliness is next to godliness.
ONE:	Now I shampoo as often as I can. Not being obsessive about it or anything. But…
TWO:	Still, you gotta wonder what's in there—what you're missing…
ONE:	It's the same with germs. They say we have the germ of pneumonia inside us all the time. They say our thoughts

	can make us sick or well. Each one of us has pneumonia right this very second, but we might not know it. (TWO *starts coughing.*) Only if you start showing the symptoms does it become…apparent.
Two:	Still, you gotta wonder what's in there—what you are missing…I used to play hide-and-go-seek. I'd hide so well no one could find me, and after a while they'd stop wondering where I was, start playing something else, and forget that I was missing.
One:	That woman in the paper. She was about my age. She sure had something inside her.
Three:	*(Speaks as though reading a news report.)* "We do not know whether there is a danger that she will spontaneously combust again. We've consulted with experts on this and they have no idea. We're hoping that it was a one-time response to a horrible situation and we are trying to calm her fears about this."
One:	She was just walking home and somebody jumped her. Boom! She burst into flames. She had all that fire inside her, just kind of smouldering. Nobody even knew. Not even her. Certainly not her assailant or he would have thought twice.
Three:	One. Two. Never mind.
One:	The woman survived and is now in hospital with third-degree burns to her entire body. Reporters say her burns are minor compared to her trauma of discovering she was capable of so much fire.
Three:	*(Sings.)* "I don't want to set the world on fire. I just want to start a flame in your heart."
Two:	My heart skipped a beat. Boomboom…Boom. Boomboom. Still, you gotta wonder what's in there. What's missing.

ONE:	Who's to say what could reignite her... Or me, for instance.
THREE:	A dirty look. One too many questions at the border. A simple phrase, "Let's just be friends."
TWO:	I remember the black-and-white days of Laurel and Hardy. They'd be in a small room with a package that was actually an uninflated life raft, and they'd end up pulling a plug or pushing a button, or doing something unintentional like that. And that tiniest gesture set off the process and the life raft would become enormous in no time. It was like the thing had all this "space" in it all along. The air had always been there; it just needed to be triggered.
THREE:	Emotions are in the body. They are in the body.
TWO:	I feel so big inside. So very big. And there's so many trigger points...so many safety valves... Still, you gotta wonder what's inside.
ONE:	Things like that really make you stop and think.
TWO:	Stop!
ONE:	I'm not sure what to think, but I can't stop thinking about it.
THREE:	Come to a complete stop. Count to three. One... Two... Three. Three-way stop. Always yield the right of way. Driving is a privilege, not a right.

ONE, TWO, and THREE: *(Together.)* Who's in the driver's seat?

MEDITATOR: I am! *(Puts hand out in front.)* Stop!

(The end.)

Notes

meditation the practice of focusing the mind through contemplation. This mental exercise has been a central component of many world religions and, in the twentieth century, a secular form was popularized as a means of reducing stress.

Activities

1. If you were the costume designer for this play, how would you dress the characters? Record your ideas in your journal and then discuss them in a group. After your discussion, reflect on the various approaches to costuming within your group and decide which of them you would choose if you were staging the play.

2. How has the author used diction and syntax to differentiate among characters One, Two, and Three? Reread the speeches by each character independent of their context and make notes on their distinctive styles and tones. By what other means does the author distinguish the characters from each other? Discuss and compare your ideas in a group.

3. If you could turn the three dominant aspects of your personality into characters, what would they be like? Imagine a conversation among these characters in a setting of your choice and write a play modelled on *Stop!* Before writing your script, make notes on the various directions the dialogue will take and identify the climax toward which you are moving. Present a dramatic reading of your play to your class.

Another Viewpoint: Critical Approaches

Psychological literary criticism often examines the author and the author's writings in the framework of Freudian psychology. Freudians divide the personality into three functional parts: id, ego, and superego. Look up these terms in several reference books and create your own definition for each. Consider which of the play's characters—One, Two, or Three—might represent the id, the ego, and the superego, respectively. How does this way of approaching the characters affect your thinking about the play?

Dead Parrot

Monty Python

Monty Python, a group of six British writers and performers, was formed in 1969 to create a comedy show for British television, *Monty Python's Flying Circus*. The result was a half-hour compilation of live sketches combined with some animation. Between 1969 and 1972, forty-five episodes of this extremely popular show were produced. The troupe also created several movies, including *And Now for Something Completely Different* (1972) and *Monty Python and the Holy Grail* (1975). To what extent is your sense of humour similar to or different from that of your friends? Are you more likely to laugh at physical comedy or a witty exchange of words? Why?

ANIMATION: including dancing Botticelli Venus, which links to pet shop. MR. PRALINE walks into the shop carrying a dead parrot in a cage. He walks to counter where SHOPKEEPER tries to hide below cash register.

PRALINE:	Hello, I wish to register a complaint... Hello? Miss?
SHOPKEEPER:	What do you mean, miss?
PRALINE:	Oh, I'm sorry, I have a cold. I wish to make a complaint.
SHOPKEEPER:	Sorry, we're closing for lunch.
PRALINE:	Never mind that, my lad, I wish to complain about this parrot that I purchased not half an hour ago from this very boutique.
SHOPKEEPER:	Oh yes, the Norwegian Blue. What's wrong with it?

PRALINE: I'll tell you what's wrong with it. It's dead, that's what's wrong with it.

SHOPKEEPER: No, no, it's resting, look!

PRALINE: Look, my lad, I know a dead parrot when I see one and I'm looking at one right now.

SHOPKEEPER: No, no sir, it's not dead. It's resting.

PRALINE: Resting?

SHOPKEEPER: Yeah, remarkable bird the Norwegian Blue, beautiful plumage, innit?

PRALINE: The plumage don't enter into it—it's stone dead.

SHOPKEEPER: No, no—it's just resting.

PRALINE: All right then, if it's resting I'll wake it up. *(shouts into cage)* Hello Polly! I've got a nice cuttlefish for you when you wake up, Polly Parrot!

SHOPKEEPER: *(jogging cage)* There, it moved.

PRALINE: No, he didn't. That was you pushing the cage.

SHOPKEEPER: I did not.

PRALINE: Yes, you did. *(takes parrot out of cage, shouts)* Hello Polly, Polly. *(bangs it against counter)* Polly Parrot, wake up, Polly. *(throws it in the air and lets it fall to the floor)* Now that's what I call a dead parrot.

SHOPKEEPER: No, no, it's stunned.

PRALINE: Look, my lad, I've had just about enough of this. That parrot is definitely deceased. And when I bought it not half an hour ago, you assured me that its lack of movement was due to it being tired and shagged out after a long squawk.

SHOPKEEPER: It's probably pining for the fiords.

PRALINE:	Pining for the fiords, what kind of talk is that? Look, why did it fall flat on its back the moment I got it home?
SHOPKEEPER:	The Norwegian Blue prefers kipping on its back. Beautiful bird, lovely plumage.
PRALINE:	Look, I took the liberty of examining that parrot, and I discovered that the only reason that it had been sitting on its perch in the first place was that it had been nailed there.
SHOPKEEPER:	Well, of course it was nailed there. Otherwise it would muscle up to those bars and voom.
PRALINE:	Look, matey *(picks up parrot),* this parrot wouldn't voom if I put four thousand volts through it. It's bleeding demised.
SHOPKEEPER:	It's not, it's pining.
PRALINE:	It's not pining, it's passed on. This parrot is no more. It has ceased to be. It's expired and gone to meet its maker. This is a late parrot. It's a stiff. Bereft of life, it rests in peace. If you hadn't nailed it to the perch, it would be pushing up the daisies. It's rung down the curtain and joined the choir invisible. This is an ex-parrot.
SHOPKEEPER:	Well, I'd better replace it then.

Notes

innit a slang expression meaning "isn't it"

shagged out a slang expression meaning "exhausted"

pining yearning; from the Old English *pīnian,* meaning "to cause to suffer"

kipping a slang expression meaning "sleeping"

Activities

1. Write a short personal response to this selection. What elements appeal or do not appeal to you? Meet with a small group to compare your reactions and identify the comedic techniques used in the script. Are there common social, cultural, personality, or demographic attributes that affect the reactions of group members? To what extent do these factors affect your response to other forms of comedy? Present your conclusions to the class.

2. Comedy relies on the actors' use of their voices and their movements, as well as the words they speak. Make a copy of the script. Work with a small group to experiment with ways of delivering the lines by focusing on volume, pitch, facial expressions, physical movements, and timing. Then insert stage directions into the script. Present the script as a readers' theatre and compare the choices you made with those of other groups. If possible, view a videotape of the original Monty Python sketch and consider the extent to which their delivery enhanced the material.

3. View several episodes of a comedy show. Write an essay analyzing the intended audience and the underlying values reflected in the material. Make connections with the social or historical context in which the programs appeared. You may choose recent episodes of a program such as *The Royal Canadian Air Farce* or *This Hour Has Twenty-Two Minutes*, or videotapes and reruns of programs such as *SCTV* or *Monty Python's Flying Circus*.

Another Viewpoint: Literary Modes and Forms

The literary mode of comedy has a rich history and tradition. Do research into this mode by focusing on such conventions of traditional comedy as the use of stock characters and situations, bombastic language, and slapstick. Then write an analytical essay in which you consider to what extent "Dead Parrot" falls within the tradition of a classic literary comedy.

wrap-up
d r a m a

1. Use the Internet or other sources to identify some well-known stage plays that have been adapted as television or feature films. Choose a film video that is easily accessible to you and find its script. Read the play and then watch the film, taking detailed notes on how the play has been interpreted on camera. Write a review that presents a strong argument for why you would or would not recommend the film. Use the Internet to look up reviews of other play adaptations for ideas on what you might include.

2. Choose one character from a dramatic work in this unit or from a story in the short fiction unit. Write and then present a monologue in which the character you have chosen reflects on her or his life ten years later. Maintain a consistent point of view in your portrayal by accurately reflecting what the character would see, know, and feel, and how he or she would speak. Rehearse your monologue aloud to yourself. Tape-record and replay it to determine whether it sounds like the voice of your chosen character. Present the monologue to your classmates and get their feedback on its effectiveness.

3. With a small group, select one or more scenes from a dramatic work in this unit, and, on chart paper, outline a plan for its set design. Be sure your plan contains the following: a clear statement of the rationale for your design, a description of the physical space you will use, rough sketches of the set, and a description of each element of the design, such as backdrops and props. Present your plan to the class and elicit their feedback on your rationale and design choices.

4. Work with a partner. Choose a dramatic selection in this anthology to convert from one dramatic form into another—for example, from a stage play into a radio play. Before you begin, study samples of the two forms you have chosen. Note the main script conventions of these forms, such as dialogue format, directions for actors' movements, use of props and sound effects, choice of camera shots, and set descriptions. Create a checklist of these conventions. Share your list with a small group and make revisions based on feedback. With your partner, write the script for your adaptation, carefully reviewing the revised checklist to make sure you have observed the conventions you identified.

Who was William Shakespeare? Today Shakespeare is considered more than just a brilliant writer from another era. Through his works, Shakespeare continues to have an influence throughout the world. In fact, his extraordinary talent has led scholars to question whether just one person of Shakespeare's background could have accomplished so many achievements. His very identity has been debated. We do know that there was a William Shakespeare who was born in Stratford-upon-Avon, England, in 1564. As a young man, he moved to London to become an actor and playwright. By 1590, he was active on the London stage. Over the next decade, he wrote such plays as *Romeo and Juliet* (1595), *A Midsummer Night's Dream* (1596), and *Julius Caesar* (1599). In 1599, Shakespeare's company, the Lord Chamberlain's Men, built their own theatre, The Globe, on the south bank of the river Thames. Works such as *Hamlet*, *King Lear*, and *Macbeth* were premiered there in the early seventeenth century.

Shakespeare's literary output was prodigious. His impact on cultural history and on the English language itself is inestimable. Many individual works of literature, contemporary drama, music and opera, dance, film, fine art, and non-fiction, and even such commercial media works as advertisements, have been inspired by or based on Shakespeare's work or contain allusions to it. At times, when Shakespeare could not come up with a suitable word, he invented one. Many of these invented words have remained within the modern English language. Phrases from his plays, such as "To be or not to be," have become very familiar. The depth with which Shakespeare's writing embodies human life and passion—our fears, hopes, frustrations, aspirations, secrets, victories, and defeats—can at times be breathtaking.

This In-Depth explores the pervasiveness of Shakespeare's influence. Included is a profile of a costume designer from the Stratford Festival in Ontario, who has created her own works of art for numerous Shakespearean play productions. An excerpt from Kenneth Branagh's screenplay of *Hamlet* allows us to experience how a screenwriter adapts an original play to bring it to life on screen. The question-and-answer format of a filmmakers' symposium offers insights by renowned film directors into their interpretations of Shakespeare's work. Examples of literary criticism—a classic segment on tragedy by A.C. Bradley and a contemporary take on comedy by Angela Pitt—allow us to enter the vibrant discipline of Shakespearean scholarship. And an anecdotal story by Stephen Leacock pokes fun at the discipline of Shakespearean criticism. As you explore some ways in which, centuries after his death, William Shakespeare continues to shape our lives, consider how other writers have had an impact on both your thinking and your decisions.

A print of a seventeenth century black-and-white engraving from a frontispiece to a published collection of Shakespeare's plays. The portrait of William Shakespeare is by Martin Droeshout.

Invisible Genius: The Quiet Talent of Tanya Moiseiwitsch

Therese Greenwood

Therese Greenwood was born in 1962 on Wolfe Island, Ontario, one of the Thousand Islands near the city of Kingston. She holds a master's degree in journalism, has worked as a reporter, editor, and journalism professor, and is a regular correspondent for CBC Radio. She has also written historical fiction set in the Kingston area. This article, which appeared in the *Kingston Whig-Standard* magazine, describes the brilliance of Tanya Moiseiwitsch, a theatrical costume designer. What do you think are the responsibilities of a costume designer when designing the clothing for characters in a play? What do the clothes you wear suggest to others about yourself? How can clothes be symbolic of specific characteristics of society?

At first glance, it seems strange that the Stratford Festival's exhibition of theatre designs by Tanya Moiseiwitsch should contain only one letter of praise from a major theatrical figure. The exhibition, after all, celebrates a 40-year association between the festival and a woman whom many theatre experts consider the world's premier designer. Somewhere, one feels sure, there must be a trunk packed with letters from the world's greatest theatrical personalities, all testifying to her talents. For Tanya Moiseiwitsch has rubbed shoulders with such people as Sir Alec Guinness, Dame Edith Evans, James Mason, Vanessa Redgrave, and Sir Ralph Richardson—costuming many of them during her work at Stratford, where she designed 29 productions including both of the festival's inaugural shows in 1953.

Surprising, then, that the exhibition at the Gallery Stratford features only one testimonial, written by Sir Laurence Olivier 20 years ago for an earlier exhibition of her work? Not really. For in fact the absence of rave reviews from celebrities is a reflection of the personality of Tanya Moiseiwitsch, an artist who was able to command all the beauty and power of the theatre without placing herself at centre stage. Indeed, it is that very ability that has made her one of the world's best designers.

"I've yet to see a designer who has bettered her," says Ronald Bryden, theatre critic and drama professor at the University of Toronto. "There are designers who are more noticeable, who make a big splash on stage. She's the only one who's too good to make the splash."

Laurence Olivier would have agreed. "Tanya Moiseiwitsch is a very wonderful designer," he wrote in his letter. "Painters are not usually so successful in so completely disguising themselves and sinking their personalities into each project as if it was the first solution they had ever found. Her voice, though excessively quiet, one might say—her manner so retiring one feared she would disappear through the wall—was always marvellously assertive and solution-finding in its own quiet way."

Ms. Moiseiwitsch, now retired from the theatre, retains her unfailing modesty. She evades questions about the impact her designs have had on Stratford and theatre in Canada by praising someone else: the curators, the actors who wore the costumes, Tyrone Guthrie. She apologizes for sounding "too serious" or a "bit solemn." She asks an interviewer if they may sit in another part of the building so she might avoid the sound of her own voice being played back to her on the videotaped interview that plays on an endless loop in one part of the exhibition.

Yet her genteel sensitivity also has an air of theatricality. It is not theatricality in the vulgar sense of striking a grandiose pose, but in the sense that certain secrets must be preserved if the theatre is to maintain its magic. Now, as she makes her annual visit to Stratford as a member of the audience, she refrains from making technical comments on the productions, determined to maintain the confederacy of silence that sustains the magic of the theatre.

"I do see that it's all so stimulating and I see the work that goes into it," she says. "I suppose anybody who's worked in the theatre sees that. But the audience isn't supposed to know that. I think a certain air of mystery should be preserved and the audience must find things out for themselves."

Helping to maintain the theatre's aura of mystery, making her brilliant contribution disappear into the overall production, is a hallmark of Moiseiwitsch design, says Mr. Bryden. Her costumes are never so flashy that they detract from the performers and always fortify the foundations of the production.

"They are never so obtrusive that they take away from the actors. She never uses a strong colour that jumps out at you. She provides the kind of clothing design that assists a director in saying that this is the central figure, these are the subordinate characters.

"She's a great researcher," says Mr. Bryden, pointing to her ability to assemble details from paintings, sculptures, and other artistic sources that give her costumes historical accuracy. If a director casts a play in the seventeenth century, Mr. Bryden says, Ms. Moiseiwitsch will not use a colour that paintings suggest had not then been invented.

"If you know your classical art, you can look at your references and you can see from some of her notes how she went around assembling her costumes from little bits of details she sketches and then uses in her designs."

Bearing out these observations are the questions carefully printed on some of the exhibition's sketches, asking "How does this fasten, hooks or eyes?" On another, of a man wearing a birdlike mask, is the note "Beak held antiseptics during the plague of 1665."

But Ms. Moiseiwitsch's greatest achievement, says Mr. Bryden, is her ability to conceive a costume as it will appear on stage, that is, as a three-dimensional product that, as an extension of the actor, will be required to physically occupy space.

"This is her great quality: she thinks in spatial terms," he says. "The clothes are always structural rather than pictorial. She doesn't choose colours that will make the costume look like an oil painting. She chooses materials that fall in structural folds. The costumes always look like sculpture rather than paintings."

The Stratford exhibition of Ms. Moiseiwitsch's work succeeds in recreating this impression by presenting her designs on faceless dummies. (The placards list the actors who wore the costumes to help the viewer envision a familiar face amid the material.) The impression is enhanced by posing the costumes on reconstructed portions of the festival's famous thrust stage designed by Ms. Moiseiwitsch and Tyrone Guthrie.

The construction of the thrust stage created the need for a designer who could think in spatial terms—and, indeed, was responsible for the initial success of the festival. It was the organizing committee's assurance that he would be allowed to construct a stage of his own design that ultimately lured the famous London director Tyrone Guthrie to the small Ontario town that dreamed of operating a world-class Shakespeare festival.

Guthrie had long argued that Shakespeare's works were not well suited to the "picture frame" proscenium stages common to most theatres. He felt that this type of stage, originally designed for performances of opera, isolated the audience from the performers and fostered the impression that the theatre was only an illusion. He championed the concept of a "thrust" stage, which literally thrusts out into the viewing area and is surrounded on three sides by the audience, allowing one scene to flow into the next without the obstruction of a curtain or scenery changes.

When the founders of the Stratford Festival gave Guthrie carte blanche to build his stage, it was natural that he ask Tanya Moiseiwitsch to take the ideas from his head and transform them into a working model. As World War II was drawing to a close, Guthrie had chosen Ms. Moiseiwitsch to work with him at the newly expanded Old Vic in Liverpool. By 1953, she had already designed more than 50 productions at Dublin's Abbey Theatre, 150 productions at the Oxford Playhouse, and productions at the Old Vic in Liverpool, Bristol, and London. Most importantly she shared his belief in the thrust stage.

"Miss Moiseiwitsch and I, who are old collaborators, had long dreamed of such a stage as was now to come into being," he wrote in his autobiography.

Writing in *The Oxford Companion to the Canadian Theatre*, Mr. Bryden sums up the effect of a platform that still dominates the style of the festival's productions:

> The novel thrust stage that Guthrie and Moiseiwitsch designed tried to recreate the original style of Shakespearean performance. It rescued the actor from painted scenery and restored the primacy of the spoken word. With the general shape and features of the Elizabethan platform stage, surrounded on three sides by an auditorium reminiscent of classical Greece, the stage also encouraged spectacle and movement, characteristics Guthrie exploited to the full as one colourful scene flowed smoothly into the next with a constant swirl of lavish costumes, eye-catching properties, and waving banners.

These eye-catching costumes and properties, necessary to create instant impressions of time, place, and mood, are essential, notes Mr. Bryden. "Guthrie said about the stage that she designed for him that it would need to be very richly furnished, that since they weren't going to have any scenery, costumes would have to do the work of the scenery." And, he adds, with the audience seated so much closer to the stage, props and costumes must look more authentic in order to bear up under closer scrutiny.

Most importantly, the thrust stage gives more "space" to actors, so that they are not seen within a frame, like pictures, but like sculptures occupying a three-dimensional space. This means it is important for a designer to think in terms of the space the actors—and their costumes—will occupy. It is a concept that Tanya Moiseiwitsch understood completely, and her grasp of it is perhaps best illustrated in this exhibition by one of the most magnificent pieces of her work, the coronation robe from the 1953 production of *Richard III* starring Alec Guinness.

Ms. Moiseiwitsch, predictably, credits Tyrone Guthrie with deciding that as Alec Guinness, weighed down by 40 yards of heavy red velvet, made the long, slow trek to his throne, his costume would telegraph a message to the audience.

"By the time he got to the throne," she says, "the whole of the stage was covered in red velvet. And that wasn't just showing-off-costume time. That was Guthrie. The thought behind it was, to get to the throne he had killed a lot of people, and this was an ocean of blood that he was carrying as a burden on his shoulders. Did everybody know what they were meant to think? No, absolutely not. But that was the thought behind it."

But the impression of this scene was much stronger than Ms. Moiseiwitsch allows, according to Ronald Bryden, who says that theatregoers still remember the scene and how a talented actor made use of this extraordinary prop.

"He used the whole stage. The cloak was designed to just about cover the entire stage," says Mr. Bryden. "Then, I'm told, Guinness turned around and walked on the velvet and it was as if he was saying, 'This is my kingdom and I can now enjoy it.' It was this feeling of royalty in space and he was taking advantage of it. Not many designers would think of that."

This careful thought, this ability to contribute to the pageantry of Shakespeare without upstaging the performer, is Ms. Moiseiwitsch's legacy to the theatre that influences how most Canadians view classical theatre. Also, the Stratford stage—since remodelled several times to incorporate minor modifications made under her supervision—has continued to define the type of performance staged at the festival. And its lavish costuming, although threatened by budgetary constraints, continues to measure up to the best in the world.

"She set a standard at Stratford," says Mr. Bryden, pointing out that from the beginning she insisted on professional standards, bringing in a staff of specialists and painstakingly training locals to carry out her designs. "Gradually all of that got built into Stratford, so that the wardrobe and properties department is superlative, one of the best in the world."

Although today's designers live up to her standards, they don't always live up to Ms. Moiseiwitsch's self-effacing approach. "Sometimes they swamp the stage and overwhelm the production," says Mr. Bryden. It is an error Ms. Moiseiwitsch never committed.

Looking over her designs, Ms. Moiseiwitsch can voice no regrets. She says she wouldn't change a thing. "If I could do it over again, I would refuse. You don't go and try to wipe up any kind of spilled milk. Just let it lie. That's the beauty of the theatre. Usually it's in people's memories rather than anything visible."

That has been Tanya Moiseiwitsch's true talent: the ability to remain invisible, her individual brilliance devoted to making others live in the memory of theatregoers.

Notes

Sir Alec Guinness, Dame Edith Evans, James Mason, Vanessa Redgrave, and Sir Ralph Richardson renowned stage and screen actors of the twentieth century

Stratford a city in Ontario, the site of the Stratford Festival of Canada; North America's largest repertory theatre, presenting the works of William Shakespeare and other playwrights

Sir Laurence Olivier (1907–1989) a renowned British actor, producer, and director, who won the Best Actor Academy Award for *Hamlet* (1948)

Plague of 1665 the London plague, also known as the Black Death, a highly contagious bacterial infection that reached epidemic proportions, killing over 100,000 people in and around London, England

"picture frame" proscenium stage a stage with an arch at the front, creating a visual frame for the theatrical audience

carte blanche unrestricted power or authority; a French-language phrase meaning literally "blank paper"

Richard III in this instance, the popular historical tragedy written by Shakespeare in 1594

Shakespeare was instrumental in building the Globe Theatre, which he described in the chorus of his play Henry V as a "wooden O." The centre of the Globe was open-air, but its perimeter had a roof over the stage and galleries. The theatre's thrust stage had no curtain and jutted from the rear wall into an open, unroofed yard that accommodated about 800 groundlings, or members of the standing audience. When the house was full, approximately 1,500 spectators sat in the galleries. By all accounts, the audiences at the Globe were very vocal and participatory, calling back to the actors and throwing objects onto the stage if they were displeased.

From

Hamlet

William Shakespeare and Kenneth Branagh

Actor, director, producer, and writer Kenneth Branagh was born in Belfast, Northern Ireland, in 1960. He studied at the Royal Academy of Dramatic Arts and joined the Royal Shakespeare Company at the age of twenty-three. In 1988, he left that company to form his own, the Renaissance Theatre Company. Often credited with creating a popular movie audience for Shakespeare, Branagh has developed and starred in a number of film adaptations of the bard's plays, including *Henry V* (1989) and *Hamlet* (1996). This excerpt, from Branagh's screenplay, corresponds to Act I, Scene 2 of *Hamlet*. In it, Hamlet has returned home to find that his father is dead and his Uncle Claudius has become both his stepfather and the new king. How might a screenplay script of a Shakespearean work differ from the original play? In what ways might these differences affect how you approach your reading of a screenplay script?

Cut to:
Interior/State Hall Day
A glorious procession of the new King Claudius: *and his* Queen Gertrude. *We move with them into a packed gathering of smiling Courtiers and Commoners. The men are crisp, sexy. The military cut—all dashing clothes and hair. The women's clothes colourful, gloriously textured, shapely and flesh-revealing.*

They walk from the enormous doors through rows of bleachers. It's like the House of Commons. Everyone stands. The guard of honour salutes.

CLAUDIUS *in full military regalia. Severe cropped hair, brushed back, standing to attention atop a striking face that bears a crisp beard.* GERTRUDE, *complete with veil and generous bosom on show, also trim and vigorous. This irresistibly sexy, confident couple reach the throne. They face their Audience of bright festive colours and supportive faces.*

The King begins to speak. Measured, compassionate, intelligent. All listen attentively, particularly the Prime Minister, POLONIUS, *his son* LAERTES, *and his beautiful daughter* OPHELIA.

CLAUDIUS
Though yet of Hamlet our dear brother's death
The memory be green, and that it us befitted
To bear our hearts in grief, and our whole Kingdom
To be contracted in one brow of woe,
Yet so far hath discretion fought with nature
That we with wisest sorrow think on him
Together with remembrance of ourselves.
>*Moist eyes. A man of genuine compassion.*

CLAUDIUS *(continuing)*
Therefore our sometime sister, now our Queen
>*She, also moved, emotions very close to the surface.*

CLAUDIUS *(continuing)*
Th' imperial jointress of this warlike state,
Have we as 'twere with a defeated joy,
With one auspicious and one dropping eye,
With mirth in funeral and with dirge in marriage,
In equal scale weighing delight and dole,
Taken to wife.
>*(He kisses her hand.)*
Nor have we herein barred
Your better wisdoms, which have freely gone
With this affair along. For all, our thanks.
>*Slow, then quickening and intense applause. He overrides this reaction with his clearly genuine gratitude to this court. Now to business and*

a serious public policy statement for a worried nation. MARCELLUS *is not alone in his fears.*

CLAUDIUS *(continuing)*
Now follows that you know young Fortinbras,
Holding a weak supposal of our worth,
Or thinking by our late dear brother's death
Our state to be disjoint and out of frame,
Co-leaguèd with the dream of his advantage,
He hath not failed to pester us with message
> *An Attendant gives him a paper.*
Importing the surrender of those lands
Lost by his father, with all bonds of law,
To our most valiant brother.
> *He tears up the paper. There is a gasp from the* CROWD, *then applause. He's playing them well.*
So much for him.
> *Now, tougher still. He's into Norman Schwarzkopf mode. There will be no messing with the Danish King. He plays it out confidently to the gallery, taking another paper.*

CLAUDIUS *(continuing)*
Now for ourself, and for this time of meeting,
Thus much the business is: we have here writ
To Norway, uncle of young Fortinbras—
> *Cut to:*
> *Interior/Bedroom Night (Flashback)*
> *We see the wizened, frightened old man.*

CLAUDIUS V/O
Who, impotent and bed-rid, scarcely hears
Of this his nephew's purpose—to suppress
> *The face grows dark. We see the surly young* FORTINBRAS, *tearing up the map.*

Claudius V/O
His further gait herein, in that the levies,
The lists, and full proportions are all made
Out of his subject;
> *Cut to:*
> *Interior/State Hall Day (Real time)*

Claudius
and we here dispatch
You, good Cornelius, and you, Voltemand,
> *The two wise men, also in military garb, move to the throne.*

Claudius
For bearers of this greeting to old Norway,
Giving to you no further personal power
To business with the King more than the scope
Of these dilated articles allow.
Farewell, and let your haste commend your duty.
> **Voltemand** *takes the papers.*

Voltemand
In that, and all things, will we show our duty.

Claudius
We doubt it nothing, heartily farewell.
> *The* **Audience** *applauds. No hysteria this time, but all are quietly
> impressed by this statesmanship. Time now to turn on the charm with
> the young aristocrats. Also a good show for the ladies, who crane their
> necks on the balconies to see which of the bright young things around
> the throne will be indulged with a public favour.*

Claudius
And now, Laertes, what's the news with you?
You told us of some suit.
> *A darkly handsome young man steps forward. In the uniform of a
> cadet.*

CLAUDIUS *(continuing)*
What is't, Laertes?
You cannot speak of reason to the Dane
And lose your voice. What wouldst thou beg, Laertes,
That shall not be my offer, not thy asking?
The head is not more native to the heart,
The hand more instrumental to the mouth,
Than is the throne of Denmark to thy father.

> *He turns to* POLONIUS, *once again letting the court know how the power structure stands. Then on with a smile.*

CLAUDIUS *(continuing)*
What wouldst thou have, Laertes?

LAERTES *(nervous)*
My dread lord,
Your leave and favour to return to France,

> *Knowing looks from around the court. The phrase "sowing wild oats" comes to people's minds.* LAERTES *responds quickly.*

LAERTES
From whence, though willingly I came to Denmark
To show my duty in your coronation,
Yet now I must confess, that duty done,
My thoughts and wishes bend again towards France
And bow them to your gracious leave and pardon.

> *The King teases it out for a moment.*

CLAUDIUS
Have you your father's leave? What says Polonius?

> *Dad joins in with the gentle ribbing.*

POLONIUS
He hath, my lord, wrung from me my slow leave
By laboursome petition and at last
Upon his will I sealed my hard consent.
I do beseech you give him leave to go.

CLAUDIUS *steps down to* LAERTES.

CLAUDIUS
Take thy fair hour, Laertes. Time be thine,
And thy best graces spend it at thy will.
> *As the* AUDIENCE *applauds, the Camera tracks slowly past them and comes to a halt under the right hand balcony. There at the other end of the hall is a black silhouette of a man. We make an abrupt Cut. The humorous applause that has greeted* LAERTES' *departure is stopped by a big Close-up on* CLAUDIUS *and his firm tone.*

CLAUDIUS *(continuing)*
But note, my cousin Hamlet, and my son—
> *We make another abrupt Cut back to the lonely figure behind the bleachers.*

HAMLET
A little more than kin, and less than kind.

CLAUDIUS
How is it that the clouds still hang on you?
> *From* CLAUDIUS' *POV we see* HAMLET *move forward and sit down.*

HAMLET
Not so, my lord, I am too much in the sun.
> *We see reaction on the* AUDIENCE'S *faces. This is embarrassing. The* QUEEN *moves away from the throne and we see her and her son in profile 2-shot. She attempts intimacy. This should not be public.*

GERTRUDE
Good Hamlet, cast thy nighted colour off,
And let thine eye look like a friend on Denmark.
Do not for ever with thy vailèd lids
Seek for thy noble father in the dust.
Thou know'st 'tis common—all that lives must die,
Passing through nature to eternity.

HAMLET
Ay, madam, it is common.

GERTRUDE
If it be,
Why seems it so particular with thee?
> *In his shocked reaction he raises his voice, so that the* CROWD *can almost hear the hissed reproaches that he shoots at her grief-free demeanour.*

HAMLET
Seems, madam? Nay, it is. I know not "seems."
'Tis not alone my inky cloak, good mother
Nor customary suits of solemn black,
Nor windy suspiration of forced breath,
No, nor the fruitful river in the eye,
Nor the dejected haviour of the visage,
Together with all forms, moods, shapes of grief
That can denote me truly. These indeed "seem,"
For they are actions that a man might play;
But I have that within which passeth show—
These but the trappings and the suits of woe.
> *There are whispers now through the* CROWD. *They're witnessing a scene that should take place behind closed doors.* CLAUDIUS *has had enough. Time for action.*

CLAUDIUS
'Tis sweet and commendable in your nature, Hamlet,
> *He goes toward the Prince bringing in the* CROWD *with his voice. This will now be a very public conversation.*

CLAUDIUS (*continuing*)
To give these mourning duties to your father;
But you must know your father lost a father;
That father lost, lost his; and the survivor bound
In filial obligation for some term
To do obsequious sorrow. But to persevere

In obstinate condolement is a course
Of impious stubbornness, 'tis unmanly grief,
It shows a will most incorrect to heaven,

> *As* CLAUDIUS *gives this rough lecture, he directs his injunctions to the physically immobile Prince. The great gallery of Courtiers behind, packed to the rafters. The power and strength of the King's position chillingly clear.*

CLAUDIUS *(continuing)*
A heart unfortified, a mind impatient.
An understanding simple and unschooled;
For what we know must be, and is as common
As any the most vulgar thing to sense,
Why should we in our peevish opposition
Take it to heart? Fie, 'tis a fault to heaven,
A fault against the dead, a fault to nature.
To reason most absurd, whose common theme
Is death of fathers, and who still hath cried
From the first corpse till he that died today,
"This must be so."

> CLAUDIUS *puts his arm around* HAMLET. *An invasion of intimacy.*

CLAUDIUS *(continuing)*
We pray you throw to earth
This unprevailing woe, and think of us
As of a father; for let the world take note

> *He drags* HAMLET *out onto the dais and produces the next information with a great Churchillian flourish.* HAMLET *eventually will be King—* CLAUDIUS *has nominated him here and now—all is well. The* CROWD *respond.*

CLAUDIUS *(continuing)*
You are the most immediate to our throne,

> *Huge applause from the* CROWD.

CLAUDIUS *(continuing)*
And with no less nobility of love

Than that which dearest father bears his son
Do I impart towards you.
Now, the atmosphere changes.

Claudius *(continuing)*
For your intent
In going back to school in Wittenberg,
The great issue comes up. Laertes, Ophelia, Gertrude *all wanting to see* Hamlet *take his rightful place.*

Claudius *(continuing)*
It is most retrograde to our desire,
And we beseech you bend you to remain
Here in the cheer and comfort of our eye,
Our chiefest courtier, cousin, and our son.
Quiet again. The Audience *straining to overhear.*

Gertrude
Let not thy mother lose her prayers, Hamlet.
I pray thee stay with us, go not to Wittenberg.
We see Hamlet's *crushed body language. The sense of a head bowed. Nevertheless he is a Prince and this is clear in the manner of his reply.*

Hamlet
I shall in all my best obey you, madam.

Claudius
Why, 'tis a loving and a fair reply.
Be as ourself in Denmark.
(To Gertrude*)* Madam, come.
He takes her hand and moves to the front of the Dais. They effectively mask Hamlet *from the Court. Peace is restored. Finally neither foreign upstarts nor truculent nephews have thrown this new King off balance, at this formal opening of his new parliament. He is intimate with her now. Happily letting the Court share their obvious intoxication with each other.*

CLAUDIUS

This gentle and unforced accord of Hamlet
Sits smiling to my heart; in grace whereof,
No jocund health that Denmark drinks today
But the great cannon to the clouds shall tell,
And the King's rouse the heavens shall bruit again,
Re-speaking earthly thunder.

Confetti begins to fall.

CLAUDIUS

Come, away.

Cheers, trumpets. The Royal Couple race out like the hungry newlyweds they are. The happy CROWD *chase them like a drunken wedding party. The huge hall empties almost by magic. We see the end doors shut and then we see* HAMLET *still standing at the throne. His body collapses, leaning on the arms of the throne. As we hear him start to speak we move slowly around him.*

HAMLET

O that this too too solid flesh would melt,
Thaw and resolve itself into a dew,
Or that the Everlasting had not fixed
His canon 'gainst self-slaughter! O God, O God,
How weary, stale, flat, and unprofitable
Seem to me all the uses of this world!
Fie on't, ah fie, fie! 'Tis an unweeded garden
That grows to seed; things rank and gross in nature
Possess it merely. That it should come to this—

The Camera moves with HAMLET *down the hall.*

HAMLET *(continuing)*

But two months dead—nay, not so much, not two—
So excellent a King, that was to this
Hyperion to a satyr, so loving to my mother
That he might not beteem the winds of heaven
Visit her face too roughly! Heaven and earth,

Must I remember? Why, she would hang on him
As if increase of appetite had grown
By what it fed on, and yet within a month—
Let me not think on't; frailty, thy name is woman—
He turns to face away from the door.

HAMLET *(continuing)*
A little month, or ere those shoes were old
With which she followed my poor father's body,
Like Niobe, all tears, why she, even she—
O God, a beast that wants discourse of reason
Would have mourned longer!—married with mine uncle,
My father's brother, but no more like my father
Than I to Hercules, within a month,
Ere yet the salt of most unrighteous tears
Had left the flushing in her gallèd eyes,
She married. O most wicked speed, to post
With such dexterity to incestuous sheets!
He looks back down the almost empty state hall. We see the melancholic profile of a young man in black military cadet uniform, flaxen hair and a single tear trailing down a face more used to smiles.

Notes

Norman Schwarzkopf the American general who was the allied commander during the Persian Gulf War (1990–91)

V/O the abbreviation for *voice-over*, a narration or commentary in a filmed work in which the viewer does not see the speaker, who is off-camera

Churchillian flourish a grand gesture; reference to Sir Winston Churchill, British prime minister during World War II, much praised for his heroic leadership and skills as an orator

Hyperion a Titan in classical Greek mythology

satyr a mythical creature that is half-human and half-goat

Niobe a character in Greek mythology who, while weeping for her slain children, is turned into a stone from which her tears continue to flow

Shakespeare in the Cinema: A Film Directors' Symposium

On December 15, 1998, the magazine editors of *Cineaste* posed several questions about cinematic adaptations of Shakespeare's plays to noted film directors Sir Peter Hall (*A Midsummer Night's Dream*, 1968), Richard Loncraine (*Richard III*, 1995), Baz Luhrmann (*William Shakespeare's Romeo + Juliet*, 1996), Trevor Nunn (*Twelfth Night*, 1996), Oliver Parker (*Othello*, 1995), Roman Polanski (*Macbeth*, 1971), and Franco Zeffirelli (*The Taming of the Shrew*, 1967; *Romeo and Juliet*, 1968; and *Hamlet*, 1990). Their intent was to gain insights into the aesthetic considerations and working methods of film directors who have adapted Shakespeare for the cinema. What is the role of a film director in the making of a movie? What do you think are the most typical modifications filmmakers make when adapting a Shakespearean play for film, and why are they made?

It is almost always necessary to make cuts and other changes in the text when cinematically adapting a Shakespeare play. What is your own philosophy or strategy for making cuts, for updating antiquarian or obscure words, or for rewriting or rearranging scenes?

Richard Loncraine: If you're making a Shakespeare film for a contemporary audience, you have to make sure that they don't get bored. Shakespeare wrote *Richard III* about 400 years ago, when people were used to words. They didn't have much visual stimulus, there was no set design, there was no television, there was no cinema obviously, so words were crucial. In our telling of the story, we have everything from special effects, to scored music and exciting imagery. We can communicate with pictures an awful lot of what Shakespeare expressed with words. I do believe that you can cut the text. Shakespeare's plays were almost never put on in their full-text form.

Baz Luhrmann: Our philosophy in adapting *Romeo and Juliet* for the screen was to reveal Shakespeare's lyrical, romantic, sweet, sexy, musical, violent, rude, rough, rowdy, rambunctious storytelling through his richly invented language. Consequently, our specific strategy was to avoid changing or adding words. We were adamant that we should maintain the colour and taste of the actual words even to the extent of the "thee" and "thou."

Setting the story in the contemporary world of urban gangs allowed us to put Shakespeare's inventive usage to work as a dexterous and ornate street rap. This game allowed us to justify all words even when the actual meaning was not immediately apparent.

Where we took significant liberty was in restructuring and cutting. We felt it was important to serve Shakespeare's ultimate goal of strong storytelling. He had to arrest the attention of a very noisy, disparate, savage yet honest audience not unlike at your local cinema. To facilitate this he used all the devices at his disposal: the clash of lowbrow comedy with high tragedy, the use of popular song (pop music), etc. Similarly, we developed a specific cinematic language for Romeo and Juliet that transformed all of these devices into cinematic equivalents in order to achieve the same goal with our noisy, disparate, savage yet honest audience.

Oliver Parker: I don't have a strategy regarding cuts. I'm sure it would vary according to the particular piece and my vision of it. To present the plays in their entirety would be a disservice to Shakespeare. I'm sure if he were alive today, he'd be radically reworking the text for a new medium, and would most likely want to direct it. His plays are colossal things, open to infinite interpretation. I'm interested in remaining true to the spirit, not to the text, of plays.

Roman Polanski: I'm definitely not for rewriting scenes, unless there's really a possibility of making them clearer by some minute change. There is so much literature written by so many scholars that, in certain cases, they have it all ready for you. If a change helps the clarity and does not spoil the verse, you may in some cases do that.

Cuts definitely have to be made, just because of length. You may also rearrange the text sometimes, film it in a different sequence, without harming the play—in fact, you can sometimes help it. The plays were written for the stage and had to take into account the rigidity of that format. The stage just doesn't allow you to tell your story in the way you would necessarily want to tell it, whereas the film allows you to tell it in any way. If there is some kind of retrospective narration, for example, you can use a flashback, which you cannot on the stage.

Franco Zeffirelli: Anything created in another medium, like a novel or a play, has to accept certain rules when it migrates into the formidable medium of cinema—the length of the film, the language of images, and so on. I cannot think of one novel or play that has been transposed entirely—apart from an exception like Branagh's *Hamlet*—because otherwise your film would last five hours. Adaptation is therefore inevitable, a necessity that no one can escape.

What is your view of the proper presentation of Shakespeare's verse in a film? Should it be delivered differently on screen than on the stage? Do you attempt to preserve the poetic and musical quality of the blank verse, or do you think it's more important for the actors to achieve a more naturalistic delivery that will not seem so alien to the ears of contemporary moviegoers, most of whom are not theatregoers?

Sir Peter Hall: The verse has to be underplayed. One of the problems about Shakespeare on screen is that he wrote for an intimate theatre, in which one could both shout and whisper, and that vocal range is part of the Shakespeare experience. If you shout in a film you look like an old ham. So half the Shakespeare dynamic range vocally goes out the window as soon as you put it on screen.

As for the musical quality of the blank verse, those are external judgments. I don't think that you can speak poetically or speak musically. You can speak with sense, with wit, and with a concrete imagination, and if you don't you're a rotten old Shakespearean ham. I detect at the back of your questions a feeling that film acting needs to be real whereas Shakespeare acting needs to be false, and that is not true.

Baz Luhrmann: One of the great things about Shakespeare's text is its musicality and rhythm. The fact is the actors learn so much about what they are doing and saying from the rhythm itself. I do believe that this rhythm should, where possible, be maintained. As far as the way in which it's delivered, again it is whatever works for a particular situation. There is no reason why an actor cannot deliver the line in a natural style while maintaining the underlying metre.

Trevor Nunn: It seems to me that the camera requires work of actors that is quite fundamentally untheatrical and unstylized. It requires actors to be as truthful as is conceivably possible. The camera is associated with eavesdropping on the real event. Consequently, what is said in front of the camera needs to convey to the cinema audience the sense that it has not been written, that the language of the screen is being invented by the character in the situation spontaneously at that moment. We must not be aware of the writer.

Oliver Parker: Shakespeare's verse is a gift to the actor. It contains great insights into the character and is an astonishing channel for emotions. Iambic pentameters have a rhythm very close to normal speech. On screen there is the opportunity to make it sound even more natural, to be even more intimate. At the same time, I find the language stylistically liberating. It challenges you to find an equivalent cinematic style.

Is it important for a director of a Shakespearean film to be knowledgeable about the history, the culture, and the cosmology of the Elizabethan world in which Shakespeare wrote his plays?

Sir Peter Hall: I think it helps, but it's much more important for him to have an imaginative response to Shakespeare's images. I don't mean his verbal images, but the image of the whole play.

Baz Luhrmann: As with any story, if you don't understand the world in which the text was generated and if you don't have an absolute, totally and utterly thorough understanding of the history, culture, and cosmology of everything about that world, then you are interpreting the text in a vacuum.

Trevor Nunn: I was taught as a young teenager by a teacher, with whom I had something bordering on idolatry, who read Shakespeare plays with us and who expanded the texts. So, from that age, I've been consumed with a desire to find out more about Shakespeare, to learn everything about his language, his vocabulary, his slang, the words he invented, the dramaturgy that he invented, things that didn't exist before Shakespeare. I can't think of starting on any of the plays without wanting to consult all of that background knowledge, and that's regardless of saying, "I concluded that I want to change the imagery of the play and set it in the nineteenth century." Every particle of its original intention needs to be understood because surely the intention of the contemporary production is to find ways of releasing the original intention more potently to an audience in our own age. I might need to represent the work differently in order to do that, but I must know everything about its original force, if I'm going to undertake that. I don't believe that one can ever say that ignorance is bliss.

Oliver Parker: Important, yes. Essential, no. It depends on the particular vision of the director and how close it is to the original play.

Franco Zeffirelli: I think it's essential, for Shakespeare, or for any great author you're dealing with. You study a lot about him, what came before, what happened around him. You can't just jump in and expect to know how a character behaves in a historical context without knowing that historical context.

What is your view of filming historically updated versions of Shakespeare's plays as opposed to period presentations?

Sir Peter Hall: Well, none of us know what "period" means, any more than we know what "update" means. Shakespeare put chimney pots and docks in Rome; it didn't bother him, he didn't know they didn't have them. I think every Shakespeare play or film has to have its own visual world, and if it makes you think, "Daddy, why are they talking about swords?" when actually all they've got is pistols, then it's rubbish. But you can't be period accurate, that's antiquarian and boring.

Richard Loncraine: I think both are valid, both have their place. Shakespeare never performed his plays in period costume, they were played in whatever actors turned up on the day in, so Shakespeare obviously didn't think it was that important, and neither do I.

Baz Luhrmann: Having directed Shakespeare in theatre, opera, and film, it's never been a question of, is there a right or a wrong method. One must simply address an audience at a particular moment in time and attempt to reveal the greater richness of the particular idea or story. Whether you do an unbelievably accurate Elizabethan version, performed on a bare stage, in the middle of the day to four thousand mostly drunk punters, with the female roles played by adolescent boys in drag and spoken in a virtually incomprehensible accent, or any other interpretation, it is correct if it reveals the heart of the story and engages and awakens the audience to the material.

Trevor Nunn: I'm all in favour of people taking a different approach to visual imagery in contemporary production, be it in the theatre or the cinema. Often what happens when strong conceptual lines are taken with Shakespeare is that things come alive in very unexpected ways and that's much more commendable than the inept version that sets out to take the play at face value.

Oliver Parker: I respect the desire to update the plays, especially when the intention is to connect with a wider audience. I don't think, though, that it necessarily makes it more relevant. Sometimes it seems just a gimmick. But when it's done wittily and thoroughly, it can be terrific. Baz Luhrmann's *Romeo + Juliet* is a case in point. I found it passionate and poignant and hugely accessible.

Roman Polanski: I absolutely hate those updated versions, I'm allergic to them. I think that Shakespeare can indeed be played like jazz—you know, there are no other directions than "enter" and "exit" or "is slain" or whatever—so you can act it and stage it any way you want, but what's the point of updating it? That's a cacophony. If filmmakers fear Shakespeare is antiquated, then leave him alone; they should look for different material.

Franco Zeffirelli: As I've said, I don't think dressing the characters in modern costumes has any advantage. When I did *Romeo and Juliet*, I did it period, but after a few minutes the audience forgot that the story took place in Verona four or five hundred years ago, and that people were dressed in a certain way. They were engaged immediately through their identification with characters they came to love. When you have the power of a character that surpasses contemporary dressing up and other references, I don't think you need to make that effort. Actually, it might misfire.

Producing a Shakespearean film is usually referred to as "popularizing" Shakespeare for a mass movie-going audience. What is your view? What sort of compromises does such "popularization" involve?

Sir Peter Hall: The fact that a lot of people are aware of *Romeo and Juliet* because of Baz's film doesn't mean, when they go to see the play of *Romeo and Juliet*, that they won't be woefully disappointed, because it's nothing like the film. I think that popularization is valuable but we shouldn't kid ourselves that it's the real thing. I'm a purist because I believe that a great artist deserves to be respected and not cut to hell.

Richard Loncraine: Shakespeare didn't write plays to be stuck in drawers or that no one went to see; he wrote them for a mass audience. He had no amplification, so with more than about five hundred people, no one could hear what the hell was going on, but if Shakespeare could have had loudspeakers he would have played to audiences in the thousands. Compromise by doing Shakespeare on film? Not at all. I think it's probably a strength. There are certainly things you have to adapt. In *Richard III*, Richard doesn't even get killed on stage. He's killed off stage and someone comes in and says, "The king is dead." Well, you certainly can't do that with a film audience, they would tear you apart. So Shakespeare certainly has to be adapted for the screen, but if you respect the man's writing and you approach it as if he is the one doing the adapting—I mean, try to think of what Shakespeare would have done—you probably won't go far wrong.

Baz Luhrmann: It is almost embarrassing to me when people start talking about Shakespeare as if his intention was not to be popular or as if he was a storyteller, playwright, poet, and actor who was not interested in the widest possible audience. Do we think Shakespeare would be turning in his grave because he beat Sylvester Stallone at the opening weekend of *Romeo and Juliet*? I don't think so.

Are we trying to say that a man who had to play to four thousand punters a day and to every kind of person from the street sweeper to the Queen of England wouldn't be interested in being successful in the multiplexes? At what time was Shakespeare only interested in playing to a small elite? I don't understand that notion. It seems the antithesis of everything Shakespeare stood for is to treat his text as high culture.

Trevor Nunn: There is this pressure, partly from film production companies and partly one's own knowledge and instincts. You want your film to play to the widest possible audience, and yet you want to be able to hold your head up amongst Shakespeare scholars and not to have to say, "I deliberately abandoned all my beliefs for that period of time," or "I wittingly vulgarized this bit of material for commercial considerations."

Shakespeare was an extraordinary example of a writer who discovered the going form. There was this huge creative energy in him, a sheer appetite for creation, and he chose the theatre. He didn't choose prose, he didn't choose long narrative poetry, he chose the theatre because it seemed to him to be the going form, where the excitement was. That was where people who could write were suddenly congregating, and where there was this huge burst of activity. I think the going form changes from age to age, and it's not an accident that in the nineteenth century, it was the novel, and the greatest writers became novelists and the less great writers continued to struggle with the theatre. There's obviously a sense in which the cinema is now the going form, and I'm convinced that, were he alive today, Shakespeare would be gravitating toward cinema.

Oliver Parker: I applaud the desire to popularize Shakespeare, to introduce him to a mass audience to prove the stories, characters, and language can be extremely entertaining and accessible. What makes him such a genius is the many layers to his work, his ability to be insightful, moving, and profound, while entertaining at the same time. Given that so many people now regard him as the province of academics, I think it is important to reclaim him as a popular artist. I don't think this need debase him. The point is to encourage people into their seats, and, as he was a shareholder in the Globe Theatre, I'm sure he would sympathize.

Roman Polanski: Whether you refer to it this way or not, it's a fact, not a matter of opinion. Certainly more people have seen Olivier's film of *Hamlet* than have seen theatrical productions of it. Whether a film adaptation of Shakespeare requires compromises depends on the standing of a director who can oppose the influence of the habitual committee that is asking him to make it for the lowest common denominator. When I shot *Macbeth*, I didn't compromise in any way. Whatever changes we made were based on research, and, as for the illustration, you can illustrate certain things in such a way that you do not need to replace antiquated words, because they become clear by the visual context or through acting.

Franco Zeffirelli: There is a preconceived attitude—Shakespeare, oh my God!—but there is also a big reward when you present a classical story straightforward, and you don't try to be literally modern with it, because people will respond. You must do everything possible to grab the audience, but convincing the audience that they are revisiting a great classic under the proper conditions is an effort we should make.

Notes

symposium a meeting or conference at which several experts discuss a topic and put forward their opinions on a subject

iambic pentameter a rhythmic pattern in poetry of ten syllables per line that comprise five beats known as *metrical feet*; each foot consists of an unstressed (short) syllable followed by a stressed (long) syllable

cosmology the study of the nature of the universe, including its origin, structure, and space-time relationships

punters a British slang term for people who bet at the racetrack

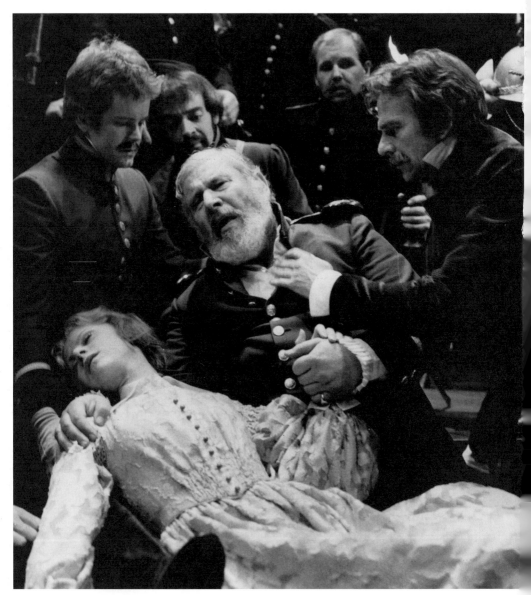

Peter Ustinov as Lear in a Stratford Festival production of King Lear, *1979*

The Shakespearean Tragic Hero

A.C. Bradley

Andrew Cecil Bradley, born in Cheltenham, England, in 1851, is considered to be the pre-eminent Shakespearean scholar of the late nineteenth and early twentieth centuries. He attended Oxford University and later held a professorship there and at the University of Liverpool and the University of Glasgow. Bradley died in 1935. This selection comes from his book *Shakespearean Tragedy* (1904), which is recognized as a classic of twentieth-century Shakespearean criticism. His work presents a psychological analysis of Shakespeare's characters, in which he deals with these characters almost as if they were real people. How would you define the word *tragedy*? What is a tragic hero? Why do you think readers like to read tragedies? What are we able to learn from reading or viewing tragedies?

Let us now turn from the "action" to the central figure in it; and, ignoring the characteristics which distinguish the heroes from one another, let us ask whether they have any common qualities which appear to be essential to the tragic effect.

One they certainly have. They are exceptional beings.... The hero, with Shakespeare, is a person of high degree or of public importance, and his actions or sufferings are of an unusual kind. But this is not all. His nature also is exceptional, and generally raises him in some respect much above the average level of humanity. This does not mean that he is an eccentric or a paragon. Shakespeare never drew monstrosities of virtue; some of his heroes are far from being "good"; and if he drew eccentrics he gave them a subordinate position in the plot. His tragic characters are made of the stuff we find within ourselves and within the persons who surround them. But, by an intensification of the life which they share with others, they are raised above them; and the greatest are raised so far that, if we fully realize all that is implied in their words and actions, we become conscious that in real life we have known scarcely anyone resembling them. Some, like Hamlet...have genius. Others, like...Lear, Macbeth...are built on the grand scale; and desire, passion, or will attains in them a terrible force. In almost all we observe a marked one-sidedness, a predisposition in some particular direction; a total incapacity, in certain circumstances, of resisting the force which draws in this direction; a fatal tendency to identify the whole being with one interest, object, passion, or habit of mind. This, it would seem, is, for Shakespeare, the fundamental tragic trait.... It is a fatal gift, but it carries with it a touch of greatness; and when there is joined to it nobility of mind, or genius, or immense force, we realize the full power and reach of the soul, and the conflict in which it engages acquires that magnitude which stirs not only sympathy and pity, but admiration, terror, and awe....

In the circumstances where we see the hero placed, his tragic trait, which is also his greatness, is fatal to him. To meet these circumstances something is required which a smaller man might have given, but which the hero cannot give. He errs, by action or omission; and his error, joining with other causes, brings on him ruin....

The tragic hero with Shakespeare, then, need not be "good," though generally he is "good" and therefore at once wins sympathy in his error. But it is necessary that he should have so much of greatness that in his error and fall we may be vividly conscious of the possibilities of human nature. Hence, in the first place, a Shakespearean tragedy is never, like some miscalled tragedies, depressing. No one ever closes the book with the feeling that man is a poor mean creature. He may be wretched and he may be awful, but he is not small. His lot may be heart-rending and mysterious, but it is not contemptible. The most confirmed of cynics ceases to be a cynic while he reads these plays. And with this greatness of the tragic hero (which is not always confined to him) is connected, secondly, what I venture to describe as the centre of the tragic impression.

This central feeling is the impression of waste. With Shakespeare, at any rate, the pity and fear which are stirred by the tragic story seem to unite with, and even to merge in, a profound sense of sadness and mystery, which is due to this impression of waste. "What a piece of work is man," we cry; "so much more beautiful and so much more terrible than we knew! Why should he be so if this beauty and greatness only tortures itself and throws itself away?" We seem to have before us a type of the mystery of the whole world, the tragic fact which extends far beyond the limits of tragedy…. Tragedy…forces the mystery upon us, and it makes us realize so vividly the worth of that which is wasted…. In this tragic world, then, where individuals, however they may be and however decisive their actions may appear, are so evidently not the ultimate power, what is this power?…

The ultimate power in the tragic world is a moral order. Let us…speak simply of good and evil. Let us understand by these words, primarily, moral good and evil, but also everything else in human beings which we take to be excellent or the reverse. Let us understand the statement that the ultimate power or order is "moral" to mean that it does not show itself indifferent to good and evil, or equally favourable or unfavourable to both, but shows itself akin to good and alien from evil. And, understanding the statement thus, let us ask what grounds it has in the tragic fact as presented by Shakespeare.

Here…I choose only two or three [grounds] out of many. And the most important is this. In Shakespearean tragedy the main source of the convulsion which produces suffering and death is never good…. The main source, on the contrary, is in every case evil; and, what is more (though this seems to have been little noticed), it is in almost every case evil in the fullest sense, not mere imperfection but plain moral evil. The love of Romeo and Juliet conducts them to death only because of the senseless hatred of their houses. Guilty ambition, seconded by diabolic malice and issuing in murder, opens the action in *Macbeth*. Iago is the main source of the convulsion in *Othello*; Goneril, Regan, and Edmund in *King Lear*. Even when this plain moral evil is not the obviously prime source within the play, it lies behind it: the situation with which Hamlet has to deal has been formed by adultery and murder…. And the inference is obvious. If it is chiefly evil that violently disturbs the order of the world, this order cannot be friendly to evil or indifferent between evil and good, any more than a body which is convulsed by poison is friendly to it or indifferent to the distinction between poison and food.

Again, if we confine our attention to the hero, and to those cases where the gross and palpable evil is not in him but elsewhere, we find that the comparatively innocent hero still shows some marked imperfection or defect—irresolution, precipitancy, pride, credulousness, excessive simplicity, excessive susceptibility to sexual emotions, and the like. These defects or imperfections are certainly, in the wide sense of the word, evil, and they contribute decisively to the conflict and catastrophe. And the inference is again obvious. The ultimate power which shows itself disturbed by this evil and reacts against it, must have a nature alien to it. Indeed its reaction is so vehement and "relentless" that it would seem to be bent on nothing short of good in perfection, and to be ruthless in its demand for it.

To this must be added another fact, or another aspect of the same fact. Evil exhibits itself everywhere as something negative, barren, weakening, destructive, a principle of death. It isolates, disunites, and tends to annihilate not only its opposite but itself. That which keeps the evil man prosperous, makes him succeed, even permits him to exist, is the good in him (I do not mean only the obviously "moral" good). When the evil in him masters the good and has its way, it destroys other people through him, but it also destroys him. At the close of the struggle he has vanished, and has left behind him nothing that can stand. What remains is a family, a city, a country, exhausted, pale, and feeble, but alive through the principle of good which animates it; and within it, individuals who, if they have not the brilliance or greatness of the tragic character, still have won our respect and confidence. And the inference would seem clear. If existence in an order depends on good, and if the presence of evil is hostile to such existence, the inner being or soul of this order must be akin to good.

These are aspects of the tragic world at least as clearly marked as those which, taken alone, suggest the idea of fate. And the idea which they in their turn, when taken alone, may suggest, is that of an order which does not indeed award "poetic justice," but which reacts through the necessity of its own "moral" nature both against attacks made upon it and against failure to conform to it. Tragedy, on this view, is the exhibition of that convulsive reaction; and the fact that the spectacle does not leave us rebellious or desperate is due to a more or less distinct impression that the tragic suffering and death arise from collision, not with a fate or blank power, but with a moral power, a power akin to all that we admire and revere in the characters themselves. This perception produces something like a feeling of acquiescence in the catastrophe, though it neither leads us to pass judgment on the characters nor diminishes the pity, the fear, and the sense of waste, which their struggle, suffering, and fall evoke. And, finally, this view seems quite able to do justice to those aspects of the tragic fact which give rise to the idea of fate. They would appear as various expressions of the fact that the moral order acts not capriciously or like a human being, but from the necessity of its nature, or, if we prefer the phrase, by general laws—a necessity or law which of course knows no exception and is as "ruthless" as fate....

Thus we are left at last with an idea showing two sides or aspects which we can neither separate nor reconcile. The whole or order against which the individual part shows itself powerless seems to be animated by a passion for perfection: we cannot otherwise explain its behaviour toward evil. Yet it appears to engender this evil within itself, and in its effort to overcome and expel it it is agonized with pain, and driven to mutilate its own substance and to lose not only evil but priceless good. That this idea, though very different from the idea of a blank fate, is no solution of the riddle of life is obvious; but why should we expect it to be such a solution? Shakespeare was not attempting to justify the ways of God to men, or to show the universe as a Divine Comedy. He was writing tragedy, and tragedy would not be tragedy if it were not a painful mystery.... We remain confronted with the inexplicable fact, or the no less inexplicable appearance, of a world travailing for perfection, but bringing to birth, together with glorious good, an evil which it is able to overcome only by self-torture and self-waste. And this fact or appearance is tragedy.

Notes

paragon a model of excellence or perfection

poetic justice an outcome in which vice is punished and virtue rewarded, often in an ironic manner

Divine Comedy a classic poem by the Italian Dante Alighieri, written from 1306 to 1321, that chronicles the main character's journey through hell, to Mount Purgatory, and finally into heaven

From

Strong Women Prevail in Shakespeare's Comedies

Angela Pitt

Angela Pitt was born in Aylesbury, Buckinghamshire, England, in 1946. She holds degrees in English from the University of London and the University of Ottawa, as well as a master's degree in archaeology from Oslo University in Norway. In the following selection, she explores the role of women in Shakespeare's comedies.

By the end of the fifth century BCE, the word *comedy* came to describe a play that was distinct from tragedy. In tragedy, the protagonist is seen to be a superior or special person in society, whereas the protagonist in comedy finds fulfillment within the existing society. A key attribute of the mode of comedy is that it always has a "happy ending." Regardless of the seriousness of the problems and situations depicted, the audience knows that everything will be joyfully resolved.

Comedy generally contains two other key characteristics. First, comedy occurs when specific events and characters of a play challenge basic assumptions about society. Traditional comic writers pit humanity's excesses, frauds, hypocrisies, and follies against a background of normality. Second, comedy often involves the suspension of the natural laws of logic and probability. Therefore, actions do not have the consequences they would have in real life. Often normal expectations are reversed.

Shakespeare wrote his comedies between 1594 and 1603. He is probably best known for his romantic comedies, such as *As You Like It* and *A Midsummer Night's Dream,* in which an idealized heroine and hero overcome impediments to be united. In romantic comedies, characters leave the troubled real world to enter a pastoral, magical world in which problems dissolve. Shakespeare also wrote comedies of manners, including *Love's Labours Lost* and *Much Ado About Nothing,* in which the intrigue between sophisticated gentlemen and ladies relies to a great extent on witty repartee. In such comedies as *The Taming of the Shrew* and *The Merry Wives of Windsor,* Shakespeare uses elements of farce. These plays have hilarious physical scenes filled with exaggerated caricatures, slapstick, and sight gags.

Note the title of Pitt's essay. Why might Shakespeare have cast women as strong characters in his comedies, but not necessarily in his tragedies? From what you know of Shakespeare's comedies, do you think his purpose in writing them was primarily to please the audience? Why or why not?

If the dark realm of Shakespeare's tragedies is essentially men's territory, pride of place in the bright panorama of his comedies must surely belong to the women. Set alongside vivacious heroines...their male counterparts pale into insignificance. The character of Beatrice, indeed, has such force and charm that interest in her eventually takes over the play, despite the fact that her fate is not an important aspect of the original plot.

Why should the women leap into prominence? One reason may be that Shakespeare found their traditional attributes of modesty, intuition, and high-spiritedness highly suitable material for his comedies, and in varying blends and degrees, all his comic heroines have these characteristics. They never go beyond the bounds of what an Elizabethan audience would have found acceptable in a woman: it is rather that Shakespeare exalts the positive, rather than the negative traits. Any women that go against prevailing conventions are redeemed by the end of the play. Thus Katharina in *The Taming of the Shrew* is forced to give in to Petruchio's will, and Helena's unfeminine pursuit of Bertram is justified by the fact that he had failed to recognize her true worth; once he does so, she is submissive.

Another reason is that Shakespeare tacitly accepts the medieval idea of a hierarchy of nature in which woman is second to man. This means that the high seriousness of tragedy, with its intense focus on the fate of the individual, is an unsatisfactory setting for all but a very few women, and even these have their destinies inescapably intertwined with those of the tragic heroes. Comedy, on the other hand, allows for a broader, more detached view of society and a lighter tone. Although moral issues are not excluded (*The Merchant of Venice* is very much concerned with the contrast between material and spiritual wealth, as well as the nature of justice), we do not become anxious or painfully involved with the characters and, as the play progresses, hints are given that everything will turn out all right in the end. The characters themselves are frequently capricious, willing to compromise, and although they may well have faults, these do not inspire *fear* in the audience, as would be the case in tragedy. The plots too are full of twists and turns, surprises and coincidences. Until the final scene makes everything clear, no decision is incapable of being changed or reversed.

The forces of charm and whimsy are so strong in his comedies as to offer a further strong indication as to why Shakespeare favoured women characters for the leading roles. His choice was not a foregone conclusion, for other Elizabethan writers of comedy—notably Ben Jonson—let men dominate the stage as in tragedy. In the sixteenth century there were two traditions of dramatic comedy. One was the satirical revelation of human errors, played out so that the audience laughed to see their own follies so skilfully exposed. The other was to use as a setting some upset, sadness, or problem that is subsequently resolved happily. Jonson wrote in the first, more hard-hitting tradition, where we laugh *at* the characters; Shakespeare in the second where we laugh *with* them. The hallmark of Shakespeare's comedies is consequently the move toward reconciliation and a restoration of order by the correct understanding of the original problem. Unlike the tragedies, which insist that chaos can be averted only by the elimination of those swept up in the catastrophe, the comedies show that problems can be solved and sorrows overcome if the situation is properly understood by those involved in it. Although we laugh at comedy, its purpose is as realistic and serious as that of tragedy: comedy shows us that happiness results from being able to face problems and put them into a balanced perspective; tragedy shows that misery and death result when dilemmas loom so large as to blot out all other aspects of life. As with the tragedies it is impossible to impose a strict formula on the construction of the comedies beyond the pattern mentioned above: that they all begin with the characters perplexed or threatened, but end happily. This general definition serves to embrace the eleven usually termed "comedies" by editors and the five "last plays."

The agents of happiness and order in Shakespeare's comedies are the heroines, and their function is therefore of supreme importance. Not only do the women have the leading roles but also they are more numerous than in the other types of plays. They cover a wide range of types and classes: a queen, a countess, princesses, dukes' daughters, a doctor's daughter, merchants' daughters, ladies-in-waiting, servants, shepherdesses, a goat-girl, nuns, and prostitutes. This rich variety gives tremendous scope for contrasts and comparisons among the women themselves, as well as between men and women. With the exception of *The Tempest*, in which Miranda is the only woman, the other comedies present women as foils to each other. At its best, use of this device not only results in the idiosyncrasies of speech and behaviour, which make the heroines so very alive and credible, but also allows Shakespeare to reveal many subtle facets of their natures....

Notes

comedy derived from the Greek word *kōmōidia*, which originally referred to a comic singer or to a celebratory song and dance performed by a chorus in a play

tragedies in this instance, refers to Shakespeare's plays that portray calamitous events, often containing a main character who has a fatal flaw that results in an unhappy ending

Beatrice a witty female character in Shakespeare's comedy *Much Ado About Nothing*

Elizabethan the time period between the mid-1500s and the early 1600s when Great Britain was ruled by Queen Elizabeth I (1533–1603)

medieval relating or belonging to the middle ages, an era in European history dating from 476 to 1453 CE

Ben Jonson an English actor and writer (1572–1637), whose best-known play is *Volpone* (1606)

foils characters who, through contrast to the main characters, either underscore or enhance the traits of the protagonists

Saloonio

Stephen Leacock

Born in Swanmore, England, in 1869, Stephen Leacock immigrated to Canada in 1876 and grew up near Lake Simcoe, Ontario. He attended Upper Canada College, the University of Toronto, and the University of Chicago, studying political science and economics and teaching these subjects at McGill University from 1903 until his retirement in 1936. Leacock was a prolific writer of humorous fiction, literary essays, and articles on social issues, politics, and other subjects. He won the Governor General's Award for Nonfiction in 1937. He died in

1944. Leacock was a master of the short sketch or extended anecdote and his writing exhibits a strong oral characteristic. Have you encountered a short story before that takes the form of an anecdotal sketch? If so, what was the piece about and why do you think the writer chose this form?

They say that young men fresh from college are pretty positive about what they know. But from my own experience of life, I should say that if you take a comfortable, elderly man who hasn't been near a college for about twenty years, who has been pretty liberally fed and dined ever since, who measures about fifty inches around the circumference, and has a complexion like a cranberry by candlelight, you will find that there is a degree of absolute certainty about what he thinks he knows that will put any young man to shame. I am specially convinced of this from the case of my friend Colonel Hogshead, a portly, choleric gentleman who made a fortune in cattle-trade out in Wyoming and who, in his later days, has acquired a chronic idea that the plays of Shakespeare are the one subject upon which he is most qualified to speak personally.

He came across me the other evening as I was sitting by the fire in the club sitting room looking over the leaves of *The Merchant of Venice*, and began to hold forth to me about the book.

"*Merchant of Venice*, eh? There's a play for you, sir! There's genius! Wonderful, sir, wonderful! You take the characters in that play and where will you find anything like them? You take Antonio, take Sherlock, take Saloonio—"

"Saloonio, Colonel?" I interposed mildly, "aren't you making a mistake? There's a Bassanio and a Salanio in the play, but I don't think there's a Saloonio, is there?"

For a moment Colonel Hogshead's eye became misty with doubt, but he was not the man to admit himself in error:

"Tut, tut! young man," he said with a frown, "don't skim through your books in that way. No Saloonio? Why, of course there's a Saloonio!"

"But I tell you, Colonel," I rejoined. "I've just been reading the play and studying it, and I know there's no such character—"

"Nonsense, sir, nonsense!" said the Colonel, "why he comes in all through; don't tell me, young man, I've read that play myself. Yes, and seen it played, too, out in Wyoming, before you were born, by fellers, sir, that could act. No Saloonio, indeed! why, who is it that is Antonio's friend all through and won't leave him when Bassoonio turns against him? Who rescues Clarissa from Sherlock, and steals the casket of flesh from the Prince of Aragon? Who shouts at the Prince of Morocco, 'Out, out, you damned candlestick'? Who loads up the jury in the trial scene and fixes the doge? No Saloonio! By gad! in my opinion, he's the most important character in the play—"

"Colonel Hogshead," I said very firmly, "there isn't any Saloonio and you know it."

But the old man had got fairly started on whatever dim recollection had given birth to Saloonio; the character seemed to grow more and more luminous in the Colonel's mind, and he continued with increasing animation:

"I'll just tell you what Saloonio is: he's a type. Shakespeare means him to embody the type of the perfect Italian gentleman. He's an idea, that's what he is, he's a symbol, he's a unit—"

Meanwhile I had been searching among the leaves of the play. "Look here," I said, "here's the list of the Dramatis Personae. There's no Saloonio there."

But this didn't dismay the Colonel one atom. "Why, of course there isn't," he said. "You don't suppose you'd find Saloonio there! That's the whole art of it! That's Shakespeare! That's the whole gist of it! He's kept clean out of the Personae—gives him scope, gives him a free hand, makes him more of a type than ever. Oh, it's a subtle thing, sir, the dramatic art!" continued the Colonel, subsiding into quiet reflection; "it takes a feller quite a time to get right into Shakespeare's mind and see what he's at all the time."

I began to see that there was no use in arguing any further with the old man. I left him with the idea that the lapse of a little time would soften his views on Saloonio. But I had not reckoned on the way in which old men hang on to a thing. Colonel Hogshead quite took up

Saloonio. From that time on Saloonio became the theme of his constant conversation. He was never tired of discussing the character of Saloonio, the wonderful art of the dramatist in creating him, Saloonio's relation to the modern life, Saloonio's attitude toward women, the ethical significance of Saloonio, Saloonio as compared with Hamlet, Hamlet as compared with Saloonio—and so on, endlessly. And the more he looked into Saloonio, the more he saw in him.

Saloonio seemed inexhaustible. There were new sides to him—new phases at every turn. The Colonel even read over the play, and finding no mention of Saloonio's name in it, he swore that the books were not the same books they had had out in Wyoming; that the whole part had been cut clean out to suit the book to the infernal public schools, Saloonio's language being—at any rate, as the Colonel quoted it—undoubtedly a trifle free. Then the Colonel took to annotating his book at the side with such remarks as, "Enter Saloonio," or "A tucket sounds; enter Saloonio, on the arm of the Prince of Morocco." When there was no reasonable excuse for bringing Saloonio on the stage the Colonel swore that he was concealed behind the arras, or feasting within with the doge.

But he got satisfaction at last. He had found that there was nobody in our part of the country who knew how to put a play of Shakespeare on the stage, and took a trip to New York to see Sir Henry Irving and Miss Terry do the play. The Colonel sat and listened all through with his face just beaming with satisfaction, and when the curtain fell at the close of Irving's grand presentation of the play, he stood up in his seat and cheered and yelled to his friends: "That's it! That's him! Didn't you see that man that came on the stage all the time and sort of put the whole play through, though you couldn't understand a word he said? Well, that's him! That's Saloonio!"

Notes

The Merchant of Venice a tragicomedy written by William Shakespeare in 1596

doge the elected chief magistrate of the former republics of Venice and Genoa; from the Latin word *dux*, meaning "leader"

Dramatis Personae a list of the characters or actors in a drama; a Latin phrase meaning "people in the drama"

tucket a fanfare on a trumpet; from the Middle English word *tukken*, meaning "to beat a drum"

arras a tapestry wall hanging or curtain; named after a city in northeastern France well known in medieval times for the manufacture of tapestries

Shakespeare: Activities

1. Some selections in this In-Depth deal with Shakespeare's relevance to today's world. Which specific issues related to relevance do these selections raise? Review the selections and, in the left-hand column of a chart, list any challenges raised about studying or staging Shakespeare today. In the right-hand column, list any solutions to these problems that the selections contain. To what extent do you agree with the solutions presented?

2. Choose a Shakespearean tragedy or comedy that you know well. How is its setting described in the original text? If you were creating a stage or film production of the play with a modern setting, what particular places would you use? What kind of costuming would you provide? Explain your decisions to the class in an oral presentation. Organize your material coherently, providing evidence for your decisions and using visual aids for support.

3. Working with a group, choose a scene from any Shakespearean play. Discuss the pros and cons of performing the scene live versus on videotape. Based on your discussion, decide which method you will pursue. Assign roles and create a brief list of the criteria you consider necessary for a good performance. Distribute your list to your classmates and present the scene to them. Collect your classmates' responses to the criteria and compare their views with your group's own assessment of the performance.

4. Write a research essay with a clearly stated thesis in which you discuss the similarities and differences between Shakespearean comedy and tragedy. Choose an example of each mode, read each play carefully, and do the research required to understand the nature and main characteristics of Shakespearean comedy and tragedy.

Glossary

act A major division in a dramatic work, larger than a **scene** or episode.

adaptation Any work that recreates or redevelops another work in a different medium (e.g., a film based on a novel, a television show based on a comic strip).

allegory A story with a literal surface meaning and a second deeper, usually moral, meaning; traditionally involves **personification** (e.g., in Dickinson's poem "Because I Could Not Stop for Death—," such objects, events, and ideas as the sun, death, and immortality have been personified into characters).

alliteration The repetition of the same sound *at the beginning of* nearby words (e.g., "Landscape-lover, lord of language"—Tennyson).

allusion A direct or indirect reference in one work to another work or to a historical person, place, or event. The essay title "Get Beyond Babel" by Ken Wiwa contains a *direct* allusion to the biblical town and story of Babel (now thought to be Babylon), where construction of a tower was halted when workers could not understand each other's language. The song title "Afternoons & Coffeespoons" by The Crash Test Dummies contains an *indirect* allusion to T.S. Eliot's poem "The Love Song of J. Alfred Prufrock." Though it does not contain the name of a person, place, or event, the title alludes to Eliot's lines: "For I have known them all already, known them all— / Have known the evenings, mornings, afternoons, / I have measured out my life with coffee spoons."

analogy A comparison based on partial similarity for the purpose of making something clearer or more powerful (e.g., comparing a telecommunications system to a spider web).

anecdote A brief story about a single humorous or interesting event (e.g., Stephen Leacock's short story "Saloonio" consists of one anecdote).

antagonist A **character** who is the **protagonist**'s main opponent.

anti-hero A **character** who is the **protagonist** of a narrative and is also obviously unheroic, or lacking typical qualities of a **hero**, but for whom an author might arouse sympathy or influence us to alter our view of his or her circumstances.

antithesis A rhetorical device that contrasts ideas that are opposite or at least very different; sometimes **parallelism** is used to heighten the contrast. In general use, something is said to be the antithesis, or direct opposite, of something else.

aphorism A brief, memorable, and often witty statement of truth or principle (e.g., Hippocrates' "Life is short, art is long, opportunity fleeting, experimenting dangerous, reasoning difficult" or George Eliot's "The happiest women, like the happiest nations, have no history").

archetypal criticism A critical approach to literature that seeks to find and understand the purpose of **archetypes** within literature. These archetypes may be themes, such as love; characterizations, such as the hero; or patterns, such as death and rebirth. Archetypal criticism draws on the works of the psychoanalyst Carl Jung, literary critic Northrop Frye, and others. Unlike **psychoanalytic** critics, archetypal critics such as Frye do not attempt to explain why archetypes exist.

archetype Something that represents the essential elements of its category or class of things; Greek for "original pattern" from which all copies are made, a prototype. Certain themes of human life (e.g., love, loss), character types (e.g., the rebel, the wise elder), animals (e.g., snake), and patterns (e.g., the quest, the descent into the underworld) are considered to be archetypal, forming a part of the collective unconscious (the sum of society's inherited mental images). For example, a character in a TV series who continuously changes careers might be said to be the archetypal "seeker."

aside A **monologue** in which a **character** speaks directly to the audience as though unheard by the other characters onstage. Often it is expressed in a "stage whisper," which is a loud whisper meant to be heard by the audience.

assonance The repetition of the same or similar vowel sounds *within* nearby words for musical effect (e.g., the three sounds repeated in "The *bows* glided *down*, and the coast/ **Blackened** with birds took a **last** look/ **At** his **thrashing** hair and whale-blue eyes;/ The <u>trodden</u> town **rang** its <u>cobbles</u> for luck" from "Ballad of the Long-Legged Bait" by Dylan Thomas).

atmosphere See **mood**.

autobiography A person's story of his or her own life. While a memoir generally contains selective recollections in no particular sequence, an autobiography generally tries to present a chronological view of one's own life, giving proportional weight to all events. A work by a person based on his or her life can be described as autobiographical, but see **biographical fallacy**.

ballad A **narrative poem** about common events and people, which in the Western tradition typically has four-line **stanzas** and a **refrain**; generally, ballads originate as songs passed by word of mouth, so their creators are unknown. The term is also used broadly to mean romantic songs.

bias Language or a thought that contains a prejudice (an inaccurate, irrational, usually negative perception) against something or someone. Bias within a text can exist when information essential to an accurate depiction of a subject has been omitted, thereby prejudicing the unwitting reader's understanding of the subject.

biographical fallacy The unwarranted interpretation of a work (e.g., a novel) based primarily on knowledge of the author's life; literally, the falsehood that a writer's work is necessarily biographical. Proponents of **New Criticism** in particular reject what they consider to be biographical fallacy in favour of viewing a work as self-contained.

biography The story of a person's life as told by another. A brief biography is often called a profile.

blank verse A type of unrhymed verse that closely resembles everyday conversation, is usually written in **iambic pentameter**, and is used in some **epics**, **lyric poems**, and drama (e.g., by Shakespeare).

byline The line near the beginning of a news or magazine article that provides the writer's name.

camera angle The relative height or position from which the camera films the subject, e.g., high (from above), low (from below), straight/flat (from the same height), etc.

caption A brief explanation or title given for a photograph, cartoon, chart, or other graphic. Some publications (e.g., a chemistry text) might use both title and explanatory captions.

caricature The depiction of a flat, one-dimensional **character**, who is often a comic, absurd, or grotesque exaggeration of characteristics. In a cartoon caricature, a person's distinguishing physical features are exaggerated.

catharsis The experience of a vicarious purification or relief. Aristotle defined tragedy as "incidents arousing pity and fear, wherewith to accomplish the catharsis of such emotions." In Aristotle's view, witnessing a tragic play provided the audience with a sort of instructive purification.

cause-and-effect organization The arrangement of ideas and information (e.g., in an essay) according to causes and effects, actions and their outcomes, or states of being and their impact (e.g., the effect of a trauma on a survivor's day-to-day habits).

character One of the people in a story, either in fiction or drama. The person may be a specific type of character, such as a **stock character**, **protagonist**, **antagonist**, **foil**, **hero**, or **anti-hero**.

characterization The techniques used to portray or describe a **character** (e.g., in a novel, through the character's **dialogue**, actions and interactions, thoughts, or through direct description).

chorus In song lyrics, the **refrain** or repeated phrases or lines. In drama, particularly Greek drama, one or more **characters** who narrate or comment on the action of the drama or voice a character's thoughts.

chronological organization The arrangement of ideas and information (e.g., in a **biography**) based on the sequential order of events (e.g., beginning with events from the subject's childhood, followed by the teen years, followed by early adulthood, etc.).

cinquain A **stanza** of five lines.

classification The arrangement of elements into classes, categories, or groups (e.g., folk tales classified according to their countries of origin; within each of these categories, they might be further classified according to era or purpose).

cliché An overused, time-worn phrase or description generally considered to be ineffective and therefore avoided. Certain uses of both **diction** and **characterization** can be considered *clichéd.*

climax In a **plot**, the height of the tension in the **conflict**. The turning point in the plot, sometimes called the *crisis.*

colloquial language Words, phrases, and expressions used in ordinary everyday, familiar conversation. **Informal language** that is typically relaxed and plain rather than formal and literary.

comedy A drama that may include misfortunes, but ends happily, intending to entertain, but sometimes also to educate or persuade. Types of comedy include **parody**, **physical comedy**, and **satire**.

comparison A consideration or description of two or more things in which similarities are identified.

conflict The central struggle or problem of a narrative, which moves the **plot** forward and motivates the **protagonist**.

connotation An implied meaning of a word or phrase that can be derived from association or frequent use. The connotation extends beyond the **denotation** of the word or phrase, providing additional meaning (e.g., the denotation of *independent* is "self-governing and free from the influence, guidance, or control of others or self-reliant, not relying on others for support"; its connotation in a letter of application, for example, would be "self-directed," "not requiring close supervision," and "able to complete tasks alone").

context In general, the surroundings or circumstances of something. In print, it refers to any element related to communication that influences the creation of a text or the understanding and interpretation of it. These elements include the purpose, the intended audience, and the circumstances including time, place, and cultural and gender issues. Examples include the words appearing before and after a phrase, the imagined world that a fiction author creates, and the cultural setting in which a writer works.

copy The text of an advertisement or, in magazines and newspapers, the matter to be printed. Thus, an advertisement can be said to consist of art and copy, created by art directors and copywriters.

couplet A pair of lines in a poem, one after the other, with rhyming ends; also known as a **rhyming couplet** (e.g., "In these deep solitudes and awful *cells,* / Where heavenly-pensive contemplation *dwells,* / And ever-musing melancholy *reigns;* / What means this tumult in a vestal's *veins?*" from "Eloisa to Abelard" by Alexander Pope).

critical approach A method or manner in which to describe, interpret, and evaluate a work such as a novel, dramatic performance, or television series, often based in a belief about the role or worth of works in the same class (e.g., **New Criticism**'s belief that each poem is self-contained and worthy, in itself, of close reading). See **archetypal criticism, cultural criticism, feminist criticism, New Criticism, New Historicism, poststructuralism, psychoanalytic criticism, reader-response criticism,** and **structuralism.** See also **literary analysis.**

cultural criticism A recent movement in criticism that is interdisciplinary by extending the range of examined texts beyond just the literary works themselves to objects or practices that can be interpreted as representative of a culture's beliefs, values, laws, etc. Practitioners of cultural criticism view a text in relation to the dominant or competing ideologies (belief systems) of the time and place in which the text was written. Works are therefore considered in light of their historical and cultural contexts (e.g., Joseph Conrad's *Heart of Darkness* may be read in terms of practices of European imperialists, race relations in Africa, or the economic history of ivory). Cultural criticism is related to *cultural studies* and shares some interests with **feminist criticism, New Historicism,** and Marxist criticism.

debate A formal or informal setting in which two or more participants discuss or argue two conflicting sides of an issue, question, or topic, with one side arguing for a particular belief or resolution and the other arguing against it.

deck In a periodical publication, a sentence or short paragraph of text explaining (and following) the **headline,** or title, of an article, thereby acting like a subtitle. It is often used to catch the reader's attention, drawing the reader into a text through the use of a dramatic, controversial, or humorous statement.

deconstructionism An approach to literary criticism that emphasizes rhetoric and the self-reference of language. See **poststructuralism.**

definition A statement of what a word or phrase means, especially in a specific **context** (e.g., a discussion of an immunization plan might require first giving definitions of *epidemiology, adverse effects, risk-benefit analysis, contra-indications, auto-immune diseases*).

denotation A literal dictionary meaning of a word or phrase (e.g., a heart as the chambered, muscular organ that pumps blood).

dénouement In a **plot,** the story's end or conclusion; also called the resolution.

description A style of writing that creates images of people, places, and objects using carefully observed, expressed, and arranged details. These details are perceived by the five senses. Description can range from objective, scientific details to subjective and impressionistic perceptions.

dialect A way of speaking or a variation on a specific language that is unique to a particular social or cultural group or to a specific region.

dialogue The conversation of two or more **characters** involving an exchange of ideas or information.

diction The choice of words and phrases by a writer or speaker.

dramatic irony A type of irony based on a situation that contrasts what a character perceives with what the audience and one or more of the other characters knows to be true (for example, a mother in a play believes her son has forgotten her birthday, whereas the audience knows that her son plans to wait until late in the day to give his mother a card and present).

dramatic monologue A poem in which the speaker addresses an unseen, silent listener. This form is related to the **soliloquy**.

elegy Traditionally, a formal poem that is a solemn meditation, written as a lament for the death of a particular person.

empathy The act of mentally identifying with a person or object, as a way of relating to and comprehending it fully (e.g., knowing a character's struggle because it echoes one's own); from the German term *Einfühlung* meaning "feeling into." In general use, sympathy is considered to be compassion, while empathy is the response to a shared or the *sense* of a shared feeling or condition.

epic A type of **narrative poem**, long and about historic or legendary people; like a legend but not prose (e.g., Virgil's *Aeneid*). In modern usage, the idea of an epic can extend beyond a poem to refer to such popular media as a film, for example.

epigram Originally (in ancient Greece) an inscription on a monument or statue, but now a short, witty statement in prose or verse. Coleridge defined it as "A dwarfish whole, / Its body brevity, and wit its soul."

epilogue A closing or concluding section of a drama.

essay development The manner in which an essay is organized, how it unfolds for the reader. Methods to develop an essay include **cause-and-effect organization**, **comparison** or contrast, **chronological organization**, spatial organization, and **classification**.

euphemism A vague, indirect term with a positive connotation, used instead of a more precise or blunt term that may offend or frighten (e.g., describing someone who has died as having "passed away" or "gone to a better place").

exposition A **style** of writing that is systematically explanatory and communicates information, primarily factual (e.g., an expository essay).

farce An obvious, unsubtle comedic drama that uses exaggeration, caricature, improbable and ludicrous happenings, absurd pretences, and physical slapstick to evoke laughter. In contemporary drama, farce is often used in television sitcoms.

feminist criticism Literary criticism based on feminist theories. It considers texts with the knowledge that societies treat men and women inequitably. Feminist criticism will analyze texts in light of patriarchal (male-dominated) cultural institutions, phallocentric (male-centred) language, masculine and feminine **stereotypes**, and the unequal treatment of male and female writers. Practitioners make use of key concepts from other approaches, such as **psychoanalytic criticism**, Marxist criticism, **cultural criticism**, and **deconstructionism**. Feminist criticism developed primarily in the 1960s and 1970s, although it is evident in earlier works as well (e.g., by Virginia Woolf).

figurative language Language that uses figures of speech, such as **simile**, **personification**, and **alliteration** to create **imagery** (e.g., "Like a student skimming reference books in a print-based library, Internet search engines systematically scour the Internet to scan site contents or summaries, flag and stockpile possibilities, and then evaluate and rank them. The effect is the same as that of someone choosing clothes for a date: a heap of clothes that won't make it out the door in a pile under those hung up for closer scrutiny.").

first-person point of view Storytelling in which one **character** of the story serves as the storyteller/**narrator**, telling the narrative from his or her **point of view**. One indication of first-person point of view is that at some point in the text, the speaker refers to herself or himself through such words as "I," "me," "my," "mine," "we," "our," or "us."

flashback A device used to depict events of the past (e.g., a biographical essay about a musician that focuses on the subject in adulthood and offers brief anecdotes about earlier performances).

foil A **character**, usually minor, who contrasts with and therefore sheds light on the **protagonist**.

foreshadowing A literary device in which a hint is provided about events that will occur later in the work (e.g., a crop that unexpectedly flourishes might foreshadow a character's personal growth against the odds).

form Broadly, the shape of a communication (e.g., one form of non-fiction is the **biography**; one form of poetry is the **ode**; one form of business communication is the sales letter). With literary texts, **genres** are the larger divisions and forms are the smaller divisions.

formal language Language that is appropriate, polite and respectful in tone, and rigorously follows conventions. It might be used, for example, in a letter of application, in a research paper, or between strangers introduced at a school ceremony.

formalism See **New Criticism**.

free verse Poetry that follows natural speech **rhythms** and has no regular pattern of line length, **rhyme**, or rhythm.

genre A type or class of literary texts (e.g., the novel) within which there are categories or **forms** (e.g., historical novel, speculative fiction, fantasy). Broadly, genre means any type or class. It can refer, for example, to media products (e.g., sitcoms, reality-based TV shows) and formal speeches (e.g., sales presentations, eulogies).

graphics Pictorial representations or other visual images (e.g., illustration, bar graph). On a Web site, for example, all that is seen can be categorized as either text or graphics.

haiku A traditional Japanese verse **form** consisting of three lines, of which the first line is five syllables, the second is seven syllables, and the third is five syllables.

head A short form for **heading** or **headline**.

heading The title for a section of a text. It is used to introduce a section of text, indicating the topic and offsetting it from other sections.

headline The title of an article in a periodical publication, sometimes called the **head**. Most often used to refer to the title of a news story, intended to both summarize the article and draw in the reader. It is sometimes followed by a **deck**.

hero A **character** who is the **protagonist** and also heroic, demonstrated by such characteristics as bravery and loyalty. Not all protagonists are heroes.

hyperbole Intended exaggeration, a device often used to create **irony**, humour, or dramatic effect.

iambic pentameter In poetry, a pattern of ten syllables (five **metrical feet**) per line, each foot (pair) beginning with an unstressed (˘), and ending with a stressed (ˊ) syllable.

idiom A form of expression, usually a phrase, in which the figurative meaning is different from the literal one (e.g., "neither here nor there" means "it doesn't matter" or "as fit as a fiddle" means "in trim, excellent shape"). Some idioms are so appealing that they become overused and therefore **clichés**.

imagery The collected images that exist in a text. These images include "mental pictures" and any other sensory perceptions that have been created in a text through its use of language. Imagery can be created through words or groups of words that evoke images that are visual (sight), auditory (hearing), tactile (touch), olfactory (taste), gustatory (smell), and kinesthetic (movement). Imagery can be descriptive (literal) or suggestive (metaphorical).

informal language Language that is familiar, intimate, casual, and sometimes includes slang terms or other **colloquial language.**

irony A literary device involving contrast; a discrepancy between the expected and the actual state of affairs. The most common type is verbal irony, a method of expression in which the actual meaning intended by a speaker is different from (and often opposite to) what she or he expresses. One famous example is the opening sentence of Jane Austen's *Pride and Prejudice*: "It is a truth universally acknowledged that a single man in possession of a good fortune must be in want of a wife."

juxtaposition The practice of placing two elements in a text side by side for the specific purpose of creating an effect through their association. Although the two items are not explicitly compared and contrasted, their proximity creates a contrast for the reader.

literary analysis A critical response to a literary text in the form of critical essay or oral commentary. It includes a thorough interpretation of the work. Such analysis may be based in a variety of critical approaches or movements, e.g., **archetypal criticism, cultural criticism, feminist criticism, New Criticism, New Historicism, poststructuralism, psychoanalytic criticism, reader-response criticism,** and **structuralism.**

logical fallacy A falsehood or misunderstanding based on flawed reasoning.

lyric poem A subjective, emotional poem with musical roots that may use **rhythm** or **rhyme** to evoke a reflective, introspective mood. Forms include **odes** and **sonnets.**

malapropism A ridiculous misuse of words, especially through confusing words that sound somewhat alike. From the French words *mal à propos*, meaning "out of place." A character in British playwright Richard Sheridan's comedy *The Rivals* (1775), noted for her speech blunders, was named Mrs. Malaprop; at one point, she is thinking of an alligator when she describes someone as being "as headstrong as an allegory on the banks of the Nile."

mass media Media that reaches a very large audience.

melodrama A sentimental drama using unrealistic **characters** and **plot** created primarily to appeal to emotions. Like a **farce** in **style**, but not humorous.

metaphor An implied **comparison** that (unlike a **simile**) does not use *like* or *as* (e.g., Walt Whitman's metaphor for grass in *Song of Myself*: "the beautiful uncut hair of graves"). The comparison connects two or more usually unlike things that have something in common (grass and hair).

metre The pattern of **rhythm** (stressed and unstressed syllables in poetry) measured and categorized in **metrical feet.**

metrical feet The units of stressed (ˊ) and unstressed (ˇ) syllables. A way of examining **metre** and identifying the feet according to type and number (e.g., **iambic pentameter**).

Middle English The language spoken and written in England from about the time of the Norman conquest (1066 CE) to the mid-fifteenth century. In contrast to **Old English**, it had a weaker and more regular inflectional system and incorporated many French and Latin words from Norman French, which was spoken in England by the ruling class after the conquest. *The Canterbury Tales, Piers Plowman,* and *Sir Gawain and the Green Knight* are surviving examples.

mode In literature, a manner, kind, method, or way of writing that brings with it certain expected customs and conventions (e.g., precise use of detail in descriptive writing, the tragic flaw in **tragedy**, the happy ending in **comedy**, the idealism in romance).

monologue In drama, a speech spoken by one **character** (e.g., a **soliloquy**, an **aside**).

mood The prevailing feeling created in or by a work, also known as the *atmosphere.*

motif An element (type of incident, device, or formula) that occurs frequently in literature and other artistic works (e.g., a child whose parents' absence or deaths leave the child unprotected and needing to fend for himself or herself). Also, a recurring image, character, or pattern of words that forms a dominant idea in one work (part of the **theme**) can be called a motif (or *Leitmotif,* German for "guiding motif"). For example, in Virginia Woolf's *Mrs. Dalloway,* a motif is the sound of clocks striking.

myth A story that involves supernatural beings or powers, that explains some aspect of nature (e.g., how the world began or the changing of the seasons) or of the human condition (e.g., romantic love, greed) *and* is part of a culture's mythology (its system of stories, often **archetypes**, passed down through generations).

narration A **style** of writing that incorporates **plot** to relay events over time by telling a story.

narrative poem A poem that tells a story (e.g., **ballad**, **epic**).

narrator The storyteller in narrative writing; a function of the **point of view**. Types include first-person, **omniscient**, and limited omniscient.

New Criticism A movement in literary criticism that proposes close reading and textual analysis of the text itself. It is referred to as "New" because it operates contrary to the previously favoured focus on the author's biography (see **biographical fallacy**), the historical **context**, and the perceived parallels between these and the text. Practitioners focus on both the "external form" (e.g., **ballad**, **ode**) and the "internal forms" (e.g., structure, repetition, patterns of figurative language, paradoxes). These practitioners reject consideration of the author's intention and the affect on the reader as illegitimate (thus coined *intentional fallacy* and *affective fallacy*). The movement is also referred to as *formalism.*

New Historicism A range of critical practices that examine works in their cultural and historical **contexts**. Practitioners of this critical movement developed it by examining a wide range of texts such as newspapers, advertisements, popular music, historical accounts, poetry, novels, and diaries. Practitioners believe that works cannot be viewed in isolation from history and culture. A reading of a work must take into account its intention, **genre**, *and* historical situation. This approach developed in reaction to both **New Criticism** and **structuralism**.

octave A **stanza** of eight lines.

ode A **lyric poem**, typically long and formal, with a complex structure, created to offer praise to a person or location.

Old English The language of the Anglo-Saxon peoples in England spoken from the mid-fifth century CE to soon after the Norman conquest in 1066 CE, at which time the language of England changed to **Middle English**. Because it dates from the first invasion of the British Isles by the continental Angles, Saxons, and Jutes, Old English is Germanic and highly inflected. "The Dream of the Rood" and the **epic** *Beowulf* are surviving examples.

omniscient narrator An all-seeing, all-knowing storyteller/**narrator** who is "outside" the **character**s; one type of third-person narrator.

onomatopoeia A device in which a word imitates the sound it represents (e.g., the *hum* of the computer, the *twitter* of sparrows, the *boom* of a building's collapse).

oral tradition A custom or long-held practice of composing and transmitting works orally; using the spoken word to create and communicate narratives.

oxymoron A device that combines contradictory words for dramatic effect (e.g., wise fool, living death, deafening silence).

page layout The physical arrangement of the text and graphics content of a page, such as a newspaper, magazine, Web site, or book (e.g., the size of type, text running in one or more columns, the placement of graphics).

parable A brief folk tale or narrative that functions as an **analogy** in order to teach an *implied* moral or lesson.

paradox An apparent contradiction or absurdity that is somehow true (e.g., "There are no errors on this page, except this one.").

parallelism Similar constructions or treatments placed side by side, for effect (e.g., grammatical parallelism in "Early in the novel, the character Piers did.... In the fifth chapter, he did.... At the climax, in the seventh chapter, he did....").

parody A humorous, exaggerated imitation of a work, **style**, or person.

pathetic fallacy A technique of attributing inanimate objects, especially parts of nature, with human feelings and capacities (e.g., flowers that are blooming with joy). It is often used in poetry and is less formal than **personification**.

pathos The quality (e.g., in a novel or play) that evokes pity, sorrow, or tenderness; the Greek word for "suffering" or "feeling."

personification A technique in which inanimate objects or concepts are given human qualities, form, or actions (e.g., "The moon is no door. It is a face in its own right, / White as a knuckle and terribly upset. / It drags the sea after it like a dark crime..." from Sylvia Plath's "The Moon and Yew Tree").

persuasion A **style** of writing that attempts to convince the audience either to act in a certain way or to adopt a certain opinion, perspective, viewpoint, or belief.

physical comedy Performed **comedy**, such as slapstick, that depends on physical jokes (e.g., one **character** making faces behind another's back) more than verbal wit or other intellectual stimulation. It typically involves unsubtle, boisterous, clownish behaviour, and so is often part of a **farce**.

plain language Clear, straightforward communication that is intended to be read by the broadest audience, uses concrete and familiar words, avoids using (or explains) jargon, and is organized for easy comprehension.

plot The series of connected actions and events in a story that includes rising (or intensified) action, **conflict**, **climax**, falling action, and a **dénouement** (or resolution).

point of view The perspective and **voice** from which information and impressions are conveyed—either physical (from a tower, from within the grass) or psychological (e.g., from that of a police officer, from that of a robber)—which, in fiction, is determined by the choice of the **narrator**. See **first-person point of view**, **second-person point of view**, and **third-person point of view**. See also **visual point of view**.

poststructuralism Refers to a critical approach to language, literature, and culture that questions or criticizes **structuralism**. Like structuralists, poststructuralists rely on close readings of texts; however, poststructuralists believe that language is inherently unstable in meaning and the meaning of a text is ultimately indecipherable. The best-known poststructuralist approach is deconstructionism. Poststructuralism is often associated with **cultural**, Marxist, **feminist**, and **psychoanalytic criticism**.

précis As an action, to precisely summarize a text in writing. The resulting text is also called a précis.

prologue An opening section of a drama, a kind of introduction.

props Objects appearing in the action of a drama and used to perform or enhance it. Props, short for *properties*, include such items as furniture or common household objects.

protagonist The narrative's main **character**.

proverb A brief, familiar saying that expresses a general truth (e.g., "We cannot step twice in the same river" or "When you want a drink of milk, you don't buy the cow"). Some proverbs are the morals of fables.

psychoanalytic criticism Literary criticism grounded in the psychoanalytic theory of the founder of psychoanalysis, Sigmund Freud (1856–1939). Practitioners attempt to psychoanalyze the author's unconscious desires, the reader's responses, and the characters in the work. The last approach involves examining the text for **symbol**s and psychological complexes. In addition to Freud, key figures are psychiatrist Carl Jung (noteworthy for his exploration of **archetype**s) and, most recently, Jacques Lacan.

pun A play on words using a word with two meanings, two words of similar meanings, or words that are similarly spelled or pronounced (e.g., in *Romeo and Juliet*, Mercutio saying as he dies, "Ask for me tomorrow and you shall find me a grave man").

quatrain A **stanza** of four lines.

reader-response criticism A critical approach that shifts the emphasis to the reader from the text or the work's author and **context**. This approach focuses on the individual reader's evolving response to the text. The reader, to a great extent, "creates" the meaning of the text and therefore there is no one correct meaning. Reader-response criticism has some basis in **deconstructionism** and disputes **New Criticism**'s notions of the text as a self-sufficient object.

refrain A phrase, a line, or lines repeated in a poem. In song lyrics, these are often called the **chorus**.

review An evaluation of another work (e.g., stage play, movie, novel) in essay or report **form** or a report on a product (e.g., a consumer report).

rhetorical question A question asked to promote thought and reflection, and for dramatic effect, not to elicit an answer.

rhyme The sound effect of words that have, or end with, the same or similar sounds. Poetry that has a strong rhyming quality may be called rhyme.

rhyme scheme The pattern of **rhyme**d line-endings in a **stanza** or entire poem, as usually indicated by letters of the alphabet. For example, a common rhyme scheme for a **quatrain** is *abab,* in which the first and third lines rhyme, as do the second and fourth. An example from "Let No Charitable Hope" by Elinor Wylie: "I was, being human, borne alone/ I am, being woman, hard beset;/ I live by squeezing from a stone/ The little nourishment I get."

rhyming couplet A pair of successive lines in a poem, grouped to accentuate the unit of thought, that have the same **metre** and rhyming ends. Also known as a **couplet**.

rhythm The sound effect of stressed (accented) and unstressed (unaccented) syllables. The pattern of rhythm is called the **metre**. It sets the beat and tempo of a poem.

romance In medieval literature, this was a verse narrative originally written in Old French or Provençal (both were "Romance" languages), which recounted the marvellous adventures of a hero of chivalry. Such medieval romances fall into three main cycles: the Arthurian, based upon the life of King Arthur; those which retell the life and deeds of Charlemagne and his most celebrated Paladin; and those devoted to the exploits of Alexander the Great.

sarcasm Language, often ironic, that is bitter or hurtful toward others. The **connotation** of sarcastic comments or phrases are distinct from their **denotation**. Often the explicit meaning is more positive, but a sneering tone or expression reveals a negative **subtext**.

satire A **form** that uses **irony**, ridicule, or **sarcasm** to expose human flaws.

scene A division within a dramatic work, usually within an **act**. Typically, a scene takes place in only one specific place and unit of time.

second-person point of view A text in which the writer refers directly to the reader(s) as "you" (or an implied "you," as in "read and analyze this text"), and does not ever refer back to the writer.

sestet A **stanza** of six lines.

set design The plan and construction for the area in which a drama takes place (e.g., a political suspense film's imitation White House, a stage play's backdrops and furniture).

setting The place and time—"where" and "when"—of a **narrative**.

sidebar A short article, often boxed, appearing beside another article, typically to supplement or provide background information for the larger, main article.

simile A definitely stated **comparison** that (unlike a **metaphor**) uses "like" or "as" in its construction (e.g., Wordsworth's "I wandered lonely as a cloud" or a software manual's "Use this e-mail program like a filter, to sort and prioritize your messages").

soliloquy A **monologue**, often long, in which the lone **character** expresses his or her thoughts and feelings.

sonnet A **lyric poem** with fourteen lines, sometimes written in **iambic pentameter**. The major types of sonnet are the Italian (Petrarchan) and the English (Shakespearean).

sound effects Any sounds other than speech or music made in a movie, stage play, etc. (e.g., footsteps of a **character** running, rumbles of a volcano erupting, the screech of airplane brakes). Sound effects are imitative and made artificially.

sound track The recorded sounds of a film; any part of this made available for sale (e.g., the recording of a song written to accompany part of a movie).

special effects Illusions created for film, television, or the stage using camera work, **props**, lighting, or computers (e.g., a woman flying out of her body, computer-generated dinosaurs, a man sawn in half).

specialized terms Words or phrases arising from or using the precise meanings of a particular field of study, work, etc. (e.g., *formalism* in literary studies, *tone colour* in music, *portico* in architecture, and *prohibition* in law).

stage An area in which actors perform, arranged for the best presentation to the audience. Types include the *proscenium stage* (a raised platform with a large, square arch at the stage edge that frames the acting area for the audience), the *thrust stage* (a stage with an extended platform that juts into the audience's area; also called the Shakespearean or Elizabethan stage), the *platform stage* (an informal raised stage, such as a parade float), and the *arena stage* (an open area at floor level that is surrounded by raised, bleacher-like seating; sometimes called theatre in the round, even if the space is not round).

stage directions In scripts, text that outlines performance requirements or suggestions (e.g., instructions to say a line angrily or to enter from stage right).

stanza A grouping of successive lines in a poem, separated on the page from other stanzas above and below it by a blank space.

stereotype A type of flat **character**, who is one-dimensional and lacks complexity, often reflecting some **bias** on the part of the person who created it.

stock character A type of flat **character**, whom the audience will immediately recognize, who serves a familiar function.

storyboard One of a sequence of pictures (sometimes with writing) used to outline or plan, for example, the shot-by-shot narrative of a TV commercial or film.

structuralism A method of intellectual inquiry (used in the study of language, literature, anthropology, etc.) based on the belief that structuring is an innate part of all human behaviour. Proponents focus on **form**, structure, and patterns of literary language and works, not their cultural **context** or an author's **biography**.

style An individual's manner of expression. In writing, style is the result of the choices the writer makes regarding such elements as **diction**, sentence structure, and **figurative language**. Style also expresses the writer's personality and way of thinking.

subhead A short form for **subheading**.

subheading A secondary or subordinate heading, title, etc., within a text (e.g., titled subsections of a proposal or research paper); also called **subhead**.

subplot A secondary course of action in a narrative. Subplots serve such purposes as providing humour in a **tragedy**, rounding out minor **characters**, or helping to tie up loose ends.

subtext In a text, a hidden meaning that is not explicit.

summary A brief account; a condensation of a work's content. Sometimes called a **synopsis**.

suspense Increasing tension in a narrative, caused by uncertainty and excitement about the conclusion that generally springs from the narrative's **conflict**.

symbol Something that represents or stands for something else (e.g., a heart shape for love, a forked road for a choice to be made). Symbolism is many symbols collectively. Symbolic language includes **figurative language** (e.g., **metaphor**, **personification**) that is metaphorical, not literal, which creates a work's **imagery**.

synopsis A brief outline, **summary**, or general account (e.g., a synopsis of a **plot**).

syntax The arrangement of words to form phrases and sentences.

tableau A "frozen" moment in a drama, in which the performers freeze in position, motionless and soundless.

tanka Considered the most important form of poetry in Japan, the tanka was invented circa 700 CE, before the **haiku** form. A tanka requires thirty-one syllables and is divided into five lines broken into the following syllables: 5-7-5-7-7. Generally, tanka poems lyrically crystallize a moment or occasion.

target audience The chosen or intended readers, viewers, or listeners (e.g., of a speech); usually a distinct demographic group.

terza rima A verse **form** consisting of tercets (three-line **stanzas**) in which the second line of a stanza sets the **rhyme** for the first line of the next stanza. Thus the **rhyme scheme** is *aba bcb cdc ded efe* etc., ending with a **rhyming couplet**. It is an effective rhyme scheme for long **narrative poems** and was invented by Dante Alighieri and used most famously in his *Divine Comedy*.

theme The central insight, idea, focus, or message of a work (especially fiction), stated indirectly or directly (e.g., the theme of jealousy in Shakespeare's *Othello*).

thesis The main idea of a work of non-fiction writing. A thesis is focused and is developed with the use of examples and evidence. A thesis is usually stated directly in a **thesis statement**.

thesis statement The **thesis** provided by the writer of a text explicitly in one or several sentences of that text.

third-person point of view Written text in which the writer never refers either to himself/herself, or directly to the reader as "you." The position from which such a text is written.

tone In a text, the creator's attitude to the subject or audience as conveyed through elements of that text. In writing, the author's tone is often conveyed through **diction** and **style**. In spoken communication, the speaker's tone can be conveyed through her or his diction, volume, pitch, and body language. In visual representations, the artist's tone can be conveyed through the choice of subject matter, medium, technique, **visual composition**, emphasis, and balance.

tragedy Traditionally, a drama that focuses on the downfall of the **protagonist** (due to a character flaw or a mistake) and ends unhappily. In the traditional tragedy, the protagonist is of high social status (e.g., a prince, a goddess), but in contemporary tragedy is often an ordinary person. In current usage, tragedy might refer broadly to events, or works including events, that are catastrophic and that seem horribly unjust or preventable.

tragic hero The heroic **protagonist** of a **tragedy**.

tragicomedy A drama that combines aspects of **tragedy** and **comedy**.

usage The customary established or common manner of using words, phrases, and expressions in a way that is not yet reflected in dictionaries (e.g., as with computer terminology or with teen slang) *or* a writer's particular choice, when an option exists, in the use of a word, phrase, or expression.

visual composition The artistic arrangement of parts in the whole visual work; the way in which parts are combined and related. For example, Hiroshige Utagawa's *Shower at Ohashi Bridge* shows a bridge with people walking over it placed diagonally in the foreground, an expanse of river and a boat in the middle ground, a shore in the background, and drenching rain over the whole.

visual point of view The position from which something is viewed; the actual, physical or imagined standpoint. For example, a painter might paint the subject for the viewer to see as though from below, from above, from a bird's-eye view (aerial), from a worm's-eye view, from outside, from inside, or as in Pieter Brueghel's *Landscape with the Fall of Icarus*, from a field far from the figure falling from the sky.

visual scale Proper proportion; proportional representation of actual objects in a visual work. The relative size of objects in a visual work (e.g., in a painting, the representation of two buildings, one near and one far, or the foreshortening of a male subject's arm stretched forward).

voice Broadly, the personality of the speaker or persona (or the author) coming through in a work, created through the combination of **diction**, **point of view**, and **tone**. Narrowly defined, voice can be described as active (e.g., I made a mistake) or passive (e.g., Mistakes were made).

voice over Narration (e.g., in film) in which the speaker is not seen.

Another Viewpoint Index

Another Viewpoint: Archetypal Patterns

The Rocking-Horse Winner 35

Outside Edges 59

Elegy in Stone 235

I, Icarus 517

Because I Could Not Stop for Death— 610

Another Viewpoint: Critical Approaches

The Death of the Moth 241

Of Youth and Age 262

Why I Write 271

The Heroes You Had as a Girl 506

foremother 510

Summer Night 529

The Love Song of J. Alfred Prufrock 538

grammar poem 547

Stop! 649

Another Viewpoint: Culture

The Shining Houses 73

A Devoted Son 86

Magpies 95

No Great Mischief 162

Call of the Weird 282

To You Who Would Wage War Against Me 514

O Can You Leave Your Native Land? 603

Another Viewpoint: History

Peace, Technology 322

Paradise, a Poet, and Promised Land 330

The Rime of the Ancient Mariner 600

Dover Beach 607

Another Viewpoint: Literary Modes and Forms

Was It a Dream? 154

A Modest Proposal 293

People on the Bridge 523

The Canterbury Tales 569

Sonnet 116 571

Dead Parrot 654

Another Viewpoint: Society

Windows 117

War 137

A Place to Stand On 223

Chameleons and Codas 228

My Mother's Blue Bowl 255

Ours by Design 363

The River 544

Beowulf 559

Author Index

Acoose, Janice 636
Akiwenzie Damm, Kateri 511
Aristotle 454
Arnold, Matthew 605
Atwood, Margaret 205
Auden, W.H. 518

Bacon, Francis 259
Bhatia, Amin 345
Blackduck, Alison 355
Blake, William 572
Bouzane, Lillian 507
Bowering, George 489
Bradley, A.C. 687
Branagh, Kenneth 666
Brewster, Elizabeth 481
Brown, Kurt 500
Brueghel, Pieter 366

Campbell, Joseph 171
Cassatt, Mary 484
CBC Television 640
Chaucer, Geoffrey 561
Chekhov, Anton 614
Clarke, George Elliott 327
Climenhage, Kate 349
Coady, Lynn 331
Coleridge, Samuel Taylor 575
Conlogue, Ray 380
Conrad, Patricia 225
Cope, Wendy 478

Dawson, C. Daniel 498
Desai, Anita 75
de Villiers, Marq 466
Dickinson, Emily 608
Dorin, Ivan 48
Dove, Rita 7
Dryden, Ken 243

Edmonton Journal 456
Eliot, T.S. 531
Elliott, Bob 446

Findley, Timothy 120
Franklin, Ursula 313
Frye, Northrop 166

Goulding, Ray 446
Government of Newfoundland and Labrador 392
Greenwood, Therese 658

Harvey, Kenneth J. 449
Heaney, Seamus 553
Heighton, Steven 229
Henley, Marian 364
Highway, Tomson 6
Hiroshige Utagawa 368
Hoffman, Eva 307
Hughes, Langston 527
Husarska, Anna 389

Joyce, James 181

Kimenye, Barbara 97
King, Thomas 87
Kingsolver, Barbara 273

Lange, Dorothea 256
LaRocque, Emma 524
Laurence, Margaret 217
Lawrence, D.H. 18
Leacock, Stephen 696
Le Guin, Ursula K. 144
Levertov, Denise 14
Lewis, Donna 642
Livesay, Dorothy 492

MacLeod, Alistair 155
Maupassant, Guy de 150
McIntyre, Lyle 60
McLuhan, Marshall 431
Milne, Courtney 370
Mitchell, Barbara 370
Mitchell, Ormond 370
Monty Python 651
Moodie, Susanna 601
Moore, Marianne 473
Morgan, Bernice 109
Morrison, Lee 459
Moyers, Bill 171
Munro, Alice 63

Neruda, Pablo 4
Ng-Chan, Taien 37
Nowlan, Alden 515

Ondaatje, Michael 486
Orwell, George 263
Ozick, Cynthia 196

Pitt, Angela 692
Postman, Neil 434
Pratt, Christopher 118
Purdy, Al 349

Quindlen, Anna 12

Rees, Ann 443
Reguly, Eric 463
Reid, Bill 142
Richler, Mordecai 10
Roberts, Brad (The Crash Test Dummies) 539
Rose, Chris 421
Ross, Val 188

Schulz Gropman, Karen 634
Scliar, Moacyr 138
Shakespeare, William 570, 656–700
Shelley, Percy Bysshe 177
Shelton, Margaret 46
Swift, Jonathan 283
Szymborska, Wislawa 521

Taylor, Drew Hayden 279
Thomas, Dylan 494
Tranchemontagne, Chantal 337

Walcott, Derek 542
Walker, Alice 251
Wallace, Bronwen 503
Watson, Patrick 300
Waytiuk, Judy 394
White, E.B. 209
Winter, Kathleen 323
Wiwa, Ken 295
Wong, Rita 545
Wood, Daniel 403
Woolf, Virginia 237

Zeman, Brenda 636

Credits

Every reasonable effort has been made to find copyright holders of the material in this anthology. The publisher would be pleased to have any errors brought to its attention.

Literary Credits

p. 4 Translation © Alastair Reid; **p. 6** From *Everybody's Favourites: Canadians Talk About Books That Changed Their Lives,* Penguin Books Canada Ltd., 1997. Copyright © Tomson Highway; **p. 7** "For the Love of Books" from *Selected Poems,* Pantheon Books, © 1993 by Rita Dove. Reprinted by permission of the author; **p. 10** From *Everybody's Favourites: Canadians Talk About Books That Changed Their Lives,* Penguin Books Canada Ltd., 1997. Copyright © Mordecai Richler; **p. 12** From *How Reading Changed My Life* by Anna Quindlen, copyright © 1998 by Anna Quindlen. Used by permission of Ballantine Books, a division of Random House, Inc.; **p. 14** "The Secret" by Denise Levertov, from *Poems 1960–1967* copyright © 1974 by Denise Levertov/Reprinted by permission of New Directions Publishing Corp.; **p. 18** Used by permission of Laurence Pollinger Limited and the Estate of Frieda Lawrence Ravagli; **p. 37** With permission of the author; **p. 48** Copyright © Ivan Dorin; **p. 63** "Shining Houses" by Alice Munro from *Dance of the Happy Shades* © 1968, Ryerson Press. Used by permission of McGraw-Hill Ryerson; **p. 75** Copyright © 1978, Anita Desai. Reproduced by permission of the author c/o Rogers, Coleridge & White Ltd., 20 Powis Mews, London W11 1JN; **p. 87** Used by permission of HarperCollins Canada; **p. 97** "The Winner" from *Kalasanda.* Copyright © 1965 by Barbara Kimenye. Used by permission of East African Educational Publishers, Kenya; **p. 109** Bernice Morgan is the author of the novels *Random Passage* and *Waiting for Time* and a short story collection *The Topography of Love.* Used by permission of the author; **p. 120** From *Dinner Along the Amazon* by Timothy Findley. Copyright © 1984 by Pebble Productions Inc. Reprinted by permission of Penguin Books Canada Limited; **p. 138** "Paz e guerra" in: Moacyr Scliar: "Contos reunidos," Companhia das Letras, 1995 © 1995 by Moacyr Scliar. Translation by Patricia Feeney. Used by permission of the author and translator; **p. 144** Copyright © 1975 by Ursula K. Le Guin; first appeared in *Epoch;* from *Buffalo Gals and Other Animal Presences;* reprinted by permission of the author and the author's agents, the Virginia Kidd Agency, Inc.; **p. 155** *No Great Mischief* by Alistair MacLeod. Used by permission of McClelland & Stewart Ltd. *The Canadian Publishers;* **p. 166** Excerpts from "The Archtypes of Literature." First published in *The Kenyon Review*—Winter 1951, OS Vol. XIII, No. 1, Copyright *The Kenyon Review;* **p. 171** From *The Power of Myth* by Joseph Campbell & Bill Moyers, copyright © 1988 by Apostrophe S Productions, Inc. and Bill Moyers and Alfred Van der Marck Editions, Inc., for itself and the estate of Joseph Campbell. Used by permission of Doubleday, a division of Random House, Inc.; **p. 181** "Araby", *Dubliners* reproduced with the permission of the Estate of James Joyce; © copyright, Estate of James Joyce (1967); **p. 188** Reprinted with permission from *The Globe and Mail;* **p. 196** "Portrait of the Essay as a Warm Body" by Cynthia Ozick, from *The Best American Essays 1988.* Copyright © 1988 by Cynthia Ozick. Reprinted by permission of Houghton Mifflin Company. All rights reserved; **p. 205** Copyright © O.W. Toad, 2001; **p. 209** All lines from "Afternoon of an American Boy" from *Essays of E.B. White* by E.B. White. Copyright 1947 by E.B. White. Originally appeared in *The New Yorker.* Reprinted by permission of HarperCollins Publishers Inc.; **p. 217** *Heart of a Stranger* by Margaret Laurence. Used by permission of McClelland & Stewart Ltd. *The Canadian Publishers;* **p. 225** Used by permission of Patricia Conrad. First appeared in *The Globe and Mail,* July 10, 2000; **p. 229** "Elegy in Stone" from *The Admen Move on Lhasa* copyright © 1997 by Steven Heighton. Reprinted by permission of Stoddart Publishing Co. Ltd.; **p. 243** From *The Game: A Reflective and Thought-Provoking Look at a Life in Hockey,* 3rd Edition. Copyright © Ken Dryden, 1983, 1993, 1999. Reprinted by permission of Macmillan Canada, an imprint of CDG Books Canada, Inc.; **p. 251** "My Mother's Blue Bowl" published in *Anything We Love Can Be Saved: A Writer's Activism,* copyright 1997. Used by permission of Wendy Weil's Agency Inc.; **p. 263** *Why I Write* (Copyright © George Orwell 1953) and reproduced by permission of A.M. Heath &

Co. Ltd. on behalf of Bill Hamilton as the Literary Executor of the Estate of the Late Sonia Brownell Orwell and Martin Secker & Warburg Ltd.; **p. 273** Pages 257–262 from *High Tide in Tucson: Essays from Now or Never* by Barbara Kingsolver. Copyright © 1995 by Barbara Kingsolver. Reprinted by permission of HarperCollins Publishers Inc.; **p. 279** Used by permission of the author; **p. 295** Originally published in *The Globe and Mail,* June 22, 2001. Copyright © 2001 Ken Wiwa. With permission of the author; **p. 300** Patrick Watson is the Creative Director of the Historical Foundation's Heritage Minutes and other Media programs. This article originally appeared in the Toronto *Globe and Mail* in September 2000; **p. 307** "Wanderers by Choice," by Eva Hoffman. Copyright ©2000 by Eva Hoffman. Reprinted by permission of Georges Borchardt, Inc., on behalf of the author; **p. 313** Used by permission of the author and *Peace Magazine,* P.O. Box 248, Stn P, Toronto, ON, M5S 2S7; **p. 323** Reprinted by permission of Kathleen Winter; **p. 327** Used by permission of the author. Published in *Canadian Geographic,* January/February 2001, p.98; **p. 331** Used by permission of the author; **p. 337** "Sixth Flight" originally appeared in *Equinox,* July 2000. Article reprinted by permission of the author; **p. 345** Reprinted from the October 2000 issue of *Canadian Musician Magazine;* **p. 349** Used by permission of the author; **p. 355** Alison Blackduck is a journalist living in Yellowknife, NWT; **p. 371** Adapted from *W.O. Mitchell Country* by Orm and Barbara Mitchell. Reprinted with permission from the publisher, McClelland and Stewart Ltd. *The Canadian Publishers;* **p. 381** Reprinted with permission of *The Globe and Mail;* **p. 390** Anna Husarska is a writer, journalist and senior Political Analyst at the International Crisis Group; **p. 395** Used by permission of Judy Waytiuk and *Marketing Magazine;* **p. 405** Used by permission of the author, Daniel Wood; **p. 422** Used by permission of the *Vancouver Sun;* **p. 431** Marshall McLuhan; **p. 434** From *Conscientious Objections* by Neil Postman, copyright © 1988 by Neil Postman. Used by permission of Alfred A. Knopf, a division of Random House, Inc.; **p. 443** Reprinted by permission of *Vancouver Province;* **p. 446** Bob Elliott and Ray Goulding; **p. 449** Kenneth J. Harvey is the author of thirteen books. He lives in Newfoundland. Used by permission of the author; **p. 456** Reprinted with permission of the *Edmonton Journal;* **p. 459** Used by permission of the author; **p. 463** Reprinted with permission from *The Globe and Mail;* **p. 466** Excerpt from *Water* by Marq de Villiers, published by Stoddart Publishing Canada © 2000, pp. 370–374; **p. 473** From *Collected Poems of Marianne Moore.* © 1935 Marianne Moore; **p. 479** "Engineers' Corner" by Wendy Cope, published in *Making Cocoa for Kingsley Amis* by Faber & Faber Ltd.; **p. 482** "Is the Pathetic Fallacy True?" by Elizabeth Brewster is reprinted from *Selected Brewster* by permission of Oberon Press; **p. 487** By permission of Michael Ondaatje; **p. 490** By permission of George Bowering; **p. 493** Reprinted with permission from *Archive for Our Times: Previously Uncollected and Unpublished Poems of Dorothy Livesay,* edited by Dean Irvine (Arsenal Pulp Press, 1998); **p. 495** "Fern Hill" taken from *Dylan Thomas: The Poems,* first published in 1971 by J.M. Dent & Sons Ltd.; **p. 500** "The Committee to Upgrade Celestial Signs" was first published in *More Things in Heaven and Earth* (Four Way Books, 2002), and is reprinted with permission of the publisher; **p. 504** "The Heroes You Had as a Girl" by Bronwen Wallace is reprinted from *Signs of the Former Tenant* by permission of Oberon Press; **p. 507** Reprinted by permission of the author; **p. 512** By permission of author. "To You Who Would Wage War Against Me" first appeared in *My Heart Is a Stray Bullet,* Kegedonce Press, 1993; **p. 516** "I, Icarus" from *Selected Poems,* copyright © 1967 by Irwin Publishing. Reprinted by permission of Stoddart Publishing Co. Ltd.; **p. 519** "Musée des Beaux Arts," copyright © 1940 and renewed 1968 by W.H. Auden, from *W.H. Auden: Collected Poems* by W.H. Auden. Used by permission of Random House, Inc.; **p. 521** "People on the Bridge" by Wislawa Szymborska, translated by Joanna Trzeciak. From *Miracle Fair: Selected Poems of Wislawa Szymborska,* May 2001; **p. 525** "Progress" first published in *Canadian Literature: A Quarterly of Criticism and Review,* No. 124–125, Spring–Summer, 1990. Used by permission of the author; **p. 528** From *The Collected Poems of Langston Hughes* by Langston Hughes, copyright © 1994 by the Estate of Langston Hughes. Used by permission of Alfred A. Knopf, a division of Random House, Inc.; **p. 532** Used by permission of the Estate of T.S. Eliot; **p. 540** From the album *God Shuffled His Feet* written by Brad Roberts, published by Polygram International Publishing, Inc. Used by permission of Universal Music Publishing; **p. 542** "The River" from *The Gulf and Other Poems* by Derek Walcott. Copyright © 1970 by Derek Walcott. Reprinted by permission of Farrar, Straus and Giroux, LLC; **p. 546** "grammar poem" by Rita Wong first published in *monkeypuzzle* by Press Gang Publishers, Vancouver © 1998. Reprinted with permission of the author; **p. 550** "Mu-lan" published in *The Flowering Plum and the Palace Lady,*

Interpretations of Chinese Poetry. Translation by Hans H. Frankel. Used by permission of Yale University Press, © 1976; **p. 555** Translation by Seamus Heaney; **p. 560** Middle English excerpt edited by John H. Fisher; **p. 561** Modern English excerpt translated by Nevill Coghill. Reproduced with permission of Curtis Brown Group Ltd., London, on behalf of the Estate of Nevill Coghill © Nevill Coghill 1951; **p. 614** From *The Brute and Other Farces* by Anton Chekhov, edited by Eric Bentley, translated by Theodore Hoffman. Applause Theatre Book Publishers, 1985. © 1958 by Eric Bentley for collection; **p. 636** Prof. Janice Acoose: citizen of the Sakimay Saulteaux First Nation and Marival Métis Community; **p. 642** Used by permission of Donna Lewis, author and performer of various Sleeping Beauty Cabaret Monologues; **p. 651** Used by permission of Methuen Publishing Ltd., London; **p. 658** Courtesy of *The Kingston Whig Standard*; **p. 666** Printed by permission of Kenneth Branagh Ltd.; **p. 677** Used by permission of *Cineaste Magazine*; **p. 692** Used by permission of Angela Pitt.

Visual Credits

p. 2 Jacob Lawrence, Smithsonian American Art Museum, Washington, DC/Art Resource, New York; **p. 11** Pablo Picasso, *Bottle, Cup and Newspaper* 1912–1913. © Estate of Pablo Picasso (Paris)/SODRAC (Montréal) 2001; **p. 16** Ryuichi Sato/Photonica; **p. 36** Corbis/Jose Luis Ortiz; **p. 47** Margaret Shelton, *Calgary from Sunnyside* (undated), Woodcut, 5/100, Carleton University Art Gallery: The Frank H. Underhill Memorial Collection of Block Prints, 1998; **p. 61** Lyle McIntyre; **p. 62** Nikolaevich/Photonica; **p. 74** Hugh Sitton/Getty Images/Stone; **p. 96** Design "Dialogue" by Nuwa Wamala Nnyanzi www.nnyanziart.com; **p. 119** Ned Pratt; **p. 143** © Ulli Steltzer, photographer from *The Black Canoe*, Douglas & McIntyre, Vancouver; **p. 164** Copyright Victoria & Albert Museum, London/Art Resource, NY; **p. 170** CORBIS/Gian Berto Vanni; **p. 189** Poster published by The National Union of Conservative and Unionist Assoc., London, 1929/Bridgeman; **p. 194** Neil Leslie/Photonica; **p. 216** Kathy Warinner; **p. 224** Gord Wiebe; **p. 236** By courtesy of the National Portrait Gallery, London; **p. 242** London Life-Portnoy Hockey Hall of Fame; **p. 257** Dorothea Lange/CORBIS; **p. 258** © Scala/Art Resource, NY; **p. 272** Chuck Rancorn; **p. 294** M.C. Escher's Tower of Babel © 2001 Cordon Art B.V.—Baarn—Holland. All rights reserved; **p. 306** Eva Rubinstein/Photonica; **p. 336** Marty McLennan; **p. 354** Reproduced with the permission of The West Baffin Eskimo Co-operative, Cape Dorset Nunavut; **p. 365** Maxine! Comix. Reprinted by permission of the artist; **p. 367** Painting by Pieter Breugel the Elder courtesy of Bridgeman Art Library; **p. 369** Painting by Utagawa Hiroshige. Courtesy of Magma Photo; **pp. 371–79** Courtney Milne; **pp. 382–387** Used by permission of CBC; **pp. 390–91** Jozef Bury. Published in *Saturday Night* magazine, August 12, 2000; **p. 393** Compliments of Newfoundland and Labrador Tourism Advertising Campaign 1993–1999, Target Marketing; **pp. 395–400** Used by permission of MTS; **p. 405** Holly Harris/Getty Images/Stone; **pp. 406, 413, 416–17** Jeff Speed Photographer; **p. 408** © Dorling Kindersley; **p. 411** UHB Trust/Getty Images/Stone; **p. 414 left** PhotoDisc; **p. 414 right** Firstlight; **p. 415 left** Roger Wright/Getty Images/Stone; **p. 415 right** Rob Gage/FPG; **p. 419** © Dorling Kindersley; **p. 423** Ian Smith/*Vancouver Sun*; **p. 443** Cameron Cardow; **p. 452** Malcolm Mayes; **p. 476** Joseph Squillante/Photonica; **p. 485** Mary Cassatt, American, 1884–1926, Evening, 1879/80, soft-ground etching and aquatint on cream laid paper, 19.7 x 22.1 cm. The Albert H. Wolf Memorial Collection, 1938.33. Photograph © 2001, The Art Institute of Chicago, All Rights Reserved; **p. 499** C. Daniel Dawson; **p. 530** Used by permission of Madame Gilberte Brassai; **p. 548** Excerpt from *100 Celebrated Chinese Women* published by Asiapac Books www.asiapacbooks.com; **p. 554** Rockwell Kent/Granger; **p. 560** Ellesmere Manuscript, Canterbury Tales, Chaucer/Bridgeman; **p. 573** Used by permission of Rare Books and Special Collections, Princeton University; **p. 574** The Watersnakes Appear, scene from *The Rime of the Ancient Mariner* by S.T. Coleridge 1877 engraving. Collection Kharbine-Tapabor, Paris France/Bridgeman; **p. 604** E.O. Hoppé/CORBIS; **p. 612** Gen Nishino/Getty Images/Stone; **p. 635** Karen Schulz Gropman—set designer; **p. 641** Photo by Justin Hall, provided by Passage Films Inc.; **p. 650** Everett Collection/Magma Photo; **p. 657** Historical Picture Archive/CORBIS; **p. 686** Scene from the 1979 Stratford Festival production of King Lear by William Shakespeare. Directed by Robin Phillips. Designed by Daphne Dare with with l–r: Gregory Wanless as Officer to Cordelia, Rod Beattie as Doctor, John Lambert as Officer, Jim McQueen as Kent, Peter Ustinov as King Lear and Ingrid Blekys as Cordelia. Photograph by Robert C. Ragsdale. Courtesy of the Stratford Festival Archives.